Prais

'A learned, wise, wonde~~~~~ ~~~~~ single volume history of a civilisation that I knew I should know more about.' **Tom Holland**

'Masterful and engrossing. Michael Wood sets out China's rich and complex past in a history that is well-paced, eminently readable and well-timed. A must-read for those who want – and need – to know about the China of yesterday, today and tomorrow.' **Peter Frankopan**

'Over 500 pages of text and not a dull one among them. The change of focus between the court and cities and the countryside means that all sides of Chinese life are portrayed. Wood explains with immense clarity how traditional culture never really went away and why it has reappeared. On gender history, on the 1989 killings, the text is lucid and immensely fair minded. What a triumph!' **Rana Mitter**

'If you're going to clearly and engagingly dissect 4,000 years of dense, sprawling saga, you need someone up to the job. Thankfully, acclaimed historian and TV documentarian Wood is able to wrangle China's uniquely epic story into one readable, relevant volume.' *Wanderlust Magazine*

THE
STORY OF CHINA

A Portrait of a Civilisation and its People

MICHAEL WOOD

**SIMON &
SCHUSTER**

London · New York · Sydney · Toronto · New Delhi

First published in Great Britain by Simon & Schuster UK Ltd, 2020
This edition published in Great Britain by Simon & Schuster UK Ltd, 2021

5 7 9 10 8 6 4

Simon & Schuster UK Ltd
1st Floor
222 Gray's Inn Road
London WC1X 8HB

www.simonandschuster.co.uk
www.simonandschuster.com.au
www.simonandschuster.co.in

Simon & Schuster Australia, Sydney
Simon & Schuster India, New Delhi

A CIP catalogue record for this book
is available from the British Library.

Paperback ISBN: 978-1-4711-7598-5
eBook ISBN: 978-1-4711-7600-5

Typeset in Sabon by M Rules

Printed in the UK by CPI Group (UK) Ltd, Croydon, CR0 4YY

MIX
Paper | Supporting
responsible forestry
FSC® C171272

謹以此書獻給親愛的Rebecca

CONTENTS

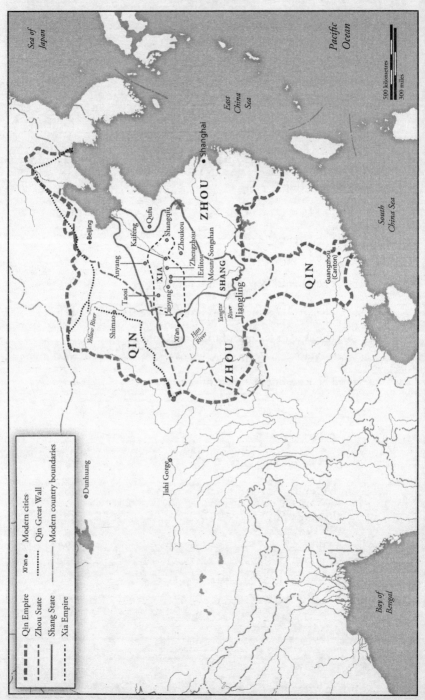

Early China *c.* 2000 BCE–206 BCE

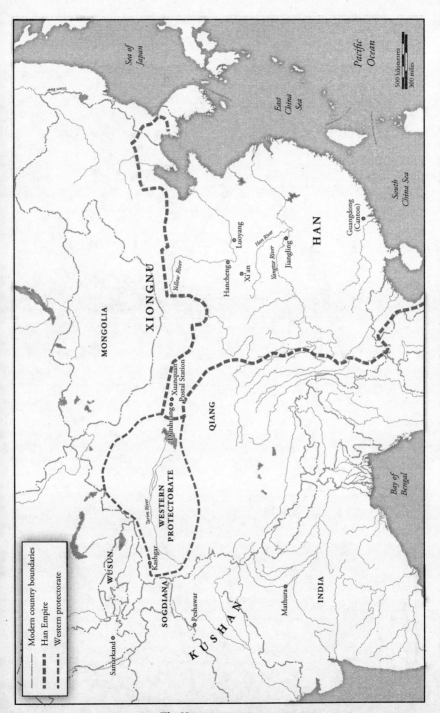

The Han 202 BCE–220 CE

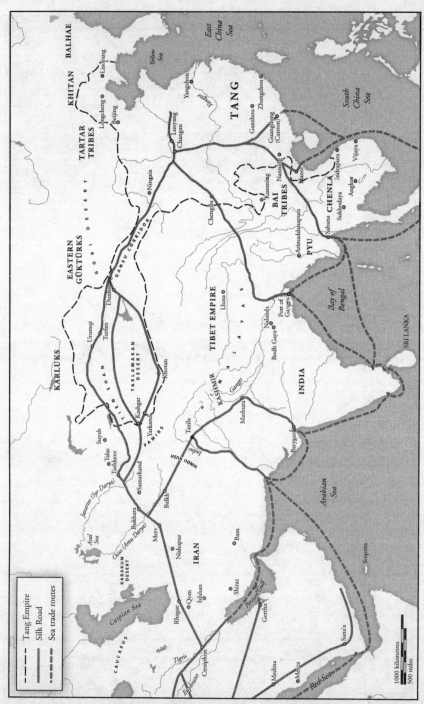

The Silk Road and world of the Tang 618–907

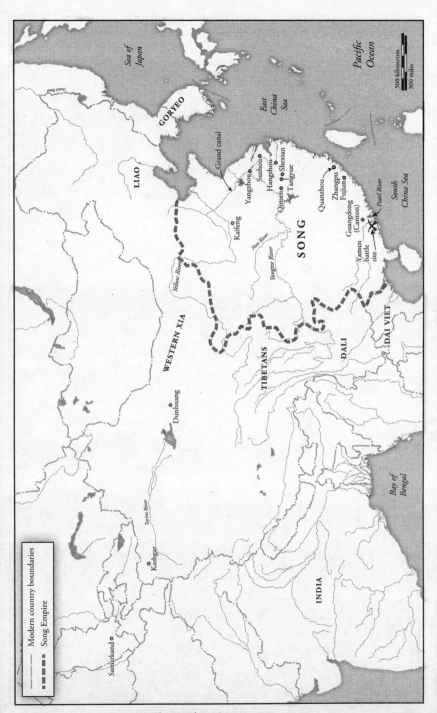

The Northern Song 960–1127

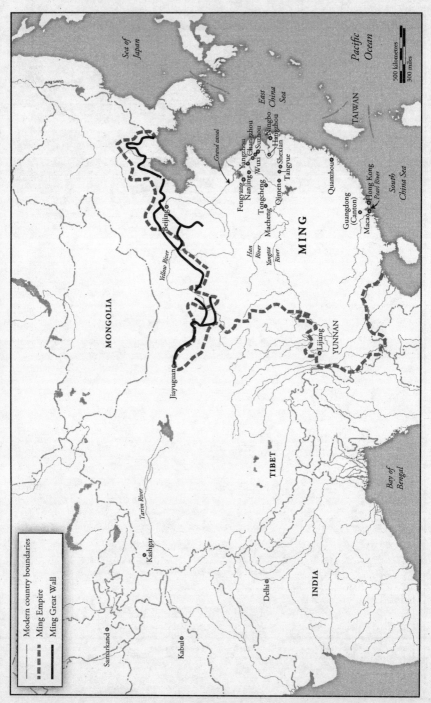

The Ming 1368–1644

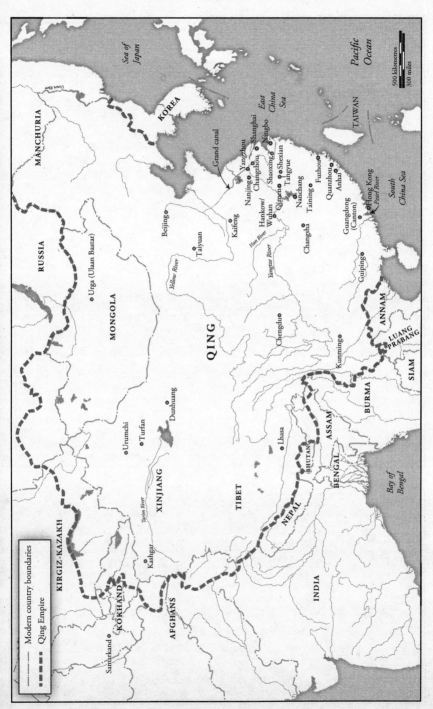

The Qing Empire 1644–1912

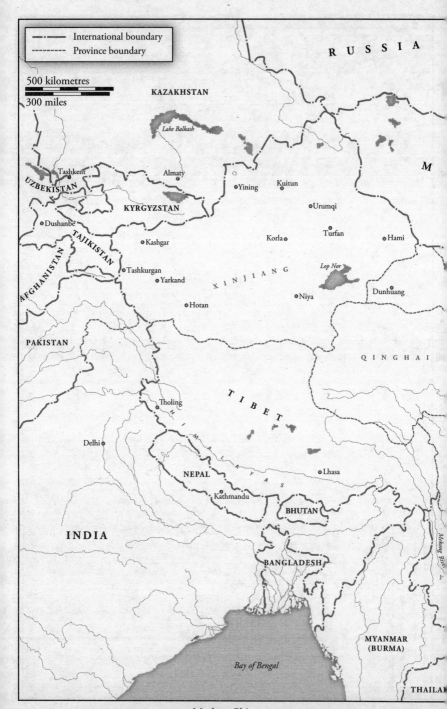

Modern China

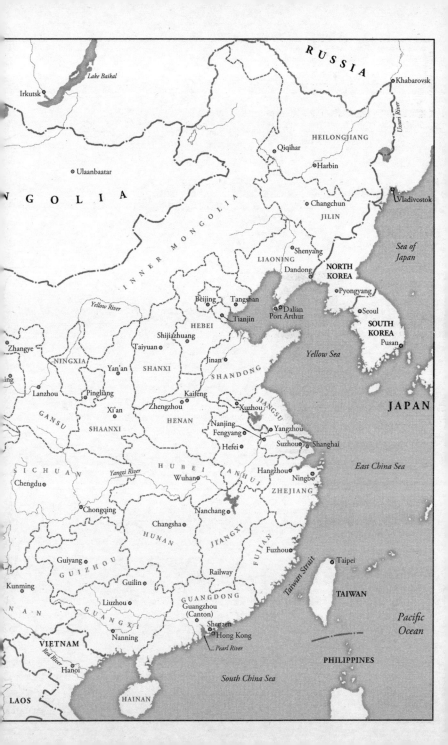

PREFACE

This book has come out of a long fascination with China which began in my schooldays in Manchester with A. C. Graham's *Poems of the Late T'ang*, one of those books that opened a window on a world one could never have dreamed existed. Later, as a graduate student in Oxford, sharing a house with a sinologist was another eye-opening time, encountering revelatory books like Arthur Waley's *Book of Songs*. At that time among the larger-than-life characters who came through our kitchen was David Hawkes, who had been in Tiananmen Square on 1 October 1949 when the People's Republic was founded, and who had latterly given up his post as professor of Chinese in order to translate 'the novel of the millennium', *Dream of the Red Chamber* (a book whose story is told below, pages 353–69). Since then my journeys in China have extended over four decades, both as a traveller and as a broadcaster; for example making *The Story of China* films, which have been seen worldwide, then in 2018 a series on the fortieth anniversary of Deng Xiaoping's 'Reform and Opening Up', one of the most significant events in modern history. Most recently, in autumn 2019, I returned to make a film on China's greatest poet, Du Fu, which, though late in the writing of this book, gave me another opportunity to think about the long vistas of Chinese culture and its enduring ideals. We filmed in Chengdu, where Du Fu stayed for nearly four years from the end of 759. Today the supposed site of his 'Thatched Cottage' is one of China's most delightful and popular tourist destinations, with its ornamental streams and gardens, stands of bamboo, peach and plum trees, and yellow splashes of wintersweet and jasmine. Its reconstructed buildings, pavilions and gift shops the visitor might think are a purely invented past; but recently, following a chance find during the laying of a drain, an excavation inside the tourist site uncovered the footings of a small Tang dynasty Buddhist monastery, with houses and brick platforms just as Du Fu describes; an inscription on a tablet from 687 even mentions 'the small tower of the senior monk', evidently the same building 'west of the stream' to which Du Fu refers as 'the tower of monk Huang'. With Tang dynasty ceramics and domestic pottery, eaves tiles and stamped bricks, the find confirms in detail a tradition passed down tenaciously over more than 1,200 years. Though destroyed and rebuilt many times, this was indeed the very spot. Nothing now survives above ground that is of any antiquity, but in China it is not the physical fabric of the building that matters; it is the sense of place that conjures the stories, songs and poems that have been handed down for so long among the people; the riches of what Confucius called 'this culture of ours'.

Writing on China's past, though, is a daunting task, all the more so if one is not a sinologist. China is a huge and incredibly rich, indeed inexhaustible, subject – 'the other pole of the human mind', as Simon Leys said in a famous essay. With more than three millennia of written records, it has a vast history – small libraries have been written about each of my individual chapters! And that history is growing by the day, with a constant flow of new discoveries in the past few years. Among a host of recent major textual finds still being evaluated and published, for example, are extraordinary collections of private letters, law codes and legal cases going back to the Qin and Han dynasties. Since the discovery of the Terracotta Army at the tomb of the First Emperor in 1974, there have also been many sensational archaeological finds, such as the remarkable prehistoric astronomical platform at Taosi, and though many are still unpublished, I have tried to give up-to-date accounts where possible – a preliminary interpretation of the exciting finds at Shimao in the first chapter, for example, was only published by the excavators in 2017. China's early history in particular is a fascinating and constantly evolving field.

As regards the form of this book, in the manner of a film maker I have tried to keep the grand sweep narrative moving along while making detours to provide close-ups, homing in on particular places, moments and individual lives, voices high and low. For ordinary lives early in the story I have gratefully used the new finds, for example letters by soldiers in the Qin military – the real-life Terracotta Army – or letters from Han garrisons on lonely watchtowers in the wilds of the Silk Road, which give us the kind of immediacy we get in Britain from the Vindolanda tablets on Hadrian's Wall. In the Tang dynasty there are letters exchanged between Buddhist monks in China and India. Later we have the correspondence of a mother and daughter caught up in the horrors of the Manchu Conquest; the diary of a child during the Taiping War; memos by loyal Confucian village officials in the declining days of the Last Empire; diaries and letters recounting tales of the Boxer Rebellion, the Japanese invasion and the Cultural Revolution. In all these cases, as the reader will see, I have used as a regular device the 'view from the village' in the belief that the big story can be fruitfully illuminated from the grassroots.

I have often been led, inevitably, by personal interests; hence my sometimes extended sections on individual people, for example on the Buddhist pilgrim Xuanzang, whose journey to India initiated one of history's great cultural exchanges; the poets Du Fu and Li Qingzhao, who lived through the cataclysms that engulfed the Tang and the Song; the 'free and easy wanderer' Xu Xiake, who saw the decline of the Ming; China's most loved novelist, the tragic Cao Xueqin, who lived during the splendours of the eighteenth century; the electrifying feminist revolutionaries Qiu Jin and He Zhen at the end of the empire. Brought to us by superb translators, such as Patricia Ebrey, Ronald Egan, Julian Ward, David Hawkes, Dorothy Ko and many others, their brilliant and powerful words enable us to weave their dramatic life stories into the tale of their times.

I have also used voices from today's families, who tell stories from their family documents and their oral traditions, describing their involvement in great historical events from the fall of the Yuan to the Taiping, the worst war of the nineteenth century, and the Cultural Revolution in the 1960s. The reader will note in my text the contributions, for example, of the Bao family of Tangyue, the Xie clan of Qimen county, the Zhaos of Fujian, the Fengs of Tongcheng; the Zhangs of Henan, Fujian and Hunan; and the Qins of Wuxi. Recorded in their precious woodblock printed family books, and still transmitted in the family memory, their stories enable us to understand something of the deep sense of cultural continuity still felt by so many Chinese people despite the vast changes of their time. In the last chapter, dealing with events since the death of Mao Zedong, I have been able to add material from interviews made in 2018 with participants in the 'Reform and Opening Up' that began forty years ago: former students from universities in Beijing and Shanghai; party officials from industrial Guangzhou; farmers from the 'badlands' of the Anhui countryside – epicentre of the dramatic events of 1978, when the people turned their backs on Maoism and embraced the market. Spending a few months in 2018, in the midst of writing this book, working on the changes of the past forty years, and talking to people who were there, I hope has given my account of that crucial period of change an immediacy that can only come from eyewitnesses.

I have also been keen to set stories in real places and landscapes, in the belief that the setting of history is always crucially important. China as an inhabited landscape has a very deep history; as the poet Du Fu wrote in 757 amid the horrors of the An Lushan Rebellion, 'the state has been destroyed, but the rivers and lakes remain' – that is, the landscape, the country as we might say. Many of China's cities have been inhabited for between two and three millennia and their changes over time can help tell the story. So I have also tried to keep that sense of place running through the narrative. After some consideration I have not compromised on the liberal use of names and place names, using them as one would refer to, say, Somerset or Sheffield in a book about England. I don't think there is any way around that; the non-Chinese reader has to trust the storyteller, and will soon, I hope, get a handle on where Henan is and where the Yellow River flows (and there is a pleasure in that!). The lovely maps, I trust, will help, depicting the expanding and contracting shape of the Middle Land almost like a living organism, which in a real sense it is; maps that show not only the great empires – Tang and Song, Ming and Qing – but the periods of breakdown and fragmentation, which can be just as illuminating. As the great novel *Romance of the Three Kingdoms* begins: 'Everything that is united will fall apart, and everything that is fallen apart will come back together again. So it has always been.'

And, finally, a reminder of where this book has come from. The inspiration for *The Story of China* was a series of films made between 2014 and 2017 for the BBC and PBS, films which have been seen in China and around the world. Of course there are great pitfalls for any foreigner, whether writer or film maker, in setting out to portray another culture, let alone a civilisation as great as China. But the films had a warm response from viewers in China, where the state news agency, Xinhua, said they had 'transcended the barriers of ethnicity and belief and brought something inexplicably powerful and touching to the TV audience', and this emboldened me to look again at my material and to write this longer account. Of course a book is a different creature to a popularisation for a mass TV audience; it allows a much 'thicker' narrative and a deeper engagement with landscapes and stories. But it still has a thrilling story to tell, one of fabulous creativity, intense drama and deep humanity, and I hope some of that filmic verve comes over in these pages. After all, there are few, if any, narratives as compelling, exciting and important in all of human history.

PROLOGUE

BEIJING, DECEMBER 1899

In the freezing December of 1899, two days before the winter solstice, the Guangxu emperor left the Forbidden City through Tiananmen Gate at the head of a huge and colourful procession. In a yellow sedan chair borne on the shoulders of sixteen scarlet-robed servants, he was carried to a curtained state carriage drawn by a caparisoned elephant. The emperor wore a yellow court gown with blue dragons and a blue overgarment; on his head a sable winter cap trimmed with crimson silk and topped by a pearl on a gilt spike. Mounted eunuchs in gorgeous silk robes stood by him, followed by an escort of Leopard Tail Guards, imperial grooms in maroon satin imperial liveries, standard bearers with triangular dragon banners, and horsemen with bows, gilded quivers and yellow saddle cloths. In all, 2,000 princes, grandees, officers, servants, musicians and attendants gathered under a steel-blue, winter twilight sky.

Escorted by this brilliant retinue, the emperor headed to the Temple of Heaven, the great imperial shrine on the southern edge of Beijing, through the central Gate of Qianmen and over the marble Bridge of Heaven, cleared of its booths and beggars, the wide street smoothed with yellow sand to stop the carriage bumping on Beijing's frozen, rutted streets. All was hushed; nothing was allowed to break the silence and profane the rites. Even Beijing's new-fangled Siemens Electric Tramway, laid to the Tartar City's south Yongdingmen Gate only months before, was stopped; its whistles and bells stilled.

Leaving the gate the procession passed into the Chinese City with its warren of alleys, temples and markets; the side streets screened by huge blue curtains. People were commanded to stay indoors, houses on the route were shuttered, and foreigners (of whom there were many now in the city) were warned in the English-language *Peking Gazette* not to approach or look at the ceremony. No one was allowed to see the emperor perform his sacred task, still less gaze on his face.

He stared impassively ahead, his long pale face with prominent cheekbones already marked by an illness, diagnosed by his French physician as chronic nephritis. To those Westerners who had seen him in public, it was a troubled face, burdened by the excruciating pressure of rulership, the fear of failure, and by his anxious desire to benefit the people. His expressed desire was 'to make the Empire wealthy and powerful again', hoping, as he said, 'if possible, to inaugurate a glorious era eclipsing our ancestors'.

If the emperor chose to reflect on it, and this was above all a ceremony for reflection, his dynasty, the Great Qing, had been on the throne since 1644, and during that time eleven Manchu emperors had restored and surpassed the glories of earlier dynasties. At the height of its prestige, in the eighteenth century, China had been the leading power in the world, with the emperor Kangxi's 61-year reign one of the greatest in Chinese history. When his great-great-grandfather, Qianlong, died in 1799, a century before, the Qing empire had unrivalled power and reach, encompassing Mongolia, Tibet, Central Asia, and reaching to the jungles of Vietnam and northern Burma. Along with the Han Chinese, 300 tribes and peoples recognised the Son of Heaven. But population growth, over-taxation, natural disasters and that indefinable loss of group feeling that can undermine even the most powerful states, had gnawed away at the dynasty's sense of self. In 1842, the Great Qing had been defeated by the British in the First Opium War, and was then shaken by the cataclysms of the sixteen-year-long Taiping rebellion, in which 20 million people died. Since the 1840s the European powers had established treaty ports and enclaves all round China's shores and had begun to undermine the old values of the empire. A brief recovery was halted by humiliation in the Sino-Japanese War in 1894, and three years later Germany exacted more concessions, eating away at the already eroded authority of the Qing. The sense of crisis grew. In 1898, progressive officials, journalists and democrats, led by the reformer Kang Youwei, began a 'Self-Strengthening Movement', and the young emperor had sided with them. But the Hundred Days' Reform (11 June–21 September) was quashed by the conservatives, led by the 'Mother Empress Dowager', and from that moment the emperor had become a prisoner of the state.

At that fateful time, the risings began. Through 1898 into 1899, famine struck Shandong. Seething at what they saw as foreign provocation, desperate peasants formed what became known as the 'Militia United in Righteousness' or the 'Society of the Righteous and Harmonious Fists' – the Boxers. In a frightening surge of violence they attacked missionary compounds, sacking churches and slaughtering Chinese Christian converts. Emboldened by a sympathetic Shandong governor, in late 1899 Boxer groups began moving north, spilling out from the countryside across the impoverished and frozen fields of Shandong and the grimy mining towns of Shaanxi to the very outskirts of the imperial city. So now, on the winter solstice, with the countryside to the east and south in flames, the ancient ritual to be performed on the Altar of Heaven carried more than its usual weight; an even more heartfelt hope for auspiciousness. Even now, perhaps, the omens might be reversed by an appeal to the old order of heaven, which had protected the Chinese state through all its triumphs and tragedies.

Since the crushing of the 1898 Reform movement, the Mother Empress Dowager, Cixi, had seized power and placed her nephew, the emperor, under house arrest. Sixty-four years old, capricious, formidably intelligent, still in full powers, the empress, too, was shaken: 'The situation is perilous,' she confided, 'and the foreign powers are glaring at us like tigers eyeing their prey ... all eager to force their way into our country.' But the great ceremonies of state must continue, and none was greater than this: the performance of the rituals on the winter solstice, when the emperor must ask for auspiciousness on behalf of 'All Under Heaven', accepting the peculiar burden of bearing the nation's sins on his shoulders, in his report to the ancestors on the state of the empire.

The procession had almost reached the southern edge of the city where, in the winter dusk, the outer wall gave way to fields, canals and pollarded willows; a brief window onto a troubled land for the troubled man in the golden carriage. The Son of Heaven was twenty-eight years old now. He'd become emperor at six, under the guardianship of the empress Cixi, and then entered long training in the ancient Confucian curriculum. He had spent a deprived childhood under his tutor, the cold and austere Weng, in the cheerless expanses of the Forbidden City, with a series of bullying eunuchs focusing his mind on the responsibilities of rulership. His duty as taught was 'to be upright, magnanimous, honourable and wise', to promote Confucian virtues and to study his ancient predecessors, good and bad, as exemplars. Now older, wiser perhaps, he found himself trapped in a gilded cage by his prisoner-guardians and by his own fearfulness and introversion: 'When we were given the prerogative of governing the empire alone, we were aware of the difficulties of statecraft accentuated by the crisis of our empire; hence our thoughts were filled night and day with the problems that beset us on all sides.'

After ten years training as a scholar he was ostensibly a sage-emperor, but in reality he was an introverted, brooding man, prone to sudden outbursts and unsuited for the task of making the empire wealthy and powerful again. His advisers, Western-minded reformers like Kang Youwei and Liang Qichao, had been condemned to death and fled to Japan, dashing the emperor's hopes of constitutional reform. As the empress dowager said, their slogan had been: 'Protect and defend China, not protect and defend the Qing dynasty ... And they still write treason from abroad making themselves out as Reformers as opposed to the Conservatives, not knowing that our Empire rests on a solid base, the sovereigns of which reverently observing the rules of government laid down by our ancestors, sit on an eternal foundation.' At this time at least, under the vast darkening dome of the winter sky with a pale waning moon rising, the foundation still seemed secure.

That very morning of 20 December, as the emperor prepared himself for the ceremony, the English version of the *Peking Gazette* carried an extraordinary account of the latest imperial edict in its 'Capital Report', reporting bluntly that it was 'what the emperor has been forced to say'. In a rambling memorial he acknowledged the many troubles that faced China and then thanked the empress dowager profusely: 'We ascended the throne when yet an infant and express gratitude to the Empress Dowager for her tender solicitude and untiring energy in trying to inculcate the tenets of orthodoxy into our receptive mind. This we must acknowledge has gone on for nearly thirty years.'

Finally the procession arrived at the shrine in the far south of the city, the precinct laid out between 1406 and 1420 by the Yongle emperor, the builder of the Forbidden City. Nearest the gate stood the Temple of Heaven itself, with its superb triple-roofed circular dome and golden pinnacle 'scintillating like a jewel' in the last light. Moving along the central path they finally reached the scene of the ritual, the Altar of Heaven. Built by the Jiajing emperor in 1530, the altar stood (as it still does) in a huge, square-walled enclosure within a park filled with ancient cypress trees. At the centre was a great three-tier altar, open to the skies, dedicated to the worship of *tian* – heaven. 'Radiant in its isolation, no other sanctuary on earth has a more profound or grandiose conception,' observed one contemporary. 'It is one of the most impressive spectacles the world can offer.'

The altar was, and still is, a huge, three-stepped circle of white marble 450 feet across, set inside a square – the ancient image of heaven and earth in primordial cosmogony; square earth and round heaven. On the west side of the courtyard is the Hall of Fasting or 'Palace of Abstinence'; here the emperor would spend the middle part of the night preparing himself for his sacred duty – 'for the idea', said one participant, 'is that if he is not filled with pious thoughts, the spirits of the unseen will not come to the sacrifice'.

By four in the afternoon the pale winter light fades and the grey line of the western mountains stands out with stark clarity. In the harsh winters of the 1890s it often snowed at the solstice; the cold so intense that, as one of the officiating priests told an English missionary, 'even high wadded boots and the thickest furs fail to keep strong men from chilling to the marrow, and even in some cases going to their graves'.

There in the great courtyard the stage was set for the thrilling drama that was about to unfold; the actors and props ready for this intense moment of imperial theatre. Below the altar, huge horn lanterns were hoisted up on tall red poles and dragon-entwined stands for the musical instruments. Wooden racks had been erected to carry the carillon of bronze bells and the set of sixteen sonorous hanging stones made of dark green nephrite, whose sounds would facilitate communication with the world of the spirits. Imperial banners were lifted amid the first flurries of snow and a shrine representing heaven was placed on the highest platform facing south, lit by hundreds of torches casting their glow over the frosted terraces.

Around the altar the priests and court officers took their places; the officers of the Board of Rites, the officials in charge of the kneeling cushions, and the incense bearers who were to present the meat and wine offerings to the emperor in exquisite lidded altar bowls of moon-white porcelain and gold lacquer inlaid with gold. By the emperor's place on the second tier, the prompter waited ready to supervise the order of service. Below in the courtyard, the great furnace prepared for the bull sacrifice was glowing, with smaller ovens for silk and other offerings. The order of the ritual was to be followed punctiliously according to the *Directory of Worship* and the *Illustrated Guide to Ceremonial Paraphernalia of the Qing Dynasty* published by the Manchus in the middle of the previous century.

Behind the closed door in the Hall of Abstinence, warmed by braziers, the emperor finished his prayers and meditations towards midnight. No image was ever sketched or photograph taken of this most sacred observance, for although the empress dowager allowed cameras into her court and was adept at collaborating in staged images, foreigners were never permitted to see these things. We know what followed, however, from surviving ritual handbooks and the accounts of participants.

At midnight the ceremony commenced. The music began with flutes, a trill of bells and a chime of musical stones. The prompter started the rite, directed by the master of ceremonies, who hoarsely called out into the darkness. The worship of heaven was first; the fires of the sacrificial ovens casting their glow over the pale marble terraces, catching the gold threads on the blue gowns of the mandarins assembled on the three great tiers of the altar.

As the music began, the emperor knelt at the foot of the steps on the second terrace leading up to the upper platform, whose central circular stone symbolised the axis mundi, the supreme yang, the centre of the universe. Facing north, he worshipped the tablet of the Lord of Heaven placed on the northern edge of the top terrace. He paid homage to the Five Founders, the primordial kings of China's deep past, and to the first ancestors.

Below on the paved stones of the courtyard, the red-clad imperial court orchestra played a stately reed concerto as the emperor bowed and prostrated himself. It was, some found, an arduous job; in his later years the emperor's great-great-grandfather Qianlong appointed a prince as his deputy. It was important, he said, that everything should be done perfectly with no errors, and Qianlong eventually bowed out, saying, 'All that ascending and descending, the prostration and bowing, it wears you out: at my age it's a mistake.'

The emperor next laid a sceptre of blue jade in front of the tablets and offered food and a libation to the tablet of heaven. Kneeling three times and kowtowing nine times, he made offerings of twelve pieces of the finest silk. This was followed by the sacrifice of burnt offerings: a bullock 'of one colour free of flaw and blemish', cleaned and prepared for burning in the oven. Two hours before dawn, at the call of the majordomo, the emperor and the officers of court kowtowed and prostrated themselves once more, and a prayer was spoken to the deified forces of nature. Then the music stopped. All was hushed. The emperor spoke:

The emperor of the illustrious dynasty, the Great Qing, has prepared this proclamation to inform the spirits of the sun, the spirits of the moon and planets, the constellations of the zodiac and all the stars in the sky, the clouds of rain, wind and thunder, the spirits of the five great sacred mountains, spirits of the four seas and the four great rivers; the intelligences which have duties assigned to them on earth; all the celestial spirits under heaven, the spirits presiding over the present year ... we ask you on our behalf to exert your spiritual power and display your most earnest endeavours, communicating our poor desire to Shang Di the Lord of Heaven, praying that he graciously grant us acceptance and regard, and be pleased with what we shall reverently present ...

The antecedents of this beautiful and archaic ritual, the incantations, the burnt offerings and the bovine sacrifices, went back more than 3,000 years to the ceremonies described in the oracle bone divinations of the Bronze Age. The whole splendid performance was designed to express the traditional Chinese relationship between humanity, the heavens, the cosmos and the earth. When the sun is at its weakest and the weather most bitter, when life is frozen in cold, it is the time for human beings to pray for renewal, good harvests and fertile soil. Throughout Chinese history such primordial beliefs were bound up with the auspiciousness of the dynasty. This was China's report to the ancestors, the state of the union as it were. And also at the core of the ritual, as shown by the exclusiveness of the ceremony, hidden from the common gaze, was the division between the rulers and the people, reinforcing a hierarchy in which the ruler-sage commanded the lives of the common people and mediated for them the relationship with the powers of the cosmos.

Encoded in the ritual, then, was a bigger truth, which reached the very heart of the beliefs of Chinese civilisation. In his use of certain words – heaven (*tian*), 'the Way' (*dao*), monarch (*wang*) – the emperor embodied Chinese ideas about order and rulership that had developed since the fourth millennium BCE, and which still persisted despite the sudden rapid inroads of Western modernity in his time;

the ancient concept of heaven as both a supreme deity that oversees the realm of human affairs, but also the ultimate cosmic reality, the impartial laws of the universe. 'The Way' contained the supreme principles that kept the cosmos in balance, and which it was the duty of the sage councillors to understand and follow. These currents came together in the person of the monarch, in the supreme political leader, the embodiment of wisdom, without whom society would fall apart. All now manifest in this frail and uncertain person.

The emperor knelt again three times and bowed nine times, then went to the firewood stove. Here all the offerings, ceremonial placards, silk scrolls and paper prayers were respectfully put inside to be burned, so that 'along with our sincere prayers they may ascend in gusts of flame to the distant azure'. While 'the Xiping chapter of music was played', the emperor silently watched as the offering prayers curled and burned away. Finally he turned to depart.

The embers settled, occasional snowflakes spinning as the first hint of dawn appeared on the horizon behind the dark cypress groves. The emperor ascended into his carriage and made his way back to the Forbidden City, where the gate closed behind him, returning him to house arrest. Heaven surely had listened. But in the days that followed, as the Europeans in Beijing's Legation Quarter spent an anxious Christmas, the revolt in the countryside grew. In the last days of 1899 more news came of the killing of Chinese Christian converts and the sacking of churches as Boxer groups moved towards the capital. On 31 December the Boxers in Shandong captured Rev. Sidney Brooks from the Missionary Society of the Church of England, paraded him with a wooden cangue round his neck and then beheaded him. He was the first foreign casualty of the rising.

A few days later, pressured by the conservatives among her ministers, the empress dowager changed her views on the Boxers and issued an edict that was widely believed to support the Boxers and their slogan 'Support the Qing, Exterminate the Foreigners'. Boxer bands on the outskirts of Beijing and Tianjin were now ripping up railway tracks, cutting telegraph wires and burning foreign homes.

Panic-stricken letters from foreign compounds spoke of the country-side 'swarming with hungry, discontented, hopeless idlers'. In the spring, allied naval commanders began attacks on Chinese forts on the coast and urgent messages were sent to Europe for armed reinforce-ments. Finally, on 21 June, the empress dowager declared war on the eight foreign powers and fled the capital. A 55-day siege of the Foreign Legation Quarter by the Boxers followed, providing the Western press with ample copy on European heroism, and what they saw as savage oriental acts of irrational barbarism against the 'civilised world'.

So the new century had arrived, on the Western calendar, and at that moment it appeared China might be dismembered as other parts of the world had been, divided between foreign powers, or broken into regional states as it was in the tenth century during the Five Dynasties, or at the end of the Yuan, the Mongol age. In May 1900 forces of the Eight Powers occupied Beijing and the sacred precinct of the Temple of Heaven became the temporary command base of the alliance, occupied by American troops. The temple and the great altar were desecrated, the buildings defaced, gardens trampled and cypresses felled for firewood. In the stores the ritual paraphernalia were looted and musical instruments broken.

So the solstice ritual of 1899 was the last time the ceremony was performed. In 1914, after the end of the empire, hoping to bolster his claims to the presidency, the warlord Yuan Shikai attempted to gather the pieces and revive it, in a vain attempt to conjure the spirits, even 'aided by a cinematograph', but by then what took place was merely a costume performance. With dramatic suddenness the mean-ing of those archaic actions, words and music had drained away.

From then on the shocks came one after another. The revolution of 1911 saw the end of the empire after more than 2,000 years, and the founding of a republic, which in its brief life knew no peace. With peasant risings, Japanese invasion, civil war and the com-munist revolution, the twentieth century was a time of trauma for China, leading on to the catastrophes of the Great Famine, and the Cultural Revolution in the 1960s. In modern times no nation has gone through so much.

All these events were part of almost two centuries of revolution since the First Opium War, out of which today's China has emerged. But they were only the latest in a series of violent ruptures that had occurred throughout China's history. The story of China since the Bronze Age is the tale of the rise and fall of many dynasties, through which the idea of a single unified state has been tenaciously maintained, underwritten by an ancient model of political power that has persisted right down to our own time. This ideal of a centralised, authoritarian bureaucracy ruled by the sage-emperor and his ministers and scholars is one, as we shall see, that continued in the psyche of Chinese culture even after the end of the empire.

In the aftermath of the communist revolution, the Altar of Heaven, that ethereal symbol of Chinese civilisation, was briefly used as a municipal rubbish dump, finally emptied, or so it seemed, of the last drop of its numinous power. Today it has been restored as a public monument, open to the sky, surrounded again by cypress trees, where on winter dawns visitors may perhaps still touch the thought world of the ancients. Coming just before the end of 2,200 years of the Chinese empire, the ceremony that took place in 1899 seems now to stand as a parable, an event that crystallises the drama of all that had come before and the questions that would follow. What happens when a great ancient civilisation, with the biggest population in the world, breaks down in giant and traumatic spasms of violence? How should it modernise? Indeed, what does modernity mean? There are no parallels in history for such a tremendous and far-reaching cycle of change. And now in the twenty-first century, as we retell this amazing story, we may also ask, what were the driving ideas of the civilisation, and what relation does today's China have to that past? Is that past still working on China's present? And how will that history continue to shape China's future in the crucial decades ahead that will determine the fate of our planet, and in which China will have such a central part to play?

1

ROOTS

The first fact of Chinese history is geography. Today's China is a vast land, stretching from the deserts of Xinjiang and the Tibetan plateau down to the mountains of Burma and Vietnam and up to the wild expanses of Manchuria and the Yalu River on the Korean border. From Kashgar in the far west of Xinjiang to the capital is 4,000 kilometres by road. North China for much of the year is cold and often grey, while the south is subtropical; one grows millet and wheat, the other rice. The oldest rice in the world has been found in the south on sites dating back to 8000 BCE. With a fundamental divide in ecology and climate, these two great zones of China have been distinct in people, language and culture for millennia, and still are.

Yet vast as these outer lands are, the historic heartland of China is much smaller, lying between the Yellow Sea and the uplands, where two great rivers come down from the high plateaux of Qinghai and Tibet. To the north is the Yellow River, where the early dynasties grew up; to the south the Yangtze valley, the great centre of population, wealth and culture in later history. Under the Han dynasty, the Roman period in the West, the Chinese state first extended its rule outward into the oases of Central Asia, and there was another period of direct rule in Xinjiang under the Tang empire in the seventh century CE. For most of its history, however, the heartland of the two rivers was China. It was only in the eighteenth century that the much bigger shape of today's People's Republic was determined by the huge multi-racial empire of the Manchus – the Qing dynasty, which spread its rule over Mongolia, Xinjiang and its Tibetan protectorate.

These days you can journey by train across that heartland, from north to south, in less than a day. Travel has been transformed by one of many amazing recent infrastructure projects, and the high-speed train covers the 2,300 kilometres from Beijing to Guangzhou in a mere eight or nine hours. At a more modest pace, twenty-four hours on the stopping train will suffice to cross the Yellow River plain down to the rich south, to Jiangnan, 'The Land South of the River', about which Chinese poets wrote with such feeling. It is a journey not only in space but in time, allowing us to look through the windows and see the deeper patterns of history, the old contours of landscape and civilisation.

The early civilisations of the Yellow River were not near the sea, but in the central plain, close to where the river emerges from the mountains. In the lower reaches were wide shifting flatlands of streams, rivulets, low-lying swamps and great lakes that were teeming with wildlife in the Bronze Age, regions only drained for farmland in the later centuries BCE. So the first centres of civilisation were inland; the sea did not feature in the imagination of early Chinese culture.

Rising in the Qinghai plateau, the Yellow River makes a huge northern arc up into Mongolia across the arid loess lands of the Ordos, the 'yellow earth' of eroded windblown silt which exerts its climatic influence on China, as does the Sahara on the Mediterranean. Then, taking a sharp turn southward, it issues from the mountains with sometimes uncontrollable power, rushing down to its confluence with the Wei River and into the plains. There it enters the 'Middle Land', where it has changed course on at least thirty occasions in the historical period, bursting its banks in violent floods more than a thousand times, shifting its mouth on the Yellow Sea by as much as 500 kilometres, so that, incredibly, its mouth has been sometimes north, sometimes south of the Shandong peninsula.

So the Yellow River is a constant, unpredictable and often ter-rifying character in the story of China, nothing like the benign life-bearing flood of the Egyptian Nile, whose rising was celebrated each year with unerring predictability on 15 August, or the Tigris in Mesopotamia, whose summer rising was greeted into the twentieth century with liturgies and food offerings, even in Muslim households. The Yellow River, too, was the focus of religious ceremonies; from the Bronze Age sacrifices and rituals were directed to the 'Yellow River Power', the 'High Ancestor River'. But these were performed out of fear, to pacify and assuage, not to welcome; 'Will there be no flood this season?' asked the anxious kings and their diviners in their oracle bone inscriptions. Vestiges of the cult of the River God survive even today, for example at the ancient village of Chayu near Heyang, next door to the Grand Historian Sima Qian's hometown, where each year in late summer, on the fifteenth day of the sixth lunar month, ceremonies are still held for the rising. Banging gongs and beating drums, the men dance in tiger headdresses and the women make huge steamed buns and elaborate food offerings for the river gods, floating twinkling lamps out onto the darkening river marshes at twilight. Today these ceremonies entertain Chinese tourists, but in the past they were a 'prayer for safety', offered up by farmers and boatmen hoping to avert loss of life and livelihood from often devastating floods. The rituals, it is said, have gone on 'since time immemorial, beyond what any elder can remember'.

Some Yellow River floods were so severe that they changed the course of Chinese history. In 1048, as we will see below (pages 204–8), a giant inundation profoundly altered the topography of the northern plain, while the catastrophe of 1099–1102 saw 'corpses of the dead filling the gullies and numbered in their millions', according to an appalled local administrator who saw 'no sign of human habitation for over a thousand *li*'. Seven million died in the 1332 flood, precipitating the disorder that hastened the fall of the Mongol dynasty; there were 2 million dead in 1887, more than that perhaps in 1931. Right up to the mid-twentieth century the Yellow River remained an unpredictable killer, and everywhere it has left the traces of its passing. The countryside around Zhengzhou is scored by a tracery of old courses, and though the main bed today is still in places five kilometres wide, even during the monsoon it now musters perhaps only a tenth of its pre-1940s flow. Indeed, in the past forty years or so the river in its lower course below Zhengzhou has dried up more years than not. At the heart of governance since the Bronze Age, then, has been the management of water, and it still is, although the problem today is no longer its barely controllable excess, but its scarcity.

So China's early civilisations grew up on the banks of the river in the middle plain, where the fear of the breakdown of society due to natural disaster was ever-present, and irrigation could only be managed by a strong state. Not surprisingly, then, the earliest Chinese myths about state origins converge on stories about the control of water, tales that focus on the mythical king Great Yu, 'the tamer of the flood'. As we shall see, these stories were perhaps handed down orally before the age of writing in the late Bronze Age, before about 1200 BCE, proof of the incredible tenacity of cultural memory in China that reaches back to the Longshan culture of the third millennium BCE. Dramatic archaeological discoveries in the twenty-first century suggest that these myths commemorate events that are still written in the landscape and that show how ecology determined the nature of political power. The ability of kings to organise labour, dig dykes to contain the water, supervise irrigation, look to the heavens for the patterns of weather and climate, and seek validation from the great ancestors, was paramount. This would be the pattern down to the end of empire in 1911, and indeed beyond.

THE ROOTS OF CHINESE CIVILISATION

There were many distinctive regional cultures in China in prehistory, but the most important grew up in the wide wheat fields of Henan, the central plain, the *zhongyuan*, of the later Middle Kingdom. The Chinese name for their country, *Zhongguo*, was first recorded by the Western Zhou in about 1000 BCE and denoted this middle land long before it came to signify the whole nation and, in time, even a China-centred world. Indeed, it is possible, as we shall see, that

A gift for you

I've really been enjoying this book so far. I wanted to give you a copy for your birthday since I'm still reading mine, but I wanted to make sure it was good before I sent it. Enjoy! From Jair Gutierrez

amazon Gift Receipt

Scan the QR code to learn more about your gift or start a return.

Story of China

Order ID: 111-3861279-8515419   Ordered on May 6, 2024

the name originally applied to one specific place. China has many cultures and many narratives, but it has one great narrative, and this is the area where Chinese history, as a shaped, structured story, handed down by the early historians, really begins.

An emerging megacity with over 10 million people today, Zhengzhou lies just south of the Yellow River, under a brown haze of pollution. Criss-crossed by huge freeway intersections are serried walls of vacant high-rises bordering the hi-tech development zones, with their electronics and vehicle plants and the world's largest smartphone production site, iPhone City. Beyond lie smoke-shrouded steel works and coal mines. But running alongside the inner expressway is a long stretch of massive, tamped-mud walls recalling the city's role as one of China's Bronze Age capitals during the Shang dynasty three and a half millennia ago. In terms of history and archaeology, Zhengzhou now promotes itself to visitors as the earliest of China's historic capitals, the focus of a local 'Ancient Capital Group' of eight neighbouring historic sites which are part of a wider 'Central Plain City Group', taking the national narrative back ever further into prehistory.

To touch on that deep past we must leave the beaten track. After an hour's drive along suburban freeways, the traveller enters a different world of long straight country roads between yellow fields, with villages every half-mile. Even up to the 1980s these were often earth-walled enclosures with tile-roofed, mud-brick communal buildings housing extended families. Still today among the gleaming silos, water tanks and warehouses of modern agribusiness one can find clan villages where people plant their strips by hand, in the age-old routine, putting sweetcorn seedlings between the rows of wheat so they have two weeks of root growth before the wheat is gathered in, but escape the scythe. At the edge of the fields are old shrines with long bamboo flagpoles; it is a world that still values auspiciousness. For a while yet these worlds coexist, especially in the minds of the older generation of Chinese people, for whom memory still reaches back before the revolution of 1949 and the brief but violent rupture of the Cultural Revolution in the 1960s and early '70s.

Two hundred kilometres south, on the central plain, at the lake of Huaiyang near Zhoukou, the crowds are gathering for a festival. A million people, ordinary farming folk from the Henan country-side, converge on a lakeside temple complex to celebrate the cult of China's primordial deities Fuxi and Nüwa. As the traveller will see everywhere these days, such local cults are part of a dramatic revival of religion in China where three or four hundred million are thought now actively to belong to the main faiths – Buddhism, Christianity and Islam – with many more participating in Daoism and folk cults. This site is one of the oldest; it was already important in the Spring and Autumn period (700 BCE). The main deity, Fuxi, is male, but for well over two millennia he has been associated with a primeval goddess, Nüwa. A thousand years ago, in the Song dynasty, the pair became the focus of an imperial ritual, which was renewed with the current buildings in the Ming dynasty and lasted up to the end of the empire at the beginning of the twentieth century. Here the emperors worshipped not only their own ancestors, but China's mythic kings and culture heroes: the Yellow Emperor, the Five Primordial Rulers, and the 'First Farmer' Shennong, the 'Divine Peasant' who taught the people agriculture and is still revered as a deity in folk religion. Here too is a shrine to Yu the Great, the legendary king who first channelled and controlled the Yellow River floods and laid the foun-dations for the first Chinese state. But behind them all are Fuxi and the goddess Nüwa, the makers of the first humans.

Popular worship here survived among the country people until the 1950s, when the temple fairs were still big events, times for buying and selling, dancing and singing, celebrating the onset of spring in the second lunar month. Then the fairs were stopped and the temples closed down during the Cultural Revolution; the cult statues were destroyed and the buildings vandalised or turned into workshops and factories. In 1980, however, religious practice was permitted again by the Communist Party, and through the '80s under Deng Xiaoping's 'Reform and Opening Up' policy, secular fairs were once more allowed, in part to encourage local economies. At first the revival came with a high degree of grassroots spontaneity, and the fairs became again places of popular performance, song and dance, storytellers, acrobats, jugglers, crafts and music, as well as gambling, games and divination. Soon popular religion revived and the temples were resacralised, their altars and cult statues restored as these big public fairs pushed the bounds of what the government was prepared to allow in the loosening up after Mao's devastating attack on 'old customs, culture, habits and ideas'.

Today this 'Farmers' Festival' is one of the big events in this part of Henan. In the town are grand new pilgrim hotels, their palatial atriums decorated with murals showing the deities and the sacred stories. A reception desk in the marble foyer greets the tour bus visitors with welcome packs, goodie bags containing a map, badges, folders and notes on rituals explaining what the participant needs to do. It is all part of the return of traditional customs to China as the people rediscover their roots. Alongside the lake, the temple complex is a vast rectangle at whose heart are the shrines to Fuxi and Nüwa, the primordial god and goddess. Fuxi is a powerful ancient deity who 'laid down the laws of humanity' in the first days of primitive humankind, when, as a Han dynasty text, the *Bai Hu Tong*, says, 'there was no moral or social order'. He is the first among the legendary primogenitors of 'Huaxia', the culture of the Chinese. The two deities are portrayed on Han dynasty steles with human faces and long snake tails intertwined. Behind the main temple hall is the legendary site of Fuxi's burial mound, where, at festival time, frenzied but good-natured crowds throw armfuls of flaming incense onto a huge fire in his honour.

Because of her influence on marriage, childbirth and auspiciousness, however, the veneration of Nüwa is the most important of the pilgrimage rituals. She has her own shrine where the cult image shows the goddess holding the chunk of stone with which she will repair the broken pillar of heaven. In her other arm she holds a baby, the first human being, which she made by mixing her own blood with the yellow clay of the Yellow River. In front of her temple a sacred stone is touched by women hoping for children – part of a deep stratum of myth to be found the world over.

Some of the women's groups in the crowds have come here from Nüwa's home shrine 20 miles away, where her newly rebuilt temple attracts 100,000 a day at festival time, the country roads blocked by crowds and tractors festooned with ribbons. Her fair takes place in what the pilgrims say was originally a female village. There, hardcore goddess followers can be seen trance dancing as Nüwa takes over the spirits of the worshippers and they sing of 'Heaven and Earth and the goddess and her daughters', speaking in tongues on her behalf, giving voice to her thoughts – 'dancing and weeping, laughing and crying, making wild movements sometimes for hours on end'. In Zhoukou, too, precedence is given to the women's groups wearing colourful costumes specially made by each local association, who dance to drums and flutes. Most revered are the old women in black jackets who sing and dance with a carrying pole over their shoulders from which hang baskets of flowers. According to these women, their dance was taught to their female ancestors by Nüwa herself and only women know and perform it. Another dance, 'The Snake Sheds Its Skin', features sinuous movements in honour of the symbol of Nüwa, like the snake goddesses in archaic Indian religion (perhaps a hint of her primitive origin?).

Their haunting creation songs are uncannily like the cosmogonies of the ancient Greeks:

> Remember when the world began and all was chaos
> No sky, no earth, no human beings.
> Then the god of the sky created sun, moon and stars
> The god of the earth created grain and grass
> And with sky and earth separated the chaos ceased.
> Then the brother and sister appeared,
> Fuxi and Nüwa, the human ancestors ...
> They gave birth to hundreds of children
> That's the origin of us – the hundred surnames –
> The people of the world
> So, people in the world may look different
> But we belong to one family.

Around the lakeside in the streets of the town, pilgrims mill around the food stalls and open-air kitchens which serve meatballs and eggs baked in incense ash – sacred food believed to have healing power. They bring with them little bags of earth from their home villages, which they empty on the tomb mound, and in return take a small amount back to bless their land. At the souvenir stands, glazed pottery images of the deities are on sale along with baskets of little clay dogs and chickens painted black, red and yellow, a reminder of the story that after she had made humans, Nüwa used the leftover clay to make these two animals. And as for the goddess herself, 'she is our mother', the women say: 'we Han people are all the same family, so this is the ancestral place of the Chinese people'.

In China today, history in all its manifestations – whether the 'glorious' new history of the Communist Party's 'China Dream', exemplified in school curricula as 'National Studies', or the deep-rooted tenacious and long-lasting culture of the people of the countryside – is on the way back. Shrines like this are being restored all over China, their rituals reconstituted by the older generation, for whom the thirty years of Maoism has turned out to be, after all, only a small period of time in Chinese history.

At first sight such festivals may appear to be merely tourist-board-sponsored spectacles. In Zhoukou the temple website frames the pilgrimage in terms of 'cultural identity and national cohesion', things the Chinese government is keen to stress these days. And, indeed, special ceremonies for today's elites have been newly invented, recycling practices from pre-1911 ritual handbooks; events for the local bigwigs conducted in private, night-time ceremonies with a prayer leader calling out movements and gestures for rows of devotees draped in yellow silk sashes, each bearing a flickering lamp. But the rituals of the ordinary people are another matter. They have been brought back to life from the memories of the older generation, carried on almost seamlessly as before, as the people fill the void left when religion was belittled and dismantled, first under the Republic, then under Mao, seeking a spiritual dimension to life at a time when materialism has swept all before it. After all the shocks and the wholesale changes of the past eighty years, these stories and myths, 'old ideas, customs and belief', are again part of the culture; not as they were once, it is true, for the break was traumatic, but nonetheless real and still evolving – new, yet still the same. A metaphor perhaps for the whole story of the survival of traditional Chinese culture in the twentieth century.

In prehistory there were many different cultures within what is now China, and many different languages, besides the still fundamental ethnic and linguistic divide between north and south. But beyond those divisions are deeply shared continuities – beliefs about ancestors and patriarchy, civility and conformity, the collective over the individual, family and auspiciousness. These come from the deep past, as far as records allow us to go. So how did China, unlike Europe, develop a sense of being a unitary civilisation, with one 'Han culture', one 'Han language', and one 'Han script', as people say today? And how did it hang on to that, even through extended and traumatic periods of breakdown, when it might have seemed that unity had been lost permanently? This process, which is fundamental to China's identity, it could be said began with the creation of one state out of many smaller states in 221 BCE under the First Emperor, Qin Shi Huangdi, who is famous today the world over for his giant tomb near Xi'an guarded by the Terracotta Army. But before the First Emperor lay a long prehistory. The story is summarised by the Qing dynasty historian and geographer Gu Zuyu (1624–80) in brilliant piece of onomastics, a philological analysis of the antiquity of Chinese place names, *Notes on the Geographical Treatises in the Histories*. Gu saw the process as the product of continuous institutionalised warfare, the conquest and annexation of one state by another, over many centuries. Adding the Western system of dating to his text, the picture of Chinese history he gives is this:

In the beginning, in the time of King Yu, that is at the beginning of the Xia, the first dynasty [c. 1900 BCE], there were ten thousand petty states. When the Shang were founded [c. 1500 BCE] there were three thousand, and when the Shang fell [1045 BCE] there were still over a thousand. But by the end of the Spring and Autumn period [476 BCE] the states of the feudal lords numbered little more than a hundred, of which only fourteen were important. Then under the Qin emperor [221 BCE] there was just one.

Gu, of course, was writing before modern archaeology and new textual discoveries revolutionised our knowledge of China's story. But he gives us a model to help us imagine the way Chinese society developed from the Neolithic down to the First Emperor, with the gradual concentration of wealth, technology, writing and coercive power in the hands of powerful lineages. In the third millennium BCE, modern archaeology has shown that there were indeed thousands of villages and dozens of small 'states' dotted across the river valleys of central China, rectangular walled towns of rammed earth, each with its own ruler. And in that period our narrative begins.

PREHISTORY: THE BEGINNINGS OF CIVILISATION

There have been human beings in China since the first spread of *Homo sapiens* into East Asia. However, the rise of villages and the development of organised societies in China took place comparatively late in the story, later than in the powerhouses of the western ancient world, Egypt and Mesopotamia, which thrived from the fourth millennium BCE with large-scale monumental architecture, writing and cities. On the Indian subcontinent, too, in the Indus Valley, there were huge cities in the third millennium BCE whose origins have been traced back to walled settlements in Balochistan as far back as the seventh millennium BCE. The growth of all three of these early civilisations, with their rapid population rise, was made possible by large-scale irrigation, which made it feasible for the first time in human history for thousands of people to be fed, and for surplus to be created. In West Asia this took place before 3000 BCE – as the Sumerian King List puts it, 'in the time when kingship first came down from Heaven'.

'Civilisation' is a problematical word these days with its conno-
tation of 'high culture' and its suggestion of the superiority of one
form of human society over another. It is worth bearing in mind,
however, the common markers of 'civilisation' as anthropologists
and archaeologists define it. For them it means cities, bronze technology, writing systems, large ceremonial buildings and temples,
monumental art and social hierarchies sanctioned by some form of
law and held together by coercive power wielded by armed elites.

These are common to almost all early civilisations across the
world; only the Inca lacked a writing system. But of course they are
material markers, which hide very different conceptions of the core
values of a culture. In China in prehistory the conditions for settled
growth were more precarious, and population groups were far more
scattered than in West Asia and the Nile Valley, so civilisation, both
in its material and cultural senses, developed later. In the fourth
millennium BCE, in what is known as the Yangshao culture, villages
appeared, often protected by large, ditched enclosures. Then, after
3000 BCE, in the so-called Longshan period, a spurt in population
growth saw an enormous number of small settlements springing up,
many of them in the uplands to the west of the Yellow River plain,
some with tamped earth walls that look like centres of local power.
In around 2300 BCE large walled settlements emerged, most tantalisingly in a spectacular, newly discovered, late Neolithic site currently
being excavated at Shimao on a tributary of the Yellow River on the
edge of the Ordos Desert, the frontier zone both ecologically and
culturally between China and Inner Asia.

Shimao is the largest walled settlement of its time in China. Back
in the 1920s and 1930s the site had become known as the source of
rare, prehistoric carved jades (some of which found their way into
Western collections), but until recently it lay unrecognised, as its
eroded and collapsed stone terraces were mistaken for sections of one
of the early Great Wall systems that run through the region. Lying
on a loess ridge looking out across the Tuwei River, just inside the
border of Inner Mongolia, the site has three enclosures – the outer
one over three miles in circuit with watchtowers and gates, another

with an elaborate barbican. Dominating the site is a pyramidal hill circled by eleven manmade terraces, which from a distance resemble the cultivation terraces of the Cycladic islands of Greece. In the drystone retaining walls across the site, jade plaques were placed between the stones, and skulls from human sacrifices were buried at key points, apparently to imbue the walls with sacral power. The stone facings of the terraces were set with blocks carrying vigorously carved faces or eye symbols, distantly recalling the decorations on stupas in later Tibetan and Nepali culture, which were evidently intended to offer magical protection. On top of the hill, reinforced with stone buttresses, was a platform of rammed earth with traces of wooden pillars that may have supported palatial buildings. Built in around 2300 BCE, this massively built inner citadel over 70 metres high is still known to the local farmers in the Tuwei valley as the 'Royal City', an oral tradition handed down for over 3,500 years after the site was abandoned.

The 'stunning monumentality' of the complex, as its excavator has described it, is without any parallel in early Chinese archaeology. Four hundred hectares in extent, in its time Shimao was politically and economically the most important centre in China, reaching its peak in 2000 BCE when the site was expanded with a second outer wall. By then the excavators conjecture it was the centre of a territory 150 miles wide controlling three or four thousand minor settlements. With evidence of metal and jade working, it was also part of a much wider trade network in raw materials and precious stone. But at its heart is a riddle. Shimao is far away from the Yellow River plain where the traditional narrative of Chinese civilisation says the first dynasties arose. So these dramatic finds, which were only announced in a provisional summary in 2014 and are yet to be fully published, call into question the long-accepted idea that Chinese civilisation spread from the central plains of the Yellow River to other regions. What we have here is another view, and a total surprise; the first state of early China may not have been in the plains, but in what is often seen as the 'barbarian' uplands. Even some of the core cultural symbols that became so important in the Chinese Bronze Age in the plains seem to be found here first – most important of all, the jade sceptre, later the great symbol of royalty, which may even have been invented here in Shimao. But what this unknown state was, and what its relation was to the later 'China', is as yet impossible to say.

THE TAOSI STAR PLATFORM: WATCHING THE HEAVENS

So the emergence of civilisation in China may be the product of an interaction between the Yellow River plain and one or more of half a dozen peripheral prehistoric cultures, among which were the 'barbarians' of the high plateau who created the extraordinary culture of Shimao. Nonetheless, the chain reaction of ideas and political power that gave birth to Chinese civilisation resolved itself in the Yellow River plain after 2000 BCE. The narrative of Chinese history was created there, and to see how that happened, we must go to a second seminal discovery at the village of Taosi in Shanxi. This is perhaps the most important Chinese archaeological discovery of the present century so far. The site lies 100 miles north of the Yellow River in the foothills northwest of Luoyang, just above the plains. Excavated since the 1980s, until the discovery of Shimao it was the largest known walled town in prehistoric China. A very large occupation site on a natural rise with a smaller raised terrace within it, it looks out over a green plain, which is intersected by a tributary of the lower Fen River. The site was occupied from 2500 to 1900 BCE, when it was violently destroyed, so it ended around the time later written traditions say the first Chinese dynasty, the Xia, began. It consisted of a huge rammed clay enclosure with outer walls more than a mile square. By far the biggest town from the third millennium BCE in the Yellow River plains, it is hard to avoid the idea that this was a major centre of royal rule, but without writing it is not yet possible to say who the rulers were.

The sequence of buildings at Taosi covers a span of 500 years, with evidence of metal working and craft production; the excavated cemeteries contained over 10,000 human remains. The archaeologists also detected clear evidence of social stratification, with a separate quarter of elite residences or palaces. In the cemetery there was an area of higher-class graves with painted wooden grave goods in what may have been a royal cemetery; one tomb, though plundered, contained jade grave goods, painted ceramics and lacquered vessels. On the basis of these finds the excavators' impression was that over 90 per cent of the wealth was concentrated in a small elite making up less than 10 per cent of the population.

At the heart of the site was a feature discovered in 2004 that has caused huge excitement among historians and archaeologists. On a raised mound was a circular platform about 50 metres in diameter, with three steps or levels, bearing a distant resemblance to the circular altars open to the sky which were constructed in later times, such as the one in Xi'an from the Sui dynasty (sixth century CE) or the Ming Altar of Heaven described in the prologue. Thirteen pillars arranged around the southeastern arc of the circle provided sight lines converging on an observation point in the centre. Here a red painted wooden pole over 7 feet long was probably used as a gnomon for measuring shadow length on the summer solstice. The archaeologists were able to prove that the platform was used to ascertain the length of the solar year. Tests showed that the architects had created the sight lines through the twelve slits between the thirteen solid pillars to align with set points on the horizon, where the sun would rise on specific dates. This way they could establish the correlation between lunar months and the solar year and create a combined lunar/solar calendar with the extra intercalary thirteenth month inserted in the year cycles.

Taosi is one of the earliest observatories confirmed by archaeology, if not the oldest – the Stonehenge complex in Britain is older and was evidently used for observational purposes at solstice rituals, but this was not its main function. Indeed, it is possible that the Taosi altar was seen as the centrepoint of the very first *zhongguo*: the original 'central state'. After the destruction of Taosi this idea of the axis mundi was transferred by the successors to the region of Luoyang, where the idea continued through history and still survives in folk belief today in the countryside near Dengfeng below the sacred mountain Songshan.

'Ever since people have existed', wrote Sima Qian, the great Han historian, in around 100 BCE, 'rulers have observed the movements of the sun, the moon, the stars and their constellations.' Now these new discoveries show that the ancient Chinese priests of Taosi were sky watchers and astronomers, observing the sunrise and the planets as early as 2100 BCE. Many scholars have argued that significant aspects of early Chinese civilisation, including notions such as the Mandate of Heaven, were linked to astronomical ideas, notably the series of Five Planet conjunctions, which the ancients believed had foretold the rise and fall of the first dynasties, beginning with the Xia in February 1953 BCE. Here perhaps is the first concrete evidence.

Taosi was the centre of a pre-dynastic kingdom where crucial developments were made in observing the heavens, bequeathing to later generations one of the fundamental ideas in Chinese civilisation that lasted until the end of the empire in the twentieth century. Indeed, Taosi is only a few miles from the ancient site of Pingyang, which is often identified with the mythical capital Youtang, home to one of the legendary founders, Emperor Yao. Fragmentary stories in later annals, including the so-called *Records of the Five Kings* in Sima Qian's *Shiji*, tell how Yao 'assigned astronomical officers to observe sunrise and sunset, and the stars and planets and to make a solar and lunar calendar with 366 days and also calculate the leap month'. The coincidence of myth and archaeology is, to say the least, very striking.

Taosi was destroyed around 1900 BCE, its last phase marked by political turmoil. The massive mud walls were breached, the palaces and state altar levelled and the population massacred. Fifty skeletons were found butchered in the palace area, the corpses in the royal cemetery were removed from their graves and a massive hole dug at the top of the observation mound, as if to destroy its numinous power. So it was a thoroughgoing destruction, and archaeologists suspect that it might have been perpetrated by people from Shimao, who had spread their power into the Yellow River plain around

Luoyang, introducing their own ritual and craft traditions and the crucial *zhang* jade sceptre that would become a core symbol of later political religious authority in China.

The date of these events, around 1900 BCE, corresponds to the traditional date given to the beginning of China's first dynasty, which historians called the Xia, but no written sources exist to help us be clearer about these events, and many scholars still doubt even the existence of the Xia. However, here again perhaps myth can help us, for according to later stories the founder of the Xia was one of the most famous of all China's legendary kings, who in a celebrated story came to power after an ecological catastrophe when he channelled the flood and ordered society: King Yu the Great.

ON THE TRACKS OF KING YU

Leaving the old walled city of Kaifeng in Henan by the south gate, a walk of a mile or so takes the visitor past the railway station through a clutter of alleyways, machine-tool factories and car-repair yards into the wooded grounds of a massive, squat, tenth-century brick pagoda, built in the days when Kaifeng was the Song capital and the largest city on earth (see below, page 191–96). Beyond it in a parkland of woods and streams is a place called Yuwang Tai, the platform of King Yu, a terrace covered with pine trees and a cluster of temple buildings. Ruined in the Cultural Revolution, the site has now been restored and hosts a small local spring festival in the gardens. The temple is dedicated to King Yu the Great – 'he who controlled the flood'. Legend says Yu stopped here to organise the local people to build the terrace above the flood plain. From the gardens a stone stairway leads to the secluded courtyards of Yu's temple, built in the Ming dynasty in 1517 after another Yellow River flood. A charming and little-visited place, it is especially atmospheric in pouring rain, as thunder rolls over the inner courtyard where the trees are wound with strips of scarlet cloth left as offerings by the locals. In the shrine in the main hall King Yu sits on a throne, wearing a yellow dragon robe and holding a green jade tablet – a ceremonial gift from the supreme deity to mark his work in making the world fit for human habitation.

The caretaker breaks off from his game of mahjong to tell the legend of the shrine. In the great flood, he begins, the terrace on which we are standing was built up by Yu with two supernatural helpers, 'Yellow Dragon, who used his long powerful tail to create water channels, and Black Turtle, who pushed river mud with his huge flippers to build up the levees'.

> Yu worked with his father for nine years rebuilding the dykes and dams, channelling the Yellow River. Then Yu continued the work for another thirteen years until his hands and feet were covered with callouses. Although he was newly married, on three occasions when he passed his own door, he didn't enter his home. The people were still suffering, so he could not rest. In the end the king was so impressed with Yu's diligence and effort that he passed the throne to him rather than to his own son, knowing that Yu was familiar with every part of the land because of his tireless work to protect the country from the flood. Yu accepted and divided the land into nine provinces, and with the bronze tribute from each of them he cast nine *ding* tripod cauldrons. These were placed in a temple to the west of here at his capital Dengfeng under the sacred mountain Songshan. We call that place the Centre of Heaven and Earth. After Yu died, his son became the first king of the first dynasty.

Of China's many myths about superhuman prehistoric culture heroes, this one above all is concerned with state foundation. Castings of the famous nine *ding* vessels, intended for the ritual preparation of food during feasts for the ancestors and deities, were passed down through the early dynasties. The focus of social relationships in the royal hall, they were symbols of legitimacy and, as later generations believed, the sign that they possessed the Mandate of Heaven.

Until recently the Yu legend was believed to be pure fable, and a late one at that. But new discoveries in texts, bronzes and archaeology suggest the story is very ancient. The recent find of a ninth-century BCE bronze tureen with an inscription describing Yu's deeds is worded in a way so close to the later Yu texts in the *Book of Documents* that it proves that the canonical story was well known at the start of the first millennium BCE. It is no doubt a Bronze Age tale.

The story takes many forms, but in all of them the beginning of ordered society is directly tied to Yu's success in dredging channels and stabilising the communities of the upper plain. The very symbols of governance, 'caps of office and formal dress for governors', are traced back to King Yu. In all versions of the tale, after he surveyed the land and created the nine provinces (the phrase will become traditional nomenclature for China), he set up a tribute system. Each region was called a *zhou* (a territory limited by water borders, usually rivers) and an early tribute list purporting to be his names all nine, with a description of the tribute from each, as well as the waterways or land routes by which the tribute was brought to the king. Though created much later than the Bronze Age, the text gives us a vivid glimpse of the produce of the prehistoric culture of the Yellow River plains: skins, hides, feathers, baskets woven in shell patterns, elephants' tusks, whetstones and cinnabar, flints to make arrowheads and bamboo for making arrows, 'and the big river turtle when it is specially required (and can be found)'.

In ancient times Yu's journey around China was celebrated in ritual dances. Nearly a century ago the French sinologist and anthropologist Marcel Granet suggested the archaic tribute text came from an orally transmitted poetic account celebrating the deeds of Great Yu, which accompanied a ritual dance performed at festival time. The performance conjured up Yu's routes across the country while the movements of the dancers imitated what was called 'the gait of Yu', shuffling and dragging one leg as if paralysed (Yu was said to have been lame). Resembling the shamanic mime dances described in early Daoist texts, these dances were already archaic in the eleventh century BCE when they were first recorded.

So, the story certainly comes from the Bronze Age. Yu's tale was told in a ritual performance, acting out a circuit of the lands of the nine provinces, linked to already existing long-distance pathways of tribute and pilgrimage and crossing its own tracks at Longmen gorge, the place legend said was cut through by Yu to channel the river, and which is still today known as the 'Gateway of Yu'. What was handed down then was not historical fact but a cultural memory of the process of early state formation. Orally transmitted for many centuries before it was eventually put down in writing, it became the mythic backdrop to the tales of the early dynasties, a model for the conception of the 'original' China: China's first great story.

A GREAT FLOOD?

So, on this hypothesis the imagined world of Yu's tracks became the overarching cultural narrative shared by early states in China. Reshaped, re-edited and rewritten in the Iron Age, it became the foundational myth: 'How beautiful are the deeds of Yu! Far reaching are the effects of his bright virtue. If not for Yu we would have become fish!' said one text of the sixth century BCE; 'Great and illustrious were my august ancestors who received Heaven's Mandate and settled on Yu's tracks.' The central plain (*zhongguo*) from then on became the theatre for China's historical story.

But could the memory of a real environmental catastrophe lie behind the myth? Very recently, and totally unexpectedly, archaeology has provided us with evidence of real events that may be distantly mirrored in these later foundation myths. In 2016 a team of geologists, geomorphologists and archaeologists identified a great flood of the Yellow River in the Jishi Gorge in Qinghai province, more than 1,000 miles upriver from the point where it enters the plain. Here the river snakes through immense canyons below towering pinnacles of red rock. In the ravine they discovered traces of an earthquake in prehistory which had caused a huge landslip at a place where the river makes a sharp turn as it winds through the gorges. Here, with still-surviving banks of sediment deposited on the sides of the gorge, scientists were able to map the landslide deposits and to identify an enormous and still visible landslide scar. Blocked to a height of maybe 240 metres, the water built up over six to nine months before it broke through in what they called 'one of the largest freshwater floods of the Holocene'. The flood, it is estimated, was felt more than 2,000 kilometres downstream, breaching natural levees, destroying Neolithic farming communities and causing a major shift in the course of the Yellow River in the plains. A close dating comes from cave dwellings just below the blockage at Lajia village, which was initially destroyed by the earthquake and within a year inundated and sealed by the flood. Carbon samples from the debris and bone samples from the victims yielded a date of 1922 BCE, plus or minus twenty-eight years.

Of course, stories of flood disasters occur in many traditions – in Mesopotamia, the Bible and ancient Greece. The Yu legend need not have been inspired by a real event, but such catastrophes in Chinese history are well documented in later times (for example the 1048 disaster which is looked at in detail below, pages 204–6). If such a flood did indeed happen, it is likely it would have survived in the collective memory over the centuries, and it is fascinating that early texts such as the *Shujing* and *Shiji*, which associate the rise of the first dynasty with King Yu's successful dredging work after the inundation, say it began at a place called Jishi, the name of the gorge where scientists think the historical flood began. While the evidence awaits full publication, what we can say for now is that a series of ecological crises between 2300 and 1900 BCE, including perhaps a great Yellow River flood, appear to coincide with dramatic political changes in the central plain. A social reconfiguration of the earlier Longshan society took place, which led to the emergence of the first dynasty in the Luoyang basin, where elements of these different regional cultures combined to create the first monarchy, the ancestor of all later Chinese dynasties.

THE FIRST DYNASTY: THE XIA

Later written histories say the first king of the first dynasty was the son of Yu, whose name was Qi ('Revelation'), and the date, it is generally thought, roughly corresponds to 1900 BCE in the modern calendar. Astronomical data have suggested a date around 1914 BCE following the Five Planet Conjunction of 1953 BCE, while the archaeology and the Jishi Gorge finds, as we have seen, suggest a date around 1900 BCE. Though all are tentative, these dates converge in a remarkable way. Twenty-nine Xia kings are named by the historian Sima Qian, who, writing in around 100 BCE, had assiduously gathered early written and oral traditions. It has often been claimed that his king list is pure invention, but he has proved remarkably accurate on the names and the order of the later Bronze Age kings of the Shang dynasty, and perhaps he was right here too.

Tradition said the centre of Xia kingdom was in the plain near the confluence of the Yellow River and the Luo River in the original 'Central Land', the region of Luoyang where several later capitals stood in the lee of Songshan, the central peak of China's five sacred mountains. Following Sima's account, archaeologists in the 1950s went looking outside Luoyang in the yellow wheat fields near the village of Erlitou. Here, as so often in China, local traditions clung to the place; the locals said it was 'the oldest place in China', the seat of the fabled Yellow Emperor. The dig here began in 1959, but the main excavations took place through the '70s and '80s and still continue. Two large, walled enclosures were uncovered with bronze casting sites and pillared halls constructed on tamped earth platforms, the ancestors of later architecture right down to the Forbidden City. There was even a triple gateway that seemed to anticipate the later imperial style. The archaeologists also uncovered a tantalisingly rich burial, set apart from the rest, with a sceptre of turquoise in the shape of a dragon – the symbol of Chinese royalty ever since. Some speculated it was the tomb of a dynastic founder, but no evidence has yet emerged from the dig at Erlitou of a unitary state, nor that it was called Xia. And though there were some suggestive marks on the pottery, there is no sign of an organised system of writing. What was clear, though, was that these first 'cities' were not where the wider population lived; they were enclosures of royal power and ritual, containing palaces, storerooms and workshops where craftsmen produced ritual vessels and weapons of war. A fundamental discovery from this and other digs in the plain is that the Bronze Age transformation in China, the emergence of civilisation, was not, as in Iraq and the Near East, due to sudden technological advances or great social change. The development of centralised power was political and based on a deep-rooted cosmology which would last until the twentieth century. All the great ancient civilisations – ancient Egypt, Iraq, India – have origin myths, foundation stories about the time and the place when political society was established for the first time. And perhaps this is the place where it happened in China, in the very centre of the 'Middle Plain' of the 'Middle Land'. It was from this archaic core that the deep ideas about Chinese society and rulership spread out across ever-widening lands over the next 3,500 years.

ANYANG: THE SHANG

In about 1550 BCE the Xia were conquered by a neighbouring people who called themselves the Shang, the second dynasty, and one of the most important in the story of China, who profoundly influenced the shape of the early state over their 500-year existence. The Shang homeland lay further down the Yellow River plain to the east, and the story of their discovery is the most exciting in Chinese archae-ology. It took place under the Republic in the 1920s and '30s as a young modern nation emerged with optimism out of the world's oldest state and sought to discover its own historical roots. In 1899, a Chinese scholar called Wang Yirong, the chancellor of the Imperial Academy in Beijing, a collector of bronzes who was interested in the earliest Chinese writing systems, fell ill with malaria. He received a traditional Chinese remedy from his local pharmacy which included 'dragon bones' to be ground up, boiled in water and drunk to alleviate the fever. To his surprise, he saw that some of the bones, which were from cows and sheep, were inscribed with primitive forms of the writing systems he knew from his ancient bronzes. The signs were predecessors of the classical and modern Chinese script. Over the first two decades of the twentieth century some of these inscriptions were published and subsequently recognised as prehistoric divination texts, earlier than any Chinese writing yet known. By 1915 the bones had been traced back to illicit digs at a little town in the northern part of the Yellow River plain, a site still known to the local people as Yinxu, 'the ruins of Yin' – the name of the last capital of the Shang. The place was Anyang.

In those days Anyang was still a small, walled and moated Ming country town with streets of single-storeyed houses, a brick factory on the outskirts, Buddhist temples and an ancient shrine to the horse god. On the northern edge of the Henan plain, Anyang was, and still is, a place with extremes of climate; thick snowfalls in winter, summers in the high forties and above all violent winds from all points of the compass, especially between April and June, when tremendous storms drive windblown sand into every building. As a 1930s traveller wrote, 'The modern visitor to that region, blinded by a pitiless and incessant hail of dust and sand with all of his exposed skin turned literally to the colour of the soil and fairly blown off his feet, wishes fervently that he possessed a charm effective to quiet that energetic demon.' As the archaeologists would soon discover, those were the conditions in the Bronze Age too.

Excavations began in 1928 and lasted up to the Japanese invasion of 1937. Carried out on a heroic scale with a huge workforce and armed guards, as nationalist armies were fighting regional warlords nearby, it was the most important excavation in Chinese archaeology and one of the most significant in the world. Trenches were dug across the flat wheat fields where the peasants had found the dragon bones and the archaeologists struck sixth-century graves only 2 feet below the plough. Below them the archaeologists dug straight into the Bronze Age. They uncovered royal tombs, huge rectangular pits over 50 feet deep accessed by long ramps. Plundered long ago, the kings' remains were gone, but from the pits the archaeologists recovered ritual bronzes, containers for food and wine for royal liturgies, bronze bells, ceremonial weapons and clan symbols, some showing almost incredible technical skill and imagination on the part of the bronze casters.

The key find was writing, in effect the archives of the Shang kings. Buried in pits were tens of thousands of oracle bones that had been used for divination – clearly a central part of royal life. In a formal ritual, questions were put to the higher powers, their answers divined from the cracks in the bone or shell. Using cow shoulder bones, or turtle shells, hollows were made at the bottom of the shell – the plastron – and a burning hot point inserted to make fine cracks. The shape, number and position of the fissures were then interpreted by the diviners and the questions and answers written on the bones. This very ancient form of divination, called scapulimancy, was once widespread. It was still practised in the twentieth century in the rural Balkans and northern Greece, and has lasted a very long time in China, where divination is used in all walks of life. Forms of tortoise shell divination still exist in rural Taiwan and in the teeming tenements of Hong Kong's New Territories.

The writing on the oracle bones allowed a full chronology to be established for the seventeen generations of the kings of the Shang dynasty, which we now know lasted from around 1553 to 1045 BCE. The traditional king list as reconstructed by the historian Sima Qian turned out to be accurate after all. Writing is only found in the late period, after about 1200 BCE, although it is likely there was a long development of which no trace survives, perhaps because earlier texts were recorded on bamboo, wood or leather. By the end of the period the king was a central figure in the divination ritual. Perhaps he even did the reading himself. The aim of the divination was to know the mind of heaven and the ancestors, and the spirits of nature, in order to understand and control future events. The form has changed today (diviners now more often use the famous *Book of Changes* and cast their horoscopes with dried yarrow stalks), but divination is still a very important part of Chinese life, and fortune-tellers are a respected part of social and business life, performing the function of psychotherapists for people in personal doubt or distress, and even helping with business decisions. And in today's modern Chinese, the two brush strokes depicting a crack still signify the word for divination.

For the Shang rulers, most questions to the gods were about practical things; the royal kin, the king's consorts and sons, campaigns and journeys, rituals, dances and sacrifices. Some ceremonies were grand rituals: sixty head of cattle, for example, were sacrificed in one ceremony for the pre-dynastic ancestors and the Yellow River 'Power Spirit'. Laconic, and at times inscrutable, the oracle bones provide us with a partial account of the daily lives of the Shang elites and even perhaps their voices. They also give us a first picture of Chinese thinking, for the Shang legacy can still be discerned in the later political culture of China, and indeed in folk religion too. In attitudes to life and death today, for example, the core belief that the ancestors live on after death and that they have the power to influence the life of the living is still widespread, as is the conviction that the ancestors need food and sustenance from the living, to keep the world on track. These beliefs came out of prehistory and have survived right down to today, despite the communist revolution's war on 'old thoughts' and 'old customs'. In that sense, then, the Shang are not only China's first political state; they are its first ancestors.

Everywhere at Anyang there was evidence of human sacrifice, piles of skulls and rows of 'beheading sacrifices' often taken from subject peoples and from enemies defeated in war. Such captives the oracle bones describe as being offered to the spirits of the deceased Shang kings: 'Offering to Da Ding, Da Jia, and Zu Yi, 100 cups of wine, 100 Qiang prisoners, 300 cattle, 300 sheep and 300 pigs'. The animals would be eaten, their bones recycled in bone workshops, while the humans were disposed of in earth pits specially prepared in one part of the royal site. More than 2,000 such pits containing human skeletons have been found around the royal tombs at Anyang. But we should not think the early Chinese were uniquely cruel in such practices. Human sacrifice is part of many early civilisations and can be found in pre-dynastic Egypt, the Royal Tombs at Ur, Bronze Age Crete, and of course the Central American and Inca civilisations. Ritual killing of human beings is part of the human story, and the priest and the executioner have gone hand in hand for much of history, indeed long after the formal end of human sacrifice as such. To understand ourselves, to see the ways in which humanity has evolved, it is something we need to see as part of the evolution of civilisation, the long, slow Ascent of Man, if such it is.

THE SOUL OF THE SHANG?

The astonishing finds at Anyang were proof that there was substance in the ancient myths, and that the early Chinese historians had passed down a picture of the Chinese past that had a firm basis in reality. By their very nature the bones do not tell us about the joyful parts of life (love, marriage, festivities, etc., on which see below, page 63), and perhaps our perception of the Shang is misleadingly weighted by their concerns. But it is hard to avoid the perception that the oracle bones are replete with what we might call a cultural anxiety; wary of threats both external and internal, excessive rain or drought, floods of the 'Great River Spirit' and blasts of the 'Great Wind', infestations of locusts and raids by hostile peoples. For all the magnificence of the royal tombs, and the enormous size of the last capital, which spread over 24 square kilometres along the Huan River, there is a lingering sense that even the city itself might be temporary. It was a feeling that their world was always in danger of disorder, and that auspiciousness had to be sought continually and earnestly in a world where the unseen was palpable, forever threatening to burst over the frontier of dreams into the land of the living. And so the questions are constant: 'Will the great waters rise? Will there be disasters? Is Di himself afflicting this settlement? Is it of this settlement's auspiciousness that Di does not approve?'

To answer these incessant enquiries, the king's own role as interpreter for the spirits was the key to his political and religious authority. He made fruitful harvests and victories in battle possible through the sacrifices he offered and the rituals and divinations he performed. The oracle bones, then, depict a kind of ritual conversation between the living and the ancestors. Just as the king's generals and officers made reports to him, so the king made reports to his dead ancestors, who acted as his intermediaries with Di, the Lord of Heaven. So the king was not only the one who governed, led the army, commanded the workforce and gave land, bronzes, slaves and treasure to his kinsmen and nobles; he was the key link to the past kings of his lineage. On him auspiciousness and order depended, through his ability to ensure good harvests, bring rain or stave off disaster. And here perhaps is the germ of the ruler's future role in Chinese history as the sage-monarch, the ultimate repository of power and wisdom. As we shall see, this way of thinking was never forsaken in Chinese civilisation, even into the twentieth century.

So, with the Shang, some of the main themes that will shape Chinese history until today begin to emerge. The Shang polity came out of the Neolithic, like its neighbours in other parts of China. But it created the model for later Chinese kingship: the central role of the king as mediator between heaven and earth; the crucial importance of lineage and ancestors; the control of shamanism and divination as a source of authority; and the monopoly of bronze technology, and of writing. In China, from the beginning civilisation was shaped by political necessity, the rituals of power and the interpretation by the elite of the will of heaven.

2

THE GREAT WAR OF THE SHANG

The Shang state lasted from the 1550s to 1045 BCE, the contemporary of Bronze Age Greece, the world of Mycenae and Troy. The first ancestors of the later Chinese state, they bequeathed central aspects of the culture: rulership, ritual, divination and, crucially, writing, the script itself, of which today's script is a direct descendant. This astounding continuity is paralleled in patterns of thought which were to prove incredibly durable in the long struggle in Chinese civilisation between the threat of chaos and the need for order. The Shang state fell in 1045 BCE in the first great war of Chinese history, which recently has been illuminated by remarkable discoveries in texts, excavations and the new science of astro-archaeology, which has established an absolute chronology from computer-derived maps of the movements of the heavens. The Shang, as we shall see, cast a long shadow, and their end was a never-to-be-forgotten drama.

Like all early historic states, the Shang were sustained only by tribute from their subject allies and from warfare against their neighbours. In 1046 BCE, a vassal kingdom, the Zhou, rose against them. As the story was told later by the victors, the last king of the Shang, Di Xin, sank into megalomania and vicious cruelty, to the point where his own ministers and family members opposed him. Di Xin was even abandoned by his brother Weizi, who, as we shall see, was a key figure in the transmission of the traditions of the Shang to later times.

The Zhou kingdom lay to the west in the Wei River valley and had long been under Shang hegemony. Their ruler was the famous King Wen, whose mother was a Shang princess, commemorated for her virtue in the *Book of Songs*. The king's wife, too, was of the Shang. So the two kingdoms had very close ties, in clan, religion and ritual practice. Finds of oracle bones in the Zhou capital Qiyi, today's Zhouyuan, show they worshipped the Shang ancestors along with their own clan. So the rebellion was not only between one state and another; it was a war between a subject king and his overlord.

Zhou tradition said that the decision to rise up was inspired by a *tian ming*, literally a heavenly sign which came to be interpreted as the Mandate of Heaven, which all Chinese rulers must possess. Recent discoveries have pinned down this celestial event with thrilling precision. In late May 1059 BCE, a remarkable astronomical phenomenon was observed by the Zhou seers: a five-planet conjunction, 'in less than the width of an outstretched hand', appeared in the northwestern sky. Visible from the Zhou capital in the foothills of the Qi mountains, this close conjunction of the five 'unblinking' planets occurs once every 516 years. One which can now be dated to February 1953 BCE was believed to have foretold the beginning of the Xia dynasty, and the next, in December 1576 BCE, marked the rise of the Shang. The next occurrence in 1059 BCE was, therefore, loaded with portent, when the five planets appeared on the horizon, with Mercury, Venus and Mars 'like a triple star' along with Saturn and Jupiter. This persisted for several days, one of the densest gatherings of planets in human history. Other omens came with it. A later chronicle known as the *Bamboo Annals* records that, in the reign of Di Xin, the last king of Shang, 'the Five Planets gathered in the constellation known as the Chamber and a great red bird alighted on the Zhou altar to the Earth'. A parallel account by the fourth-century BCE writer Mozi, using an ancient source, is explicit: 'A crimson bird clasping a jade sceptre in its beak descended on the Zhou altar to the Earth at Mount Qi saying, "Heaven commands King Wen of Zhou to attack Shang and take possession of the state."'

The omen was understood by the Zhou diviners as a sign that

Heaven's approval had left the Shang and gone to the Zhou. King Wen then declared that the kingship of Zhou had separated from the Shang regime and prepared to challenge his overlord. He inaugurated a new calendar marking 'the first year of the receipt of Heaven's Mandate'. He also expanded his power, subdued more lands and tribes to the east, laid out a new capital at Zongzhou in the Wei River plain and prepared his army for the task ahead. Still, the final confrontation did not happen while Wen was alive. He died in 1049 BCE, while the Shang were embroiled in campaigns in the northeast. Finally, after an abortive campaign was called off in 1048 BCE due to torrential storms and inauspicious omens, his son, King Wu, 'the martial king', launched the attack in winter 1046 BCE.

The story of what followed is the first great historical narrative of Chinese history. It comes from an account of the Zhou conquest, known as the *Yi Zhou Shu*, the 'Lost Book of Zhou'. In ancient times this text was excluded from the canon, but it has recently been reclaimed as one of the key sources of Chinese history. Long dismissed as a later reconstruction, its rejection began with early historians such as Confucius' follower Mencius, whose idealised view of Zhou history could not accept the gruesome evidence of cruelty and mass human sacrifice that attended the victory. This did not fit with the later portrait of the noble and pacifist Zhou king, the exemplar of China's monarchical culture. Mencius in particular thought a moral imperative governed the Zhou conquest, which had laid a template for the future:

> If we believe everything in the *Book of History* it would have been better for it not to have existed at all. In the text I can only accept two or three sections. A benevolent man that has no match in the empire! How could it be that he was swimming in blood [literally 'the flow of blood floated pestles'] when the most benevolent waged war against the most cruel?

However, it is now clear from linguistic analysis that the core of the 'Lost Book' was specifically composed at the behest of King

Wu immediately after the war. The bloody story of the Zhou conquest can now be told, with the help of this and other modern discoveries, including astronomical data, which have now given us an exact chronology. (The translations that follow are by Edward Shaughnessy.)

When the time for a final confrontation with the Shang tyrant had arrived, fortified by new divinations, the Zhou army departed on foot from their capital on 16 November 1046 BCE, marching under their commander-in-chief, General Wang. The king left on horseback, or by chariot, on 15 December, 'the Day of Expanding Brightness', and after two weeks' travel caught up with the army on 28 December. On 9 January 1045 BCE, the army crossed the Yellow River at Mengjin. From there, a six-day march brought them to Muye on 14 January, in today's Xinxiang county, north of Zhengzhou. There they deployed, ready to face the Shang army the next day in the first great battle of Chinese history.

The Zhou and their allies were outnumbered, but the loyalty of the Shang army wavered and their enslaved or press-ganged forces gave way under the massed chariot attacks of the Zhou. The pursuit went on into darkness, and by sunrise the Shang capital was in their grasp. The Shang king retreated to his palace, where he donned his jade suit and, according to the 'Lost Book', took his most precious treasure, the 'Heaven's Wisdom' jade, along with other jewels and 'wrapped them thickly round his body'. Then he immolated himself and his concubines, setting the palace on fire. 'On the fifth day', said the 'Lost Book', 'when the fire had died down, King Wu then sent a thousand men to seek them in the debris, where the "Heaven's Wisdom" jade was found to have been unburnt in the fire.' He then shared out all of the pieces of the 'Heaven's Wisdom' jade. In all, he had captured thousands of pieces of precious Shang jade, the ancestral treasures of the dynasty.

The Battle of Muye was fought on 15 January 1045 BCE. After four days mopping up resistance around the capital, King Wu declared 'the establishment of government'. Then he held victory ceremonies at an important temple near the Shang capital, rewarding his loyal leaders with captured treasures and metals, out of which they would cast bronzes for the use of their own clans at commemoration feasts. Amazingly, one of these was discovered near Xi'an in 1976, a sacrificial vessel known as the Li Gui. One of China's greatest treasures, it was made of bronze melted down from Shang weapons after the victory, and its inscription mentions the Zhou victory. It records the astrological conjunction with spine-tingling immediacy:

> King Wu attacked Shang. On the morning of *jiazi* day, planet Jupiter was rising and we defeated them by dusk. By the next dawn we had occupied Shang. On the *xinwei* day the king was at Jian encampment and rewarded Marshal Li with metal and Li herewith makes for Lord Zhan his esteemed ancestor this treasured sacrificial vessel.

The surviving Shang leaders were then hunted down by the Zhou generals with attacks on outlying regions and subsidiary capitals. Each returned with captives and tallies of 'ears taken', the left ear cut off the dead. In early March a great triumphal ceremony took place with the presentation of the captured nine tripods from the Shang royal temple, denoting the nine provinces of China. These were the symbolic vessels said to have been handed down from the time of Yu the Great: 'At this time the king reverently displayed the jade tablet and made an announcement to the heavenly ancestor Shangdi.' The king also held a series of great royal hunts over several days, a custom after military victories. Even if the figures are exaggerated, it was a killing spree: 'King Wu hunted and netted 22 tigers, 2 panthers, 5,235 stags, 12 rhinoceros, 721 yaks, 151 bears, 118 yellow bears, 353 boar, 18 badgers, 16 king-stags, 50 musk deer, 30 tailed deer and 3,508 deer.'

King Wu's account also summarises the war of conquest by 'countries', meaning anything from small kingdoms to tribal groupings: 'King Wu had pursued and campaigned in the four directions. In all, there were 99 recalcitrant countries, 177,779 ears were taken and registered and 310,230 men captured. In all, there were 652 countries that willingly submitted.' These figures approach, but perhaps do not quite reach, the incredible.

Finally, fifteen weeks after the battle, with the Shang lands now pacified, the king returned to Zhou with his captives from the Shang royal family, their ministers and generals. On 30 April came the terrible denouement, a carefully prepared and dramatically orchestrated ritual on a grand scale, accompanied by solemn ritual music, bells, flautists and sung refrains. King Wu arrived in the morning and performed a burnt-offering sacrifice in the Zhou temple. Then followed a grim and sombre scene, the Zhou ancestral temple prepared for human sacrifice, smoking with incense, banners hung outside the city gates. In what follows, the reference to a written document is especially notable. Later historians and philosophers brought up on the virtue of Zhou refused to believe this could be genuine:

King Wu descended from his chariot and caused scribe Yi to intone the document in the declaration to Heaven. King Wu then deposed the hundred evil ministers of the Shang King. He beheaded and offered [as sacrifice] their little prince and the great master of the cauldron [the chief ritualist] and beheaded the leaders of their forty families and the masters of the cauldron. The commander of the foot soldiers and the commander of horses first attended to their declaration of the sacrifice outside the city, then the southern gate was flanked with the captives to be sacrificed, all of whom were given sashes and clothes to wear. The ears taken were first brought in. King Wu attended the sacrifice and the Great Master shouldered the white banner from which the head of the Shang king was suspended, and the red pennant with the heads of his two chief consorts. Then with the first scalps he entered and performed the burnt-offering sacrifice in the Zhou temple.

Six days later, in the Zhou temple, King Wu offered as a sacrifice the ears taken in the war: 'Reverently I the small one slaughter six oxen and slaughter two sheep. I have brought peace to the glorious ancestors. The many states are now at an end.'

Even in this abbreviated form there are few more dramatic historical narratives. Later Confucians rejected the 'Lost Book of Zhou', believing the founding fathers of the Zhou were too virtuous to engage in such violence. Still, the text leaves no doubt that they practised human sacrifice on the scale, and with all the formal liturgical precision, of the Shang. In time they would be transformed by their own archivists, and then by Confucian philosophers, into the virtuous founders, exemplars for every dynasty that followed. It was a watershed moment in Chinese history, not so much for how it was seen at the time, but for how this great turning point was construed and interpreted over the next three millennia. As King Wu had declared, 'the rule was established'. From now on we are dealing with the history of China.

PASSING ON THE LEGACY: THE 'PLACE OF THE ANCESTORS'

The overthrow of the Shang was a turning point in Chinese history to which all later dynasties would look back. The key to this was the Mandate of Heaven: the idea of the succession of dynasties, each of which was believed to have received divinely ordained authority, which in due time was passed on. The cyclical pattern of the narrative of China's history was set.

First, the Zhou had to make provision for the Shang ancestors. After their defeat, the surviving members of the Shang royal lineage, led by Weizi, the good brother of the last king, were permitted to stay on the site of their ancestral cult centre, the place of their dynastic origin. They were to be loyal to the new dynasty, but still perform the rituals for their ancient kings. That site still survives, and so, incredibly in the twenty-first century, do traces of the cult of the Shang ancestors.

One hundred and forty miles down the Yellow River plain from Zhengzhou, on an old track of the Yellow River, lies the city of Shangqiu in Henan, a crossroads on the old land route, now the G35, which goes from the North China Plain down to the Yangtze and on into south China. Shangqiu stands at the intersection of the east–west prehistoric route from Luoyang down the Yellow River to the vast low-lying tracts of marshes and lakes, from which in the early Bronze Age the Shang had emerged from the Neolithic cultures of the eastern seaboard.

Today, outside the ramshackle entrance to the old town, bustling rickshaws weave among the crowds around the wheeled food stalls under their bright sun umbrellas. Packed collective taxis ferry commuters back and forth and country buses blare their horns as they swerve through the cavernous entrance arch into the town bus stand. On the outside of the old bus station, above signs for cheap hostels and restaurants, are two huge Chinese characters. The first is derived from the sign for an offering table; the second is a pictograph of a mound. Together they spell a name to tantalise the seeker after China's early history: Shangqiu – 'the Ruins of Shang'.

The word *shang* is still commonplace in ordinary speech, its meanings embracing a wide sematic cluster centring on words for commerce, trade, merchants and business – *shang chang*, for example, is a shopping mall. Legend indeed told how, after their defeat, the royal clan were thenceforth allowed to be merchants, but the character 'shang' carries its prehistory in the makeup of its brush strokes. Originally it appears to have designated the act of performing a ritual to the ancestors. As far back as the oracle bones, the character signifies an ancestral image set on a table, with a mouth and a tongue to represent communication. So the name came from the place where the ancestors were worshipped. Later, the character's meaning extended to refer to the Shang ancestral shrine in the sacred Mulberry Grove, then to the city where the ancestral temple was located, and finally to the dynasty or the group of rulers who originated there. The original meaning in the early Bronze Age, then, was, perhaps, 'the place where we communicate with the ancestors'.

Until recently, Shangqiu was a small, down-at-heel, out-of-the-way country town. However, in the past twenty years or so, it has been transformed by gleaming new rail junctions at the intersection of the high-speed link between Beijing and the south and the revamped east–west Longhai railway. Now a rail crossroads of China, there are well over a million people in the shiny new urban zone. Beyond the high-rise apartment blocks, the new hotels and car showrooms, is a Ming dynasty walled town built in 1513, after one of many destructive floods of the Yellow River, which in these parts have overlaid the physical remains of several millennia of history. Below the Ming walls, a wide moat that once circled the whole town opens to a lake, on whose banks the townsfolk take the air on muggy summer evenings in the plain.

Though Anyang was the administrative and ritual centre for the last 200 years of the Shang dynasty, it was one of several capitals. Over the 500 years of the dynasty, the Shang had moved capital several times in response to strategic necessities, wars, floods, or internecine struggles between branches of the royal kin; but also, perhaps, driven by fears expressed in the oracle bones of the withdrawal of auspiciousness. Over that time, though, they retained the memory of their ancestral home, 'Great City Shang', *Da Yi Shang*, which remained a special place in their ritual universe. From time to time they returned there for what the oracle bones call 'telling' rituals to the pre-dynastic founders. Since the decipherment of the oracle bones in the 1930s, there has been a big debate about the site of 'Great City Shang'. Evidence from the campaigns recorded on the oracle bones seemed to point towards Shangqiu, but searches there in the 1930s found no clue and an expedition in the 1970s also drew a blank. There things stood until recently, when discoveries both above and below ground dramatically changed the picture.

Like so many of China's ancient cities today, Shangqiu's old city is being modernised. The cavernous ramshackle market with its stone lions and canopied alleys of cheap clothes and the decaying lanes of low-rise Qing dynasty houses are soon to be 'upgraded', to the regret of many locals, who still prefer its homely, old-world charm. To the traveller wandering its streets and alleys, nothing visible above ground today appears earlier than the Ming town, built after its predecessor was destroyed by flood. In the northwest corner inside the walls, however, stood a small Ming temple which was demolished in the 1950s. Now only a stone stele survives recording its rebuilding in 1527, and again by the Kangxi emperor in 1681, along with the history of its Yuan and Song predecessors, going back a thousand years. The inscription tells us that the temple was dedicated to none other than Weizi, the virtuous brother of the last king of the Shang, who went into exile to resist the wicked and dissolute tyrant. After the fall of the Shang in 1045 BCE, it had been Weizi who was charged by the victorious Zhou with continuing the rituals to the ancestors in their origin place.

A short bus journey south into the town's dusty hinterland is Weizi's tomb, a grand complex recently restored with three temples and a memorial hall with steles from the Ming dynasty. The inscriptions record that the complex was rebuilt under the great Tang emperor Xuanzong in the eighth century. It reached its present form in 1612, according to a battered stele in front of the tomb mound. Though destroyed in the Cultural Revolution, it was rebuilt in 2002 by a wealthy and famous overseas Chinese family, the Soongs, who claim descent from Weizi and now come back on the Qingming Festival, Tomb-Sweeping Day to perform rituals at their ancestors' grave.

A little further south, down a small country road, is another amazing survival. A cluster of pillared halls and shrines lie at the end of a Ming spirit way, a sacred path. Around them is a grove of nearly 200 cypress trees, which were planted in the Tang dynasty, according to the custodian, who can recite the ancient names of the most venerable ones. Mercifully unmodernised, unprepossessing local shrines like this can be seen all over the deep countryside in China these days, open for worship once more. A seventeenth-century restoration of a Tang shrine, this one is still an auspicious place, where the local people hang the trees with offerings and leave clumps of incense smoking at the tangled roots. This is the tomb of Yi Yin, a former slave who legend says became a royal cook and then chief minister of the first king of the Shang, back in the sixteenth century BCE. He sits in the main hall, a painted wooden statue in a dusty imperial blue robe and scarlet cloak. Yi

Yin is a man celebrated in later myths for his sense of justice and equity, qualities especially prized and remembered down the ages in China. These stories are still well known among the older generation here. At the shrine to Yi Yin's wife, the custodian and his neighbours tell her story:

> She was a virtuous woman, her spirit of helping her husband and running things with her good advice is still admired by the people. She was known as 'Auntie Xian' and she had been a servant. She found a baby in the hollow trunk of a mulberry tree when she went to feed the silkworms and she took him home and raised him as his foster mother. He became the first Shang king. So all of their achievements would be impossible without her: that's why there's a memorial hall here for her too.

Again, this is a reinvention of tradition, like so much in China today, as they retie the broken thread of their historical narrative. Nevertheless, it could not better illustrate the fact that in China the physical fabric of buildings is of less importance than the sense of place. They may be rebuilt many times, but the key thing is to hand on the stories.

Astonishingly, then, although invisible to the casual visitor, the Shang ancestors and their stories are still commemorated over 3,000 years after the dynasty's fall. These are not, of course, real monuments from the Bronze Age, for pre-Han sites like 'Great City Shang' are buried deep under the river silt. But still, these sites go back at least 2,000 years, and the commemoration has been maintained by each dynasty, and by the locals themselves. It is, let us say, as if the hero cults of Nestor and Achilles still drew pilgrims in today's Greece.

The story of Shangqiu does not end there. One of the key royal cults of the Shang age still survives on the south side of old Shangqiu. Standing on a huge artificial mound is a temple built at the end of the thirteenth century in the Yuan dynasty, the replacement of earlier shrines. It is called Ebo Tai: the temple of Ebo, an archaic culture hero who is both the Chinese Noah and the Chinese Prometheus. Since the '80s the site has gathered huge crowds at festival times, and the complex below the hill has been modernised with a car park and an open plaza, with outbuildings and stalls selling incense, garlands and ceramic statues of the deities. The mound itself was here in the Han dynasty and may be much more ancient. It is 30 metres high today, but with aggregation of the plain clearly it was once much higher. Inside the temple, the cult statues, restored after the Cultural Revolution, personify several ancient myths surrounding Ebo, who survived the Great Flood and gave fire to humanity. His cult is specifically linked to Antares, the Fire Star, the tutelary star of the Shang. It is tied to an ancient myth of the origins of the dynasty, who, when they established themselves here, took over the duties of Ebo. These legends are only recorded in the Han dynasty, but archaeology and texts again suggest a very archaic connection with the myths of the prehistoric world.

So, was this mound once part of 'Great City Shang', the original cult place by the sacred mulberry grove? Despite these tantalising stories, nothing of the Bronze Age has yet been found here. Over the millennia, the flood sediments of the Yellow River have sealed its many earlier histories deep below ground. However, recently, a new attempt was made using resistivity and magnetometry, which revealed the outline of the walls of a late Bronze Age city of far greater extent than the Ming settlement, nearly 20 feet below the surface. A rhomboid of rammed earth walls, 2,900 metres by 3,600 metres on its longer sides. Test cores found this buried wall was still some 6 metres high. With several construction phases it was not securely datable, but certainly existed in the eleventh century BCE. Without a massive excavation it will not be possible to establish whether this lay on the lines of an earlier city still. What is certain, though, is that in no other place in China is such a concentrated group of cults and traditions connected with the Shang. The city lasted some 700 years and is described by many later sources, with its palaces and markets, and its temple with the sacred mulberry tree, the axis mundi of the Shang world.

PRAYING FOR THE ANCESTORS

So, with a combination of local legends, inscriptions, texts and archaeology, Shangqiu is a test case for how traditions have been passed down in China. How the scholars and seers and ritualists of previous dynasties transmit their ideas of kingship and history to their descendants, underwriting their legitimacy with the royal ancestors. After their fall, the surviving Shang clan were coopted by the Zhou into their picture of the way Chinese kingship was understood and handed down. Indeed, the recent discovery not far from Shangqiu, of a remarkable and, so far, unique tomb from the period following the fall of the Shang, shows us the transition in the material culture. Here, a man called Changzikou, a former Shang official in the Zhou state, was buried in a large pit 50 metres long and 8 metres deep, with a mix of new Zhou and old Shang practices. Four hundred artefacts were found, including bronzes, jade, ceramics, shells, Shang bone panpipes, wine vessels and musical bells. The sixty-year-old had served in the Zhou court after the conquest, but was buried with ancestral Shang rites, including human sacrifice – thirteen people and a dog, which was buried under the coffin with one of the humans. Changzikou, perhaps, was the last of the Shang lords.

The ideals that had shaped the Shang state for the 500 years of its existence, and come into the full light of history in the oracle bones, would continue to run under the surface of later Chinese history. Many later ideas of Chinese governance were shaped by their Zhou conquerors, but the foundations were laid by the Shang, whose legacy in customs, rituals and beliefs would persist in so many areas. Indeed, as we shall see, Confucius himself, the greatest cultural influence in Chinese civilisation, will claim descent from Weizi's clan at Shangqiu. As he said five centuries later: 'The Zhou based themselves on the rites of Yin [Shang], what they discarded and what they added can be known.'

3

THE MANDATE OF HEAVEN

In the eight centuries between the fall of the Shang and the rise of the First Emperor, there were many important developments in Chinese civilisation as a patchwork of kingdoms coalesced towards a single state. The period saw the emergence of a distinctive political philosophy based on older historical traditions and rituals of rulership. At its heart was one great and enduring idea, that of the king who ruled by virtue, the sage-monarch mandated by heaven, to whom all allegiance was due. The key figure in shaping this ideology, the most important person in Chinese civilisation, was Confucius. Seeing himself simply as a codifier, a transmitter of much older traditions, Confucius had an incalculable influence on Chinese culture, and still does today, even though China ceased to be a Confucian state in 1911. This move towards a unified state came out of a period of incessant internecine fighting, which has been illuminated in the past few years by fascinating archaeological and textual discoveries.

In 2003, shoppers in the middle of the bustling city of Luoyang were able to watch an extraordinary excavation unfold. During digging for a new underground station, a huge pit was uncovered containing eighteen chariots with ornamented chariot boxes and spoked wheels, the horses still harnessed to their yokes and draft poles. Pride of place was a six-horse span pulling a magnificent imperial chariot. The pit was one of seventeen that have been excavated in recent years in the 'eastern capital' of the Zhou, outliers of the tombs of the kings of the Eastern Zhou, the rulers of the central plain from the eighth century BCE until their destruction by the Qin in 256 BCE. The chariots were buried in what the Chinese call the Spring and Autumn period (c. 700–600 BCE), and they belong to the Iron Age warrior culture that flourished here at the time Homer composed the *Iliad*. During that period there were still over 100 states, large and small, often in conflict with each other. Like Homer's Agamemnon, their warrior kings relied on the petty states and tribes under their overlordship to provide chariots and infantry for the army to fight their enemies for land, tribute, treasure, slaves and women. They mustered armies of many thousands of men and a big kingdom could deploy 7,000 chariots in battle. In the Luoyang pit, then, is graphic evidence of a hierarchical warrior aristocracy, manifested in death as in life. This incredible expenditure of valuable resources reflects early Chinese social structure, ritual order, and military and economic power.

Horses were introduced into the Bronze Age cultures of Eurasia at the start of the second millennium BCE, from the Central Asian steppe. Chariot warfare rapidly spread west, all the way to Ireland, Mycenaean Greece, Pharaonic Egypt and Vedic India. In China, the use of chariots in war began under the Shang, when they simply carried kings and nobles into battle. In the Spring and Autumn period, chariot warfare came into its own, when thousands of chariots were deployed in big battles. This continued until they were made obsolete by new forms of warfare, including the mass-produced mechanical crossbow in the Qin period. The chariots themselves were very high-status pieces of equipment, carefully itemised in Zhou kings' dedication inscriptions to their warriors:

I confer on you a chariot with bronze fittings, trappings of soft leather painted red for the horses, a canopy of tiger skin with red lining, bronze bells for the yoke bar, gilded bow holder and fish scale quiver, a team of four horses with their bits and bridles and bronze ornaments, gilt girth straps and a scarlet banner with two bells.

There we have the Chinese equivalent of Hector and Achilles in the Trojan War. In Zhou heroic poetry, chariot warfare is as lovingly described as in the hymns of the Rig Veda, the Mahabharata or in Homer. During a mass chariot attack, with the noise of spinning chariot wheels 'rumbling like a roll of thunder' on the plain, we have flashes of a Chinese *Iliad*:

> The hero Fang-shu came
> Driving his four dappled greys so obedient,
> In his big chariot painted red,
> With his awning of lacquered bamboo
> And his fish scale quiver;
> Breast guards and metal-headed reins ...
> Banners shining bright
> Eight bells jingling,
> Showing off his insignia,
> With red greaves so splendid
> Soaring as a hawk does
> Straight up into the sky
> Then swooping down.
> The hero has come with three thousand chariots
> And a host of battle-trained foot soldiers
> With his bandsmen beating the drums,
> Illustrious truly is the hero;
> Deep is the roll of his drums,
> Shaking the host with its din.
> His war chariots rumble,
> Rumble and crash
> Like a roll of thunder.
> Illustrious truly is the hero
> Who filled the tribes with fear.

Writing about this period down to the unification of China in 221 BCE, the historian Sima Qian said that 'the ages before the Qin dynasty are too far away and the material on them too scanty to permit a detailed account of them'. Remarkably, though, discoveries over the past forty years have revolutionised the picture. Some of the discoveries include texts on bamboo strips, turtle shell archives, an astounding series of inscribed bronzes and, above all, the Zhou royal cemetery. These have shed light on their wars, but also their court culture, with its feasting ceremonies, sacrifices, games, archery contests, feats of strength, ritual dances and musical audiences. New texts of land grants have revealed the workings of their aristocratic culture and, indeed, the beginnings of Chinese bureaucracy, with Ministries of Land, Construction and War, staffed by professional scribes and document makers. In this period, too, are the origins of the county system that still exists today.

The Zhou dynasty is the first period of Chinese history from which extended texts have survived. Among them are the canonical classics of Chinese culture, which were collected and preserved at this time. The oldest of these is the famous divination text: the *Book of Changes* (*I Ching*). Riddling and ruminative, it is one of the great works of world literature and is still used as a practical guide by the people of China and East Asia today. The *Book of Songs* (*Shijing*) is a poetic anthology, containing the earliest texts from the world's oldest living poetic tradition, going back to 1000 BCE, or even before. Its 305 songs are about love, courtship and marriage, agriculture, feasting and dancing, sacrifice, hunting and warfare. Among them beautiful lyrics about the joys of life and the pain of loss anticipate some of the great poetry we will encounter later in our story, suffused with a humanity that opens a window on the feelings of the Chinese people so long ago. On the other hand, the *Book of Documents* (*Shujing*) preserves key historical documents and claims to contain, and perhaps does, texts from the early Zhou, after the conquest of the Shang in the eleventh century BCE, including the famous narrative of the fall of the Shang (see above, page 52). These texts frame the Zhou claim to rule and would influence the whole of the Chinese tradition. They describe the conquest of the Shang as a victory of a just ruler over a wicked and decadent king and show the Zhou dynasty as legitimate successors. History itself in the *Shujing* then is seen as a crucial tool in validating power. From now on, the control of history is linked to the control of writing, which the state monopolised through its scribes and ritual specialists. Through the written word came the possession of history.

A second key idea is bound to this: the Zhou conception of the Mandate of Heaven. As we have seen, originally the *tian ming*, the celestial mandate, was literally an astronomical sign seen in the sky in 1059 BCE during the reign of King Wen, whose son, Wu, founded the Zhou dynasty. The interpretation of the sign by King Wu and his diviners was that this was the celestial mandate given by the Lord of Heaven and was a 'great command in the sky ... so Heaven [*tian*] will protect and watch over me, its child, in the manner it had protected the former kings extending to the four quarters'.

The rule of the Zhou, then, was linked to heaven. A king and his dynasty could only rule so long as they had heaven's favour. A king who neglected his sacred duties, or who acted tyrannically, would arouse the displeasure of heaven, disturbing cosmic harmony. Disorder would follow and society would descend into chaos: the great fear of Chinese culture even today. In the end, heaven could withdraw its mandate and eventually reveal a new mandate, usually by a visible sign.

The Western Zhou lasted 400 years. During this time, the concept of the Heavenly Sign or Mandate developed from a specific event in 1059 BCE, during the reign of King Wen, to the broad conception of a changing mandate tied to a theory of dynastic cycles. It was validated by Shang Di, the old Lord of Heaven and supreme deity of the Shang, who in this period becomes elided with *tian*, heaven, the supreme deity of the Zhou. So what we see in this period is the creation of a paradigm. Political ideology and, indeed, political philosophy begin to be shaped in the service of a monarchical idea, that of the sage-king. Hence, influential thinkers from Confucius to Wang Anshi and Sima Guang in the eleventh century looked back on the Zhou as the ideal. For Confucius, 'follow the Duke of Zhou' becomes a mantra, a golden age to be emulated rather like resetting a clock. Indeed, the high status accorded to the Zhou is shown by the use of their name in dynastic titles by other kingdoms in later Chinese history, including the 'Later Zhou' in the 950s and the 'Great Zhou' in the 1350s. All these kingdoms declared themselves revivals of the Zhou, the model to which they aspired.

So the cosmos was perceived as a moral order, and moral values were built into the way the earthly order worked. The virtuous ruler would mediate between heaven and the realm of humans, as the Shang king had done with his diviners. Now, though, there was a moral contract. Of course, in any culture the gap between the ideal and the reality of rulership is often wide, and in China, it was dependent on the success of the king's ministers and philosophers to steer the guiding principles of governance. These ideas would play out over the next two and a half millennia. The ceremony of 1899, with which this book began, was still a living expression of this in the age of telephone and automobile. And, as we shall see, the end of the empire was not the end of this powerful idea. Even in the communist era, the Mandate remained an invisible presence behind the autocracy of the party. The figure of the sage-king could still be seen in the figure of Chairman Mao, whose calligraphy was even inscribed on the boulders of the sacred mountain Taishan. Mao's personality cult in the Cultural Revolution still invited the people to trust in the virtue of the Great Helmsman and Teacher.

KONG QIU: CONFUCIUS

In the sixth century BCE, the Zhou state fell into decline as rival regional powers fought for supremacy. Order broke down. Violence and war became endemic – so much so that later centuries called this the Zhanguo period: the Warring States. Still, out of this age of conflict and political instability arose a golden age of Chinese philosophy that would define the Chinese political tradition. Among many great thinkers wrestling with the fundamental issues of order, virtue and justice was the most celebrated person in Chinese civilisation. This great figure who codified these ideas in the sixth century BCE was called Kong Qiu, but in later times became known as Kongfuzi,

'Master Kong'. The name was Latinised by Jesuit missionaries in seventeenth-century China as Confucius (c. 551–479 BCE). 'A transmitter who invented nothing', as he described himself, Confucius is one of the most influential and famous figures in history. It has been said that no book, not even the Bible, has influenced so many people for so long as his *Analects*, his 'Sayings', which have shaped the intellectual and cultural life of the whole of East Asia, Japan and Korea.

Confucius is such a famous figure, who has gathered so many accretions from the past, that it is very difficult to see him as a man of his time – as Kong Qiu, an Iron Age thinker in a regional culture of the Eastern Zhou, in the time of Warring States. In an attempt to see him afresh it is best, first, to go to his origin place in the northeastern province of Shandong, an easy journey by train these days from Beijing, to Qufu.

From the gleaming new high-speed station the visitor may still approach Qufu through the countryside, a rarity in today's China, leaving the main highway along long tree-lined country roads, through wheat fields and past small villages. Trains were kept away from the centre of Qufu when railways first opened up in China at the express wish of the Kong clan, who were and continue to be powerful in the town. The extended lineage of the descendants still make up half the population of Qufu and clan members on the street will proudly show their ID bearing the Kong name. In the centre of the city, inside the walls, is the sprawling complex of the Kong ancestral mansion, with its 480 rooms and courtyards. The magnificent temple to the Master is one of the most splendid buildings in China, its gardens full of steles and memorial arches commemorating the visits of generations of Chinese emperors. Beyond the north gate is the fabulously atmospheric 'Forest of the Exalted Sage', the walled family burial ground with its tangled thickets, overgrown hillocks and fallen tomb monuments of thousands of long-forgotten Kongs.

Qufu itself is still a small, charming walled town, where costumed gate ceremonies with pikes and drums are put on every night for tourists. By day it bustles with cycle rickshaws and horse-drawn carriages. Today, the presence of Confucius is everywhere, despite being execrated by the communists during the Cultural Revolution. Exhorted by Mao, the Red Guards vandalised the cemetery and dug up Kong graves, proclaiming that to smash Confucius was 'the most important thing for the whole party, the whole army and the whole nation'. Nevertheless, the Master had his revenge and he is now thoroughly rehabilitated. Recently, President Xi cited him in his keynote address to the party and provided a recommendation for the latest Chinese popular edition on a wrap-around cover. The book was a bestseller. Confucius' statue stands at the entrance to Qufu's poshest hotel, where a copy of the *Analects* lies in the bedside drawer, like the Gideon Bible.

Qufu was the capital of a small Eastern Zhou tributary state called Lu. The town had a 6-mile circuit between the Zhushui and Si Rivers. Founded in the eighth century BCE, the Archaic period in ancient Greece, it contained the palace of the kings of Lu from the Spring and Autumn period down to the Western Han, the time of the Roman republic in the West. Qufu has been rebuilt many times. Today's Ming walled city only occupies the southwest quarter of the ancient city, which once included the Kong cemetery. Fragments of the ancient walls survive, in places, up to 30 feet high. Inside the walls no major digs have ever taken place, but a number of test soundings have revealed platforms of rammed earth for large buildings along the main axis of the town. Presumably, these were part of the royal palace. Outside the southern gate was another platform, forming a huge open-air altar on which dances and prayers for rain were performed and which still survives out in the fields, topped by trees. Traces of bronze and iron foundries, as well as workshops for ceramics and working bone, have also been discovered. Cemeteries of the Zhou period lay inside the walls on the west side. In the sixth–fifth century BCE, therefore, Qufu was recognisably descended from the city planning of the old Shang world, with royal and ducal palaces and workshops.

This, then, is the background of Confucius. He came from a provincial Iron Age city-state and his origins offer clues to who he was.

In the family mansion, today's Kong family have a long-preserved genealogy extending back fifteen generations from the Master, to the eleventh century BCE. It contains the intriguing claim that Confucius' Qufu forebear, his great-grandfather who first came to Qufu, was a 'Man of the state of Song', descended from the brother of the last Shang king, Weizi, who was left to rule the state of Song in Henan. If so, this would be a fascinating clue to Confucius' psychological and cultural makeup. An alternative early tradition, however, says Confucius was actually a 'man of the wilds', from the countryside south of Lu. His father, it is said, was an old warrior of the Zang family, who had had several wives and concubines, his mother a young girl of the indigenous Yan clan. If this is so, the young Confucius was a cultural outsider, not actually of the Zhou, and there is a tradition that he was once mocked and disparaged for it. Still, on his father's side the Zang family were famous for stead-fastly maintaining the ancient rituals. The teaching Confucius got from his family may account for the intense loyalty he felt, all his life, to the ancient ideal of Zhou kingship, though his fate was to be 'a wanderer in many lands'.

Confucius showed talent early, but did not have a successful career as a young member of the elite and never rose high in the state, pos-sibly because he was a minor son of Zang outsiders. He remained poor all his life, though his scholarship and knowledge of the ritual tradition of Zhou helped him, for a time, to stand out at court. On one occasion, he confronted three powerful rival clans in Lu and got them to agree to a plan to demolish their fortifications; he was even responsible for sending troops to crush a rebellious minister. Yet in 497 BCE, if the traditional dates are correct, when Confucius was already in his fifties, he lost his position and was ousted. With a group of followers, he began a fourteen-year journey around China, before finally returning to Lu to study and teach. This journey is a crucial part of the biography – a mind-changing experience he shares with other great figures in Chinese history, such as the historian Sima Qian and the poet Du Fu. Perhaps the breadth of his mind and universality of his views were reinforced by seeing a wider world.

For the remarkable thing about Kong, as a man from a small East Asian city-state, is that he did acquire a universal sense of humanity, or 'humaneness'. How much he ever knew of the world beyond East Asia, though, is doubtful, and 'humanity' to him, perhaps, still comprised 'All Under Heaven': China.

We have no contemporary picture of Confucius. The conventional image, used in later times, is of a frail old man with a smiling face and a wispy beard, his character a bit pompous and boring. Despite this, his own view of himself, as preserved by his disciples, was that enthusiasm was his main characteristic: 'Why didn't you say how passionate I am?' At times it would appear almost on the autistic spectrum, and he could be physically overwhelmed by music. Even into middle age he was a man of action, adept at the outdoor activities of a cultivated man: an expert with horses, good at outdoor sports, archery, hunting and fishing. He was a tireless and bold traveller in a period when one had to travel everywhere armed. Often in great physical peril, he evaded several attempts by his enemies to kill him. In dangerous times tough young disciples are useful people to have around.

THE QUEST FOR UNITY

In Confucius' lifetime, the war-torn multi-state system under Zhou lordship was breaking down, and it became clear that long-term stability lay in some kind of political unity. It is in this context that Confucius' career as a thinker is to be understood. He was probably the first to suggest the advantages of a unified rule over 'All Under Heaven'. Referring to a violent usurpation in his native state of Lu in 505–502 BCE, Confucius said this:

When the Way prevails under Heaven, rites, music and punitive expeditions are ordered by the Son of Heaven. When there is no Way under Heaven, rites, music and punitive expeditions are directed by overlords. But if they are directed by overlords, within ten generations most states will be lost; if they are directed by

the nobles, they will be lost within five generations; when mere
retainers hold the destiny of the state, they will be gone within
three generations.

This is the nub of Confucius' message. He was undoubtedly not the
only one to come to this conclusion, but his specific message was
to restore the potency of the kingship of the 'Son of Heaven' by
concentrating power in a single, wise, legitimate monarch. This was
the way to stop the turmoil and the breakdown of society. How to
achieve it practically, he doesn't say. He is talking about principles,
but ideologically the blueprint is clear: a single monarch using the
restored ritual norms of the Western Zhou. At the core of royal
conduct is virtue (*de* in Chinese), so the ideal ruler must be humane
and learned – a sage in fact. It was an ideal, of course, a utopian
dream, unattainable in reality, though Chinese historical tradition
always insisted it was attainable, and had been, once upon a time,
in the founding moment of the Zhou, which was Confucius' model.

As for the role of the intellectual, the key was to determine the
Way (*dao*). When the Way is lost, the sage has a moral duty, above
all else, to reform society, to set the Way back on track, to define the
tradition and advise the prince. Politics, then, was Confucius' first
and foremost concern, which is also true of Chinese philosophy as a
whole. Chinese thought, it might be said, has revolved around two
central questions: the harmony of the universe and the harmony of
society, cosmology and politics. Hence, the central vision of Chinese
philosophy for 2,500 years has been political and ethical. It was very
different from the post-Classical West where until the Enlightenment
and the Scientific Revolution, monotheism took things on a very different conceptual path. In Europe, shaped by Roman and Germanic
law, the institution of kingship developed a legal custom separate
from political authority. These two paths have marked the traditions
of the East and West to this day.

We know Confucius' voice through the *Analects*, a compilation
of his sayings and anecdotes as reported by his pupils. Although
linguistic evidence suggests some of the later ones are not by him,

the main body of the text conveys one voice, which is forceful, idiosyncratic and, as Elias Canetti has written, 'the oldest complete intellectual and spiritual portrait of a man'. Just as Marx warned his followers he was not Marxist, Confucius certainly was not a Confucian in the way that Chinese civilisation eventually enshrined him, and indeed as the Mao age vilified and dethroned him. He was often called a teacher, but he was also a political agitator with a sense of mission. This was part of his strange mental makeup, from watching the collapse of a civilisation that had been built up over the previous 500 years. He was driven by an unshakeable belief in his own divinely inspired calling to reform the political order in China and seems to have believed that heaven had chosen him to bring people back to the path of righteousness, as defined by the first Zhou kings, and reunify the civilised world.

And the downside? It is easy, of course, to use conformity to reinforce a repressive system, even though Confucius was adamant that the sage's duty was also to oppose unjust rule. Yet the idea of just rule depended on moral education, and Confucius was not an advocate of a legal system, let alone of separating executive and legislature. When all power is in the hands of the ruler and there is no independent legal system, the intellectuals place themselves in the hands of the ruler, as they have done in China right through its history down to the People's Republic. Confucius believed in human nature and mistrusted laws. Legal rules, he thought, were not the best way of creating a just order. This was best achieved through a matrix of ritual and moral conventions, inculcated through education. But a small Iron Age city-state is one thing – a great empire quite another. That conundrum will be confronted later by progressive Chinese thinkers, for example in the seventeenth century (below pages 299–304), as they attempted to negotiate changes in the imperial system and the role of the sage-king, then again in the 'Self-Strengthening Movement' of the nineteenth century, and indeed even in our own time.

In the West, the inheritors of Roman law and Germanic custom came to believe that the government of men is always flawed, unless limited by a strong legal system. They gradually developed the idea that states should be ruled with the informed consent of the governed. This is a major divergence, even by the time of the Song dynasty, when in England, for example, the law was already something the king should obey. Governing a state the size of medieval England with a few million, as opposed to 100 million in China, of course required a different attitude to freedom. Still, failure to establish the rule of law would remain one of the most intractable problems in the Chinese political tradition until the end of the empire. Since then, it would be partially addressed under the Republic, trampled by Mao, revived in the 1980s, but has stalled since the early 2000s.

Confucius himself had always insisted on the duty of intellectuals to oppose arbitrary and unjust power. That is easier said than done, as the whole of Chinese history will show. Like many great books, though, many of Confucius' profound insights have stood the test of time. Confucian humanistic ideals were eventually written into the Chinese state's educational system in the tenth century and over the next centuries spread to Korea, Japan, Vietnam and Southeast Asia. During a special ceremony at the Master's grave in Qufu in 2016, a group of Korean Confucian teachers in traditional gowns and high scholars' hats summed up his message for the twenty-first century: 'He defined our collective values of hard work, duty and benevolence; his belief in universal brotherhood in this age of individualism makes his message still true after 2,500 years, for all the world!'

THE AXIAL AGE

At this point in the story, a final intriguing question should be asked – one that chimes with the transnational perceptions of our own time: How do we set Confucius and the Chinese age of philosophers into the bigger picture of what we might call the global cultural history of Eurasia, in the sixth–fifth century BCE? Writing in 1949, in the bitter aftermath of the Second World War, when total conflict and the Holocaust had cast a deep shadow over the achievements of Western civilisation, the German philosopher Karl Jaspers made a great claim for the age of Confucius. This was a crucial moment in the history of humanity, an 'Axial Age', he said, when 'the spiritual foundations of humanity were laid simultaneously and independently in China, India, Persia, Judea and Greece; and these are the foundations upon which humanity still subsists today'.

It was not, in fact, a new idea. In eighteenth-century India the pioneering French Indologist Anquetil-Duperron had spoken of a revolutionary transformation in thinking in different parts of the world around 500 BCE. He said that 'this century can be seen as a major epoch in the history of humanity ... a kind of revolution, which produced at the same time in several parts of the world geniuses, Greeks, Persians, Jews and Indians, who set the tone for the future'. Anquetil-Duperron had read the Latin 'Life of Confucius' published in Paris, as a preface to the translation of his works in 1687, which hailed him as 'wisest of philosophers who purely by the light of natural reason' had constructed 'an infinitely sublime moral system'. Fired by this Enlightenment idea, Anquetil-Duperron included Confucius among the three greatest figures who had changed the face of history and was still 'an oracle', a fount of wisdom for the whole of the Eastern world.

So was this extraordinary simultaneity mere coincidence? In the mid-first millennium BCE, across Eurasia, there were certain common experiences in material culture, societies in transition from Bronze to Iron Age culture that developed powerful monarchies and large-scale cities. Mercantile classes appear and with them writing becomes more widespread, for the first time out of the hands of religious and political elites. Ways of thinking about the world arise that feel different from anything that had gone before. These key figures all lived within a handful of generations, between the 550s and the fourth century BCE. Some, like Confucius, the Buddha and some of the great pre-Socratics, may even have been alive at the same time.

What we can say, then, is this: that Confucius and his disciples lived in a period of history when the great Bronze Age civilisations had gone. In their place were competing Iron Age city-states, in Archaic Greece, the Ganges valley and the Warring States of China.

All of them show the beginnings of social diversification, and in all there were thinkers of genius. There were the philosophers and scientists in Ionia: Heraclitus, Pythagoras and Anaxagoras. The Buddha's contemporaries included Jains, Ajivikas, sceptics, rationalists and atomists. All of them question the nature of the mind and the physical universe. In China, too, this is the period known as the Age of Philosophers, the 'Hundred Schools of Thought', with Daoists, Mohists and Confucius' followers such as Mencius. Among them, as in Greece and India, there were many different views about humanity and the cosmos. The parallels perhaps are only general. It would be stretching things to suggest the political concerns of Confucius had much in common with the Buddha's disputes about karma with other religious groups in the Ganges plain. The key point is that their preoccupations are about human beings and their place in the cosmos.

The deal that Confucius offered local ruling elites in Warring States China was a challenge: to live up to his exacting standards of virtue and wisdom, and, for the good of humanity, work towards the 'great unity' (*da yitong*). But no matter how well he and his itinerant band of disciples were first received on their travels, they made enemies among palace cliques and corrupt ministers and were usually forced out. In the end, Confucius' failed mission brought him back to Lu, where he spent the rest of his days in obscurity. For all his later fame, Confucius was a failure in his own lifetime. Nobody took up his offer to remodel their state on the lines of *de*, virtue, despite the Zhou's formulation of the Heavenly Mandate that united 'All Under Heaven'. And why should they? Despite China's sense of a common culture and script, and the deep myth of unity that went back to the prehistoric legends of Yu the Great, no one was going to cede power to the declining Zhou order, the mediocre contemporary heirs of the noble duke of Zhou. So how would unification come about? As it happened, it would be achieved not by agreement, but by force, by one of the most remarkable rulers in Chinese history: Qin Shi Huangdi, the First Emperor.

4

THE FIRST EMPEROR AND
THE UNIFICATION OF CHINA

The rise of the Qin empire has been justly called 'one of the greatest epics in human history'. Like their contemporaries, the Macedonians before the age of Alexander the Great, the Qin state was a 'barbarian' kingdom on the edge of mainstream civilisation and was seen by its neighbours as a 'land of wolves and jackals'. But in the 240s BCE, under their leader King Zheng, they burst onto the stage of history, ended Zhou rule and unified China. Zheng then became the First Emperor. Though they only ruled all China for fifteen years, the Qin were the superpower that changed the story of China for ever, leaving structures of governance and contours of thought that still exist today. Over the past few years a series of sensational archaeological and textual discoveries have given us totally new insights into their brilliant and violent world.

The path to China's unification had been laid over the previous two centuries during the age of the Warring States (480s–221 BCE), a time that had also seen intense battles of ideas. As we have seen, back in Confucius' lifetime (551–479 BCE) no one had been convinced by his idea of uniting the states under an overarching sage-ruler, who would uphold the values of the Zhou and rule by both exemplifying and encouraging good behaviour. In the 'universal disorder' of the time, nobody was willing to cede power to the waning Zhou rulers, or to embrace the notion of virtue – *de* – when realpolitik was a necessity. The resolution to these contradictions emerged later among the thinkers who came after Confucius.

The philosopher Mozi (468–390 BCE) first proposed that the remedy for universal disorder was the establishment of a universal ruler. He envisioned meritocratic appointments of state officers, supervision of office holders and the unification of thought and behaviour, but with ideological conformity enforced within a strongly ordered society. Even the famous *Dao De Jing*, written by Laozi around the sixth century BCE, saw the logical extension of the vision of unity as a correspondence between the political and metaphysical orders: 'The Dao is great, Heaven is great, Earth is Great, and the King is great. There are four greats in the state and the King is one of these.' With that we are on the way to the intellectual formulation of a vision of imperial kingship, a oneness both cosmic and political. When asked how to stabilise 'All Under Heaven', Mencius, China's second sage, replied: 'Stability is in unity.' If the ruler is humane and just, 'nobody will not follow him: if this really happens the people will go over to him as water flows downward. Who will stop it?'

And so it proved to be. By the third century BCE, all agreed that unity of government was the precondition to implementing the principles of the Way, and hence the path to peace and the Great Unity. But how was it to happen? Of course philosophers, especially Confucian ones, could not advocate that it should come about through violence. It was impossible to contemplate a just prince killing his way to power. But nor was it likely that any of the big states would voluntarily surrender power. In the end, as so often in history, change was brought about by war. China was united by the sword and by a ruling ideology very different from the Confucian ideal.

The key text that underwrote the unification is *The Book of Lord Shang*. Written by a Qin dynasty thinker of the fourth century BCE, it is one of the most remarkable books of the ancient world, East or West. It has been called the first totalitarian manifesto in history and a 'blatant assault on traditional culture and moral values'. In

China, it was despised in some quarters as a shameful argument for despotism through a cynical Machiavellian use of power. For others, though, it was a supremely useful tool. It has even been praised in our own time, when totalitarian rule was justified as 'the first stage of socialism', a temporary phase on the path to a Marxist utopia. *The Book of Lord Shang*, however, is the original.

The core of the book was written around the 340s BCE, though parts of the text were added in the next century. The book advances a legalist argument for a new form of state in which governmental power penetrates right to the base of social order, creating a society wherein every peasant is a diligent tiller of the soil, every soldier a brave and loyal supporter of the state, and every official an unswerving enforcer of a harsh code of retributive law. To facilitate this new order, Lord Shang recommended practical reforms which, in essence, have survived through Chinese history. First was the division of society into counties, districts and villages. At the base, the smallest unit was a grouping of five families mutually responsible for each other's conduct, with the deputed head member personally liable for any crime. This was linked to a system of universal registration for all people, from birth to death. There were thirteen categories of quantifiable data, including name, place of origin, gender, names and number of children, whether too old or young to work, social ranking (as defined in the lawbooks) and holdings of animals such as horses and oxen. The whole population, therefore, could be strictly controlled through a pyramid of government and harshly enforced law. Benevolence, in fact, was not the answer to attaining 'the Great Harmony' as Confucius had thought, though it might be workable in the future, when unity and obedience had been fully established. For now, though, a harsh law would prevail. Even the virtuous King Wu, Lord Shang wrote, 'seized the world by force, though he later held it by righteousness. But now none of the states of ten thousand chariots is not at war. Things have been blocked up for a long time.'

Warfare, then, was the way to establish effective kingship, and severity was the way to hold it. From family registration to the over-arching conception of rulership, this was the blueprint for a total state. Lord Shang's injunction to create a 'rich state and a strong army' would be the template in Chinese history down to the present People's Republic and the 'four modernisations' of Zhou Enlai and Deng Xiaoping.

By the third century BCE, there was also a revolution in military technology. High-grade weaponry and mechanical crossbows were developed, and the ability to put huge, highly disciplined armies into the field was one of the reasons unification finally became a possibility. The Qin lived west of the Zhou heartland and up to that point had been one of the many peoples who had acknowledged the earlier kings of the Zhou. They had long shared in Zhou culture and intermarried with the royal family. Yet as the Zhou declined over a century or so, the Qin developed a strong sense of their own separate cultural identity as well as a certain Spartan toughness. In 255 BCE, the Qin annexed the Zhou royal lands, the last symbol of the old political order that had endured since the eleventh century BCE. 'These are dark times: there is no limit to the sufferings of the ordinary people,' one old loyalist wrote. 'The house of Zhou is destroyed. The line of the Sons of Heaven is broken ... nothing can be worse than the absence of the Son of Heaven.'

In a series of rapid shock assaults, the Qin overcame their six main rivals, the 'ten thousand chariot states'. Chinese imperial history had begun. The speed of success was amazing. Between 230 and 221 BCE, they swallowed up the kingdoms of the old Warring States and followed up their military triumphs with measures to fulfil the legalist blueprint. The Qin legal system was introduced with reformed weights and measures, coinage and script. There were new state rites aimed at unifying the realm. Draconian population swaps and ethnic cleansing brought 120,000 families of the 'rich and powerful' from recently conquered states to be resettled in the region around the capital. To commemorate his stunning victories, the emperor had giant bronze statues made for his palace, with inscriptions announcing the establishment of the 'Great Unity'. A generation later, the statesman Jia Yi explained how the dynasty came to power:

The Qin took over all within the seas and annexed the neighbouring states; he faced south and called himself emperor. Thus,
he nourished all within the four seas and the gentlemen of 'All
Under Heaven' docilely bowed before his wind. Why did this
happen? I would reply that then, the world had been a long time
without a ruler. The Zhou house had sunk into insignificance,
the strong were lording it over the weak and the few over the
many. Arms and armour were never set aside and the people
were exhausted and impoverished. The masses hoped they would
obtain peace and security and there was nobody who did not
wholeheartedly look up in reverence. This was the moment to
preserve authority and stabilise achievements and lay the foundations of lasting peace.

Recently, remarkable archaeological discoveries have given us fresh
insights into the Qin hegemony and its institutions. For administrative purposes, the country was divided into thirty-six commanderies
linked by a 6,800km road system. A series of long walls was constructed across north and northwest China, joining up the border
walls of earlier states and adding up to 4,000 kilometres – the forerunner of the 'Great Wall'. An 800km superhighway ran between the
capital (near today's Xi'an) and the northern military bases, where
armies totalling 300,000 men were stationed. All these grand projects were driven by conscripted labour, much to the resentment of
the people, according to later historians. These developments were
so swift and so far-reaching that they can only be compared with
those introduced after the revolution of 1949 and the still-continuing
counter revolution, which began after 1979.

Bringing order then was at the centre of Qin propaganda, and popular support for the unification was a major factor and a justification
for the regime's ruthless severity. It was clear to all at the time that
this was a moment of profound change. On inscriptions erected in
the conquered lands and on the sacred mountains, the First Emperor
announced that he had 'brought peace to All Under Heaven ... the
black headed people are at peace and never need again to take up

arms'. He had 'wiped out the powerful and rebellious and brought stability to the four quarters'. Henceforth, only the unified empire would be the legitimate form of rule. In the future, even when the state fell apart, (as after the Tang, Song and Ming) a centripetal force pulled it back together again. From then on, unity was legitimisation.

Yet, given so many differences in regions, cultures and languages, why was the idea of China's unity so strong that it could be restored time and again? Indeed, the remarkable fact is not that at times it disintegrated, but that it always came back together. In Europe, there were periods, under Charlemagne for example, when large parts of the continent were under a single ruler, but it always split apart again into nation states. The Arab Caliphate also attempted to impose political unity over a vast and heterogeneous area, but regional cultures and identities proved too strong. India, perhaps, is a closer parallel, because of the deep cultural unity across the sub-continent provided by the indigenous religious systems. Nevertheless, even though there were large Indian states under the Mauryans, Guptas and Moghuls, and in the south under the Cholas, there was never political unity from the Himalayas to Cape Comorin until it was imposed by the British outsiders. In China, however, the 'Great Unity' was an almost inbred ideological myth from the pre-Qin past, which was never abandoned, even in times of catastrophic breakdown.

THE FIRST EMPEROR

As for the man himself, Prince Zheng became king of Qin in his teens in 247 BCE. In 221 BCE, after the Qin had conquered all the other Warring States and unified China, using the title of the myth-ical primeval rulers, he called himself Qin Shi Huangdi, 'the first Emperor of the Qin'. The most remarkable and controversial leader in Chinese history, later Confucian scholars were deeply hostile to him, saying that he 'relied solely on mutilation punishments and pen-alties ... while the master wielded textbook and ink'. One famous story alleged that he burned the history books and buried 460 scholars and historians alive. But, harsh as he undoubtedly was, this negative picture has been transformed by new archaeological finds which allow us for the first time to get behind the lurid accounts of the First Emperor and begin to see the workings of the Qin empire at grassroots at this fundamental turning point in Chinese history. And, to begin with, it is worth remembering that for all the images we have of the brutality of the Qin, their rule was based on law.

In the past few years, enormous quantities of documents from local Qin centres of administration have come to light. In December 2007, for example, more than 2,000 bamboo strips turned up in a Hong Kong antiques market. Belonging to one of the Qin prefectures in the Yangtze valley, the documents contained a series of exemplary criminal cases handled by local 'justice secretaries'. These had been kept as an archive source to illustrate good legal practice for magistrates. There are cases about banditry, rape, robbery and grave robbing, a sexual consent case and even petitions for retrial. For all the reported ferocity of the Qin legal system, here we get an insight into legal procedures and even the conduct of local magistrates. These magistrates interviewed witnesses, listened carefully to evidence and had graded punishments, where discretion and mercy could, in theory, play a part.

In practice, though, application of the law was severe. Take the example of a newly discovered legal case from 219 BCE during the Qin army's conquest of the southern Chu kingdom. It concerns a Qin magistrate, Mr Tui, who was accused of being too lenient. In a war situation, he tried to reduce the punishments of conscripted local militia deserters, who faced the death sentence. This was tantamount to 'releasing and letting guilty people go', as these were men who had broken the Qin statutes on soldiers 'lacking courage and not fighting' – a capital offence. Convicted of being soft on crime, indeed of being effectively a closet Confucian, Tui's sentence was to be 'shaved as a criminal and made a gatherer of fuel'. (Higher up the list of Qin punishments were mutilation, cutting in half at the waist, beheading and 'slicing' – Death by a Thousand Cuts – a penalty only abolished in 1905.) It is likely that Magistrate Tui's wife, children and property were impounded too. Such was the fate of a loyal Qin law officer who strayed too far towards mercy.

The case of Mr Tui highlights the use of a written code of law and show us that later imperial codes go back much further in time. In these legal documents there are training tips on how to ask questions in cases, and a guide to right practice to help good justice rise in the system. Of course the gap between theory and practice is as interesting as it is in early medieval Europe. With another of these newly discovered documents in hand, let us go to the Qin countryside near the Wei River, northeast of Xi'an, during the winter of 242 BCE, the fifth year of King Zheng of Qin (the man who will become the First Emperor).

The fields of wheat are divided by baulks and dotted with little huts and cottages where many of the poor workforce live. The tiny plots are tilled by families or single men and sometimes women on their own. Two men are sleeping in their hut: An, 'a penal labourer', and Yi, a 'rank and file man'. During the night they are attacked, stabbed and killed. The murderer steals their clothes and tools and leaves no clues at the scene 'except for the red garb of a penal labour convict'. What follows comes from newly published documents translated by Ulrich Lau and Thies Staack.

Three local law secretaries go to the scene to inspect the bodies and call in the magistrate. Mr Chu, a man in his early forties, has loyally served in the local office for twenty years. First, he consults the record of registered convicts within the prefecture, interviews those he can and makes a list on writing tablets of the names of those who had absconded. Next Chu and two helpers from his office split up and interview all the people working the fields adjoining An's holding. They even put guards on the main field paths at night to check comings and goings and question anyone acting suspiciously. Drawing a blank, Chu takes another look at the red clothes found at the scene. Was the murderer a convict labourer or was he laying a false trail? Chu now instigates a search in the floating population of the neighbouring walled town, Liyang. There, five days later, attention is drawn to a man called Tong who has suddenly come into a bit of wealth: 'at his belt a great new sheath and knife'. When brought in for questioning, 'something about his manners created a bad impression', Chu wrote; 'there was an evasive look in his eyes'. Tong's stories began to contradict. He first said he was a bond servant at the local government, then a servant in the neighbouring prefecture. Their records are checked, too, and his story begins to unravel:

'My registered name is Wei. I'm originally from Yancheng. When I surrendered at the end of the war I was made a bond servant of convict rank and I was deported to Sicong prefecture, but I left and absconded.'

'Where did you get the money to have your coat patched and to buy the sheath and knife?' Chu asks.

'I earned the money from hired work,' the suspect replies.

Eventually trapped by inconsistencies, Tong admits he is a career criminal, planning other robberies to support his family: 'I have a mother, wife and children at Wei, I am guilty and liable to punishment. I can say no more.'

The story is followed on the next bamboo strip, with a note on the character of the criminal, written by the investigating officials:

Wei is a man from Jin. He has an aggressive disposition. He planned his crime buying the red clothes of a convict and used them to throw officials off the scent. A man who kills people in the fields and then goes off to stay in a market guesthouse within the city is brazen-faced. He is not a normal person. He bought the knife quite prepared to kill people in the act of committing a robbery. This all shows he is a real danger to society.

Tong was sentenced to execution, but the case ended with a recommendation for Mr Chu, the investigating magistrate:

This case was extremely obscure and difficult to solve. Mr Chu and his colleagues tested these obscurities with cleverness. Mr Chu became secretary in prefecture when he was twenty-two years old. He is now forty-three years old, Peng Ju and Zhong, his colleagues,

likewise are senior in office and age. They are all officeholders
who have personal integrity and moral purity, they are impeccable
and dutiful. In their hearts they are impartial, upright and act in
accordance with the rites. We recommend them and stand guaran-
tee for them and request evaluation of their performance in order to
promote them to the ranks of provincial clerks-in-chief so that their
example may be an encouragement to other officials ...

The account, as we have it handed down, is an 'exemplary case',
mediated, of course, by local officials and their regional boss. Yet
in the images it gives us, of the poor village huts in the countryside,
the shifting population of the small town with its guest house in
the market, the pattern of rural smallholders, convicts and bonded
servants, vividly evoke the local world of the Qin. Set against the
wider background of war and disruption, in the period of the Qin
conquests, we learn of the enslavement of captive populations, the
movement of bonded labourers to different estates, and we hear for
the first time the voices of the lower ranks of Chinese society. All of
it is seen in astonishing detail through the files in the magistrates'
office with their registers of the whole population.

THE LIVES OF THE PEOPLE:
NEW EVIDENCE FROM THE LIYE STRIPS

During the Qin age, more than 90 per cent of China's population
were people like the poor farm labourers in Chu's murder case, working in the fields to pay taxes and to feed themselves. For more details
of the lives of such people, we now have an amazing set of data from
what has been called the most important archaeological discovery in
China in the twenty-first century. In June 2002, an excavation was
conducted at a moated site on the north bank of the You River, on
the ruins of the ancient city of Liye in Hunan province. Inside the
circuit of walls, several old wells were found 10 feet below present
ground surface. One of them, 45 feet deep, had been used as a dump
and contained an abandoned Qin government local archive on more

than 37,000 bamboo strips. This incredible cache includes registers, letters, tax calculations, data from the postal service, monthly consumption figures for army provisions and the issue of military gear. There are even notes on ethnic groups. On the slips, we meet the figures of authority in the county, the ministers of public works and defence, and local law officers.

What this treasure reveals is the crucial importance of information gathering to the Qin state. Now we actually meet the five-family groupings, the basic unit of Qin society as proposed by legalist philosophers like Lord Shang. The emperor's minister Li Si had put theory into practice by registering everybody, and in one example from a population register, a single wooden strip lists the owner of the house and his wife and children. From it we learn that the householder Huang De's place of origin is Nanyang, he is ethnically from the Chu state and his status is fourth rank. He has a wife called Qian and four children. He is the head of his five-family grouping.

As a head of a five-household unit, Mr De probably had some level of literacy, the basic reading needed to confirm and sign off the data. Some things are not recorded, including age and occupation. Health status is assumed, because scribes elsewhere record chronic illness or disability if it affected ability to work, so evidently the De family were able-bodied. Family records were probably updated every year, with verification through personal contact by local officials. A little later, under the Western Han, the government directly employed 130,285 officials who were fully literate, but there must have been far more people who were able to read, extending right down to local level, including the village teacher – long a mainstay of grassroots education in China. In the Qin era, government depended on broad-based basic writing skills, as well as on professional scribes. Under the Western Han, scribes in training had to pass a written test that included recognising 5,000 characters to qualify for a post. This is the number that, in today's China, pupils are expected to recognise by the time they are twelve years old.

So, writing and information were essential tools of the Qin autocracy. In the third century BCE, the government was already developing standardised population data for use in taxation, crime and labour conscription and a system of village registration we see again in later periods, in the Yellow Registers of the Ming dynasty, or even the present Resident Identity Card system introduced by the PRC (People's Republic of China) in 1984.

THE REAL-LIFE TERRACOTTA ARMY: BROTHERS IN ARMS

Along with the written word, the other great pillar of the Qin state was the army, and their image is now known across the world thanks to the astonishing find of the Terracotta Warriors. They were discovered in 1974, close to Xi'an, at the vast site of the Qin emperor's tomb complex, which is still being excavated. They appear to us as massed ranks, faceless and regimented. Though, again, remarkable recent discoveries from tombs at Shuihudi, near Wuhan in the Yangtze valley, have turned those assumptions upside down.

One tomb contained letters, written on wooden boards, by two brothers: Heifu and Jing. Ordinary soldiers in the all-conquering Qin army, they fought in the campaign against the southern state of Chu in 224–223 BCE that brought about the unification of China. Their mother, wives and younger brother were back home in Anlu town near Yunmeng in northwest Hubei. Deployed several hundred kilometres from home, the brothers express themselves in a personal and straightforward way, with all the vivacity found in the Roman period tablets from Vindolanda on Hadrian's Wall in Britain. Writing to their brother Zhong, they ask for cash to be sent and for their mother to make clothing for them and send it to them at the front. The following translation is by Enno Giele.

On 6 April, Heifu and Jing send best greetings to their brother Zhong:

How is Mother? We are fine. Recently we were split up, but we're back together again now. Heifu has entrusted me to beg you for help, and putting this into writing … Send me cash, don't bring summer clothes. Now when you get this letter, Mother, look in Anlu for silk cloth that is cheap. If there is some that can be made into an unlined skirt and shirt, can you make that and send it with the cash? If the cloth is too dear, just send the cash and I'll make the clothes myself with hemp cloth.

Then war intrudes, and the First Emperor's army is on constant campaign footing: 'I and my unit are about to help in attacks on rebel cities at Huaiyang in Henan. How long it will take, and how many will be captured or wounded no one knows . . .'

Then come questions about the family: 'How are Auntie, sister Kangle and Aunt Gushu? Send best wishes. To our young Ying Fan, best regards. And what about *that* business? Is it settled yet?' (Perhaps a forthcoming marriage?) And there is a note to one of the wives to look after their parents well: 'new sister in law . . . give your best'. The letter ends with a list of regards to old neighbours and friends, not forgetting 'old Yan Zheng from Bin neighbourhood'.

The second letter, from Jing to his young brother at home, repeats the request for money and clothes, suggesting that their situation had become a little desperate (the brothers perhaps were in debt), and asks that money be sent speedily. Jing asks whether their aunt's childbirth has gone successfully, and shares his worries about the security situation with many rebels on the prowl on the roads.

Finally Jing sends good wishes to the wives, asking them to look after the old parents, and tells his young brother to make sure that his new wife takes care not to go too far away when she's gathering firewood, 'and do the shrine sacrifices for me, if they are not being done for me it's because I'm tied up in a rebel city'. 'PS: Robbers have entered the new territories,' he ends. 'So, Zhong, I wish that right now you weren't going there. Take great care!'

These letters give us a glimpse into the real lives behind the Terracotta Army. They show ordinary Qin soldiers writing to their families, sharing their feelings and worries, and that the army allowed this kind of private communication. Even in times of war, it seems that the postal service from the front line was sufficiently well organised to enable regular contact, and family members could visit the camp to deliver clothing, food and money.

But did Jing write the letters himself? The script on the bamboo strip is fine and regular and looks scribal. Maybe the brothers asked a literate colleague to help, or even paid a scribe. Yet the letter says, 'Heifu has entrusted me' – Jing – 'to beg you for help', and it is clearly possible that people of his rank in the army were literate. Later Han documents suggest writing skills were fairly widespread outside the civil service. One soldier, for example, is described as 'capable of writing reports to higher authorities and managing official business and people. He is somewhat familiar with the texts of the statutes and ordinances. He is thirty-two years old.' Evidently there were many like him already in the Qin empire, so perhaps Jing was such a literate soldier. These discoveries were only fully published in 2015 and underline the pace at which our knowledge of early China is changing.

Though women were not part of the Qin army, they did accompany their husbands stationed out west in the following century. Women also appear as heads of households in Qin and Han surveys, so we must assume they too had some writing skills if they were part of the government's system of registration. Women in the Qin empire could also be in business. The historian Sima Qian mentions the business acumen of a widow named Mrs Qing, from Ba county, who took over the family cinnabar-mining firm. This was dangerous, toxic work, especially if she was also involved in the distillation process. They mainly produced mercury sulphide ore for vermilion used in face makeup, for adorning precious objects and making paint for ceramics. Cinnabar was used as early as the prehistoric Yangshao culture, for decorative purposes. Indeed, in traditional medicine it is still used today, in popular insomnia remedies, for example. It was especially in demand during the Qin era, however, as large quantities of mercury had to be produced for the First Emperor's tomb.

THE FIRST EMPEROR'S BUILDING PROJECTS

Like all great autocrats in history, the First Emperor created grandiose monuments to himself. The historian Sima Qian tells the story that Shi Huangdi had palaces and pavilions built to symbolise each of the conquered nations, full of their treasures, artefacts and women, so the emperor could revisit each of his conquests:

> Whenever Qin wiped out one of the feudal states, he would recreate its halls and palaces and reconstruct them on the slope north of Xianyang facing south over the Wei River. From Yongmen east to the Jing and the Wei Rivers, mansions, elevated walks and fenced pavilions succeeded one another, all filled with beautiful women and the bells and drums that Qin had taken from the feudal rulers.

The emperor's conquests, then, were mapped onto the landscape of the capital as a kind of vast memory room. The scale was such that it enabled the emperor to walk among these models of the defeated states, contemplating his triumphs in the looted bronzes, bells and royal regalia. It also allowed him to possess the captive women of the former royal families as he wished.

Most celebrated in later poetry and painting was the Epang Palace, south of the Wei River, which was said to be the most richly decorated of all. The throne room, as determined by archaeologists from surviving traces of the huge earth platforms, was 690 metres by 115 metres. Under its giant roof, 10,000 people could be seated. Covered walkways joined it to the administrative palace at Xianyang 6 miles away. They were connected by a bridge over the Wei River, which was itself imagined as an earthly twin of the Milky Way in a vast symbolic landscape mirroring the heavenly order, at the centre of which was the 'palace of the celestial pole'.

INSPIRED BY THE GREEKS?

These staggering constructions, which were never completed, drew on an eclectic range of models which open up fascinating perspectives on the Qin dynasty's relation to the outside world. One of the most controversial is the description by Sima Qian of twelve huge bronze figures which were cast for the emperor: 'Weapons from all over the empire were confiscated, brought to Xianyang and melted down to be used in casting bells, bell stands and twelve men made of metal. These last weighed a thousand piculs each and were set up in the palace.'

One picul, notionally, was what a man could carry on a shoulder pole, 60 kilograms. So the figure is an impossibility, a statue of a thousand piculs would weigh 60 tons. But did the statues exist? And, if so, what was the inspiration behind them? Large-scale figural sculpture, indeed any kind of naturalistic representation of the human body, was unknown at that time in the heartland of China. The recent sensational finds at Sanxingdui of highly stylised, life-sized bronze figures are from much earlier and left no discernible artistic legacy. So what was the inspiration for this very brief flowering of large-scale figurative art? Recently, intriguing claims have been made of Hellenistic Greek influence from across the deserts of Central Asia. The Terracotta Warriors themselves are stiff and anatomically inaccurate. However, the eleven figures of acrobats, weightlifters or dancers, discovered in a separate pit in 1999 (dozens more are still being restored), are a different matter. Only the Greeks at this time were capable of such anatomically well-observed renderings of the human body.

In the late fourth century BCE, in the very years when the Qin were beginning their expansion in China, Alexander the Great had conquered Iran and burst into India and Central Asia. Over the next two centuries his successors moved down the Ganges valley almost to the Bay of Bengal and colonised Bactria and Sogdiana. That they had contact with China across Central Asia seems certain, even though direct evidence is so far lacking. Hellenistic finds in the far west of China include textiles, two small statues of soldiers in Xinjiang and a beautiful Hellenistic bowl from Gansu. Ideas came eastwards, too: the theorem of Pythagoras reached China within a couple of generations of Alexander's death. The first known Chinese mission to the Hellenistic cities of Central Asia took place a century later, but there is no difficulty at all in pushing such contacts back earlier. Among the cities Alexander founded in Central Asia, Khodjent still exists on the Syr Darya river in Tajikistan, 150 miles west of Ferghana. On the Amu Darya (Oxus) in northern Afghanistan, Ai Khanoum, with its agora, theatre and gymnasium, survived until it was destroyed in the second century BCE. Between the 250s and 230s, these cities were part of a powerful Hellenistic kingdom in Bactria that ruled as far east as the Fergana valley in the very time when the Greeks believed contact with the 'Seres' began.

It is fascinating, then, that the story told by Sima Qian was that the Qin emperor had been inspired by the descriptions of 'palaces far to the west' when commissioning his twelve statues of 'big men' in foreign robes for his own residence at Xianyang. We have no good description; according to one later source they were 11 metres tall, and though this is probably an exaggeration, it seems likely that they were larger than life-size. They also carried an inscription: 'In the twenty-sixth year of the emperor when the emperor for the first time unified All Under Heaven and first divided China into provinces and unified the weights and measures'. Hollow and cast in pieces, other evidence suggests the statues were fashioned after non-Chinese prototypes – 'foreign models'. In this case it seems certain the ideas came from the Hellenistic world of Central Asia. There, the techniques of large-scale bronze statuary had been refined, and Greek art and sculpture had become the pictorial language of half the world. It is therefore quite possible that Chinese merchants or ambassadors had seen such statues out to the west. During the lifetime of Qin Shi Huangdi, the Indian Emperor Asoka of the Mauryan dynasty (268–232 BCE) sent ambassadors to West Asia, Syria and the Greek Mediterranean. There are also Indian traditions that he sent relics of the Buddha to China. It is probable that the Mauryans at least knew of the existence of the Qin and called them by that name. (The Western name for China is derived from the word Qin, and it was most likely transmitted via the Mauryans through Sanskrit and Persian into Greek.)

The twelve great Qin bronzes were lost in antiquity. Ten were melted down in 190 CE; two we know survived until the fourth century; but no trace of that astonishing Hellenistic–Qin hybrid survives today – except perhaps the Terracotta Army itself.

THE MAKERS OF THE TOMB: BELLE THE POTTER

On the making of the Terracotta Army, recent archaeological discoveries have given us fascinating new insights into the craftspeople who actually worked on the figures for the tomb complex. About ninety names have been found on figures of humans and horses. These are mainly men, though lacquer painters were more likely to be women, and some of the terracotta potters were women too. They were state artisans, employed by palace ceramic workshops, with separate groups responsible for the water pipes, roof tiles and figures. Artisans who normally worked for private workshops in the Xi'an area were also conscripted to work on the project, inscribing their names into the clay of the figures, sometimes prefixed by a county of residence and job description. Some of the items are also inscribed with numerals, which appear to be job numbers. Other markings suggest the composition of the workshops, with a master potter or foreman as head of a work brigade of at least ten potters and apprentices. This suggests a possible workforce of around a thousand artisans working on the terracotta figures. The potters were mostly men, but one potter is called Yue, her name written with a sign containing a female semantic classifier, used only in phrases describing female beauty. We might call her Belle – a literate, female master potter who may have been the head of her workshop, perhaps the daughter of a master potter trained in the family business, just as professional scribes were sometimes daughters of scribes. So Belle could have been brought up in the workshop, where she learned her trade along with basic literacy and numeracy skills. These enabled her to inscribe her name, rank, county and job number in the standard orthography onto the objects she was making. A quality-control exercise at the time, but for later archaeologists a delightful insight into one of many craftspeople conscripted to the huge task of tomb construction.

THE FIRST EMPEROR'S TOMB

Qin Shi Huangdi initiated the construction project for his own tomb when he took the Qin throne, aged only thirteen, but once he became emperor, in 221 BCE, gigantic resources were devoted to its planning and completion. The hard labour of digging out the immense vault and creating the artificial mountain above it was done by penal slaves and conscripted labour. Fragments of ceramics from the workers' cemeteries enable us to pinpoint some of them by name and place of origin. One slave worker on the imperial mausoleum was called Yu. His title was *bugeng*, denoting a low-ranking civil servant, and his place of origin was Bochang, a village more than 1,000 kilometres from Xi'an towards the northeastern edge of the empire. An educated man, an ex-civil servant, perhaps Yu had been an officer for the former Qi state. Sentenced to hard labour for an unknown crime, he had been part of a chain gang, led along the road routes up the Yellow River valley to the huge construction site under Mount Li. He never returned to his homeland. It is possible he was even killed when the work was completed.

The slave Yu was one of hundreds of thousands who worked on the insatiable construction projects of the Qin empire. The most famous, of course, was the royal the tomb itself, built underneath Mount Li at Lintong, 25 kilometres west of today's Xi'an, one of the most famous archaeological sites in the world. Writing a century or so after the emperor's death, Sima Qian tells the tale of its construction in an unforgettable passage:

When the First Emperor ascended the throne, the digging and preparation at Mount Li began. After he unified his empire, 700,000 men were sent there from all over his empire. They dug down deep to underground springs, pouring copper to place the outer casing of the coffin. Palaces and viewing towers housing 100 officials were built and filled with treasures and rare artefacts. Workmen were instructed to make automatic crossbows primed to shoot at intruders. Mercury was used to simulate the hundred rivers, the Yangtze and Yellow River, and the great sea and set to flow mechanically. Above, the heaven is depicted, below, the geographical features of the land. Candles were made of 'mermaid's fat', which is calculated to burn and not extinguish for a long time. The Second Emperor (his son) said: 'It is inappropriate for the wives of the late emperor who have no sons to be free.' He then ordered that they should accompany the dead, and a great many died. After the burial, it was suggested that it would be a serious breach if the craftsmen who constructed the tomb and knew of its treasure were to divulge those secrets. Therefore, after the funeral ceremonies, the inner passages and doorways were blocked, and the exit sealed, trapping the workers and craftsmen inside. None could escape. Trees and vegetation were then planted on the tomb mound such that it resembled a hill.

This, then, was to be a tomb for eternity. Here, the emperor's spirit would be guarded by spectral armies and attendants in a labyrinthine complex. Above ground, rituals for the founding ancestor would be carried out forever by his later descendants. The site extends over 100 square kilometres and is still not entirely mapped, let alone wholly excavated. Pits bordering the tomb complex have so far yielded over 8,000 terracotta soldiers, 130 chariots with 520 horses, 150 cavalry horses, acrobats, officials, musicians and even a strongman. Other pits recently uncovered include dismembered remains. These may be the remains of childless concubines who Sima Qian says were killed when the emperor was entombed.

The tomb itself, under its enormous mound, remains unopened. The archaeologists fear they may not have the resources or the expertise to deal with the sheer quantity of fragile material which may still lie inside, and that once exposed to the air may be lost. They are proceeding carefully, therefore, though the use of geophysical surveys has brought fascinating new insights. We now know, for example, that the whole mound, flattened and eroded over so many centuries, originally measured 515 metres from north to south and 485 metres from east to west. The plan included underground dams with sealed tiled channels to divert subterranean springs and water systems. The designers were apparently successful in doing this as the tomb seems to have escaped flooding. The underground palace was rectangular in shape, rather like the great royal tombs of earlier epochs, going back to the grave pits of the Shang, but on an even bigger scale. An immense pit was dug to a depth of at least 30 metres below the original ground level. This was then lined with a massive burned-brick perimeter wall, 460 metres by 390 metres and about 4 metres high. Inside this rectangle, a huge brick structure was built, with a hollow interior to surround the actual burial chamber.

In 2003, geophysical and geochemical analysis of the soil found unusually high levels of mercury concentrated in one area. Its distribution suggests a vestige of the model of China's great rivers laid down on the floor of the tomb, confirming Sima's account of its design and construction. The quantity of mercury needed to achieve this, industrially reduced from mined cinnabar in workshops run by the likes of Widow Qing in Ba county, is little short of mind-boggling.

The buildings on the surface of the site were destroyed in the great revolt that overthrew the dynasty after the emperor's death and the grave pit may have been plundered at that time. But the main body of the tomb chamber has not collapsed and the massive wooden structure still exists underneath the tomb mound. The large concentrations of mercury might also suggest that the burial chamber was not open to the elements. It is possible, then, that the First Emperor still lies entombed in his underground palace, surrounded by the bones of his servants.

THE FALL OF THE QIN

The great tomb was to be a ritual centre that would perpetuate the emperor's authority over the world even after his death: a memory palace for 'ten thousand generations'. Yet for all the emperor's hopes that his empire would last for all time, the collapse was extraordinarily swift.

Within six years, like several great dynasties in Chinese history, the Qin was overthrown by massive peasant rebellions. As always, heaven announced the changing mandate with signs and omens. In 211 BCE, a meteor fell in the lower reaches of the Yellow River.

When the stone was recovered, someone had inscribed on it: 'The First Emperor will die and his lands shall be divided.' According to Sima Qian, the event was frantically investigated by the now dying emperor. When no culprit was found, the local people living where the meteor fell were killed and the stone was burned and pulverised. By this point in his reign, later historians claimed, the emperor had become mentally unbalanced. Increasingly drawn to megalomaniac schemes, he climbed sacred mountains to distil the dew of dawn and sent young girls and boys on sea journeys seeking the mythical Isles of the Blessed. Finally, debilitated by alchemical concoctions devised by his physicians as pills of immortality, he died on 10 September 210 BCE, still not fifty years old.

The first political genius of Chinese history, Qin Shi Huangdi bequeathed China the template of a state unified by force. He also passed on the dark model of the 'all-powerful emperor', in whose person coercive power, morality and law were all combined. These two legacies would provide a continuing tension in the heart of China's political culture. As the later poet Du Mu said:

> If Qin could have loved its people,
> Then the Qin dynasty could have lasted not three but a
>   thousand generations.
> If the later generations only lamented Qin's tragic ending,
> But failed to learn a lesson from it,
> Then the vicious cycle would repeat itself . . .

THE FIRST CHINESE REVOLUTION?

The reign of the First Emperor is one of the most important moments in the history of China. The transformation of society and culture under the Qin was so great that it can only be described as a thoroughgoing revolution, perhaps the only real revolution until the twentieth century. Qin Shi Huangdi began a new epoch and put the ruler at the centre of the historical narrative. He created a unified territory and introduced a centralised bureaucracy. His government controlled people right down to the family group and measured land to the last *mu*, helping to reinforce the idea of one polity subordinate to the emperor's will. Short-lived as it was, the Qin empire bequeathed a legacy that has informed every period of government that followed, through many dynasties, down to the Republic, to Mao and even today's People's Republic: the principle that authority over a united China stems from a single source of power, which is both the executive and the dispenser of law.

The Qin's way of thought has always met with approval in periods of Chinese history when disorder threatened. Mao described himself as a mixture of Marx and Qin Shi Huangdi. The seductive image of Confucius' 'sage-ruler' and the coercive power recommended by the legalist Lord Shang, it would turn out, were both tools in the hands of an autocrat. But the Qin unified China. From then on, for all its ups and downs, the idea of China as a unitary civilisation persisted as the goal to return to; in the opening words of the famous Ming novel *Romance of the Three Kingdoms*, written more than fifteen centuries later: 'The empire that is united will one day fall apart, and what is divided will come back together again. So it has always been.'

5

THE HAN EMPIRE

Founded by a peasant rebel, Liu Bang, the Han is one of the great dynasties of China. Their influence on later history was profound – so much so that the Chinese still call themselves 'Han' today. Covering a 400-year period, there were many great achievements in Han governance and culture. Their empire spans the period of the later Roman Republic and the early empire in the West, with whom China had diplomatic and commercial relations for the first time. In recent years, as with the Qin, astonishing archaeological discoveries have opened up their world to us, including even letters by ordinary people in government offices and soldiers and administrators at watchtowers and way stations out on the Silk Road in Central Asia. Their story begins with the turmoil that followed the sudden death of the First Emperor and the swift dissolution of his hated rule.

THE FALL OF THE QIN

The First Emperor of Qin had died in northeast China on one of his grand royal tours on 10 September 210 BCE and was succeeded by his son. It was only eleven years after the unification. Aware of seething resentment among the people and fearing a general uprising, his ministers concealed the emperor's death for the two-month journey back to the capital. Legend says the royal procession was accompanied by carts of fish to conceal the stink of the decomposing body. As ministers and the royal clan disputed the succession, the atmosphere built up like an electrical storm heavy with the charge of revolt. The following summer, chaos was unleashed.

The scene is one of extraordinary drama, even by the standards of the time. With the 'god-like and vicious' First Emperor dead, the net of fear cast by his rule began to unravel. In the muggy monsoon heat of July 209 BCE, an army of 900 press-ganged peasants headed through Anhui, up the old north road, led by Qin army officers. When they reached the Huai River, the summer rains burst in a torrential downpour, reducing the countryside to a lake. Faced with rising waters at the way station of Dazexiang, 'Big Swamp Village', they could go no further. The harsh Qin law, however, decreed the death penalty for failure to fulfil orders, no matter what the excuse. The officers leading the peasants were two obscure men long remembered in Chinese history: Chen Sheng and Wu Guang. Both of these Qin army captains decided to fight rather than meekly give up their lives. They knew that the state was already in turmoil, that the emperor's eldest son and heir had been forced to commit suicide on his father's orders, and that though the younger son was now on the throne, allegiance was haemorrhaging in the provinces. So Chen fabricated a prophecy written on a piece of cloth, which he pulled theatrically from the entrails of a fish taken from the floodwaters: the Qin would be overthrown, the old kingdoms restored, and Chen would be king. They then killed any officers who stood in their way and began the revolt. Joined by disaffected local officials and rebellious farmers, they soon numbered 10,000 strong. It was the first rising against the hitherto invincible Qin empire.

During the following year, rebellion broke out in many places. Joined by more disgruntled farmers and local garrisons, Chen Sheng and Wu Guang marched their peasant army on the capital, but were crushed by the disciplined Qin army with its chariots and mechanical crossbows. In the aftermath, the two were killed by their own men. They were remembered in folk stories and are still found among the plethora of characters portrayed as door gods in Daoist shrines and village temples, for whom incense is lit at the threshold. Nor was their watchword forgotten: 'Are kings and nobles given their status by birth?'

The risings against the Qin now coalesced into two main rebel movements. The first was led by a former peasant, Liu Bang, who had risen to be a county scribe and a local magistrate. Liu is one of the most remarkable figures in Chinese history and many legends gathered around him in later times, which are still told today in folk tradition and in the storytelling houses. It was said that his mother had given birth to him in a tremendous lightning storm, while sheltering under a bridge. Above the bridge, her husband saw an omen, a dragon hovering in the clouds. Towards the end of the First Emperor's reign, Liu had been ordered to escort a party of convicts to join the labour gangs working on the First Emperor's mausoleum, but on the road some broke their chains and escaped. As Liu was responsible, the penalty was death under Qin law. So he decided to release the rest of the prisoners and became a fugitive himself, with a price on his head. He fled to a land of rocky wooded outcrops around Mangdang, down the Henan plain. There, Liu took refuge in an abandoned fort where other outlaws had gathered, including a former local magistrate who was his old patron. They patiently waited for their chance and, the following year, as central China rose up in arms, they took it.

Liu joined up with a bigger rebel army under a charismatic and violent warlord, Xiang Yu. Together the two coordinated an attack on the Qin capital. After many reverses, Xiang defeated the Qin army, killed the new emperor and sacked the capital. They burned the First Emperor's splendid palaces, among them the unfinished Epang Palace, which was subsequently remembered as the most glamorous in all of history. (Portrayed in dream-like paintings and poems as a world of the immortals, it has been recycled in the modern age across East Asia in movies, TV shows and theme parks.)

Xiang was now in control of a huge swathe of central China and announced himself as the paramount ruler, the 'Hegemon King'. He made his subordinate, Liu, 'Lord of Han', that is, of the valley of the Han River, which meets the Yangtze at Wuhan. Tensions between the two soon escalated, however, and eventually the erstwhile allies fought a bitter war for the imperial throne. After three years of conflict, Liu defeated Xiang, who committed suicide. Xiang's almost supernatural bravery and cruelty ensured him a long afterlife as a hero and villain in folk tales, poetry, novels, opera, and latterly in films, comics and video games.

So Liu was proclaimed emperor. Seeking validation from heaven, the court astrologers announced that the five-planet alignment of May 205 BCE had announced the conferral of the Mandate on the Han, just as it had the Xia, Shang and Zhou dynasties. In 202 BCE, Liu was declared emperor of the new dynasty, which he named after his own lordship, the Han.

THE MAKING OF THE HAN

Despite his peasant origins, Liu Bang had some experience in law and administration. Therefore, as emperor, he began by abolishing the most repressive Qin laws, while keeping their bureaucratic structures. Like the other great peasant emperor, Zhu Yuanzhang, of the Ming, he instituted changes to help the poor, with land reforms, reduction of land taxes and lessening the hated burden of forced labour. Gradually the Han accrued huge power. Under his successors, new capitals were laid out at Chang'an (today's Xi'an) and Luoyang with imperial architecture on a vast scale. The high point of Han military power and cultural achievement came under Emperor Wu (ruled 141–87 BCE), a contemporary of the later Roman Republic in the West.

In terms of the broad ethos of governance, the early Han rulers had followed the legalist leanings of the Qin. However, under Wu and his successors, Confucius was rehabilitated and imperial scholars were entrusted with devising a new curriculum that would serve the state. They collated and reconstructed the classics banned by the Qin and added more, with commentaries on the canon created by Confucius. They also included history, notably the *Spring and Autumn Annals*, traditionally attributed to the Master himself.

These texts received official status as textbooks for schools and civil service examinations. And so began what would turn out to be a two-millennia-long linkage between the Confucian classics and Chinese political discourse that exerted huge influence over political ideas and personal behaviour in traditional China. The Han scholar Dong Zhongshu argued that the Han had proved themselves the legitimate successors to the true models of kingship, the Zhou. Their mixture of Confucian humanism and legalist harshness, empowered by Confucius' vision of history, would survive to the twentieth century.

WARS WITH THE XIONGNU

Like the Roman Empire with its defended frontiers in North Britain, on the Rhine, Danube and Euphrates, the big geopolitical issue for the Han was their relations with people beyond their borders who did not acknowledge Han rule and Han law. Throughout its history, the Chinese state shared the lands of East Asia with other powers, which sometimes (as under the Song) ruled only part of China proper and sometimes (as with the Yuan and the Qing) ruled all of China. In the Han period, this perennial historic confrontation between the sedentary and nomadic focused on the vast semi-nomadic confederation of the Xiongnu.

The Xiongnu extended along the northern edge of the empire in an immense arc from the Irtysh River in today's Kazakhstan to the Amur River in the northeast, and from Lake Baikal in the north to the middle stretches of the Yellow River where it crosses the Ordos plateau. In 201 BCE, the newly inaugurated Liu Bang suffered a heavy defeat in northern Shaanxi. After that, the Chinese adopted a policy of 'peace and alliance', with diplomacy instead of war. This would be accomplished through dynastic marriage and gift giving, in effect a tributary relationship. Still, there were many attacks, and in the late second century BCE, after decades of conflict, Emperor Wu determined to force them to acknowledge his supremacy. From the 130s BCE, Wu mounted several huge military expeditions into

Xiongnu territory, with massive attacks by tens of thousands of cavalry, forcing his enemies to retreat beyond the Gobi Desert. These 'Northern Desert Wars' were on a scale never seen before in world history, dwarfing the armies with which Alexander the Great invaded Persia and India. From then on, the upper hand lay with the Han.

THE BIRTH OF HISTORY

In spring 110 BCE, led by the emperor himself, a 'colossal' Han force of twelve army groups assembled at Yunyang on the Hanshui River in Hubei, 200 miles southwest of Xi'an. From there, they marched up the Yellow River valley to the top of the great bend of the river in the Ordos, beyond the Qin Long Walls, past Lake Juyan, skirting the edge of the Gobi Desert, to the 'Chanyu plateau'. This was an important Xiongnu campsite, near one of the headwaters of the Tuul River that flows into Lake Baikal, not far from the present-day Ulaanbaatar. Having demonstrated their overwhelming force, the army finally returned to the north bank of the Yellow River. 'As a piece of logistics this was a tour de force', noted a later writer, 'though in reality it did not achieve very much.'

A 35-year-old newly married scholar was with the expedition, on the royal staff as a ritualist and archive keeper. This man was the future Grand Historian of China, Sima Qian. For Sima, this spectacle of the realities of war and of the military power of the Han must have been a telling and exhilarating experience, providing him with raw material and an exemplar that would help shape his approach to writing a new kind of history. History is one of the keys to Chinese culture; in all states, the rulers create the narrative of a common past with which people can identify and which helps create allegiance, but in no state has this been more important. The famous story of the Qin emperor killing historians and burning books was emblematic: 'fearing the power of the past to discredit the present'.

History was political in the truest sense. In no Chinese epoch of imperial times, therefore, are there historians like Herodotus or

Thucydides, who were writing for themselves. In China, history was written to endorse the assumption of the Mandate of Heaven. It was also written to uphold the timeless values of the canonical tradition, as determined by Confucius and his followers, at the centre of which were ritual, morality and history. It is no accident, then, that recent finds excavated in Han tombs have yielded bamboo strips that include excerpts from the *Spring and Autumn Annals* in the hands of local magistrates and administrators. This was the core of the historical canon and was part of the official's training. Sima Qian would bring together these earlier ideas in a great synthesis, which would determine the future path of historical writing and interpretation in China, with its exemplary Confucian moral voice.

A younger contemporary of the Greek historian Polybius, Sima was born in around 145 BCE, seventy-five years after the death of the Qin emperor. So his time was almost within living memory, but certainly within accurate second-hand tradition. His family home was a gentry estate outside the town of Hancheng, northeast of Xi'an – a wonderfully atmospheric place where the Yellow River completes its great arc south, through a steep gorge, before entering the plains. (The landscape there has deep associations with the tales of Yu the Great, a story with which the young Sima grew up.)

Still a small town by Chinese standards, Hancheng has so far escaped the devastation of modernity and still has scores of historic houses in its narrow alleys. Sima's tomb is reached by a steep stairway under brick and wood memorial arches, up a wooded hillside with magnificent views over the river. A place of pilgrimage for centuries, the complex with its ancestral temple was refurbished under every dynasty since the Tang. At the circular brick tomb, where an ancient cypress tree grows out of the roof, a stele written by an official of the Qing dynasty salutes Sima not as a historian, but as 'Keeper of the Calendar and the Astronomy of the Han'.

Sima's father had been a court servant under Emperor Wu, but had fallen from favour. He too is often called 'Grand Historian', but that is to give the wrong impression of what his job was. The Sima family were descended from ritualists who, from the Zhou period, had recorded royal deeds, sacrifices and omens. They played an important role in interpreting and predicting the course of government, according to the influence of the sun, moon and stars. In other words, they were interpreters of the fluid relationship between humanity and the cosmos; court astrologers akin to Roman augurs. Since the early days of the Zhou, the keepers of the calendar had recorded the deeds and journeys, the proclamations and sacrifices of the kings, and these were read out at ritual occasions. Such was the job Sima would inherit from his father, in the end producing the defining text on early Chinese history.

THE JOURNEY OF SIMA QIAN

In his vast book *Historical Records*, the most famous of all works of Chinese history and one of the great products of the Han age, Sima gives a laconic summary of his own life in the third person. Turned into a first-person narrative, it is a fascinating biographical record of the intellectual, emotional and cultural roots of one of the great figures in Chinese civilisation:

> I was born at Longmen [Hancheng], I ploughed and kept flocks on the sunny side of the hills along the Yellow River. By the age of ten I could read aloud the classical texts. When I was twenty I travelled south to the Yangtze and Huai Rivers, I climbed Mount Kuaiji [near Shaoxing], looked for the cave of King Yu and I saw the Nine Peaks of Jiuyi [in Henan, the burial place of the primordial ruler, the first farmer Shun]. I sailed down the Yuan and Xiang Rivers and in the north forded the Wen and Si Rivers [in Shandong]. I studied the learning of the cities of Qi [Yingqiu-Linzi in Shandong] and Lu [Qufu]. I observed the customs and practices inherited from Confucius and took part in the archery contest at Mount Yi in Zou [Shandong]. I met with trouble and danger in Po and Xie and Pengcheng. Then I passed through Liang and Chu [Xuzhou, Jiangsu] and returned home. Afterwards I served as a palace gentleman ...

Aged twenty, that journey around China was of crucial importance in Sima's life, as a similar journey had been to Confucius. Travelling gave Sima a feeling for the diverse culture and geography of China and for the antiquity of its story. He visited the burial places of legendary founders like King Yu and King Shun, but also the sites of recent history, including Qufu, the birthplace of Confucius, where he immersed himself in the living Confucian tradition first hand through the Kong clan. All the way, he asked questions of old people about their stories and traditions, which as he discovered were often diametrically opposed to received versions in official texts.

After his return home, Sima married and had two sons and a daughter. His job, as a palace attendant, included duties on inspection tours with the emperor Wu – among them, as we saw, the military expedition into Mongolia. Then Sima Qian's father, Sima Tan, fell ill. On his desk Sima Tan left unfinished, or in note form, a privately compiled work of history. It was intended to be not simply a list of records, but an interpretation of the records, involving those key aspects of historical writing: judgement and critical selection. The aim, he told his son, was to continue 'a thread that has been handed on for a thousand years'. The issue, Sima's father said, was that over recent times 'some states have annexed others, historical records have been lost, and excised', most famously in the book burnings of the Qin emperor. 'But now', he continued, contemplating his unfulfilled plans, 'the Han has risen up and all within the seas is united and though I became Grand Historian, I have not placed on record the enlightened rulers, loyal ministers and public servants who would have given their lives out of their sense of duty. And now I fear that the historical writings of All Under Heaven will be discarded.' Exactly how much Sima Tan had already written is not known. Nevertheless, at this point, 'grasping my hands with tears in his eyes', Sima Tan made his son swear to complete it: 'Don't forget what I intended to argue and set down in writing!'

Sima started his task after his father's death in 109 BCE. Three years later he was made court astrologer. In 105 BCE, he was also one of the scholars chosen to reform the Qin calendar and produce a new Han calendar. Sima Qian's learning was being recognised by all, and he was a valued councillor of the great emperor, who was now in his mid-fifties and had been on the throne for forty-one years. But then came a fateful change in his fortunes.

THE SILKWORM CHAMBER

In 99 BCE, Sima was caught up in an affair of state when a General Li Ling was condemned for a military failure against the Xiongnu. Li was not a friend, but Sima respected him as a loyal servant and defended him. However, he was alone in doing so. A man swift to anger, Emperor Wu was enraged at Sima's boldness in speaking out and sentenced him to death. The sentence could only be commuted by an enormous sum of money, or by castration, faced with which any gentleman would ask to be 'permitted to commit suicide'. Sima, though, had sworn an inviolable oath to his father that he would finish his great work of history. So, in filial piety, he 'submitted to the knife' in the hothouse warmth of the 'Silkworm Chamber'. After that pain and humiliation and three years in prison, Sima chose to live as a palace eunuch in the imperial administration, while working on his history in private. He was 'driven by the fear that the deeds of the great people of the past would be forgotten and that my writings would be lost to posterity', as he put it in writing to his friend Ren An, in one of the most famous letters in Chinese history:

> I too have ventured not to be modest, but have entrusted myself to my useless writings. I have gathered up and brought together the old traditions of the world, which were scattered and lost. I have examined the deeds and events of the past and investigated the principles behind their success and failure, their rise and decay, in 130 chapters. I wished to examine all that concerns heaven and man, to penetrate the changes of the past and present, completing all as the work of one family. But before I had finished my rough manuscript, I met with this calamity. It is because I regretted that it had not been completed that I submitted to the extreme penalty

without rancour. When I have truly completed this work, I shall deposit it in the Famous Mountain. If it may be handed down to men who will appreciate it and penetrate to the villages and great cities, then though I should suffer a thousand mutilations, what regret should I have?

Already in draft when disaster struck, the book was finished in 94 BCE. Despite its great fame as the foundation of the historical record of China, until recently most of its 130 chapters were untranslated outside East Asia, with only certain treatises, the key biographies and the annals on the Qin being well known beyond China. The problem for Sima Qian, as for all historians, was how to organise his picture of the past. To use Western analogies, should it use narrative like Herodotus or Polybius, biography like Plutarch, or analysis of institutions like Aristotle? If those comparisons seem to exaggerate the intellectual originality of a writer two millennia ago, they are there simply to point out that intuitively, and perhaps consciously, Sima perceived that, in history, no one approach will do. The complexity of events and historical process cannot be rendered in one straight narrative, but must mix between those different elements. Sima solved the problem for himself by forsaking an integrated narrative for five main sections in an encyclopaedic form which consider the calendar, religion and music, as well as biography. That said, we should be wary of assuming that anyone in China before the middle of the first millennium CE had any sense of history in a modern sense. In Sima's writings, the religious and mythic element is very strong, and so too is the moral. Indeed, for him, history is a prime source of morality. At a basic level, too, as Sima himself tells it, a further key motivation was filial piety. Sima Qian wanted to pass down the memory of his disparaged father through his great passage on the value of history, even if the words, in fact, are Sima's own.

In the aftermath of the Second World War and the Holocaust, Hannah Arendt wrote that good is on the limited scale in history, evil on the unlimited. In China, history is mainly optimistic, even if the lesson of history was that disorder, cruelty and violence were more the norm than periods of peace. For Sima Qian, if evil may triumph in the short term, it is the historians who ensure that in the long term the record of good deeds, human values and justice is passed on. Preserving the memory, then, is also a moral task. In that, Confucius was a big influence on Sima's world view, with his insistence on humanity and virtue. Sima's own story, his own sufferings, and the honesty of his *Letter to Ren*, made later generations think his way.

Sima's legacy was a base text on which later Chinese historians would build. First there was the conceptual framework, the narrative of prehistory and the first three dynasties painstakingly reconstructed from pre-Qin sources, oral tradition and even material survivals, including bronzes. Then there was the history of the successive dynasties which followed, culminating in the Han peace. Following that was the idea of morality as the driving force of history. So the Zhou conception of history was now the model. Heaven-inspired, the Mandate was working itself out in history and can be understood in the past and defined by the historian as a model for the future. For Sima Qian, then, as for Confucius, history becomes a guide to the present, as it still is in China, more than in any other country.

LIFE UNDER HAN RULE: THE VIEW FROM ZHENG VILLAGE

In recent years, remarkable archaeological discoveries have begun to reveal details of the Han order at the grassroots level. Han China was an agricultural civilisation, as it was up to the late twentieth century (in the 1980s, four fifths of the population was still rural, compared to only one quarter today). In agriculture, the legacy of the brutal extortion and exploitation under the Qin had been widespread rural unrest. The punishments in the Han lawbook would remain, essentially, the same as what we saw in the Qin. However, statesmen in the Han tried to ameliorate conditions for the peasants by cutting the land tax, improving forced labour laws and freeing people who had sold themselves into slavery during the massive disorder that had accompanied the fall of the Qin. The new documentary finds allow us to see the lives of such peasants in some detail for the first time in Chinese history.

In the excavation of a Han cemetery by the Yangtze, at Jiangling in Hubei, the tomb of Zhang Yan was uncovered. Mr Zhang was a landowner and local official in Jianglingxian town, who died in 153 CE. His job was to collect the local taxes from the farmers and, like the Qin local official we met earlier, Zhang's tomb contained his reference works as a civil servant, including the wooden slips that were the records of local administration. Among them is a group of bamboo slips called the 'Granary records of Zheng village'. These are as mesmerising a record of subjection as the fragmentary Roman estate surveys, or Domesday Book from the medieval West.

Zheng village lay on the right bank of the Yangtze, in lands liable to flood, on the great curve of the river in northern Hubei. In the Han period, this was a region of agricultural colonisation, with the extension of irrigation systems and the building of new river dykes to protect from summer floods. The workforce lived in villages and communal households, cultivating for their lord. The lord held their estate from the emperor as a fiefdom and part of it, 'private fields', was used by peasant families for their own sustenance. The bamboo strips that were found included local government receipts for grain seeds loaned to the twenty-five farming families of Zheng village. These people laboured, like most of the poor through history, to feed the rich before they could feed themselves. The receipts record the amount of cultivated land and the complete population of the village, enabling us to take one community in the heyday of the Han and see the subsistence level of its ordinary people.

Excluding infants, the twenty-five families of Zheng village added up to 105 persons, of whom sixty-nine were capable of doing agricultural labour. Excluding the lord's land, from which a portion of the produce came to the workforce, the village had a total of 617 *mou* of land. A *mou* varied in size, but was roughly 800 square yards, a sixth of an acre. So the total area of cultivable land in Zheng village was over 100 acres. Each family, though, had just under 25 *mou* per household, about 4 acres. The average Han farmer, then, if this is anything to go by, had a small amount of land by Western standards, especially if compared with the Roman estate surveys or Anglo-Saxon England, where, though admittedly in a much more sparsely populated land, one family had a notional 120 acres. With such pressure on people in daily life in Han China, there was no room for failure, especially in times of famine.

The receipts found in Mr Zhang's tomb name one farmer called Mr Ye, whose family consisted of eight people, perhaps wife, children and parents. Ye had 15 *mou* of land, 6,840 square yards, less than an acre and a half. The dark soil of Jiangling was, and still is, rich and intensely irrigated from the river floods that had built up fertility over the centuries. This made multiple cropping possible. In the south, as many as three or even four crops may be grown simultaneously. No doubt that was how farmer Ye and his family survived, along with selling or bartering their tiny surplus, but living conditions and labour must have been harsh indeed.

Like later Chinese farmers before modern agribusiness took over the countryside, the Chinese system of agriculture was more like market gardening. Everywhere the landscape was a pattern of small-holdings, as still can be seen in parts of the Yangtze delta, with the fields divided into gardens rather than what might be called farms. Paintings in Han tombs show how rural estates included ploughing with oxen and tilling, but also vegetable gardens where farmers do hoeing surrounded by mud-brick walls with chickens and pigs, mulberry groves and fruit trees. This system of small farms was always intensive, aimed at feeding the greatest number of mouths on the spot.

'FARMERS OF FORTY CENTURIES'

The extraordinary thing is how little some of these factors changed over Chinese history. In 1909, the American soil scientist and agronomist Franklin King made a nine-month tour of the Far East, with a longer stay in Shandong. There he looked closely at the lives of what he called the 'Farmers of Forty Centuries'. Among the farmers he interviewed was one man with a family of twelve that included parents, his wife and children along with a working donkey, a cow and two pigs. He farmed 2½ acres, where he grew wheat, millet, sweet potatoes and beans. Another holding of 1⅔ acres supported a family of ten.

On average, a well-to-do peasant farmer might have 15–20 *mu* of land for eight people. A less well-off cultivator might have 2–5 *mu*, with a couple of cows, a donkey and eight to ten pigs. These are exactly the figures in the Han documents. Obviously, late imperial China had a far bigger population than in the Han, and much more land was under cultivation at the start of the twentieth century. King's estimate, though, by averaging the seven holdings he recorded, was a density of nearly 1,800 people per square mile, excluding animals. This shows why governments from the Han onwards attempted to relieve the pressure on farming that had existed throughout Chinese history. As King observed, 'the remarkable maintenance of efficiency attained by Chinese farmers centuries ago and projected into the present, with little apparent decadence, merits the most profound study', and with such huge population density, 'it is clear that either very effective agricultural methods are practiced or else extreme economy is exercised'. The answer, of course, was that both were true.

From his observations in the field, King also drew some conclusions about the character of Chinese rural culture, which we may well imagine were shared by Mr Ye in the Han:

Nothing jars more than incurring needless expense, extravagance of any form, or poor judgement in making purchases. Daily we became more and more impressed by the evidence of the intense and incessant stress imposed by the dense population through centuries and how, under it, the laws of heredity have wrought upon the people, affecting constitution, habits and character. Even the cattle and sheep have not escaped its irresistible power.

Such observations lie behind the revelation of the newly discovered Qin and Han farming documents, an entirely new source for the story of China, that bring to life the summaries, statutes and management texts of the literati. With the experience of centuries behind them, Han dynasty farmers, like Mr Ye in Zheng village, used their skills, ingenuity and energy to wrest a living from the soil. Constant attention to detail, unremitting toil and infinite patience provided them with a means of subsistence in normal times. Still, the equilibrium was always fragile and easily wiped away in times of disaster, especially in flood and famine, which bred a stoicism and fatalism that can already be seen in the peasant songs from the eighth-century BCE *Book of Songs*.

From ancient times to today, many observers of the Chinese people have remarked that 'certain human qualities such as their optimism and fortitude and their honesty and community spirit' also helped them to face recurrent calamities. As a European traveller of the 1920s observed:

No other peasantry in the world gives such an impression of belonging, so much, to the soil. Here the whole of life and the whole of death takes place on the inherited ground. Man belongs to the soil not the soil to the man; it will never let its children go. However much they may increase in numbers they remain upon it, 'wringing from nature her scanty gifts by ever more assiduous labour'.

For Farmer Ye and his neighbours, who were still responsible for taxes and forced labour dues, it was easy to be driven into bankruptcy. When big landowners bought up the farmland of bankrupt tenants, the landless men had to become hired labourers, a pattern to be seen throughout Chinese history. It was the same, of course, in medieval Europe, on the great estates on the plains of Iraq in the Caliphate, and in the rice villages of southern India in the Cholan Empire. In all early agricultural societies this was the condition of the masses, whose labour sustained the incredible riches of the upper classes. By the end of the Han era, wealthy families had come to own huge numbers of once independent small farms. Some of these are depicted on the walls of Han tombs, with their manor house, barns and stables, fruit and vegetable gardens, industrial workshops and outhouses making beer and wine. The spread of these private manors begin to mark the rise of a landed aristocracy who will become powerful over the next few centuries and dominate the heartland of China until their demise at the end of the Tang dynasty.

THE LIFE OF HU SHENG, THE SLAVE

As for the poor, the people glimpsed in narrative accounts of peasant risings, their simple graves have yielded a coin or two, wooden tools, simple unglazed pottery. At the very bottom were the penal slaves, 'earth pounders' or 'wall builders', and the convict work gangs made up of bankrupted farmers and enslaved prisoners. They provided the forced labour on state projects, palaces, city walls and road and bridge construction. An extraordinary excavation in 1972, near the imperial tomb of the Han emperor Jingdi in Shaanxi, gives us an insight into the lives of such people.

In a satellite cemetery of about 20 acres, 10,000 or more prisoner labourers were buried, some with chains still on their feet or neck. These were people who laboured with shackles on. Another cemetery was found just outside the walls of Luoyang, in a place local farmers had long called 'Skeleton Gully'. The whole area is some 12 acres. One section, which was dug in 1964, had 500 graves. These rectangular pits were long, narrow and less than a metre deep; in them were crammed together mostly men, but there were also a few women. Most of these people were in their youth or early adulthood and many showed signs of war wounds on their bones. Some had a few coins, but most of the graves were empty.

One or two broken bricks were found with each skeleton, with crudely incised inscriptions. These recorded the name of the supervising unit, the skill, if any, of the prisoner, the presence of shackles or not, the name of the original prison from which they had been brought to Luoyang, the organisational unit to which they belonged, the date of death and the category of the penalty. The majority were labouring people, very few upper-class or officials. They had come from all over Luoyang and from prisons across the country to work as forced labourers, building city walls on two massive construction campaigns. The 500-plus tombs date from 107 CE to 121 CE. Their occupants probably died of hard labour, poor conditions, bad food and maltreatment. Graves were often turned over to make room for new dead prisoners. Many of the inscriptions are in unintelligible Chinese, but a precious few give some sense. One brick names a slave who came from Nanyang, south of Luoyang, one of the oldest continuously used city names in China:

(Grave 39, row 11)
Name: Hu Sheng
Date of death: beginning of the leap month, 119 CE
He is skilled in five areas: he can work with wood, metal, leather, making ink and making something from plants [the Chinese at this point is so obscure modern commentators are unable to determine his exact job, but perhaps he worked with hemp for rope textiles and clothing]. The prison he came from is Nanyang Lu. The sentence is third degree, *guixin*, the penalty is labour work such as logging for men, milling for women.

Others faced a harsher fate. Grave number 7, row 8, names a slave called Shi Shuyong, whose date of death was 28 January 108 CE, a time of year when frosts are often severe in the Luoyang basin. He came from Rencheng prison, much further away down the Yellow River, by modern Jining. He was unskilled and had a fifth-degree sentence, the most severe. He was shaved clean, that is, his hair was shaved off, and he wore a pincer around the neck with a chain. This was worn while doing hard labour, like a chain gang member in the Antebellum southern States.

This is the unseen presence behind the great empire visited by the Antonines in the 160s, though we should not pretend that slaves on estates in Roman Britain, or under the Saca in India, or the Kushans, were any less severely treated. Indeed, parallel texts to that of Hu Sheng, listing their various skills along with names, survive from as late as the eighteenth century in the Caribbean and the nineteenth century in the Southern United States.

EMPIRE OF THE SCRIBES

The government of the Han was therefore a continuation of the Qin, albeit less oppressive. If Confucius and his followers had laid down the ideal of moral rulership, and if the Qin had created a model of administration run on legalist principles, then the Han rulers took these ideas and bent them to their will over a 400-year period, and all later empires rested on its foundation.

Such a far-reaching administration, that could extend down to and record the lives of Farmer Ye and the slave Hu Sheng, was only made possible by writing. As standardised by the Qin, writing was now used by the state at every level, and so scribes were essential components of an increasingly complex bureaucracy. They were the people who carried the reach of the government into the provinces, towns and villages of the empire. Through them, the state could supervise the population, exploit its labour, control and punish.

New documentary discoveries show that there were scribal schools under the Han and that the office of scribe often ran in families, handed down from generation to generation, similar to diviners and keepers of the calendar. As the empire expanded to a population of 60 million, far more scribes were required than could be provided by the hereditary system. Specifically, more than 120,000 professional scribes were needed in the Han, all of whom had to be trained and examined. Already literate at home by seventeen years old, they would then go to school for three years of formal study. If a pupil failed, the teacher was fined. There were written and oral tests in mid-autumn, and this is the first evidence for any kind of 'civil service examination' in China, where men of skill and merit were recruited for government service. Candidates were tested to recite from memory, to write out 5,000 words from a scribal primer, and to brush characters in eight different calligraphy styles.

For divination candidates, the form was slightly different. A prospective diviner had to read and write 3,000 words from the same scribal primer, but also chant 3,000 words from a diviner's book and then perform six test divinations for the examiners using yarrow stalks. They had to get at least one accurate to pass. That was at a beginner's level. For the upper grades, a top diviner had to know 30,000 words, almost on the level of a leading scholar in later times.

The control of writing as an instrument of governance, therefore, was central to the Han system of rule. In early China, as anthropologists and social scientists have often noted in all early societies, 'writing favoured the exploitation rather than the enlightenment of mankind ... its primary function, as a means of communication, being to facilitate the enslavement of other human beings'.

RELATIONS WITH THE WEST: THE SILK ROAD

It was in Sima Qian's lifetime that the first direct contacts took place between Han China and the West. The Greek historian Polybius of Megalopolis, who had been an eyewitness to the sack of Carthage by the Romans and who died in around 125 BCE, suggests a growing awareness of this changing world in a prophetic passage:

In earlier times, the world's history had been a series of unrelated episodes, but from now on history becomes an organic whole. The affairs of Europe and Africa are connected with those of Asia and those of Asia with Africa and Europe and all events bear a relationship and contribute to a single end.

Chinese contacts with West Asia, as we have seen, had probably already taken place during the Qin. The Central Asian world had been opened up by the conquests of Alexander the Great and his successors, spreading Greek culture into Central Asia. The Hellenistic age was cosmopolitan, multi-lingual and multi-ethnic. Greek cities with mixed populations were founded on the Amu Darya (Oxus) in northern Afghanistan and on the Syr Darya in Tajikistan. The geographer Strabo says eighty cities in that region had Greek foundations. Great Silk Road oases like Samarkand were vectors of Greek culture and goods, easily reachable from the Tarim basin on the western edge of the Han world. It was inevitable that they would make contact with the Han in Central Asia, and from now on, continuous links begin that would bring Roman embassies to China in the Antonine period.

'From that time the journey to the western regions became an open passage,' wrote the later historian Sima Guang, using Han sources. Han diplomacy began to put feelers out to the many kingdoms in the vast tracts of Central Asia, between the Iranian plateau and Xinjiang, across the Pamirs to Samarkand and Parthia. The leader of the first embassies to the West was the diplomat Zhang Qian. After an initial exploratory mission and a period of captivity by the Xiongnu, Zhang led a lavish train with 300 men, 2,000 horses, cattle, sheep, and gifts of gold, silver and silk brocades. With a commission from the emperor to visit other kingdoms in the western regions, he travelled to Wusun, near Lake Issyk-Kul in today's Kyrgyzstan, where he stayed as a guest of the ruler and recruited translators. He sent subsidiary embassies out to Kokand (in modern-day Uzbekistan), Samarkand, Kunduz (in northern Afghanistan) and Persia. They gathered information about the routes down into India and across to the Near East. Henceforth, the western regions started to make commerce with the Han. For all this, Zhang Qian 'became a much respected celebrity at the Han court'.

'Henceforth the kingdoms in the western regions began to commence trading activities with the Han,' wrote Sima Guang. The Han envoy groups that travelled west to Central Asia varied in size, some of them numbering over several hundred, the smallest ones made up 100 or so. Later, when the Han court became more familiar with the regions, the number of envoys decreased; only some ten or more groups departed to the West, sometimes as few as five or six. These envoys, travelling long distances to the 'Far West', possibly the Mediterranean, could take as long as eight or nine years to complete a round trip, 'even the shortest ones could take several years to accomplish'. But the opening of what would later be known as the Silk Road changed the geopolitics of Eurasia. From then on, contacts were unbroken with the lands of West Asia.

RUNNING THE HAN EMPIRE:

LIFE ON A SILK ROAD POST STATION

From the western end of the Ming Great Wall, at the Jiayuguan Pass in Gansu, the westernmost point of traditional China, the traveller can look out from the ramparts to where the mud-brick Han dynasty frontier wall snakes off into the sand dunes westwards. There, dust storms frequently roll menacingly across the desert. Out on the old route west are the ruined mud-brick remains of forts, stations and watchtowers connecting the oases into Central Asia. All these were linked by the imperial post system, and here again recent documentary discoveries have brought vivid insights into people's lives out on the edge of the Han imperium.

The postal system already existed under the Qin, but by the Han it extended across vast distances into Xinjiang and Inner Mongolia. The network of postal stations delivered official documents and private mail by relays of runners and mounted carriers. The letters were of bamboo or wooden slips and boards, but also paper and silk. Letters in silk envelopes have been found in the dry climate with the address and delivery instructions still on the package. The wealth of new finds out here in the past twenty years is still being processed, but they give us a remarkable insight into the feelings of people billeted at the edges of the Han world. These people lived in Silk Road Xinjiang, but also at Jiyan in Inner Mongolia, where 20,000 documents have been recovered in a series of digs since the 1930s. From them we can appreciate the day-to-day routine, the tedium and the dust; a Han dynasty *Plain Tales from the Hills*.

Xuanquan postal relay station lay on the Silk Road, 40 miles east of Dunhuang. It was a jumping-off place for the Yumen Pass frontier in the west, a distance of 270 kilometres as the crow flies. Nine postal stations on this sector have been identified, with two beacon watchtower sites and three horse stations. Yumen was the final stop leaving Han China to the fifty or so kingdoms or small city-states of Central Asia that are named in the Han documents. Excavations in the early 1990s exposed the site of a Han dynasty postal station used from a little before 100 BCE to the fourth century CE. The main building had a square compound 55 yards square, with 7-metre-square turrets on two corners, one of which was probably a beacon tower. The central complex had twenty-seven rooms that included a hostel for travellers with kitchen facilities. The documents name cooks among the staff, as the local commander had to entertain official travellers, Chinese and foreign, going east or west. Most visiting groups were small, but some were large. On one occasion, the king of Khotan came with 1,700 people, most of whom must have stayed in tents. To host such a large company, supplies and personnel were sent forward in advance. In the station there were also rooms for the post courier personnel and the garrison, and stables for horses.

The letters and administration documents had been thrown out as rubbish, along with coins, tools, old weapons, cart parts, combs and lacquered chopsticks, as well as the remains of foodstuffs, grain and animal bones. In all, an astonishing 35,000 discarded documents were discovered. Twenty-three thousand of these were mainly wooden tablets and boards along with 12,000 bamboo slips and fragments, only a handful of which (a few hundred so far) have been transcribed and published. Newly translated by Enno Giele they date, mainly, from the first century BCE up to 107 CE.

The letters are about the business of daily life, asking favours, enquiring about deliveries of goods, swapping news, and also, perhaps, asking for promotions. Some official post was carried by travellers and merchants. In one letter a man named Yuan, a storekeeper in an outlying fort, writes to Xuanquan station and addresses someone who is apparently an old friend, but perhaps of higher rank. His friend, Zifang, is off on a big journey east, evidently to a much bigger and richer place, where the shops are better stocked. Yuan sends him a shopping list of goods that were hard to get out there. Maybe Yuan is also not well off and is cadging from his friend. He asks for some new shoes 'of thin but strong silk and soft leather', for which he gives size measurements (1 foot 2 inches; around 28 centimetres, so today a UK size 8). He also requests five fine calligraphy brushes, offering to 'pay at your home when next convenient'. He is anxious, though, as currently he has no good shoes, which is not ideal in the desert conditions of the Taklamakan to say the least:

> Can you please pay attention to the shoes? I want to get strong ones which are good for travelling on foot. Sorry to bother you again, but it's so hard to get good shoes. Please ask the next officer who comes out here to look after them and bring them so they arrive in time to be used. That would be great. I send my best regards!

Other letters are about festivals and celebration days, just like the Roman birthday party invitations from Hadrian's Wall. Chinese New Year in the Han was evidently the great festival it always has been and the garrisons get New Year's allowances from the authorities, while friends exchange gifts with each other. As might be expected, good clothes, food and drink are perennial themes, as in this letter from a soldier based at a Han border town in Inner Mongolia. He writes to his younger brother, who is on a lonely posting 200 kilometres to the south of Juyan oasis in Gansu, at a fort with a garrison of about 100 men:

> Dear Yousun and the young lady, life here on the frontier is very hard. I hope that in the hot season you both have the right clothing and good food and take great care on the frontier. I was glad to see you are well when I stopped by on my way to the border. I am well too. I am hoping that Xing, the supervisor of the station here, will deliver this letter to the tower captain at Linqu, he will call at your office. The letters will be sent out today, the company

is forwarding it but the post messenger Xing hasn't arrived yet.
I hope that you are getting on well in your own affairs, don't let
yourself be the last among all the sections! And don't let yourself
lag behind in promotion stakes!

One letter on silk, which was found in its envelope at a beacon
tower site in Dunhuang, gives an insight into the huge distances of
the empire at its height. If correctly understood, the sender, Zheng,
was living at an outpost near Hohhot in Inner Mongolia, astonishingly 2,000 kilometres from Dunhuang, where the letter was
found. Not surprisingly, Zheng is feeling cut off after five years on
duty, his social contacts confined to a small group of local regional
military elite and the occasional merchant or traveller, as it was not
a major trade route. Writing to his old friend Youqing and his wife
Junming, Zheng gives an impression of the boredom and heat out
on the northern frontier:

> Zheng sends his best regards. My dear friend You and Lady Ming.
> How are you? We haven't heard from you or seen each other.
> During this hot season I dearly hope that you, my friend, and
> Lady Ming can dress comfortably and eat well while getting on
> with provincial business. I have lived in Chengle for more than
> five years now and have not been transferred. The roads leading
> here are long and far off, traffic is rare. My official position is
> inconsequential and my status is low. Letters don't get through.
> Kindly allow me to rely on my young colleague Wang Zifang, who
> has been appointed as the probationary deputy to the commander
> of Yuze company of Dunhuang province, to deliver this letter to
> you and allow me to express the wish that you may be so kind as
> to inquire with Yang Junquian ...

The letter is incomplete, but Zheng evidently wants his friend to
intervene with his superiors and complain about life in these 'shabby
quarters on the northern frontier'. Zheng also sounds down. He is
apologetic about being late with his accounts and gives us a sense

of torpor, compounded by the recent death of his governor. (As this post was now empty, was he, perhaps, hoping for a promotion?) He concludes: 'If I could obtain enlightening news from you, my friend and Lady Ming, and learn how your children at home are, that would make me very happy ... My dear friend You and Lady Ming! Please give my regards to your young lads Zhangshi, Zichong and Shaoshi.'

With that the dust storms of the edge of the Gobi swirl around the little outpost and Zheng vanishes from his brief moment in the eye of history. No more letters in the cache carry his name. Perhaps he fulfilled the term of his service and was able to return home and eke out his retirement with a little garden back home in the Middle Land?

FROM THE THREE KINGDOMS TO THE SUI TRANSITION

'It is a truth universally acknowledged', as we might loosely paraphrase the famous opening of the novel *Romance of the Three Kingdoms*, 'that an empire long united will fall apart.' In around 200 CE, the Han fell apart in civil war. Rather like Napoleon's Russian campaign in Tolstoy's *War and Peace*, the war is the centrepiece of the great fourteenth-century novel, which is set in the time of the Han collapse. The climactic Battle of the Red Cliffs was fought in the winter of 208/9 CE between a divided north and south. In the south were the warlords Sun Quan and Liu Bei, and in the north the generalissimo Cao Cao, who had attempted to conquer the lands south of the Yangtze and reunite the Han. The battle has been claimed as the largest naval battle in history in terms of numbers. Its location, which is still hotly disputed, was somewhere on the Yangtze, southwest of Wuhan, perhaps at the Red Cliff at Chibi in Hubei, where a carved inscription from the eighth or ninth century is still visible above the river waters. Defeated in a huge naval engagement, Cao Cao made a disastrous retreat northwards to the Han River, where his remaining fleet was destroyed by fireships. Then a desperate retreat through the marshlands north of the Yangtze incurred huge losses through famine and disease. The Red Cliffs battle would go down in legend as the end of the Han dynasty.

This is another of those moments when China threatened to break apart for ever. When the warlord Cao Cao died, he left instructions that he should be buried with no treasures and no ceremony, 'for the country is not at peace'.

China broke into two on the old north and south divide, initiating the longest period of division in its history, over 350 years. Wei, Jin, Northern and Southern dynasties – there is no agreed name for this time of disunity. But during this time important developments took place. First was demographic change. Under the Han, the bulk of the population had been in the lower Yellow River valley. Now the colonisation of the subtropical lands of the Yangtze valley begins, filling unoccupied land, clearing hillsides and forests, draining marshes and developing and expanding the southern rice culture. China's population rose perhaps as much as four- or fivefold between 280 and 464 CE. By the 500s, the south was the rice basket of China and a major centre of culture, with 40 per cent of the registered population now living in the Yangtze valley.

In the sixth century, China was reunited by a powerful former administrator in the north, Yang Jian, who became Emperor Wen of Sui. An unfamiliar name outside China, Wen was one of its great rulers. An extraordinarily interesting man, frugal, abstemious in his private life, he was a 'cautious, solemn, hardworking, conscientious worker' who decreased tax burdens on the poor and introduced a scheme to compensate families whose sons had died in war. However, he was also suspicious, critical and picky, which lost him many allies and friends, and in the end even his own sons.

The Sui inaugurated a period of prosperity unseen for three or four centuries. The imperial granaries, it was said, were stocked up with fifty years' worth of supplies, to meet any crisis of drought, flood or famine. The population continued to rise. According to Sima Guang, 'at the beginning of the reign, the census rolls recorded less than 4 million households, but by the end 9 million. Ji province alone [Hengshui Hebei], had 1 million households'. So this is another case in China's history where a dynasty that was short-lived but full of innovation laid the foundations for the success of a much longer-lived and more glamorous period, in this case the Tang. Emperor Wen ruled from 581 CE in the north. Then, to reunite China, he began a massive campaign of conquest in 587 CE with fleets on the great rivers and down the coast in a triple-pronged assault. In 588 CE, he occupied present-day Nanjing in one of the most important campaigns in Chinese history. News of these events even reached the Mediterranean, where the capture of the south was described in Constantinople.

The Sui lasted only three and a half decades, but in this short time they reunited the northern and southern lands after the civil wars of the sixth century and pushed out along the Silk Road into Central Asia, where they encouraged the spread of Buddhism, which Emperor Wen himself embraced. It was perhaps at this point that he made contacts with the Byzantine world. At home, he introduced a renewed examination system for the empire, which would be the model for all future dynasties, creating the *jinshi*, the most prestigious degree. Emperor Wen also built a new capital near the site of the ancient Qin and Han capitals, linking his dynasty to the Han legacy. This would be the great metropolis that became a world city under the Tang: Chang'an (Xi'an).

The Sui also instituted far-reaching economic reforms in agriculture and carried through a gigantic infrastructure project which would have a huge impact on the whole of Chinese history: the construction of the Grand Canal. Beginning in 584 CE in the north and expanded between 605 CE and 609 CE, the canal crossed the countryside from north to south. It involved the labour of up to 5 million conscripts, men and women. The largest manmade waterway in history, the canal would be a major factor in joining the north and south. It also accelerated the shift in the economy and population from the traditional heartland of the Yellow River to the Yangtze valley and the south, linking their river systems, which would be such an important feature of China's economic and social history during the next three centuries.

However, for all their achievements, the Sui were brought down as they overextended the empire. Wen's successor was drawn into disastrous wars against Korea, where he was defeated in 614 CE.

Rebellions also broke out back home, exacerbated by overexpenditure on extravagant palaces and other vanity building projects. After that, the dynasty rapidly disintegrated and a series of popular revolts led to the assassination of Emperor Yang by his ministers in 618 CE.

It was at this point that Li Yuan, who had been a governor in northern China, declared himself the new emperor, taking the reign name Gaozu, 'the Great Founder'. He was a member of the Li family, one of the military clans from the far northwest – tough, horse-riding frontier people. Though he had to fight off rivals in the aftermath of the Sui, by his death in 626 CE he had reunited the country. It would be the beginning of one of the most brilliant epochs in Chinese history: the Tang.

In terms of the culture and history of Eurasia, it is as if a light had been switched on. The impact of the new dynasty was such that, even far away in the Mediterranean world, the last historian of late antiquity, Theophylact Simocatta, writing in Constantinople in around 630 CE, on the eve of the Arab conquests, wrote about China's reunification, 'in the time of our emperor Maurice under the Sui emperor Wen, with their conquest of the rival Chen dynasty in southern China, 'when the northerners crossed the Great River [Yangtze] southwards.'

Theophylact also adds information about Chinese geography and culture, which he brings up to date to his own time, portraying China as a great state, 'idolatrous but wise in government, under their great emperor *Taisson*, the meaning of which is Son of God'. This is the first Western mention of a Chinese emperor: Taizong of the Tang. It could not be more appropriate. Taizong was one of the great figures in seventh-century world history, the sponsor of a dynamic and confident age in which Tang China pushed its influence into Central Asia along the Silk Road, through the oases and signal stations which had been occupied briefly under the Han, but which now became a part of China's western provinces. Reaching out almost as far west as the Aral Sea and the Karakoram, down to Vietnam and up to the northern part of the Korean peninsula, the Tang represented a new orientation in Chinese history: China's first cosmopolitan age.

6

The Glory of the Tang

In the seventh century CE, the axis of China's history shifted as new elements came into Chinese civilisation from other cultures, from the Near East, Persia and Central Asia, and from India. Japan, too, was now drawn into the Chinese orbit. The Tang dynasty created the largest Chinese empire before the eighteenth century. Building on the administrative reforms of their Sui predecessors, they created a centralised empire, with a postal system and an extensive network of roads and canals, radiating from the capital to the far west and the northeast. Their cultural achievements, in the arts, literature and history, were extraordinary; humane and self-aware, full of empathy for the world and for people, their poetry is still regarded as China's greatest. The arrival of Buddhism was perhaps the most important and long-lasting of the foreign influences that came from the Tang opening up to the world. With Buddhism came trade, ideas, art and different conceptions of philosophy and spirituality, by sea and by land, but especially along the Silk Road from Central Asia and India. And there this part of the story begins, with one of the most celebrated figures in the history of China, the monk Xuanzang.

In the summer of 632 CE, a Chinese traveller looked out from the Jayendra Vihara monastery, across the soft green Vale of Kashmir and the blue expanses of its lakes, to the sparkling snow peaks of the Himalayas. Even to his Chinese compatriots he was an imposing figure: over 6 feet tall, he wore his customary brown wool robe and broad belt, now with perhaps an extra layer, as even in summer Kashmir can be chilly. He was twenty-eight, with bright clear eyes and a fine face burnished by long desert journeys. An exceptionally handsome and graceful young man, eyes turned as he passed by, looking straight ahead 'with a clear level gaze'. And he was no less impressive in conversation. Trained since childhood as a precocious Buddhist oblate in Luoyang, his voice was 'clear and sonorous', his speech elegant. His intellectual mastery of the quiddities of the Idealistic philosophy and the schools of Buddhism, in their own language, had astonished and delighted the old monks of Kashmir and, along with 'a certain sweetness of manner', caused even kings to seek his company.

For nearly twenty years Xuanzang had dreamed of India. Born in a village near Luoyang, his family had visited the White Horse monastery during temple fairs and festivals, and he had grown up with magical tales of how Buddhism first came to China more than 500 years before he was born. Especially tantalising was the story of the Han emperor's dream in which a strange man appeared, 'twelve feet tall with his skin the colour of gold, his glowing head framed by the sun, the moon and stars'. The court astrologers and diviners had pronounced that the golden man had come from the west and must be the Buddha himself. The emperor was fascinated and sent an expedition to find out more. Eighteen courtiers and scholars, with their attendants journeyed out to the west, travelling beyond the watchtowers and beacons at the end of the Han Long Walls and through the oases skirting the vast deserts of the Taklamakan. Finally, in a monastery in Afghanistan, they met two Indian monks who agreed to come back with them to China. They arrived in Luoyang on two white horses, carrying their bags of scriptures and precious relics, and were established in what became known as the White Horse Pagoda. There they translated the first Buddhist text to be rendered into Chinese: *The Sutra of Forty-Two Chapters*, which has had a special place in the hearts of Chinese Buddhists ever since. The Indian monks died and were

The Altar of Heaven, Beijing: built in 1530 on the pattern of an ancient circular mound altar; up until 1899 it was the scene of the annual midwinter imperial ceremony, which renewed the link between humanity, earth and cosmos.

From the Bronze Age, such rituals were determined by observation of the stars.

The emperor was the intercessor with the heavens, the guarantor of harmonious order – the fundamental goal of Chinese rulership.

One of the five sacred mountains that are the cardinal points of China's spiritual geography, and today once again places of mass pilgrimage.

Landscapes, real and imagined, play a central role in Chinese culture: Huangshan, left, in a painting *c.* 1930.

The immense variety of Chinese geography and landscapes: rice terraces of the south; deserts of the Silk Road; the Yangtze Gorges and the wheat fields of the Yellow River plain where civilisation arose in the Bronze Age.

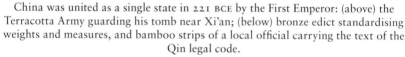

China was united as a single state in 221 BCE by the First Emperor: (above) the Terracotta Army guarding his tomb near Xi'an; (below) bronze edict standardising weights and measures, and bamboo strips of a local official carrying the text of the Qin legal code.

The visionary art of the Dunhuang caves from the Silk Road in the Tang dynasty, mixing Indian, Persian and Central Asian themes and styles.

The monk Xuanzang, who travelled to India in the seventh century; later a folk hero, with his supernatural companions, he is still celebrated in movies, novels and in the festival of 'Hungry Ghosts'.

The Song capital Kaifeng in *c.* 1120, depicted in one of China's most famous works of art.

Camels go through the city gate, one of seventeen in the outer walls; inside, a shopping district with Dr Yang's clinic and Shenyang's Licensed Tavern (see p. 193).

'Rainbow Bridge' crammed with street vendors; in front, a big inn, guests on the balcony, waiters serving dishes.

Luxury passenger boats on the Bian River with cabins, washrooms and mat awnings fore and aft; the kind of vessel taken in 1127 by Li Qingzhao (p. 225).

The Song achievement: rational governance, scientific invention and brilliant arts and crafts, including ceramics and silk painting.

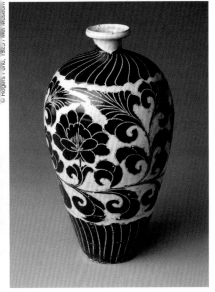

The spirit of the land: *Travellers among Mountains and Stream* by Fan Kuan (*c.* 950–1032): a packhorse train on the path below giant crags; 'he not only painted mountains, but more important, their soul.'

buried in the monastery, where their tomb mound still stands today in a small garden. It was not the first exchange between India and China, but from that moment onwards the dialogue of civilisations would be continuous.

Xuanzang grew up with these tales; a serious, studious boy, he followed his elder brother as a convert to Buddhism. However, in his late teens, the breakdown of the Sui dynasty cast a shadow over his future. China was in chaos, 'the Sui had lost the empire and the whole kingdom was in confusion, with riot and famine,' he remembered; 'there was no regular government and troops were under arms everywhere . . . The books of Confucius and the sacred pages of the Buddha were forgotten, for everyone was occupied with war.' The situation around Luoyang was especially desperate. In winter 618 CE, near his native village, there were horrendous stories of cannibalism as famine took hold. Along with many refugees, he escaped with his brother over the mountains to Chengdu, where he continued his studies. But the more his knowledge grew, the more he realised that to understand the Buddhist tradition he had to go back to the original texts, a task that could only be undertaken in India.

At the time, the Tang under the emperor Taizong were fighting wars out in the northwest and there was a ban on foreign travel for Chinese people, though merchants from Central Asia, Sogdiana and Tibet with travel documents could pass without hindrance. In April 629 CE, with the help of friendly Buddhist guards, Xuanzang slipped through Gansu and Qinghai, across the Yumen Pass, 'the key to the Western frontiers', and made his way to Turfan, where the local king helped him with letters of introduction in the Sogdian language, gifting him textiles and valuables he could convert into cash en route. Following the Tian Shan mountains westwards, he went around the Taklamakan desert, where he nearly lost his life in a nightmare five days and four nights after spilling his precious supply of drinking water. There were many adventures and close shaves; sometimes it was Xuanzang's charm as much as his nerve and physical courage that got him through. Across Kyrgyzstan and

Uzbekistan, friendly courts under Turkic rule helped him on the way from one caravan city to the next. From Samarkand he turned south, crossing the edge of the Pamirs, through the canyon of the Iron Gates at Derbent and down to the ferry crossing of the Amu Darya (Oxus) river at Termez.

At that time Afghanistan was still a stronghold of Buddhism, though many places Xuanzang visited were in ruins after the invasions by the Huns in the late fifth century. Crossing the mountains of the Hindu Kush, at the end of April 630 CE, he reached the fertile valley of Bamiyan, in whose pink sandstone cliffs were the famous giant Buddha statues carved in the Kushan age. The greater one was the largest standing Buddha in the world: 55 metres high, and still in its glory then, with huge Kushan boots, a carmine red coat and long blue cloak. Its chalk-white face, black hair and top knot presented a spell-binding image of the Master that seemed to beckon Xuanzang into a new world.

Bamiyan was a crossroads of Asia, the meeting place of Hellenistic, Central Asian and Indian cultural traditions. Alexander the Great had come this way, establishing Greek cities on the Oxus and in the Kabul plain with their agoras and gymnasiums. Xuanzang stayed in the Maha Sanghika monastery, whose library had texts going back to the roots of the Mahayana Buddhist tradition from the Kushan era in the second and third centuries CE. Recently, the remains of birch-bark and palm-leaf texts from this library have been excavated; the earliest surviving manuscripts of the 'Dead Sea Scrolls of Buddhism', some of these had hitherto only been known in Chinese translations, many were completely unknown. Perhaps this gives us a sense of the excitement Xuanzang felt when he saw and handled them. It was a foretaste of the wonders that lay ahead.

Coming from the Kabul plain down the Khyber Pass, Xuanzang now entered the heartland of Gandhara. Here, fabulously rich artistic traditions had developed depicting the mythical life of the Buddha, mingling Greek, Persian and Indian themes and symbols, for example creating the image of the Buddha in a Greek toga that is known across the world today. At Peshawar he feasted his eyes on the famous pilgrimage sights – the sacred pipal tree, the temple of the Buddha's begging bowl and the giant stupa erected by the Kushan king Kanishka, a contemporary of Emperor Hadrian. Some 400 feet high, this was the foremost wonder of the Buddhist world; its huge plinth nearly 300 feet square, covered with sculptures, its burnished copper umbrellas glinting in the sun. With silk flags snapping from the apex like dragon's tails – the biggest of them said to be a gift from a Han queen – it was 'the highest of all towers on this earth'.

Xuanzang was now on the great route later known as the Grand Trunk Road. He crossed the Indus and entered the plains of India, pushing on to reach Kashmir at the end of 630 CE. The valley was a great centre of Buddhist studies, with over 100 monasteries and more than 5,000 monks. By then, his name and story had gone before him, so when he approached the capital the king came out to greet him, his retainers carrying parasols and waving royal standards, lighting incense and scattering flowers before Xuanzang. Like a visitor from another world, he was invited to ride with the king into town on a richly caparisoned elephant.

Xuanzang was given lodgings at the Jayendra monastery, where the remains of the great stupa are still to be seen today on a terrace overlooking the Vale. To help him on his mission, he was allotted servants and twenty scribes to copy some of the sacred books, embodying centuries of teaching: not only in the shastras, but in logic, epistemology and learned commentaries on the ancient canon. It was an intensely productive time for him. A time, too, for refining his understanding of Sanskrit so he could read, write and speak it fluently. Through 631 and 632 CE he studied in Kashmir with the great teachers. Seminars with senior monks helped him assimilate the traditional exegesis. He needed to master the complex and often conflicting ideas behind the different traditions; the Great Vehicle and Lesser Vehicle, the exoteric and the esoteric. All this was preparation for the grand translation project he had in mind for when he got back to China (he seems to have never doubted that he would return).

THE SEVENTH-CENTURY REVOLUTION ACROSS EURASIA

Sometimes the synchronicities of history are eye-catching. That same summer of 632 the Prophet Muhammad died in Medina, enjoining his followers to 'seek knowledge even as far as China'. Within three years Arab armies burst out of the Arabian Peninsula, across Syria and North Africa. In China, the Tang dynasty was about to expand westwards into Central Asia and to spread Chinese culture eastwards to Japan and Korea and into Southeast Asia. Though he could hardly have known it, Xuanzang was living across a cusp of history.

This was a transformative period right across Eurasia. In the Eastern Mediterranean heartland of Western Classical civilisation, the Byzantine Empire would soon be fighting desperate wars of survival against Arab armies, which expanded Islamic civilisation as far as Spain and Central Asia in less than a century. Indeed, in the eighth century, the Arabs would clash with the Tang on the Talas River in Kazakhstan. Meanwhile, out on the far edge of Eurasia in the 'Barbarian West', beyond the limits of civilisation (as it might have appeared to people then), Germanic-speaking Angles and Saxons, Franks, Visigoths and Ostrogoths settled in the ruins of Rome. There they built their kingdoms, making their first steps to restore Roman Christian civilisation through Latin culture, script and texts. At home in China, the Tang, with their capital at Chang'an (today's Xi'an), became perhaps the greatest and most cosmopolitan civilisation on earth. They welcomed Persians, Indians, Sogdians and Arabs, Christians, Jews, Zoroastrians and Muslims, along with their goods and luxuries, their food and fashions, and their religions, art and ideas.

Indeed, in this next part of the story of China, we will see one of the great epochs of civilisation that laid the foundations of the medieval and early modern world, driving social and economic, as well as cultural, change. The Tang bequeathed to the modern world a Chinese cultural empire across East Asia, Korea and Japan, as Rome would hand down Latin culture across the West. This, it might be said, is the age in which the modern pattern of human cultures across the Eurasian landmass began to crystallise.

AN INWARD-LOOKING CIVILISATION?

It is an extraordinary fact, then, that in the modern Western world an idea has taken root that China has been a monolithic and unchanging civilisation, inward-looking and resistant to outside influence. Despite being a historical construct created by Western historians, politicians and missionaries, this idea gave birth to a perception of China insulated from the outside world as a matter of policy, incapable of self-development and isolated by choice. A civilisation, as it were, confined behind a Great Wall, built as a barrier to shut out people and ideas.

Such assumptions are flawed. In the Tang, for example, international links in diplomacy and trade were extraordinarily wide. Temples and monasteries were built in China for Buddhists, Christians, Muslims and Manichaeans. On the Silk Road, manuscript finds have been made in Persian, Sogdian, Syriac and even Hebrew; in the other direction, in Japanese and Korean. Though, like all cultures, it knew periods of retrenchment, China, in fact, has always been a civilisation open to outside influences. During the Tang, the Silk Road extended west to the Mediterranean and east to Japan. Its influence on later East Asian civilisations was profound, and continues to this day in culture, script and language.

ON THE SILK ROAD

Out on the northernmost edge of Kyrgyzstan, a mile or two from the Chuy River and the Kazakh border, overlooked by the snow-capped ranges of the Tian Shan, is the site of Suyab, a caravan city founded sometime in the fifth century CE by Sogdian merchants who came from the region of Samarkand. The Sogdians were the great intermediaries on the Tang Silk Road, and their letters give us a vivid sense of daily life in this vast region. Their trade networks survived the shifts of regimes and reached into Persia, India and the heartland of China. The site of Suyab lies on the road and rail route to Bishkek, the narrow point on the east–west corridor of the Silk Road, beyond the steel-blue lake of Issyk-Kul.

Xuanzang describes Suyab as:

> the city of the Suye River: a couple of miles in circuit, various Hu [foreign] merchants from the surrounding nations gather and live here; the soil is favourable for red millet and for grapes; the climate windy and cold, so people wear garments of twilled wool ... Travelling from here westwards are a great number of isolated towns each with a chief, not dependent on one another but with allegiance to the Khan of the Turks.

In the 640s, the Tang emperor Taizong sent his armies out west. The long-distance caravan trade was becoming so important to the empire that their routes had to be secured and protected. First they ventured into Xinjiang, then, in the 650s, they pushed beyond the old Han network of fortified towns, with their beacons and watchtowers, out into Central Asia on the merchant routes to Fergana and Samarkand. By now, the Chinese could not allow trade, run by Sogdian middlemen, to be disrupted. In the new world of Tang urban civilisation, with enormous consumption in the capital and other great cities, important trade was not in essentials, but in luxuries. The Silk Road through Xinjiang came under Tang rule in 648 CE when the Chinese established their 'Protectorate General to Pacify the West'. Their aim was to control the Tarim basin oases, with the key Chinese army bases at Kucha, Kashgar, Turfan and Khotan. Then, in 658 CE, troops were sent further west to Suyab, where new fortress defences were dug in 679 CE. So Suyab was absorbed into the loose suzerainty of the Tang empire as a western military outpost, and Chinese civilians along with garrison soldiers moved out beyond the long walls to populate it.

The Tang poet Cen Shen, who had a government job in the garrison towns around Turfan, describes such a place in the mid-700s. He tells us about parties held by military commanders with 'wine set in the inner room; brocade mats spread; singing girls freshly rouged all looking their best ... drunk in front of red candles', feastings that took place as winter set in 'in a warm room with embroidered curtains and a glowing ground stove; the walls covered with woven stuffs, the floor with patterned rugs'. Cen's view of expatriate life out in Central Asia was realistic; his enthusiasm for the place always tempered by the harshness of conditions; the monotony of sunrise and sunset over the featureless desert. Life on such army bases was tough, sweltering in a summer heat that can reach 60 degrees, with 'a flaming wind sweeping sandy dust'. The pleasure of having a visitor was grasped with both hands, and departure a cause for sadness:

> Here in the camp we set wine and drink for the
> departing guests,
> The lute sounds, the violin and the Tibetan flute,
> Thick, thick the evening snow falls at the camp gate,
> The wind tears at the red banners frozen too stiff to flap.
> At the east gate of Luntai we come to see you off
> And as you go snow fills the road to the Tian Shan.
> A turn of the hill, a bend of the road and you are
> lost to sight;
> And all that is left is the track on the snow of your
> horse's hooves.

This, then, was the world at the outer reaches of empire. The wild frontier world of the Sogdian merchants is revealed in documents and letters found by archaeologists in Turfan. Riding the shifts in regime as middlemen is always a precarious existence. Yet their riches in jade, nephrite, silks, carpets, embroideries, herbs, spices and dried fruits flowed into the markets of the Tang capital, where in the dynasty's heyday there were perhaps as many as 30,000 Sogdian residents.

THE TANG: THE STATE AND THE CAPITAL

These western landscapes were the familiar world of the Tang dynasty rulers. Three generations back they came from Gansu on the edge of mainland China, so they were authentic northwesterners.

They came from a horse culture; a military aristocracy under the Sui, on the one hand pretending a descent from the legendary Daoist sage Laozi himself, on the other hand claiming, more plausibly, kinship with the Khan of the Kyrgyz. When their clan rose to prominence out of the fighting of 617 CE, they deposed and killed the last of the Sui and announced their new dynasty, naming it after the region in Shanxi, which legend said had been bequeathed to them by the Yellow Emperor himself. With that, the centre of gravity of the empire began to shift away from the Yellow River heartland of Chinese history to the Taklamakan and Central Asia. The Silk Road became the natural axis of their mental map. From the Qin Long Walls and Han beacon sites and postal stations; beyond the deserts of Xinjiang and the high plateau of Qinghai and Tibet; past the great mountain chains of the Himalayas and the Pamirs, whose passes lead to the plains of India, China's horizons were opening out. By the late eighth century, the population numbered 50 million people, by far the world's biggest state. Even into the ninth century, when the situation at the centre was less stable, it was a well-governed country with complex long-distance supply chains for food and raw materials, where life and property were protected by a code of law administered by trained local magistrates; one could travel the length and breadth of the land on reliable roads, or using the canal system, and always find a place to stay at night and a meal to eat, the administration providing service industries and security from bandits and violence. And, ultimately, all roads led to the capital, Chang'an, today's Xi'an.

Chang'an lay at the Chinese end of the Silk Road; the first of the five great capitals that have exerted such an influence in the story of China. A political and ritual centre for over 1,000 years, it was the centre of the bureaucracy, the headquarters of main army units and the place where the examinations for entry to the Tang civil service were held. Home to nearly a million people, according to the Tang censuses, the great city of Chang'an was an agent of change, giving birth to a new kind of urban life.

The construction of the city had been begun by the Sui in the

580s, the layout astrologically determined in the ancient tradition of auspicious architecture for royal cities in China. Replicating the shape of the asterism of the Big Dipper constellation, it formed a huge rectangle 5 miles across with a 200-metre-wide imperial boulevard running south from the palace enclosure to the South Gate, known as the 'Zhuquemen' (Vermilion Bird). In the northern enclosure were gigantic pillared palaces set on platforms, the biggest wooden buildings in the world, with gardens and a great ornamental lake, whose outline can still be seen in the fields outside the modern city.

The main part of the city was divided by a grid pattern into 108 wards, each of which had its own walls. Inside the walls, straight lanes divided the wards, with smaller winding alleys between the temples and houses. On the east side were the grand aristocratic houses, with multiple courtyards sometimes taking up several blocks. There were gardens and trees everywhere. The guidebooks to the Tang dynasty city describe scenic beauty spots adorned with peonies and peaches, lotus and apricot gardens, fruit orchards and parks that ran along the Serpentine River and lake. On the low-lying south and southeast sides, liable to flood in heavy rains, were the poorest areas, with the homes of minor officials, merchants and migrants. There were also large areas of cultivation inside the walls, gardens, orchards and farm fields. To one Tang poet the city's 'hundreds and thousands of houses seemed like pieces on a chessboard. The twelve great streets like the orderly paths laid out between a giant vegetable garden. In the distance I see the faint and small torches of the riders to the palace, like a single constellation of stars lying to the west of the Five Gates.'

The city's two huge markets, east and west, were each about a kilometre square with a big open space in the middle for ceremonies, festivals, military shows and public executions. In their streets you could buy almost anything. In the East Market there were more than 200 lanes and alleys, each surrounded by warehouses that held 'rare and curious goods from all over the country'. There were ironmongers, cloth dealers, butchers, wine shops, brush and ink sellers, not to mention travelling musicians, jugglers, acrobats and storytellers.

The West Market was in the part of the city inhabited by foreign communities; Arabs, Persians, Indians, Tibetans and Turks. The Tang dynasty Chinese were fascinated by the different peoples and ethnic groups with whom they came into contact. They depict them in their paintings and describe them in their novels, even carving their life-size images in stone. In front of the imperial mausoleum, outside the city, are 122 stone ambassadors, lined up as if to pay homage to the Tang throne. Among them are men from Xinjiang, a Sogdian from Suyab and Turkic nobles, whose flamboyant costumes were a big hit in the capital; even the fashion-conscious Tang princes wore Turkic clothes and did their hair up Turkic-style. Reflecting the tastes and contacts of the citizens, the West Market offered a huge array of goods and services: caravan equipment, saddle gear, scales, measures and tools, foreign jewellery and clothes from the Silk Road. On the other side of the city, by the East Market, were the wards where high officials and nobles congregated; in Anyi ward, for example, was the grand city mansion of the Li family, whom we will meet later in our story (below page 169), with its courtyards and ornamental gardens and the 'Pergola of Brilliant Ideas' where Chief Minister Li wrote his memoranda. Here on the east side one could also find the houses of scholars and court musicians, a high-class wedding hall, and residences for lesser members of the royal family.

In Chinese urban history the Tang dynasty marks the beginning of the transformation of the city from a royal enclosure for the imperial family, their servants, craftsmen and women, to a more open metropolis where ordinary lives are lived, freedoms found and fortunes made.

A typical example was Pingkang ward, between the imperial enclosure and the East Market. Among the landmarks here was a Buddhist temple with famous murals by a great Tang painter; a sixth-century temple for the royal family stood at the southern gate. Above all, however, it was most famous for the 'blue houses' – the residences of the high-class courtesans of the city. Like everything in Tang Chang'an, the world of these women was highly regulated. They were licensed, inspected and taxed. Following the official edicts and timetables they were careful to observe all the big feast days and imperial ceremonies, with painted panels hung in their entrance halls marking the death days of emperors when no music could be played. They were experts in the calendar, accomplished in the *I Ching*, trained in music, poetry, dance and the preparation of wine, food and tea. In a world where, in traditional Confucian society, women were rigorously segregated, many courtesans became published writers and poets. But there was a dark side to the life they lived. Many of the girls and women in the entertainment quarters were the daughters of concubines. Many were purchased when children and brought up in that world, first simply serving tea to clients, then, aged twelve or thirteen, given the clothes and adornments of a concubine and initiated with older men. It is a typical feature of the traditional civilisations across the world, from the Arabs to the Tang, that for men, sex with young girls, including children, was considered the norm.

XUANZANG RETURNS

This teeming urban life was the world to which Xuanzang returned in 645 CE. From Kashmir where we left him, he had made his way down to the Ganges plain and then by boat to Patna, the old Mauryan capital. Then in 637 he finally walked by the wide sandy bed of the Falgu River to Bodh Gaya and, eight years after he left China, finally came to the tree under which the Buddha had sat and received illumination. He could not contain his feelings: 'I simply sat down and wept.'

Xuanzang spent two years at the university of Nalanda, which in the Tang era became the international university of Buddhism, drawing scholars and pilgrims from all over South and East Asia. By now he was fluent in the native Indian languages and able to read Sanskrit and Pali, the language of the Indian schools of Buddhism. He had, as it were, become 'the Other'. He undertook further journeys to find and copy texts he was still missing, travelling to Bengal, today's Bangladesh, where Buddhism was a major presence, and journeying down to Kanchi in south India, and to the great Buddhist centres in western India, in Malva, Gujarat and Sind. Only then, finally, did he begin the long journey back through the Khyber and eastwards to

China. He arrived in Chang'an in the early spring of 645 CE, more than sixteen years after he left. News of his approach was carried to the capital in advance and a huge procession greeted him with excited crowds in the streets, gawping to see this traveller who had set his eyes on other worlds. Then, as the court was in Luoyang, he went by road to meet the emperor Taizong, whose first words to Xuanzang were: 'Welcome back after seventeen years, Xuanzang. But you never asked permission to go!'

'Well,' Xuanzang replied, 'I applied for a permit for foreign travel on several occasions, but had no luck.' The emperor didn't reproach him, instead expressing surprise to see him alive after such a long time and congratulating him for having risked his life 'for the benefit of the whole of humanity'. Impressed by Xuanzang's bearing, intelligence and his knowledge of the world, the emperor asked him to hang up his Buddhist robes and to become his prime minister, to use his wisdom to help him run the country. But Xuanzang turned him down: 'it would', he said, 'be like taking a boat out of water. Not only would it cease to be useful, but in time it would just rot away …'

CODE SWITCHING: THE OPENING OF THE CHINESE MIND

Xuanzang's packloads of Buddhist sutras, holy texts, figurines, statues and antiquities were one of the most precious cultural cargoes ever taken from one civilisation to another. It had been a journey of exploration, not so much into unknown lands – though the physical adventure was daring enough – but into what one might call new territories of the mind. With him Xuanzang brought back the accumulated wisdom of Buddhist India to China. He would then follow up, as he had planned, with a translation project that can only be compared with that of Greek into Arabic and Persian in the Islamic Caliphate, or Greek into Latin during Europe's three renaissances between the eighth and fifteenth centuries.

A note in the biography of Xuanzang, written by one of his disciples, sums it up. He returned with 657 separate Buddhist manuscript rolls, along with portable relics, statues and figurines, carried on twenty packhorses. For the rest of his life he devoted his energies to his translation project. With imperial patronage, a translation bureau was set up where he credited himself with translating 1,330 separate texts, long and short. Still more significant was what it meant for the opening up of relationships between civilisations. The next few decades saw the coming into being of what has been called the 'Buddhist cosmopolis' of Central Asia, India, China, Korea and Japan. In that time many hundreds of monks travelled between these countries, along with countless more merchants and diplomats. They made boat journeys via Sumatra, Sri Lanka, Tamil India and Bengal, and land journeys to India through Central Asia, Tibet and Burma. The spacious seventh century brought a new sense of geography to their world.

Reflecting on the previous thousand years or more of Chinese history, Xuanzang saw that the ancients had built the Chinese state on the foundations of a Confucian ethos whose ideology was key to an ordered cosmos, while Daoism had given them the spiritual dimension of a traditional religion, and that these twin pillars had served the country well. 'In my country the magistrates are clothed with dignity and the laws are everywhere respected,' he wrote:

The emperor is virtuous and the subjects loyal, parents are loving and sons are obedient, humanity and justice are highly esteemed and old men and sages are held in honour. Moreover how deep and mysterious is their knowledge; their wisdom equals that of the spirits. They have taken the Heavens as their model, and they know how to calculate the movements of the seven luminaries; they have invented all kinds of instruments, fixed the seasons of the year and discovered the hidden properties of the six tones and of music, calming the contrary influence of the Yin and the Yang and thus procuring peace and happiness for all beings.

But both Confucianism and Daoism were uniquely Chinese. Buddhism, on the other hand, was a transnational, universal faith, which opened China to the wider world intellectually, as well as in its spiritual life, directly questioning the hitherto assumed centrality of Chinese culture and her unique civilising mission.

Although there had been many travellers in previous centuries, going all the way back to the Han, and there had been earlier translators, Xuanzang, with the help of lavish and enthusiastic imperial patronage, had initiated a great civilisational shift. Buddhism in China grew in the later seventh and eighth centuries, particularly under the remarkable Empress Wu, who was a great patron of literature, art, sculpture and temples. So, by the ninth century, China was a holy land too; Indian and Japanese travellers came to China to see the sacred sites, Mount Wutai became a great pilgrimage centre and 'the Great River of China united its pure stream with the sacred waters of Bodhgaya'.

People and ideas flowed east to Japan and Korea too. This was the time when Japan began its assimilation of the Chinese cultural tradition. Direct relations under the Tang from the early seventh century saw the wholesale importation of Chinese ideas, culture, language and texts. From 700 CE the sons of the Japanese aristocracy were trained in Chinese, and Japanese pilgrims went to China. Standing back from Western-centric views of history, the establishment of this Buddhist culture over East Asia is one of the most important stories in the history of civilisation.

This was reflected, too, in the status and glamour of Chang'an as a great international city. In Japan, the new capital of Nara was laid out between 710 and 784 CE and modelled on Tang Chang'an. Indeed, today, Nara is the best place to see what a great Tang royal city actually looked like. Within the complex is the Great Prayer Hall, until recently the largest wooden building in the world. It also houses the Shoso-in temple, a treasury full of the riches that travelled as gifts down the Silk Road to its far eastern end. This astonishing collection of thousands of eighth-century artefacts was until recently conserved in cedar chests in a wooden treasury, inside Japan's oldest archive and the world's oldest surviving museum. Here one may see Tang lutes and wind instruments, lacquer work, silk and textiles, glass bowls, cups and pitchers from Persia and Alexandria, Roman glass, Persian brocade, Indian carvings, Chinese rugs, clothing and weaponry, and Buddhist scrolls from Sui and Tang China. Among the treasures are also costumes, masks and instruments used for eighth-century ceremonies that show the faces of different peoples along the Silk Road. Few artefacts as astounding as this have survived the vagaries of war and revolution in China, but here in Nara in Japan is the single most powerful symbol of Tang cultural exchanges along the Silk Road during this expansive time.

In this age of world empires, therefore, there was extraordinary opening up, a shift in mental horizons that can be seen as the distant beginning of the globalisation of ideas. But what we might call China's main cultural strands are in place now. There is the deep prehistoric 'political' and cultural substrate, with the role of the sage-monarch, the ritual and familial traditions including reverence for the ancestors, the moral order of Confucius and the new influence of metaphysical Buddhism. The interplay of these elements has been at the heart of Chinese civilisation to this day.

The older patterns of Chinese history were shifting. In Xuanzang's lifetime Muslims would set foot in China, traders who came on the maritime route to Canton where Arabs and Persians had long been in residence. At this time, too, the first Christian mission came to China from the Byzantine world of the Eastern Mediterranean and Syria. There had already been Nestorian Christians from Persia and Central Asia living along the Silk Road. However, the first formal mission to China is described in extraordinary, indeed mesmerising detail on one of the country's greatest treasures, a stone stele preserved today in Xi'an.

The inscription is titled in nine Chinese characters: 'A monument commemorating the propagation of the Luminous Religion of the West'. It was carved in 781 CE and looks back over nearly 150 years of Christian missionary enterprise into China. Depicted above the title is a Nestorian Eastern Christian cross rising out of the clouds of Daoism, and on either side of that are the lotus flowers of Buddhism – a perfect image of the Chinese world view. The account begins with a summary of Christianity, looking at Genesis and the Fall and the coming of Christ, but expressed in Daoist Chinese terms – the Yin and Yang and the eight principal virtues of Buddhism. The cross becomes a symbol of the Chinese cosmos, the four quarters. The stele even quotes the *Dao De Jing*, the great Daoist classic of Laozi: 'The ever truthful and ever unchanging way is mysterious and almost unnameable.'

The stele tells the story of the mission of 635 CE: how a man from the west, a Christian monk called Rabban Olopun, brought the Christian scriptures to China, and how, 'following the direction of the winds through great perils and difficulties', he arrived in Chang'an. There followed an audience with Emperor Taizong in which the monk explained the Christian message and the emperor ordered the Christian scriptures to be translated in the imperial library.

After reading them, Taizong issued an imperial proclamation with a remarkable statement on the comparative values of different civilisations:

> Right principles have no invariable name, holy men have no invariable station; teachings are established in accordance with the values of their own regions, and with the object of benefiting the people at large. The greatly virtuous Olopun, of the kingdom of Syria, has brought his sacred books and images from that distant part, and has presented them at our chief capital. Having examined the principles of this religion, we find them to be purely excellent and natural; investigating its originating source, we find it has taken its rise from the establishment of important truths; its ritual is free from perplexing expressions, its principles will survive when the framework is forgotten; it is beneficial to all creatures; it is advantageous to mankind. Let it be published throughout the Empire, and let the proper authority build a Syrian church in the capital which shall be governed by twenty-one priests.

It is hard to imagine a Daoist or Buddhist embassy arriving in Constantinople in 635 CE being allowed to build a temple in such an open-handed spirit. But, for Taizong, Christianity was beneficial to all human beings and could be propagated in the empire. One of the most extraordinary documents in the history of religions, the stele inscription ends in verse:

> When the pure, bright Illustrious Religion
> Was introduced to our Tang dynasty,
> The Scriptures were translated, and churches built,
> And the vessel set in motion for the living and the dead;
> Every kind of blessing was then obtained,
> And all the kingdoms enjoyed a state of peace.

The Christians in Chang'an were soon followed by Muslim merchants who came to Canton and Quanzhou, both of which today claim China's oldest mosque. In the eighth century, two mosques were built in Chang'an: the magnificent East mosque, which stands today, with its Ming pavilions, gardens and wooden prayer hall, and the West mosque, a treasure house of Ming and Qing architecture.

AN AGE OF INVENTION

As so often in history, the Tang dynasty's opening up to the world led to a transformation in the mentalities of the civilisation in its own lands. The Tang was an age of high culture: in poetry, novels, art, architecture and ceramics. There were also great scientific advances, including cast iron technology, long before the Western world. The period also saw the growth of civic life, with guilds and merchant associations. One crucial development was the invention of woodblock printing, which would reach its fruition with mass printing in the tenth century, making books available to larger numbers of people than at any time before.

The world's first book about the writing of history was written in the eighth century by Liu Zhiji in his *General Remarks on History* (710 CE). In reaction to the traditional tight political control over the drafting of history, controlled, censored and redacted by those in power, Liu's book marks the start of a long tradition of reflection on the problem of writing history. Liu's interest in the accurate recording of words, his critical attitude to the classics and his insistence that history should not deal in myths, but only take in human factors, economics, climate and geography, were part of a core concern for objectivity, which would be a recurring issue in Chinese historiography until the present day.

So the Tang saw the beginning of a revolution in thought, with an increased self-reflexivity that runs through every form of literary endeavour. This period also saw big material changes in society, in the demography and economy of China. The Yellow River valley had been the heartland of prehistoric Chinese civilisation since the Shang. But between the 600s and the 900s the Tang dynasty saw a major shift to the south; in economy, population, food and culture. The subtropical south was opened up to colonisation. Many Tang families moved there at this time and developed rice culture over the wheat and millet diet of the north. From now on in Chinese history, the south would be the dominant part of China. Data from the Tang censuses suggest that by the tenth century China's population had halved in the north and more than doubled in the south. This was facilitated after 605 CE by the building of the Grand Canal to link the two and bring the agricultural produce of the south to the north.

This is also the beginning of China as a commercial society and of Chinese cities as great trading places rather than as centres of royal power. In the Tang, no city was more important in shifting this urban paradigm than Yangzhou, which grew up at the junction of the Grand Canal and the Yangtze River. The 'number one trading city' of the Tang dynasty, in contrast to the imperial capital with its regulated streets and curfews, Yangzhou was a commercial city, the first in history to be lit by artificial light at night. There commerce drove growth and the old, strictly controlled idea of urban society began to change into something more akin to an early modern city, where all classes and trades mixed together. By the eighth century, a Chinese official wrote that 'every stream in the empire was full of ships, moving constantly back and forth, always circulating. And if they stopped for a single moment ten thousand merchants would be bankrupted.'

THE FALL OF THE TANG

In the mid-eighth century, then, China was at the height of its power, wealth and culture under a great emperor: Tang Xuanzong. Tang ships sailed from Canton to the Persian Gulf, merchants from Central Asia thronged into the capital. In the far west, a network of fortified towns, beacons and watchtowers stretched out into Central Asia to protect the trade routes. But disaster was looming. There were two ill-advised wars in 751 CE. The poet Li Bai, a native of Central Asia, was incensed at the risk of it all. 'In Heaven and Earth all was unity,' he wrote, 'it was all peaceful within the four seas: so why send a levy of conscripts to campaign down in Yunnan?' The ensuing defeat in the tropical landscape of the southwest, compounded by disease and malaria, was costly in men and materials:

> The summer campaign south of the Yangtze ...
> [were] told to march into Yunnan
> They were frightened creatures not fighting men
> In that hot climate the long marches were gruelling ...
> Of a thousand that went out hardly one came back.

That same year, 751 CE, another military disaster took place thousands of miles to the northwest on the Talas River, at today's Taraz in Kazakhstan, an ancient Sogdian trading city. An ill-prepared Chinese expedition was caught between the forces of the Caliphate and their Turkic allies and suffered a heavy defeat that led to the Tang drawing back on their ambitions in the west. Li Bai's famous poem 'Fighting South of the Ramparts' was written in response to the news:

> Last year we were fighting at the source of the Sanggan
> This year we are fighting on Onion River [Kashgar Darya]
> We have washed our swords in the surf of the Parthian seas

We have pastured our horses among the snows of Tian
      Shan ...
The beacons are always alight, the fighting and marching
      never stop.
Men die in the field, slashing sword to sword ...
Generals schemed in vain.
Know therefore war is a cursed thing
Which the wise man uses only if he must.

Sometimes there is no one cause for great changes in history. However, from that moment, things went precipitously from bad to worse in a way that shows how even an advanced state can find itself unable to cope with a combination of natural and manmade disasters. The early 750s saw an unprecedented series of calamities, which, in the end, for all its administrative solidity, undermined the state. In 750, a severe drought led to poor harvests. In spring 751, the imperial grain fleet caught fire in harbour and 200 shiploads of grain were destroyed, so the government storehouses were ill stocked to meet the supply crisis. Later that same year a typhoon destroyed thousands of boats, large and small, at Yangzhou where the Grand Canal intersects with the Yangtze, losing more precious grain and rice. Almost incredibly, at that same time, a fire in the capital's main weapons arsenal destroyed 500,000 weapons, crossbows, swords and spears. In the autumn it rained for weeks on end and floods caused havoc as far inland as the Wei River and the environs of Chang'an. As the people faced food shortages, the government found it impossible to respond effectively. In the capital, the population of nearly a million stared starvation in the face. In summer 752, a great hurricane caused huge damage in Luoyang, followed by more floods in the autumn.

THE CONCUBINE LADY YANG

In the first half of his reign, Emperor Xuanzong had been a brilliant and gifted leader, a patron of artists and writers, and was credited with bringing Tang China to the pinnacle of its power and achievements. But after a glorious reign of forty-two years, at nearly seventy years old, his powers were fading, and he was finally brought down by his weakness for women. His impetuous love for Lady Yang Guifei became legendary, and the famous tale of the emperor's concubine is known to every Chinese person from childhood. It was said that the emperor had sent his men over the whole of the land to find the most beautiful woman in China. Then, when he was bathing at the Huaqing hot springs, he saw the eighteen-year-old daughter of a high official – 'the hot water running down her glistening jade-like body', as the poet Bai Juyi tells the tale. It was love at first sight, and although Yang was already a concubine of one of Xuanzong's sons, the emperor took her as a consort and became besotted with her. He neglected the duties of government to spend time with her, favouring her clan.

A perfect storm was unfolding on a scale which could have shaken even a modern state. Then, in autumn 755 it rained for sixty days. In Chang'an, the lower part of the city, where the poorest lived, was under water; in Luoyang, nineteen wards were flooded and huge numbers were housed in temporary camps. With the destruction of the harvest, prices soared. The government was forced to empty its grain stores to help alleviate the suffering.

The poet Du Fu, then a lower-grade civil servant, captured that precise moment in the freezing and wet November of 755. Setting out from Chang'an in the dead of night to visit his family, his fingers were so cold that, when his frozen belt string snapped, he could not retie it. At dawn, Du Fu saw the imperial war flag 'blocking out the pale sun' as he passed the Huaqing hot springs. The Emperor had arrived with his courtiers and his concubine Lady Yang the week before. While the nation froze and starved, staring into an ever-grimmer winter, the court enjoyed the hot springs and ate the finest food. 'From the Vermilion Gates', Du Fu wrote, 'comes the smell of wine and cooked flesh; in the road, the bones of men who froze to death.' On arriving where his family were staying, he writes, 'when I entered the gates, I heard the sound of weeping. My little boy had died of starvation.'

Though the government had tried its best to deal with the food shortages, fury with the luxury of the court intensified. Worse was to follow. In mid-December 755, a huge rebellion broke out under a renegade general called An Lushan that would devastate China. The son of a central Asian sorceress, stepson of a Turkic Sogdian general, An Lushan marched down from the north and proclaimed a new dynasty at Luoyang on New Year's Day, 5 February 756. All-out war broke out with the beleaguered emperor Xuanzong. Over the next eight years China was criss-crossed by armies, the land plundered and ravaged. The disruption and loss of life was huge. Movement in the countryside was disrupted as marauding armies tramped to and fro, farmers' carts commandeered to transport the living and the dead. River and canal travel was also curtailed, attacks from bandits an ever-present fear. Half the nation, it seemed, was on the road, coping with the breakdown of the state, caught up in the swirling vortices of violence. With no means of support and little private wealth, Du Fu and his young family were swept up in these disasters. They took to the road and river with refugees, moving from place to place, often reduced to taking charity. No great poet in the history of the world perhaps had such experiences. 'Thinking on what I myself have lived through,' he wrote, 'I have lived a life of privilege ... but if even I have known such suffering, then the common man must indeed have been shaken by these storms.'

Running through his poems is a constant critique of corruption and incompetence, but always from the idealist standpoint of a loyal Confucian. 'This was a time', he wrote, 'when the powerful indulged in murder and plunder, the military used up the tax grain in the stores: the imperial fighting cocks had to be fed. Many warnings could have been obtained from history about why a dynasty falls ...'

Some of the poems have fantastic immediacy, with a sense of heart-pumping panic as the family struggle through the night, dodging bandits and wolves. Recalling what we see on television in Syria, Yemen, North Africa and so many other places in the modern world, perhaps no other great artist or poet has ever portrayed what it is like to be a refugee on the road in such conditions:

> I remember when we first fled the rebellion
> Hurrying north, passing through hardship and danger,
> The night was deep on the Pengya Road ...
> We clung together pulling through mud and mire
> And having made no provision against the rain
> The paths were slippery, our clothes were cold.
> At times we went through agonies
> Making only a few miles in a whole day,
> Fruits of the wilds our only provisions ...

In 756, with An Lushan's forces advancing on Chang'an, the emperor and his entourage fled, but his troops mutinied on the road west. Among their demands was the death of Lady Yang, she of the 'moth-like eyebrows'. In the end the emperor gave in and she was strangled in the courtyard of a small Buddhist temple, out in the countryside, at the Mawei postal station on the main road towards the west. The emperor's heart was broken. Later, in extreme grief, he had her exhumed, but her body had decayed and was kept from him. Instead, a perfumed pomade buried with her was sent back to him.

One of the most famous stories in Chinese culture, the tale was immortalised in poetry, even during the Tang, and has been the subject of countless books, films and operas. Today there is even a grandiose 'son et lumière' on the site of the hot springs, outside whose gates, as Du Fu wrote, lay the bones of the poor who had frozen to death.

A month later the emperor abdicated and was succeeded by his son, and Chang'an was captured and sacked by the rebels. Despite An Lushan's death, the war carried on, but the Tang fought back and eventually recaptured the city. The war ended in 763, but the massive disruption to the country lasted much longer. The national census of 754 had recorded 52.9 million people in nearly 9 million taxpaying households. Ten years later, it counted 16.9 million in nearly 3 million. This suggests that more than 30 million people had been displaced as refugees, killed in war or died of famine. If so, it was one of the deadliest wars in history.

Looking back from later times to the eighth century, the reign of 'the Brilliant Emperor' Xuanzong, the besotted lover of Lady Yang and the fatally flawed protagonist of the An Lushan war, was seen as one of cultural greatness and legendary splendour, despite its tragic denouement. At the heart of this collective memory was Du Fu's poetry, which came to be seen as the touchstone of the Confucian voice that speaks with unwavering moral integrity, the embodiment of China's moral conscience, as it has been for the past 1,000 years. Indeed, to call Du Fu China's greatest poet is to underestimate his importance in Chinese civilisation, for it limits his role merely to that of a poet. Why that should be is an interesting question. He died in complete obscurity, believing his name would be forgotten. But in the Confucian revival of the Song dynasty, his voice became the one that spoke for the nation, in its combination of sympathy for the people and Confucian loyalty to the state, and as such he is still taught in the national school curriculum today. His universal appeal in modern times, though, perhaps derives from something more. His writings are a sustained articulation of remembrance in the face of loss that that runs right through Chinese literary history: Li Qingzhao at the fall of the Song, a refugee still guarding her precious scrolls of his poetry; Fang Weiyi, another great female writer and educator who wrote of the fall of the Ming with Du Fu in mind; Zheng Zhen, the greatest of the moderns, who made a pilgrimage to Du Fu's Thatched Cottage in Chengdu amid the horrors of the Taiping; even during the Rape of Nanjing in 1937 the poet's words appeared in graffiti on fire-scorched walls: 'the state is destroyed but the country remains'. At the heart of his poetry was grief for what was, and for what could have been.

The year 755, then, would turn out to be a catastrophic break in Chinese history. To seek a psychological parallel in Western culture we must turn to the First World War – for example to the French, German and English poets; to Apollinaire's anguished understanding that on 4 August 1914 a new world had been born. A year or so later, Sigmund Freud wrote his great essay on 'Mourning and Melancholia', arguing that one may mourn for a culture, a civilisation, as for a beloved. Du Fu's grief, which perplexed even him ('why do I still mourn?'), is shot through with this bigger sense not only of personal grief, but of cultural sorrow.

Weeping in the wilderness, how many families
know of war and loss,
Barbarian songs in scattered places
rise from fishermen and woodcutters.
Sleeping Dragon Zhuge Liang,
Leaping Horse Gongsun Shu,
heroes turned to brown dust.
All word of events in the human world
lost in these vast silent spaces.

7

DECLINE AND FALL

The eight-year An Lushan Rebellion was a turning point in the story of China. Censuses suggest that as many as 30 million people died, comparable to figures from the First World War, and it was accompanied by similar institutional crisis and societal and governmental breakdown. But its effects on the culture were also psychological. The dynasty continued, but in a very different, more embattled, mood. Over the next century the Tang faced floods, famines and further rebellions; the progressive eroding of central government and the gradual loss of provinces saw marauding armies at times threatening the heartland. Meanwhile, new ideas crept like a damp stain into the very fabric of Tang culture, casting a shadow across the world of the old aristocratic clans that had survived. Over its huge span of time Chinese history had experienced periods like this before, and would do so again, but this period was remembered with peculiar intensity. Now we enter – though of course they could not have seen it this way – the Late Tang.

AT HOME WITH THE DU FAMILY

In the beautiful valleys south of the capital, the rich aristocratic families that had been the upholders of order for hundreds of years rebuilt their mansions after the devastations of An Lushan's armies. They replanted fruit trees, repaired their barns and houses and continued to live a life of privilege. One such was the Du family, not related to the great poet, who had the finest estate in Chengnan, the area south of Chang'an. The house lay in the valley of the Fanchuan River, below a long ridge called Red Slope that ran south away from the capital above the valley, where landscaped gardens and rockeries, artificial grottos and streams were laid out with gazebos and pavilions. As their grandson would later write, 'Our home and gardens at Xia Du are old, lying by the river, a ridge of red leaves, of green willows stretching away to a shrine.' The clan's connection to the area went back to the Han dynasty, when they had first settled here, and the place was still soaked in their history, with memorials of the past all around them. After dinner or music and poetry recitals in the house, the visitor could inspect the family's collection of paintings, bronzes and manuscripts, or go for walks to the crumbling Han temple and inspect antiquities going back to the time of the Zhou. It was a period that in Chinese poetry evokes (to use a very loose analogy from Western literature) something of the air of 1913, of the country estates of Alain-Fournier's *Lost Domain*, or the glamorous aristocrats of the Guermantes family in Proust's *Lost Time*; a world – and a millennium – away, but sharing an extraordinary refinement of high culture and also a sense of living on the edge in a time of 'no longer and not yet'.

On the Du estate the family retired for leisure and to study politics, history, literature and poetry, all of which were in the family's blood. Only a few miles out of the city, within easy reach by horseback or the family horse-drawn carriage appropriate to ministerial rank, this in the late eighth century was the home of a famous figure in the Tang government, Du You, who, for reasons that will become apparent, we will call 'Grandad Du'.

Born in 735, Grandad Du was a great minister of an old family; three generations of his ancestors had served the Tang state in high office. He traced his ancestry back to the Han, and even, it was claimed, to the Qin and Chu. Families like his were the backbone of the bureaucracy; Du had been chancellor and three times prime minister. As a teenager and young man he had lived through the terrors of An Lushan, and it was that shattering experience that led him to devote over thirty-five years to a personal literary project: the *Tongdian*, 'A Comprehensive Study of Our Institutions'. Completed in 801 in his retirement, it was a grand work of synthesis, reflecting on the continuities and ruptures in Chinese history and economics, state organisation, law and ritual.

The book was the first great history of institutions since Aristotle, and the first in China, a work little known outside the country (indeed it still awaits a full translation) but one that has been compared to Ibn Khaldun's *Introduction to History*, written six centuries later. Following the new historiography of the Tang historian Li Zhiji, the *Tongdian* is realistic in a way that was beyond medieval, Western Christian or Muslim writers, whose narratives and conception of the past were perforce shaped by monotheism and the teleology of salvational history. In its scope and method Du's work shows yet again how an outsiders' view of China is often flawed, partial and monolithic; the keys to understanding the civilisation may be the Confucian classics, but there were always counter thinkers, some of whom we will meet in later chapters. Brilliant and innovative as the civilisation was in so many ways, China's political problems were structural, and thus had a habit of recurring.

Like most of the great panoramic surveys of Chinese history, the *Tongdian* involved a huge amount of (to our Western mind) over-detailed recapitulation, but then codification was the key. The aim was to select and systematise knowledge and hand on an expanded and annotated sum of the past, incorporating for example an officially commissioned text from 738 on the six main institutions of the Tang. The work was privately published, but it was intended for the eyes of the emperor, aimed as a wake-up call. In an increasingly troubled epoch where the future was insecure, the government had to move with the times and change its ways. Optimism was a key theme in the book, along with a Confucian belief in the moral advancement of society by 'transformative education' and a faith in what we would describe today as consultative autocracy – 'despotism with Chinese characteristics'. For Du, institutional history was indispensable for good governance because good institutions run by properly qualified civil servants were the very embodiment of Confucian teaching. So his was a work of transition in more ways than one, emphasising the political and moral importance of the ritual tradition, sceptical of cosmological justifications of state power, preferring instead material and institutional validation. It was a new type of historical writing, looking at the perennial tension in classical Chinese culture between eternal principles and present realities. And these could not have been more dramatically opposed in the last years of Du's life as he looked out from Red Slope to a darkening horizon.

CHANGING TIMES: LOSS OF NERVE

When he presented the book to the emperor in 801, Grandad Du was still optimistic, but the strains in Chinese society he reflected were evident for all to see. After Du died at the end of 812, China had a series of short-lived, dissolute rulers, and then in 827 the emperor Jingzong was murdered by a cabal of eunuchs. In the grand mansions of the old lineages there was a sense of their world changing for the worst. As Du's grandson would observe in a telling image of an imagined hall of high culture and ritual, 'rainwater is leaking down moss-damp walls, autumn leaves blowing along the table'.

What went wrong? Why is it that great ages decline? The historian Ibn Khaldun thought the key was the loss of the ethos that binds the rulers to their aristocracies; that luxury, wealth and overconsumption fatally undermine 'group feeling'. For Gibbon it had been the Christian religion, with its otherworldly eschatology, that eroded the old virtues of Rome. In China, too, there were some, like Du and his contemporary Han Yu, who felt that the ethos had been eroded and that religion was the problem. For Du, the country needed a sense of shared culture, transmitted through institutions run by qualified people, but the institutions were not finding the right men. Equally, however, the huge royal investment in 'non-Chinese' institutions and beliefs was undermining the country. Buddhism, so enthusiastically embraced in the first Tang century, with vast investment in land, buildings, art and treasure, was actually an alien intrusion. Its intellectual and spiritual influence on Chinese culture was regarded by Du as ultimately negative, the product of a 'Western barbarian' whose core ideas were 'nihilistic'. It went against the grain of Chinese civilisation, whose world view was essentially practical and optimistic, as long as the state was governed justly. This was not how Buddhism's relationship to China had been defined for the previous 700 years. Du and Han Yu were calling for China to return to its roots and to throw off foreign influence – the kind of rhetoric we see in our politics today in times of disturbing change. Chinese tradition was the path to renewal, they said; Confucianism and Daoism should be the new axis, while Buddhism – the scapegoat – was the enemy within. And so the ecumenical view of the Early Tang was abandoned.

THE PERSECUTION

The new emperor Wuzong came to the throne in 840 and ran with the new policy, much as in the sixteenth century Henry VIII and his successors moved against the vast inherited wealth of the Catholic Church in England. In the early 840s, a massive campaign of temple closures began. It was brutal, sweeping and destructive. The government's persecution of the Buddhists between 842 and 846 came at time of growing internal and external threats, when marauding private armies threatened the Yellow River heartland and pirate fleets plundered the coasts. In the far west, Turkic and Uighur kings and warlords overran the frontier provinces. It was in this troubled time that Wuzong launched 'the great anti-Buddhist persecution'.

Capricious, unpredictable and cruel, the emperor was probably mad, though his detractors were quick to invent preposterous tales of his excesses. A vivid, contemporary diary gives the mood of the time as the clampdown began. It was written by a Japanese pilgrim by the name of Ennin, a Buddhist monk who in 838 had accompanied the Japanese ambassador to the Tang court. His journal is shot through with anxiety as an increasingly authoritarian ruler gave way to irrational prejudices and deranged beliefs, watched with growing alarm by the Japanese visitors.

After arriving in China, Ennin had studied at the complex of Buddhist monasteries on Mount Wutai in the forested hills of Shanxi. Travelling there today, one may still see something of what Tang dynasty pilgrims saw, from China's oldest wooden buildings to the 'marvellous flowers of the rarest kinds in bloom all over the mountain from the bottom of the valleys spread on the hillsides like brocade, their scent so strong, even our clothes were perfumed by it'.

Over three years of journeying in China, Ennin had sailed the Grand Canal and travelled the road and river systems, admiring the network of inns and hostels, and the post stations and the burgeoning markets en route. Negotiating the many practicalities, the red tape of permits and travel documents, he gives us a vivid portrait of a still-functioning great power. But Uighur armies were on the rampage in the far west, and even as he journeyed, events began to acquire a grim momentum as heterodox sects were singled out one by one and the pogroms began.

First the Uighur residents in the big cities were accused of belonging to the proscribed Manichaean sect, rounded up and executed in a gruesome sacrificial parody. Then, in the summer and autumn of 842, as he travelled overland to Chang'an, Ennin noticed that Buddhist monks were being excluded from the customary rituals of state. In his diary on 14 November he recorded that an imperial edict had been issued that all monks and nuns in the empire should be forced to return to lay life. Money, estates and grain stocks were to be surrendered. Monastic gates in the capital were sealed and stock-taking begun. By early February the next year, Ennin noted that nearly 2,500 monks and nuns had been returned to the lay life, temple treasures confiscated and melted down, books burned.

There were exceptions, however. By then Buddhism was so ingrained in popular culture that people often refused to do the emperor's bidding. In autumn 845, Ennin was told some had refused to attend imperial Daoist ceremonies: 'They have stolen offerings made to Buddha and are using them for worship of demons. Who wants to go and look at such a show?' Students in the university in the capital had refused to obey the new laws. In some provinces feelings ran so high that local governors refused to put the edict into action and continued to receive Buddhist pilgrims. In Hubei and Shanxi, north of the river, 'no monasteries have been destroyed: things are continuing as before,' Ennin confided in his diary; 'message after message has been sent but the threats of punishment have been ignored. The people simply say, "If the Son of Heaven wants the monasteries destroyed let him come and do it himself. None of us can bring ourselves to do such a thing."'

The situation worsened. In May 846 the Uighurs of Central Asia threatened the Silk Road frontiers and the government issued another edict ordering the killing of all Manichaean priests. In Chang'an, the great circular Altar of Heaven dating from the Sui dynasty was rebuilt. China was to go back to its roots. In June, Daoist priests attended grand celebrations for the emperor's birthday. Megalomaniac projects ran in parallel with massacres. And so China gradually sank into an era of darkness.

DU MU: AT THE FAMILY VILLAGE

Ironically, one great Late Tang figure who lived through all this was the grandson of Du You, the very man who had argued that Buddhism was un-Chinese – an alien importation. A historian and civil servant, Du Mu had five generations of ancestors who had been high ministers in the Tang state, eminent literary men and statesmen. Today he is best known as one of the great Late Tang poets, but he also wrote on governance and composed an influential handbook on the conduct of war. His poetry, though, conveys with thrilling immediacy those years of persecution. As an increasingly disillusioned, peripatetic civil servant, the younger Du saw Buddhist persecutions first hand. In his poem on the transience of civilisation, 'Ice-Blocked Bian River', the image of the water flowing 'eastwards day and night under the ice while no one notices' became a metaphor that would be refracted through the whole of later Chinese literature. 'This floating life is but a dream: how much longer can we enjoy our happiness?' would be the theme of the literati of the ninth century.

On the eve of the Buddhist persecution, frustrated in his career and always looking for preferment, Du Mu had taken a job in Huangzhou in the prefecture of Qian on the north bank of the Yangtze, where the river makes its great bend south. It was a small, poor prefecture, 'the place where I got enough sleep', he wrote, wryly observing his own predilection for the 'blue houses'. Even the accommodation was primitive: 'the governor's house,' he wrote, 'is the kind of place where you'd live if you were out in the wilds'. But it was a place with deep historical associations, for it was believed to be the site of the great Battle of the Red Cliffs in the time of the Three Kingdoms at the end of the Han dynasty in 208 CE, which presaged the breakdown of China (above page 123). In his spare time Du rode out on trips, to think on past glories, reflecting on a battle relic, a broken halberd in the sand, with the fabulous receptivity to the past that is characteristic of Tang poets:

> I find it poignant that at Red Cliff, the crossing where
>   heroes contended,
>   there is now only an old man in a raincoat, sitting and
>   fishing ...

In the early autumn of 844, Emperor Wuzong issued the last of his series of edicts, closing down all but a few Buddhist temples in the empire, with thousands of monks and nuns now forced to leave their calling, grow their hair and dress as lay people. A blanket ban was announced on 'superstitious offerings to relics and mystical false-hoods of the barbarian from the West which delude the common people'. In the capital alone 300 Buddha halls and local shrines were closed and looted. As a public official, Du Mu had to approve and enact policy, but as a poet he was deeply troubled by the disruption, destruction and social dislocation. He composed poems on an abandoned temple in Chizhou, 'imagining its bell still ringing still', and an old monk stripped of his Buddhist robes and bell. Sent south to another poor prefecture at Muzhou in Zhejiang, he conjures a haunting moment as the bell rings time for prayer and he scrutinises the old lined Buddha-face across the refectory table:

> Once you were a novice on Mount Jin. The Buddhist way we all know takes a thousand years but do not spurn me for my big city dust: I too was once inspired by higher ideals.

Meantime internal rebellions and frontier wars increased. In autumn 843, imperial troops clashed with rebel armies and extra taxes were levied for massive new military expenditure. The Japanese pilgrim Ennin, still marooned in China, now confounded by police orders and new visa restrictions, watched huge wagon trains carrying grain supplies heading west and heard rumours that military costs there were so great that the equivalent of 200 million coins were needed every day to pay the imperial armies. The looting of the temples and their treasures and estates would help. With a paranoid and unpopular government, suspicions of disloyalty were rife. When one escaped guard officer sheltered 300 former monks, all were summarily killed. There were reports of massacres of civilian populations, even common peasants out in the west, while among the imperial armies cannibalism reared its head. In 844, 3,000 disaffected troops, who had fought continuously for three years and now asked to be relieved, were disarmed and executed in the East Market in Chang'an, blood drenching the sandy plaza between the market streets. Not for the first, or last, time in its history, the country under Wuzong was now in the grip of tyranny.

A MEETING ON THE ROAD

Ennin and his companions were forced to leave the capital and make their way out of China. In summer 845, at the hottest time of year, 'mosquitoes and horse flies making clouds like rain', they travelled along the main highway eastwards. There they saw signs of the destruction of the Buddhist order all around them: temples looted, buildings destroyed, monks and nuns sent back to their places of origin, their shaven heads wrapped. At every stopping point the refrain from local officials was: 'The destruction of the monasteries has started.' In the wayside taverns, too, the phrase 'the monasteries are to be destroyed' was on everyone's lips.

Now formally expelled and defrocked, Ennin and the others headed for the coast to find a boat home. Before he left, however, he bumped into a local official who had once shown him kindness:

> We took tea with him in a wayside store and talked for a long time. When we parted he said this: 'Buddhism no longer exists in this land. But Buddhism flows on towards the East. So it has been since ancient times. I hope you will do your best to reach your homeland and propagate Buddhism there. Your disciple has been very fortunate to have seen you on many occasions. Today we part, and in this life we are not likely to meet again. When you have attained Buddhahood, I hope you will not abandon your disciple.'

THE LOST DOMAIN

By the time Ennin and his companions reached Japan in 847, the revolts in the north of China had been defeated. The emperor himself had died in 846, his health destroyed by the elixirs his Daoist alchemists thought would procure long life. More than quarter of a million monks and nuns had been removed and around 5,000 temples destroyed, along with countless smaller shrines. The destruction of cultural treasures was vast: an incalculable wealth of bronzes, art and manuscripts. Today in Chinese Buddhist temples, very little statuary and art has survived from before this time – a measure of the extent of the vandalism. But Buddhism would at least survive in China, and, as we shall see, thrive again under the Song dynasty. Zoroastrianism and Manichaeism, on the other hand, were virtually destroyed, and for Nestorian Christianity, too, Wuzong's persecutions would prove to be a near-fatal blow, though it would revive for a time under the Mongols.

By then, Du Mu was disillusioned with politics, old enough to see his government career was a failure, and still young enough to feel bitter about it. Over the years he had frequently resigned and asked for transfers, and in autumn 848 he was moved back to the capital as vice-director of the Bureau of Merit Titles and awarded his old post in the History Office. At least with history he could feel like a fish back in water; in Chinese culture, poets have always been historians too.

At this point in his life – disappointed, prematurely white-haired though only in his mid-forties – he went home to Grandad Du's house on Red Slope south of Chang'an, to walk again in the garden where he remembered such happiness in childhood, in a world in which natural beauty and social order seemed in harmony. In good times, 'go out and change the world', Grandad Du had recommended. Now, in bad times, his grandson returned to the symbolic landscapes of his child-hood. His last verses written here are interiorised; the poet wrapped in on himself 'like the horns of a snail'.

Du Mu died before the end of 852 and was buried on the estate near the Du family village. In the 1960s the funeral mound was lev-elled and carted off for topsoil, and the site today is a faint hollow in a cabbage patch in a field bordered by crumbling red-brick barn walls and sheds. Its inscription, broken in Mao's day, has been recently replaced by a new memorial stone. Perhaps egged on by modern researchers, the locals have not forgotten him, even though his reputation ranks him below the greatest of the Tang poets. His poem for the day of the ancestors, 'A Drizzling Rain Falls on Tomb Sweeping Day', is still especially loved. After his death, his nephew put his poetry together in print; a vision of the transformation of the Tang world which is shot through with a sense of transience, ruin and loss. More than any other Tang writer he is the poet of lost idyll: the world as it might have been. How that moment arrives in a civilisation, with the loss of group feeling, is often a mystery until it suddenly becomes visible to all. It is hard for the historian, working through administrative documents, memorials and annals, to touch on the real lived experience, but poets can. Like Milton and his friends after the bloodshed and rupture of the seventeenth-century civil wars in Britain, Du Mu's poetry captures the experience of defeat.

ENDGAME: THE HUANG CHAO REBELLION

For families like the Du clan, the end came in the 870s and '80s as the Tang entered its last decades with a series of hammer blows. The plunder of the immense wealth of the Buddhist establishment had helped the imperial family and the nobility pay their armies and survive in the short term, but it did not address the continuing economic crisis. In 860, there were mutinies of the army on the frontiers, while at home unrelentingly heavy taxes and labour burdens provoked rural revolt. One peasant uprising, terming itself the 'Righteous Army', gathered over 200,000 peasants, vagrants, beggars and pirates. The empire was now hugely overstretched geographically and secession wars began in frontier provinces. Then droughts, floods and famine struck. In the 870s and '80s, there was widespread belief that heaven was displeased, that the dynasty had lost its Mandate. The coup de grâce was the rebellion of Huang Chao, a final brutal spasm of almost unimaginable violence with many parallels to the Taiping, the bloodiest war of the nineteenth century, as this was of the ninth. In the 870s, several large bandit armies had risen up, fired by a succession of massive harvest failures and the government's continued intransigence over tax relief. In the past when this happened, Tang governments had been able to combat famine by distributing grain from a network of state granaries with surplus food stocks alongside an aggressive policy of price regulation, but not now.

Huang began his revolt in 874 in Henan, a hotbed of peasant rebellion from early times to the twentieth century. Charismatic, swaggering, an expert with crossbow and weapons, Huang had some skill as a writer as well as a swordsman. He came from the coast of Shandong, where his family had been salt smugglers and privateers for several generations – effectively a wide and powerful mafia clan. One of eight brothers, Huang had several times sat and failed the imperial examinations, again curiously foreshadowing Hong, the nineteenth-century Taiping leader who turned his fury against the very establishment he had hoped to join. In the beginning Huang's motivation was hunger. Looking back, the next generation remembered those days as a time of desperate famine, when hordes of famished people, from the subtropical south up the eastern coast to the central plains of Henan, became robbers, and bands of robbers coalesced into armies.

Huang's rebels were well organised and motivated; in the new world of Tang literacy, they distributed leaflets printed on woodblock presses, railing against corrupt and greedy local officials, excessive taxes and unfair punishments. Their anger turned against the 'worthy and outstanding talents who instead of showing anger retreated to their private estates'.

Over the next few years Huang fought devastating wars from the central plain down to the Pearl River: a Tang Spartacus leading his forces against local governors and imperial armies. Though he suffered defeats, over seven years of campaigning he proved very hard to corner, and his troops stuck with him. Then, in winter 879, claiming the title of the 'Heaven-Storming Generalissimo', he attacked the Tang's richest port of Canton, whose warehouses were crammed with the accumulated goods of merchants who traded with Sumatra, India and the Persian Gulf. After a prolonged siege, the city's resistance was broken and punished by a horrendous massacre, the death toll estimated at 120,000 by Arab chroniclers, who noted the deliberate targeting of resident aliens, foreign merchants, Arabs, Persians and Jews. But above all this was a class war. Increasingly the peasant armies took revenge on the scholar classes and the old landed families whose estates and prosperous farmlands, like those of the Du clan, clustered around the wealthiest towns and cities, making them easy targets. Many people were forced to flee to poorer, more isolated areas like Huizhou near the sacred mountain of Huangshan. Today the printed genealogies of old medieval merchant families whose descendants still live there claim their original migration to this region occurred during and after the upheavals of the Huang Chao rebellion.

In summer 880, Huang's terrifying caravan of death and destruction recrossed the Yangtze and marched north, press-ganging young men everywhere in a devastated countryside. They were 150,000 strong now, though some said their armies eventually reached more than half a million. They camped in the lower Yellow River plain and proclaimed their intention to topple the dynasty, capture the young emperor Xixong and make him and his family 'pay for their crimes'. Pushing west, they captured the eastern capital Luoyang and broke through the Tang defence line, the historic fortifications in the Tong pass, and descended on the capital, Chang'an. On 8 January 881, the emperor Xixong abandoned his capital and fled over mountains to Chengdu, the demoralised imperial troops plundering and setting fire to the West Market before they left. Huang's soldiers entered the city shouting the name of 'King Huang', who they promised 'will make life good, not like the Li family [the royal clan], who had no sympathy for your lives'.

A leading Tang general welcomed Huang in a ceremony of submission at the city gate. The rebels issued printed proclamations declaring Huang's love for the people, urging the citizens to carry on with their daily routine and assuring them that their shops and properties would not be looted. But the riches on view in the markets and mansions of the capital turned the heads of Huang's raggletaggle army of peasant soldiers, and from the beginning looting was the order of the day. Huang based himself in the mansion of a Tang minister, but several days later he moved into the Tang palace in the imperial city. He then ordered the execution of all captured members of the imperial clan and proclaimed himself Emperor of Qi, as if the Mandate had passed on.

What followed is one of the grimmest moments in Chinese history. Supplies for the huge rebel army were hard to come by as civil order in the countryside collapsed, and in 883, faced with starvation, they turned to cannibalism as a deliberate policy. As famine gripped the countryside, it was later claimed that Huang's army killed more than 1,000 people every day for food. An exaggeration? A lurid tale to make monsters of the rebels? In Chinese history, cannibalism casts a long and dark shadow, but no society in history is immune to it, especially in times of starvation. Sometimes in Tang China it had occurred as a grim act of vengeance or of punishment, but when the rebels ran out of food it is said captives were killed, chopped up, cooked and eaten, sometimes salted or pickled to preserve them: 'In some places', wrote one contemporary, 'it was said human flesh was more plentiful than dog meat. Eating it was known as the "unnatural practices of bandits".'

And so, after achieving such greatness, the Way was lost in a miasma of cruelty and horror. The Tang court took refuge in Sichuan, and over the next year their armies launched counter attacks. In Chang'an, the people rose against the rebels and Tang forces briefly retook the city before Huang retaliated, regained the city and massacred the civilian population. The capital was now thoroughly looted and wrecked as rebel troops ran amok killing the wealthy and officials in a rage against the rich. It was the end for the old landed aristocracy in the countryside around Chang'an and Luoyang. Perhaps it was then that the Du mansion was plundered and the garden on Red Slope lost forever. The poet Wei Zhuang, who was in the capital at the time of Huang's occupation, described the scene: 'in house after house the blood flowed ... my neighbour had a young daughter, lovely as a goddess ... her lustrous flashing eyes, the very image of spring in her mirror, but she was murdered in her house ... as women across the city were violated ... fires burning across a vast landscape ... ashes spinning in the wind ...'

All remaining members of the Tang royal family the rebels could lay their hands on were now killed, any Tang official who refused to submit and serve the rebel state executed. Among the famous cases of scholar-officials asked to serve Huang was Li Dao, who announced to his tormentors, 'My knee can be cut off but a memorial I cannot draft.'

As so often in history, at first rebellions are borne on a high tide of rage, class hatred and a sense of injustice, but once power is gained, what then is to be done? There were many possible lessons from Chinese history. The peasant Li Bang, after all, had founded the Han, and, later, the illiterate Zhu Yuanzhang the Ming. Both had commanded allegiance by sheer force of personality and military prowess, but in the end Huang did not. A concerted counter attack finally drove him out of Chang'an, and as his army broke up in disarray, he was ambushed and killed by his own clan while crossing the Yellow River in July 884.

So ended the career of one of the most famous rebels in Chinese history. Many myths and stories later attached themselves to him, and there were persistent legends that he had survived – that he became a Buddhist monk and was later recognised by one of the Tang leaders in a monastery in Luoyang. Despite the staggering violence, modern communist historians found it easy to excuse mass killing in the name of what they saw as class war, and praised Huang as a champion of the peasants against the rulers.

The revolution had a devastating effect on the several hundred old families who had been the ruling aristocracy of China for 300 years or more. Among them was the Li family from Zhaocun in Hebei, whom we met more than a century before during the An Lushan Rebellion. Since then they had known only success: eight chief ministers in the past century. Their fine city mansion in Anyi ward in Chang'an had been one of the most splendid of the residences in the capital, so grand that they became known as Li of Anyi. The house was destroyed in the rebellions of the 880s along with the family's country property outside Luoyang, mirroring the experience of many of the old families of the empire. It was a real watershed. Not only because of the violence and destruction, but because the institutions, customs and rituals which had ensured clan identity and allegiance to the state were destroyed. These, as we shall see, were created anew in the Song dynasty in ways that would influence the whole of later Chinese history. But for the old Tang families, it was too late. In the countryside after Huang's rebellion, one witness described 'roads overgrown, households wrecked, deserted fields and gardens, trees cut down and taken away by woodcutters, gardens and pavilions levelled, and everything ownerless'. On the road, an old beggar portrayed in a famous poem is typical of the time: 'Look at me, I had lands 200 *ch'an* in extent, 2,500 acres ... my tax bill was a million in silver cash a year' – he points to the hills – 'and up there, there are thousands like me.'

The intense drama of the Tang's final decline is overshadowed by the sheer violence of the events, but deeper causes lie in what historians and anthropologists have termed systems collapse, pointing to the other great breakdowns in Chinese history: the collapse of the Mongol Yuan dynasty in the early fourteenth century; the decline and fall of the Ming between the late sixteenth and mid-seventeenth centuries; and the fall of the Qing which led to China's twentieth-century revolutions. These four giant crises are deep-rooted in China's cultural memory, in historiography, literature, poetry and in popular culture.

What happens when things fall apart? We know that the dissolution of complex societies, such as the Roman Empire in Western history, has multiple causes, but often stems from the decline of strong authority at the centre with the concomitant loss of power in the periphery. As the tenth century dawned, central order fragmented, local self-defence militias proliferated, the provinces were militarised and regional armies formed. As local generalissimos vied to found dynasties, north and south China split apart. This breakdown brought an end to the great era of the Tang, a period in which for over 1,000 years Chang'an in its various incarnations had been China's capital. The centre of gravity of Chinese history was about to shift again.

Chang'an was finally sacked and levelled in 904, its great buildings dismantled and their timbers removed. The last Tang emperor was overthrown in 907. But though the Great Tang ended in breakdown and chaos, the dynasty had seen tremendous economic and cultural achievements, including a permanent shift of China's demographic and economic centre of gravity to the south, setting the stage for new social, political, economic and educational institutions that would shape the future later in the tenth century.

So we draw a line under the glorious age of the Tang, a time by which the Chinese still define themselves, especially in the south, where the visitor today is as likely to hear someone call themselves Tang as Han. It is a time admired for its cosmopolitan reach and cultural, artistic and scientific achievements, when Chang'an matched and in some respects surpassed Baghdad and Constantinople as a world city. After the Tang, the pattern of the Chinese past reasserted itself – great order followed by disorder, with some eighteen kingdoms and dynasties supplanting each other, or uneasily coexisting, in a mere seventy years. In the era of the Tang, however, the path was laid for the future – if 'All Under Heaven' could be reunited.

8

THE FIVE DYNASTIES

Historical narratives sometimes resist easy divisions into periods and dynasties. The histories tell us the Tang dynasty ended in 907 and that the Song was proclaimed in 960, consolidated its grip by 979, and announced its final victory in 1005. In between, however, was a prolonged and violent hiatus. The Five Dynasties, by which the epoch is known today, were – the Later Liang (907–23), Later Tang (923–36), Later Jin (936–47), Later Han (947–51), and the Later Zhou (951–60). All were large, state-sized entities, with millions of people, armies and civil services, which tried to promote commerce, a favourable climate for the arts and learning, all making serious efforts to pass on 'this culture of ours'. But there were also a dozen smaller kingdoms with imperial clans, generals, mutineers, warlords and satraps who all declared that they would 'restore the world'. Out of these divisions, early modern China would emerge, but at the time it was by no means certain that there would again be a united kingdom under a sage-ruler who possessed the Mandate of Heaven. That age of division has found few admirers among historians, but is as fascinating as any in China's story.

Among individual people there were many reactions to the end of the Tang; some even rejected the world altogether. The political chaos saw the artist Jing Hao, for example, taking refuge in the Zhongtiao Mountains north of the Yellow River in Shanxi, where he lived as a farmer. There he painted and wrote on the Chinese landscape, depicting its grandeur and immemorial beauty, its precipitous crags, waterfalls and rushing streams; a natural world in which human beings are so tiny as to be almost invisible and their deeds merely transient. It was here that Jing developed the ideas that would underpin China's most influential school of painting, articulating a debate on the nature of reality and the rejection of worldly desires in sublime landscapes. It would become a key theme in Chinese art from then until today; as the poet Du Fu had written, 'the state is destroyed, but the country remains'.

For others, despite the uncertainties of the future, the only right action was to stay engaged, to be a Confucian gentleman and to strive for the preservation of the ideals of 'this culture of ours'. A case in point, recovered from fragments only recently, is the story of a remarkable man who lived from 880 to 956, through the period of breakdown. Working for four of the Five Dynasties, 'his reputation shining in seven courts' as his grandson said, Wang Renyu was an eyewitness who saw himself as representing the old virtues of the state rather as 'the last of the Romans', Brutus, in the horrors of the Roman civil war. But Wang's life also pointed the way to a new age: the end of the old world of the Tang and the rise of a new, more egalitarian and meritocratic world that not only brought new rulers but new forms of society, where loyalty to dynasty was superseded by a bigger allegiance – to China itself.

'THE OFFICIAL WHO TOWERED ABOVE HIS TIME'

To trace Wang's life we must travel 350 kilometres west of Xi'an, on the ancient route from Gansu down into Sichuan. Lixian is an old garrison town at the confluence of the western Han and Yangtze rivers, where crumbling forts perched on crags command the valley that links the Yangtze and Yellow River systems. First established under the Qin, today Lixian is a desultory modern city in a flat plain between brown terraced hills backed by ridge after ridge of rugged mountain ranges that rise towards the Tibetan plateau. A fissured landscape where, as the British orientalist Eric Teichman 100 years ago described, 'the bare loess hills of central Gansu with their waterless valleys give way to jungle-covered mountains, with abundance of water'. This is the 'Land West of the Pass' – for much of early Chinese history a frontier world, far from the centre, offering a different perspective on the 'Middle Land'.

Here in Zhanlong village a few miles further on up the valley from Lixian stands Wang's memorial stele, his 'Spirit Road Epitaph'. Carved with the story of his life composed by a loyal pupil, it was erected by his grandson in 984 in his hometown, and today stands on its battered tortoise plinth, in a small walled enclosure. Now weathered but still legible (its text long since transcribed by loyal local antiquarians), it opens an electrifying, first-hand window into the age of chaos that followed the Tang. It begins by quoting Wang's grandson: 'My grandfather was renowned for generations as a man of wisdom ... his service extended through several regimes ... he gained the respect of the highest in the land and maintained the highest standards of the grand secretariat ...'

Wang Renyu was born in 880 in the middle of the Huang rebellion. His clan were originally from Taiyuan, an old landed family who had hitched their fortunes to the Tang star and were part of the migration south into border prefectures during the empire's heyday. His autobiography, lost for centuries, has recently been partially reconstructed from fragments by Glen Dudbridge (who made the translations that follow) and it offers an intimate portrait of a tenth-century man, a warrior, a governor, who lived a life of scholarship, poetry, music and war. A rarity from anywhere in history at this time, it gives details of manners and inner beliefs, the world of signs and symbols, sensibility and memory – in other words, a person's hinterland. Its subjectivity is not a literary construct but a record of real feeling – what we really hope for when we study the people of the past.

Wang was an orphan, raised by an elder brother in a time when 'the Tang era had brought chaos and grief'. He was unusual in that he came from out on the edge of China, not from the capital, and that gave him a unique outsider's perspective on events. Nor was he typical of the scholarly governing class; in his early years, as his grandson tells us, he was a wild youth who learned the hard way the value of education:

> Lacking the discipline of teachers and friends he spent his time solely with hunting and amusement. At the age of twenty-five he had not the slightest knowledge of book learning. But then in a dream he saw pebbles in the West River covered in writing. He picked them up and swallowed them and when he awoke, his mental faculties had opened up to insight ...

The haunting dream of the pebbles in the West River, Wang tells us, stayed with him all his life. From then he felt the importance of learning and began 'eagerly exerting himself' in the Confucian scriptures – 'and with one reading it was as if he had always known them'. So, although late in the day, the path of his life was set: to become a 'gentleman' (a word bound up with Confucian connotations of culture and humanity). Picked out by a local military commander, he rose to a series of top posts, embarking on a life of action and contemplation marked by steadfast loyalty and integrity. But, as his grandson put it, it was a time 'when good governance and instruction were deeply damaged'. The issue, then, for the educated classes was how should that damage be remedied? How should a traditional Confucian follow the Way when the state no longer cohered? How should one's talents be used to serve the state and hand on the values of civilisation?

Wang worked for ten years as a minister in the state of Shu in Sichuan. There, in 907, with the last Tang emperor gone, a local hard man, smuggler and bandit claimed imperial power and fought his way to control of the whole region of the southwest, ending up with his own kingdom with its capital at Chengdu. Wang served this kingdom for a decade, rising from local military command to the very centre of court life. A close friend of a later ruler, Wang helped set up a replica Tang court with a scholarly academy imitating the Tang's famous national academy, the Hanlin.

A person of great physical toughness and tireless curiosity, on campaigns and government journeys Wang developed a deep sense of the landscape and people of China. When time allowed he climbed mountains and explored the wild routes of western China. The surviving fragments of his memoirs are distinguished by his wide intellectual interests, including a remarkable and even philosophical concern about the life of animals.

One story concerns a monkey given to him by a trapper, which he kept and attempted to tame. Intrigued by its 'sly intelligence', he named the monkey Ye Ke, 'Wild Guest'. But at his HQ, where Wang was adjutant to the military commissioner, the monkey proved disruptive, screeching and biting, throwing tiles, and on one occasion wrecking the commissioner's kitchen. Wang was the only human he would obey. Eventually running out of patience with his feral companion, Wang had him released into the countryside, 30 miles away, only for Ye Ke to return to his door within hours. Then Wang took him up to the headwaters of the Han River, so far away that he couldn't find his way back. Tying a red silk string round his neck, Wang composed a poem about their relationship before the final parting. Then, a year later, at the end of his time of service, on his way up the Han River valley, Wang encountered a troop of monkeys drinking in a stream; and there, hanging in a tree, was Ye Ke, still wearing the tattered strip of red silk. In a riveting passage, Wang describes the moment of recognition, the reactions of Ye Ke, and his haunting moan as they parted.

I called to him and he answered with repeated cries. I kept my horse standing there for a while, and gradually he took on an anguished look. When I stirred the reins to go, he departed with cries of lament. And as I climbed the mountain road, winding among the valleys and streams, I could still hear his sobbing sounds, which I suspect, came from his broken heart. So I composed a second poem about him . . .

> As he sleeps in the moonlight he dreams in freedom of a
>   tethered life ...
> Heartbroken cries echo to the clouds:
> Who is his old master from a year gone by?

Wang's description of the monkey's behaviour is typical of his sensibility, not only to human feelings but to the feelings of animals. Here we
enter a tone in human discourse not heard perhaps since late Roman
Neo-Platonists like Porphyry. In the West, Aristotle had earlier denied
any kind of moral equivalence between humans and animals, as did
the Hebrew Bible, saying that 'animals exist for human use as plants
do for animals'. But in ancient China there were other views. Mencius
himself had thought that a humane person's attitude to animals should
be that 'once having seen them alive he cannot bear to see them die,
and once having heard their cry he cannot bear to eat their flesh'.
Wang found himself observing the habits of primates as he would
humans, and interrogating his own fellow feeling across the species
barrier, making analogies, for example, between primates' family
bonds and those of human society. What is it to be human? What
separates us humans from animals? In western China on a hunt for the
golden snub-nosed monkey, whose fine skins were coveted as cushion
covers by high officials, Wang tells the story of a male monkey struck
by a poisoned arrow, its reactions to the fatal shot, 'his wrinkled brows
and downcast look, retching and moaning just like a human being'.
Especially haunting to him was the image of frightened infants 'clinging inseparably' to their dying mother. Family bonds among animals,
then, were analogous to those of humans: 'If a humane person were
to behold this he could not bring himself to sleep on their skins or eat
their meat. And anyone who felt no compassion would have a heart
of iron or stone: such humans are no better than beasts.'

HISTORY

Most of all, however, Wang was an observer of history; it is his sharp
powers of observation as an eyewitness that help us catch the mood

of this momentous time of change. Wang served where he could work for 'this culture of ours': for the Qin kingdom from 915; the Shu from 925 to 935; then successively the Later Tang, Later Jin, the Khitan, Later Han and Later Zhou. Sometimes his survival was almost miraculous. When the Later Tang fell, the captured royal family were dispatched on a safe conduct which was actually a death warrant for the whole party, not just the royal clan – in all, a couple of thousand people. Wang was in their service and survived execution only because a benevolent minister changed a single character on the warrant so only the royal clan were executed. On another occasion, at the fall of the Later Jin, Wang was captured and prepared for execution, but his speech was so admired that he was spared.

He had hoped in the end to retire back to his native Gansu, but he came out of retirement and in his sixties rose in the Later Zhou state to be minister of finance and then minister of war. Still anxious to widen educational opportunities, he was most proud of his appointment to examinations minister. Looking back on his legacy from the 980s, his grandson reflected, 'the general opinion is unanimous that now the most talented in learning, even among orphans and commoners would all achieve careers', a hint perhaps of the more meritocratic and even egalitarian currents of the age that would follow.

CIVILISATION AND BARBARIANS/THE MEANING OF HISTORY

In the 940s, barbarian armies criss-crossed the Chinese heartland, and in 947 the old eastern capital of Luoyang was sacked. The event was attended by signs in the heavens, always in traditional China thought to indicate a coming change of Mandate, as Wang's grandson recalled, translated again by Glen Dudbridge:

Towards the end of the Jin dynasty, powerful officials took over control and dynastic governance was shared among many. There was a succession of poor harvests, as well as incessant warfare. Regional warlords forcibly occupied territories and lands, but with his time occupied with ritual and music, no military leadership came forth from the emperor. Wang grieved that good order had fallen into destruction and disarray. He submitted papers and documents setting forth his advice. Repeatedly he bowed before the palace gates to offer the strongest possible views on current affairs. But as he wrote, 'when a river breaks out in spate it cannot be blocked in with handfuls of soil; once a great tree has toppled it cannot be controlled with a single rope'. So it came to pass that the barbarian forces flared up fiercely, and the sacred vessels of Jin changed hands.

Reflecting on the broader pattern of China's relations with the barbarians, Wang himself wrote (in Glen Dudbridge's translation):

Let us come now to recent times, when among the many barbarians the most fierce are the Khitan: with them we have reached the point where only an enlightened and worthy ruler with divine backing and great virtue and wisdom will be able to withstand those who bring disorder and treachery to China. Over the past few decades the barbarians have annexed the countries round us, in the last decade they marched over the central plain, and falsely usurped the title of emperor. Many of our provinces are under their control, the deserts are filled with Chinese jades, silks and brocades. The government lost control as treacherous ministers sold out their country and fierce Chinese armies and valiant warriors were tamely surrendered. The emperor, his generals and ministers became prisoners of war and the common people were slaughtered. Thorns and brambles grew in the palaces, vermin roamed the temple yards, clouds cast gloom, the sun was dimmed. Since the beginning of civilisation there has never been disorder like this. We have fallen into dark times.

How could Heaven allow scheming shysters and vicious gangsters to carve China up, or tribal chiefs to indulge in their mindless violence? Now that a million people have died in war, will the great Monarch of Heaven still not extend his protection to us?

Look at the omens of the thunder and the ice, the falling star, the death of the barbarian king. None of this was by chance! Hardly by chance! Things cannot be negative for all time. The Way cannot finally be exhausted. A true man will arise ... Heaven I believe will announce a new Han dynasty.

THE REUNIFICATION OF CHINA

When Wang died in 956, the warfare was already advanced that would bring the 'new Han' he had hoped for: a dynasty in the central plain based around Kaifeng on the Yellow River in the historic heartland of China. The triumph of the Song, led by two brothers who became the first two emperors, was seen in retrospect as inevitable, destined by heaven, and the omens that preceded the rise of the Song were famous. One tale in particular is still told by the older generation in Kaifeng. Today in Twin Dragon Alley, the old tiled courtyard houses are to soon be redeveloped and everywhere demolition signs are daubed in red on their doors, but under a pillared veranda the mahjong players were only too happy to tell the tale. Though just a fairy story, it was first recorded in the Song, and it catches the atmosphere of the time. Warming to his tale, the old man rose and waved his arms; gesticulating down the street, he was soon in full flow:

The story goes like this. Back at the time of chaos and destruction, after the Tang dynasty fell, a hermit called Chen Tuan who had acquired prophetic powers came down from the sacred mountain of Hua Shan. On the road he ran into crowds of refugees pouring down the highway from Luoyang, fleeing from the fighting. Swept up in the hurly-burly was a poor man carrying two baskets on a pole across his shoulders, inside each basket was a baby boy. But when the hermit looked inside he saw two little dragons! Roaring with laughter he exclaimed, 'I never expected that the Mandate of Heaven would come back to earth so quickly. This time of disasters will be over very soon.' Now, Chen Tuan told the man with the baskets, 'You must look after these two little boys very carefully.' So the poor man came here to Kaifeng, and put the two boys into the care of a Buddhist monastery in this street, which was known as Chicken Lane then. The monks brought them up and those babies grew up to be the first emperors of the Song dynasty. So that's how Kaifeng became the next great capital of China. And that's why this place is called Twin Dragon Alley today.

Charming as the story is, there was nothing preordained about the arrival of the Song dynasty. Reunification happened through prolonged warfare, the accidents of history and strokes of luck in battle at crucial moments. Official narratives were created later to make it seem inevitable and relatively bloodless. But bloodless it certainly wasn't. There were years of fighting before the decisive battle at Gaoping in Henan on 24 April 954. The military leader of the so-called Later Zhou, Shizong, had pronounced himself emperor. His kingdom based in the Kaifeng region faced hostile states on all sides and in 954 it was invaded by an alliance of its northern enemies, the Northern Han and the Liao. The battle was fought on the old north–south route (today's G55) between the Yellow River and north China. It changed the course of Chinese history, breaking the cycle of chaos that had persisted for over a century.

Victory was only just snatched from the jaws of defeat by a general who showed exemplary nerve and leadership. At a crucial moment one wing of the army gave way, most of its leaders fled and 1,000 troops surrendered. General Zhao, the commander of the other wing, fought on and finally swung the balance the other way; by nightfall the roads north were blocked with thousands of fugitives. Afterwards, in a ruthless collective act of military discipline, Zhao ordered all those on his own side who fled to be beheaded, along with cavalry and infantry commanders who had failed, and seventy-two senior commanders of the imperial guard. In all, 2,000 men were killed. Akin to the decimation practices in the Roman army, and in

Europe in the Thirty Years War, this punishment was intended to 'stir imposing awe'. It also allowed Zhao to replace the purged officer corps, so now his own officers were the power behind the throne.

After the battle there were still powerful, independent kingdoms to the north and south, but it was a huge moment in Chinese history, for Shizong's army had defeated the combined force of his two most powerful enemies. He now asked to see plans for military campaigns to eliminate the many individual kingdoms and recreate one unified empire. The issue for Shizong was whether to strike north first or to move south, but in April 955 he announced the plan proposed by his chancellor; after limited operations to the north they would focus their attack on the south. The grand strategy was already unfolding when, after a five-year reign, the emperor, still in his thirties, died in 959. At his death, Shizong left a six-year-old son, but the succession was resolved in a carefully prepared coup led by the officer corps. The army was camped at Chenqiao on the north bank of the Yellow River near Kaifeng (a shrine by an ancient tree still marks the spot). There 'to his surprise', General Zhao was proclaimed emperor by his troops and donned the conveniently prepared yellow robe.

THE SONG PROCLAIMED

On 3 February 960, a new dynasty was proclaimed. General Zhao – one of the mythical dragon babies in the baskets in Twin Dragon Alley – became Song Taizu, the first emperor of the new dynasty. 'A man of few words', it was said – a canny military man, not an innovator, still less a man of high culture – he had only 'basic conversance command of the classics'. At that point, of course, it was by no means certain that the Song would be any longer-lasting than the Five Dynasties, but once their power was consolidated in their heartland of the Yellow River, a new order was imposed over much of southern and central China. As always in Chinese history, the name taken by the new dynasty was of great historical significance. Song (as we saw above pages 53–8) was the name of the regional state that ruled the Yellow River plain after the defeat of the Shang dynasty in 1045 BCE. The place was the Shang ancestral heartland, where surviving members of the Shang royal clan had been permitted to continue the rituals to ancestors, carrying on the dynastic tradition of prehistory. In that choice they were stating their aim to go back to their roots, and to initiate what their contemporaries in Europe would have called a *renovatio*.

The new emperor was inaugurated in February 960 and heavy fighting continued north and south as he consolidated his power. Then, in 967, the court astrologers observed a confirming omen. 'In the fifth year of Emperor Taizu's reign in the third month (13 April–11 May), the Five Planets gathered like linked pearls in Ares.' What they had seen was the same five-planet conjunction, which only happens once every 516 years, that had confirmed the triumph of the Zhou two millennia before.

As the great Song philosopher Zhu Xi observed, the cycle of Chinese history had been re-established: 'The transmission of the Dao had arrived at the Sage Ancestor Taizu of our Song dynasty.'

So the new dynasty was to be not simply a continuation of the dynastic cycle, but a revival of Confucian teaching, a return to the eternal wisdom of the Chinese state. The restoration of the Mandate of Heaven was not only about temporal rule but the transmission of the Dao itself, the Way. This idea came to be seen by Song philosophers as transcending the mechanisms of earthly rule, and the prospect of the renaissance of the long-neglected learning of the Dao energised thinkers and rulers in the new era. It would take two more decades to crush their surrounding enemies, culminating in the conquest of the powerful 'Later Tang' state in the south in the winter of 975, although the true founding was only celebrated in 1005, almost a century after the fall of the Great Tang.

Despite the Song dynasty's reputation as an age of peace and cultural brilliance, therefore, its foundation was achieved by relentless warfare. In every year of the 960s their armies mounted campaigns north and south from the central plain, with tens of thousands of troops out in the field. Everywhere there were savage reprisals, the mass execution of prisoners and suicides of entire garrisons. In one notorious example of psychological warfare south of the Yangtze, one Song general had a group of 'fat prisoners' shared out, killed and eaten by his forces in front of his captives, who were then freed to take back the news of the chilling show of terror. As often in history, the great achievements of civilisation have been underpinned by shocking violence, and China was no exception.

The Song achieved power after decades of relentless warfare. Emperor Taizu died in November 976 and the final victories to consolidate the empire were achieved by his younger brother Taizong (the other baby in the basket in the legend from Twin Dragon Alley). The Southern Tang kingdom in Nanjing surrendered in 976, the Northern Han in 979, and by 982 Song power extended over most of south China. But north China was never brought under their rule, the powerful Liao kingdom's capital remaining near the site later known as Beijing. So Song supremacy would always be contingent on treaties, forced to coexist with other major political groupings on the landmass we know as China. The decisions taken in 955, important as they were, never led to the retaking of the so-called 'Sixteen Provinces' in the north. But by 979 the Song was well and truly established as the next great dynasty, and vast resources were being poured into what has become known as China's Renaissance. The Song would preside over one of the most brilliant epochs in Chinese history, one that has often been compared with ancient Athens for its cultural, artistic and scientific achievements, not to mention its remarkable experiments in governance. To tell that story, we must now travel to the city that had been the Song base for their military campaigns against the north in the 930s and '40s, one of China's five great historic capitals: Kaifeng.

9

THE SONG RENAISSANCE

In the late tenth century, China emerged again as the greatest civilisation on earth. Its cities were the world's largest, and its artists, craftsmen and scientists were unsurpassed. The population doubled in a century – over a quarter of the world may have lived in China at this time; some have thought as many as one third. In viewing the pattern of global history, Europeans have always brought their own preconceptions. They call the time in Europe from the fourteenth to the sixteenth centuries the Renaissance, when classical humanism was rediscovered after it had been lost, when modern scientific ideas began to develop, and when new conceptions of society and the individual emerged. China, though, never lost touch with its 'classical' past, the cultural bedrock laid down under the Han, nor its great 'medieval' flowering under the Tang. In China, what might be termed a Renaissance took place from the tenth to the twelfth centuries, as the Song recovered from the disasters of the Late Tang and created an astonishingly civilised new Confucian age.

Many of the features of the Song Renaissance will seem familiar. Just as in Europe, there was a rediscovery of the 'classical past' and the spread of printing, enabling mass production of books, encyclopaedias, works of science and medicine; epigraphical and philological studies began to analyse the remains of the ancient past in inscriptions on bronze and stone and in manuscript evidence. Catalogues were produced of ancient bronzes and there were even archaeological excavations at famous historic sites like Anyang. In the writing of history, too, great achievements were made in codifying the tradition and critically examining the sources for the past. In the Song, China's commercial economy and technological achievements far outstripped the medieval West. Song advances in science in particular were unrivalled between the Hellenistic Age and the eighteenth-century European Enlightenment.

But, as we have already seen, the Song was created by warfare, and the cultural achievements of the eleventh century rested on the battles of the tenth. It was a time when China might have broken apart for good, leaving a patchwork of states akin to medieval and modern Europe. The big question, then, is why, unlike the Roman Empire and every other empire of the ancient world or the Middle Ages, did China stay together in the tenth century and not break up? How are we to explain the revolutionary changes that happened under the Song, in economy, science, society and culture? Part of the answer lies in the strategic decisions made in 955, to concentrate efforts on the conquest of the south, so large parts of northern China were left under the rule of the neighbouring Liao kingdom, whose territory extended right into the heart of China. In the northwest, too, the Song state never reached out along the Silk Road into Central Asia, and left powerful neighbours like the Tanguts over the Amur River. Necessarily the Chinese had to cultivate close diplomatic relations with these border states, and regular exchanges took place with ambassadors bringing gifts, celebrating birthdays and giving condolences at the time of deaths. Relations with the Liao, it was said, were warm, 'like one family'.

This brought a change in the world view of the Chinese: 'All Under Heaven' now shared a landmass with other states, and interaction was not limited to diplomacy; in this period there was a fertile exchange of people, goods and ideas. As happened later in Western history, increased knowledge of the Other helped to define the meaning of the state to its citizens and developed loyalty to the newly defined idea of China. And it was not just the borders that were redrawn; governance itself was changing. The old aristocracy had been destroyed and its place was filled by professional bureaucrats, chosen through a meritocratic entry system of imperial examinations. Knowledge was also shared at this time through the widespread availability of print – it was even the first real age of travel literature. This encouraged a very different view of Chinese identity. We have seen fascinating accounts of foreigners at the Tang court, but the cosmopolitanism of the Song was of a different order. Forced to look out beyond their frontiers, they came to see themselves as one great state among many, albeit at the centre of all they surveyed.

Within a few years the Taizu emperor and his advisers began a major cultural project, which over time developed into one of the great creative epochs in the story of China. It was in particular an age of invention: from science and technology to steel production and cast iron; from pharmacology and medicine to astronomy and mineralogy; not to mention paper money, playing cards and pulp novels. There was even a book printed in 1085 entitled *How to Make Sure that the Elderly Have Happy, Healthy Retirements* – perhaps the first of its kind in history and, astonishingly, still in print. In all respects the Song was an era of groundbreaking innovation: the world's first national library, the first national university, the first print culture. Many of the Song achievements would not occur again anywhere until the early modern age in Europe.

Unfortunately for China, the long diplomatic balance they achieved with their Liao neighbours didn't extend to the Tanguts, and in the late eleventh century they found themselves embroiled in wars on the northern frontier, which were very expensive in men and materials, and which contributed to the catastrophe of 1127. But that is to jump ahead of ourselves. The Song may not have ruled all of what is China today, or the China of the Manchus or the Tang, but the empire they brought into being was a polity of astonishing cultural brilliance. At the height of its prosperity in the eleventh century, the Song was one of the most humane, cultured and intellectual societies in Chinese history – even, it may be said, in all world history. At the centre was the capital, Kaifeng; it is time for us to enter its streets.

THE NEW CAPITAL: KAIFENG

It is sunset at the crossroads on Book Street, in the centre of town. From the side lanes, food stalls are being wheeled in, kerosene lamps lit, and soon kebabs are sizzling in yellow pools of light. Here, today's traveller to Kaifeng may get her bearings, gratified to find that something of the old town's topography of streets and lanes is still visible. The city wall forms a parallelogram, most of it on the line of the inner wall of the Song city. The northern sector was once the royal city, with lakes, parks and palaces, where there is still the great artificial hill on which stands the Dragon Pavilion. Around us are rows of reconstructed two-storey shops with lanterned balconies; a warren of narrow alleys lined with houses, and the huge open-air food market by the Drum Tower. None of the alleys is earlier than the late Qing dynasty, but Song paintings show this part of the old city is what it looked like 1,000 years ago, with shops, shrines and the courtyard compounds of the leading families. The low-rise architecture is still the same; halls and temples built of brick, with elegantly curving tiled roofs and decorated finials.

In the lanes near East Gate Alley the visitor can get a taste, however distant, of the Song's cosmopolitanism. Persians, Arabs and Central Asians resided here then; Nestorian Christians, Zoroastrians, Muslims and even Jews. Today, they, or their traces, are still here. The site of the old synagogue, which survived until 1855, is in 'Teaching the Torah Lane', where the Jewish community have lived in the past few centuries. A fifteenth-century stone stele says the synagogue was built in the Song in 1163. Here a few hundred people still live who bear the seven clan names of the Jewish community listed in their seventeenth-century memorial book. At its height, then, they comprised maybe four or five thousand people. They may have first come in the Song, bringing with them the customs of circumcision, abjuring pork and praying to Jerusalem, which were still followed in the nineteenth century, by which time no one was left who could read their Hebrew Torah scrolls and manuscripts. Their last teacher of Hebrew died in the late eighteenth century.

Small though it may be, Kaifeng's Jewish community has left a magical trail like the strands of historical DNA. Their stone inscriptions say they came from India; their language, with its Farsi words mixed with Hebrew and Chinese, suggests the roots of community really lay in Persia or Central Asia, along the Silk Road; but some of their prayers may be Yemeni; and their Bible text suggests an even older Babylonian connection. The mysterious ways of history!

Until recent times, little was known about the Chinese Jews, although far to the west in the Library Cave in Dunhuang a Hebrew document was discovered a century ago with a prayer using lines from the Psalms. More recently, fascinating new discoveries in Hotan have helped to bring to life the Jewish merchants who left Persia after the Arab Conquest to make their fortunes in the East. They include letters from a Persian-speaking Jew living in the city in the early ninth century, written to another Persian-speaking Jew residing in an oasis town in the Taklamakan Desert. Part of a regular correspondence with the wider clan, the Hotan letters include references to 'my dear brother Shavapardar' and name eight family members including Isaac, 'my little sister Khudenak', and his brother, whom he calls rabbi. In the community there is a dispute with a landlord about sheep grazing; he gives a list of gifts, including silk and cane sugar, that the merchants must pay to the local king to oil the wheels of trade. And, as always, there is evidence of the uncertainties of the outside world, in this case the defeat of a Tibetan incursion into Hotan: 'The news from Kashgar is this: They killed and captured all the Tibetans. I donated for the war a sum worth a hundred strings of coins. And as for your advice – however much money they ask, don't hold back anything, I followed this, as did David and your nephew.'

These letters give us a sense of the stories that lie behind the dimly known history of the early Chinese Jewish communities, who came by sea to Canton and by land through the Silk Road cities of Central Asia, and of which today the Kaifeng Jews appear to be the only survivors. Until the 1980s they were reluctant to advertise themselves, but now links with American Jewry and Israel are growing, their inscriptions have been published, and with international interest in their culture, they themselves are re-engaging with their rituals. On the festival of Rosh Hashana, the Jewish New Year, at a family house in one of the alleys, a small knot of Chinese Jews celebrates with traditional food and prayers; fish cooking in the pan, apples dipped in honey on the table, and the squeal of the Ram's horn floating over Teaching the Torah Lane. Another case of the reinvention of tradition in today's China, and yet also of an unlikely and tenacious survival.

The Kaifeng Muslim community was much bigger: they also came in the Song, again, so far as we can tell, both by land on the Silk Road to Chang'an and by sea through Canton, China's earliest centre of Muslim culture. They were already well established here before the sack of 1127; many left then in the general mass exodus, but there were still more than 800 families here in the following century. Today there are 10,000 Muslims in Kaifeng, with a big congregational mosque on the east side of the walled city, surrounded by Muslim cafés and restaurants. There are also some thirty smaller mosques and prayer halls, half of which are for women only and, still more remarkably, with women imams, a tradition whose origins are obscure but which seems to have arisen in the Qing dynasty. It all seems a long way from the world of international Wahhabism, but Chinese Islam took root in those expansive times when people, goods, foods, ideas and religions passed along the Silk Road, and when China, though always wary of outsiders, welcomed 'the teachings of the barbarians as useful to mankind'.

Tang Chang'an (Xi'an) had been a place of palaces and government offices, a highly regulated conurbation, with the people confined by walled wards and curfews and restrictions of class and rank. Kaifeng was a different thing altogether, a new kind of Chinese city. Originally about a mile and a half square, on the line of the old walls which still surround the inner city today, in 955, after the victory at the Battle of Gaoping, a great outer circuit was built, 27 kilometres long. Once peace had been established, people crowded in, encouraged by preferential property and tax rates, and the huge space was soon filled with new streets, shops and houses. Wells were sunk everywhere, haulage firms and construction companies set up business, hiring bricklayers, carpenters and crafts-men from far and wide. Soon, illustrated woodblock-printed books were mass-produced as guides to system-building fine homes and housing estates, temples and palaces. New kinds of social relations developed and a new kind of urban society was born, an open-all-hours, vibrant and commercially minded consumer paradise, with restaurant quarters, shopping streets and busy wharves beyond the palaces and government offices. The path shown by Tang Yangzhou was followed by Song Kaifeng.

But, as so often in China, the essential survival of a great historic city is not so much in buildings, in bricks and stone, but in prose, poetry and paint. In the history of the world, few places perhaps have a richer memory in words and in paintings than China. And more than any other Chinese city, perhaps, just as Alexandria and Constantinople are to the Greeks, Kaifeng is a 'capital of memory'.

CITY OF FESTIVALS, CITY OF DREAMS

Pride of place is a scroll, the *Festival on the River* (*Qingming shanghe tu*). It is China's most famous work of art and, as historical sources go, it is one of the most arresting anywhere in the world. Nearly 20 feet long, it was painted only ten years or so before the fall of Kaifeng to northern barbarians in 1127, a date as etched in Chinese history as the Sack of Rome is in the West. Painted by a court artist in Kaifeng, it is so fascinating, so original, that it has been annotated by emperors, poets, painters and connoisseurs ever since. It is nothing less than an image of what urban life can be in time of peace.

The scroll depicts Song Kaifeng on a spring day around the year 1120. It begins in the countryside along a lane lined with leafless trees. Visible through misty groves are thatched cottages, small footbridges, rippling creeks and ancient gnarled trees. Beyond, we glimpse lines of irrigation, canals, fields and ditches. The wintry landscape of Henan is coming back to life, travellers are setting out on journeys, ladies in sedan chairs are returning from visiting the ancestral graves. As we walk into the suburbs, people are preparing their houses and businesses for the early spring Qingming Festival. Big wicker frames for the decorations have been erected over taverns and houses, just as is done today, but they are not yet hung with their colourful paper and cloth hangings: the festival is clearly still a few days off. Around us is bustling city life: there are no government officials, no aristocrats, let alone royals; before us is a world of teashops and wine bars, barbers and boatmen, physicians and fortune-tellers.

Let us look closely. We pass Wang's Funeral Store, hung with paper horses, flower arrangements and other funeral offerings. Further along the street are tea houses and bakeries, and a huge restaurant decked out with flags and banners. There's a sesame pancake stand under a big umbrella with hot pancakes waiting on the tray, just as any traveller in China would see today. Soon our stroll brings us to the bank of the Bian River, which carries cargo and passenger boats right into the middle of the city. The artist follows it now, as a camera might pan across a teeming market scene (to achieve this we must imagine the artist made his scroll from a dozen images taken from separate viewpoints). At the wharves there are boats unloading stone, timber and building materials; a camel caravan enters the gates; in the travellers' inns and tea houses, diners crowd around the tables. In front, the river now opens out into a basin where wide-bellied passenger boats are moored. There are latticed windows in their cabins and roofs of matting, with private rooms for well-to-do passengers, storage for their baggage, a small galley for cooking food, even a writing table with brush and ink; the kind of boat the poet Li Qingzhao will take later in our story (below page 215). Further on, a crowd of boatmen are hauling a barge upstream, straining on the long ropes, while two sailboats bump together, their crews shouting at each other as they swing perilously close in the swirling current.

Heading deeper into the city there are more teashops and restaurants – the artist leaves us in no doubt of the importance of food to the citizens. There is a wheelwright and carpenter's workshop, food and industry cheek by jowl, as you will still see today in China's old towns. Then we emerge into a wide, tree-lined street. We pass a

Buddhist temple, a fine courtyard house, and a fortune-teller with his charts, divination manuals and advertising placards: 'Your Fortunes Told Here'; 'Accurate Psychic'; 'Your Uncertainties Resolved'. This you will still see in any Chinese city: even today, few people in Kaifeng – few in China for that matter – would do without their fortune-teller.

The road crosses the moat and passes through the city gate, one of sixteen in the outer wall. We are now inside the city proper, in a broad thoroughfare thronging with shoppers. Here are businesses for the better-off middle-class citizen, a rising class in Song China: Dr Yang's Medical Clinic, a herbal drinks stand, and a butcher's shop (whose sign boasts, 'We don't cheat on weight here'). There is a posh fabric retailer – 'Wang's Brocade, Silk Satin and Cloth Emporium' – and Liu's Spice Store, outside which Buddhist and Daoist monks walk in the crowd. Dr Zhao's residence has a public area in the front, as traditional chemist's shops do today, with consultation rooms behind where clients come for diagnosis and prescriptions. Here too are some of the seventy or so big restaurants for which Kaifeng was famous. Among them Shenyang's Tavern is a huge two-storey establishment, its upper floor packed with customers as the holiday approaches – a good place to stop and take stock of the alluring new world of urban life in the Song.

The people of Song-dynasty Kaifeng were probably the best-fed citizens on earth, and perhaps the best-fed people who had lived so far in history. Thanks to improved farming and distribution, Song cooks had a bigger range of ingredients than ever before, and they developed the first great restaurant culture in the world, complete with cookbooks, gourmet diaries and guides to dining etiquette. There were even restaurants here advertising regional cuisines, especially the spicier foods of the south. Not surprisingly, then, Song writers discussed food at length; poets wrote about food and even philosophers considered food high and low, the raw and the cooked.

Eating out was part of city life in the Song, as it has been ever since in Chinese culture. Among several accounts written about the city in its heyday, the most famous was by a minor official called Meng

Yuanlao. Meng's book, *Dreams of Splendour of the Eastern Capital*, is that rare thing among historical sources – recalling street-corner conversations, feelings and even tastes. One of his big interests was food. Food and diet, of course, are one of the distinctive qualities of any civilisation, but especially so with China. In establishments like Shenyang's Tavern, Meng wrote like a gushing restaurant reviewer:

> When guests arrived, a single person holding chopsticks and a menu questioned all of the seated guests. Customers here in the capital would be very demanding, asking for a hundred different things – some hot, some cold, some warm, some regular, some iced, as well as special orders, like noodles laced with lean and streaky meat. Everyone would order something different. The waiter took the orders and went to a counter, where he would reel the orders off ... Then, in no time he would be back, carrying three dishes in his left hand, and on his right arm, from hand to shoulder about twenty bowls, which he would distribute precisely as everyone ordered, without an omission or mistake.

There were also cheap stalls for urban workers, as there still are today in the night market in Kaifeng, where one can find every conceivable kind of food, including scorpions and millipedes: famine food in the old days. For all the sophistication of the cuisine, the dishes even in good times were often made of the very simplest, inexpensive ingredients. And although the imperial table was much richer, well-to-do Song-period writers counselled against overconsumption and the wastage of food. Even the discerning wealthy shared the pleasure of simple food, simply prepared. The eleventh-century historian and diplomat Sima Guang, for example, looked back to his own childhood and the family ethos:

> Whenever a guest came to visit my father, he would always serve wine, sometimes there were three rounds of drinking, sometimes five, but never more than seven; the wine was bought from the common market. The only sweets were pears, nuts, dates and

persimmons, the only dishes were dried or hashed meats, vegetables and thick soup. That was the way officials of that time entertained their guests. They met often and were courteous to each other. Though the food was cheap, their friendships were deep.

Such, too, was Meng's recollection in his nostalgic memoir:

The people of Kaifeng were kind and friendly. A family newly arrived in the city would always find their neighbours quick to help: kindly souls would bring tea and hot water, offer to lend them things, run errands for them and give them practical tips. In every neighbourhood there were people who would go around with a kettle of tea and go from door to door every day, inquiring after the health of the members of the household, and having a chat over a cup of tea.

The *Festival* scroll and Meng's *Dreams* were both idealised views of a city as a well-governed place – flourishing, humane and harmonious. Again, a comparison with Renaissance Europe is telling. Take Lorenzetti's great fresco in Siena, 'The Effects of Good Government'. This was also an idealised view of city life, but there, good governance was the responsibility of a 'Council of Nine': bankers, rich burghers and businessmen. The medieval City of London was essentially the same, with its Corporation, its financiers and its merchant and crafts guilds. Song Kaifeng, by contrast, was not run by bankers or merchants but by Confucian scholar-officials who had passed stringent national exams and together formed a highly educated professional bureaucracy inculcated with Confucian ethics. 'My chief councillors', said the first Song emperor, Taizu (not himself, it may be remembered, a bookish man), 'should be men who read books.' Uppermost in the emperor's mind was the fact that China had gone through a turbulent century, ending in a prolonged time of violence at the end of the Tang when things had fallen apart, aided and abetted by dissension and disloyalty among the armed forces.

He himself was a military man, who had come to power in a coup, and knew that as long as the generals remained powerful, his new regime would be insecure. So he retired the old army leadership on comfortable pensions, and then restructured the government so that the armed forces were subordinated to a well-trained civilian bureaucracy. 'Demilitarise, stress the civilian' would be a crucial development in Chinese history.

THE IMPERIAL EXAMINATIONS

To recruit an adequate number of such civilian officials, and ensure they were the best candidates, the Song emperors radically expanded China's civil service examination system. As we have seen, the Sui emperors nearly 400 years before had initiated this meritocratic process for selecting men for office on the basis of their literary skills and their knowledge of the Confucian classics. The Song emperors hugely extended this system, which would essentially direct Chinese government until the beginning of the twentieth century and, indeed, leave its mark up until the present day. A young man who wanted to get on in Song China had to find a teacher and textbooks, and study for up to ten years, sometimes longer. The civil service exams tested literary ability, mastery of the Confucian classics, and the degree to which the pupil had imbibed the guiding principles of virtuous conduct, the ruling ethos of 'this culture of ours'. If he passed the prefectural-level examinations, his first civil service job would probably be as an administrator in a distant county town. Over his career he might travel widely across China, transferring from one assignment to the next, acquiring valuable knowledge about the land of China and its people, until perhaps ending up in a job in central government in the capital. The most ambitious men could attempt the highest metropolitan exams, which were held once every three years in the capital. The pass rates were dauntingly low; in 1002, only 219 passed the metropolitan exams out of 14,000 entrants. But success in the civil service exams ensured prestige for the candidate and his proud family: he (and they were only open to men) immediately entered the ranks of the great and the good. A successful graduate would be welcomed home in style, it was said, 'in a horse-drawn carriage, flag bearers in front, and a mounted escort at the rear, with people gathered along both sides of the road to watch – and to sigh!'

Unlike the Tang, then, the elite of Song China were not hereditary nobles, or warlords, or bankers or merchants (although of course only better-off families could afford to have their young men dedicate themselves to long years of study). They were the Confucian 'scholar-officials', a governing elite that was unique in world history and would be for centuries. As the Jesuit Matteo Ricci observed in the early seventeenth century, echoing Plato, 'it is the best system of governance in the world, for here they really do have the rule of the philosophers'.

The expansion of the examination system under the Song created a huge new demand for learning, and for books. In the Late Tang period, as we have seen, the invention of woodblock printing had made the production of books cheaper and faster than ever before. A family in Song China could now more easily purchase copies of the Confucian classics for their sons who were studying for the exams, as well as dictionaries and reference works, books on history and ritual. In the late tenth century, the Song rulers presided over the first great flowering of printing in China – and the world. It had massive repercussions on the culture, helping to develop and spread a national consciousness in the Song just as the availability of mass-printed books in nineteenth-century Europe would be a major factor in creating European nationalism.

It was the second emperor of the Song, Taizong, who reigned from 976 to 997, who began this movement. After two decades of battles to consolidate the Song hold over south China, he entitled his rule 'Taiping xingguo' – 'Supreme Peace and Nation Restored'. China was to enter a new age of peace, and there were three key developments in this cultural revival. First was the reassembling of the imperial library collection after its great losses through war. Second, a planned codifying of knowledge by commissioning huge compendia, encyclopaedic compilations containing a vast amount of

material from earlier literature, much of it thought lost. Third was
a crucial technological change: the transition from manuscript culture to the age of print – a change that only began in the West with
Gutenberg, Aldus Manutius and Caxton in the fifteenth century.
Just as later in the West, these changes in the technology of writing
from manuscript to print culture mark a major civilisational shift
that was crucial in shaping Chinese identity.

Nothing better illustrates the traditional Chinese reverence for the
written word than the way Taizong went about the task of restoring
the imperial library, which had been founded 1,000 years earlier.
When his predecessor, his brother Taizu, came to the throne, there
had been 12,000 scrolls in the imperial collection. Now, as Song
rule expanded into the Yangtze valley in the 960s, though by no
means a learned man himself, in the wake of his armies Taizong
sent commissioners to towns and noble houses to save manuscripts,
expanding the collection by four times. Then, in 976, Taizong built
a new imperial library with a staff and a directorate of books. He
then instituted a nationwide search for books containing the lost
learning of classical China. He told his librarians: 'When we consider
the old imperial catalogue (from the Tang in 721, it listed 60,000
manuscripts) the losses have been great. A wide search is in order.
We must look for the missing books; the message must be announced
far and wide that if any government official has books we lack, he
must bring them to the throne.'

It was the beginning of a cultural project that might justly be
compared with the Renaissance humanists in Europe who collected
manuscripts of the Greek and Latin classics and made them available
through the medium of the printing press. Taizong's aim, too, was to
show that the Song was not just another short-lived regime founded
by warlords, but one whose rulers had inherited the responsibility for
the sacred cultural tradition of the Han and the Tang. The imperial
library, then, was both a symbol of national unity and culture, and
an affirmation of the dynasty's legitimacy.

Moreover, the Song rulers were able do something that previous
dynasties could not: they could use the new technology of printing

to spread learning far and wide. Gathering and collating manuscripts from the four corners of the land, the government engaged
in a massive publishing effort through the 970s and 980s. The
Confucian classics, such as the *Book of Songs* and the *Book of
Documents*, were reprinted, along with Sima Qian's *Records of the
Grand Historian of China* and Du You's *Tongdian*. Dictionaries and
grammars came off the presses, as well as the complete Buddhist
canon, for which it took twelve years to prepare the wooden blocks
(a complete set of which still survives in Korea, engraved on 81,000
woodblocks).

The Song government also commissioned huge anthologies, which
were to include everything that China's cultural tradition had to
offer, on any topic. The *Reader for the Time of Supreme Peace*,
for example, was an encyclopaedic gathering-together of key works
about heaven, earth and man. The *Extensive Records for the Time
of Supreme Peace* collected all known texts on more mysterious
matters, such as ghosts, spirits and immortals, as well as the ideas
of monks, priests and doctors. Then came the thousand chapters
of the *Finest Blooms in the Garden of Literature*, as well as a comprehensive account of government affairs, and *The Prescriptions by
Imperial Grace*, which was a collection of public and private medical
knowledge.

The era advanced scientific research and invention in many areas,
both practical and theoretical. The Song, for example, pioneered
water-driven spinning machines, coke-fired blast furnaces and the
steel smelting process. The scientist Shen Kuo (1031–95) established
True North and fixed the position of the Pole Star – a major contribu-
tion to navigation along with another Song innovation: the magnetic
compass. Shen was also a pioneer in physiology, using dissection
to understand the workings of the human body. His speculations
about the origin of mountains posited physical changes in the geol-
ogy of the earth over enormous periods of time, through uplifting,
erosion and sedimentary deposition, as Leonardo was to conjecture
four centuries later in the West. The most famous scientist, Su Song
(1020–1101), was a polymath typical of his time; in addition to his

classical learning, Su wrote on metallurgy, pharmacology, botany and zoology, and compiled a celestial atlas with star maps – the first ever to be printed. A distinguished diplomat, he was on a mission to the Liao dynasty in the north in 1077 when he realised the calendar was more accurate there, and so returned to build an astronomical clock, which was erected in Kaifeng in 1094. More than 40 feet high, this was a water clock driven by an endless chain drive with an escapement mechanism. Su Song is often called the Chinese Leonardo, but in fairness it might be said more accurately that Leonardo is the European Su Song.

The Song government also wanted to spread practical know-how, such as information about the latest technology and tools. The Directorate of Education printed and circulated practical, illustrated handbooks on topics such as mathematics, medicine, agriculture, warfare and architecture. And alongside the official presses, across the empire commercial presses also flourished, printing books on religion, divination and geomancy; books containing legal forms and methods, self-help reference works, as well as cheap editions of the classics and commentaries. There were even collections of model exam answers to help the aspiring provincial exam candidate and his anxious family.

As a renaissance of learning and culture through the means of print and education, it was an age without parallel so far in human history. The Song spread of books and of learning had a profound influence on the society of China, making widespread literacy more attainable for the first time. Not just the administrators, the Confucian elite, but the traders, craftsmen and even well-to-do farmers in the Song empire could use manuals and almanacs to help them in business. As we have seen, there were self-help manuals for the urban elite, too, on how to have a happy and healthy retirement, and even handbooks on how to plan weddings and funerals.

And so, over 400 years before Gutenberg and Caxton began a similar process in Europe, printing revolutionised the spread of ideas in China. Moveable type was also invented first in China under the Song, but while that would be transformational in the West, with its small alphabet, in China, moveable type never took off to any great extent, its use limited by the nature of Chinese script, which required thousands of individual pieces of type. Woodblock printing continued to be widely used up until the end of the nineteenth century, and even today is still used in China for prestigious texts, deluxe productions and family genealogies, which are currently experiencing a revival.

In the upper levels of society, the university and school systems were also greatly expanded under the Song rulers. Scribal schools had existed in China from the Han period, as we saw in Chapter 5, but by 1103 the number of students at university in Kaifeng had grown to 4,000, and there were around 200,000 students at schools empire-wide. Entry to these was also by examination, so the numbers of people reading and writing, and hence imbued with the Confucian culture of the Song national curriculum, was larger still. The old examination system ended in 1904, but its influence was transmitted down the generations across the revolutionary period and can still be seen today in modern China in the huge respect given to examinations as the path to betterment.

So as Sima Guang, the great eleventh-century statesman and scholar put it, the Song dynasty had set out 'to restore learning and teaching, and to decrease the influence of military affairs'. But what would prove to be the price? By 1100, China had developed many of the characteristics that would later constitute early modern society as we in the West define it. It had reunited and achieved revolutionary changes in technology, education and the arts. But why, then, did it not become the first modern society? And why after the Song did China fail to maintain the incredible pace of technological and societal advance? Did the real divergence between China and the West attributed by Western commentators to the period of the Industrial Revolution and European imperialism actually begin much earlier?

To that fundamental question we will return.

10

THE FALL OF THE
NORTHERN SONG

In the eleventh and twelfth centuries, the age of the Fatimid Caliphate in the Mediterranean, the Cholans in India, and the beginnings of the Gothic in Europe, China stood at the centre of civilisation. But it faced many threats. Throughout its history China has had to cope with problems of governance on a scale beyond any other state. There were the perennial pressures of population, challenges from neighbouring powers with whom it shared the East Asian landmass; its geography, too, made it particularly prone to floods and natural disasters, and the attendant famines and social dislocation. While China can be seen as the most successful political entity in human history, its failures – if we may call them that – were often the product of these factors, compounded by its rulers' inability to shake off deep-rooted tendencies towards a centralised despotism. The brilliance of the Song Renaissance, with so many achievements unrivalled so far in history, was undermined in the end by a perfect storm of these factors: natural disasters, foreign invasion, and failures of leadership. These issues were wrestled with at the time by some of the most gifted and fascinating characters in our story, the charismatic statesman Wang Anshi, the historian Sima Guang, and China's greatest female poet, Li Qingzhao. This part of the story starts with the mid-eleventh-century crises that began to cast a shadow over their world.

The Song dynasty had been created by war, and for all its societal and cultural ambitions it was maintained by military power.
From the mid-eleventh century the economic revolution that
underpinned the Song state allowed it to maintain a huge army –
perhaps the biggest the world had yet seen. By 1040, the regular
army comprised 1.4 million men – over three times the size of
the Roman army at its peak in the third century CE. The central
army in the plains numbered 300,000, while regional forces were
stationed on the frontiers. Three hundred thousand were based in
Hubei to face the Khitan across the northern lakes and an enormous 450,000 men across Shanxi to counter threats from the west
and northwest. The scale of military planning was on another
level from that in the Han and Tang dynasties. Mass production
of weaponry now involved separate departments responsible for
millions of weapons and suits of armour; more than 16 million
arrowheads a year were produced by government foundries. One
of the keys to the smelting industry, centuries before its mass use
in Europe, was coal, which was used for high-quality iron casting.
The great Song poet Su Dongpo mentions the opening up of new
coal reserves in northern Jiangsu in 1079: 'In times past the place
had lacked a supply of coal so in New Year 1079 men were sent
out to look for it. They found it to the southwest of the prefectural city of Xuzhou, and to the north of Paitu town. It was used
for smelting iron ore and for making extraordinarily fine sharp-
edged weapons.'

For a time, Chinese advances in military technology kept them
ahead. China, after all, was the leader in mechanical siege engines,
rocket and projectile launchers and flame throwers and the like. But
in the course of the eleventh century these technologies inevitably
crossed frontiers, and, as in today's world, once that happened, the
advantage of being the sole possessor of certain hardware was wiped
out. Meanwhile, the maintenance of such vast forces over the long
term put huge strains on the economy. Then, in the mid-eleventh
century, Song China encountered the first of a series of huge and
unforeseeable crises.

THE 1048 ENVIRONMENTAL DISASTER

Through China's history the decline of dynasties has been as much due to climate and environmental change as civil war or foreign invasion. Back in the Bronze Age, the foundational myth of the state told of the great king who constructed channels and dykes to harness a cataclysmic flood and make the land cultivable. The very basis of political power, the Mandate of Heaven, rested on the king's ability to feed the people. And as we can see from the prayers to the Great River on Shàng oracle bones to the reports of Communist Party hydraulic engineers, for a state based in the Yellow River plain, the control of the rivers and water systems was absolutely central. But from the 1040s an unstable environment began to exert pressure on the Song state and eventually played a huge role in undermining the dynasty. One natural disaster in particular, which has recently been reconstructed from local gazetteers and memorial inscriptions by Ling Zhang, had massive long-term effects.

On 19 July 1048, the towns and villages of the middle plain were preparing to celebrate a national festival. In the streets of Kaifeng, lanterns were being hung out, marquees put up, wine and food prepared; the city was in a holiday mood. Since the declaration in 1041 of the 'Festive Era' of the longest-reigning Song ruler, Emperor Renzong, it had been a time of plenty, and the people had many things for which to be grateful. The dynasty was now in its eighth decade, the land had been free of war for a generation or more and the standard of living continued to rise, the census of 1040 revealing a population increase of two thirds over sixty years. All this was the fruit of good government and diplomacy, keeping the peace on the northern Liao frontier with a massive military presence, along with annual payments and regular diplomatic contacts. Even in the northern Hebei frontier zone, long damaged by attacks, agriculture was thriving, and the population had seen a huge rise in two generations. So, the public holiday of 1048 was anticipated in a happy mood.

By mid-July the heat had clamped on the river plain and was stuck at well over thirty degrees. Many now slept in the open air on roofs or out of doors. Just beyond the northern suburbs the Yellow River had been rising for many days, swelled by the snow melt a thousand miles away on the vast plateau of Tibet and Qinhai. Then, on 19 July, at Puyang to the northeast of the capital, a 700-metre stretch of the embankments on the northern bank broke, unleashing a vast torrent that surged northwards over the wheat fields of Henan, obliterating all before it. Over the next days it widened northwards across the plain into Hebei, opening a new main channel and subsidiary flows, entering the sea nearly 700 kilometres away, near today's Tianjin in the Gulf of Bohai, turning the course of the river thirty degrees counter-clockwise; one degree of latitude.

'The people were swept away like fish,' it was said; 100 miles to the north, the people of Hebei, for whom the river had never featured in their lives save in myths, were caught completely by surprise – 'Flushed away, turned into food for fish and turtles.' It was a natural disaster on a huge scale, flattening and sweeping away thousands of homes and villages; over a million people were killed or became refugees. 'For over 1,000 *li* [over 300 miles] the roads are full of corpses', wrote the essayist and poet Ouyang Xiu, then a local prefect in Hebei: the damage was so comprehensive that when the waters subsided 'eight or nine households out of ten migrated out of Hebei'.

From autumn 1048 through 1049, standing waters were left in so many places that three seasons of crops were ruined; three harvest failures that led to apocalyptic stories of starvation and cannibalism. The historian Sima Guang, who was thirty at the time, recalled the horror when 'fathers and sons ate each other'. The government immediately ordered state granaries to be opened and supplies were sent to relieve the poor. Provincial governments gathered refugees in temporary camps, setting up stoves and collective soup kitchens, creating shanty towns outside undamaged towns and cities on the edge of the flooded zones. But the numbers were too great to cope with, and as the squalor of the camps grew, sickness was rife, and outbreaks of disease soon added to the horror: as the local prefect in Qingzhou observed, 'relief operations done in the name of saving people ended up killing them'. The central government began a recruitment drive to bring unemployed young men into the military, take them out of the area and feed them. The rest of the civilian population – women, old people and children – were reduced to begging, even selling themselves into slavery, as rich families were encouraged to 'adopt refugees as servants'. The immediate impact of the disaster was so huge that for several years the government had to ship grain from the south to help the starving north. As a former chief minister, then a local prefect in Daming, wrote: 'Yellow river floods have damaged us since ancient times, but never like this.'

AFTER THE FLOOD

The long-term effects of the disaster on the Song state were huge. Though we single out wars and rebellions as changers of history, the effects of environmental disaster can be no less long-lasting. The 1048 flood destroyed the indigenous water systems of huge swathes of northern China, in places erasing centuries of communal channel and dyke building, and in the end undermining the stability of the Song state. Even today, south of Beijing, a string of lakes stretches across to the Gulf of Bohai, part of the biggest freshwater wetlands in northern China. The government is planning a new eco-city near one of them – Lake Baoding, a huge public works project, built around the environmental legacy of the flood of 1048.

Rebuilding, where it was possible, took an enormous effort, and it was the local authorities who took the initiative to try to mitigate the succession of disasters: rebuilding towns and villages; organising the locals to dig relief canals and construct embankments. Typical was the small town of Quzhou in the central plain of Hebei, where the flow of rivers from the mountains to the west collided with the new course of the Yellow River, causing heavy damage and loss of life. Linghu Duanfu was a local official in the aftermath of the 1048 flood, whose instructions were to safeguard the town and its remaining inhabitants as best he could from further crises. Hoping to mobilise the gentry and their supporters, he asked his superiors in the local government in Mingzhou to allow him to construct a new dyke to shield Quzhou from the Zhang River, which still flows past the town today.

This request was turned down on the grounds that, though it might help Quzhou, it was in danger of deflecting waters elsewhere in the prefecture and damaging other counties. The local landowners, the rich and powerful, refused to cooperate with their magistrate, not wanting to expend a huge effort for regional infrastructure when they could protect themselves with local defences. So Linghu now held meetings with the smaller people, the local landowners and poorer farmers, and they agreed to build the proposed dyke themselves, maintaining it for years after Linghu had gone. Looking back, the locals felt the magistrate had done well, for 'without this dyke there would no longer be a Quzhou county'.

Aside from the loss of life, the cost of restoring the infrastructure and rebuilding ruined settlements, canals and embankments was huge. The millions of bundles of wood, clay and straw that were used like sandbags to block breaches in the dykes accelerated local deforestation. The 1048 flood also had a massive effect on taxation: in the northern provinces tax revenues were reduced to a fifth of their pre-disaster levels. But, little known to them, this was not the end, for the 1048 flood was the beginning of a cycle of natural disasters. Longer term, the issue was not only a problem of flooding, but of soil fertility. It might have been thought that the silt was good for the fields, but the Yellow River's silt contains a huge amount of desert sand from the rocky landscapes of the loess plateau, not thick rich black soil as for example in Egypt. An eleventh-century document gives a graphic account of what that meant for farmers: 'After the Yellow River's waters recede sediments are a fertile glutinous soil in the summer. But then it turns into a yellowish dead soil in the early autumn, quite loose in texture. Later, it turns into a whiteish dead soil in the late autumn. Then after the first frost it becomes sand completely.'

From that point, so locals judged, a heavy silt cover can make the land sterile for twenty years. This disastrous situation only began to change for the people of the Hebei region in 1128, when the dykes were deliberately broken as a defence measure by the Song government and the river shifted its course again southwards. But the longer-term effects persisted down the centuries. In places in the north, twelfth-century travellers had the impression of journeying through a desert, and even two centuries later some counties were still struggling with salinisation and sand. In the late fifteenth century a Korean visitor encountered blinding spring sandstorms, and in 1549 a Japanese pilgrim in southwest Hebei described strong winds darkening the sky as fierce gusts whirled up the sand, conditions that are still encountered today in the hinterland of Tianjin. The once rich city Daming is now one of the poorest districts in China, as the environmental disaster of the eleventh century has continued to influence later generations, something today's world will find easier to understand as climate events become more and more frequent.

Conventional explanations of the fall of dynasties and kingdoms tend to highlight revolts and wars, but often take no stock of such cataclysmic natural changes in which society is shaken and the basic capacity of government is undermined. South of the river, untouched by the flood, the capital of Kaifeng was still the golden city, its markets overflowing, festivals lighting the streets, though its population was now swelled by thousands of refugees. Increasingly there were major incidents of social unrest, which, coupled with falling taxes and military threats on the frontier, began to suggest a gathering storm. It was therefore a period of urgent argument about the workings of the state and the nature of governance: Where should resources best be allocated? How could they lessen the burdens on the poorest? Did the whole system need change? In the second half of the eleventh century, such questions preoccupied two of the greatest figures in Chinese history.

WANG ANSHI: CHANGING THE STATE'S COURSE?

In the late 1070s and early 1080s, while the Normans were tightening their brutal grip over England, a traveller approaching the walls of Nanjing, the 'Serene River City', from the wooded mountains on the east might have noticed an eccentric local with unkempt hair and soiled clothes, on his donkey a bag of books and a picnic bag with flat bread and wine. Unwrapping inkstone, brush and paper, he would sit in silence by a stream, marking the signs as he composed airy, alchemically distilled poems, shot through with Daoist mysticism.

After a lifetime of government service, Wang Anshi had resigned at the age of fifty-five. A blunt man of no social niceties, he had been the most powerful man in China after the emperor, and the emperor at that time had been a mere boy. His tale has a Shakespearean grandeur: Wang had effectively ruled China, accepting his Confucian responsibility to help the emperor care for the people, and had spent his life working in public service. Then, however, disillusioned, he devoted his last years to a search for inner truth. A mind once occupied with great issues of the day now sought a Zen amalgam of Daoism and Buddhism: emptiness, extinction, calm.

Wang had been born in 1021, his father an official in Nanjing who died when Wang was eighteen. Wang followed in his footsteps and became an official there. At this point the country was enjoying a long period of prosperity, but the unresolved tensions were there to be seen. Keeping the barbarians at bay involved enormous military expenditure. Taxes were unequal and small farmers and merchants were suffering in the aftermath of the environmental disaster of 1048. Wang's early life travelling the country had opened his eyes. One poem (translated by Burton Watson) sounds very much like personal experience as a district officer:

> Before I ever took up office
> I grieved for the common people:
> If a year of plenty cannot fill their bellies
> What must become of them in flood or drought?
> Though no brigands molest them
> How long can they last out?
> Above all they dread the officials
> Who ruin eight or nine households out of ten

More when the millet and wheat fail in the fields,
Without money for a bribe they cannot appeal for relief,
And those trudging to town to plead with the magistrate
Are whipped away from his gate. [...]
But since I came to help govern this poor district
My heart fails me, shame overwhelms me,
For today I am the one responsible
For all that once appalled me.
Self-reproach spurs me on to do my best
And I share my worries with my colleagues.

Wang decided that serious reforms were needed if the nation was to progress, and sent a memo to the government: the *Ten Thousand Word Memorial*. One of the most famous documents in Chinese history, it was debated even during the communist period, as it called for the wholesale restructuring of government and society. The state, Wang thought, should take over the management of commerce, industry and agriculture in order to support the working classes and 'prevent them being ground into dust by the rich'. He found himself an instant celebrity, reformers applauded his boldness, but the emperor rejected the appeal. Then, in 1063, Wang's mother died and he returned to the south to do the customary three years of mourning – a huge time to take out of the career of a man at the top. But in 1065, the new emperor, Yingzong, was young, reform-minded and open to listening to modernisers. Wang was made governor of his home province and then summoned back to the capital, Kaifeng, where he was made an imperial scholar and chief adviser, one of three Grand Councillors, eventually becoming prime minister, in effect the most powerful man in China. The reforms he instituted were the most radical in the whole of the pre-twentieth-century history of China, and they ran right across the board. He tackled education, the economy, taxation, trade and the examination system. He looked at practical subjects too, providing loans to farmers and heavier taxes for wealthy landowners. There was also a war on corruption, that perennial issue in Chinese bureaucracies of

THE STORY OF CHINA

every period. The efficacy and legacy of Wang's ideas were bitterly contested then, as they still are today. Though most were only ever petitioners, Wang was one of several great reformers in Chinese history who went against the tide; unlike them, he had the chance put his ideas into practice.

After eight years of almost unbounded energy, his already strange traits became more marked; he often forgot to bathe or eat, had unkempt hair and clothes, and avoided grand banquets. A whirlwind of intellectual force, he rubbed many up the wrong way with his abruptness and singlemindedness. Maybe his health was already undermined by the pressure of pushing through the reforms; as Deng Xiaoping remarked, ruefully, after listening to Jimmy Carter's remarks about the knotty problems of American politics: 'You should try ruling China!'

In 1074, in the continuing aftermath of the great flood, north China was hit by another huge famine. Many farmers were driven off their lands and the debts incurred from seasonal loans piled up: local officials still tried to collect the money owed, and amid the anger fingers were pointed at Wang. The emperor supported him, but attacks by conservatives grew, and in 1076, at fifty-five years old, Wang decided he had discharged his duties and retired to the cluster of Zen monasteries on the wooded slopes of Purple Mountain above his 'Serene River City'. The emperor made him governor there, but he soon resigned that too, choosing to live in what the Buddhists called Samadhi Forest, meaning the mind in its most concentrated state: meditative absorption – in the oldest Buddhist sutras, the development of a luminous mind, last of the eight elements of the eightfold path.

He lived on Purple Mountain with his wife, in a simple house he called 'The Half Way Garden' (the site is still to be seen inside the Naval College). There amid woods and streams he wrote poetry, scripted commentaries on Buddhist sutras and compiled a dictionary probing the philosophical underpinning of the pictographs in the Chinese writing system. Distanced from the capital, his critics and enemies now gathered against his reforms. In 1085, the emperor died, and the new regime began reversing his policies. Wang died a year later. Unwavering, exhausting, brilliant, exasperating, in his thwarted attempt to reset China's way of doing things, he was one of the country's most memorable failures. In his own life the contradictions at the heart of Chinese civilisation were played out; the fight between order and disorder, the nature of just rule, the plight of the many, the personal quest for happiness and transcendence. Among his last poems is this one, entitled 'Reading History':

> Fame and achievement are a bitter business from the
>   beginning.
> Who can you trust to tell the story of all you've done
>   and not done?
> Whatever happens is already murky enough, and full of
>   distortion,
> Then small minds muddle the truth further and it's utter
>   confusion.
> They only hand down dregs. Their green-azure and
>   cinnabar inks
> Can't capture that fresh kernel of things, that
>   quintessential spirit,
> And how could they fathom a lofty sage's mind, those
>   witless sentinels guarding thousand-autumn dust on
>   their pages of paper?

SIMA GUANG

Wang's chief opponent through the late 1060s, the leader of the 'Conservative Faction' resolutely opposed to Wang, was a no less monumental figure in China's history. Sima Guang came from southeast Henan where his father had served as county magistrate. His was an old family that still survives in the clan village near Yuncheng in the corner of Shanxi where the Yellow River makes the great curve which is such a pronounced feature of the map of China.

There a lovely Buddhist temple alongside his tomb is still maintained by his descendants. Sima is a towering figure in Chinese culture. His *Comprehensive Mirror of History*, commissioned in 1065 and finished nineteen years later, was presented to Shenzong in 1084 in a time of growing economic crisis. The book was a vast survey in 354 chapters, extending from 403 BCE to 959 CE, intended as a study of history but also as an aid to government in the present. As he said in his preface to the emperor and the heir apparent:

> This work is prepared with an aim to examine the vicissitudes of our forebears, hence to reflect and verify the merits and deficiencies of the present time ... With it we hope the governance of our kingdom shall excel and transcend beyond what has been accomplished before, so that the common people living within the realms of the four seas may profit from benevolent rule.

It was a big claim for the educative power of history. Sadly the emperor who commissioned it died the following year and the work fell on deaf ears. Yet it remains China's greatest single piece of historical writing. In a culture where exemplars of history are still everything, it had enormous influence as the fundamental narrative of 1,500 years of Chinese history until the story was transformed by archaeology in the twentieth century. Though Sima Qian back in the Han dynasty is viewed as the founding father of Chinese historiography, his namesake Sima Guang's scope and influence make him the greatest of all Chinese historians. And while his impact on scholarship has been huge over the past 900 years, what is really remarkable is the standing his book has had in the eyes of the general readership, in its many abridgements, new editions and commentaries. It was practically the only general history with which most of the reading public of pre-Republican China were familiar, its regular reprints culminating in a great eighty-volume woodblock edition in the late nineteenth century, which was reprinted through the Republican period. Such is the continuing power of history in China, it is no accident that

Mao in his last days was photographed reading it, and that Deng Xiaoping is described by his daughter as having also studied Sima during his time in exile.

The book also gives us clues to the broader understanding of Chinese history. It was, said a twelfth-century commentator, a book 'compiling the records of good political order, and of chaos'. But of course, like almost every other great thinker in China until the twentieth-century reformers, Sima never contested the core narrative: the monarchical system. The issue for him was not to change it but to find out how best to make it work. 'You will see in these pages,' he wrote to the emperor, 'over these 1,400 years, that the history of China has been a story of violence and disorder in which periods of good order and harmony have been short, less than 300 years in all this span: and even then, not free of violence. Harmony in the state is therefore a very difficult thing to establish – and needs to be very carefully tended once it has been achieved.'

Such concerns drove his history, but also his politics, especially in his bitter rift with the reformers led by Wang Anshi. After fourteen years of being sidelined, working on his history, he suddenly found himself in demand. The last eighteen months of his life were the pinnacle of his political career, launched into the forefront of politics, appointed prime minister and chief adviser to the emperor. His abolition of Wang's reforms did the state's finances no good, but was well received among the people: sales of small portraits of him to have on household altars were big enough for some painters and craftsmen to get rich from, in the way of populist politicians today.

When his patron the emperor died, leaving a nine-year-old heir, Sima's world was upturned. He had burned the candle at both ends overworking on his giant project. Walking with a stick now, he couldn't ride, or kneel before the imperial throne, although he still insisted on trying. Writing by lamplight had made him very nearsighted, he had lost most of his teeth and, most dreaded of all for a historian, over the past couple of years his memory was starting to falter. The fact was he was finished; he knew he was dying, but was so desperate to reverse Wang's new reforms that he acted and spoke less cautiously than he would have. He died still at work; in his last few days he was losing awareness of his surroundings, 'as if in a dream still mumbled about affairs of state'. As a pupil said: 'He wanted to sacrifice himself for All Under Heaven.'

The two great opponents, Wang Anshi and Sima Guang, died within months of each other; Wang on 21 May 1086, Sima on 11 October, just as concerns about the state of the nation and the security of the frontiers were growing more insistent. Wang had given up on politics, but right to the end Sima's concern was how to ensure the stability of the state and society. Sima was a conservative where Wang was a radical innovator, but both had seriously tried to engage with China's future.

THE FALL

The brilliant world of Song China was now beginning to sink into financial trouble. Increasingly pressured by aggressive neighbouring states, the government was persuaded to massively boost the size of the military. This started with a misjudged change in foreign policy that led to border wars with the Tanguts. Up to the 1040s relations had been good, but when the Tangut ruler claimed the title of emperor, tensions grew until they developed into outright war. Military expenditures, as well as the ongoing cost of the payments which Song China continued to make to her other neighbours, eventually absorbed up to three quarters of the government's annual cash income. So, despite the flourishing economy, the government began to run out of money. As Sima Guang had written in his dedicatory letter to the emperor: 'Governing a state is like maintaining an old house that's fallen into disrepair. You don't just tear the whole thing apart and start again ... To demolish an old house and build a new one, excellent craftsmen and quality materials are needed. I am afraid that we lack both. I fear that the house we have may not shelter our nation from the wind and the rain.'

A VOICE FROM THE 'WOMEN'S CHAMBERS' – LI QINGZHAO

And wind, rain and storms would indeed come. But not quite yet. When Sima wrote those words in 1070, the golden age of Kaifeng had little over a half a century still to run. One of our most important witnesses for that time is also one of the most distinctive voices in Chinese history, the poet Li Qingzhao. She lived in an age of change when urban women were playing an expanding role in the economy, running shops and retail businesses in Song cities, as indeed they appear in the Kaifeng scroll, though only as a small minority in the crowds of male traders and shoppers. They managed their household finances and taught their children while their husbands studied and pursued their careers. But they were published as writers and could own property. And yet, paradoxically, it was in this age that Chinese women in the upper levels of society began increasingly to be confined to the home, and when footbinding began to spread for the first time. This painful practice, intended to emphasise a woman's physical delicacy, as a rich woman didn't need to walk, persisted into the twentieth century. And yet the Song was the time when women's voices start to be heard, and for the first time in Chinese history we can explore in detail the stories of women below the ranks of the royal family.

Li Qingzhao was a woman from a middling family who rose to fame because of her poetry and her writing. She is also an extraordinary eyewitness to the events of history as a participant, a commentator and an artist. Born in 1084 in Kaifeng, in the view of most Chinese people, she is one of China's greatest poets. She is also still widely misunderstood, defined in the past by patriarchal assumptions about her story which have in some important ways denied her true voice. The chief witness to her tale is in her own words, her poetry, and also the first autobiography from a woman in Chinese history (and perhaps the first in the world?). Her father had encouraged her to join male poetry gatherings when she was young, and she was already a poet of repute by the time she was seventeen, when she married a student at the university in Kaifeng. Here is Li

Qingzhao writing about herself, in her intriguingly 'modern' tone, translated, as are all her words here, by her biographer Ronald Egan:

> Insight, they say, leads to understanding ... Concentration leads to refined skill, and with refined skill, everything you do can reach a level of real excellence ... For example, by nature I am fond of board games. I can lose myself in board games and play all night long without thought of food or sleep. All my life I have played such games – and I usually win! Why? Because of my level of refined skill.

Li Qingzhao's marriage has for so long been portrayed in Chinese culture as the ideal devoted marriage. When they were young, she tells us, she and her husband were soul mates who loved literature and history. She recollects how they liked to pass the time in Kaifeng's Da Xiangguo Temple, wandering the courtyards, buying antiquities at the stalls, making rubbings of the inscriptions, munching fruit from the little side cafés. As one walks even today in the little market inside the temple precinct, or in the lanes of food stalls outside the university, thronging with students after classes, it is easy to imagine them. They built an enviable collection of books, enjoying the pleasures of the moneyed middle class in the Song with access to the best paper and writing materials. They were wealthy enough to own fine things, although not always so rich they could buy the very best, once having to give back an antique scroll because they couldn't afford it. Li Qingzhao's first married years, as she paints them, were an idyll: 'We lived happy together those years. By the fire we made tea ... and were untroubled by sudden storms ... so long as we could share a cup of wine, and a sheet of fine paper ...'

After twenty years of marriage, however, a chill descends on her life. Reading between the lines, her marriage seems increasingly fraught. Li Qingzhao, it appears, had no children, and new evidence suggests her husband may have had sons by a concubine. In one famous poem, which she introduces in prose, Li writes with powerful understatement but unmistakeable feeling, of travelling to join him.

Husband and wife had been apart for several months; his government posting had taken him to Laizhou on the coast of Shandong, an important shipping place for travellers and traders to Korea and Japan and cargo boats moving south to the Yangtze. But when she arrived, he was not there to greet her. Instead she was taken by the servants to her room.

> I arrived in Laizhou on the tenth day of the eighth month in 1121, and found myself alone in a single room. Nothing of what I was used to seeing all my life was there before my eyes. On the table was a copy of a book of rhymes and I opened it at random, having decided to use whatever rhyme I opened it at to write a poem. By chance there was the character depicting son, so I used that for my rhyme, and composed a poem called 'Stirred by Emotions':

> > A cold window, broken table, and no books.
> > How pitiful to be brought to this ...
> > Writing poetry, I turn down all invitations, shutting my
> >   door for now
> > In my isolation I have found perfect friends:
> > Mr Nobody and Sir Emptiness.

A shadow had fallen across Li Qingzhao's charmed life. But now a shadow was falling across her China too, troubles into which, as we shall see, she would herself soon be swept up in the most dramatic circumstances. Only five years after that lonely summer, the storms of war would gather to wreck her world.

DECLINE AND FALL: THE EMPEROR HUIZONG

The ruler of her world was the Song emperor, Huizong. On the throne since 1101, he would be the last great emperor to rule from Kaifeng. Huizong, as even his chief councillor said, was 'careless and frivolous, and not cut out for ruling All Under Heaven'. Paintings of him show us a man who looks sensitive and learned, retiring and somewhat unworldly, and so he was. A Renaissance prince, he surrounded himself with poets, artists and philosophers. His collection of paintings and antiquities would have put that of the Medicis in the shade. He was an accomplished artist himself; his surviving scrolls of exquisite blossoms and exotic birds are visions of beauty. Music was another delight; he employed hundreds of musicians, and spent his evenings listening to Daoist and Buddhist orchestras. He built palaces, temples and gardens of unsurpassed splendour. In his spiritual inclinations, he was above all a Daoist; he conferred with Daoist masters, wrote on the ancient texts of Daoism, and urged his subjects to follow their precepts.

In summer 1119 he had a stone tablet set up in the Imperial Temple and copied across the empire. It was entitled 'The Jade Purity in the Divine Empyrean'. Drafted and written by the emperor himself, it effectively announced a Daoist renewal movement under the influence of Daoist mystics; a remaking of a nation sunk in error and cut off from the Way. The message was clear: 'Return to the pure ways of magnificent antiquity, consider exclusively the mystery of what cannot be seen and heard.' He announced eleven great festivals, national services of worship so 'people of this entire generation sunk in error for so long, can uphold the truth'.

But his vision of sacred kingship tragically compromised his ability to rule. He lost touch with reality in his mystical flights of divine kingship when much harder choices were needed on military expenditure and defence planning. When the crisis came, he finally lost everything.

In a remarkably short space of time in the early 1100s, the precarious stability the Song had won by war, and by a network of diplomacy and tribute, collapsed. A new enemy now emerged in the north. The Jurchen Jin were a people originally from beyond the Amur River, in what is now Russia. They had moved south, annexing smaller states and tribes and uniting to form a powerful and populous state. In 1122 they defeated the Song's long-time tributary state in northern China, the Liao-Khitans, and made the Tanguts their vassals. Their empire now ruled a vast area between Manchuria and the Mongolian steppe.

This was a very dangerous moment for the Song dynasty. Stable relations with the Liao through the eleventh century had been one of the factors that both kept stability and shifted the Chinese self-centred view of themselves. The Chinese had sent embassies most years, which were well received. Acknowledging the facts on the ground: China was no longer 'All Under Heaven', but *primus inter pares*, in a real world balanced by diplomacy. Suddenly this new eruption from outside the world of the Song diplomats presented a massive threat ...

Sensing military weakness, and a failure of will and nerve in the Song government, the Jurchen moved south. Their mounted armies and siege trains were equipped with all the modern technology, weapons of war invented by Song scientists – bombs, gunpowder, flame throwers and wheeled armoured vehicles – and they now had the immense wealth of China in their sights. Having overwhelmed the Song northern defences, in 1126 they built bridges of boats, swept over the Yellow River, and surrounded Kaifeng, an army of 100,000 men with vast supply trains, siege engines and towers threatening the capital's 17-mile outer circuit. The Chinese court paid them off to buy time, but within the year the Jurchen came back to find that the Song government had made no real effort to regroup. And the tale of what then befell them, at the close of 1127, is another never-to-be-forgotten story in the many tragedies of Chinese history.

That bitter winter of 1127, when the Jurchen Jin armies came, thick snow was swirling across the city of Kaifeng. From the Dragon pavilion with its hundred steps, on the darkening horizon the gate-houses of the outer city were on fire and many of the houses and shops were burning along the road in from the East Water Gate – the road portrayed bursting with life in the Qingming scroll. Hordes of attackers were already surging through the outer suburbs, looting Shenyang's tavern and wine store, smashing Dr Zhao's dispensary. And here, in the inner city, thousands of terrified citizens of Kaifeng were still resisting, hopelessly. There was no food, the markets were empty, and there were even rumours that human flesh was being eaten in the streets – here of all places, the culinary capital of the world. The government had again tried to buy off the invaders, but, of course, every time they gave gold, the invaders wanted more. They wanted millions of ounces of gold and silver. They wanted precious gems, antiques and temple bells. They wanted ritual vessels and the musical instruments played by the court orchestras. And they wanted people, craftsmen, artisans, carpenters and metalworkers, musicians, acrobats, entertainers; and, above all, they wanted women. They wanted the hundreds of ladies in waiting from the imperial palace and the 1,500 female musicians who used to play before the emperor. They wanted the wives and daughters of the royal family and of the courtiers and the leading citizens, thousands of them to be delivered to the two great camps of the invaders stretched over snow-streaked fields north and south of the city. Many of those women committed suicide rather than submit to that. And so the city that had stood for many of the best achievements so far in civilisation was brought to nothing. The Song government surrendered and began the grim negotiations to give up everything.

THE MARCH NORTH

Abused and mocked, his yellow imperial gown stained, the captive emperor now began a journey north with his wives and thousands of courtiers on a hellish forced march to the Jurchen homeland in Manchuria. Fourteen thousand officials, court women and servants went with the royal family. Mocked, beaten and raped, forced to cook and to serve at Jurchen banquets, the women of the imperial family were shared out among the Jurchen leaders. They would never see their homeland again. A brief diary of a Chinese interpreter on the convoy has survived, compelling in its brevity and immediacy: a grim recital of hardships through snow and heavy rains. The imperial consort Zhu was raped only four days after a miscarriage when she had gone off the road to relieve herself. 'The sufferings of hell can hardly be worse than this,' wrote the interpreter, as they marched on in mud and torrential rain. The translation is by Patricia Ebrey:

11 April. Noon. A meal was prepared for the Jurchen commander Shaohe ... Since Consort Zhu and Consort Zhu Shen were good at songs, the commander told them to compose some new songs. After he repeatedly insisted, Consort Zhu composed this: 'Once I lived in heaven above, in pearl palaces and jade towers. Now I live among grass and brambles, my blue robe soaked in tears. My body is bent and my will humbled. I hate the drifts of snow. Not till I arrive at the spring will my grief end.'

'She composed the song,' added the interpreter. 'But she would not sing it.'

Among the vast tide of loot that the Jurchens took with them – jades, silks, musical instruments, gold, silver and artworks – was Su Song's 45-foot astronomical clock, which they dismantled and transported north on carts, intending to re-erect it as a trophy of war in their capital. However, with its intricate mechanisms and finely calibrated cogs and wheels, the task proved beyond them.

The survivors ended up at a place called the Fort of the Five Nations near Harbin in Manchuria. Few signs remain of the place in the fields today. There are the outer ditches, hummocks grassed over, bleak and snow-blanketed in winter. This is one of the less well-known sites in the Chinese story. But there the courtiers of the Northern Song spent their last days, the three or four thousand survivors of the march. The emperor died here in 1139, the most aesthetic, intellectual and artistic of all emperors; a broken man who found no more solace in his Daoist introspections. As he himself admitted, 'I inherited a great and flourishing empire, but I myself was a mediocre person, not up to the job. And in the end, I failed the nation.' The return of his coffin is commemorated in a painting of solemn and fantastic grandeur which survives today in Shanghai.

Unsparing in her anger, the poet Li Qingzhao responded to the disaster with one of the greatest political poems in Chinese literature, which ends with these lines:

And you should have been more cautious,
better educated by the past.
The ancient bamboo books of history
Were there for you to study.
But you didn't see ...
Times change, power passes;
It is the pity of the world.
And the hearts of the vicious were
Deep chasms of evil.

Almost miraculously, the famous scroll of Kaifeng, with which we began this chapter, also survived. Among many marginal annotations to the painting which were made in later times, a Song poet has added:

A million people once thronged these streets, there were restaurants as far as the eye could see, and music in the air. Who would have thought it could all be brought to ruin. And what would we not give to be able to visit that golden time just once more?

11

THE SOUTHERN SONG 1127–1279

In the twelfth century, China was divided along its age-old fault line, the fundamental north–south divide in landscape, climate and language which still persists today. And now the shift in the nation's economic and social centre of gravity, which had begun in the Tang, became permanent. The south became the richest and most populous region of China, probably unrivalled anywhere on earth for its prosperity. Over the next 150 years the dynasty which we know as the Southern Song reached a standard of living not yet achieved in human history, with huge agricultural productivity, commercial wealth and cultural resources. The first Western accounts of China come from this time, among them Marco Polo, who gives a dazzling, breathless account of urban life in the capital, Hangzhou: 'the greatest city that may be found in this world'. But this next chapter of the story begins in the chaotic aftermath of 1127, when we rejoin the poet Li Qingzhao.

After the fall of Kaifeng, Li Qingzhao fled south by boat, one of millions on the move, hoping to meet up with her husband. He now sent news by letter that he was seriously ill. They were reunited at a port on the lower Yangtze, but there he died. Qingzhao was now a widow in a time of war, and, worse, she now discovered that her husband had left no provision for her support. Perversely, however, before he died he had left her with a troubling injunction. She must protect with her life their art and manuscript collection, together with the antique bronze ritual vessels they had collected: 'Live or die with them!' It was a strange, disturbing command, as if the collection had replaced her; as if it had acquired greater value than her. And the collection was valuable. As she continues the story, we realise that she's a rich woman, travelling in some state: by land with a carriage and drivers and her faithful retainers; by water on a sturdy river boat with a cabin and a covered cargo hold. An aristocrat fleeing the tide of war with her household valuables, like the Rostovs after Borodino.

'After I buried my husband', she wrote, 'I had nowhere to go.'

They said that the crossings of the Yangtze would soon be blocked. At that time I still had our library, 20,000 books and manuscripts, folios of inscriptions, bronzes, all the kitchen utensils and bedding enough for 100 guests, and many other now superfluous things. I was by now very sick, my breathing very weak. I put half the stuff into storage in Hongzhou but bandits sacked the city and it all went up in smoke and flame. All I had left with me now were a few treasured scrolls, some manuscripts of Li Bai and Du Fu. I couldn't get further upriver, and the movements of the invading armies were unpredictable, so I got to the coast, left my clothes and bedding, and hired space on a boat heading down the coast to try to take refuge with the court.

Over the next three years she moved from place to place as a refugee, still trying to hang on to their precious manuscripts, art and bronzes, one of the finest private collections in China, as if in loyalty to the Chinese past as well as to her own now lost life with her late husband. In the end, however, she lost everything, robbed by bandits, local bosses, landlords, fellow travellers, and even in the end by officials in the Southern imperial court. The whole collection of books and paintings they had built up together and treasured was stolen or burned. 'But in the end', she said, ever acute and self-reflexive, and stripped now of all illusion, 'I understood that that is in the very nature of things.'

A WORLD MADE BY MEN

As her story unfolds through these personal and national disasters, she begins to talk in a way that perhaps no woman has done hitherto in Chinese literature: not only about her inner life, but about the world, and the incompetence and treachery that has betrayed China; the failure of governance, and of nerve, in public life; the failure of *men*; 'a century of achievement and we lost it all'.

In the end, inevitably, the collection had become a dangerous liability; with her life constantly threatened, she decided to give what survived to the new emperor, but before she could it was stolen by one of his generals. She finally escaped to safety with her younger brother. By now she had completed the customary two years of mourning for her husband, but then, out of the blue that spring, at the age of forty-eight, she remarried. This story became very contentious in later literature. For centuries afterwards male literary critics rejected the idea that a loyal widow like Li could have remarried at all, let alone that she could then have publicly pilloried her second husband in public. But Li Qingzhao was always her own woman.

The marriage lasted only 'one hundred days'. Risking prison (she was actually detained for a few days) and courting public censure and humiliation, she took her new husband to court, and made a graphic submission against him, detailing his private behaviour, showing precisely why the marriage was so short-lived. Again, the translation is by Ronald Egan:

All my life I have tried hard to see right from wrong ... Recently I contracted an illness that was nearly fatal. I was delirious at one point and my coffin nails were made ready. Though I had my younger brother with me, there was only one old retainer to answer the door. In my dire straits I became imprudent. I trusted fine words and was beguiled by beautiful speeches. My brother was tricked into believing the man was who he said he was. It all happened so fast you wouldn't believe it. I was dithering and indecisive; still ill and fraught, when he pressed me to be his wife. But as soon as I regained my sight and hearing I knew we could never live together. To my dismay I realised that at my advanced age I had married a worthless shyster of a man. I sought only to break away but he began to abuse me freely, raining blows on me daily.

Before the judge she proved her case and got a divorce; not because of her husband's physical abuse, but because he had lied to her about his social rank and his examination record. For that he was demoted and exiled to a far-off posting. She won her case, but for her outspokenness she was condemned and disparaged by most male commentators. Later, in the Ming and Qing dynasties, and even in the twentieth century, her story would be reshaped by critics who claimed her autobiography could not be genuine and that her second marriage never happened; her words against her marriage were never spoken. Even today the several memorial halls and 'former residences' that tell her tale to modern tourists do not give the full story.

A WOMAN THINKING ON THE TIMES

In the aftermath, she became a commentator on history, a critic of the men who had betrayed China. The next few years after her divorce were very difficult. Hangzhou, the new capital south of the river, was frequently threatened by raids from the north. Life was lived on the edge. In 1134, Jurchen armies surged south through Anhui, and again there was a mass flight of refugees. Li was swept along in the panic of the times, in an exodus which in her words echoes the Chinese experience from ancient times to the Japanese invasion and the Huai River battles of the civil war in the late 1940s:

Since crossing the Yangtze southwards I have been separated from my loved ones and forced to wander here and there. This year at the start of winter we heard that military emergencies were reported along the Huai River. Those who lived in the Yangtze River basin fled westwards from the east, and southwards from the north. Those who lived in the forests and hills made plans to flee into the cities; those who lived in the cities made plans to flee into the hills and forests. In all this protracted flight, with everyone hurrying this way and that, there was no one in the end who was not displaced.

For a time Li stayed in the Zhejiang coastal plain, south of Hangzhou, at the house of the Chen family. 'Having recently swapped the comforts of verandas and windows for the hardship of boats and oars, I feel quite content now. But the nights are long: how to pass the nights?'

Hard as the times were, for her these were the most productive. Now in her fifties, with no illusions, she addressed the political and military issues of the day, as well as writing poems and prose, song lyrics, a dissection of prosody, and her memoir. In all this, as she tells it, she recovered her sense of self, moving from the crippling sense of loss and the crushing humiliation described in her memoir to develop new ways in which she could get her ideas across and project herself as a woman of self-confidence and principle. At times, like so many women writers throughout history, she felt she had to play down her extraordinary intelligence – 'the burden of female talent' as her greatest modern biographer has put it. Even modern critics have thought it 'astounding and unprecedented' that a woman could have entered the debate about the government's policy of appeasement. She wrote political poems to the peace envoys that the Southern government sent to the Northerners, even addressing herself to the commissioner of the army and the chief minister. One poem is a detailed examination of the issues, one a pithy dismissal of the 'peace party' at court and their posturing but ineffectual diplomacy: 'Cheered as they go off to conferences, applauded in their fine robes, but how come all these negotiations just make things worse?'

She concluded with verses referring to Mulan, the famous woman warrior who disguised herself as a man and joined the campaigns against the northern barbarians in the fifth century:

Our high-ranking ministers still run away in all directions;
Images of the great steed of the old heroes fill my eyes.
In these dangerous times where can we find real horses
    like them?
Mulan holds her lance firmly, a fine woman warrior!
I am old now but I still have ambitions that stretch a
    thousand miles.
All I want is with others like me to cross the Huai
    River once more

Such, then, were the struggles of a woman of genius in medieval China: a scintillating window on women's real experience. In the Song, as we saw, most men considered published writing, let alone commenting on politics, inappropriate for women. The historian Sima Guang thought that they could compose poetry, but it should not be seen in print. Li Qingzhao, however, refused to conform, and has been a model for women poets for the past 1,000 years, read by women of all backgrounds in many situations, in war and in peace.

THE CAPITAL MOVES SOUTH: HANGZHOU

Though divided, the empire was not yet lost. The dynasty survived. After the fall of Kaifeng, some of the imperial family fled south to a new capital, and a new destiny. The new order they created south of the Yangtze is known as the Southern Song, and that dynasty ruled south China until the Mongol conquest in the late thirteenth century. Their northern frontier was now the Huai River, and though the Jurchen wars continued, the south was too powerful, too populous, and too far away, for the Jurchen to conquer, even though their armies made predatory raids across the Yangtze for several years. As for Kaifeng, Meng's city of dreams, its days as the metropolis of the world were gone: the city was not destroyed, but the great phase of its history was over. The end of the Northern Song in Kaifeng, however, signalled the rise of the next of China's great capitals. In spring 1132, the Southern court was re-established 200 miles south of today's Shanghai, in a place that would be immortalised in the pages of the Italian traveller Marco Polo: Hangzhou.

The landscape was proverbial in its beauty. 'Above there is paradise,' as the saying went, 'below there are Suzhou and Hangzhou.' The city stands on the Qiantang River, about 50 miles inland from a great bay of the South China Sea, about as far as London is from the Thames estuary. It is bordered on its western side by emerald green hills and the beautiful expanse of West Lake, whose shores and islands are dotted by temples and fairytale pagodas linked by causeways 'in situations of unbelievable beauty', as a British intelligence officer in the Second World War wrote, allowing himself a brief moment of emotion in an austerely factual report. An unimportant place in earlier history, Hangzhou had been walled in the Late Tang; a long rectangle between the river and the lake. Now, in the Southern Song, it would grow to become, as Marco Polo remarked in the 1270s, the 'finest and noblest city in all the world'.

After the fall of Kaifeng, thousands of refugees fled south to join the remnant of the imperial clan who set up the kingdom of the Southern Song with a new emperor, a kinsman of the deposed Huizong. While Huizong himself and his captive courtiers shivered in misery in the winter rains and snows of Manchuria, cooking their rice in soiled robes, a vast flood of displaced people was on the move south of the river. Their stories are preserved not in the accounts of historians but in clan books, woodblock-printed genealogies and family histories. The Zhaos were one such lineage. Claiming descent from the general who became the first Song emperor, Taizu, one branch of the Zhao clan took a boat from the Yangtze to Hangzhou and then moved on down the coast of Fujian. There in the coastal plain opposite Taiwan they settled and built a stone-walled village whose plan was laid out 'like a miniature Kaifeng', so the golden city, their ancestral home, would never be forgotten. The clan village is still there (below page 322) and continues to be inhabited by the Zhaos, who tell their tale today from their woodblock-printed family history and their oral traditions of 'the days when we were emperors'.

Among the many who made a new life in Hangzhou itself was

Meng, the author of the nostalgic *Dreams of Splendour* about old Kaifeng. With other old-timers Meng would reminisce over the next forty years in Hangzhou wine bars, taverns and tea houses, telling their children and grandchildren, and fellow bar haunters, about the good old days when Kaifeng was the shining city on the plain. Among them were even some of the Jews of Kaifeng who had fled to Hangzhou with their Torah scrolls and traditions, and we may perhaps imagine that they too, faced with the loss of their Chinese Jerusalem, sat down by the banks of the Qiantang river and wept.

THE LATE SONG TRANSFORMATION

The great characters in the story of the Song – Sima Guang and Wang Anshi for example in the eleventh century, Li Qingzhao in the twelfth – were driven by what we would call patriotism, a sense of the Chinese nation as an idea worth fighting for. This very distinctive development in Chinese culture will have great importance for the future. During the Tang, the interests of the great aristocratic families had been paramount, but now the old medieval aristocracy was gone, replaced by a governing class chosen on merit, men with a national sensibility that went beyond clan or even dynastic loyalty. Among these people there was an agreed and overarching set of civilisational values that had to be protected and passed on. As the poet Lu You, who was born on the eve of the fall, wrote to his son at the end of his life:

> Death ends it all, that's for sure
> But what grieves me is not to have seen our land united.
> That day when the emperor wins back the central plain
> Make sure you come to my tomb and let your
>   old dad know!

But the south thrived. The population of China had already doubled in size during the tenth and eleventh centuries to about 100 million. In the twelfth century it may have exceeded 120 million, of whom the larger part was in the south, in the Yangtze valley and delta, with the southern coastal plain perhaps accounting for as many as 50 million people. These increases were made possible by many factors, but especially by improved food production and better diet. Rice cultivation in the south was expanded, and new, early-ripening rice species imported from Southeast Asia enabled two, and in some places even three, harvests a year.

To defend their prosperity, and mindful of previous military failures, the Southern Song under the emperor Gaozong (1127–62) initiated new programmes of arms manufacture, and a massive programme of shipbuilding. He oversaw the improvement of harbour defences and the creation of a coastal beacon system; China's first standing navy was created in 1132. After the disasters of the past decades, China would be able to defend itself. A writer of the early thirteenth century summed up the economic and demographic changes of the era with a palpable sense of historic achievement:

> Our dynasty possesses southern China, and so south of the Yangtze all is calm and under control. The amount of cultivated land in southern China constitutes two thirds of the empire. With respect to geographical extent and wealth it is three quarters. The northwest now it is but one quarter. In terms of food production, tea and textiles, southern specialities give the richest returns. So, though the population living to the south of the great river only occupies a part of all China, it has two thirds of its total wealth. At the present time the profits of both land and sea are to be found first and foremost in the Yangtze delta. The use of irrigation today is most developed there around Lake Tai than anywhere else in the empire. The northwest comes nowhere near.

THE NEW CAPITAL

Hangzhou itself was now transformed into an imperial capital. Hitherto a small city in the subtropical landscapes of the lower Yangtze valley, to some of those who arrived from the north it had felt 'a lost corner' of the empire. The tranquil waters of the lake and the circling hills beyond were beguiling, but the city itself was crowded and narrow, a noisy place filled with traders and craftsmen. The street plan did not present the grand formal layout of a traditional Chinese capital, following as it did the natural curve of the land between the lake and the hills. In the early days it was swamped with refugees from the north who were lodged in military camps, in shanties outside the gates, or in the city's hundreds of Buddhist monasteries. At first the emperor and the court moved into the prefectural offices in the southern corner of town, as it was assumed that they would at some point retake the north and this would therefore only be a temporary measure. But as the division of the country soon began to look more permanent, the city was provided with grander buildings. An immense processional way running for 3 miles from north to south was laid out with a huge new palace in a walled enclosure overlooking the river. Within just a few decades, at least a million people were living inside the new capital. And as all the available space became filled with streets, the city planners began to build upwards. So, as Kaifeng represented a change in urban living from the ritual space and tightly regulated wards of Xi'an, Hangzhou in its turn was another new phase of urban history in China: a commercial city. In the thirteenth century, Marco Polo describes a jam-packed high-rise city with houses of six, eight and even ten storeys. 'Green mountains surround the still waters of the lake,' one resident said, 'one would say a landscape composed by a painter. And towards the east, where there are no hills, the land opens out, and there, sparkling like fish scales, the bright-coloured tiles of a myriad rooftops.'

Urban life in Song Hangzhou was different from that in China's previous capitals. Rather than being dominated by government establishments and the institutions of imperial bureaucracy, it was pre-eminently a trading city. Family-owned businesses were the backbone of city life. 'If one views all the guilds and the hundred markets,' said a Hangzhou resident in the 1200s, 'from outside the roadblock at the Gate of Tranquillity all the way to the Bridge of Inspection, there is not a single family that is not in the trading business.' There were the Chen and Zhang family banks, the Xu and the Zhai families who ran haberdasheries, the Li family's silk shoe shop, the Pengs who dealt in waterproof boots, the Kongs who specialised in hats, and the Nius who sold woven belts. There were beauty parlours where you could have facials, or buy makeup and face cream, eyeliner and false hair; shops specialising in flutes and others in bamboo whistles; shops for incense and candles, for gold-spotted writing paper and for ivory combs. There were even pet shops. 'This is the hub of the universe,' our author said. And if, after a day of shopping in Hangzhou, one was not yet worn out, the visitor could repair to teashops or wine bars, or public theatres large and small, where a new southern brand of musical drama had developed out of the old Kaifeng style.

Such wealth made Hangzhou a great centre of international trade. The city itself was not easily accessible to ocean-going ships because of the famous tidal bore; but standing at the southern end of the Grand Canal it was linked by waterways to Ningbo, 100 miles away on the Bay of Hangzhou, which, along with Canton and Quanzhou, became one of Song China's biggest ports. From these places wide-bellied merchant ships sailed to India, Africa and the Persian Gulf. 'According to government maritime regulations concerning seagoing ships,' says Zhu Yu, whose father had been commissioner of shipping in Canton, 'the larger ones can carry several hundred men, and even the smaller ones may have more than one hundred crew on board.' On long-distance voyages, some had palatial private cabins and saloons for richer passengers. An impression of such vessels is provided by the archaeological discovery of a thirteenth-century three-masted ocean-going junk from Quanzhou that worked the Thai and Indonesian trade routes with cargoes of incense, wood and pepper. Nearly 120 feet long with a 32-foot beam, divided by watertight bulkheads into thirteen compartments, this was a typical general-purpose 'tramp' of the age. There were guilds of merchant adventurers who owned many such ships, organised in a company structure with CEOs, business managers and shareholders. Accounts from the Arab world describe Chinese vessels as major players in the

THE STORY OF CHINA 235

Indian Ocean trade, each year using the monsoon winds to cross to Aden, Yemen, the Indus Valley and the Persian Gulf, bringing iron, swords, porcelain and silk.

The wealth and fashionable lifestyle of merchants began to outpace that of officials. Lu You, whom we last met writing to his son lamenting the loss of the middle plain, penned a poem about the high-rolling, luxury-filled lives of the merchants:

> In singing-girl towers they play at dice, a million on
> one throw,
> In flag-decorated pavilions, calling for wine, ten
> thousand a cask.
> They say: 'The Mayor? The Governor? We don't even
> know their names!
> What's it to us who wields power in the palace?!'
> But look what heaven gives me, an official: luck
> thin as paper.
> Now I know that merchants are the happiest of men.

HANDING ON 'THIS CULTURE OF OURS'

The increased commercialisation of society saw the spread of a mercantile ethos across south China, from ports like Ningbo and Quanzhou to the great cities of Yangzhou and Suzhou. Smaller towns in the hinterland also saw the rise of new merchant elites supplying the capital with food, coal, grain and timber. Some of the most famous clans of traders came from the Huizhou region, 200 miles inland from the capital. 'Wherever there is commerce', it was said, 'you will find a Huizhou merchant.' In this thickly forested countryside cut by many rivers and overlooked by the beautiful peaks of the sacred mountain Huangshan, there are many families today that can trace their ancestry back to that period. Their clan documents chart cultural change at the grassroots and give an insight into processes that often go unnoticed in the official histories.

The county seat is the picturesque old walled town of Huizhou, today known as Shexian, on the Xin'an River. The port here, created by a Song-dynasty dam which still exists, had two or three hundred river boats large and small, ferrying timber and raw materials downriver to Hangzhou. From the middle ages to the end of the empire its merchants were famed for their business acumen. Today, in the hinterland of the town, well-built clan villages survive, their fine houses with whitewashed walls and grey tiled roofs clustered together along stone-paved streets and alleys. Inside the houses, the exquisite stone carving, painted beams, carved wooden screens and panels attest to the wealth and taste of their owners. Clans like the Hu in Xidi, the Wangs of Hongcun and the Baos of Tangyue rose to become some of the richest families in China by the eighteenth century. They were merchants in timber, salt, rice and grain, in coal and tea; some traded overseas, such as the Xu lineage of Xucun, who had business interests in the Malacca Straits and Japan.

A SONG FAMILY

One Huizhou clan came from a town 40 miles west of Huizhou, across the watershed of the Chang River, which flows down from the mountains of Huangshan to the Yangtze near Wuhan. Founded back in the Tang, the old town has had a huge makeover since the turn of our millennium. The charming river frontage with its stone steps and piers, where boats began their journey downstream to Hangzhou, still partially survives, along with the medieval, five-arched bridge. In the centre of the old town, the main commercial street ran down to quays lined with cavernous shuttered wooden shops and store-houses for grain and tea. A century ago, when it thronged with traders, the locals called Qimen a 'mini Shanghai'; even in the 1940s today's older generation remember the quays were piled with timber ready to be shipped down to Jingdezhen in Jiangxi, the centre of the ceramic industry. They exported tea and timber and brought in cotton cloth, sugar, salt and oil. But in 2004 much of the old town was swept away for a new shopping centre with department stores, fashion shops and fast-food bars. Behind the modern shops, though, down a maze of twisting alleys, a few old gentry houses survive. One of them is the house of the Xie family. Over the doorway is an ornately carved stone frieze featuring auspicious plump fish with dragon fins and mythical birds with scaly feet. Through the gate, a worn wooden threshold leads into a late sixteenth-century house, with a central courtyard open to the skies. Red lanterns hang from the eaves alongside clothes on the washing line and a joint of meat seasoning on a string from the balcony.

The head of the family, Xie Youcai, a sprightly man in his seventies, has an encyclopaedic memory of the family story. On the table is a nineteenth-century woodblock-printed account of the genealogy of his clan, the precious record of the family hidden by his grandfather during the turmoil of the 1960s. Hanging from the walls are faded signboards also saved from destruction, advertising the scholars of the clan who achieved the top degree, the *jinshi*, in the Song dynasty. The family to say the least has a long and proud record of service to the country, and a loyalty to an older world that still seems a natural part of the family story.

'We were local officials, people of substance here from the Song dynasty,' says Mr Xie, his recall instant and fluent, internalised in way that brings his ancestors to life as real people not just names on a family tree: 'The house is about 500 years old but our history goes back much further than that.' The family were originally from the North China Plain, but in the early tenth century, after the wars of the Five Dynasties, one of them fled into these hills, bringing his whole family with him. 'He was our first ancestor here in Huizhou.'

At first we were farmers. But the land here in Qimen county is poor and hilly, all mountain with few fields for cultivation. So over time we spread out across the valleys in search of enough land to grow food and to try to find a livelihood. People round here sold timber and tea, and manufactured paper, ink and lacquer to make a living. By the end of the Northern Song, branches of the Xie family lived across this county, one group settled here in the

county town and became merchants. Later we moved into the salt
trade; we owned a landing stage on the river, but mostly we had
careers in government.

They were also beneficiaries of the expanded education system under
the Southern Song which enabled the gentry to rise in the world, not
just as traders but as gentlemen, their sons passing the provincial and
national examinations. 'In 1173, a man of our family came first in
the upper metropolitan degree,' Mr Xie continued. 'His name was
Xie Anbang. Half a dozen other Xie men also then passed the upper
exams during the Southern Song. One served as a county military
officer, the other graduates did government jobs in different parts
of the empire.'

Back home in the town, the clan founded and supported local institutions: schools, granaries, charitable estates, hospitals and orphanages,
all organised by local families rather than by the state. Such was the
Confucian ethos of one leading gentry family who rose in the Song.

AT HOME WITH THE ANCESTORS: NEW CONFUCIANS

The old world of the Huizhou gentry which carried down to the
Second World War is perforce almost gone now, but in the person of
Mr Xie, who was born before the revolution, we may still touch on
the old Confucian values of his class in a way that is becoming less
and less possible in the new China. In the clan house, a ramshackle
wooden staircase leads onto the balcony, with the upper chambers
looking down on the inner courtyard. In a spare bedroom old
furniture is piled up: winnowing baskets, dusty lattice screens and
a cracked enamel bowl containing tiny silk shoes for bound feet.
Through a door is the altar room. There Mr Xie carefully folded
back the wooden screens to reveal a deep cupboard containing
dozens of spirit tablets – wooden plaques, each inscribed with the
name of a Xie ancestor; each one prepared after the funeral and
inscribed with the dead man's name and the name of his descent-line
heir. Mr Xie lit incense and offered a prayer.

'There are thirty-seven spirit tablets in here. We are one of the oldest lineages in China. Each represents a member of the family. Each is marked to show to which generation the person belonged.' He pointed to the name, and the dates of birth and death, before carefully setting the spirit tablet back in its place. 'That was my grandfather,' he said, indicating a hand-drawn picture done in charcoal. 'Grandfather saved our family records from the Red Guards in 1966, hiding the plaques in the roof space. And here's my father.' He gestured to a photograph, cracked across the frame. 'Now once more I can do the rituals for them, as my son will for me. As for me,' he said, 'I am the thirty-fifth generation since Xie Xuan. And after me, my sons will make sure the house and the tablets are cared for. It is in our blood.'

THE SONG CONFUCIAN REVIVAL: 'FOLLOWING MASTER ZHU'

Back in the thirteenth century, the ethos of the Huizhou merchant clans, and indeed of later Song China, was shaped by the most famous thinker of the age, one of the greatest figures in Chinese civilisation: the philosopher and teacher Zhu Xi. 'Back then,' Mr Xie reflected, 'it was customary to form clan associations committed to Master Zhu's "School of Moral Learning". The gentry read his books, followed his instructions to hold onto the liturgical rites, and tried to live according to the custom of Zoulu – Confucius' homeland. He was the great teacher and they taught the descendants these same ways.'

Born in 1130 in the aftermath of the fall of Kaifeng, Zhu Xi grew up as part of the generation moulded by the experience of defeat. Influenced by an eclectic range of teachings, including Buddhism, the core of his work sought to re-establish the fundamental concepts and values of Confucianism and to restore the cultural and political integrity of Southern Song China, as he put it, 'to celebrate the cosmic legacy far back to Fuxi and Huang Di'. With China divided, it was a powerful message of renewal, especially when Confucianism was perceived simply as a state ideology, a lifeless orthodoxy that had lost its spiritual and ethical heart.

Very soon after his death in 1200, Zhu Xi's reinterpretation of the fundamental concepts of Confucius began to be taught nationwide in private academies and public schools. It then became the basis of the imperial civil service examinations from 1313 until their end in 1905, making Zhu one of the most influential of all the world's philosophers.

Central to his teaching was the idea of moral improvement; how human beings can be helped to live a better life. He was interested in what we would call behavioural psychology and his simple breakthrough was to stress mindfulness in society, 'reverential attention' as he put it. For Zhu, empathy, an understanding of the interconnectedness of life, was the basis of good human interaction. In this, as so often in Chinese culture, the family was the starting point. His practical guide, *A Book on Family Rituals*, could be found in every household in China in the late empire. It was a huge influence, too, in Japan, Vietnam and Korea, though his work is still little known today in the Western world. Zhu is the most important Chinese thinker after Confucius, and is enjoying a major revival today; indeed it has been said that his range of inquiry from the philosophical to the scientific is unmatched in the whole Chinese intellectual tradition, and in the West is comparable only to that of Aristotle.

But his appeal was not just philosophical. For Zhu, taking a leaf out of the Buddhist scriptures, emotions are the key to finding the meaning of the ancients in oneself. Parts of his handbooks on ritual are beautifully expressed, as he attempted to create a musical, poetic, magical language to communicate with the dead. This is not dry scholarship, otherwise it would never have survived so long or still be capable of reinvention today. It examines the place of human beings in the universe, and the continuing presence of the ancestors in the lives of living, conjured through ritual:

Your filial son, because now is the end of autumn when things begin to ripen, performs this service to your honour, our late father, and our late mother.

Your filial son presumes to report to his late father and his late
mother. Now because it is the end of autumn when things begin
to ripen, we feel the passing of time, and think back with longing.
Vast heaven is limitless ...

THE MONGOLS: THE FALL OF THE SOUTHERN SONG

So the neo-Confucian movement, with its alliance of gentry and
literati, was crucial in passing the ethos of Chinese civilisation on
in the era of the Southern Song, providing a compelling answer
to those who feared the heart of the old culture had been lost.
The Confucian ideal was given new life, and later under Mongol
occupation it became the core component in the imperial examinations, as it would be to the end of the empire in the early twentieth
century. Books, schools and literacy spread enormously with the
greater availability of mass printing, and in the streets of Hangzhou
and in the hills of south China, families like the Xies flourished
during the twelfth and thirteenth centuries. In local communities
all across the Southern Song, these gentry families were the essential link between the centre and the locality, and men from the
provinces came to play an increasingly important role in national
politics too. So, in the south, the values of traditional China, codified in the Han and Tang dynasties, were preserved, transformed
and handed on.

In the north, however, a new storm was gathering. In the vast
plains beyond the Great Wall and the mountains edging the North
China Plain, a huge confederation of nomadic tribes had come
together in the Mongolian homeland. Their charismatic leader,
Genghis Khan, was proclaimed ruler of all the Mongols in 1206.
With mobile, mounted armies they launched fast attacks on states
along their borders, eventually reaching all the way into Central
Europe. The Mongol attacks on the heartland of China began in
the first decade of the thirteenth century. In 1209 they overwhelmed
the Tangut Western Xia empire, and then destroyed the Jurchen
Jin, eliminating the old enemies of the Song who had conquered

Kaifeng the previous century. In 1215, breaking through the passes in the Yanshan mountains, they came down into the northern plain and made their new capital of Dadu, on the site of today's Beijing. The Mongols were effectively ruling northern China, and soon they began to spread into the lands of the Southern Song, recruiting Chinese generals and troops in their captured territories and using Chinese military technology including firebombs and gunpowder.

For a while the Song were able to put large forces into the field against the invaders, and even defeated them in battle. But in the 1260s the Mongols pushed south with huge mounted armies while simultaneously deploying captured naval forces. In 1268, Kublai Khan, the grandson of Ghengis, blockaded the mouth of the Yangtze, and in 1271, with the net tightening around what remained of the Southern Song, he declared the foundation of a new dynasty in China, the Great Yuan – the 'Primal Force'.

Now the final assault began. The Mongol land armies overran the great cities that guarded the central basin of the Yangtze. With the help of Chinese generals and engineers who had abandoned the regime, the Song forces at Yangzhou were smashed. The royal family, with its loyal advisers and the core of the imperial army, fled further south. In 1275, the Song armies were heavily defeated and most of their territory surrendered. In 1276, the Mongols massed a huge fleet in the Yangtze estuary, crossed the river and besieged and sacked Suzhou. Hangzhou itself was now defenceless and soon surrendered. The Mongol army then pursued the refugee Song court deeper into the remote corners of the empire, until finally, in the swamps of the Pearl River delta, the final remnants of the Song forces were cornered in one last, terrible battle.

It was 19 March 1279: a dark day in the story of China. On the coast south of Canton, the Song generals had moored their fleet in a remote lagoon in the Pearl River delta. They had cut down trees from the hillsides around and put up a makeshift wooden palace for the court, with barracks and huts surrounding it. But as the Mongol fleet massed at the mouth of the estuary, supplies of fresh water were running out and their situation soon became desperate.

The battle was fought behind the narrows at a place called Yamen. To visit the site today at the time of the anniversary, with the air chilly and the mist clinging and damp, is to imagine something of what the last Song loyalists must have felt that day. By late afternoon, going into dusk, the mist descended and the far shore almost disappeared.

The Song commanders decided not to defend the narrows, so the Mongol fleet sailed through into the lagoon. And there the Song navy faced them. They had about a thousand ships, which they had lashed together to form a floating fortress. The decks were protected with wet mud to stop the effects of the fire projectiles from the Mongol catapults. When the battle began, an eyewitness describes the air full of the flaming tracers of firebombs; the tumult reverberating into the sky and across the sea. But when the tide rose, the Mongols were able to encircle the Song forces and the royal family was trapped.

The emperor Huaizong, a seven-year-old child, was on a large junk flying the imperial flag, at the very centre of the fleet. Understanding that all was lost, the emperor's loyal minister Lu Xiufu made a famous speech to the little boy. 'The affairs of our state have come to this,' he said, 'we must not disgrace the nation.' Then, taking the boy in his arms, he jumped into the sea, to commit suicide. On the deck, so it was said, the little boy's pet white parrot began to screech and beat its wings, until its cage worked loose from its hook and fell into the water, the loyal bird perishing with its master.

The glory of the Song had ended in shattering defeat. Its achievements had been huge and its inventions had outstripped those of the West. Its artists and scientists were without rival in the world, while mass printing had spread its ethos and its ideas as never before in history. It had been poised, or so it appears today, to become the world's first modern society. But, as so often in Chinese history, before and since, the world beyond China burst over her frontiers and disrupted the development of civilisation and society. Mongol dominion, the first completely foreign rule in Chinese history, was such a shock to the Chinese psyche that when it ended in the fourteenth century, as we shall see, it was followed by a native dynasty, the Ming, which retreated from the open society of the Song, turned its back on the commercialisation of China, and created a bureaucratic autocracy that looked back to older despotisms, setting China on a course that would cast its shadow until the present day.

12

The Yuan: China Under the Mongol Empire

In the thirteenth century, China was conquered by the Mongols and became part of a world empire that extended from the Gobi to the Black Sea. To the Chinese literati and governing class, alien rule was a profound shock. This experience would lead to a deeply conservative and inward-looking reaction in the later fourteenth century, under the Ming dynasty. What then could have been a post-Song early modernity would turn out to be Ming despotism, shaped by the experience of conquest and foreign occupation. This would have long-term consequences, bequeathing a model of governance that would last down to today's People's Republic. However, though brief, the Mongol age would be another one of those interstitial periods between great epochs in Chinese history that was extraordinarily creative, laying markers for the future in governance, and in particular seeing a great opening up across the Eurasian world, with the first direct contacts between Western Europe and China.

THE PRIMAL FORCE

In 1271 the Mongols announced the new dynasty in the Chinese language as the 'Great Qian Yuan'. This ancient name meaning 'Origin' or 'Primal Force' enabled the founder, Kublai Khan, not only to show respect for China's classical antiquity, but also to set the universalist pretensions of Chinese monarchy within even wider geographical limits. The Yuan ruled the Middle Kingdom through the Confucian officials of the former Southern Song governing class, along with many foreigners in their multi-racial, multi-lingual empire. The young Marco Polo, for example, seems to have served in the Yangzhou local government for two or three years, perhaps with the Italian merchant community in the city. If so, then he was just one of many outsiders making their fortune in the Mongol imperium. Yet the contacts also went the other way. The first Chinese person to go to Western Europe travelled from Beijing to Bordeaux in the 1280s, attempting to negotiate an alliance between the rulers of Christian Europe and the Mongols against the Muslim Caliphate. So the Mongol empire stirred up world history as never before. Whether in Plantagenet England or Yuan Dadu, it was a time of rich new possibilities.

The Mongols' first great achievement was to reunite China, which had long been divided. As we have seen, from the Tang onwards, the Chinese had been compelled to share the landmass of China proper with other powers. Even at their height, the Song emperors did not control the north, and after 1127 they had to content themselves with a Southern Song state ruled from Hangzhou. However, while the Mongols reunited traditional China, the conquest was a huge blow to the traditional elites. Northern China had been under non-Chinese rule for 300 years, but the south had never experienced foreign government and not once had China, in its entirety, been conquered by a foreign people.

So how did Chinese culture fare under the Mongols? Of course, to the Chinese scholar-bureaucrats, the main issue was how to instruct the Mongols in the ways of the Middle Kingdom, which, it went without saying, was the superior civilisation. The Yuan historian Ma Duanlin, for example, like many Chinese literati, laid great stress on institutional continuity and on the vital task of transmitting the values of Confucian culture. The national imperial examination system was resumed in 1315 and for the first time, the interpretations of the great Song philosopher Zhu Xi (above page 239) were made the orthodox guidelines for the education system. Neo-Confucian philosophy and political autocracy were therefore brought together through the examinations for the bureaucracy, and would remain so until the end of the empire.

Many other scholars accepted that Heaven's Mandate had passed to the Mongols and put their efforts into working with the new regime. A scholar from north China, Xu Heng, was the leader of a group dedicated to 'rescuing the times'. He became the first head of Kublai's National Academy, striving to teach the new Mongol rulers how to run the nation with Confucian ideals. Xu Heng also became a mentor to Kublai Khan at the court in Beijing and was tutor to the emperor's sons, preparing short summaries, in simple language, to teach the Mongols about Chinese government; a core message for hearts and minds. 'In the past and present, the models and regulations upon which the state was established have varied from dynasty to dynasty,' Xu wrote in a memorial to Kublai called *Five Measures Required by the Times*. 'But the most important thing', Xu went on, 'was always to win the hearts of All Under Heaven. And to win the hearts of All Under Heaven is nothing other than to show love and an impartial devotion to the common good. If you love the people, their hearts become compliant. And if you are impartially devoted to the common good, the people become willing to serve. Compliance, and willingness to serve are what makes good government.'

A typical old-fashioned Confucian, Xu Heng stressed to Kublai the importance of a proper school system, with a strong focus on public morality. He wrote:

If there are schools everywhere, from the capital to the local districts, everyone can engage in study – from the princes of the palace, to the sons of the common people. And if every day the people are taught about the virtue of proper relationships between parents and children, and between the ruler and his ministers, then after ten years, those above will know how to guide and those below will know how to serve.

IN XANADU: MONGOL BEIJING

It was not, however, all a matter of self-preservation. In many areas, including popular culture, the Mongol period was an extraordinarily expansive time. In the great capital of Dadu, immortalised later in Europe as Xanadu, one could meet merchants, ambassadors and travellers literally from the other side of the world. Built between 1267 and 1285, Dadu swiftly became one of the largest and grandest cities in the world. Almost completely vanished today, overlaid by the centre of modern Beijing, it was surrounded by an immense outer square of walls that were built of pounded earth, with eleven gates and a deep moat. Its residential districts were laid out with wide avenues, between which were lanes that are still today called by their Mongol name, '*hutongs*'. Of the palace itself, swept away in the early fifteenth century by the Ming, only fragments have been found. Its giant base was of white marble, carved with dragons and phoenixes. Its roofs were covered with glazed tiles and its carved wooden brackets, beams and lintels were painted in dazzling colours and picked out in gold. The private rooms had walls lined with silk and decorated with landscape paintings, their floors painted green to remind the rulers of the grass of their native steppes. To the west of the palace was the lake, where Kublai had stayed on his first visit to Beijing. This area became a green and pleasant pleasure garden, with clusters of exotic rocks and rare trees and plants from foreign lands. This was the real landscape behind Coleridge's stately pleasure dome, with its 'gardens bright where blossomed many an incense-bearing tree'.

In the streets outside the palace enclosure, in the 'Chinese city', were houses, shops, stalls, inns, teahouses and several markets. To feed the city's fast-expanding population, the Grand Canal was extended in 1293. A branch canal was formed, allowing barge traffic that brought grain from the south, to sail from the main northern depot at Tongzhou right to a terminal at the Rear Lake, at the gates of the imperial palace. Here, merchants gathered from every part of the country. This world can still be glimpsed in photographs of nineteenth-century Beijing streets, peopled by Mongol craftsmen and women, cooks and traders, and caravaneers with their huge trains winding through the streets on their way out to Mongolia.

Like all international ages, the Yuan was also a very creative time in art, culture and, in particular, drama. There were many playhouses in the entertainment districts, some holding audiences of two or three thousand. There, the citizens of the capital could watch plays by their favourite writers and applaud their star actors. Perhaps influenced by models from India and Iran, writers began to produce dramas in four or five acts, with dialogue in language that was close to the daily speech of the people. Over a hundred Yuan playwrights are known by name, as well as a host of anonymous dramatists whose unsigned works have been preserved. The best-known Yuan playwright was Guan Hanqing, who was active either side of the year 1300. He wrote over sixty plays, of which fourteen survive, including the famous *Snow in Midsummer*. Quarrying the big social issues of the day, including court corruption, Guan was particularly well known for his strong female roles that were 'high-spirited, self-willed, sharp-tongued, outspoken, unafraid, salty, yet loveable', as a contemporary said. His female characters include prostitutes and servants, child brides in forced marriages, poverty-stricken and destitute mothers and widows. Often, like the heroine Dou E, these characters highlighted the burning social issues of the day. For example, the phrase 'snow in June' is still in common speech today, used to describe the corrupt miscarriage of justice.

In the huge multi-racial Yuan empire, all religions were accepted. Edward Gibbon made a telling comparison between the cruelty and irrationality of the Catholic inquisition in Europe and the 'pure theism and perfect toleration of the religious laws of Zingis Khan'. Genghis Khan himself had followed the shamanic cults of Mongolia, while Kublai favoured Buddhism, and some later khans converted to Islam. Nestorian Christians were also influential among the ruling class and several khans were brought up by Christian mothers and educated by Christian tutors. The Mongols favoured Muslims from Central Asia as administrators in many cities, especially the big ports. In Beijing, several great mosques and temples still standing today owe their origins to the Mongols. The large mosque on Niujie Street was a major site of Muslim worship. There was also an Islamic observatory and an Islamic academy. People could worship at around 100 Buddhist and Daoist temples across the city. The White Stupa Temple was commissioned by Kublai and designed by a Nepali architect. There were also Christian places of worship, including a Franciscan church that could seat more than 200 people, with a tower and three bells that rang across Dadu at prayer time.

Among the great popular shrines of the city built under the Mongols was the sprawling complex of the God of the Eastern Peak. This temple was an amalgam of Daoist, Tibetan, Buddhist and shamanic deities and cults and was typical of the syncretist mood of the time (on its later role in China's most famous novel, see below page 367). The Mongols also oversaw the construction of a state shrine, the famous Confucius Temple, which still stands next to the Yuan Imperial College. Inside its courtyards is a forest of 200 steles recording the names of more than 50,000 *jinshi* scholars who took the imperial exams for the highest final degree from the Yuan period until 1905; testimony to a world restored.

THE VIEW FROM THE VILLAGE: TANGYUE IN ANHUI

At a local level, the Mongol conquest had often come with violence and chaos. Later lineage documents from Huizhou in Anhui, south of the Yangtze, suggest how people responded. One family forced to adjust to the times was the Bao clan of Tangyue, a hamlet in a fertile plain edged by forested hills in the south of the province. The Bao family had moved here during the Song dynasty and established a farming village a few miles from the prefectural town. After the founding of the Southern Song in 1127, with Hangzhou only a few days' journey downriver, these Huizhou villages found themselves perfectly placed to supply the new capital with their produce: tea, grain, lacquerware and, especially, almost limitless supplies of timber. The clan moved up in the world, marrying the daughters of officials and gentry. Soon

they were able to educate their sons. Bao Zongyan, born in 1224, was
taught by his mother and became an avid book reader. Then, at the
time of the Mongol conquest of the south, law and order broke down
and armies of bandits roamed the county.

A later local gazetteer tells the story, drawing on Bao family tradition: 'I am Bao Shousun, son of Bao Zongyan. In the Bingzi year of
the Deyou reign period of the Song (1276), General Li Shida's troops
broke into the villages to the north and west, many bandits emerged
and the white blades of weapons were like a forest; our villages were
burned and plundered.' Father and son narrowly escaped death at
the hands of robbers, but the family survived. The Baos seized the
opportunity to better themselves. Young Bao Shousun accepted
a government job as a salt field inspector. In 1324 his son, Bao
Tongren, passed gloriously in the Yuan state examinations, having
'learned Mongol speech and writing'.

TRAVEL: OPENING THE WORLD

The Mongol period left many important legacies in the arts and
painting, in philosophy and history. One area of especial interest
was astronomy. Since the Tang dynasty the Chinese had been influenced by Indian and Islamic science, and under the Mongols Persian
astronomers came to China and Chinese scientists went to study
in Iran. Kublai Khan founded the predecessor of today's Beijing
observatory under the mathematician and scientist Guo Shoujing,
who founded many observation sites across China. The Mongol
rulers were also tolerant in religion, promoting Tibetan Buddhism,
Nestorian Christianity and Islam. Perhaps the biggest influence came
from its very nature as a vast transnational empire. The Yuan era
gave a huge impetus to travel across the whole of Eurasia: embassies,
long-distance contacts, merchant journeys and pilgrimages. This
is the period of the first regular missions between East and West,
and many Westerners left their accounts. Among these are John of
Plano Carpini, who came overland in 1246; William of Rubruck,
who travelled to Mongolia in 1254; and Odoric of Pordonone, who,

in the 1320s, spent three years with a mysterious Franciscan, 'James of Ireland'. A Christian church was established in Beijing in 1308 by John of Montecorvino and there were embassies the other way, one led by Genoese merchants resident in Beijing. The world was opening up – so much so that in 1339 Francesco Balducci Pegolotti, a Florentine merchant who worked in Antwerp and London, produced an itinerary of travel, a handbook on the 'Practice of Commerce' from Fife in Scotland and across Europe to Asia. The handbook included a route map to Beijing, details of business practice terminology and data on the comparative value of money. For the first time in world history, Scotland and China were part of the same story.

One fascinating aspect of these exchanges was the creation of more accurate maps. In the Song dynasty the Chinese had already developed exceptional mapping techniques for China and its provinces, with accurate grids. They were the best maps yet produced in world history. Now, in the fourteenth century, Islamic maps of Europe, West Asia and Africa became available in China. Kublai Khan sponsored the compilation of an imperial geography and a Mongol world map by the geographer Li Zemin. This became the source of later maps, including the magnificent 1389 'Composite Map of the Ming Empire', which survives in a later copy. This curiosity about the world never stopped. The accession of the Ming dynasty in 1368 curtailed such freedom of movement. Still, the Yuan legacy in mapmaking and geographical knowledge can be seen in Ming diplomatic missions across Central Asia and Afghanistan, such as the embassy to Herat in 1406. As we shall see, the accumulated Yuan knowledge of the world lay behind the seven voyages of Admiral Zheng He, between 1405 and 1433. During the Yuan, China had become part of the wider world, and Zheng knew where he was going.

MARCO POLO: AN ITALIAN IN THE MONGOL EMPIRE

For the first time in history, under the Mongols, China was part of a new global world. The Mongol rulers controlled a vast arc of land across the continent of Eurasia, from Baghdad in the west to Beijing in the east. There was often warfare between the Mongols' various khanates, but they provided a favourable commercial environment, and contacts between China and the rest of the world flourished. Foreigners from the West visited China in unprecedented numbers, not only missionaries but merchants. Among the Europeans who spent time in Mongol China, one in particular would become famous worldwide.

Born into a merchant family in Venice, Marco Polo set off to China in 1271, when he was seventeen. During the 1260s, his father Niccolo and uncle Maffeo had pioneered a commercial route to the Mongol capital, Karakorum, to which they returned with the young Marco in 1273–75, intending to train him in the China trade. They were tough, experienced men, brave travellers and skilful traders. Uncle Maffeo had a house in the Genoese colony on the Black Sea at Sudak in the Crimea, from where he mounted his journeys to Iran, Central Asia and Mongolia. With his father and uncle, Marco travelled overland along the Silk Road, visiting cities such as Kashgar along the way. If we can believe his account, he lived in China for twenty years and may have become a low-level official in the Yuan bureaucracy in the Yangtze valley. Marco marvelled at China's wealth and the splendour of its cities. He travelled on the Grand Canal and visited Hangzhou, a city he thought so grand, so beautiful and so full of abundant delights that it 'might lead an inhabitant to think himself in paradise'.

In modern times doubts have been cast on Marco's book, with some scholars believing that he never went to China, or at least never went beyond Beijing. Persuasive arguments have been put forward that he cobbled the story together back in Italy from popular travellers' tales and fantasy literature. However, new research might suggest otherwise. His descriptions of the postal system, with its stations every three miles, and his observations on the various denominations of paper money and the different currencies in use in the regions, including cowry shells in Yunnan, are all remarkably well informed. Most convincing is the information he gives on the salt industry in Yunnan, worked by the indigenous people who extracted the salt from brine hoisted in buckets from wells. This was a land where salt was so scarce that it could be used as currency, a custom carried right down into the mid-twentieth century. Marco's account of the techniques of salt production is closely echoed in many later sources and illustrated in numerous Chinese technology treatises, and, although rejected by earlier generations of scholars, it is accurate and unique.

Marco also mentions the salt industry in the eastern coastal lands, south of the Huai River in Jiangsu, which produced over a third of all China's salt and raised rich revenues for the Yuan government. Here he travels down the Grand Canal from Gaoyou to Taizhou and Tongzhou:

> When you leave Gaoyou, you ride another day to the south-east through a constant succession of villages and fields and fine farms until you come to Taizhou, which is a city of no great size but abounding in everything ... There is a great amount of trade and they have many vessels. And you must know that on your left hand, that is towards the east, and three days' journey distant, is the Ocean Sea. At every place between the sea and the city, salt is made in great quantities. And there is a rich and noble city called Tongzhou, at which there is produced salt enough to supply the whole province, and I can tell you it brings the Great Khan an incredible revenue.

The next point of Marco's journey was the 'very great and noble city' of Yangzhou on the Grand Canal. As we saw earlier, Yangzhou had been the hub of the booming economy of the Tang dynasty, with a sizeable foreign community of Arabs and Persians. Here, remarkably, Marco claims that he 'governed', *seignora*, for three years. This has often been rejected as fantasy, though it might conceivably be a simple garbling of a text that originally said that Marco had 'stayed', *sejourna*, in Yangzhou, probably between 1282 and 1284. Still, the idea that he had some kind of government post in Yangzhou, perhaps as an overseer or low-level local official, is not entirely impossible. Marco even tells us about the post stations in that part of the Yangtze valley and accurately gives us the number of towns (twenty-seven) that were administered from Yangzhou.

There are only a few remnants today of the Yangzhou that Marco Polo knew. Among these is a much-restored Yuan dynasty pagoda in one of the old shopping streets and the ornate tomb of a Muslim merchant in a big unkempt garden and cemetery by the Grand Canal. On the south and east sides the canal forms the city's moat, as it did in his day, intersected by smaller canals enclosing old quarters of narrow alleys lined with houses, shops and markets. As interest in his adventures grows in China, a lifesize equestrian statue has recently been erected outside the rebuilt East Gate, looking out over the old Grand Canal. It is there, as he described, that 'vast amounts of shipping transport immense quantities of merchandise and many cities send their produce to be distributed in every direction ... bringing huge revenue to the Great Khan'.

THE ITALIAN COMMUNITY OF YANGZHOU

If Marco Polo stayed in Yangzhou for three years, we may well ask, why there? And with whom? In 1951, a chance find opened an unexpected window on Yangzhou's Italian community in his day. An army work group, demolishing the old city walls of Yangzhou, found a tombstone cut in grey marble. At the top was an image of a Madonna and child, sitting not on a Gothic throne but on a round Chinese-style table with curved legs. Angels fluttered round the mother and child, plump Italian putti, but wearing trailing gowns like the Buddhist spirits that fly across the painted caves of the Silk Road. Beneath the angels was an image of Saint Catherine with two wheels, but not like those to be seen on the walls of a medieval European church – more like the dharma wheels from a Buddhist sutra. At the bottom of the slab, hacking down a kneeling martyr, was a man with a sword, clothed like a Mongol soldier.

The Latin inscription is still clear: 'In the name of God, Amen. Here lies Katerina, once the daughter of the deceased Dominico de Yllionis, who died in the Year of Our Lord 1342, in the month of June.'

So who was Katerina Ilioni, and why was she here in China? Like the Polos, her family were old Silk Road merchants. One Pietro Ilioni appears in 1264 as a trader in Tabriz in northern Iran. Katerina's father Domenico, we know, was a friend of merchants who travelled to China from Genoa, in Italy. He is listed in a Genoese record of 1348 as the executor, at some point in the past, of the merchant Jacopo de Oliverio, who had lived 'in the Kingdom of Cathay'.

These were people of some status, the kind of merchants trusted by the Mongols to carry out embassies to the West. Yangzhou, with its overseas commercial links, had long had its foreign communities. The Franciscans had come here in the thirteenth century and by 1322 there were three churches serving the 200 or so Christians who lived here. The tombstone must have come from one of them. Katerina died still bearing her father's surname, Ilioni. Evidently she was not married and had been living in Yangzhou up to 1342. Perhaps she was even born on Chinese soil. Indeed, since the discovery of her tombstone a plaque has been found commemorating the death in November 1344 of Antonio, her brother. These were families with a long-term commitment to the China trade, lasting several generations. Their father's Genoese friend Jacopo, it was said, had multiplied his capital fivefold during his time out there. Go east, young man!

Marco Polo returned to Europe in 1295 and dictated the story of his adventures from memory, while in prison in Genoa. The version we have is often garbled and embellished but it was the first detailed description of China available to Europeans, and Marco's story became a bestseller, translated into many European languages. The book was widely read and shaped Europeans' image of China for centuries, inspiring others, including Christopher Columbus, to seek new sea routes for trade with the wealthy and sophisticated world that Marco had described.

THE FIRST VISITOR FROM CHINA TO EUROPE

To people in the West, the most famous travellers who were involved with China during the Mongol empire were the Europeans, like

Marco Polo, who travelled from Europe to the East, and came home to tell the tale. But travellers also made the journey the other way round, from China to the West. Indeed, among the Mongol embassies to the West, one to Italy and France in 1336 was led by Genoese merchants in the service of the Great Khan, people like the Ilioni family.

The most extraordinary was Rabban Sawma. A Mongolian convert to Nestorian Christianity, Sawma travelled from China nearly 8,000 miles by land and sea across the entire Eurasian world. His journey began in 1280, as a pilgrimage to Jerusalem from his birthplace in Beijing. Carrying an official travel permit from Kublai himself, Sawma's dream as a Chinese Christian had been to see Jerusalem and the holy places, just as the Chinese Buddhist pilgrim Xuanzang had been driven by the desire to see the sacred sites of India centuries before. Travelling by horse and camel, Sawma went all the way through Central Asia to the Caspian Sea. He risked his life time and again, but escaped unscathed thanks to his resourcefulness, linguistic skills and personal charm. By 1286 he was in Iran, and there Sawma's pilgrimage turned into an extraordinary diplomatic mission. By then, the western part of the Mongol empire had broken up into separate khanates, and he was asked by the khan in Persia to head a mission to the Pope and the kings of Europe. The goal was to persuade the Europeans to ally with the Mongols, to launch a crusade against their common enemy: the Muslim Caliphate, which controlled the Holy Land, Egypt and Syria.

Sawma went on to Constantinople and thence by sea to Rome. There, Pope Honorius had just died, but Sawma was welcomed by the conclave of cardinals and travelled on to the court of Philip the Fair of France. Then he journeyed south to meet King Edward I of England, who by chance was in Gascony. In Bordeaux Cathedral, at the king's request, Sawma performed the mass in the Nestorian ritual, surely one of the most extraordinary meetings in history. On his return to Rome, Sawma met the newly elected Pope Nicholas IV. France, England and the Pope all gave their backing to the planned grand Christian–Mongol alliance, which in the event never materialised.

So far as we know, Rabban Sawma was the first person from China to visit the West. He never made it home to China. He returned through Greece, to Iraq, and died in spring 1294 in Baghdad, where he was buried in the great church of Darath Rhomaye, in the old Christian quarter, east of the river, outside the walls of the medieval city. A former companion wrote down his story in Iraq, and the only manuscript, a copy in Syriac, was discovered in the 1890s, in a small Christian town near Lake Urmia in northwest Iran. Sawma's amazing story was a dead end in Chinese history, as his account lay undiscovered for so long and so never entered the mainstream of Chinese history and literature, never inspiring others to go in his footsteps. Nevertheless, as a symbol of how the world opened up under the Mongol empire, his story is without rival.

THE FALL OF THE YUAN

The founder of the Yuan, the great Kublai Khan, died in 1292 in the Mongol capital. Once a master of half the world, he had spent his last years increasingly isolated, grieving for his beloved wife, alone in the palace by Beijing's North Lake, overweight, morose and ill. After his death, factions split the court. His successors lacked his iron will, his guile and his energy. Increasingly distracted by the international geopolitics of their far-flung dominions, from the 1300s onwards, the overextended Mongol empire began to break down into warring khanates. Rebellions broke out inside China as claimants to the dragon throne jostled for power. The situation came to resemble the breakdowns of earlier times, in the Five Dynasties, or further back at the end of the Han in the days of the Three Kingdoms; another one of the periods of dissolution that have marked Chinese history. Chaotic, terrifying and dangerous times, yet catalysts for a new era, when, almost as if by a centripetal force, the broken fragments of old worlds are drawn back together to create a new one.

This was a troubled period across Eurasia, as climate change exacerbated political instability. A mini ice age brought unheard-of conditions from lowland England to rural Anhui. In Europe, the

Great Famine of 1314–22 killed a tenth of the population. In China, beginning in the 1320s, repeated Yellow River floods caused failed harvests, famines and massive movements of refugees. The Yuan government insisted on calling the refugees 'bandits', the nomen-clature for enemies of the state right down to the 1950s. After a catastrophic Yellow River flood in 1344, increased taxation and a vast conscription project to mend the river dykes caused fury. Soon local revolts turned into full-scale rebellions as regional warlords declared themselves king, proclaimed new dynasties and began new calendars for a new time. These are old themes in Chinese history, where revolution is a simple fact of life, a recurring cycle whenever powerful central authority loses its grip.

THE BLACK DEATH

The omens and signs came thick and fast. This was a culture that implicitly believed in the power of the unseen to burst across the threshold of the real. In 1339, a series of terrifying visions was reported. Monstrous dragons swooping out of the storm clouds, on the coast of Fujian, unleashed tornadoes and torrents of rain, flooding and devastation. Prophecies ran like wildfire through the cities of the south. The heavens were disturbed. It was said that in 1349 five more dragons materialised out of giant waterspouts over the sea in the Yangtze delta, harbingers from the unseen realms of chaos. From then on, almost every year, the dragons were more and more insistent in their messages to humanity. Dragon sightings were made even in Beijing itself, one whirling in a fiery flash out of a well within the imperial Mongol palaces. The Chinese people, of course, understood these communications from the other world all too well, especially coming from the most meaning-laden supernatural creature of them all. The world was out of balance, the Mandate of Heaven in abeyance. 'Gazing on these sights,' wrote one scholar, 'the prosperity of former days felt like a dream.'

In the early 1330s the famines and floods were followed by a deadly outbreak of plague. It began in the northern province of

Hebei, where, one source claims, nine tenths of the people died. It is still uncertain whether this marks the beginning of the Black Death in China, or whether it was simply one of several local outbreaks. It has long been believed that the great fourteenth-century pandemic originated in Chinese Central Asia, where the *Yersinia pestis* bacillus is endemic in the rodent population. The very latest studies by medical geneticists, who have compared DNA extracted from archaeological remains with living strains, suggest the genetic family tree of *Yersinia pestis* did indeed originate in western China. There, for example, in a Nestorian cemetery near Issyk-Kul lake, are more than 100 grave markers from the late 1330s, some specifically speaking of 'pestilence'. From these regions, in the last years of the Pax Mongolica, plague seems to have been carried west on the Silk Road to the shores of the Black Sea and the Crimea by armies and traders. In 1347 it went from there to Constantinople via the port of Kaffa and on, by sea, to Venice and Sicily. Like a slow-burning fuse, by the late 1340s it reached the British Isles, and Ireland and Iceland by 1350.

Much remains to be understood about the Chinese outbreak. Imperfect estimates from censuses suggest a third of the Chinese population died in the crisis of the fourteenth century. Many of these deaths must be attributed to disease. Voluminous records survive from Yuan and Early Ming China, though none have yet been studied in sufficient depth to give a picture as comprehensive as that available for Western Europe. In 1334, 13 million people died, according to an official government source. Further outbreaks of a 'great pestilence' occurred in 1344–6 down the coast, from Shandong to Fujian. This was in the aftermath of a huge Yellow River flood which shifted its course from north to south of the Shandong peninsula, where it would remain for the next 500 years. Then, in the early 1350s, most of north and central China was affected, across the central plain of Henan, down into Hunan, Jiangxi and the southeast. In Jiangsu, 900,000 deaths were reported, with pestilence every year from 1356 to 1362. These are huge losses. The general consensus is that, though China's population was around 120 million on the eve of the

Mongol conquest around 1200, it was only half that number by the late 1300s. Data from Mongol censuses suggest the main losses took place after 1290. So the population loss in the last three decades of Mongol rule could easily have matched the estimate that one third of the population died during the Black Death in Europe.

Faced with these multiple challenges, Mongol power in southern China began to disintegrate. Armies of farmers and rural bandits rose up, often moved by millenarian religious ideas in such apocalyptic times. Rival rebellions coalesced in the different regions. There were various sects like the White Lotus, the Red Turbans, the Holy Lodge and the followers of the Kingdom of Light, some touched by the strange afterglow of Manichaeism, the Near Eastern sect which had become the state religion of the Uighur kingdom in the seventh century. It had vanished as an organised religion in the ninth century during the Buddhist persecutions, but still survived in the countryside during the Yuan, when Marco Polo reported 700,000 followers in Fujian (where a Manichaean temple with its cult image still survives near Quanzhou). Though long gone now, Manichaeism left a persistent marker in the psychology of popular revolt in south China, with its vision of a cosmic split between good and evil, yin and yang. Even the greatest nineteenth-century rebellion, the Taiping, though influenced by Christian eschatology, had its Manichaean strain. All these sects were millennial in the true sense of the word, believing that a divinely inspired leader would arise to save China from chaos.

THE VIEW FROM THE VILLAGE

How that leader arose is one of the most extraordinary stories in Chinese history. It takes us first to the northern edge of Hubei and the mountain range that runs along the border with Henan, the 'great divide' between the Yangtze and the North China Plain. Here, on the south side of the picturesque Dabie Mountains, are vast, tangled thickets of ancient azaleas. In the spring and early summer these flowers carpet Tortoise Mountain with red, to the delight of today's tourists. Yet in grey light, under storm clouds, the blossom can look like a blood red snowfall, staining the hillsides crimson, conjuring the old nickname 'Bloody Dabieshan', which comes not from flowers but from killing.

Out here there is a long history of civil conflict and rebellion, a persistent strand of extreme cruelty and violence. From the fourteenth to the nineteenth centuries the area was a hotbed of revolt, an out-of-the-way place that the government always found hard to control. In the hills to the east, along the Jiangxi border, the 1906 rising took place, and the Jiangxi Soviet in 1931. These were the scene of murderous purges against the indigenous Hakka people and brutal suppression by the nationalists. The hills were again the scene of savage conflicts between 1949 and 1953, when the communists waged their war against the remnants of the nationalists and local allies, the 'bandits of Dabieshan'. As a Ming dynasty local historian put it: 'Macheng has always been a battleground.'

In these hills was old Macheng, today a sizeable city. A walled county town, with its drum tower and market, it had maybe 10,000 people in the fourteenth century, more in the surrounding hill villages. In the early 1350s, a devastating drought, which lasted for three years, brought famine and virulent plague epidemics. The situation was so bad that people resorted to cannibalism. Soon the hills were awash with bloodshed as competing clans and local warlords fought each other. In this fevered environment, forces crystallised that would end the Yuan and usher in a new dynasty.

In 1338 a rebellion broke out just over the mountain passes to the north. Its leader was a peasant called Peng Hu, 'Peng the Virtuous'. Another self-proclaimed, righteous leader to the south in Hunan called Zhou Ziwang raised a 5,000-strong army and proclaimed himself king. Here in Macheng village, the people were soon caught up in these events. A local blacksmith calling himself Pusheng, 'all triumphant', became military leader in the area and in 1338 founded a religious military sect called 'the Lodge of the Holy One'. Over the next decade the sect grew and chose Peng as its spiritual leader.

Peng came from the highlands on the Jiangxi–Hunan border. He'd been a monk in a local temple and became an expert in the occult arts, sorcery, healing medicine and prophecy. He had wandered the highlands as a young man, a travelling healer, marked down as a sorcerer in the eyes of the authorities who tried to hunt him down. Preaching the coming of a new age, he made converts and led a failed revolt. He managed to escape execution and moved on, distributing sutras in woodblock printed texts and establishing local lodges across the area. The situation was ripe for revolution.

In this seething atmosphere of discontent, one of Peng's converts was another itinerant monk, a son of poor peasants from the famine lands of Anhui. This convert would become the founder of the Ming dynasty, one of the most remarkable figures in Chinese history: Zhu Yuanzhang (to whom we will return in due course).

Warlords arose carving up the south out of this maelstrom of prophecies, social protest and anger at the venality of those who ran the Mongol state. Some of them combined forces to make military alliances. In the Macheng region, the wandering healer Peng and the monk beggar Zhu were joined by a third, the self-proclaimed emperor Xu Shouhui. Xu Shouhui was a former cloth vendor who claimed to be Maitreya, the Buddha of future times, and promised to 'destroy the rich to help the poor'. Reacting to oppressive levies and the huge conscription drive by the Mongol government in Beijing, together they launched a rebellion and soon gathered an army of 10,000 men.

At the same time, other leaders arose to the east claiming descent from the Song royal family. Han Shantong's Red Turban Army, 'the Greater King of Light', made a confederation with 'the Southern Red Turbans', or the 'Red Army'. In 1351 they launched attacks that led to the collapse of Yuan power in the Yangtze valley. Another perfect storm of revolt had arisen, driven by poverty and resentment, but also by religion. It was not only directed against the Mongol state, but also attacked the Confucian elites, smashing their temples and schools, as they claimed to usher in the earthly rule of a divine saviour: 'The King of Light will appear'.

This was not only a class war, poor against rich, but also a Han nationalist revolt against alien rule, and it was waged with extreme violence and cruelty. When the 'Red Army' swept into Macheng, they killed every Yuan official they could lay their hands on, most of them Han Chinese not ethnic Mongolian. They were killed with great savagery, flaying alive, disembowelling and even, it was said, 'mincing and pickling' them. This might be taken as a grim metaphor, were it not for the insistence in our sources that cannibalism did indeed take place in the Macheng region during the famines and wars of the 1350s. Once the fuse was lit, it did not take long to spill over, exploiting smouldering resentments and antagonisms of class, wealth, religion and lineage ties, the stark divisions between rich and poor, the haves and have-nots.

This would happen again, in the same region, at the fall of the Ming in the seventeenth century and in the savage pogroms against the communists in the 1930s. Though let us not think it was only in China that such atrocities happened in history, when people turn against their neighbours with such savagery, exterminating whole elements of the population. In the twentieth century, too, there were the horrors of the Holocaust in the shtetls of Eastern Europe, the burnings and disembowellings during the Partition of India, and even the lynchings and burnings in the American Deep South.

As Yuan Mongol rule collapsed, eight rival contenders for power grew powerful enough to challenge for the throne of China. For seventeen years, there would be civil war. At root these were essentially class wars, eyewitnesses speaking of a consistent thread of the peasants waging war against the rich and powerful. The Red Army's constituency was the poor and landless, their rallying cry: 'Take from the rich to relieve the poor'. It would not be the last time.

In the dragon-scorched southern landscape of the 1350s and '60s, in the rich rice country of the lower Yangtze, fierce battles were fought as rival armies criss-crossed the delta and the fecund plains round Lake Tai. They sacked the mansions of the rich, looted villages, plundered crops and cut down mulberry groves. The fleets of a former local official, Chen Youliang, now calling himself 'King of the Han', terrorised the lower Yangtze. The victor would be the one who could offer a resolution to the violence with greater violence and thereby create a new allegiance.

PROSPEROUS SUZHOU

The climax of this battle for China took place in the lower Yangtze valley, along the north–south axis of the Grand Canal, between Yangzhou and Suzhou. Here, a former salt smuggler and some-time Mongol official, Zhang Shicheng, now called himself Duke of Wu and King of Dazhou. Zhang raised the standard of revolt against the Yuan around Yangzhou on the Grand Canal and the flat saltlands stretching round Gaoyou Lake to the Jiangsu coast. A one-time salt worker and boatman himself, Zhang knew the land and its people well. As the Yuan government control weakened, the people of these flatlands and canals had found themselves vic-tims of corrupt officials, greedy merchants and transport workers who turned to smuggling, ruffians and bandits. From these people Zhang quickly raised a large following, which he organised into a personal army. His troops plundered the towns of the region and captured the rich town of Gaoyou, on the Grand Canal. Zhang now declared a new dynasty, 'Utmost Orthodoxy'. This was a bold gesture indeed, as he controlled so little territory. Zhang knew, however, that the countryside all the way north up to the capital in Beijing was now in chaos as the dynasty's control weakened. Poor and desperate farming people who bound their heads with red cloth headbands, hence their name 'the Red Turbans', came in their thousands flocking to his banners.

The Yuan government sent a force from Yangzhou to crush the rebellion, but Zhang murdered their envoys. Reinforced, the Mongols then cornered Zhang's army in Gaoyou, but suddenly their commander was recalled north. The Mongol forces retreated in disorder, leaving Zhang to pursue his ambition of becoming emperor and creating a dynasty, just as the Song had been founded four centuries before. In 1356, Zhang ferried his army over to the south bank of the Yangtze and marched into the rich and densely populated agricultural lands around Lake Tai. That March, Zhang's forces began the siege of the biggest and most prosperous city of the region: Suzhou.

To go to Suzhou today takes an hour and a half, by road, from Shanghai. There have been big changes in the landscape since the Yuan. Today it is more than 30 miles from the sea, but then the city of Suzhou was at the mouth of the Yangtze estuary and controlled the coastal lands to the south. Over the centuries, with the huge amounts of silt carried downriver, the mouth has shifted and the vast conurbation of Shanghai now lies between Suzhou and the sea on reclaimed land. The wide fish-rich shoals controlled by the city in the Middle Ages are now Chongming island. Suzhou itself, though, is still a beautiful city despite being surrounded by serried rows of high-rise apartment blocks thrown up in the property boom of the past twenty years.

Suzhou was probably the largest non-capital city anywhere in the world between the fourteenth and eighteenth centuries. The signs of its former grandeur are still everywhere in its canals, bridges, pagodas, temples and more than 100 private gardens, mainly laid out under the Ming. Sacked in the Jurchen Wars of the twelfth century, it had been lavishly rebuilt by Han merchants and gentry classes, which had thrived under Mongol rule. Even then it was already proverbially famous for its beauties. An *Illustrated Guide to Suzhou* from the Song dynasty quotes the poet Bai Juyi on the '390 bridges with their vermilion railings', and explains that 'since his day many more have been built, all of very fine workmanship ... and all of stone or brick so you don't see red wooden railings anymore'. As for their names, noted a supplement to a guide for the traveller or antiquarian, 'there has never been a complete record ... the famous ones with either ancient or modern stories to tell about them are recorded here'. It was in truth a heavenly place: 'Look out towards Lake Tai from the Song River bridge', recommended the author, 'standing in the Suspended Rainbow Pavilion, and experience the light shining off the lake and the fresh breezes from the ocean and the waters rippling delightfully: this is one of the most beautiful sights in all the Suzhou region.' Now the city was surrounded by an enormous rebel army, a quarter of a million strong, with siege engines and rams, sappers and rocket launchers.

'SPEAKING MY FEELINGS'

Among the wealthy families who had settled in 'prosperous Suzhou'
during the Mongol peace, and who now waited for the outcome of
the siege with deep anxiety, were the Zhengs. An ancient lineage
of gentry, scholars and administrators, the Zhengs had originally
come from the town of Xingyang, near Zhengzou in Henan. They
had migrated south after the fall of the Northern Song in 1127 and
their ancestors had included a prime minister during the Southern
Song. Early in the Yuan dynasty, a Zheng had been assistant prefect
in Suzhou, where it was said the family 'owned half the prefecture'
and he had made his retirement home in one of the elegant water-
side mansions of the city. This man's granddaughter was Zheng
Yunduan. In her mid-teens she had married into a local gentry clan,
but in the past few years had fallen on hard times, 'poverty and bad
health fuelling constant worry', as she said. Thirty years old now
and mother of at least four young children, Yunduan is a poignant
eyewitness to the struggle that now unfolded in the south, in this
decisive moment in the history of China.

> I was born to a noble family that for generations has revered the
> Confucian studies. My father and elder brother instructed stu-
> dents in the classics and made a name for themselves throughout
> Suzhou. Because I was taught by my father, from my earliest
> years, I was able to read and recognise the written characters.
> Later my mind became set on study and by pilfering and stealing
> my father's leftover books, I acquired a rough understanding of
> duty and principle.

Growing up in this lovely place, with such a rich cultural life,
where the tradition of women poets and writers went back centuries, Zheng Yunduan had grown to love art and literature and
began to write poetry in her spare time. In her mid-teens, 'when
I came of age', as she says, she married a young scholar from a
local gentry family who became a local official. His ancestors also

had a long tradition of involvement in the arts. They had sons and daughters:

> My husband was a man of Confucian culture and our interests were very much alike. In the leisure allowed by my wifely duties I had an even greater opportunity to play and sport with writing brush and ink, to chant and *express my feelings and my inner nature* …

Under the Yuan, women's position in gentry society had taken a step backward from the Song. Indeed, for women it would prove to be something of a turning point in Chinese history. Their legal and social status declined and, in the middle classes, the kind of segregation we first saw in the Kaifeng scroll becomes more the norm. Women's rights to property and remarriage were weakened. The traditional Confucian view that a woman's place was in the home was reinforced. In everyday life the bondage was twofold: upper- and middle-class women were confined to the 'inner quarters', the women's chambers, and footbinding became more widespread, reinforced by a patriarchal ideology that stressed female fidelity.

Zheng was not the only woman to write against these conservative forces in fourteenth-century China, though rarely were women so explicit about their feelings, frustrations and their sense of injustice. In her poetry she deliberately sets out to subvert traditional literature by women, what women were expected to write about. She complains that much of contemporary women's poetry is sentimental and cliché-ridden, that she wants to 'do away with old habits in women's writing and reject the popular trends of the day'. Her own reading was wide, from philosophy and literature to history. She read the female Han historian Ban Zhao, as well as Du Fu and Li Qingzhao. She also read literature about women, for example Ban Zhao's *Seven Chapters of Precepts for My Daughters*, which, as a mother with daughters, Zheng saw as almost a feminist manifesto and read again and again. In her poetry, though expressing the habitual female deference to male critics as the arbiters of taste and style, she often adopts an unusual tone of authority and an awareness of her transgressive stance. Some women writers, she notes, will destroy their poems in deference to their subservient role, but she leaves clear instructions for her work to be preserved after her death.

Her confinement to the 'inner quarters' is a source of bitterness and frustration to her, but through art her mind can escape. The same goes for dreams. In her poem 'Writing My Feelings', Zheng recounts a dream in which she was in another life, in the Isles of Immortals over the Eastern Ocean, and had tended on the Queen Mother of the West, the ruler of female immortals. She was a woman who had 'fallen by accident into this vulgar world, this dusty net': a moving insight into the psychology of a woman artist of that time, whose guardian angels, as we might put it, are specifically empowering supernatural females.

From her poems we also learn about Yunduan's attitudes to the visual arts. At least thirty of her poems are about painting. One of them references a famous landscape painter of the Song dynasty and is placed at the start of her collection, which, as she says, she put 'in proper order' and must therefore have programmatic significance to her. It is a poem about the fate of a woman caught between home, marriage, the patriarchal male world and the possibilities of freedom outside. Playfully riffing on a poem by Du Fu, she scrutinises painted landscapes like those of the famous tenth-century artist Li Cheng, 'of layered hills and stacked peaks ... strange rocks and tall pines'. Apparently, on a folding screen, the painting is so finely executed in its illusory receding horizons in diluted ink that it acts in her imagination as a portkey to the outside world. Inside it she imagines she can hear the rushing water, transported to the sylvan glades of Mount Lu with its Buddhist and Daoist temples, which had attracted famous Tang poets like Bai Juyi.

The magical beauty of the landscape only intensifies her feelings of being trapped, for she then tells us that her feet are bound. Essentially, she is handicapped and cannot go out to seek fresh experiences. Here, translated by Peter Sturman, she describes the landscape in the painting:

> Revealed, I feel as if there, seated under Mount Lu,
> And feel as if all worldly dust has been cleansed
>   from my heart.
> But this body is destined to grow old in the inner quarters
> I hate not being able to go out in search of hidden places
> My stockings and linen and my black shoes have
>   ruined my life:
> Facing this painting I am filled with helpless frustration

Her writings are full of such sensitivity to women's experiences, and encourage women to write poetry for women. She even writes a warning, perhaps to her own daughters, about making unhappy arranged marriages above one's station. Like other women poets of the period, she speaks for equality and affection in companionate marriages. Zheng wants women to express their 'feelings and inner nature'. She also gives us a graphic insight, as Li Qingzhao did two centuries before, of women's fate in war:

> My Younger Sister followed her husband
> when he took up his post near Mount Lu.
> That was more than a year ago,
> we have yet to receive a letter with news.
> Recently we learned news of travellers and merchants
>   of bandits and robbers throughout the Jiangxi
>   province ...
> wherever they go they plunder the cities
> The blood of the butchered stains the streets
> ... with the Post service collapsed
> I do not know whether she is still alive
> Or has died in the midst of these disasters.

Over 1355–6, as the war unfolded, her health suddenly collapsed. She spent much of her last year stricken, in bed, suffering from extreme exhaustion and loss of weight; she became unsteady on her feet. Her illness sounds very much like cancer. Certainly, she knew she was dying, watching her body fall to pieces at the same time as her country, in a 'ten-year chill of death'. The deep psychological anguish caused by her sickness, which she shares with the reader, was disapproved of by later literary critics as a sign of female weakness. For us, it gives a precious glimpse into what she really felt in desperate times, both personal and political. We can well imagine her state intensified her depression in an extraordinarily sensitive and intelligent person who felt trapped by her physical situation, an incapacitating anxiety alleviated only by putting her brush to scroll.

In 1356 the Red Turban armies broke into Suzhou and began the sack of the city. Trapped in her family mansion, Zheng was unable to flee because of her bad health and her bound feet. In any case, presumably her male guardians would have preferred she commit suicide than compromise her position as a high-born woman. One of her last poems, 'The Mirror', is about her old 'bright shiny mirror in its case'. She had had this mirror since she was a fifteen-year-old, first wearing makeup. Remembering her glowing complexion at fifteen, 'fresh as a flower', she now scrutinises the face of this prematurely ageing thirty-year-old, already careworn and lined through illness and poverty. 'This morning the mirror too has grown dim, dusty and dirty, speckled with rust: we look into each other and sink into darkness,' she writes.

On the city walls the Yuan garrison fought with the local gentry, but in the end Suzhou fell and Zheng's home was ransacked and burned. The disaster broke her already frail health. That spring, on Tomb-Sweeping Day, knowing she had only months to live, she wrote a brief account of her life, translated by Peter Sturman:

Whenever I would write songs and poems, I would lock them away in chests and baskets, waiting for a master wordsmith to correct them and only later would I show them to other people. However, now I have been ill for many years and I may die at any time. Afraid that these poems might be lost without leaving a trace, I have copied them out once again and put them in proper order. I will place them in the family schoolroom so they may be shown to later generations . . .

She went on: 'Long ago, a Tang-dynasty hermit had a poetry gourd inscribed with the words: "only the one who finds this will understand my bitter heart". I could say the same. Zheng Yunduan, First Year of the Reign of Utmost Orthodoxy, April 1356.'

With the Red Turbans in charge in Suzhou and her estate in ruins, Zheng Yunduan died that year, at the age of thirty. As she had hoped, her works survived, preserved by her husband with a preface by a renowned Yuan scholar and artist, Qian Weishan. They were published by a fifth-generation descendent, in a woodblock edition, during the reign of the Jiajing emperor (1521–67). Without that, her works, her experience and her feelings would be lost to us. Remarkably, Zheng's memory is still guarded by the Zheng family today; as a clanswoman says, 'because she married out she does not appear in the Zheng family genealogy, but her poetry is still treasured by our women'.

THE KING OF DAZHOU: THE FALL OF THE YUAN AND THE RISE OF THE MING

When the siege of Suzhou was over, the rebel leader Zhang, 'King of Dazhou', entered the city and made it the seat of his new regime, as he bid to be the ruler of all China. Zhang was already master of the agricultural resources of the city's hinterland and of the salt revenues of his old home country, the coastal plain north of the Yangtze. So Zhang became the richest of all the contenders for power, and among the people of Suzhou he was long remembered for his just rule.

Zhang's kingdom in Suzhou lasted eleven years. His forces were slowly ground down by bigger and better-organised armies. Slowly, his territories were reduced. By now events were moving with unstoppable momentum. In 1367, the great-grandson of Kublai Khan abandoned Beijing and fled over the mountains back to the steppes of Mongolia, leaving the Chinese to fight it out among themselves. The Yuan dynasty was finished. That same year Zhang's capital in Suzhou was besieged by the Red Turbans' great rival: a brutal and charismatic generalissimo who had gathered huge support to his name. Zhu Yuanzhang, a sometime beggar, the follower of 'Peng the Virtuous' whom we met in the azalea-clad mountains of Dabieshan, was now poised to take centre stage in Chinese history.

After amassing his power south of the river in Nanjing, Zhu marched on Suzhou to fight Zhang, 'King of Dazhou', for the lordship of mid-China. The city fell on 1 October 1367 after a ten-month siege; by then packed with refugees, its population inside the walls was more than a million starving people. Zhu strictly ordered no plunder, no rape. Zhang was captured and killed. However, his tomb is still pointed in Suzhou today, in an industrial park outside the South West Gate. Every year on his birthday, 30 July, he is remembered by the locals for his generosity and good governance. They still make straw toys in his name and hang them at the doors of their houses, in the shape of dragons.

The victor at Suzhou, however, the winner in the civil wars and in the expulsion of the Mongols, Zhu Yuanzhang was destined to become one of the greatest figures in Chinese history. A peasant by birth, like Liu Bang, the founder of the Han, Zhu had been merely one of several warlords, self-proclaimed emperors, who had founded new dynasties during the chaotic days of the fall of the Mongols; but his was the one that endured. Suspicious, coarse, cruel, utterly ruthless but a creative genius, he would found one of the great eras of stability of Chinese history. In an echo of the ancient millennial cults out of which his movement had grown, the new dynasty was to be called 'the Bringer of Light': the Ming.

13

THE MING

The Ming dynasty still defines our popular image of Chinese civilisation: the Forbidden City, the Temple of Heaven, the Great Wall, Ming porcelain and painting. Together they speak of high culture, exquisite sensibility and the dazzling glamour of empire. This was a crucial period in Chinese history, which established a bureaucratic despotism under the first Ming emperor that would have great repercussions for the later Chinese state. But it was also the time of the famous voyages of Zheng He to India, the Persian Gulf and Africa. In the Late Ming period, too, a rich middle-class culture arose with many achievements in the arts and literature. New intellectual currents also arose, contesting autocracy with arguments about China's political culture that are still alive today. We start with the amazing story of the founder of the Ming, the peasant emperor Zhu Yuanzhang.

We have already met Zhu, the poor farmer's son from Anhui who fought with peasant rebels in the hills of Henan in the dark days at the end of the Yuan. He had been a follower of 'Peng the Virtuous' and his motley crew of visionaries, mystics and rebels, fired by the strange swirling soup of peasant mythologies, Buddhist eschatology and prophecies of the 'King of Light' who would come to cleanse the earth. Out of all this Zhu emerged as one of the most important figures in Chinese history, whose revolutionary rule still casts its shadow over China today. Seldom has one individual had such an impact on history.

By an extraordinary chance we have the emperor's own story of his early life, composed in 1378 for a stele at his parents' tomb. He also related the tale of his rise to power in a fascinating text called *The Story of a Dream*, one of the most remarkable of all ruler auto-biographies. Zhu was born in 1328, in a small village in the Huai River valley near Fengyang. As he himself tells us, his father was a peasant, 'enduring all the hardships of agriculture, working day and night, always worrying'. The Zhu family had six children, but were too poor to feed so many mouths, so the second and third sons were given away to other families, and the girls were married off. The youngest boy, Zhu worked as a shepherd and migrant farmhand. In spring 1344, he was an already intimidating teenager: 'tall and strongly built with a great nose and a bulging forehead'. In later imperial portraits, his face suggests a man of extraordinary and implacable will.

During this time, the Anhui dustbowl was swept by drought and the fields were so dry that the earth became patterned 'with cracks like the back of a tortoise'. The millet seedlings yellowed and with-ered and the people prayed for rain. They flocked to the temple of the dragon god, the deity of waters. There, the old people knelt in the hot sun and the children wore crowns of willow. Despite their efforts, no rain came. Instead of rain, the locusts swarmed the area, 'rising and circling in the air', their sound drowning out the birds. Facing starvation and reduced to eating grass and insects, the locals were laid low by dysentery and disease. Then the plague struck. 'All at once calamities gripped the land and my family met with disaster,' Zhu said. His father fell sick and died. Soon after, his elder brother followed, then his mother. The family were even turned away by their landlord, Liu De, when they begged for land for graves. Zhu never forgot their landlord's response: 'he did not care about our needs, but just carried on with arrogant shouting'. The landlord's brother, however, 'showing heart, kindness and benevolence, offered us some yellow earth'. In the end, Zhu's family were buried without coffins or burial clothes. It was an inciting incident in his life. When he became emperor, in vengeful filial piety, Zhu built a mausoleum for his parents. It still stands outside Fengyang, with a long spirit way lined by stone figures and a huge stele that stands over 7 metres high, bearing Zhu's deeply personal account of his own life.

'In my village', as Zhu tells the tale, 'food was scarce, with grasses and bark serving as nourishment. As for myself, what did I have but fear to the point of madness?' Searching for odd jobs, he tearfully separated from his brother: 'under the bright sun in Heaven, sorrow split our innards open'. Zhu then entered a local Buddhist monastery, the Temple of the Tiger Empress, which still survives today near Fengyang. There, at least, one might get a bowl of rice a day. Yet after two months in the 'fearsome drought' the monks also ran out of food and Zhu was forced on the road with a begging bowl. He roamed for three years, 'my shadow my companion'. As the clouds of war gathered in 1348, he returned to the monastery. Mongol rule was collapsing, warlords were on the rise, rebels were massing under the banners of the 'White Lotus' and the 'Red Turban'. Local militias had banded together in the Huai River region to defend their communities. The rebel groups were loosely coordinated, inspired by millenarian hopes for the coming of the Maitreya Buddha and Manichaean-tinged beliefs about the imminent arrival of a saviour, a prince of light, who would defeat the powers of darkness.

The story of the war is recounted in Zhu's *Story of a Dream*. Zhu tells us that in 1351 'the Yuan Zhizheng emperor was the ruler; but they were weak and failed to do their job ... officials usurped the rulers' prerogatives, their powers of "terrors and blessings". For the net ropes of sovereign rule had come untied and there was confusion throughout the world.' In the next year, 1352, a great rebellion broke out in Anhui 'like raging fire, burning villages, killing people like cutting hemp and decent people could not protect themselves between dawn and dusk'. For Zhu it was a day of destiny. On 15 April he cast a divination with wooden yin-yang oyster shells and left his monastery to join the Red Turban rebels. He was twenty-four, and because of his intelligence and courage Zhu rapidly rose through the ranks to become a commander: 'in less than a month I gathered a multitude and our red banners covered the countryside

and spilled over the ridges'. He then married the adopted daughter
of the Red Turban leader, called Miss Ma. A nineteen-year-old refugee from the same county as Zhu, Ma had been brought into the
leader's household as a servant and could read and write. She would
become Zhu's loyal supporter, going on campaigns with him and
even, on occasion, rallying the troops in his absence. Later, it was
said, she was his adviser and, as empress, would manage his papers
and handle investigations in her own right. Though Zhu had many
consorts as emperor, this was the partnership that mattered.

With war sweeping the south, Zhu now had an army. He captured the city of Nanjing, which became his base for wars against
his rivals. By now, he said, it was clear to all that the Yuan dynasty
had lost the Mandate of Heaven. 'The guide rope of the Yuan could
no longer be restored and its leaders had not consulted the Founding
Ancestor's Laws while the other warlords and rebels lacked all
benevolence,' Zhu said. Then came the battle for Suzhou and the
defeat of Zhang Shicheng (above page 272), at which point Zhu's
followers called on him to be the emperor.

Just before dawn on 23 January 1368, he performed the rituals
to inaugurate a new dynasty with the city inauspiciously blanketed
in snow: 'At the hour of my sacrificial ritual and the assumption
of the throne, a fragrant mist arose, coalesced in the heavens and
then came down again, enveloping the earth in a bright cloud.
Only the middle star was still exposed to view. I then proceeded to
adopt the reign title "Hongwu".' The grandiose reign title may be
translated as meaning 'Abundant Martial Virtue' or 'Great in War'
(The Terminator?). The name Zhu took for his dynasty reflected the
Manichean cosmology of the rebels from whose forces he had arisen.
He chose the word for 'brightness': Ming.

ZHU THE TERMINATOR

A peasant, then, had become a dynastic founder, like a number of
great figures in Chinese history, such as Liu Bang of the Han and, of
course, Mao Zedong himself. Though poorly educated, Zhu was a

man of action, a bold and shrewd tactician, with a visionary mind. He was also hard-bitten and utterly ruthless. Like many tyrants in history he would ultimately descend into paranoia, gathering power more and more into his own hands and eventually ordering the murder of thousands.

As soon as his rule was established, Zhu suppressed pockets of resistance in the south and sent his armies north to chase the Mongols out of China. When he took Beijing he noted that 'the markets did not fall into chaos, and brave officials came forward to reveal their skills and shining qualities'. Many Mongols stayed on after the fall of the Yuan, in the military and as translators and interpreters. Still, Zhu ordered the removal of outward traces of the Mongol presence in China. His subjects were forbidden to speak Mongolian or to use Mongolian dress and hats, to practise rituals or perform Mongolian marriages. The new China was to be a revival of Han culture. And to create a secure and stable society, the state apparatus would be all-powerful. Never again was China to suffer the horrors of the chaos Zhu had lived through. How he achieved this would leave its mark on China to this day.

NANJING: THE 'SOUTHERN CAPITAL'

Zhu made Nanjing his new capital, the fifth of China's great historic capitals. The city would be transformed into a magnificent imperial centre, a symbol of the might and legitimacy of Ming rule. Twenty thousand families were ordered to move there to augment a population badly depleted by war. An immense circuit of walls was constructed, which still stands today. Twenty-two miles long and up to 60 feet high, it is the longest set of city walls in the world. Of the original thirteen gates, the giant 'China Gate' survives intact; a fortress in itself with three barbicans and four separate sets of gateways in huge tunnels, in all, 420 feet deep. The work to build the walls took approximately twenty years and involved communities in nearly 200 counties across the south of Hongwu's empire. Hundreds of local work gangs manufactured the 350 million bricks and transported them to the building sites in Nanjing. The names of each community and even of the officials who were responsible were stamped onto the bricks, which can still be seen today in the city wall. Here is just one example:

PREFECTURE – Nankang
COUNTY – Du Chang
BRICK DESPATCHER – Zhao Bin
SUPERVISOR – You Qing
TITHING HEAD – Fang Chaozhang
KILNMASTER – Lu Li
BRICK MAKERS – Guangfu Monastery

The labour involved to build the walls, as well as a thousand other projects across the new empire, was organised through the '*lijia*', or 'hundreds and tithings' system that Hongwu established and which was a key part of his plan for China. A peasant himself, the emperor had a vision of China as a giant community of village-based peasants, peacefully engaged in farming and textile production. It would be a world where everyone knew their place. He did not favour commerce; indeed, he issued edicts against it. The common people of the villages, Hongwu thought, should provide the bulk of the products and services required by the state: rendering their taxes, giving grain and rice, making bricks, raising levies for dyke construction and filling army quotas.

To facilitate this, Hongwu organised local communities across China into village groups of 110 households each. The largest ten households were to ensure the whole group fulfilled its tax levies and organise labour gangs for public works. Each of the ten 'large households' took responsibility in turn, with one of their men becoming 'tax captain' on a ten-year rota. To set up the system, Hongwu needed a register of all households in his empire. So he ordered a new census to be carried out along with a land survey. The census noted down the names of each family, the numbers of able-bodied men in the household and how many women and children there were. This became known as the Yellow Register. The land survey noted down each plot, who owned it and the size and quality of the land. The land register became known as the Fishscale Register, because the maps of all the small plots of land looked like the scales of a fish. However, it was also called the 'watertight' register, because 'not a drop of land' was to escape its reach. On a far bigger scale, this was the Chinese equivalent of England's Domesday Book.

TANGYUE: THE VIEW FROM THE VILLAGE

In their village of Tangyue, deep in the Huizhou hills, lived the Bao family. We previously met them working for the Mongols, with one son even learning to speak and write their language. Now the Baos were recorded in the Yellow Register as a large household and were made responsible for tax levies and public works in their locality.

Today, in the family's old courtyard house up the narrow alleys of Tangyue, the head of the clan, Bao Xunsheng, still keeps the woodblock-printed family genealogy. Originally compiled in Late Ming times, it records their family traditions as drawn up in the seventeenth century, added to in successive editions over time. Thread-bound on soft, yellowing paper, with neat rows of characters, the book tells the story of each generation of the Bao lineage, with imaginary woodcut portraits. Bao Xunsheng, the current head of Tangyue village, reads some of the story, offering a vivid glimpse of Hongwu's revolution at grassroots:

When Bao Jibao was just eighteen years old he became tax captain in our community. There had been much destruction in the local area during the chaos at the end of the Yuan period, county offices destroyed, weeds sprouting everywhere, bridges damaged. When the bandits came everyone had scattered into the hills. The local magistrate called for a census to ascertain the labour gangs of the hundreds and tithings, who would take on the reconstruction. So Bao Jibao had to undertake the heavy task of compiling the Yellow Registers. Because there was no fixed format at this

time, Bao Jibao ended up compiling records in the morning and
then having to change them at night. He became exhausted with
the documenting and calculating, and there was no end to the
frustration. The following year, discrepancies were found in the
register and Bao Jibao had to go to the capital in Nanjing to make
the corrections and deal with the legal punishment. This kept him
from paying attention to his own livelihood, tending farm fields.
He had to pay a fine, as well as cover the costs of travelling there
and back. The whole thing was a headache from beginning to end!

REBUILDING DESPOTISM: THE YELLOW REGISTERS

Hongwu's tax system did indeed generate gigantic amounts of
paperwork. The records for the entire population were stored by the
Finance Ministry on three islands in the Xuanwu lake in Nanjing,
curated by Finance Ministry staff. Each time the national census
was carried out, thirty rooms had to be added to the archives to
accommodate the new records. Though largely destroyed at the time
of the Manchu conquest in 1645, it was perhaps the greatest archival
project in history before modern times.

The first census was done in 1391, with standardised question
forms printed out and distributed to the masses through local officials. One thousand university students helped with the filing, under
the supervision of revenue officers. Four copies of each survey were
made; three for local and provincial government offices and the
fourth under yellow covers for the national archives. After the first
survey it is estimated that they expanded at 60,000 volumes per
survey. By the end of the dynasty the archive stood at 1.7 million
volumes stored in 700 storage rooms, representing twenty-seven
surveys, the last one in 1642.

After Hongwu's day, however, accuracy declined rapidly through
abuse, corruption and sheer exhaustion. In the county gazetteers,
some communities were still recording the fourteenth-century
figures 200 years on. The ambition of it all was astounding. Every
ten years they produced statistics on population, birth and death

for every household in China, with widows, minors, old-aged and handicapped people exempted from tax. Even ethnic minorities in the remote south had their own sections. To take one sample year, in 1542 the data came from 1,139 counties, 230 subprefectures and 240 prefectures. It was so vast an enterprise that there were cases of insanity and suicide among the staff, the burden too much for overloaded brains. Battling with the limits of technology, human frailty and dishonesty, not to mention the depredations of nature, Hongwu's desire for absolute control was an impossible dream. In 1609 the editor of one local gazetteer condemned the whole enterprise as 'a waste of paper and writing brushes'. Now, with plastic identity cards, today's Chinese government can do what Hongwu wanted with the click of a computer key.

THE ACCESSION OF YONGLE: DESPOTISM ENTHRONED

In his later years, Hongwu became increasingly suspicious and paranoid. He instigated murderous purges in which thousands died. Trusting no one, he executed anyone that he suspected to be corrupt or treasonous, even nine of the twenty-four 'heroes' who had been with him since the beginning of his amazing rise to power. He flew into uncontrollable rages, from which only Empress Ma dared to restrain him. Eventually he got rid of the post of prime minister and took on the work himself. The reign would be a turning point in Chinese history, concentrating power in the person of the emperor. It would prove a dangerous legacy.

Hongwu died in 1398. His eldest son was already dead and he had decided that the throne should be inherited by his grandson. The new emperor was twenty years old, a bookish and gentle young man who was concerned about the harshness of his grandfather's rule. He took the reign name Jianwen, meaning 'establishing civility', and began to promote more benevolent Confucian governance.

Jianwen also moved to curb the power of his uncles, the imperial princes. One of these men was the energetic and ambitious Prince of Yan, Hongwu's fourth son. Schooled in horsemanship and the handling of firearms, swords and crossbows, the Prince of Yan had grown up an excellent soldier, who, when he was twenty, had been sent north to Beijing, charged with defending China against renewed Mongol incursions. When the new emperor began to implement a more Confucian style of government, the Prince of Yan became concerned that his nephew's policies were endangering the state. He rose in revolt and, after a three-year civil war, Yan captured Nanjing in 1402 and seized the throne for himself. The emperor, his consort and the crown prince died in the burning palace.

The new reign was to be called 'Yongle' – 'Everlasting Happiness'. Of course, when an autocrat takes a name like that, the people must beware. Yongle executed or imprisoned thousands who had opposed him. One of the most famous was a senior official called Fang Xiaoru, who refused to draft the proclamation of Yongle's succession to the throne. Yongle was so infuriated that he ordered the punishment of 'nine degrees'. This meant not only Fang's execution, but that of his whole family, in-laws, friends and students to nine degrees of relationship. In Fang's case, however, Yongle ordered 'make it ten'. In a society where kinship and ancestors are so central, there was no more cruel a penalty. Fang was forced to watch his brother's execution before his own, when it is said that he wrote, in his own blood, the word 'usurper'. In the end, 873 people were killed. Dozens more officials were tortured and killed or banished, while others committed suicide as a protest against the usurpation. Conscious that many questioned his right to the throne, Yongle was determined to expunge the memory of his accession.

One of his early decisions as emperor was to move the capital to the north, to his own power base. There, razing the old Mongol capital, he laid out a vast new city called Beijing, 'North Capital'. The construction of Beijing took twenty years. At its heart was a vast theatre for imperial ritual, with huge temples, a processional way, and the enormous precinct of the Forbidden City. The Forbidden City was built as a compound of more than 800 rooms, including three main receiving halls, three palaces, a hundred chambers for offices, archives, libraries, factories, artisans' studios and storerooms. For this project over a million labourers felled thousands of logs, quarried rocks, manufactured bricks and tiles, burned lime and dredged the Grand Canal to bring raw materials into the new capital. The construction was not finished until 1421. On New Year's Day, in a great ceremony before the Tiananmen Gate, Yongle was greeted by thousands of foreign envoys, officials and military officers saluting his rule as 'Lord of the World'. Save for a brief period under the Republic, Beijing has been the capital of China ever since.

THE GREAT CHINESE VOYAGES

Just underneath the northwest walls of Nanjing, a kilometre from the banks of the Yangtze River, stands the temple of Tianfei, the goddess of the sea. In her sanctum she sits enthroned in all her glory, with a yellow silk cloak and a golden crown, framed by gilded columns and huge yellow silk curtains that billow like ships' sails. In front of her pavilion is an enormous stone stele resting on a giant tortoise, and on it is carved a thrilling summary of the Chinese voyages:

> The countries beyond the horizon and at the ends of the earth have acknowledged our hegemony. As far as the most westerly horizon and the most northerly of the northern countries, however far they may be, we have calculated the distances and the routes ... we have traversed more than 100,000 *li* of immense spaces of water and have beheld in the ocean huge waves like mountains rising sky high. We have set eyes on barbarian regions hidden far away in the blue translucency of light vapours, while our sails, loftily unfurled like clouds, continued their course day and night with starry speed, breasting the awesome waves as if we were treading a public highway. Truly we were under the protection of the goddess of the sea ...

Between 1405 and 1433, initiated by Yongle, the Chinese sent seven great voyages to Southeast Asia and across the Indian Ocean, visiting the Persian Gulf, India and East Africa. Their leader, Zheng He, was a high-ranking Muslim courtier, a eunuch of huge diplomatic experience. They brought back new knowledge, rare foods and plants, spices, pepper in huge quantities and even exotic animals, including a giraffe, which the Chinese identified with the mythical unicorn – an auspicious sign for the Yongle emperor.

Zheng He's fleets are thought to have included the biggest wooden vessels yet built, dwarfing the tiny ships which would later take Columbus and Magellan on their journeys. The fleets were so huge that the first one alone, of sixty-two ships, was crewed by 27,000 men. They took teams of specialists with them, including doctors, naturalists, botanists and scientists. For fresh food they even carried vegetable gardens on board.

Why Yongle commanded this enormous expenditure of resources is still the subject of much controversy. Today in China the journeys are characterised as peaceable missions to show the flag, encourage trade and wield Chinese soft power, but the idea that Zheng He's huge expeditions were done for no real political, economic or practical gain is, on the face of it, unlikely. The missions carried troops, and in Kerala it was long remembered that they came ashore with weapons, body armour and helmets. They certainly engaged in warfare, destroying pirate fleets near Palembang and intervening in civil wars to establish friendly regimes in Sri Lanka and Sumatra.

Although Zheng He was not trying to colonise or to conquer, it would appear that his goal was to establish a network of power and control between China and the Indian Ocean, over those who, in the words of his Nanjing inscription, 'resisted the transforming influence of Chinese culture'. He gave lavish gifts and received tribute, and each embassy brought back envoys who returned on later journeys or on separate smaller voyages. The tomb of a king of Borneo, who died in China, can still be seen in a leafy corner of Nanjing, a surviving trace of these far-flung contacts.

The aim of the voyages, then, was to establish or reinforce trading relations mutually beneficial to China and its various tributary states and kingdoms, and to ensure stability along its maritime trade routes: 'the sea routes were cleaned up and made peaceful so the natives were able to pursue their vocations in peace'. But over the three decades these goals seem to have expanded. Of the seven 'foreign expeditionary armadas', the first three went via Southeast Asia to the Malabar coast of south India, 'the great land of the western ocean'. By the fourth voyage, the scope of trade and diplomatic activity had expanded to West Asia, to Hormuz and the Persian Gulf, employing Arab and Persian interpreters and pilots. The last three voyages pushed further still, to the Arabian Peninsula and the Red Sea, Aden, Mogadishu, and East Africa down to Malindi. Many of these sites, from Kenya to the island of Hormuz, have yielded Ming pottery. In the Red Sea, in the old port of Suakin in Sudan, Yongle-period ceramics have recently been excavated. An Arab account of two Chinese ships arriving in Jeddah in 1432 suggests that the Muslim Zheng He, or some of his officers, also made the journey to Mecca.

Among other Arab accounts, one from the Yemeni kingdom describes the arrival of 'Dragon-ships' in the city of Aden 'with messengers from the ruler of China bearing brilliant gifts for the Sultan, including the finest silk woven with golden threads and exquisite ceramics'. On a second visit in 1420, it was reported that the Chinese greeted the sultan without kissing the ground in front of him, but after receiving their salutations the sultan replied: 'Welcome, and how nice of you to come!'

None of this should be seen as exploration. All these routes had long been travelled by Arab navigators. The Chinese themselves had first gone to East Africa as early as the Tang dynasty. In some places, such as the Straits of Malacca, there was a deliberate effort to develop commercial entrepots. Palembang was an important trading post and way station for the Chinese, but also a base for journeys into the Indian Ocean. The voyages, then, were to advertise Chinese power, exact tribute and open up new trade routes, and in particular, to get the states of Southeast Asia to acknowledge the power and majesty of the Ming.

Recent discoveries regarding the ships themselves have cast new light on this famous moment in maritime history. In 2018, the Ming civil dockyards were definitively located for the first time, during urban developments in Nanjing. As for the site of the naval dockyards, the construction site of the big 'treasure ships', this remained well known, west of the city walls on a tributary of the Yangtze, and was marked on early maps with its waterlogged basins. In the late twentieth century, it was still possible to ask local taxi drivers for the 'old Ming dockyard'. There in 2003, during the preparations for the Olympic Games, the site was drained and excavated, with an anchor and tools, adzes, hammers, rope, tackle, shoes and weapons among the objects recovered.

There is still much controversy about the size of the boats. It is generally assumed that Zheng He's biggest ships were simply larger versions of the ocean-going junks that had plied between China and the Persian Gulf during the Song and Yuan dynasties and which are described by Marco Polo and other European writers. The last of these seagoing boats, which still after the Second World War sailed up to Shandong and Korea and down to Vietnam, were known as Pechili traders. They could be up to 180 feet long with five masts and high ornamented sterns. Such ships appear in photographs of the late nineteenth century, moored in rows like old tramp steamers – perhaps the boats described as 'ocean traders' on Zheng He's third voyage were of this type. Modern theories that the Ming 'treasure ships' could have exceeded 400 feet in length are rejected by all experts in naval technology, as the size of wooden ships was always limited by the length of trees available for the keel. For sailing in heavy seas, a single strongly protected scarf-jointed keel is the most that shipwrights judge acceptable for safety. According to today's traditional shipbuilders in Fujian, this would allow a boat, in Chinese junk style, to be between 200 and 240 feet long, a size that would fit with the find in one of the Nanjing basins, of a 35-foot stern rudder post.

'TO BOLDLY GO ...'

At Point Pedro on the northern tip of Ceylon, in a typical piece of ecumenical thinking, Zheng He left a trilingual inscription to the deities of what he thought were the three great religions of the world: Allah, the Buddha and the Hindu Shiva, in Persian, Chinese and Tamil. At this moment, it might seem, China was poised to dominate much of the world. In 1433, however, the voyages abruptly ceased. In a memorable advert for the aerospace company Lockheed in the 1980s, this decision was compared to giving up the moon programme after Apollo 8. That, though, is to misunderstand the concerns of Chinese civilisation. The Confucian ethic was the cultivation of the Middle Kingdom, not the conquest or domination of other peoples. China was civilisation. Why go to all this effort and expense to make contact with, say, Africa?

In the end, the Confucian bureaucracy and the Ministry of Finance complained that the enterprise brought no profit and was enormously expensive. For all the treasure lavished, 'many perished by shipwreck or [were] marooned in foreign lands, so that after twenty years those who returned [were] no more than two in ten'. That is probably the exaggeration of a hostile party. Still, after Yongle's death the voyages were stopped immediately upon the accession of Hongxi in 1424. They were resumed under Xuande, but after the seventh voyage and the death of Zheng He, the government banned further voyages and dismantled the ships. Unfortunately for later historians, they even confiscated and destroyed the logbooks on the grounds that they could be 'dangerous to thinking'. According to a fifteenth-century account:

> Documents of the treasure voyages were removed from the archives of the Ministry of War and destroyed on the basis that they were 'deceitful exaggerations of bizarre things far removed from the testimony of people's ears and eyes' and that the expeditions of Zheng He to the Western Ocean wasted tens of myriads of money and grain and moreover the people who met their deaths [on these expeditions] may be counted in myriads. Although he returned with wonderful precious things, what benefit was it to the state? This was merely an action of bad government of which ministers should severely disapprove. Even if the old archives were still preserved they should be destroyed in order to suppress [knowledge of these things] at the root.

In 1492, Vasco da Gama sailed into Cochin, where the locals told him of the great Chinese fleets that had come seventy years before. This is a symbolic moment in world history, when the technological lead would pass to the Europeans, who would rise to world domination using Chinese inventions that Zheng He had carried with him: gunpowder, the stern rudder, the magnetic compass and paper charts.

Nevertheless, Zheng He's voyages left many legacies. Commerce was certainly one. A Ming writer attributed the flourishing state of the country during the fifteenth century to the commercial expansion in this period. It was even suggested that the enormous quantities of luxuries, spices and pepper that were imported loosened up the economy, opened up longer-term trading relations with the countries of South Asia and increased the market for foreign goods in China, even liberating productive forces among the lower classes:

> From the time when the Yongle emperor ascended to the throne, messengers were sent to every country and the tribute poured in. Precious merchandise in unprecedented quantities, as compared with former dynasties, filled the warehouses to overflowing. The poor undertook to act as sellers, occasionally making a great fortune through it and as a result the empire's wealth increased immensely.

So we should see the voyages as motivated neither by exploration, nor by conquest; let alone as mere flag waving. Instead, they were part of a sustained attempt to establish China as a maritime power with a network of commercial links across the South China Sea and into the Indian Ocean. And today, as China reaches out westwards once more on the Belt and Road, Zheng He has become a national hero, a symbol for the new self-confident world of Chinese expansionism and naval might.

'CONFUSIONS OF PLEASURE'

There were also pressing political and military reasons for giving up on sea power. In the 1430s, the threat was growing by land from China's old enemies, the Mongols. Out to the north, Ming armies made almost annual expeditions beyond the mountains into the vast steppe lands of Mongolia. Then, in 1449, the Zhengtong emperor was defeated in battle near Beijing and captured by the Mongols. The greatest military fiasco in the Ming period, this led to a massive rebuilding of the Great Wall into the form we see today, as well as a new mood of defensiveness and retrenchment. The great era of expansion was over and would not be repeated until the eighteenth century, when the Qing dynasty expanded into Xinjiang and Mongolia and once more addressed the *nanyang*, the southern sea.

At home, though, China was changing, reaping the benefits of decades of stability. In the fifteenth century, small market towns began to spring up everywhere, and China's economy began to grow and diversify. The population rose to upwards of 200 million. Incredibly, when three million lived in Tudor England, between a quarter and a third of the people of the world lived under Ming rule.

In the south, the populous lands of the delta had recovered from the wars of the fourteenth century, especially in rich cities like Suzhou. Ming China had begun as an agricultural state with a stifling command economy, fulfilling Hongwu's blueprint for a nation sustained by an obedient peasantry. Now the growth of markets gave birth to a new urban moneyed class who would begin to loosen the grip of Ming autocracy. From a starting point in which merchants occupied the lowest rung of the ideal social structure propounded by the Ming's founding emperor, by the seventeenth century commerce was a profession in its own right and all aspects of culture, from artworks, ceramics, books and fashion, to education and leisure services, were commercial commodities.

There is nowhere better to see how this worked than in the city of Suzhou. Before there was Shanghai, it has been said, there was Suzhou. With its canals and workshops, gardens and scholars, Suzhou was the largest non-capital city in the world between 1400 and 1800. It was a place whose wealth grew not from politics, but from commerce and manufacture, where 'grain transports and merchant ships gather like clouds'. During the Yuan dynasty, Marco Polo thought Suzhou was 'a large and magnificent city ... the number of its inhabitants so great as to be the subject of astonishment'. The city had entered the Ming defeated and mistrusted after its battle against the Ming founder. Yet thriving on the Yangtze River trade and the silk industry round Lake Tai, high-quality local specialisation soon made the city prosper once more. In the Ming, they said, Suzhou was heaven on earth, like Renaissance Florence with its high culture, palaces and mansions and its flourishing print culture. Political, cultural and economic success brought spectacular success in the imperial exams, too. The long lists of the top degrees won by Suzhou scholars are still proudly displayed on the walls of the shrine to the god of learning, in the Xuanmiao temple in the centre of town.

Even today, in Suzhou's temples, gardens and family mansions, the visitor can sense the new world of conspicuous consumption, of middle-class private wealth and taste, during the later Ming. On their table was the finest blue-glaze porcelain, bought by the new rich from their local art dealers and made by thousands of indentured workers in the state pottery kilns. Soon, they would be exporting these to Europe. To meet consumer demand, old arts like lacquer and silk reached new heights, the best work so coveted that collectors travelled hundreds of miles to buy the top brand names from the most famous houses.

Through the sixteenth century, then, China shook off the commercial ban by the first Ming emperor and got used to a flood of new commodities. Even the poor could rise, through commerce, to wear silk and educate their children. The strict agricultural order of the first Ming emperor was being loosened by the creative energies of the Chinese people.

These changes were visible in the countryside too. In little Tangyue, in Anhui, the Bao family had by now joined the rural gentry and their village had a fine main street, paved with stone slabs. It also had a beautiful clan hall for worship of the ancestors, with elegant memorial arches commemorating family members, including women, who had benefited society with their charity. In the sixteenth century, they also had several successful exam graduates. In the 1520s, after ten years of study, Bao Xiangxian went to the capital and passed the metropolitan exams, a great academic achievement for a man from a small rural place. He served as a senior official as far away as Yunnan, where he helped defuse a rebellion by the local Miao people. After his retirement at around sixty, Xiangxian came home to Tangyue and built a clan hall. He published a rule book in 1567, which listed the rituals and sacrifices to honour the virtuous ancestors. But, Bao added, 'we should also sacrifice to those who make money, because they establish wealth on behalf of all the descendants'. It was a sign of the times.

'Back in the late 1400s', the Tangyue local gazetteer reflected, 'in the Huizhou area every family was self-sufficient with a house to live in, land to cultivate, mountains to log and a garden to plant.' In the 1520s the sources of wealth began to diversify and merchants and traders became more numerous. By the 1570s, 'the number of those who gained wealth from trade had increased still more ... Now it is the god of gold that rules the heavens and the god of money which rules the earth.' China was on the cusp of change.

MATTEO RICCI

In 1580 a European visitor arrived in the trading post of Macao on the South China Sea, where for the past thirty years the Portuguese had been allowed to engage in seasonal trade up the Pearl River. Matteo Ricci belonged to the Society of Jesus, the Jesuits, the shock troops of the Catholic Counter Reformation in Europe. Ricci's goal, incredibly, was to convert the Chinese to Christianity. He hoped to find a Chinese Constantine who would accept the Christian message and propagate it to his people. Using Confucian ideas to interpret Christianity to the Chinese, Ricci argued that China was a deeply moral civilisation, which had always believed in God as *Tianshen*, 'the Lord of Heaven', but that the redemptive message of Christianity would be the completion of their faith. Ricci, too, was happy to accept Chinese beliefs and rituals for the veneration of the dead, though other missionaries thought he had gone too far in his affection for Chinese culture and religion.

It was a problem encountered by the Catholic Church in many places across the world in the era of European conquest and colonialism. The difference was that China was a great and ancient civilisation; its learning, social customs and traditions far older and more rooted than those in Europe. Ricci would spend the rest of his life there, until his death in 1610, and in the end things went the other way round; one might say he was converted by China. The Vatican refused his attempts to bridge civilisations by accepting the spiritual basis of the cult of ancestors, but Ricci had come to love and admire the Chinese and what he called their 4,000-year-old tradition. In his Chinese diary he makes some thought-provoking comparisons between the Chinese and the Europeans which have relevance to the whole of Chinese history:

It seems worthwhile to record a few more ways in which the Chinese differ from the Europeans. It is remarkable when we stop to consider it that in a kingdom of almost limitless expanse and innumerable population, abounding in resources of every kind, although they have a well-equipped army and navy that could easily conquer neighbouring nations, neither the emperor nor his people ever think of waging wars of aggression. They are quite content with what they have, and have no ambitions of conquest. In this respect they seem to me very different from the Europeans who frequently disturb their neighbours and are covetous of what others enjoy. While the nations of the west seem to be entirely consumed with the idea of supreme domination, they cannot even preserve what their ancestors have bequeathed them, as the Chinese have done for thousands of years.

Following Ricci, the Jesuits would hold their position in the Chinese court for over a century, as mathematicians, scientists, astronomers and medical experts. Christianity itself, as a philosophy, left a smaller mark in Chinese culture. Chinese scholars were deeply impressed by Ricci, by his personal warmth and intelligence, and by his ability in written and spoken Chinese. Most of all, though, they were impressed by his scientific knowledge, especially his translation of Euclid into Chinese. There were a few conversions; notably, Xu Guangqi, the scholar, astronomer and agronomist who helped Ricci with his Euclid and other translations from Chinese into Latin. Most Chinese scholars, though, were more interested in Ricci's new science than in what one described as 'this strange and shallow creed'.

In 1602 Ricci prepared a map of the world for the emperor. The map was 5½ by 12½ feet, and on it the Chinese saw the shape of new continents. It was another powerful symbolic moment. As we have seen, it would be a mistake to think the Chinese were unaware of the world beyond East Asia, but the centre of gravity of world history was shifting in response to the European discovery of the New World. For now, at least, it was moving away from the great powers of Asia, to small aggressive maritime nations on the Atlantic seaboard. Never before in history had one civilisation taken a whole continent, dispossessed and enslaved its people and appropriated its natural resources. Even Late Ming China was already caught up in the tentacles of the emerging new global order. In the Anhui countryside, as the Bao family had noticed, 'Lord Silver' was king now.

Slowly, then, the map of the world was being redrawn. The whole thrust of Chinese civilisation had been that they were at the centre, under the circle of heaven, the connecting point to the divine cosmos. Since even before the Shang, their ritual tradition had existed to mediate between mankind, heaven and the ancestors. To them, their traditional learning and writing enabled them to control that relationship. Their geographical horizons had widened. They knew something of the Western world and, by now, the New World too; but the centre was still the Middle Land. Ricci and his followers, though, claimed to speak for a new vision of history, purposive and redemptive; a history that led to an appointed end. Whether the mandarins considered the Christian narrative hard to grasp, their view of history misguided or even their monotheism as a moral error, these were questions to think hard on. The extraordinary depth, longevity and subtlety of Chinese thought would not be overturned overnight, but still, Ricci's map was a shock to the cosmology of the Confucian scholars and bureaucrats. Some, like Xu Guangqi, embraced the new knowledge, complaining that practical science in China was in decline. Others resisted the lure and stuck to what they knew, perplexed by the whole idea of conversion. One of Ricci's Chinese friends, who admired him greatly, could not believe that he had come all the way to China to convert its people to this 'facile doctrine'. It was simply incredible; he must have come for some other reason. For the writer Zhang Dai, on the other hand, whose grandfather knew Ricci, 'these westerners have great knowledge: they believe that the earth is a sphere hanging in the firmament, that it goes round the sun, and if you go all the way round the earth you come back to the same place'.

So in this encounter was the seed of something disturbing. The monotheism of European civilisation was not only a theological construct; it was a civilisational and cultural order, a completely different way of seeing not just the divine, but the whole relationship of humanity to the world and the universe. The very idea of a creator-god, after all, was alien to the Chinese – as it is, indeed, to all Eastern religions. But they also, for the first time, saw a superior science. On the map, the world was no longer shaped as they had believed: a square earth beneath a round sky. And they were no longer the centre of that world, closest to heaven. In a civilisation so rich, so ancient, it was not as if their conceptual framework was unable to cope with these ideas, so long as the leadership was intelligent and flexible. In Late Ming China, however, that became the issue.

THE MING DECLINE

Through the sixteenth century the empire's economy went into decline. Already in 1502, 120 years after the first census, the taxable farmlands had sunk by more than half, while the government's tax demands remained what they were. Only the lands seized by nobles, officials or princelings and their families got tax exemptions. Ordinary farmers had to shoulder a much heavier tax burden than in the early years of the Ming.

Natural disasters, too, had shaken the Ming state's ability to cope, as they had so often in the past. There were big floods and famines, and in Shaanxi in 1556 the deadliest earthquake in Chinese history. Even a well-ordered early modern state like the Ming, with massive reach in government agencies, in charity and relief provisions, started to struggle across its vast extent from Manchuria to the subtropical lands of Yunnan. There were rebellions out in the west and the northeast. Things were becoming overstretched.

Other signs of decline were evident at the centre. China's misfortune was that, during the difficult times, one of its worst rulers was on the throne. The Wanli emperor (1573–1619) suffered from poor health, exacerbated by overuse of palliative opium. In the 1580s, those present at imperial audiences found him a self-obsessed hypochondriac, endlessly complaining about loyal and well-meaning remonstrances. Meanwhile, incursions by Uighurs, Tibetans and Mongols were threatening the frontiers, and Japanese pirates were plundering the east coast at will. Cosseted in the Forbidden City, unable or unwilling to get out for the big public celebrations like the New Year, Wanli was the very epitome of failure at the top. The foreigner Ricci in Beijing heard all this from his friends:

The emperors in modern times had abandoned the custom of going out in public and when they did [there were] a thousand preliminary precautions ... under military guard, with the secret police placed along the route the emperor was to travel. He was not only hidden from view but the public never knew in which of the palanquins he was actually riding. One would think he was going through an enemy country rather than the multitudes of his own subjects.

The truth was the Wanli emperor, in his long reign, had become increasingly divorced from reality. He ruled through officials and eunuchs, was unresponsive to appeals for help from the often hard-pressed periphery, and was conspicuous in his inattention to the duties of government. This trend for emperors to become increasingly remote and inaccessible was in contrast to some of the great rulers of the past, who had regularly met their ministers. For example, Emperor Wu far back in the Han dynasty or Tang Taizong, who even had officials below ministerial level come in for interviews. During Wanli's time, the practice of full communication, which was fundamental to good governance, had not been kept up. By the end of his reign, local officials out on the edges were finding it increasingly hard to cope.

THE REVOLT AGAINST DESPOTISM

By the early 1600s, local district officers were reporting disaffection in 'the popular sentiment of the people'. As a result of the wider dissemination of higher learning during the Late Ming, schools and academies in the empire had opened the path to an enlarged educated middle class. These people felt they were entitled to a voice in how local communities were run and how they related to the centre. There was also a rising tide of dissatisfaction among professional scholars, a reformist agenda that we might say signified the point when a civilisation begins to outgrow the boundaries of the political order it has created. The problem was the Chinese system of despotism itself.

The pathway to getting criticisms and grievances heard was difficult and fraught with danger. Under Ming law, anyone, even a commoner, could make a petition to the emperor. Back at the start of the dynasty, Hongwu himself had insisted that the channels of complaint should always be open. This way corrupt practices could be exposed and the ruler would know the feelings of the ruled. This principle, which lay behind Mao Zedong's famous 'Hundred Flowers' campaign in 1957, was a fundamental part of the Ming system. Indeed, promising scholars might even hope that by presenting a good submission, even more by writing a whole book to be weighed up by the mandarins, they might attract attention from the top and launch a high-flying career. The most famous example of this, as we saw, was in the Song dynasty, when Wang Anshi submitted his famous *Ten Thousand Word Memorial* with due deference as a matter of loyalty for the national good. The memorial had been the key to Wang's rise.

In reality, however, no matter how it was expressed, and no matter how well intentioned, the chances of a critical and even frank memorial being accepted during the Ming were slight. Such reprovals were considered the work of 'embittered sour old men sending up sealed memorials to disturb the afternoons of the court'. They were often deemed to be self-serving, driven by animosity and rivalry. Petitioners were regularly subject to harsh punishment.

So there was very good reason to think that honest advice might invite a heavy and even brutal response. The physical dangers of serving the Ming government were well known. Corporal punishment of officials was an established practice. One could be beaten savagely in court and, on occasion, even deliberately beaten to death. Sometimes this happened in front of the throne, in the presence of the court, as a measure of public humiliation. Just criticism of the emperor's conduct, even implied, was enough reason to be flogged.

Back in the reign of the Jiajing emperor (1522–66), severe physical punishment became a way of keeping the scholar-bureaucracy in subservience. In 1524, after protesting against the emperor's plan to grant imperial honours posthumously to his own mother and father, 134 officials were flogged and sixteen killed. In the middle decades of the sixteenth century, many more were beaten to death. So the precedent was established that the official scholar who spoke out to advise the emperor, or recommend a change of policy, risked physical punishment, exile, hard labour or execution. Even texts that broke the taboo of naming the emperor or that were construed as insulting him, inadvertently or not, invited the death penalty. This idea had a long life. It would be the same under Mao Zedong in the Cultural Revolution of the 1960s, when people could be condemned for inadvertently soiling a statue of Mao, or destroying his image in a printed newspaper.

There were precedents for the wider use of terror against free speech. The Hongwu emperor had carried out two massive purges of the civil service, when thousands of officials were executed, having been accused of plotting against him a dozen years earlier. Fifteen thousand executions followed another denunciation of a leading general. By then, Hongwu, for all the good intentions of his initial laws, had become a megalomaniac in whom paranoia, rapacity and realpolitik combined to savagely attack any independent thought by his officials. The result was an increasingly demoralised intelligentsia that, as one noted, blurred the distinction between good and bad 'so less worthy officials do not seek to better themselves and good ones keep their heads down'.

Later reigns were less savage than the first two, but the precedent was there. Remonstration was at one's own risk. History gave ample proof that the top jobs, the goal of all high examination candidates, came at great personal risk. But as Wanli's rule drew to a close, men of conscience became more and more agitated as the emperor withdrew from public life, ruling through his eunuchs, led by the sinister Wei Zhongxian. Finally, in 1604, in Wuxi, near Suzhou, there was an attempt to organise a resistance movement by what one might call the Late Ming republic of letters, for whom independent discourse on politics was the way not just to preserve the world, but to change it.

THE DONGLIN ACADEMY

With more than 8 million people today, Wuxi is huge by European standards, but a middling city in China. At night, its gleaming skyline looks like quintessential Chinese modernity, but it is in fact older than Rome. Located on the Grand Canal, between the great cultural centre of Changzhou to the northwest and Suzhou prefecture to the southeast, it had been renowned as a market for textiles and other products since the Song dynasty. During the Late Ming, however, Wuxi became an important cultural and intellectual centre. In the Yangtze delta, the scholars in Wuxi rivalled the Suzhou and Yangzhou literati for pre-eminence, and in the early seventeenth century its Donglin Academy found a national fame that has never been forgotten.

Founded by dissident intellectuals in 1604, the site of the academy lies over the Grand Canal, east of the cobbled streets of the old town. Once the teaching centre of the most prominent intellectual opposition movement under the Late Ming despotism, there is now a museum on the site entered through an old stone memorial arch, which was all that remained after the suppression of the movement in the seventeenth century. It was in the mid-1980s that the Communist Party decided on its restoration as a memorial to the movement, though the stalwarts of the Donglin would surely have taken as icy a view of the party as they did of Ming autocracy, and, in the present climate, the party would have given the Donglin scholars short shrift indeed. Four hundred years on, true independence of thought is still a charged issue.

The Donglin story is a landmark in Chinese intellectual history. An academy was originally built here in the early twelfth century, in the golden time of intellectual inquiry during the Song, a period of wide-ranging debate about governance. Here, soon after 1600, intellectual resistance to the Ming tyranny coalesced in a protest by southern gentry, scholars and officials. Corruption, indolence, overcentralisation and the unwillingness of the emperor to engage in the business of government had begun to have a disastrous effect on the morale of governance. Infused with Neo-Confucian ideas, the renewal soon became a nationwide movement linked to many other literary societies and movements, with two or three thousand active members and tens of thousands of supporters, many of them young.

Then, in 1604, the grand secretary, Gu Xiancheng, along with other like-minded scholars, restored the Donglin Academy on its old site as a deliberate protest against government corruption, the rule of the eunuchs, dowagers and in-laws and the contagious torpor of the Wanli emperor. Financial backing came from local gentry officials, scholars and county magistrates. It was a movement with many parallels in Chinese history, where virtue is set against corruption, and, as in 1976, 1989 and 2008, it was in the deepest sense about loyalty to the culture.

The Donglin agenda also reflected social and economic forces that had been brewing for more than a century. The hegemony of the state in local matters was challenged by reformist gentry who sought to curtail the absolute power of the emperor in favour of local initiative at the provincial, prefectural and county levels. They were not against the imperial system as such – they still believed in the institution of monarchy and the person of the sage-emperor – but the Donglin followers called for devolution of power from the imperial court. Among their supporters was one of the most remarkable gentry families in China's story, one that has produced many thinkers, scientists and poets, both men and women (as we shall see below pages 324–5): the Fang clan of Tongcheng, and among their backers in Wuxi were the Qin family, whose involvement in the movement is recorded in their woodblock-printed family genealogy, as the current clan historian describes:

Our ancestor Qin Ercai was a disciple of the Donglin movement and gave his son to the academy to be tutored in high Confucian moral tone. They disseminated their ideas through widely attended lecture sessions, open to officials and students from all over China, anyone who supported the 'public spirited party'. It was a kind of ethically intense and militant Confucianism, a pursuit of truth regardless of the consequences. According to our family history and the local gazetteer of Wuxi, our ancestor Ercai was a follower of Gu Xiancheng. They worked hard to get followers in government positions to influence politics: to remodel the leadership with a moral basis, to communicate sincere moral feelings, which they expected the government would and should listen to. They were the nation's moral elite.

It is easy to see striking parallels with later times. Not that the Donglin reformers were democrats; they were traditional Confucians who believed in the emperor. They thought they should speak out with moral force, even at the cost of their lives, and that if only they could reach the emperor, he would change his ways. So it was with the letters sent to Mao during the Hundred Flowers campaign in 1957, when some critics of Mao specifically called on the model of Donglin. For any Chinese person, the lessons of history are so self-evident and so permanent, they hardly need pointing out. They are the currency of political debate. Even now, to talk of Donglin in relation to, say, June 1989, the meaning is clear.

Such critiques, however, were an invitation to be crushed by the government, especially by the eunuch dictator Wei Zhongxian. The Wanli emperor died in 1620 and his successor, the Taichang emperor, was found dead within a month of his coronation. Rumblings of discontent grew as the news spread. In Hebei, in the village of Macheng, Donglin loyalists boldly produced a manifesto dated the first year of the new emperor, even though he was already dead, refusing to accept the actions of the Beijing court as legitimate. In the event the Taichang emperor was succeeded by his son, an incompetent teenager, in the pocket of powerful vested interests at court, led by Wei, who now turned on the members of the Donglin movement. In 1625, allies of the academy were tortured, murdered or exiled. In 1626, the chief agitators were arrested. Their leader, Gao Panlong, committed suicide by drowning himself in a pond dressed in his scholar's robes. Popular protests followed. Shopkeepers, labourers and commoners blocked the streets in rain-soaked Suzhou when the police came to arrest one of the key leaders, who was tortured and executed. The eunuch Wei then ordered the Wuxi academy to be completely destroyed, and the buildings were demolished, leaving only the fragment of the stone archway that stands today.

Perhaps what was new in this ongoing conflict was not the extremes to which the state would go to defend itself (that was common enough in Chinese history), but rather the openness and determination of the resistance by the literati. And, though suppressed across the empire, the ideals of Donglin were not lost. The scholarly underground continued in the Lower Yangtze region in cities like Changzhou and Suzhou, where the Fushe movement, 'the Revival Society', was founded in the aftermath of 1628, linking up with several national literary societies to form a network of tens of thousands of local gentry and scholars who kept the flag of intellectual resistance flying.

It would be the son of one of the Donglin members who died in prison, Huang Zongxi, who wrote the single most remarkable political tract in Chinese history, the anti-authoritarian *Waiting for the Dawn*, whose central idea was that 'All Under Heaven' should belong to the people. One day, Huang even suggested, the imperial system might be replaced. It has been said of Huang's book that, since the time of Confucius and Mencius, no other work in the Confucian tradition stands out as such a thoroughgoing critique of Chinese dynastic institutions, or, indeed, of the imperial system itself, 'the most powerful affirmation of a liberal Chinese political vision before the nineteenth century'. In the final analysis, Huang said, the fundamental problem in Chinese political life lay in the very structure of the imperial state. For him, the origin of despotic misrule under the Ming lay back at the very beginning, when, in 1380, the Hongwu emperor abolished the prime ministership and began the overconcentration of power. What was needed now, Huang said, was a reformed system of decentralised government, based on classical principles, that would address the legitimate private interests of local societies:

> The rationale for public officials lies in the fact that the empire is too big for one man to govern and that it is necessary to share the work with others. Therefore, when I [an official] come to serve, it is for the sake of the whole empire and not just the ruler. It is for the sake of all the people and not just for one family name [that is, the imperial lineage]. When one acts for the sake of 'All Under Heaven' and its people, one cannot agree to do anything contrary to the Way, even if the prince explicitly forces one to do so. A true minister, then, will not obey a bad prince: if ministers ignore the plight of the people to raise their prince's rise to power, they violate the true Way.

These ideas for a decentralised and more consultative Chinese state will come back in the late nineteenth century, when Huang's book was rediscovered. His ideas may appear impossibly modern, equating traditional Chinese scholarship anachronistically with Western democratic values and processes. If they appear so, perhaps this is because we overestimate the uniqueness of Early Modern modes of thought in the West, and at the same time underestimate the possibilities of intellectual reformation and revival within traditional Chinese thinking?

As for the Donglin Academy, the memory was revived in the Cultural Revolution of the 1960s by intellectuals, writers and historians resisting Mao's tyranny. The site, as we saw, was restored in the early 1980s, in the heady days of increased openness before 1989. This was a time when the party, under Deng Xiaoping, encouraged open speech and had ignored, for a moment, how dangerous history can be. Today the arch in Wuxi stands as a visible reminder, both of the nature of Ming despotism and of the old adage: 'Fear the power of the past to discredit the present.'

14

THE LAST DAYS OF THE MING

The Ming dynasty lasted for the best part of 300 years, and its material legacy is still there for all to see. But to see the Ming only from the top down, through the glamour of the great rulers and their high culture, is to miss a sense of a dynamically changing society over that period, especially in the later years of the dynasty, when urban life was bursting with energy and new possibilities. In the last years of the Ming, our view of China opens up from below, and from the fringes and the provinces; seen through the lives of individuals, men and women, writers and travellers, all of whom experienced and reflected on their world, and its embarrassment of riches, before the Manchu conquest of 1645. This part of the story begins with journeys that are symptomatic of this outward-looking time: Mrs Wang and her children on a southern river odyssey; the Ming loyalist Zhang Dai on his night ferry; and China's greatest traveller, Xu Xiake, with his fascinating portrait of the outer reaches of the Ming world on the very eve of its fall.

The later years of the Ming dynasty are portrayed as a time of dynastic decline, but they saw the beginnings of far-reaching changes in Chinese society. With dramatic population growth and the expansion of markets and market towns, China no less than Europe was on the path to modernity. There was much more movement between social classes, and also more geographic mobility; people travelled more, the world was opening up. And to travel in the Late Ming world was to encounter a civilisation of huge vitality and insatiable curiosity about the world. All this was encouraged by a boom in printing that made cheap books available to the middle classes, and below. The centre of the popular printing industry was Jianyang in Fujian, where families of book cutters used locally made bamboo paper to serve a wider public than ever, with a huge appetite to know about the wider world. They printed novels, gazetteers, guidebooks, self-help manuals, epitomes of the classics and guides to the civil service exams; their printers' lists offered *A Hundred Questions on Bringing Up Children, The Board of Health Published Remedies on Women's Health, A Li-Du Commentary* (on the two great Tang poets Li Bai and Du Fu) *for the General Reader, Danxi's Guide to Actualising the Mind,* and *Zhang's Complete Guide to Positive Thinking.* An embarrassment of riches.

The Ming was also a heyday for women writers, hundreds of whom appear now in printed anthologies; and they were not only publishing poetry, the age-old consolation of literary women, but writing about the world around them. In around 1600, for example, Wang Fengxian wrote a vivid winter travelogue sailing the Gan River through Jiangxi, with 'endless encounters ... truly a superb journey in this floating life!' A rarity was that she travelled with her children, through wild countryside, over dangerous rapids and in violent storms, sometimes camping out on frost-filled meadows under starry skies. Wang was evidently a wonderful travelling companion, a highly educated woman composing poetry as she went, recording her feelings and the sights on the journey, noting the historic spots that evoked the 'rise and fall of dynasties', and on one night witnessing 'a moon so beautiful that the children pushed open the boat cover to admire it. Somewhere in the dark a distant flute was playing and we forgot the dusty world and felt as if we were in the land of the immortals.' What also comes out of Wang's journey is her formidable strength of character and her courageous good spirits in negotiating, hiring boats and boat pullers, and facing real dangers: 'words cannot describe how unpleasant it was. Luckily my temperament is such that I am not disturbed by toil and hardship; I just have a good laugh at things.' Finally, when she reaches the family home of her in-laws: 'Tonight we'll get drunk to our heart's content' – concluding, though, with an inevitable nod to 'superior' male literary judgements: 'I have recorded the events right when they happened. I am ashamed that this does not make for refined writing.'

Wang's travelogue was part of a growing popular genre of travel writing for the tastes of the new middle class, effectively the birth of tourism in China. Not that the Chinese hadn't travelled before now; indeed, as we have seen, as far back as the Song dynasty, travellers' diaries, along with landscape painting, gave an insight into the way the lettered classes thought about their nation. But from the later sixteenth century, in 'this time of peace', writers found new audiences, describing the sights and sensations but also the concrete reality of actual places, especially out in the southwest where the scale, remoteness and unfamiliarity for most readers made it easier to tap the exotic and the sublime. Books explored what might be called the psycho-geography of China, the sacred mountains (Daoist and Buddhist), the sites of history and legend, and the famous temple sites. By the Late Ming you could buy books about these alien lands and strange peoples, and even go there by reliable transport. The growth of market towns everywhere made it easy to travel and find home comforts in tourist inns and taverns. So the motivation was no longer just religious pilgrimage but a desire to experience cultural feasts, natural wonders, and to encounter the sheer exuberance of Late Ming urban life, when China itself, with its many regional cultures, was the object of desire.

THE NIGHT FERRY: TRAVEL AND TOURISM IN THE MING

By the early 1600s, the Yangtze delta and its coastal plain was the richest and most cultured part of China: half of the population of 160 million or more lived there. Its main cities – Yangzhou, Zhenjiang, Changzhou, Wuxi and Suzhou, down to Shaoxing and Hangzhou – were among the most prosperous in the world. As a European traveller of the time wrote:

This province far exceeds all others in Goodness and richness of Soil, so likewise in trade and Commerce, for here are the chiefest Cities of all China, each whereof famous for Traffick; no less does this Kingdom abound in Shipping above all the rest, for the number of all manner of Vessels is so great that it seems as if all the Ships of the whole World were harboured here.

Official documents from the time listed fourteen chief cities and 110 smaller towns in the south, whose population exceeded that of Europe. In scholarship and the arts, too, European visitors noted, the Yangtze delta was comparable to Renaissance Italy, with 'very learned men brought up in their schools of literature'. Suzhou, in particular, 'where the goods of all provinces flow', was the centre of what was known then as 'Suzhou style'. Booksellers, printers, fashion, food, racy novels – that was Suzhou style; for with wealth and peace came cultural creativity and an outpouring of the visual arts, music, literature, medicine and science.

The sharpest and most engaging chronicler of this time was the essayist and historian Zhang Dai. Zhang came from a Shaoxing landed family. When he was born in 1597, the Ming dynasty had been ruling for well over two centuries, and for the well-off and rising middle class it was a good time to be alive, as he remarked: 'those days were a time of peace and the whole world seemed at ease'.

With Zhang as our guide, we may descend into the crowds of early seventeenth-century China. The scene is uncannily like our accounts of Elizabethan and Stuart London. A hundred miles south of the Yangtze estuary was the port of Ningbo, China's richest entrepot under the Ming. From here, ocean-going traders sailed to Japan, Korea and Vietnam; ferries plied their trade up and down the coast, and a 20,000-strong fishing fleet operated from the landing stages at Qinghai, the out-port at the river mouth. The city itself lay 12 miles upriver, surrounded by low hills in a magnificent location above the junction of the Yuyao and Fenghua Rivers. From the tower of the Tianyi pagoda one could (and to a degree, still can) take in the whole setting, a splendid natural theatre opening northwards to the sea, southwards to the wooded mountains of Simingshanzhen, and to the east the blue expanse of Dongqian Lake and the estuary on Hangzhou Bay. Ningbo would be overtaken by Shanghai in the nineteenth century, but is now rising again in the twenty-first to be China's biggest container port. Lower down the river outside the moated oval of the old city are landing stages still crammed with fishing boats, and still today the ferry boats sail to Shanghai, and to the pilgrimage sites on Putuo island, just as Zhang describes.

It is a summer evening in 1630. As night comes on there is a crush at the jetties on the riverside below the boat bridge; the narrow alleys running down to the water crowded with passengers, hawkers, travelling salesmen, beggars, thieves and vagabonds. There are little wheeled kitchens everywhere with charcoal burners to heat a kettle and fry hot snacks. There are cheap booksellers selling pulp fiction and self-help manuals: flimsy booklets strung on bamboo stands with strings through the bindings. There are Buddhist monks telling stories; apothecaries with strange roots, dried snakes, frogs and deer horn laid out on sheets on the ground; barbers sit with their basins and razors at the ready. Back from the quayside are professional scribes, their little folding tables arranged with ink stone, brushes and paper; for a few coppers they will write letters for the illiterate. There are fortune-tellers (as one may still see today in the lanes round the city's Daoist temple) with their divination books and jars full of numbered strips of bamboo to be selected at random by the client to tally with a prophecy read out from the book. In front of the tables, painted placards warn against carelessness or complacency: life is imponderable, and to be on the safe side it is best to consult the diviner before undertaking anything of importance – especially a sea voyage.

Moored out on the river beyond a forest of smaller masts, junks, sampans and fishing boats are the big ocean-going traders, up to 180 feet long, with five masts, painted eyes on their prows and huge ornate painted sterns rearing high above the water; these could still be seen coasting down to Vietnam up to the middle of the twentieth century. The workhorses of the coasts and estuaries were smaller, 70 feet long, with cabins on the upper deck. These could take up to 200 passengers with a crew of a ship master, two deck hands, two collectors of money and two tea boys. The crew lived in the baggage room where they camped out on passengers' boxes and bundles. There was a galley 'the size of a cabin trunk', with a stove for tea and hot water; meals were available at a price. As the boat readies to sail, the tea boys scurry through the crowds on deck with big brass kettles, refilling battered teapots, stepping over trussed-up pigs, baskets of fruit and vegetables, pushing past hawkers selling fruit, nuts and sunflower seeds. The less wealthy lie on deck, head to head, wrapped up against cool night breezes. Better-off travellers share a private cabin with flat wooden shelves as bunks and wooden latticed windows to let in the night breeze.

Sharing Zhang Dai's cabin is a Buddhist monk, travelling back to his monastery, and a rather pompous local official who is proud of his learning and keen to let his fellow travellers know it. With a jug of wine, observing it all with a raised eyebrow, is Zhang Dai: writer, traveller, aesthete, bon viveur; a man with insatiable curiosity about human nature. As they sail downriver, the scholar is holding forth on the classics, 'talking big and wide' from poorly digested reading. The monk is curled up on his bunk trying to sleep, but eventually, irritated by the scholar's inflated view of himself, asks a question:

'May I ask your honour, is Tantai Mieming one person or two?' (Tantai was a disciple of Confucius.)

'Two people of course,' he replies.

'And Yaoshun?' the monk continues, slyly conflating two famous mythical kings: 'one person or two?'

'One person of course.'

The monk laughs. 'OK, that said, it's time for this novice to go on deck.' With that he stood up, smiled and excused himself and went out to stretch his legs and take the night air.

'Thinking of that night', Zhang Dai wrote, 'gave me an idea for this book. It's all very obvious and superficial, you might think. But had my fellow traveller known some of it, then the little monk might not have needed to stretch his legs. I've called it "The Night Ferry".'

It was a rather modern idea – a 'Ming China in your Pocket', a high-brow *Reader's Digest*. It also opens a window on the literacy of ordinary folk in the early seventeenth century. In Zhang's hometown of Shaoxing, almost everyone above the peasantry was literate. By the age of twenty, some went into government careers and continued their life of reading and scholarship, while others went off to apprentice in manual trades. In his region, especially in the big towns, even artisans and craftspeople were expected to have some book learning. Yet book learning from popular books, Zhang says, was not deep or fundamental knowledge, so he set himself the task of writing a 'high popularisation' to bridge the gap. 'Those conversations on night boats are sometimes hardest to handle,' he wrote: 'you want to be seen as a cultivated person, to be well informed on various subjects, and be seen as a scholar. Some people know a million facts, they can list a myriad people, positions, ranks, dates and places like a bookcase on legs, but they are not really any smarter than someone who can't even spell.'

So here was, as it were, a 'History of the World in a Hundred Stories': an anthology introducing the reader to deeper knowledge, from astronomy and geography to history, politics, customs, medicine and foreign lands. This was a potted compendium of Chinese culture for the new middle class; not civil-service-exam-level, university-educated people, but those curious to know, and to be more cultured themselves. Even Zheng He's voyages two centuries ago offered content: the flora and fauna of the Straits of Hormuz and East African exotica; strange customs and landscapes were all grist to the mill for a modern readership in the expanding world of the Late Ming heartland of civilisation.

AN AGE OF CURIOSITY

Travel, indeed, was one of the central themes of Zhang's huge output. Travel to the famous places that attracted package tours, and cultural and even literary pilgrimage. Pilgrimages to the sacred mountains were especially popular, above all to the 'King of Mountains', Taishan. This could be coupled with a visit to Confucius' hometown of Qufu, a tourist trap where the Master's descendants charged a fee to enter the precinct of the family mansion. Close by in the town of Tai'an were taverns, hostels and a dozen huge hotel complexes: 'I'll never again think of the inns of Tai'an as mere inns,' Zhang wrote, stunned by the size of these tourist establishments:

> The approach road is lined with stabling for horses and mules, houses for actors and performers who entertain the pilgrims, and houses for courtesans and prostitutes ... I thought these must serve the entire subprefecture – I didn't realise they were for a single inn! There were more than twenty kitchens preparing food and between one and two hundred servants running about serving the guests. Yet the rooms of the new and departed guests are never confused, the veg and non-veg meals are never mixed up, and the staff who welcome the guests and see them off are each different. How they get it all right is beyond me. And in the town of Tai'an alone there are half a dozen inns just like this one!

Supervised by local travel agents and tour guides, the inns offered private rooms and public restaurants with three levels of charges. There were inclusive meal deals with fixed menus; the most expensive came with a full-scale opera performance with musicians, while packed lunches were provided for the ascent of the mountain. In season, thousands made the climb every day, all paying a 'Mountain Ascent Tax' creamed off by the provincial government with a cut to the local Ming princely families. When you came down from the climb after watching the dawn – as is still the case – there was a celebration meal with gourmet food and opera by professional performers, after which the red-light district offered further worldly delights after filling one's senses on the 'King of Mountains'.

THE GREAT CHINESE TRAVELLER

That mood of curiosity about the Chinese world, its landscape, history and culture, inspired many writers. 'What's the point of living in a little street,' wrote one, 'and growing old looking out of the window?' Such wanderlust is exemplified by one of the most distinctive voices of the Late Ming, China's most famous traveller, Xu Xiake. When we first we meet him, he is on the Zhejiang coast, south of Ningbo:

> The last day of the third lunar month, 1613. I went out of the West Gate of Ninghai County Town Zhenjiang. It was a cloudless and sunny day, and I had the feeling that the mountains were sharing my happiness. Having covered thirty *li* [ten miles], I reached the Lianghuang Mountain. Upon being told that the region was haunted by tigers, and that dozens of people had been injured in the last month, I decided to stop there for the night ...

Xu Xiake came from a little village in the flatlands near Wuxi, where his ancestral home is still preserved. He was twenty-five, and already on an extraordinary career which took him on horseback and by boat, but above all on foot, across much of the heartland of China. With his literary nom-de-plume 'Traveller in the Sunset Clouds', he had made his pact with nature – 'swearing allegiance to the great mountains'– and set off on a lifetime pilgrimage whose goal was China itself. It was in one sense a metaphysical search for the sublime, a spiritual quest to attain oneness with nature through seeing and feeling. But his travels were also driven by culture, history and myth, as was only possible perhaps in an old country. Initially encouraged and supported in his wanderlust by his ageing mother, he continued until his death at fifty-two from malaria, contracted on the road in 1641, on the very eve of the Ming fall.

Xu was unrivalled in his productivity. Diaries and notes survive totalling over 600,000 characters, which were later edited by his family but printed only in the eighteenth century. Very likely the notes were not intended for publication, but with a view to a grand work on China and its landscape, which never came to fruition due to his early death. What is left gives us one of China's most distinctive voices – one that has enjoyed a recent resurgence of interest, on stamps, in potted editions and graphic novels for children, and even a biopic; so much so that now he is the patron saint of China's tourism industry: the start of his first dated journey, 19 May 1613, is now celebrated annually as National Tourism Day.

A mix of the romantic poet and the natural scientist, Xu's writing owes much to earlier Chinese travel writers. His spontaneous style of observation goes back to Song-dynasty essayists, sometimes pausing to sit for a day, just watching nature, and writing up where possible at night or first thing next day. Nothing escaped his eye. On Tiantai Mountain, today a pretty tourist spot outside Ningbo with a well-marked path, he abandoned his horse because of the mud and advanced on a circuitous route along the ridges:

> The rain had just stopped and the sky was clearing up. I was intoxicated by the magnificent scenery: the gurgling of the spring streams, the beauty of the mountains, the shifting perspective of the scenery, and the full crimson bloom of the azaleas on the verdant hillsides. As far as the eye could see, all was delight, and it made me forget the laborious climb.

His travels over the next twenty-seven years took him to the Yellow River and the Yangtze, the Five Sacred Mountains, the glorious wooded hills around Huangshan, and the coasts of Fujian, where in the troubled days of the Ming decline between the 1610s and 1630s reports of pirate raids and rampaging gangs of bandits led to cancelled local coastal ferries and disrupted journeys. But he also went down into the borderlands of Burma, Laos and Vietnam, 2,000 miles from Beijing, where he gives us a unique insight into the indigenous peoples on the very edge of the Ming world, the exotic Other.

Xu wanted to go beyond where other writers had gone, though as he never synthesised his notes we cannot know the full scope of his planned great work. These were not only travels but also explorations; for example, he attempted to resolve debates about the location of the headwaters of the Yangtze. What comes through is his incredible bravery and independence of thought. Tall, rangy and physically tough, he was a big man: 'strong as an ox but nimble as a monkey'. All who met him recognised 'a great ascetic ... he has no interest in office and a disdain for money. When it comes to the landscape he is prepared to risk his own safety; for the sake of his writing he is willing to sell himself.' Another reported:

> When I questioned him his voice was clear as a bell, his words as true as the hub of a wheel. He spoke incisively and inexhausti-bly ... his bright green eyes flash day or night and his voice is clear as a bell. As spare as a Daoist priest, his outward deportment is that of a mountain recluse, but there resides in him a rich spirit and the essence of courage. Speaking with him his words were upright and lofty, full of the stuff of strange journeys and extreme danger.

In all that, there is perhaps a touch of madness, as a friend observed: 'He is neither a Buddhist nor a Daoist Immortal, but half stubborn, half deranged.' His resilience was legendary:

> He could endure hunger for several days, keep walking for several hundred *li*. Ascending sheer cliffs and braving bamboo thickets, hanging over precipices on a rope ... He found companionship amongst fairies, trolls, apes and baboons, with the result that sometimes he could not think straight and could not speak. However as soon as we talked about mountain paths, explored water courses or sought out some challenging geographical ter-rain, then his mind suddenly became crystal clear.

THE VIEW FROM THE EDGE: AMONG THE BARBARIANS

Xu's last big journey came at the very moment that Ming rule at the centre was collapsing in the face of peasant rebellions. In 1639, now fifty years old, he went down to Yunnan and the precipitous river gorges of the Mekong and Salween; a land of stunning beauty and extraordinary flora and fauna. It had been nominally a part of China for many centuries, but large-scale Chinese settlement only started in the fourteenth century when the Mongols sent garrisons down there as military settlers. In the Ming, Han Chinese followed, but their influence was minimal: governance was through native headmen or tusis from powerful local families: non-Han peoples who had adopted Chinese culture. Among the Muslim Yi people, for example, 'in the midst of deep and remote mountains', Xu met a man so civilised 'it was truly like meeting an immortal'. In other areas along the edge of Burma, on the other hand, he met 'wild men clad only in loincloths ... people who had never heard of China. Formerly under Chinese rule, today they are untouched by imperial rule and orthodox culture.' Out here there were frequent revolts; only the return of direct Chinese rule, Xu thought, would mean the return of civilisation.

In Yunnan he explored the headwaters of the Mekong and the Salween, heading for Lijiang where he went to Jade Snow Mountain and Mount Chickenfoot (Jizu Shan), the site of a famous Buddhist shrine. This area was inhabited by Naxi and other indigenous peoples who spoke Tibeto-Burmese languages. Lijiang was an old town founded back in the Song, and when Xu came it was already a tourist destination, though much harder to reach, with a laborious overland journey of many weeks. A colourful outpost on the very edge of the Ming empire, even then the town had tour guides and sedan chair bearers, with extra fees to cross bridges and ascend rope ladders to its famous caves. There the local 'king' received Xu well and treated him to a banquet of exotic foodstuffs. At nearby Dali – today a charming hippie lakeside town with vegetarian cafés and Daoist fortune-tellers – Xu stayed for a few months after the death of the monk Jingwen, his long-time travelling companion.

The region had been loosely under Chinese control since 1382 – 'on a light rein' through local chiefs. The ruling Mu family had taken a Chinese name to demonstrate their desire to adopt Chinese culture, and their armed retinues were a barrier against the Tibetan warlords beyond the mountains. Xu stayed in the cobbled streets of the old town at the Mufu palace in a big temple-like precinct, which survives today, largely restored after the Muslim uprising here in 1873. A family inscription from the sixteenth century commemorates the defeat of a Tibetan raid with a eulogy to Confucian virtues. Here Xu's host, Mu Zeng, 'the Loyal and Righteous', was a highly cultured man, a devout Buddhist 'with a thirst to welcome noble people'. The translations from Xu's Yunnan diary are by Julian Ward.

'The Mu family have been here for two thousand years,' he wrote, 'their mansions are as beautiful as the ruler's.' They were canny operators 'Should the imperial army come near, the family meekly submit to being subdued. When the army retreats they reassert their power. So the Mu family have not suffered the ravages of the imperial army for generations. Moreover thanks to the uniquely prosperous [gold and silver] mining production, their region is the wealthiest of all the non-Han regions.'

Xu was treated to banquets on a scale that became a real challenge; one of them of eighty dishes, with delicacies including yak tongue and lychees. The headman Mu gave a warm welcome to this unusual literary traveller from the heartland of Chinese culture, and they later exchanged letters while Mu was on his rounds of the kingdom. Mu was anxious to learn more about Chinese civilisation; he asked Xu to revise his own Chinese verse and Xu spent several days 'introducing more variety into the poetry and correcting many incorrect characters'. Mu asked him to stay on to write a gazetteer of Buddhist sites around Mount Chickenfoot, and also to educate Mu's fourth son: 'The boy is interested in writing but because there are no good teachers here he has been unable to get even a glimpse of the culture of the Central plains. So I hereby ask you to instruct him: were he to learn the basic rules you would have my eternal respect.' Xu agreed and gave the boy good marks: 'his work is very clear'.

Xu's travels around the empire give us an extraordinarily vivid picture of the reality of Ming rule on the edges. They tell us about security, transport and civic order; but they also reveal the limits of

Ming autocracy. His travels in Fujian were more than once curtailed by piracy on the coasts, with ferries suspended in the estuaries. In southeast Guangxi and Guizhou he records many rebellions since the 1620s, and down towards the Vietnam border he met people who 'knew only barbarian customs and were not even aware of China', in towns and regions so lawless that they left him literally 'terrified'. In some areas of Yunnan the local headmen had only a tenuous connection with the centre: in the 1630s, Xu reported:

> Many local chiefs simply oppress the local people ... the result-
> ant chaos reaching the imperial frontiers cannot be allowed to
> continue. The suffering of the various Yi peoples, stemming
> from their abuse at the hands of the tribal chiefs is really
> heart-breaking and nauseating ... The reason the situation
> has worsened is that the Yi are only concerned with their own
> survival – so there is no question of them being unbendingly
> loyal to their distant masters. So they can be incited to rebel by
> troublemakers. They don't practice the Chinese language and are
> familiar only with Yi customs.

In the huge areas between Burma and Vietnam in the south, and the lands that touch on Tibet, he concluded that there were 'a string of towns and prefectures held together merely by the fame of the emperor's name and influence, and the policy of the "light rein"'.

Such was the reality of the Ming empire out on the edges; though there were exceptions. Two thousand miles from Beijing, down in the far south of Yunnan on the border with Burma and Laos, Xu stayed with a Mr Zao at Longjiang in the wooded mountains around Mengla, where snow-capped peaks ring the horizon. Zao was a local tusi, a tribal chief, and a member of the Yi ethnic group. He invited Xu Xiake to his house, where Zao greeted him in traditional Yi clothes, with a red cloth band round his head, then changing his clothes before greeting him again in the Chinese manner. After the evening meal (and perhaps we may imagine Xu sampling the distinctive cuisine of this part of Yunnan, flavoured with coconut and coriander), Xu's bed was prepared in the main hall, but before they turned in the two men sat up talking about the world, in Chinese. In many areas, Yunnan was lawless, and the reputation of its chiefs was poor, especially after a revolt in 1621. Zao was anxious to tell Xu that it was not so in his far-flung but loyal outpost of the empire: 'In times gone by,' Zao told Xu, perhaps thinking of the 1621 revolt, 'this place was a battleground, and a nest of thieves.'

> Today, under the power and authority of the Son of Heaven, everywhere is at peace; we have bountiful produce, better than other places. Other parts of the region are suffering droughts while here the rain doesn't stop. Other places have begun planting while here the new crops [are] already climbing [and] shooting up; other places are full of thieves and robbers whereas here we leave our doors unlocked all night. We may be on the impoverished frontier of the kingdom, but this is a happy place. All we lack is the occasional visit of a noble person. And now we have you: are not the rivers and mountains fortunate?

This was perhaps the exception. In reality, the outer reaches of the empire were no longer controlled by the centre; it was a long time since they had seen imperial troops here, let alone a scholar-bureaucrat from Beijing. Xu's last writings link this local, close-up reportage with wider political concerns. The southwest was a hotbed of revolt, where one could see the Ming's loosening grip on the periphery. Xu was aware of this, but he knew what was happening at the centre too; his friendships included members of the Donglin movement from his native Wuxi and he sympathised with the contemporary critics of the imperial system. Writing in his diaries of the immensely powerful eunuch Wei Zhongxian, Xu implies that Wei's tyranny at court had a direct relation to the widespread and growing disturbances elsewhere in the country: 'At that time Wei was in power stirring up trouble and stopping decrees', while out in Yunnan there were powerful local chiefs becoming 'even more crazed and uncontrollable'. The intoxicating sense of freedom of travel that had given Xu such joy in his earlier years was now curtailed not only by local conditions, but by a bigger sense of drift.

On Xu's second and last Yunnan adventure over 1638–40, he fell ill with malaria and became so poorly that his royal patron the Naxi king provided him with companions and a sedan to get him home, a journey that took six months. He died on 8 March 1641 and was buried outside the old house near Wuxi, at the ancestral graves, where today a memorial hall stands decorated with the huge collection of stone-cut epigraphs that Xu had dutifully gathered to honour his mother, the inspiration for his travels. His tomb still stands in front of a huge clump of bamboo in a lovely brick-paved garden; the affection he inspired in his friends is shared by the current custodian, who loved him from her schooldays when she first came here: 'to me he is almost a saint'.

Xu had embodied the old idea of *xiao yao you*, of the ancient philosopher Zhuangzi: 'the free and easy wanderer'. He had sought the sublime, but also scientific truth; he had displayed Confucian humanity, benevolence and rectitude while drawn by the freedom and nature mysticism of Daoism, and the spiritual horizons of Buddhism. In that, Xu is an eccentric representative of the syncretic spirit of his age, but in the path he chose, 'looking for the supernatural marvels of our rivers and mountains', he is truly a one-off, as a friend observed: 'To sum up, there was absolute need in the universe for such a remarkable man, and an absolute need in the annals of literature for his book. [I feel] great shame that I am too old to follow in his hallowed path which made this person unique among remarkable peoples.'

Xu's own verdict on himself is in character:

My greatest regrets are to have explored fully neither the distant obscurities of the heavens above, nor the profundities of human life below, nor the patterns of the lives of current generations. All I have achieved is what I have picked out with my eyes and examined on foot between these highs and lows.

The Ming Dynasty: (above) the Temple of Heaven, built 1406–20; here the emperor prayed for good harvests. (Below) The Great Wall: an expansion of earlier systems of the Qin and the Han, a symbol of retrenchment after the Mongol occupation.

'The Confusions of Pleasure': later Ming society saw the rise of middle-class consumption, luxuries, silk, porcelain and novels; (below) voyages in huge ocean-going ships to India, East Africa and the Red Sea brought back to China pepper and spices, and even exotica like this giraffe.

Apogee of the imperial system: the Qing dynasty. While Europe tore itself apart in internecine wars, three great Manchu emperors brought enviable stability to China for 133 years.

Kangxi.

The young Qianlong, portrayed by a European artist.

The brooding Yongle.

The 'noble consort' (Huixian) who died aged thirty-four in 1745: her real name is unknown.

During the Qing, women's voices were heard in all walks of life: as poets, writers and publishers, and also as the subject of literature such as *The Dream of the Red Chamber* (c. 1745–64), China's most famous novel.

'Prosperous Suzhou', the biggest non-capital in the world: in the Qing, China grew to over 300 million people, with hundreds of new towns and markets.

'The Chinese people are patient and industrious ... cheerful and loquacious', noted the British in 1793. These portraits taken by the Scottish photographer John Thomson give us the faces of ordinary Qing people: a Quanzhou boatwoman; street sellers in Beijing; a Muslim cook and his assistant; and the poignant face of a Manchu bride.

The coming of the British.

The foreign concession in Canton in the late eighteenth century.

Qianlong, now eighty-two,
though the British thought him
'a very fine old gentleman'.

An affectionate sketch by
one of the British of their
Chinese cook.

The first meeting in
the woods at Chengde,
14 September 1793.

The First Opium War, January 1841.

The British ship *Nemesis* destroys Qing war junks with rockets.

The Chinese surrender, on board HMS *Cornwallis* 29 August 1842.

The grim aftermath of the Second Opium War – Chinese
dead at the Taku forts, taken by Felice Beato 1860.

'Self strengthening' after the opium wars: American Gatling
guns on the walls of Nanjing arsenal.

'China, the cake of Kings – and of Emperors', a French cartoon, 1898.
A British observer had thought the break-up of China 'no improbable event',
but China's sense of unity proved more durable.

ENDGAME: WITH THE ZHAO FAMILY

As the ailing Xu was carried home on his litter to the old house near Lake Tai where he died in spring 1641, storm clouds were gathering. The main provinces facing the sea were encountering the increasing disorder he had reported on his travels over the past thirty years. On the coast of Fujian, where Xu had travelled in the 1630s, the problems were not all manmade. The weather patterns had seen serious ups and downs: in the early years of the century there had been severe droughts, with district officers in Fujian reduced to performing rain rituals to avert disaster. But the 1630s were a time of floods and famine. In Zhangpu county, heavy rains caused inundations, many houses were destroyed, grain stores ruined, and famine and pestilence followed. Then came the pirates; three or four times a year, hundreds of people were abducted. Some said it was 'the worst since the 1540s'; to those with very long family memories, it was 'even worse than the plunderings by the Mongols'. The provincial government responded where it could with new barracks, signal stations, warships and detachments of marines. In the late 1630s, county magistrate Yu reported:

> The pirate fleets are banding together to inflict local damage and have been already for a long time. When I first came to the district I saw disused armour and unprepared soldiers, all very out of use and incapable. They were old and weak and lacked courage; proper customs had fallen into abeyance. There was not one quiet day when the people did not come to my compound to complain ...

These were perennial problems for any Chinese government, even in the best of times. In Fujian, sixteen fortified towns were built in a few years in one coastal county as local society militarised. Where effective governance or charity worked, the people were grateful. In 1628, after the pirates had killed and plundered along the coast, the elders of Guanling came together as a group and requested a tablet be put up to a local philanthropist who had raised supplies, gathered troops and defeated the bandits. Then they built a fortified village to protect the villagers, 'so they could sleep in peace'. That man was Zhao Qihou.

The Zhao clan were major figures in this southern reach of the province. Though ordinary country folk today, by no means wealthy, their story goes back to one branch of the imperial family who fled Kaifeng after the disaster of 1127 and made their home here (above page 230). The Zhao village still exists, just a mile off the new coastal highway, a few miles from the sea. The buildings were erected in 1600; then, in 1604, a wall 1,000 metres long and 6 metres high. The massive fortified tower house for communal refuge stands in the centre of the village, commanding views over the countryside. Many of the 150 flat-roofed dwelling places built then are still inhabited. At the bottom of the village is a newly painted Daoist temple of Guan Yu, the loyal, righteous hero of *Romance of the Three Kingdoms*, for whom shrines are ubiquitous in shops, restaurants and police stations in today's China. The cult received a boost in 1614 when he was proclaimed not just duke or warrior but a god: 'Wanli Subduer of Demons whose awe spreads far and moves heaven'. But by the 1640s, in a threatened country, he was emphatically a god of war.

The temple lamp is lit as night falls. Close by at the lower gate an inscribed stele recounts the story of the village from that time; a story that the Zhao family proudly tell over tea with their geneal-ogy, the old woodblock copy superseded by the latest glossy print edition updated with colour photos. Their ancestor Zhao Fan was a distinguished graduate and philanthropist, whose charitable projects 'provided relief which kept thousands of people alive'. After a long career as an administrator up the coast, he came home in retirement in 1600, and with his energy and cash restored the family village. The local inspector handled his petition:

Recently I received a petition from Mr Zhao in the 18th district of this county saying this: 'The authorities permit villages to build fortifications to protect themselves against danger and to secure people's lives. I remember that my adopted father Zhao Fan after his retirement from high office in Zhejiang moved to Guantang, which lies deep in the mountains, and bought land and arranged labour to build a fortified village. Having gained permission he constructed a wall to ward off thieves and robbers. Last year heavy rains caused floods and wall collapses. I am very afraid that in the event of rebellion and mishaps they will have no place to go for protection. I therefore want to open up a site along the lines of the old fortification, to reconstruct the foundation of the stone wall and add a road and battlements. In time of peace we shall have mutual aid and protection; in cases of emergency everybody can be on guard. With such arrangements we can avoid calamity, our property will be protected and we will come to no harm. This matter is of great concern to the local people, so I have filed this request that we may be permitted to go ahead with this construction . . .'

The local officer reported:

We can see the situation with the Japanese pirates is very unpredictable. We must have adequate measures for the protection of our land. It has truly been a long time since the days of peace. How can we rely on fortified villages in case of sudden emergencies if their defences are in a state of disrepair? Now as for Mr Zhao's petition to permit the construction of fortifications to protect his clan members against unpleasant occurrences, it seems that one should therefore allow it.

The judicial officer agreed, concluding: 'Truly it is a long time since the days of peace.'

The story of the Zhao clan village is just one of many tales from the edges of the empire: those of pirates, peasant risings and clan feuds, but most of all the failure of governance. The Ming was in trouble all round its edges, while at court, the centre would not hold. And now events began to move with growing speed.

REBELLIONS: WITH THE FANG FAMILY, ANHUI

In the midwinter of 1632, snow lay thick on Anhui countryside. A lone rider on his way home crossed the Yangtze by ferry and rode into the countryside north of the river. Anxious to be home, he rode on through the night past frozen lakes, the landscape scarred by peasant risings which had flared up everywhere since the 1620s. His thoughts as he rode, he later turned into verse (here adapted from a translation by Willard Pederson):

I travelled home in the winter cold, towards the solstice, the north wind blew bitter both day and night: why is the cold so piercing? Snow blanketing the fields. At Curled Mallow Village there were cries of despair in the night; they'd had to chop their mulberry trees down for fuel. In the night air I could hear the sound of rain turning into sleet ... the whip in my hand was as cold as iron.

The man, named Fang, saw himself as a prodigal son: 'away from home and now grown low in spirits ... Why did I choose to live so far away, to become so "valiant"?' he asked himself. In the deserted fields left unploughed and seamed with snow, there were few signs of life:

The streams in the countryside were covered with ice. I galloped a hundred *li* to return home for the very first time and entered the gate still in the dead of the night, lamps still burning. And I felt a sadness when we met, unable to find the words. Then my family and the rest of the household all laughed at me: 'Year after year, year after year: you are always apart from us.'

Fang was twenty-one, and his family were an old clan of great standing in Anhui. He'd lived the golden life of money and privilege in Nanjing, studying for the triennial provincial exams, reading the classics and history, buying antiques from the Song and Yuan, and visiting rare book collectors in some of the city's stunning private libraries. More interested in science than religion and moral philosophy, he had also looked at Western learning as transmitted through the Jesuits. The faded glory of the southern capital had been left behind by the power, politics and bureaucracy in Beijing, but here things were more laissez faire – and the entertainments were legendary: friendship, food, music and sex in the fleshpots under the east walls. Across the wooded slopes of Purple Mountain stood 'a glittering ten *li* of riverside mansions with richly carved painted balconies and gorgeous silk curtains', where, a friend remembered, 'as night falls the lanterned boats gathered together in a shimmering mass of lights, like the wriggling of a disorderly dragon, so bright as to light up the night; the throbbing drums to set the rhythm for the rowers setting the heart pounding. Along the watergates of the East Side the din goes on till dawn ...'

Back home, the family didn't approve of such dissipation. Criticisms surface in the county gazetteers at this time; the ordinary people, it was said, disapproved of how the rich young men of the county's old families had abandoned their ancestral habits of thrift and frugality, and were living hedonistic lifestyles. The family were worried too by Fang's alienated student attitude, the streak of discontent: 'No one understands me,' he would say, and rail about the current political and intellectual climate. To them, his mood of disaffected youth, his cynical humour, his 'depressed and embittered feelings', were not the Confucian way, not conducive to developing the skills for passing the higher exams and giving service to the state. His father and mother, his sisters and Aunt Weiyi, were people of high moral purpose from a clan of administrators, writers and artists. His great-grandfather (whom he'd known in his childhood) had built a hall with a shrine to Confucius and founded a lecture series where he encouraged debates on morality, on the 'innate goodness of human nature'. Grandad had even lectured at the Donglin Academy, so the family credentials were long in place. Indeed, his ancestor Fang Fa, an eminent judge, had been one of those who, in 1403, at the time of the usurpation of Yongle, had refused the summons and committed suicide, drowning himself rather than serve an illegitimate ruler. So the family had long held firm to its ideals, but now felt threatened by events in the wider world. At home in Anhui, bandit gangs were harassing the province, and even the regular Ming army was to be feared: 'Murder and robberies and pillaging by government troops never ceased.' The young man later wrote of that time, describing himself in the third person:

And now the family were becoming impoverished, unable to entertain guests save with a small meal, the kind of 'three dishes' as one would offer old folk at a village festivity. For generations the family had been devoted to moral good. But good now was impossible. The family had devoted generations to learning, but now learning in many quarters was despised. He wrote criticism of contemporary politics, but burned them. Did he dare let men of the present age see them? The times were not right for that.

In the early hours Fang finally arrived home at the estate in Tongcheng. The servants opened the gate and took his horse. His family greeted him, including his beloved Aunt Weiyi, who had brought him up after his mother had died when he was twelve. There was much to talk about: the almost imperceptible diminishing of the confidence of the culture among those most charged with maintaining it. They were old landowners of long standing who exported their produce and rice to Nanjing; they had many workers and were pillars of local society. Like their neighbours and friends, they traced the local troubles back to the summer of 1618, when everyone had been shocked by a sudden violent local riot: 'a mean-spirited, deeply resentful current had been changing things for a long while'. Now the pressure was building, and in the wider empire too. Beyond the Ming's northern borders in Manchuria, a powerful state had arisen. In 1629, the Manchus had attacked Beijing, causing shock and alarm among rulers and citizens alike, who watched powerless as a mounted raiding party, frighteningly caparisoned with their plumed helmets, paraded outside the city walls and plundered the suburbs. The signs were not good.

Fang's father had been a departmental head official in the Ministry of War until the previous year, and his reports were printed in the *Capital Gazette*, whose provincial editions the student Fang read in Nanjing. He had not been reappointed, but remained 'rightly apprehensive about ill-conceived military planning'. Grandma was especially concerned about the general lawlessness and banditry, the breakdown of order: 'We have to prepare for the times,' she would say, 'accustom ourselves to toil and hardship, be frugal and hard-working: don't be self-satisfied or think of yourself as high and mighty: this cannot be forgotten for a single day: we must be prepared for the times.'

The dynasty had been on the throne for more than 250 years, but in the 1620s and 1630s a series of peasant risings precipitated its fall. Desperate conditions in the countryside led to local famines; there were outbreaks of smallpox and plague, which spread from the Yangtze region into the north. Then came another of these great surges of rebellion that mark Chinese history. Like Liu Bang who brought down the Qin, or Huang Chao who almost felled the Tang, rebel bands joined together in protest over taxation and starvation and moved from Shaanxi into Henan and the central plain. In 1635, led by Li Zicheng and Gao Yingxiang, the rebels entered Anhui province, first desecrating the ancestral tombs of the first Ming emperor in Fengyang, then moving on to the towns of Luzhou (Hefei) and Anqing. Between them lay Tongcheng and the Fang estate. No wonder anxieties were so high at home in the family compound.

The rebels' motivations deeply perturbed old landed families like the Fangs. According to the local gazetteer, these 'popular risings' were inflamed by secret societies that preached class war. The growing disparity between landlords and labourers, rich and poor, had ratcheted up tensions. It was said, too, that some powerful clans were known for 'licentious, extravagant behaviour ... their sons, younger brothers, young male servants and retinues have continually been plundering poor commoners and breaking the law at will'. Grievances were simmering. There were rumours that the peasant leaders had made alliances across the region, and that the common people were going to rise up en masse. In Tongcheng, placards calling for rebellion had been posted on the front of the government compound and one night a peasant mob led by local desperadoes cut off the town and burned and looted hundreds of houses, waving flags and setting fires in the night 'like a cauldron boiling over'.

'This was a disturbance such as the town had never experienced before,' young Fang wrote. 'Though the place was prosperous, a bitterly antagonistic mood had been changing things for a long while. But who would have thought it would come to an outbreak with armed men?' His father used all his energies to raise funds to repair the town's defences and arm a local militia. As the situation worsened, they took the decision to send the women – Fang's sister, cousins and Aunt Weiyi – to safety in Nanjing with their elderly mother and some of the household. It was sign of the times: 'nine out of ten of the rich and powerful families north of the river came south here'. In winter 1634, the rebels sieged Tongcheng but were driven off; there were richer pickings elsewhere. By then, Grandma and the women of the family had set up house in Nanjing. Among them was Aunt Weiyi.

AUNT WEIYI: WOMEN UPHOLDING THE CULTURE

Poet, calligrapher, artist, literary historian and critic, Aunt Weiyi (Fang Weiyi 1585–1668) was one of the most remarkable women of the century. A member of the Late Ming gentry and a Buddhist in her private life, she saw it as her duty to pass on Confucian beliefs in humanity to her family. Among her pupils was her nephew. Fang later recalled his beloved aunt 'looking after him as if he were her own son for eight years'. Then in her late forties, she came from a family that for 400 years had provided thinkers, writers and scientists. The women were especially talented; the sisters, cousins and daughters were all writers, and as a painter it was said that Weiyi had few rivals among men in the whole of the Ming period. The life of the family, though, was marked by tragedy. Her sister Mengshi, an accomplished poet, would commit suicide when her husband died fighting the Manchu invasion in 1645. Weiyi herself had been widowed young, losing her husband and baby daughter. Despite these tragic circumstances she lived a long and exemplary life, writing poetry, commenting on texts, and producing anthologies of women's writings. She published her late sister Mengshi's poetry and was tirelessly supportive of the women in her family – her younger sister, her niece and her in-laws. She was especially close to her sister-in-law Wu Lingyi, whose son she helped to raise after Wu was widowed, 'sharing all household duties as well as her interest in literature and history'. Firmly committed to the culture through her parents and grandparents, Aunt Weiyi had had a fine education and was well equipped to teach the young traditional Confucian values. Indeed, she was scathing about 'Suzhou superficiality' among the nouveaux riches, especially women with pretensions to learning. These were just tricks of style, not the 'real thing', as she put it. Women, too, should espouse Confucian values.

A lost figure in Chinese literature, Aunt Weiyi published three anthologies of poetry for women; she wrote a volume specifically for women readers and also a work of criticism on women's literary history. True to the values of her grandfather, she also wrote a work on modern women's place in a revived Confucianism. But it is her poems about war that best reflect the times; reminiscent of Du Fu, but with the same clarity as Li Qingzhao's political poems (Weiyi of course was familiar with both). Her voice as a writer is etched with suffering, like so many gifted women in Chinese history who through poetry found some distance from the burden placed on them, especially in troubled times. It is easy to see such a focus on transmitting Confucian values as proof of the extent of the victimisation of women in a patriarchal culture, given that those values assigned an inferior position to women. But that of course is to see her with 21st-century values: to her they were a source of pride and identity. Like earlier generations of women writers, though, she was not without an overt political voice, as can be seen in such verses as these, which are translated by Paula Varsano:

Left home for an outpost ten thousand *li* away.
Where the mountain roads are severed by wind and
         smoke ...
taxes too heavy, the food run out ...
The frontier is barren – no planting of fields.
Our foot soldiers ever mindful of death ...
But grasping officials still demanding their sum ...
                              ['*Setting Out from the Passes*']

No need to ask about my old hometown,
Arms of war torment it without rest.
Our family is poor, no use in making plans any more
The taxes multiply and add to my grief
                    ['*Returning Alone to My Childhood Home*']

In my declining years I've run into troubled times
When will I return to my native land?
Bandits invade the southern cities,
Military orders are dispatched to the northern passes,
Human horror is at its height:
Blood smears our swords to the hilt.
                              ['*Travelling in the Autumn:*
                              Hearing News of the Invaders']

Like Li Qingzhao, then, Weiyi was a very remarkable woman. Her family made great cultural contributions to the Ming, and they have continued to do so ever since: China's greatest twentieth-century philosopher was a clan member, and the Fangs still live in Tongcheng today. Her nephew Fang Yizhi (to whose story we will return below) became one of most significant philosophers and scientists of the seventeenth century, melding Western and Chinese learning in science and medicine, writing for example on the functioning of the brain. But the women in the household were slow to get recognition. Her nephew wrote of Weiyi: 'She had the ambition of being a "true man" – that is, fully the equal of a man – and always regretted that she was not made so she could have had a career in the world at large.' It was the plea of so many brilliant women in the Chinese story who were confined to the 'inner quarters'. Though Fang Yizhi published some of his aunt's writings, her three books – her studies of women's poetry, of women's literature, and her critique of women's writing – all appear to have been lost. When in the nineteenth century the family published a grand anthology, 'The Literary Inheritance from Seven Generations of the Fang Family of Tongzheng', it contained only men. Today, however, her poems have an honoured place in the collected works of the family; her grave, with its tombstone carved with Buddhist images, which was lost in the Cultural Revolution, is tended once more; and the family once again do their prayers on Tomb-Sweeping Day, when two or three hundred gather at the ancestral graves just outside the town on Moon Mountain.

THE FALL OF THE MING

In 1635, a rebel army 30,000 strong, commanded by Li Zicheng, defeated the Ming governors in the central provinces and proclaimed a new order with a communistic slogan: 'Be kind to the poor, divide the land equally and abolish the grain tax.' The tide of anger and violence grew in momentum. In 1642, both sides breached the dykes during heavy fighting around Kaifeng, causing terrible floods in which as many as 300,000 people were said to have died. Refugees fled, swelling the population of the southern capital in Nanjing. People waited with growing horror for the outcome.

In February 1644, in Xi'an, Li proclaimed himself king and advanced on Beijing. The rebels sacked the capital and the Chongzhen emperor, the last of the Ming, committed suicide, hanging himself from a tree on Coal Hill overlooking the Forbidden City. (The tree still stands, marked by a monument.) Li now proclaimed himself emperor of the Shun dynasty, meaning 'Obedient to Heaven'. In May, however, taking advantage of the chaos, Manchu invaders swept south, combining with defecting Ming generals, and on 27 May Li was defeated at the Shanhai Pass at the eastern end of the

Great Wall. On 6 June, the Manchu army entered Beijing, and finally on 8 November a six-year-old Manchu prince was enthroned as the first ruler of a new dynasty: the Great Qing, or the 'Purity'. No one could have foreseen it then, but the dynasty would last for 267 years, almost to within living memory in our own time. It would also be the Last Empire.

In the summer of 1645, when temperatures were in the thirties and humidity high, Manchu armies attacked Yangzhou. When the city resisted, they subjected it to a ten-day reign of terror, plundering and burning the old town and killing up to 300,000 citizens and refugees who had taken shelter within the walls. Crossing the Yangtze they seized Nanjing, captured the new emperor Hongguang and prepared to advance on the big mercantile cities of Suzhou, Ningbo and Hangzhou. On 21 July, a proclamation was issued warning all Chinese males to shave their heads and cultivate the *queue*: the Manchu-style pigtail. Loyal Ming local governors fought on, but resistance met massive force. One of many disasters occurred in the old city of Changshu on the south bank of the estuary, which was pillaged and burned, its men massacred, its women and children carried off. The story is recorded in memoirs by locals, including a chronicle by a retired elderly gentleman who noted events in his neighbourhoods with gripping immediacy. In the suburbs, the local resistance was fighting street by street:

> In the night the wind came up so the fires lit up the sky and spread over several dozen *li*. Of all the people's homes and palanquins not a whole beam or half a pole was left ... On the fourteenth day in the early morning the city was broken into. The Manchu army regrouped below the south wall and began firing towards the southwest corner of the city. From daybreak through the early morning, cannon fire blasted the sky and bullets flew wildly without pause.

Eventually the breaches in the city wall were widened, and as Manchu troops rampaged through the streets, the city fathers decided to capitulate. Like the Burghers of Calais, a group of citizens came forward

bearing smoking incense to kneel before the attackers and offer surrender. Their spokesperson was a distinguished old actor called Laojiang.
In a wide-brimmed straw hat with tassels and a long blue-green
gown, he bowed and spoke. The Manchus then in their own language
demanded money. Laojiang replied: 'Ah treasure: you'll find that down
the street in the temple.' 'The words hardly out of his mouth', recorded
his old neighbour, 'than his head was on the floor. He was beheaded
there in the street, killed for making a joke ... Even in death an old
actor didn't drop his irony; to the very end he thought he was in a play.'
In the end the Manchu army withdrew, leaving streets full of bodies,
the city moat red with blood from floating corpses. Five thousand
people were killed according to the locals, and more than 3,000 men,
women, boys and girls were taken captive. Their fate, especially that
of the women, is another story.

THE TALE OF MADAME LIU

Perhaps the most remarkable of these Late Ming voices is one such
woman who survived the murder and mass rape of the conquest.
Madame Liu was a widow taken with many women by the Qing
armies who eventually became the concubine and wife of a Manchu
prince. Her narrative is revealing not only about the times but also
about the culture of middle-class women in the seventeenth century.
The account was composed twenty years later by Liu's maidservant
or close companion, and it includes Liu's letters – though whether
these are the verbatim texts or have been reworked is not certain.
This unique survival of a mother–daughter narrative shows us how
women's voices had grown in the world of Late Ming literature and
were now an accepted part of literary discourse.

   The tale of Madame Liu, as told through her maid's eyes and her
own letters, can be set alongside that of any seventeenth-century
female writer in Europe, indeed it might be seen as a precursor of the
epistolary texts published in Europe at that time that flowered in the
eighteenth-century novel. The scene is Jiading county, next door to
the town of Changshu, in the aftermath of its sacking. The Manchu

general had ravaged and plundered every town he had gone through, seizing 'ten boatloads of women'. When the resistance burned his boats, he vowed to seize the most beautiful women of the region in reprisal. This is the setting for Liu's story. She lived in a fine house in a walled compound in the countryside outside Changshu. She had been married when she was fourteen to a wealthy but miserly widower three times her age. He had died just before the Manchu attack, however, leaving her with their young daughter. Liu was at home, 'wearing a plain gown and light makeup', when a detachment of a thousand Manchu troops arrived. They blasted open the gates in the outer wall of her compound and plundered her granaries, storerooms and even her private chests and cabinets. Then they killed her late husband's son and set fire to the building, before Liu and her maidservant were taken away with hundreds of other captives. They were first moved to a camp along the coast near Shanghai, then all the women were taken to the Manchu headquarters in Nanjing. There, as translated by Lynn Struve, a chilling narrative unfolds:

> An area was cleared behind the official compound in an empty yard behind the horse stables, and there a crowd of over three hundred women were housed in several tents made of matting. It was almost like living in the open. The stench of horse manure and urine was so pervasive that one could hardly stand it for more than a quarter-hour. So the women wailed tearfully, unwilling to live any longer. Then a Manchu woman of authority came; she was over seventy and wore a flower clipped at one temple. Her garments and shoes were masculine in style ... She spoke Chinese very well. When they led her into the tents to look around, she spoke in Chinese to the women, sidestepping through the crowd of women, selecting those who she thought appropriate. She picked over thirty. Of them the 'best four' were taken to the prince's mansion, including Madame Liu, who went with her maidservant.

Meanwhile, back in the devastated Changshu, her daughter Zhen was desperately trying to find her mother, enquiring after her in the

Manchu camp, only to discover that Liu had been chosen to enter the prince's mansion. There follows an extraordinary exchange of letters between mother and daughter, which has the power of a novel but the immediacy of real experience. Letters had long been a very important medium of personal communication for educated women, all the more so given how enclosed they were compared to men, confined to the 'inner chambers', the women's quarters, as was customary in middle- and upper-class society. The literary quality of Liu's letters places them squarely in the surge of letter writing among women in the mid-seventeenth century, instigated in part by the scattering of families and friends during the disruption of the Qing conquest. (Women's literary clubs were active at this time, three women's letter collections came out in the 1660s alone; a new readership for a new age.)

To her daughter, whom she had no doubt helped to educate, Liu writes: 'If my letter arrives and you write back in your own hand, then I will know that you have survived.' The position of women in Chinese society once widowed, if they had no legitimate male support, could be perilous, but, Liu wrote, 'if I am to be a desolate widow in service to a barbarian court, then I have long since decided what to do. By nature I am high minded and uncompromising, unwilling to subordinate myself to others. If I stake everything and lose, what will death matter to me? My Zhen, my Zhen. For my sake do not worry.'

In the end, Liu became a concubine of the Manchu prince. Her acceptance of her fate is the subject of another anguished letter to her daughter: 'Alas my daughter, neither now nor hereafter can I live with you again. What else is there to say?' With that she departed for the north, where, aged thirty-five, she gave birth to a boy and found herself elevated to principal consort. At forty she became pregnant a second time. Subsequently she was reconciled with her Chinese family, even helping to place one of her young male relatives in the Manchu civil service, and finally she was reunited with her daughter: 'When they met again they embraced each other and cried, but before long were as happy as before.'

As can be seen from just this one example, the conquest brought huge suffering and left deep resentments among the Chinese that were never forgotten. But as the Qing rulers continued the long struggle with the resistance, in October 1648, only months after the union of Liu and the Manchu prince, the court formally announced that marriages between Manchus and Han Chinese were not only permissible, but desirable, as they provided a means to overcome the division between the conquered and conqueror. Perhaps this is the chief reason that Liu's remarkable memoir and letters were ever published.

THE HUNTING OF FANG YIZHI

For the intellectuals who had been engaged in an attempt to rethink China's culture in the first half of the sixteenth century, the issue had been how to do this without being a government mouthpiece and simply underwriting Ming despotism, as the Donglin reformers had found out to their cost. Was a learned and humane man to be a 'bitter gourd' as Confucius had said, 'hung up but never eaten'? The Manchu conquest, however, placed all of them in a new dilemma: to serve the new Manchu regime, or to drop out altogether? Many who lived through the cataclysm simply retreated into nostalgia: Zhang Dai, for example, finished his Ming history and wrote backward-looking, self-recriminatory accounts of the good old days; while Yu Huai, a friend in his salad days in the 'blue houses' of Nanjing, penned a tearful memoir of the girls of the Qinhuai quarter and their exquisite culture, replete with lashings of their poetry. But intellectuals like Fang Yizhi left that world behind. For them, the Manchu conquest brought a deeper disillusionment with politics but a continuing commitment to the new currents of scholarship. Aunt Weiyi's protégé, the party boy of 1630s Nanjing, became the greatest scientific thinker of the age, writing on subjects as diverse as the brain and optics. Appointed to the top academy in Beijing in 1643, Fang was still there when the rebel army took the capital and Ming officials were rounded up and told at sword point to support the new regime or to ransom themselves with huge sums. Fang was arrested and threatened with death, his seven-year-old son taken as a hostage. Leaving behind his family, he went back to their home in Anhui to raise the ransom. In the summer of 1645 he was in Nanjing when Beijing fell to the Manchus and a new emperor was declared.

At that point the Ming rump government in the south had a new emperor too, but the resistance was falling apart in enmities and conflicting factions. Friends of Fang's were tortured and broken. Accused of treason for siding with the rebels, Fang was sentenced to banishment and, though he was pardoned, realising things were getting too hot, fled south to Fujian, where his father had been magistrate twenty-five years before. There, in 1645, a new Ming court was set up in Fuzhou, but within the year, as the Manchu net closed on the new emperor, Fang dressed as a commoner and, using his mother's surname as an alias, fled further south to Canton, where he was joined by his wife and son.

At that point Fang had intended to avoid further involvement in politics, but in China that is always hard. In the event, his love of books caught up with him. One day, visiting a bookseller in Canton, he was recognised by a Ming official on his sedan chair with his retinue. They'd known each other in Beijing back in 1640 when they had both passed the higher exams. Now, meeting again, and confronted by the parlous state of the nation, they both burst into tears. Fang was now urged in the strongest terms to help the Ming and to show loyalty to the dynasty. Cornered, he gave in, and, leaving his family behind once again, he went down to Guangdong, to the capital of the southern Ming resistance led by the Prince of Gui. There he stayed for several months working for the resistance, until the Qing armies closed in and he was forced to move on, heading further south into eastern Guangxi.

He could see that his career as a high-flying civil servant was over now, and as Manchu armies poured into the south with columns of heavily armed mounted troops, his troubles grew. His health worsening, he lived for a while in the mountains near the court in Guilin, then for three years in a village further south near Pingluo. Declining offers of appointments to the rump Ming state as 'General

Secretary and Minister of Rites', he wore rough clothes and lived incognito among the indigenous Miao people until a Manchu thrust south forced him to flee again. Marked out as a Ming collaborator, he retreated to a village in the wooded mountains near Pingluo. There, in the winter of 1650, he was captured by Manchu troops. He had shaved his head like a monk and put on Buddhist robes to avoid arrest, but he was recognised nonetheless and brought before a Manchu general who threatened to execute him unless he agreed to serve the Qing. He refused, but somehow talked his way out of execution on the grounds that he had now renounced the world and wanted only to live as a monk.

Amazingly, all this time on the road, while living hand to mouth, he had continued to pursue scholarship, and was able to take books with him. He added to his manuscripts of philosophical and scientific materials *On the Principle of Things* and *On the Laws of Nature*, attempting to amalgamate Western Jesuit science and Chinese learning. Exchanging letters and receiving money even while living among the Miao in 1650, he was able to send a box of manuscript material back to the family in Tongcheng.

The world was changing fast. The Manchu conquest was by no means yet complete (there would be a grim eight-year war against the rebellious 'Three Feudatories' in the south), but their military power was so great, with Chinese troops now incorporated under Manchu banners, that the end was inevitable. In late 1652, Fang wandered back up to the Yangtze valley and met his aged father on the river at Jiujiang. He stayed at a Buddhist temple in the mountains nearby, completing a manuscript work dated that autumn 'at the peaks known as the Five Old Men', where a friend stayed with him at the famous Five Cascades, a beauty spot which had been visited by Xu Xiake. The manuscript, *Dongxi Jun*, 'On Speculative Philosophy', crystallised twenty years of thinking about the aftermath of the introduction into China of Euclidean science and Jesuit cosmography. But it was a demanding intellectual task even if he had had all the support in the world; for a man on the run, it could only ever have been interim and contingent.

In 1653, Fang returned finally to the haunts of his youth in Nanjing. The capital had been damaged after the Manchu sacking; the gorgeous riverine quarter with its mansions, gardens and fairy grottoes where he had misspent his youth was now reduced to workshops and shanties. The world of the Late Ming was already fading. Finally he made his commitment to the Buddhist way under a leading master of Zen. By the winter of 1654 he was living in a temple near Xincheng in the mountains of northern Jiangxi. Friends and family did not welcome the life change, his sons complaining that 'Father was once an expert in astronomy but now has retired from the world, he has not spoken a word about it'.

At the same time he received a study by his father on the *Book of Changes*, yet again contemplating the experience of defeat. After his father's death he mourned for three years before finally returning to Tongcheng where his wife and three sons were living. Yet he never renounced the Buddhist life, even writing a Buddhist commentary on the sage Zhuangzi. In later life he was invited to take charge of a temple in the south where his sons visited him and visitors remarked on his literary abilities, the profundity of his thought, and especially his 'detailed mastery and broad grasp of knowledge of heaven and earth, man and things, images and numbers, astronomy and harmonies, medicine and divination'. He had become a great teacher: 'tireless in his efforts to instruct others'.

In old age some of Fang's manuscripts, including scientific, philosophical works and assorted prose, were published, woodblock-cut, at least one prepared by his three sons. But fatefully this flurry of publishing drew the attention of the authorities to the continued existence of a man who had been living under a series of Buddhist pseudonyms for twenty years. There were accusations that he had worked for the southern Ming court and that he harboured anti-Manchu sentiments. In 1671, legal proceedings were started against him and his arrest was ordered. That autumn, heading up the Gan River by boat, he drowned at 'Fear and Trembling Rapids', an extremely dangerous stretch of the waterway (where Matteo Ricci and his party had been thrown overboard back in 1595). One son was with him, and his second son soon joined; they retrieved his body but were unable to take him home before officials made enquiries into his works. His elder son paints a vivid picture of being held in the governor's compound, 'day after day underlings scrutinising a huge pile of documents, brush and ink at the ready; officials and sub officials scurrying about, making notes of everything while his sons slept in the room with their father's coffin':

> My straw bed is at the side of the coffin
> The cloth for mourning tugs at me.
> Morning and evening are like before:
> I serve him as his child
> With his manuscripts crammed on the bed,
> Leave-taking is over and done
> The wick of the pottery lamp is used up.
> But I do not fall asleep.

The inquiry turned up nothing of anti-Manchu sentiment, the government 'readers' allowed his manuscripts to be returned, and the family eventually took the body back home to the graveyard at Tongcheng. Though many of his books were later published, some remain unprinted, preserved by the family through the Cultural Revolution.

Fang's extraordinary status as a thinker in the seventeenth century highlights once again the issue of the intellectual in Chinese society, from then until now. Outside the state, may one be a free thinker? Or must one be, as Confucius had said, a bitter gourd? 'How regrettable it is', wrote his son, 'that in his lifetime my father was ensnared in fame. The difficulties and troubles after his death have been that much more difficult to endure.'

15

THE GREAT QING: THE LONG
EIGHTEENTH CENTURY

China's last empire, the Qing (1644–1911), has been ill served until
recently in historical writing, and in the popular imagination, especially in the West. The predominant image is one of decline in the
face of European industry and innovation; of an inability to meet
the demands of modernity as it is defined by Western culture. Yet,
in the eighteenth century, foreign travellers and writers described
China as the most prosperous and best-governed state on earth. They
may have been right. The dynasty lasted 267 years. In the middle of
that time, with over a quarter of the world's population, under three
great emperors, China reached its highest level of material success
and political stability before its fateful confrontation with the West.
Qing society had many features of the European Enlightenment:
banks, trading guilds, charitable institutions, widespread access
to education, scientific and literary clubs. It was a time of extraordinary riches in the arts, in poetry and the novel, and in women's
literature. This chapter looks at the period through stories of real
lives: the emperor Kangxi himself, perhaps China's greatest ruler;
Cao Xueqin, the ill-fated writer whose family saga inspired China's
best-loved novel; and 'goodwife Xun', an ordinary woman in the
backstreets of the capital, sustaining her family in difficult times.
Our story begins after the Manchu conquest with the essayist Zhang

Dai, whom we last met on the night ferry, returning crestfallen to the haunts of his youth.

DREAMS OF WEST LAKE

As shadows creep across the emerald green hills, the setting sun turns West Lake into a golden pond. Out on the shimmering water, in a rowing boat, wearing coarse wool clothes, is Zhang Dai. He is nearly sixty now. A chastened man since the old days of the Ming, when, as he ruefully admitted, he was a 'silk-stocking dandy incurably addicted to luxurious living, fine mansions, pretty girls, handsome boys, gorgeous clothes, choice food, bright lanterns, fireworks, theatre, music, antiques, flowers and birds'. The war, at least here, is long over. Round the shore of West Lake, the familiar landmarks are no more. The lakeside villages, mansions and villas of the big families are gone: 'Even our own family's garden and summer house ... all have been reduced to rubble ... all the bending willows and lush peach trees and the towers and concert pavilions looked as if they have been inundated in a great flood.' The old life of bandstands, dance floors and evening concerts had disappeared.

Driven from his estate below Dragon Mountain in Shaoxing, Zhang had spent time as a wandering Buddhist monk, reduced to begging, later half-starving in poor lodgings, 'with a rickety bed and a cracked bronze cooking pot'. As a Ming loyalist he would never reconcile to Manchu rule and devoted the later years of his literary career to a huge history of the Ming. Now, returning to West Lake brought to mind the larger-than-life characters of his lost past: 'pock-marked Liu', the storyteller, with his scarred face and 'his voice like a big bronze bell'; old Pop Min with his tea house; Wang Yuesheng, the self-assured courtesan, 'aloof and remote', who 'would not socialise with philistines' and held her rich suitors in thrall. Yet now the Manchus were the possessors of his world. 'I've lived as a tenant in someone else's house for twenty-three years now,' he wrote in the summer of 1671; 'when I was fifty my country lay shattered and I took refuge in the mountains. Since 1644 I have lived as if in a daze. Looking back, those days of two decades ago seem to have belonged to another incarnation. It is as if my life in the Ming had been a dream.'

'There was something wrong with the timing of my birth,' he concluded.

I have so long been separated from West Lake – some twenty-eight years now – but every day West Lake has emerged in my dreams and the West Lake of my dreams has never left me, not even for a single day. So I have written seventy-two stories in a book called *Searching for West Lake in Dreams* to be passed on to future generations as my reflections on West Lake. I am like an explorer who has returned from a long sea voyage ...

Having finally returned to his beloved West Lake, Zhang 'hurried away from the sight': 'I'd made the journey because of *Searching for West Lake in Dreams*, but considering what I saw there it would have been better had I simply kept West Lake only in my dreams, which would have been left intact.'

THE MANCHU RESTORATION

China was now under a new dynasty, the great Qing. Yet for all their subsequent achievements, the bitterness of the conquest would never be extinguished; its wounds took a long time to heal. Indeed, it could be said, they never quite did. Like the Mongols, the Manchus would always be seen as foreigners, and there would be risings urging the restoration of the Ming until the very end of the Qing empire. Among the secret societies behind many of the peasant revolts of the Qing period – the White Turbans, the Red Scarves, the White Lotus, the Boxers, or the 1910 rising in Changsha witnessed by Mao Zedong – the watchword was still 'Restore the Ming'.

In one important sense, though, the Ming would be restored. The Manchus' great project would be not only the creation of China's largest empire, but the re-establishment of the Confucian ethos of

China. They would rebuild the state and its culture by being almost more Chinese than the Chinese. The Manchus were northerners and kept the capital at Beijing. From there they administered a vast empire that, by the eighteenth century, extended to Mongolia, Xinjiang and Tibet. They built fortresses in all the cities across China, garrisoned by their military orders, their bannermen. The emperors made frequent grand inspection tours to keep an eye on the 'prosperous and immoral' south, which was now unequivocally the heartland of Chinese civilisation. The great southern centres of Yangzhou, Wuxi, Suzhou, Zhenjiang, Changzhou, Nanjing and Hangzhou were powerhouses of culture, with academies of literati financed by the immense wealth of the merchant classes and the textile and salt traders. Here, under Manchu rule, China's thinkers were once again forced to think about the meaning of 'this culture of ours'. So, in an attempt to repair the physical and psychological damage of the conquest, the Manchus formed a cultural alliance with these elites. They sponsored the arts, publishing and scholarship, and oversaw an age of Chinese civilisation comparable to the Tang and Song dynasties. This especially took place under three great emperors who, between them, ruled for 135 years: Kangxi (1661–1722), Yongzheng (1722–35) and Qianlong (1735–96).

THE QING EMPIRE AND THE WIDER WORLD

Many factors had hastened the fall of the Ming, not only peasant risings and the Manchu invasion. China was now becoming part of a fast-changing wider world. A global economic crisis in the seventeenth century had weakened China, as European maritime powers spread their influence into the *nanyang,* the southern sea. Climate change also played its part in the 'Little Ice Age' of the early years of the century, when, as we have seen, floods, droughts and famine exacerbated the troubles of the dynasty. China's population had declined sharply between the end of the sixteenth century and the middle of the seventeenth. All these factors, economic, environmental and demographic, had played their part in the huge crisis that unfolded in the relationship between society and the state under the Late Ming.

From the mid-seventeenth century, however, the Qing restoration brought about a dramatic recovery. By the 1660s, the population rose again. Textile manufacture in the south recovered from the ravages of the conquest. Crucially, too, in the last decades of the seventeenth century, there was a big increase in land opened up for cultivation. Overall, between the 1650s and 1770, government statistics show that there was a staggering 50 per cent more land under cultivation. This sustained the population rise and brought a massive increase in tax revenues. Here, then, was the governmental and fiscal basis of the High Qing heyday, which was the envy of European visitors.

On these foundations, the first Qing emperors built an imperial superstructure of unrivalled reach, clothed in awesome ceremonial and royal ritual. The traditional rites were all recodified in a new Directory of Worship during the eighteenth century, and there was a huge range of cultural expression that dwarfed most other cultures at this time. The early Qing empire was a colossal engine of war and governance, with a standing army of 800,000 men, armed with European-style artillery. It would last as long as the vigour of its leadership and so long as the Chinese civil service were prepared loyally to serve their Manchu rulers. Over this time, China's borders expanded to incorporate nearly twice as much territory as the Ming dynasty had ruled, making it the largest unitary empire in history. And there were no serious domestic or external rivals to challenge Manchu rule. However, paradoxically, there would be a price to pay for that.

Opening our view to what was happening in the wider world at this time, Europe had been devastated by the Thirty Years War. In the 1640s and '50s, the British civil wars had engulfed mainland Britain and Ireland with huge loss of life, both military and civilian. During the early Qing period, the wars of the Spanish succession led to a series of European conflicts, from the Seven Years War to the Napoleonic Wars, devastating civilian populations from the Spanish peninsula to Moscow. These rivalries also spread abroad to the nascent European empires in the New World, and wars were fought in India between the colonial powers. Western technology and industry advanced hand in hand to feed this arms race, developing and improving their weaponry by land and sea. The naval rivalry of the British, French and Spanish saw the building of huge fleets with ever greater firepower; the biggest ships giant three-deckers mounting up to 120 cannon. These conflicts were fought between combatants who, technologically, were roughly equal and had to keep updating their military and naval science. In the 1700s, the British were able to leap ahead with an industrial revolution that had been driven by military needs from the civil wars onwards. By 1805, the British had the biggest and most professional navy in the world, and the British state, though tiny compared with China, had become a society geared to war and industrial expansion. They experienced a rapid demographic shift as agriculture began to mechanise, and the bulk of the population became employed in industry and mining, along with the army and navy. Backed by enormous financial power, they could now also raise armies from the peoples under their control. For one late eighteenth-century campaign in south India, for example, the East India Company put 50,000 men into the field, most of whom were native troops under British officers.

While all this was happening in the west of Eurasia, and in India, at home the Qing lacked competitive contenders. They had fought many regional wars around their borders from Mongolia to Burma, but had no overwhelming need to improve their military technology to conquer relatively backward inner Asian peoples and to enforce their hegemony over parts of Korea, Tibet, Xinjiang and Greater Mongolia. Now, however, the increasingly aggressive maritime powers of Western Europe were expanding into what the Chinese called the *nanyang*, the southeastern seas bounded by Taiwan, the Philippines and Vietnam. The centre of gravity of global politics was beginning to shift. It was inevitable that at some point the Qing would have to engage with them. But what would be the nature of that meeting? For now, though, that moment would be put off.

THE KANGXI EMPEROR

The first of the three great Qing emperors was Kangxi, the longest ruling of all China's emperors (1661–1722) and perhaps the greatest. Physically fearless, he was a true Manchu; a horseman, fighter and hunter: 'When Manchus go out to hunt in the north', he wrote, 'the riders mass like storm clouds, the mounted archers are as one with their horses, they fly together and their arrows bring down the fleeing game. And heart and eye are gladdened to see it!'

Kangxi's autobiographical writings, letters and memoranda include an astonishing cache of hundreds of letters and notes discovered by chance in 1911, sealed in a box in the Forbidden City. Nothing like them survives for any other ruler in Chinese history. Especially riveting is his valedictory reflection on the nature of rulership. In it he bares his soul, consumed by his bitter sense of failure regarding the son who plotted against him: 'As I was yielding he remained unchanging in his wickedness; my heart turned to ash, all hope gone.' Seldom has the burden of rulership been more powerfully expressed. Taken together, these documents, which have been translated by Jonathan Spence, amount to one of the greatest of all ruler autobiographies:

Before I die I am letting you know my sincerest feelings. The rulers of the past all took reverence for Heaven's laws and reverence for the ancestors, as the fundamental way in ruling the country. To be sincere in reverence for Heaven and ancestors entails the following: be kind to men from afar and keep the able ones near; nourish the people; think of the profit of all as being the real profit and the mind of the whole country as being the real mind; be considerate to officials and act as a father to the people; protect the state before danger appears and govern well before there is any disturbance; be always diligent and always careful, and maintain the balance between principle and expedience, so that long-range plans can be made for the country. That's all there is to it.

Of course such a demanding vision needed almost boundless personal energy, and Kangxi certainly had that. He was exceptionally curious about the world. Interested in scientific experiments, he had long conversations about Western science with the Jesuit missionaries who stayed in his court. He was also eager to learn about music, astronomy, poetry and medicine. Kangxi had an engaging sense of humour, a down-to-earth realism and a feel for the lives of ordinary people. Since childhood he had been hardened in the ways of the world and intuitively understood what was needed in a ruler. 'Giving life to people and killing people. Those are the powers an emperor has,' he wrote. There is indeed a lot of killing in the imperial memos, but he knew that 'there must be clarity and care in punishing'. He even supervised sentencing reviews for the Board of Punishments, checking cases thoroughly:

> Errors are inexcusable in matters of life and death. Naturally I could not go through every case in detail. Nevertheless I got into the habit of reading through the lists, checking the name and registration and status of each man condemned to death and the reason given for the death penalty. Then I would go through the list again with the Grand Secretaries and their staff and we would decide who should be spared.

Trained by his Han Chinese teachers in Confucian morality, Kangxi was assiduous in his work. He regularly burned the midnight oil, so that by his thirties he complained that his sight had already deteriorated after so many late nights working by lamplight on official documents. Sixteen thousand memoranda still survive today from his own daily official duties, annotated in his characteristic hand in red ink. For Kangxi, detail was everything. He knew that the greatest failure of the last Ming rulers had been a failure in leadership. Therefore, as he prosecuted wars in the south to subdue his enemies, the last Ming resistance and his own rebel feudatories, Kangxi and his advisers, Manchu and Chinese, set about the Great Restoration.

THE SACRED EDICT

Some native Chinese scholars who were Ming loyalists opted out and refused to serve the new order. For many others, however, buying into the Manchu project was a matter of 'saving the world'. The seriousness with which they viewed the propagation of morality and the cultivation of Confucian civility and humanity was evident through the founding of new schools, establishing curricula, writing and copying texts for guidance on education, for men as well as women. Among them was Chen Hongmou. The most famous Chinese official of the eighteenth century, Chen has left us a rich collection of writings that show his belief in the fundamental civilising mission of Han Chinese culture. Like Chinese educators under the Mongols, the task was to pass on 'this culture of ours'.

The first step was to reinvigorate Confucian values at the grassroots, and so the Manchus revived the old custom of regular readings of key government educational edicts. Such readings had a long history. Village lectures enunciating the government's ideals at village level were given during the Song. Schoolchildren were gathered in a circle to hear local Confucian scholars, or educated village gentry, read the edicts (rather like the national anthem at school) and give lectures on community solidarity and morality. In the fourteenth century, rather like the biblical Ten Commandments, the Hongwu emperor had enunciated his Six Maxims, centring on filial respect, neighbourly cooperation, self-cultivation and doing no evil.

In 1670, the Kangxi emperor and his advisers issued the famous *Sacred Edict*. Comprising just sixteen lines, each of seven characters, it was intended to instruct the ordinary citizen, especially children, in what today we would call good citizenship. The edict would be copied and posted everywhere, neatly written on small slips of wood and placed on public view in local government offices and public places. It spoke of filial and brotherly love, generosity to the family, keeping peace with neighbours, respecting farming, being frugal and not wasting valuable resources. People were enjoined to support schools and colleges to promote education, and encouraged to reject 'strange beliefs', including Buddhism and Christianity. The edict encouraged the well-educated to elucidate the law to instruct and warn the ignorant. It spoke of how one should always show courtesy, good manners and work diligently, instructing the young to stop them from doing wrong. It told the people not to bear false witness, not to shelter deserters, to pay their taxes promptly and fully, and to work together to stop theft and robbery. Finally, in a spirit of self-help long encouraged in popular literature, the edict announced that you should 'free yourself from enmity and anger to show respect for your person and for life'.

The *Sacred Edict* was read out in every town and village twice a month in the eighteenth century, at the beginning and middle of each moon. Local scholars would explain what the lines meant to the assembled village community in their own dialect. In 1724, Kangxi's successor, Yongzheng, issued an expanded version in 10,000 characters with explanatory stories and anecdotes, which could be amplified as people saw fit. The edict was also to be delivered to non-Chinese peoples, in their own languages, to help convince them of the benefits of Chinese rule. This was part of a huge educative programme under the Qing, as their power spread over non-Han Chinese territories and peoples.

This didactic articulation of the core ideas of rulership and 'civic values' was still custom and practice in the nineteenth century. While travelling in China in the 1870s, the English sinologist Herbert Giles reported that after the catastrophic Taiping rebellion there was a renewed push at the grassroots for the recital of the *Sacred Edict*. This was to help pull the country together and also to work against the inroads being made by Christian missionaries. Indeed, the tradition carried on well into the twentieth century. The famous New Culture radical Guo Moruo, who was born in 1892, wrote in his autobiography that in his youth, in a small town in Sichuan, he and other villagers loved to hear the lectures on the *Sacred Edict*. The lecturer would come around the villages, setting up a table on a street corner and lighting incense and candles, almost like an altar as offerings to the book. He would bow and kneel, knocking his forehead on the ground four times in the kowtow, and then recite the sixteen maxims, explaining them with stories, sometimes from famous folk tales or novels. It was a form of storytelling, integrating the ethos of government with tales from popular culture – and for that, perhaps, more effective in transmitting the Confucian ethos of Manchu rule than the elevated classical language of bureaucrats and scholar-officials.

This tradition of didactic political moralising did not die out with the end of the empire. It continued into the mid-twentieth century in the village lectures adopted by the Communist Party – to the dismay of many required to listen to Marxist jargon after a day of back-breaking toil! Indeed, not long ago, sixteen points of good citizenship were published by the government of Xi Jinping and are now available on a mobile phone app called 'Study Xi, Strong Nation'. How to rule such a huge population, and how to hold their allegiance, is still the key issue for any government of China.

In the eighteenth century, these ideas percolated to the grassroots, as Kangxi had intended, and were especially useful in the Qing civilising mission on its frontiers. One example is Yunnan in the far southwest, where the celebrated administrator Chen Hongmou was commissioner in the 1730s. A century after the traveller Xu Xiake explored these wild frontier lands in the company of its native head-men (above pages 315–20), the Qing ploughed enormous military resources to subdue the region and now sought to impose direct Chinese rule. They aimed to integrate the area into the Chinese state with ambitious educational projects. Chinese language schools were founded with the goal of genuine mass literacy training; curriculum books were provided for hundreds of new schools. Among these were works in classical prose, histories and anthologies, works of filial piety and Zhu Xi's rules on the management of the household. Along with the *Sacred Edict*, these were provided for each elementary school in Yunnan, of which there were 200 before the 1730s, but 700 after Chen Hongmou's term as provincial commissioner. 'Our nation offers the model of proper human behaviour', Chen wrote, 'by means of which all others can be instructed.'

There were many achievements in the Great Restoration of the Manchus and their effort to bring good governance and justice. The argument of administrators like Chen was simple: how was China to rule, feed and protect a population that was now rising past 200 million? The task had been no less difficult when Wang Anshi and Sima Guang debated the New Policies in the eleventh century. The problems of governance in China were, and are, on a scale different to anywhere else in the world.

It was perforce a deeply authoritarian state culture that had resisted the movement for intellectual freedoms which had briefly flowered in the Late Ming. Hugely ambitious publishing projects were initiated under Kangxi, but they were conservative in the true sense of the word. The great *Kangxi Dictionary* of 1710, for example, which explained some 49,000 characters with copious quotations and citations, was one of the most remarkable publishing projects of the age, East or West, a precursor of Samuel Johnson's *Dictionary of the English Language* of 1755.

Still, there were many persecutions of writers, book burnings and executions throughout the Qing period. These inquisitions began with the case of an unauthorised *History of the Ming Dynasty* in 1661. The Qing government was paranoid about any vestige of Ming loyalism, and families closely involved with the publication, including printers, booksellers and the officials who had failed to report the book, were executed or exiled. The writer's family was wiped out and seventy others were killed. Late in Kangxi's reign, Dai Mingshi (1653–1713), from Tongcheng in Anhui province (the seat of an influential literary movement we have already encountered above, pages 299–302), was condemned for anti-Manchu writing. Kangxi himself felt obliged to justify this case: 'He was the only scholar I executed for treasonous writings during my reign.' The emperor cited his 'wild and reckless writings' and his connections with the Fang family (above pages 324–5), and singled out the printing of the reign-titles of the three Ming claimants who continued to fight after the Manchus founded the new dynasty. Dai had argued that, following Confucian principles in the writing of history, the Ming claimants should be properly recorded. He also said that 'the government has imposed censorship, that people still avoided the subject of the Ming fall as a taboo and that evidence of the conquest was being destroyed and covered up'. As Kangxi saw it, he had been merciful:

> The Board of Punishments recommended that Dai be put to the lingering death, and that all his male relations over sixteen be executed, and all the female relatives and children be enslaved. But I was merciful and lowered his sentence to beheading, while sparing the relatives. History may be written by officials, but it is the emperor in whose reign the history is written who is finally responsible, and it is he who will be blamed by posterity if there are distortions and errors. I refuse to allow that.

Such literary persecutions would confront Chinese writers for as long as the empire lasted and still do today. In the mid-eighteenth century they reached a head in the wide-ranging literary inquisition that surrounded the emperor Qianlong's *Complete Library of the Four Branches of Literature* of 1772. Indeed, the greatest of all Chinese novels would arouse the attention of the censors – and, it was said, even of the emperor himself. That story takes us to the very heart of court, society and literature at the height of the Qing.

AN EIGHTEENTH-CENTURY FAMILY SAGA

On a clear autumn day the grey ridges of the Western Hills can be seen from Tiananmen Square and the Forbidden City in Beijing. Out there, near the Zoological Gardens 15 miles out of town, is a place called Fragrant Hills. Nowadays, crowds of Beijingers come up there to see the spectacular spring peach and cherry blossoms and the autumn Red Leaf Festival, when the hillsides are a riot of burnished copper, orange, red, gold and crimson. From the mid 1740s, the impoverished hero of our story, Cao Xueqin, lived out here in a place which his friends called 'Yellow Leaves Hamlet', on a wooded slope where the wind ruffles the lake and stirs the willows round its shore. His lodgings, as he said, were in a 'thatched cottage with matting windows, an earthen stove and rope bed', the shuttered windows poor protection against Beijing's bitter winters.

A friend sketched Cao Xueqin at the time, maybe here, in this very place. He is sitting by a stream, leaning on a rock, in a landscape with stands of bamboo. At his side is a musical instrument, a *qin*, in its cloth bag and a satchel of scrolls and brushes. Although swiftly drawn, the face is unmistakably a real portrait of a man who looks in early middle age. He is short and a little plump. His balding head still has a little hair above the ears, his eyes are widely spaced, eyebrows sloping like a clown's mask. If it is not reading too much into the sketch, it is a wry, quizzical face: a moustache and shaved chin, a drinker's nose. The expression is humorous, the eyes twinkly, suggesting a wit that would lighten up any gathering. He was such an entertaining storyteller, especially with drink, that, as a friend said of him, 'wherever he was, he made it spring'.

The scion of a family once highly favoured by the Kangxi emperor, Cao Xueqin had failed in life by the time he was washed up here in the Western Hills. He had done many odd jobs, for a time in a government office, but he gave that up. He had been a private tutor and a painter, selling his pictures to pay his drinking debts. He had even managed a wine shop and a hut dispensing hot water for tea, having been thrown out by a princely family who had employed him as a tutor only to see him get a maid pregnant. Now he was in trouble, drinking too much. Yet he was writing a novel, the idea for which had obsessed him for over ten years. It was written in instalments and circulated in copies to friends, often in exchange for a square meal and a pitcher of wine. 'If you want to know what happens next,' he would say, 'keep me supplied with roast duck and good Shaoxing wine and I'll be happy to oblige!'

He got the cottage here with help from the White Banner, the Manchu military order to which his ancestors had belonged. This is where he resided for the last six years of his life, perhaps with his second wife, 'living on porridge', borrowing money to keep the alcohol flowing. At least there was some consolation in the view down to the capital: 'Reminders of my poverty were all about me,' he wrote, 'the thatched roofs, the wattle walls, the rope bed. But these did not need to be an impediment to the imagination. Indeed the beauties of nature outside my door, the morning breeze, the evening dew, the flowers and trees, were a positive encouragement to write. What was to stop me turning the whole thing into a story, in the language of the people?'

His project was nothing less than the Great Chinese Novel. The story of a family over 100 years at the height of the world of the Manchus: the palace intrigues, the fear, the love, the disappointed dreams. For the Chinese it would become their best-loved book. In the modern world, cinema and television versions have made it known to every household. Behind it, however, is a real story of a real clan: the author's family. Their rise and fall over four generations opens a window on Chinese politics and culture in the golden age of the Qing dynasty. To tell that tale, we first need to go back in time to Cao Xueqin's ancestors over a century earlier.

The Cao clan were Han Chinese from the northeast of China. In the late 1610s, as the Ming empire declined, their ancestral lands had fallen under Manchu rule, and great-grandfather Cao Xi became a slave of the Manchus. After the Manchu conquest of China proper in 1645, the old bureaucracy in Beijing headed by eunuchs was abolished and a new department of the imperial household was set up staffed by Han Chinese. Among them were the Caos, who became bondservants of the most powerful Manchu prince, Dorgon, in the White Banner order of the Manchu military system. Because his nephew Shunzi, the first Manchu emperor, was too young to rule, Dorgon became the key player in the court, and through Dorgon's patronage the Cao family rose.

All official bondservants tied to the royal clan were ethnic Han, from important families who had been captured, imprisoned or enslaved during the conquest. So the position was low, but it was special. The Caos, too, had a special pride in their ancestry. They had helped the rise of the Song in the tenth century, which meant they had a stake in Chinese history long before the Manchus. The family steadily rose in the Manchu world, hunting and riding with the court, joining in its military culture, but also acting as sensitive interpreters of traditional Chinese culture to the Manchu foreigners.

The key to the relationship lay in great-grandfather Cao's wife, Lady Sun. Sun was a wet nurse in the royal household and their son, Cao Yin, was brought up from childhood with the boy who would become the Kangxi emperor. More than a nurse, Sun had been a 'teaching and guiding mother' and was a great influence on the young emperor's development. That link would see the family projected into the stratosphere of preferment. The first Manchu emperor died of smallpox, still in his twenties. His third son, an eight-year-old who providentially had already survived smallpox, became the Kangxi emperor in 1661. As a trusted friend, Cao Xi was promoted, and his son Cao Yin became an intimate of the emperor, the young emperor's 'milk brother' and boyhood study companion. Eventually, Kangxi appointed Cao Xi as the imperial textile commissioner in Suzhou, a much-coveted and very lucrative post, overseeing silk factories with thousands of skilled employees. Later, the adult Cao Yin followed his father, moving to Nanjing as commissioner for the South, with a personal staff of 300 people. He was now disposing of vast sums of money in the 'diamond of China', as a visitor described the city. The family's rise had been meteoric.

Today nothing remains of the Cao family's grand mansion in Nanjing. It lay outside the north wall, across the bridge at Qingliangmen. Now there is a big park and garden on the spot with views over the Qinhuai River and across to Purple Mountain. It was there that Cao Xi built 'imposing halls and pavilions, gardens full of trees and rockeries' for imperial visits, as well as a theatre and an archery field (Kangxi was a keen archer and loved to go on mounted hunts). The hall and pavilion where Kangxi stayed on his visits were treasured as family heirlooms. In the west garden they planted pear trees, magnolias and handsome willows, creating a dream-like world that would be recreated in the great-grandson's novel.

For thirty years the family lived and worked in the great southern cities that were then among the most cultured places on earth. Relatively undamaged in the Manchu wars, Suzhou was 'one of the most fashionable centres of wealth and nobility in the world of men', as Cao Xi's great-grandson would describe it. With its literary salons and printing presses, it was a magnet for poets and writers. In Yangzhou, too, the centre of the salt industry (which also came under the family's supervision), poets and littérateurs, patrons and book collectors congregated. His job of commissioner plugged Cao Yin into all these networks.

In 1705, the Kangxi emperor announced a huge cultural project: to produce an edition of the complete poems of the Tang dynasty, the greatest age of Chinese literature. To do it, he turned to Cao Yin who could mobilise his literary friends in the south – the scholars and collectors of rare books, the expert woodblock cutters and bookmakers in Yangzhou. These were the people with access to the old printed editions and rare manuscripts. Here were the printing houses with the technical means to produce such a work. Kangxi's *Complete Tang Poems* would be a Manchu monument to Han Chinese culture, the defining of a canon, a recognition that the Qing literati class looked back to this age as the peak of Chinese literature. Cao Yin would be the chief collector, publisher and organiser of the woodblock cutting. Published in 1712, the edition contained 50,000 poems by 2,200 poets. To his great joy and pride, when the edition was published, Cao Yin's name appeared on the frontispiece. 'I don't not know what happiness could exceed this,' he said.

Those were golden days for the Cao family. The emperor's visits to their house in Nanjing were never to be forgotten. Indeed, even today among old families in the cities of the Yangtze valley, the stories of those southern tours by the Qing emperors are still recounted by elders as if they occurred yesterday. They can still recite their words and quote the poems they left behind as gifts. To host the emperor was to experience pure elation, like the arrival of a deity. Gardens were reshaped, new pavilions and marquees built, trees strung with fairy lights, the garden paths and rockeries lined with lanterns for night strolls, with live entertainments by musicians, singers and dancers. What a time for the family, at the centre of this exhilarating melding of Manchu and Han culture.

On his six southern tours, Kangxi stayed with the Cao family four times, in a tented residence in the grounds of the Cao estate. The family basked in his glow. On one visit, in 1699, Kangxi greeted Cao Yin's mother, Lady Sun, his old wet nurse, with real affection: 'You are the senior lady of our house!' The emperor wrote an epigraph commemorating his visit and the family made sure it would always be remembered, reproducing it as an inscription on a large, curved, wooden plaque for public display. Painted 'bright azure with letters finished in dark paint, on the edges nine golden dragons with intertwining heads which seemed to move', it was a work of art that symbolised the 'sacred and incomparable power of the emperor'. Kangxi even arranged the marriage of two of Cao Yin's daughters to royal princes, sealing the family's ties with the imperial court.

But, as the old proverb went, 'misfortune can strike at any time'. Or, as Grandad Cao Yin used to say, 'When the tree falls, the monkeys will be scattered.' Scarcely had the great work been published than, in July 1712, Cao Yin was taken ill with malaria, aged only fifty-one. The last exchange of letters between him and Kangxi survives. The emperor recommends quinine, a remedy he had learned from the Jesuits in his court. 'Take care, take care!' he urged his old friend. The dose was sent, but too late. On 24 August, Cao Yin died of malaria. His estates and titles were passed on to his only son, Cao Yong, who became his successor as the imperial textile commissioner. But he was a nineteen-year-old youth with no experience, unqualified for the position. Then, fatefully, in 1715, Yong also died suddenly, still in his early twenties, and without a son. The family's position was suddenly under serious threat. Who would be the head? To carry on the line, out of his old affection for the clan, the emperor allowed a paternal nephew to be adopted as 'Yin's posthumous son': but this man, Cao Fu, was a far less capable person.

It was around this time that Cao Yin's grandson, Cao Xueqin, with whom we began this story at the hut in the hills, was born. When exactly this was has never been determined, but 1715 seems likeliest.

It is still unclear who his father was. Whether he was the posthumous son of Yong, whose widow was pregnant when he died, or whether he was the son of the adopted Fu, is not known. Most likely it was the latter. On this reckoning, in his early years, young Xueqin still knew the family at the height of its fortune, but when he was almost thirteen (the age he would later give his hero in the novel), the axe fell.

The family's precipitous decline began when the emperor Kangxi died in 1722, aged sixty-eight, after a reign of sixty-one years, first as ward and then as sole ruler. The last years of the great emperor had been troubled by palace intrigues and anguished talk of betrayal by his sons. The emperor descended into paranoia and cruelty amid bitter factional feuds, suspicious of even those closest to him. 'If I can die without there being an outbreak of trouble,' he wrote near the end, 'my desires will have been fulfilled.' Any change of ruler in Chinese history was a dangerous moment, but with such a big royal family, this time it was especially so. Kangxi had fathered many children by his wives and concubines, twenty-four sons all told, and the senior ones were fighting for the throne even before his death.

The victor was not the named successor, but a usurper. Yinzhen, one of the younger sons, took power, proclaiming himself the Yongzheng emperor, 'Blessed with Sincerity'. Vengeful, cunning and vicious, Yongzheng was determined to root out corruption, which was draining the treasury. For the bondservants he harboured a particular resentment. As soon as he had power, he moved against his father's old friends and their allies, among them the Caos. His method was to pursue them for debts and procure their financial ruin. Yongzheng seized property, possessions and lands, haranguing them with his 'gangster tone': 'never before had such vulgar language been used in imperial edicts'. First to go was Cao Fu's brother-in-law. Then the emperor closed in on Cao Fu himself, who had huge debts mainly incurred by Grandad Cao Yin over a lifetime of lavish patronage and charity. Fu responded to the emperor's charges with a memo whose courtly conventions do not disguise the fear of the writer. Evidently, he could hardly hold his brush steady:

Your respected eminence. I previously wrote to you about the financial deficits of the Imperial Textile Factory and in this report I begged you to allow me three years to balance the books. Today, after receiving the documents from your office, I understand that you have accepted this plan with the great generosity characteristic of your majesty. I, your ever deferential servant, realise I have failed in my duty and deserve to be torn to pieces without complaint. Yet unexpectedly I am blessed by heaven, and saved from harm, by your grace. I, your humble slave, indeed now a reborn person, shall gratefully await any punishment.

Cao Fu was now criticised out in the open, and in June 1722 the court stopped his salary on the grounds that his cloth was not of high enough quality. His enemies gathered round him, accusing him of hiding his assets and of corruption. In early December he was charged with taking bribes and designated a 'criminal official'. Then, on 24 December, the emperor sealed his ruin:

The Nanjing Textile Commissioner Cao Fu has mismanaged his office and put the department into considerable debt. I frequently delayed his debt repayment, but rather than work to clear it, Cao Fu secretly transferred property and hid his assets. What disgusting behaviour, completely devoid of gratitude! I hereby order the governor of the Southern Yangtze region to seal off all of Cao Fu's properties and arrest the main servants. The servants' properties must also be sealed until the new textile commissioner deals with them. I also understand that Cao Fu may try to send servants to the southern Yangtze region to transfer his properties before the confiscation is complete: be sure to investigate every visitor.

Government agents and soldiers descended on the family house in Nanjing. The family and their servants were arrested. The contents of every room were itemised, sealed with paper strips and stamped with the official seal. The confiscation inventory of all their houses listed 483 rooms, in a dozen locations, including the main house, the scene of their golden days in the old reign, those breathless lamplit nights when Kangxi had come to stay. There were lands and gardens totalling around 50 acres and 114 staff – cooks, stablemen and maids – who now became property of the state. On a separate list were furniture, 'old clothing and other odds and ends', even 100 pawn-shop tickets worth 1,000 *tael* of silver. When questioned, the staff and servants stated that their master owed them 32,000 *liang* of silver. Clearly the family had been unable to pay the bills for a while in the lead-up to the final denouement. A later document states that when the family's straits were eventually revealed and it became clear that they had not concealed hidden wealth, as their accusers had alleged, 'even the emperor felt pity for them'.

Perhaps that was why, in 1729, the emperor, having forced the family to relocate to Beijing, allowed them to retain a modest house outside the Tartar walls. There Grandma, the widow of Cao Yin, was allowed six servants, 'to support herself'. The family house lay just outside the Chongwenmen Gate in the so-called 'Chinese town', halfway between the Temple of Heaven and the main city wall of the Tartar City. The great government street map of the city, prepared in the eighteenth century, shows the house in a dense pattern of alleys and houses, around a single-storey, tiled courtyard, at the junction of the main road from the city gate. There were five main rooms to the north, three down each side, with a kitchen, bathroom and storerooms for rice and grain to the south. The house survived until the area was levelled for road widening in 2003. Still inside were four screen doors carved with the characters *duan*, *fang*, *zheng* and *zhi*. These four characters made up the family motto – 'virtuous, honest, decent and just' – which was not forgotten by Yin's grandson in his novel, where it is used by the fictional family.

IN THE STREETS OF OLD BEIJING

By now, in 1729, Cao Xueqin was fourteen, beginning a new life with his grandmother and extended family in the suburbs of the capital. After a pampered and privileged childhood, he was a wary teenager in anxious times, mistrustful of all power. Later on, in his persona as 'author', he offers a self-deprecating *captatio* about his wasted education: 'In defiance of my family's attempts to bring me up properly and all the warnings and advice of my friends, I had brought myself to this present wretched state in which, having frittered away half a lifetime, I find myself without a single skill with which I could earn a decent living.'

He was, however, good with the brush, both with paint and with words, and he found other inspiration in the streets around him. In the mid-eighteenth century, Beijing was the place to be. The famous aphorism by Cao Xueqin's contemporary Dr Johnson, 'When a man is tired of London, he is tired of life', was true, too, of Qing Beijing. This is one of those times in Chinese history, like Tang Xi'an, Song Kaifeng or Southern Song Hangzhou, when urban life simply over-flowed with vitality. In the eighteenth century, with over a million people, Beijing was one of the world's most vibrant cities. Xueqin lived in the centre of a vast multi-racial, multi-lingual empire, its teeming streets right outside his front door. He saw huge caravans heading out to Mongolia, sometimes 2,000 camels at a time, car-rying brick tea across the Gobi, or coal to Russia. The goods of the Silk Road poured in from Central Asia – gems, spices, woven cloths, leather and metalwork, melons and dried fruits of all kinds. Looking out from his street corner, over the rooftops towered the Chongwenmen, 'the Gate of Excellent Scholarship', a big brick arch with a huge superstructure of wood with triple eaves and balcony guard rooms. Its big bell announced the closing of the gate at the end of the day, and nearby were crowded night markets. The acrid smell of many small distilleries wafted over the houses, and brewers' carts rumbled along rutted streets. Living cheek by jowl with ordinary people, Xueqin often saw actors, jugglers and storytellers on street corners. Beijing was also a city of temples, huge state institutions and small local shrines. It was only a short walk into the Tartar City and its suburbs for the big temple festivals. One can see in his book that he was enraptured by the traditions and customs of the peoples from all over China who gathered at such times.

The most loved shrine for the people of the city, and surely for Xueqin himself, was the great Daoist temple, Dongyue, also known as 'The God of the Eastern Peak', the patron deity of the sacred Mount Tai. The temple had been built in the Yuan, when Tibetan Buddhism came to the fore in China out of an older mix of Buddhist beliefs and folk religion. It stood a mile out of the East Gate of the Tartar walls, where it still stands today. Despite being trashed and gutted in the Cultural Revolution, it has made a hesitant recovery in recent years, but back in Xueqin's day, it was a little city on its own, with its stands of ancient cypress trees and its spacious courtyards – a centre of the social life of the city. There were special cults for the guilds of tile workers, carpenters, masons, lime manufacturers, decorators, butchers, miners, bathhouse proprietors and midwives. The city's actors put on shows at festival times and even the street beggars had their own associations here. All ages, all classes – men and women, old and young, urban and rural, elite and commoners – rubbed shoulders during festivals in an 'unbroken stream'. This was the world of popular Chinese religion that survived everywhere up to the 1949 revolution.

The liturgical layout of the shrine represented a symbolic universe. It included a series of seventy-two chapels, dusty cubicles depicting all the 'departments' of Yama, the god of the dead, borrowed from Tibetan Buddhism. 'When you go into the Dongyue Temple', it was said, 'you are confronted by the gates of the seventy-two offices and you are immediately filled with fear.' Here, laid out as a kind of infernal bureaucracy, were the circles of the underworld that punished human sins: the Department for Determining Destiny, the Office of Life or Death, the Department of Wandering Ghosts, the Department of Timely Retribution. Here the pilgrim could also find the gods of childbirth, eyesight, promotion and plague, as well as the old man of the moon, who was the much-sought-after god of marriage. In the main hall sat the statue of the god of Mount Tai himself, with all his maids, servants, ministers, celestial officials and generals. He was accompanied too by the primordial deities of China: Fuxi Shennong, the first farmer; and the Yellow Emperor.

With such an all-inclusive pantheon, the temple was a memory room of the Chinese story, much as one might find in India in popular Hinduism today. In the teeming courtyards of Beijing's most popular shrine, all human life was there.

THE WORLD AS FICTION: WRITER AND THE CENSOR

This was the city in which Cao Xueqin grew up in the 1730s and '40s. It is easy to see how the flood of sensory impressions, the stories and spiritual topographies, gave the budding writer a rich source of metaphor and symbolic landscapes. It is rather similar to how, in Europe, the spiritual topographies of High Medieval Christian scholastic theology, with its nine circles of purgatory and its gradations of punishments, gave Dante the imaginative structure for his *Divine Comedy*. A key element of Xueqin's book would be the satirising of traditional religion with the eye of what we might term a magical realist, beginning by taking us through the great gate of the Land of Illusion to his imagined offices of the heart, 'the Department of Fond Infatuation', the 'Department of Ill-Fated Unions' and the 'Department of Spring Fever and Autumn Grief'.

Any satire, however, was dangerous in the eighteenth-century literary world. Xueqin's formative years as a writer in Beijing were years of literary purges. By the 1730s, the Yongzheng emperor had established his power on all fronts. In the outside world he had consolidated the empire to an unrivalled extent, including Xinjiang, Mongolia and Tibet. 'Since our dynasty began to rule China,' he pronounced in a royal memorandum, 'the Mongols and other tribes living in extremely remote regions have been integrated into our territory. This is the great expansion of China's lands.'

At home in the 1730s, Yongzheng launched a five-year literary persecution which included 'word prison cases' for any writer who was thought to have intentionally slandered or criticised the emperor. Several writers were killed. Then, in 1736, Yongzheng suddenly died, still only fifty-six, his health undermined by elixirs intended to prolong his life, though there were rumours that he had been assassinated by a woman whose family had been executed in his literary purges. He was succeeded by his son, Hongli, who came to the throne at the age of twenty-five. Hongli took the reign name Qianlong: 'Lasting Pre-eminence'. Incredibly, he would live until the last year of the century and met the first British embassy to China in 1793. Qianlong began his rule with pardons to many who had been purged by his father. In the amnesty, Cao Fu was acquitted, and though his branch of the clan never recovered its position in Qing society, the family was released from further punishment.

During these years, Xueqin learned to be a writer and found his path. While he painted and wrote poetry to earn money, the Great Chinese Novel was the thing, and would occupy his thinking from the age of thirty. *Dream of the Red Chamber* was to be an eighteenth-century saga, the tale of a noble family that falls from great heights. A friend who annotated his manuscript in 1754 speaks of 'ten years of blood and sweat', so Xueqin was already writing the book when he was around thirty, and it went through many drafts.

It was a time when the role of popular literature in China was going through revaluation. Effectively, there are two canons in Chinese literature. Each is defined by the language in which it is written: the classical literary language of China, and the vernacular. Xueqin was a champion of vernacular literature. His ambition for the tale was 'to turn it all into a story in the vernacular'. In his time, there were new developments in Chinese literary education. These followed critics in the last century who had argued for a revision of the canon, retaining some of the classical greats like Du Fu, but replacing others by vernacular works that drew on 'the life of streets and the marketplace'. Texts would be chosen on literary merit, not moral value or canonical status. Some were ancient, for example the writings of the philosopher Zhuangzi (fourth century BCE), humorous, irreverent fables and parables in a sparkling, riddling tone. Others were more recent, such as the colourful Ming dynasty novel *Outlaws of the Marsh*. These were both a big influence on Xueqin, but especially the novel. The eighteenth-century literary world, then, was moving away from the Confucian classics to a purely literary canon. The novel, the great literary form of the Ming, had come into its own. Works like the scandalous *Plum in Golden Vase*, with its mix of satire, lurid sex and social commentary, showed what a novelist could do. New possibilities were opening up for an ambitious writer and thinker.

Xueqin left few clues about the last phase of his life. For a time, as we saw, he lived out in the Western Hills above Beijing. In the 1960s, redologists (as *Red Chamber* obsessives are known in China) were hunting his trail up near the Zoological Gardens and were directed to a semi-derelict row of cottages. Locals said he had lived there for a while, where eighteenth-century graffiti and wall paintings remained on the plastered walls. It is likely the story was true. The property had belonged to Cao's White Bannermen Manchu order, so perhaps a kindly clansman had helped him out, seeing he was down on his luck. Sympathetically restored, there's a little 'Red Stone' post office there now where one may send specially franked postcards showing the novel's main characters.

A different kind of novel from the earlier Chinese classics like *Romance of the Three Kingdoms*, *The Water Margin* or *Monkey*, *Dream of the Red Chamber* is a vast, sprawling narrative, surreal and poignant, full of songs and poems – a Chinese remembrance of things past. The story is about three generations of a family who rose to dizzying heights (one daughter even becomes an imperial consort). Then it tells of their fall from grace. In the end, their house is raided and their wealth confiscated: 'In the hundred years since the foundation of the present dynasty, several generations of our house have distinguished themselves by their service to the throne and have covered themselves with riches and honours; but now the stock of good fortune has run out and nothing can be done to replenish it.'

Among the galaxy of characters is the grandmother, who holds the family together, and the adolescent hero, carefree and sensitive, born with a silver spoon in his mouth (in his case, a piece of magic jade). At the centre of the plot is his love for his fated cousin, who shares his love of poetry and music, but who dies of a broken heart after his arranged marriage to another cousin, a girl of ideal female virtue, but with whom he lacks a true emotional bond. The troubled boy is surely autobiographical, with his 'perverse, intractable nature, eccentric and emotionally unstable, whose natural brightness and intelligence augur well, but we fear that owing to the fated eclipse of our family's fortunes there will be no one at hand to give the lad proper guidance and start him off on the right path'. Initiated by the fairy Disenchantment, he enters the gate to the Buddhist- and Daoist-tinged Land of Illusion, in which is inscribed a sphinx-like riddle: 'Truth becomes fiction when the fiction's true; real becomes not-real when the unreal's real.'

Xueqin probably died on 1 February 1764, heartbroken, it is said, by the death of his only son in a smallpox outbreak. His second wife survived him. The book was finally published in print only in 1792. The last forty of its 120 chapters are a patchwork of different fragments collected over the years by his friends. Clearly something happened in the intervening time. Possibly one of his readers confiscated or destroyed parts, believing them to be dangerous. The poet's uncle, it is said, declined to read it, fearing 'indiscretions'. The story picked up in the nineteenth century by the British missionary Arthur Cornaby was that the book had been 'altered and toned down' because eminent people it satirised had been too thinly disguised.

This may be true. Writing in Qing China was always dangerous, with censorship, book burnings and executions of authors who strayed too far in their freedom of speech. Even their bones could be disinterred and destroyed. The beginning of the 1770s in particular coincided with a major literary inquisition around the collection of books for the huge Qing encyclopaedia the *Siku Quanshu*, or the *Complete Library of the Four Branches of Literature*. This giant work contained an annotated catalogue of over 10,000 key works in classics, philosophy, history and literature, with the full texts of over 3,500 literary works in more than 36,000 volumes. In a project unparalleled in world history, collectors were ordered to hand in written works, on condition they would be returned so long as the books were free of anti-Manchu sentiment. It is possible that *Dream of the Red Chamber* was caught up in that after the author's death, especially with its underground fame. There was a story that Qianlong himself was shown a copy of the manuscript by a member of the royal family and pronounced it obscene, enquiring after the real family behind the fiction. The text, as we have it, ends with fulsome praise of the emperor. A darker ending, with criticism of the emperor who had ordered the family's downfall, it is said, was removed. Perhaps reshaped after his death, then, the rewritten book took no risks; it was 'not against Confucian morals', Cornaby's informants told him a century or so on. 'We can well understand why,' he wrote, 'apart from the disclosure of family secrets and [the fact that] the writer evidently drew from life, such a work should have been proscribed by the authorities for fifty years after its publication; and that it should have been again proscribed in the 1830s when manuscript copies sold in temple book markets for a small fortune.'

From its first publication in 1792, the novel's fame was assured. 'Written by a great artist with his very lifeblood,' as its translator David Hawkes said, *Dream of the Red Chamber*, also known as *The Story of the Stone*, is now seen as one of the great novels of world literature, 'a candidate for the Book of the Millennium'. 'To the Chinese', it has been said, it is 'as Proust is to the French or Karamazov to the Russians'. Particularly striking in a work of the mid-eighteenth century is the preponderance of female characters, and, in that sense, the book is part of a surge in interest in women's voices by writers of both sexes. The female voice, as we have seen throughout this book, was always constrained by China's patriarchal society. Here, though, the boy hero says 'the pure essence of human-ity was all concentrated in the female of the species, and the males were its mere dregs'. This is the first great work of art in China where women are at the centre, which helps explain its enduring popularity today among female readers. On the strength of the female charac-ters, Cao Xueqin himself as 'author' is illuminating:

Having made an utter failure of my life, one day I found myself in the midst of my poverty and wretchedness, thinking about the female companions of my youth. As I went over them in my mind's eye, one by one, it suddenly came over me that those slips of girls, which is all they were then, were in every way, both morally and intellectually, superior to the 'grave and mustachioed signior' I am now supposed to have become. The realisation brought with it an overpowering sense of shame and remorse and for a while I was plunged in the deepest despair ... there and then I resolved to make a record of all the recollections of those days I could muster, those golden days when I dressed in silk and ate delicately, when we still nestled in the protecting shadow of the Ancestors and Heaven that still smiled on us. I resolved that however unsightly my shortcomings might be, I must not, for the sake of keeping them hidden, allow those wonderful girls to pass into oblivion without a memorial.

THE WORLD AS FACT: THE TALE OF 'THE GOODWIFE XUN'

The depiction of women in *The Dream of the Red Chamber* is one aspect of the rise of women in Chinese literature, of whom thousands appear as authors in seventeenth- and eighteenth-century poetic anthologies. The Cao family, of course, inhabited the world of high society and elite culture, with their immense household and their retinue of servants entertaining the emperor himself. They lived in a world where even a woman might have a writing room that could be mistaken by a visitor for 'the master gentleman's room'.

The private lives of less highly placed women are harder to touch. In the late eighteenth century, however, there is much more writing by and about women and their predicament, the abuses of marriage, the concubine system and footbinding. The historian and philosopher Zhang Xuecheng, for example, wrote a series of biographies of women he knew, which give intimate glimpses into the lives of the impoverished middle class, who often struggled to make ends meet. Such women were often the earliest teachers of their sons and daughters and would support their sons' higher education with earnings from spinning and weaving. In the biographies of successful men, the debt to their mothers' sacrifices is a common theme, but of their mothers' lives and feelings less is known. Seldom, save sometimes in their private poetry, do we hear their own voices.

Zhang had been brought up surrounded by women. An only son with several sisters, he had been educated by his mother and from his teens developed close friendships with older women. His intimate knowledge of the reality of women's lives made him impatient with the conventional stereotypes of womanhood honoured in imperial commendations, on clan monuments to chaste wives in standard histories written by men for men. This affected Zhang's attitude as a historian to his craft. Though a conservative Confucian, he argued that mothers and daughters transmitted the learning and traditions of families and at crucial times were often the ones who preserved bodies of knowledge that war or death would have otherwise wiped out. Within the constraints of Chinese society, then, though confined to the 'inner chambers', as Zhang saw it, women were vital transmitters of history, as well as of custom and family ritual.

Zhang wrote about several women in his immediate family, including his mother who came from a well-known family of scholar-officials. A woman of great acuteness, she once bailed her husband out of financial troubles through her own care with the family budget. She held the family together in adversity and was the real fount of wisdom and good counsel. A poet herself, she had a role in her only son's early education. When he left home as a young man, Zhang also seems to have been drawn to surrogate mothers and sisters, with whom he was at ease, coming from a family of women. Women, it should be said, were also a very strong cultural influence in his native Shaoxing and in eastern Zhejiang, an area whose distinctive literary culture produced far more women writers than any other in the eighteenth century.

Among Zhang's narratives about women, some of the most moving and intimate concern women in his wider circle; one particularly long and affectionate account of one was called *A Factual Record of the Deeds of the Goodwife Xun*. It was drawn from his own memories and from those of Xun's daughters, family members and friends, and has been translated by Lynn Struve. As a work of history by a great historian, it is without parallel in literature. In its way, it is as memorable a portrait of a woman as those to be found in eighteenth and nineteenth-century European novels. Zhang says he pieced together the story after knowing Xun for over thirty years, and it includes interviews with her daughters, whom he sometimes asked 'to come over by carriage to the family *yamen* to tell him their life stories'.

Lady Xun was the wife of Zhang's elder paternal cousin. Born in 1715 (the thirtieth year of Kangxi as Zhang dates it), Xun was twenty-three years older than Zhang. Her life spanned the century. So, when Zhang's intimacy with her began, he was in his early twenties, she in her mid-forties. She was the seventh child of a well-to-do family, but her husband was negligent and irresponsible, hopeless at managing money and providing for his family, 'so they became very poor'. She had seven children. The first, a son, died in infancy, and none of the next four, all girls, survived to adulthood. Only the youngest, the two girls whom Zhang came to love, grew to adulthood. They were born when Xun was in her mid-thirties. In 1751, when she was thirty-six, the elder girl was a toddler, the younger only five months old. With no surviving sons, her biographer, Zhang, gave one of his sons to the family after her death as he had promised.

The family were not like the Caos. Being 'very poor', they had to live a frugal life, but never complained. They rented a house in Beijing in the southern 'Chinese city', beyond the main wall in the outer quarter, an area inhabited by low-level officialdom, traders and shopkeepers. It was a neighbourhood of *hutongs* outside the southern precincts of the Temple of Heaven, near a market, a cluster of decaying Daoist temples and a Buddhist nunnery.

It is there, Zhang says, that Xun and her husband were regular hosts of four generations of the Zhang clan in town to sit the examinations, on business trips or doing government jobs in Yongzheng's time and through the long reign of Qianlong. Xun was always washing, sewing and repairing clothes for them and cooking food. Her husband's parents also lived with her. They were demanding in-laws who expected Xun to do everything for them, and yet she 'always tried to please her mother-in-law'. The household accounts had to be carefully managed, as her husband was so irresponsible with his family duties, and Xun had to stretch the family budget further to feed scores of unpredictable visitors, even lending money to hard-up students. Zhang's picture of her is as the head of the household, a person of fortitude, ingenuity and dedication to the family, though hers was far from a love marriage. Zhang himself in his younger days had spent months relying on her because, despite his huge talent, he never got a good government job. When he talked about her life with his cousins, in the writings of the memoir, they all shed tears: 'My visits to her home spanned more than thirty years from the time my father got his *jinshi* degree till I myself became an academy student . . . that's how I came to know her so well. I knew her better than anyone.'

Women at this level of society generally only had a basic education, though there were moves to change that in the middle of the century by forward-looking educationalists. Xun was not classically educated. Indeed, Zhang says 'she was not terribly at home with books'. Still, she loved popular novels and tales from heroic operas, especially stories of faithful widows and loyal ministers who stood fast in the face of adversity. Sometimes these stories were told in her neighbourhood by blind storytellers, drumming and strumming to accompany their performances. Xun resembles medieval women in Europe who derived great comfort from saints' lives, tales of constancy in the face of cruelty, abuse and attacks on their honour – tales that, for all their fantasy, in their directness validated their experience as women. Whenever Xun read that kind of book, says her nephew, or when she saw those plays, 'she seemed transported to the scene herself, carried away by their example'.

Most importantly, 'goodwife Xun' was inculcated with a Confucian moral sensibility from her own parents. She believed this should determine how a woman lived her life. As the family's fortunes fell, she tried to protect her parents-in-law from the poverty that the rest of the family suffered. She even pawned her jewels from her dowry so she could still serve them their favourite dish of pork. When her mother-in-law was dying, she couldn't open her mouth and chew her food, and for the last six months Xun would get up early every day to prepare special dishes that could be easily swallowed and digested. She would then spend hours patiently feeding her mother-in-law, 'opening her mouth and gently putting each spoonful between her lips'. Her life had many trials and tribulations, all of which she met with resolution. Her father-in-law, for example, took an overbearing concubine who drank and cursed, but when the woman grew ill and incontinent, Xun still tended her and cleaned her, as Zhang describes in graphic detail. In her resolute public humanity, Xun was a Confucian, but in her spiritual life she was a Buddhist and, it appears, a vegetarian. All this and much else she did while still raising her own daughters. Zhang also describes her sense of humour. On one occasion her husband went away for a three-year journey to the south, leaving her with six dependants. When he returned, she kidded him that in order to raise cash to feed her impoverished family and the unending flow of guests, she had sold his precious library of rare books. In fact, she had carefully saved them while still making ends meet.

'She loved to talk with me,' Zhang remembered. She even told him about her dreams. On one occasion she brought her old account books out to show him how she had managed the finances all these years. This was something for which she got no credit from her indifferent and feckless husband. 'In the end the toll of it all showed in her care-worn face,' Zhang said. Later, she also gave Zhang material for her biography, as did her daughters, one of whom also wrote an account of her mother for him. When he read it after her death, her husband wept at his realisation of her nobility of character and his own thoughtlessness and inadequacy. 'How I failed you! How I failed you!' he cried.

In 1768, aged fifty-four, Goodwife Xun died. She had been ill for a while, worn down and broken-hearted over the death of her elder daughter. Her story is a small domestic tragedy amid the grandeur of Qianlong's reign. The position of women in imperial China would begin to change in the next century. Mother Xun and her daughters were women of moral courage and high sensibility, which is why Zhang felt privileged to have been the recipient of their true friendship, affection and intimacy, and felt impelled to write of them, as well as of more fortunate women in his family. In the same sentiment, Cao Xueqin had written of the women of his family, the women who had inspired his writing, though Xueqin turned them into fiction. There was a wider import in Zhang's arguments about women's learning: that women were no less than men; indeed, in some ways they were more important in carrying down 'this culture of ours'. What he admired in the women he knew, as his modern translator has written, was 'their intuitive ability to sense what they ought to do in every demanding situation and to act on it with alacrity, competence and consummate grace ... the demands were overwhelming, the toll was enormous, yet their capacity to meet the demands and absorb the toll appeared to him to be infinite'. Zhang was well aware that very few women escaped suffering in marriage, that even what promised to be a good marriage might turn sour, and then no one could set it right.

These profound lessons, which are so central to our historiography in the twenty-first century, also informed Zhang's work as a professional historian. Though today he is compared to historians of the European Enlightenment such as Giambattista Vico, he never made it as a great figure in the Qing state, instead carrying out provincial jobs and working on local histories. While compiling one such history of Hebei, he paid special attention to the biographies of living women. Even though he was a traditional Confucian who saw a woman's place as at home, rather than in the public culture, it was a remarkable innovation based on his close relations with women.

This still seems very topical in the modern-day plea for forgotten lives and the erasure of women's history. As we see it now, it is part of the long lead-in to the modernisation debates that arose in the second half of the nineteenth century. 'What of the clever spouse who is a companion to her husband?' wrote Zhang. 'Or the wise mother who teaches her son? Or the far-sighted wife who sustains the family? Women like these are praised to the skies in surviving family memoirs, but the history books relegate them to a short sentence. How are we to uncover their hidden virtues and display their obscured deeds to influence those who will come later?'

We should not conclude, though, that Xun's life was the fate of all educated women in the eighteenth century. The huge growth of published literature saw countless female writers in print who talked positively about women's experiences. Among the next generation, for example, Gan Lirou (born 1743) was a gentry wife who wrote a remarkable autobiography and thousands of poems. The concubine Shen Cai (born 1752) composed a startlingly assured rejoinder in a public letter to male critics of her verse. These women, in their battles for the female voice to be heard, are comparable to Britain's Jane Austen, first publishing anonymously and with trepidation as 'a lady', or the Brontë sisters, who used male pseudonyms for fear of the judgement of their male peers, and the effect of their gender on their readership.

THE QING ACHIEVEMENT

The Qing dynasty, though long underestimated at least by Western historians, is now receiving richly rewarding reconsideration. The irony is that, in the eighteenth century, European Enlightenment writers such as Montesquieu and the contributors to Diderot's *Encyclopaedia* were positively influenced by travellers' accounts and by reports from Jesuit missionaries in the Chinese court. They saw Qing China as a model for a stable monarchical order based on reason and *civilité*, and the Qing emperors as rulers were held up as exemplars of the cultivation of civilised behaviour as the basis of statecraft. Of course, they were seen differently in the following century, and are viewed differently today. Though perhaps when we look at great Qing administrators and teachers like Chen Hongmou, such judgements at least help us to understand the nature of a state ruled by the principles of *wenli:* the rule of reason and civility. In China, this was society's response to profound social, cultural and demographic change. In such a populous, diverse and meritocratic society, there was an erosion of status and distinctions, along with growing social and geographical mobility and cultural pluralism that we began to glimpse in the Late Ming. The need, then, was both to redefine the world and to get back to basics.

Despite the enormous burden of rulership with a population that passed 300 million in the eighteenth century, the Qing state achieved an extraordinary level of success. This was the world's biggest economy and multi-racial empire. Away from Beijing, in the prosperous cities of the south, complex urban societies flourished with many of the characteristics of the European Enlightenment: banks, trading guilds, charitable institutions, widespread literacy, publishing and print cultures, scientific and literary clubs, poetry circles and even a measure of 'public opinion'. In Yangzhou, for example, the great salt merchants like Bao Zhidao, a member of the Bao family of Tangyue, whose story we have followed above, was a major patron of charity and culture who involved himself in issues of what we might call workers' rights. Women, too, were now a major voice: modern studies list 4,000 women poets whose collected works existed at one time or another during the Qing, even if they do not survive, or have yet to be located, today. After small beginnings in the Ming, the eighteenth century also saw the start of a societal reaction against the traditional treatment of women – including footbinding, concubinage and social seclusion – which would grow in the late nineteenth- and early twentieth-century feminist movement and come into the open under the People's Republic. That said, then, may we even say that Qing China was developing what we would call a civil society? If we look at these markers, to some extent we might answer yes. Left to its own devices, eighteenth-century China would surely have evolved its own distinctive forms of modernity. But, in the event, the outside world would have its own say on that question.

WAITING FOR THE BARBARIANS

In 1751, Emperor Qianlong commissioned a set of *Illustrations of the Tributary Peoples* (*Huang Qing Zhigong Tu*). Published in 1761, the scrolls carried illustrations of 303 different peoples of the known world, including Mongols, Tibetans and ethnic minorities of the southwest and southeast, with whom the Qing came into contact. Among them were also thumbnails of Westerners, including a small island nation 7,000 miles away at the other end of Eurasia. The scroll has illustrations, copied from a Western source, of a man with a cocked hat and breeches clutching a bottle of drink and a woman in a fine gown with a box of snuff, in the act of pinching her nose. The British.

Fighting wars in south India and Bengal, in America and Canada, the British were slowly extending their power, mercantile and military, across the world. However, in the 1750s they were still a people about whom the Qing Foreign Office had only a few vague ideas. Indeed, in Qianlong's *Tributaries* scrolls, there is a strange absence of any attempt to conceptualise or order the outer world as a whole in a way which might have helped as they attempted to adapt to swiftly changing geopolitics over the next decades. 'Britain is quite rich', wrote the scroll compiler, 'their women, when unmarried, bind their waists tightly as they like them really narrow.' After talking about hairstyles, fashion in clothes and British women's taste for snuff, the text concludes: 'They greatly enjoy drinking alcohol.'

Soon enough, fate would bring the Chinese and the British together in a way that could never have been imagined by either side.

16

THE OPIUM WARS
AND THE TAIPING

In the eighteenth century, in the middle years of the Qing dynasty, the Chinese empire reached its greatest extent. With Mongolia, Xinjiang and the protectorate of Tibet, it was China's largest land empire and the world's biggest economy, though the weight of its GDP was generated by the immense internal market. From 1735 the emperor was Qianlong (died 1799), whose long reign saw immense cultural achievements but growing problems in the economy and society. His predecessor, Yongzheng, had battled corruption and tax evasion, but Qianlong reversed his prudent fiscal policies, and with tax levels frozen since Kangxi's days, from the 1780s the state's finances became precarious while it experienced a rapid population rise. Civil servants and magistrates were underpaid, bribery and extortion were habitual, and rebellions in the outer provinces now began to occur with growing frequency. Fatefully, this is the moment the British appear in the Chinese story.

THE MACARTNEY EMBASSY

On 25 July 1793, after a nine-month journey from Britain, HMS *Lion* anchored in the mouth of the Hai River. In the somnolent heat, junks and sampans rowed round its ornamented stern under

the windows of captain's cabins, their curious crews crowding the
rail to see the visitors from the other side of the world. With a main
mast towering almost 60 metres over the local craft, the *Lion* was
bigger than any Chinese ship. Weighing nearly 400 tons unladen, her
gundeck was 50 metres long and carried sixty-four guns. Though
only a third-rate man of war (the biggest British warships were huge
floating castles with three decks and 100 guns), she was equipped
with all the modern European technology of naval warfare. Close by
at anchor, accompanying the *Lion*, was the *Hindostan*, a new East
India Company vessel chartered by the British government to take
its embassy and their staff on their two-year journey to open trade
negotiations with the imperial government in Beijing. On the deck
in parade dress with his spyglass was Britain's ambassador, George,
Earl Macartney of Lissanoure KB.

Macartney was fifty-six years old, and already famous for his
observation that Britain controlled 'a vast empire on which the sun
never sets'. From an old Scottish family settled in County Antrim
since the seventeenth century, he had been ambassador to Russia,
governor in the West Indies, and governor in Madras, where the Fort
St George we see today was largely his creation. An affable exponent
of what today we would call realpolitik, in 1784 he had negotiated
the Treaty of Mangalore, ending the Second Anglo-Mysore War,
after which he refused the position of governor general of India and
returned to Britain with thirty-two years of world travels behind
him. Few people in the late eighteenth century had seen more of
the world, still less possessed a better strategic grasp of the British
Empire, its far-flung possessions, and the links that held it together.
Few too had a better sense of the economic necessities that drove the
British expansion and the pressures which might facilitate its rise or
precipitate its fall. Now, with growing confusion in Europe in the
wake of the French Revolution, Britain was using its naval power to
move outwards, acquiring an empire, as was said later, 'in a fit of
absence of mind'. In reality it was surely more calculating than that,
but nonetheless contingent, responsive to changing situations, and
certainly at times improvised. The timing of the Chinese encounter,

however, was no accident, and the key to the British move east was India.

In 1765 the British victory at Plassey in Bengal had detached the most populous part of India from the Moghul empire and appropriated its tax revenues. The British hold over the south was strengthened in four Mysore wars between 1767 and 1799, the third of which ended in 1792 with the defeat of Tipu Sultan of Mysore, who ceded half his territory to the British East India Company, a joint stock company formed in 1600 to trade in the Indian Ocean which in time would control half the world's trade. With its Indian conquests Britain was now a global player, with a powerful navy, able to move forces across the world, armed with the latest mass-produced weaponry from arms factories of Birmingham and the Midlands.

The East India Company had traded with Chinese merchants for over a century, but in a strictly limited way. Foreign traders were only allowed into the port of Canton (today's Guangzhou) for five months of the year, and all transactions had to be carried out through Chinese officials, who imposed high taxes on foreign commerce. This is what Macartney sought to change. His goal was to meet the Qianlong emperor and to obtain cessions of Chinese territory near the tea- and silk-producing and textile-consuming areas of the country, where English traders could reside and where English jurisdiction might be exercised. He wanted to establish a resident minister at Peking and to extend British trade and commerce throughout China by negotiating a commercial treaty and opening new ports under more favourable conditions than those in Canton. He also had a wider eye on developing British trade with Japan, eastern China and the islands of the South China Sea.

Qianlong was now eighty-two, a ruler of immense experience, affable and masterful, cunning and sophisticated. He was already familiar with aspects of European culture through missionaries and artists at the Qing court and traders in Canton. But since the beginning of the eighteenth century the Chinese had been wary of European approaches in the South China Sea, and the emperor's own merchants and diplomats had warned him that, elsewhere in the world, trade came with settlement, backed by force where necessary, as recent events in India had shown.

In order to travel upriver to Beijing, the British embassy had to leave their ocean-going ships, transferring to junks for the journey to Dagu and then smaller boats to get to the end of the Grand Canal. They then travelled overland and reached Beijing on 21 August, where they were conveyed to a residence near the Old Summer Palace. Throughout these journeys the members of the Macartney embassy had been concerned to protect their gifts, which were intended to showcase British scientific and artistic achievements and to encourage interest in British trade. They were carrying exotica such as amber, coral and ivory, along with European manufac- tures including woven cloth from Bolton, brass from Birmingham and linen from Ireland. In pride of place was a planetarium and a Herschel telescope, along with Wedgwood pottery, chandeliers, clocks and watches. To avoid damage, they had been carefully transferred from vessel to vessel along the journey, but the last stage into Beijing along bumpy roads caused the already exhausted British some anxiety. On arrival, the gifts were stored in the throne room at the Summer Palace close to their residence; the construction of the planetarium was so complicated that it took eighteen days to reassemble. When they arrived, however, the emperor was not in Beijing; he was on a hunting expedition north of the Great Wall, and the embassy was instructed to travel a further 120 miles for an audi- ence at Jehol (Chengde). Leaving the planetarium and other large and fragile presents in Beijing, Macartney, his secretary George Staunton and some seventy members of the party duly travelled north. They met the emperor in the 'Garden of Ten Thousand Trees' in the great imperial mountain resort at Chengde on Saturday 14 September 1793, after lengthy deliberations on whether Macartney would or could kowtow to the emperor – that is, go down on both knees and touch his head on the ground in respect, as was customary in the Qing court. (In the event Macartney compromised by genuflecting, as he would to his own sovereign King George).

The British were very impressed by Qianlong. He was 'a very fine old gentleman', they said, vigorous and in good health at eighty-two, but he looked 'not a day over sixty'. Dignified and affable, Qianlong had the common touch, too. When he asked whether anybody in the embassy spoke Chinese, Staunton's twelve-year-old son stepped forward. He had learned some Chinese on the long voyage, and the emperor was so delighted that he gave Staunton the yellow silk purse that hung on his belt containing his favourite areca nuts. (The purse survives today in the Royal Collections.) The British took that friendly exchange as an optimistic sign, but in truth the Chinese had been playing the British, and would continue to do so, drawing them into a web of protocol, ceremony and fine dining while ignoring all requests for meaningful discussion.

The emperor received the delegation along with other tribute envoys from Burma, such was the status of the British in the eyes of the Chinese. To mark the day, the emperor composed a poem, 'The envoy of the king of the red-haired English arrived bringing a message and tribute':

> Formerly Portugal presented tribute
> Now England is paying homage.
> My ancestors' merit and virtue must have reached
> distant shores
> Though their tribute is commonplace, my heart approves
> sincerely.
> Curios and the boasted ingenuity of their devices I
> prize not.
> Though what they bring is meagre, yet,
> In my kindness to men from afar make generous return,
> Wanting to preserve my good health and power

Things did not improve. After a frustrating time in Jehol, Macartney was told that the emperor would be travelling back to Beijing, so the British contingent had to leave in order to be in the city to meet him. They left Jehol on 21 September. Macartney now fell ill and was in bed in Beijing on 1 October when the emperor arrived at the Summer Palace unannounced to view his gifts which had been laid out there. The emperor looked at the lenses for less than two minutes, rejected the camera obscura and declared that the air pump was only 'good enough to amuse children'. Of the three horse-drawn ceremonial coaches that were presented, one was rejected immediately as the driver and postillion would be positioned higher that the emperor himself – something the British had not taken into account.

The British were dismayed and exasperated. The Chinese, of course, had decided on their response to the mission long before, as was underlined by the missive that was sent to Macartney to take back to King George. The British, they acknowledged, had come thousands of miles across the wild seas out of respect for Chinese civilisation; but their demands, their diplomatic requests, were completely impossible. Commercial missions, trading towns, an island offshore that they could use as a mercantile base – it was all out of the question. The emperor explained that the Chinese had no wish to 'change our way of doing things, which we have done for so long in our empire'. The imperial reply framed by his mandarins accordingly first outlined the Qing empire's principles of diplomacy, which were of the utmost importance in China's relations with the world. In the eyes of the Chinese emperor, the British had come to pay tribute to him rather than to establish diplomatic relations as understood in the West. In a lengthy edict addressed to George III, the emperor said:

Yesterday your ambassador petitioned my ministers to memorialise me regarding your trade with China, but his proposal is not consistent with our dynastic usage and cannot be entertained. Hitherto, all European nations, including your own country's barbarian merchants, have carried on their trade with our Celestial Empire at Canton. Such has been the procedure for many years, although our Celestial Empire possesses all things in prolific abundance and lacks no product within its own borders. There was therefore no need to import the manufactures of outside barbarians in exchange for our own produce. But as the tea, silk and porcelain which the Celestial Empire produces are absolute necessities to European nations and to yourselves, we have permitted, as a signal mark of favor, that foreign *hongs* [merchant houses] should be established at Canton, so that your wants might be supplied and your country thus participate in our beneficence.

Nothing would change. The Chinese had no need of British products and saw no reason to give them special treatment. The regulations governing trade between the two countries should stay as they are. The concluding part of Qianlong's missive contained a remarkable restatement of China's cultural integrity, which gives a sense of how Chinese intellectuals in the Qing saw the Europeans, with a robust assertion of Confucian ethics:

Regarding your nation's worship of the Lord of Heaven, it is the same religion as that of other European nations. Ever since the beginning of history, sage-emperors and wise rulers have bestowed on China a moral system and inculcated a code, which from time immemorial has been religiously observed by the myriads of my subjects. There has been no hankering after heterodox doctrines . . . your ambassador's request that barbarians shall be given full liberty to disseminate their religion is utterly unreasonable.

Qianlong ended with a sharp warning to King George:

It may be, O King, that you yourself are ignorant of our dynastic regulations and had no intention of transgressing them when you expressed these wild ideas and hopes . . . If, after the receipt of this explicit decree, you lightly give ear to the representations of your subordinates and allow your barbarian merchants to proceed to Zhejiang and Tianjin with the object of landing and trading there, the ordinances of my Celestial Empire are strict in the extreme, and should your vessels touch the shore, your merchants will assuredly be subject to instant expulsion. In that event your barbarian merchants will have had a long journey for nothing. Do not say that you were not warned in due time! Tremblingly obey and show no negligence! A special mandate!

As diplomatic rebuffs go, it was crushing – or so it seems. Qianlong's rejection of Macartney, or at least the diplomatic language in which it was expressed, was seen as arrogance by the British, and no doubt the Chinese mandarins did still think they were the centre of the world. But it should not be thought that the Chinese were uninterested in European culture. In the eighteenth century they had enthusiastically engaged with Western ideas in science and art; emperors had even had their portraits painted by European artists. They were especially interested in military technology; indeed, perhaps what the emperor really wanted was guns and artillery, which were not on offer. But Chinese wariness of European trade, and the fear of importing European ideas, cosmologies and morals, seem to have outweighed other considerations. The emperor, after all, was predominantly a moral figure, guided by Confucian ethics; undesirable change and innovation were a threat to harmony and stability, and to the emperor's status as the ruler of 'All Under Heaven'.

The mission, then, was a failure in its stated goals, but for Macartney it raised big questions. China, he understood, was an archaic civilisation of extraordinary accomplishment that had by a quirk of history come through to the verge of the nineteenth century possessed of many great inventions of modernity, yet with a cosmology and imperial ideology still linked to its Bronze Age origins. It was, let us say, as if Pharaonic Egypt had come through to the eighteenth century still worshipping Amon, its bureaucracy still skilled in hieroglyphs, while having invented the steam engine and Euclidian science centuries before Europe.

The British in the Age of Enlightenment were a realistic people, in many ways attractively open-minded; but in their dealings with the world they were driven by economic realities. They were predatory – if not militarily, then at least economically – and their appraisal of the

Chinese empire was bluntly realistic. For all its evident greatness and extraordinary longevity, China, they thought, carried all the indications of its own decline. The English had no need of omens, divinations and hexagrams; as modern people, they could read the signs before them.

On their return, the British sailed from Tianjin to Hangzhou, from where they made their way overland to Canton. This allowed them to see the country for themselves. In the rich south there were exquisite landscapes to delight the expedition illustrator: 'The scene was picturesque beyond comparison with its fields of rice, plantations of sugar cane, orange trees, tea bushes, camphor and bamboo.' The opportunity to travel by road also enabled them to observe the people of China. 'The common people of China are a strong and hardy race,' wrote Macartney, 'patient and industrious and much given to commerce and the art of gain. They are cheerful and loquacious under the severest labour but by no means that sedate tranquil people they have been represented.' Indeed, the British saw signs of social unrest on the journey south to Canton through Fujian, where local reports from the time show that coastal counties and inland districts were plagued by bandits, ruffians and armed gangs. In Canton, the British learned through their interpreters and their merchant contacts of an increasingly volatile situation in the countryside, which became fully apparent only after Qianlong's death.

For all its glories, therefore, the empire was not in good shape. Population rise, inflation and a decrease in tax revenues, combined with the enormous cost of maintaining the ruling class and the imperial structure in days of rampant corruption, created a tough situation for the many local governors, clerks and magistrates. These were the loyal officials on whom the empire rested, but they were paid 'starvation salaries'. In the south, then, where the people had never fully reconciled to Manchu rule, the British soon became aware of the cracks behind the grand façade of the empire, the class tensions and the huge inequalities. 'The lower sort most heartily detest the mandarins, and persons in authority,' wrote Macartney, 'whose arbitrary powers to punish, oppress and insult them, they fear, whose injustice they feel, and whose rapacity they must feed.'

Resting in Macao before he sailed back home, and reflecting on his whole experience, Macartney framed his report with the kind of breezy nautical metaphor that came naturally to a late eighteenth-century British imperialist whose travels had spanned half the world:

> The Empire of China is an old, crazy, first-rate Man of War, which a fortunate succession of vigilant officers has contrived to keep afloat for these 150 years past, and to overawe their neighbours merely by her bulk and appearance. But whenever an insufficient man happens to have the command on deck, adieu to the discipline and safety of the ship. She may, perhaps, not sink outright; she may drift some time as a wreck, and will then be dashed to pieces on the shore; but she can never be rebuilt on the old base.

As it seems now, it was a harsh but perceptive judgement. But however it played out, Macartney's concern was the role the British could play in that future. He felt the Chinese would trust the British, as they had never acted aggressively towards the Middle Kingdom. In terms of international geopolitics, the British observed that the Manchus ruled a vast multi-national empire, but the huge territories they had recently acquired – Mongolia, Xinjiang and the protectorate of Tibet – might not necessarily adhere in the long term. And if the Manchu empire did not hold together under pressures from elsewhere, especially from the Russians on their northern frontiers, the question for Macartney was what new China would emerge, and how could Britain take advantage? To conclude, he projected his mind forward, into the new century:

> The breaking-up of the power of China (no improbable event) would occasion a complete subversion of the commerce, not only of Asia, but a very sensible change in the other quarters of the world. The industry and the ingenuity of the Chinese would be checked and enfeebled, but they would not be annihilated. Her ports would no longer be barricaded; they would be attempted

by the adventures of all trading nations, who would search every channel, creek and cranny of China for a market, and for some time be the cause of much rivalry and disorder. Nevertheless, as Great Britain, from the weight of her riches and the genius and spirit of her people, has become the first political, marine, and commercial power on the globe, it is reasonable to think that she would prove the greatest gainer by such a revolution as I have alluded to, and rise superior over every competitor.

There were other grand geopolitical considerations for the British; the loss of the American colonies and the very real prospect of a forthcoming war with France had focused minds on new markets. The British economy was already deeply tied to its international trade triangles, across the Atlantic westwards, and eastwards through the new territories in India. As a result, the textile industry in England in particular was now such an important part of the national economy that any threat would be so catastrophic that it literally could not be allowed to happen. Looking ahead, he concluded:

The aim is gradually to mould the China trade to the shape that might best suit us. Our settlements in India would suffer most severely by any interruption of the China traffic which is infinitely valuable to them, whether considered singly as a market for cotton and opium, or as connected with their adventures in the Philippines or Malaya. To Great Britain the blow would be immediate and heavy. Our great woollen manufacture, the ancient staple of England[,] and our other growing exports and imports would be instantly convulsed ... and not soon recover.

If the British economy was already tied to China, when it came to diplomatic relations, the goal was not aggression but cooperation, which the British believed would be to China's great advantage too. As Macartney saw it, modernisation would bring the Chinese the benefits of the West, the fruits of modern civilisation, 'the arts and accomplishments of civilised life'. The Qing government was holding the Chinese back, and 'a nation that does not advance must retrograde, and finally fall back to barbarism and misery ...'

But as the living incarnation of the Chinese tradition, the emperor was not concerned with the future. Nor was he contemplating change. His sacred duty as the ruler of All Under Heaven was to maintain the order that he had inherited from the ancestors. And on that difference of perceptions, together with the failure to reach an understanding on trade, would hang the convulsions that lay ahead. And those in turn would shape not only China's relations with the outside world, but also the struggle for modernisation within China, from then until today.

QIANLONG RESIGNS

In China, though, these were still clouds on the horizon. For those with power, wealth or position, especially the middle classes in the prosperous heartland of the Yangtze valley, life could not have been better. The writer Shen Fu, born to a family of officials in the delightful and cultured city of Suzhou, saw no clouds. In his famous book *Six Records of a Floating Life*, he notes that to have been born into the gentry class in 1763, or, as he put it, in the twenty-seventh year of the Qianlong emperor, was to have been truly privileged – indeed, to have won the lottery of life: 'Heaven blessed me, and life then could not have been more full. It was a time of great peace and plenty.'

That's how it looked from the rich cities of the Yangtze valley, whose citizens enjoyed as high a standard of living as any on the planet. Out in the wilds, especially on the frontiers, it was a different picture. An inscription set up by the local community in 1783 in front of the Matsu Temple in Meishan gives another view. Meishan lies in one of the twenty or so main bays along the coast of Fujian, used by fishing fleets and traders who dealt with foreign ships on their way into the port of Quanzhou; it had an official for customs examinations. From the 1760s there were growing troubles; the garrison mutinied because of lack of pay, and as pirates and 'ruffians of the coast' moved in, extorting illegal levies from the merchants, trade deteriorated. Then, in 1781, the government was forced to act against its own garrison at Chongwu in Hui-'an county, a major naval defence post in the area, one of the bases for the 62,000 troops garrisoned in these harbours along the Fujian coast. Eight hundred and fifty men were stationed in the town to protect the great port of Quanzhou upriver, but instead they were demanding illegal levies, hurting the local traders and endangering the timely supply of grain, so the authorities were forced to send in fresh troops to arrest the entire garrison.

The problem was not just confined to the coast, either. Beggars and bandits in organised groups plagued the interior of Fujian, extorting food from the locals. In the late eighteenth century, banditry, rural unrest and local uprisings increased all over the country, especially in the frontier regions. As one British observer put it, local poorly paid magistrates were overwhelmed by their tasks; they needed help from the centre at a time when the centre was leaving more and more locals to their own devices. Of course, these were tasks on a scale faced by no other government on earth, but just as had happened in the Late Ming, the ethos transmitted from the centre to the periphery was failing.

Many issues then came together to threaten the secure world of the High Qing, some of them almost perennial in Chinese history. In the countryside, they faced several revolts in the later 1700s as millennial cults and secret societies fanned the flames of discontent that rapidly flared up in response to local conditions. These rebel groups could raise armies big enough to threaten local county authorities, and even whole provinces.

In 1796, when he was eighty-four, Qianlong abdicated on the grounds that after celebrating the sixtieth year of his reign it would be disrespectful to rule longer than his revered grandfather Kangxi, who had ruled for sixty-one years and who was universally seen as the pre-eminent ruler of the dynasty. Qianlong gave up the throne in favour of a son who took the name Jiaqing. For his first three years he was ruler in name only, as Qianlong still held power behind the throne as 'Emperor Emeritus'. Jiaqing came to full power only after

Qianlong's death in early 1799, the year the British consolidated their power in south India at the Battle of Seringapatam and, with the East India Company's profits almost doubling in four years, turned their gaze eastwards to the trade with China.

From this point, China increasingly became immersed in troubles. There were revolts in the south among ethnic minorities (one among the Miao lasted ten years), and even attempts to kill the emperor, who had many enemies among disaffected exiles. The economy was suffering, with a huge outflow of silver to pay for imported goods like opium and cotton. The Middle Kingdom was now part of the world economy, even though as yet it had not formally agreed to be so.

The imperial advisers, however, continued to insist on the use of the ancient teachings of Confucius to promote harmony, stability and the eternal hierarchy, and to recruit the bureaucracy using the old examination system as set down in the fourteenth century. For them, change and innovation were a threat to the ancient moral order and the traditions of imperial rulership in the person of the sage-emperor. Heterodox ideas and the customs of foreign peoples were not the Chinese way, even if their technology was useful. But that opened up questions that will mark the next 200 years. Could a great traditional civilisation incorporate some of the benefits of modernity without the wholesale acceptance of modernity itself? Or were the habits of the civilisation so ingrained that only wholesale revolution could bring about that change?

In the early nineteenth century, few went so far as to ask that question; the imperial monarchy was still the model. But for the intellectuals in the cultural powerhouses of the Yangtze delta and in Guizhou, modernity was becoming a concern. In the 1780s, government book burnings, censorship and attacks on intellectuals accused of anti-Manchu sentiments had fostered an atmosphere of real anxiety among the intellectual class.

As we have seen, back in the Late Ming, the rise of private academies saw a convergence between Confucian philosophy and political activism – a direct response to the failure of Ming emperors to live up to the ideals of the empire. It was the same again now.

Scholars and thinkers with strong links to the southern mercantile elites responded to the social, intellectual and economic forces that had been brewing for over a century. They suggested there should be a limit on imperial power in favour of more freedom to debate governance through local initiative at the provincial level; a devolution of power so that local regions had a say in the affairs of empire. They wanted to curb the imperial restraints on trade and industry and stop arbitrary taxation. Though the Donglin reform movement had been suppressed in the seventeenth century across the empire, its arguments against despotism had been continued underground in the Lower Yangtze region in rich cities like Suzhou and Changzhou after the Manchu conquest, which many Han Chinese intellectuals saw as a restored despotism. And now the movement rose again as a forum for political and social protest among reform-minded gentry and scholars.

In his 1793 essay *On the Governance and the Well-Being of the Empire*, the Changzhou scholar Hong Liangji (1746–1809) looked at population growth and its socio-political consequences, his concerns precisely shadowing those raised by Malthus writing a little later in England. Hong pointed to the tension between the rate of growth of the means of subsistence and the growing population. Taking a somewhat exaggerated Malthusian perspective, he wrote that the tension would only be relieved by disasters, famine and plagues:

Speaking of households, there are twenty times more than there were a hundred years ago. Some people may propose that there is wild land to cultivate and spare space for housing. But the available land can only be doubled or tripled, or at most increased five times, whereas the population over the same period could be ten to twenty times larger. Therefore housing and crop fields tend to be in scarcity, while the population tends to be excessive at all time. Given the fact that some households become monopolists, there is no wonder that so many have suffered cold and hunger and even died. How does Heaven deal with the tension? Flood, drought and pestilence are the means of Heaven to temper the problem.

Born in 1746, Hong had lived through the later stage of the huge growth of population from Kangxi's reign up to 1790, when the number of people doubled from 150 million to well over 300 million, with an even higher rate of rise in the rich lands of the Yangtze delta, which to locals seemed to have become crowded with people in a mere handful of generations. Hong pointed out that government could try to mediate the problem by adjusting tax, encouraging colonisation in unpopulated lands, and enhancing the social safety net. However, he expressed his concern about the limits of government policy in addressing such an inherent, structural issue. Could the old imperial state ever cope with the pressures on it in this new age?

The protest came to a head after the death of Qianlong in 1799. Hong now boldly wrote a letter 'To Prince Cheng Earnestly Discussing the Political Affairs of the Time', which directly implied criticism of the throne. It was the opening salvo. The new emperor pondered his response to the challenge, enraged by its audacity and even more by the fact that copies had been printed and disseminated behind his back. He demoted those who received it and recommended that Hong be executed. Hong in reply reaffirmed the right of a dutiful Confucian official to engage in 'loyal remonstrance and public debate', asserting the 'public responsibility' of the intellectual. His sentence was commuted to exile in Xinjiang in the far west of China, but he was treated as a hero in the delta, with crowds cheering him on his journey. The emperor, though, later claimed he had kept Hong's letter by his bedside as a constant reminder to himself of a ruler's obligations in affairs of state.

In 1800, during a prolonged drought in Beijing, the emperor granted amnesties and performed archaic rituals for rain to propitiate heaven. Hong was pardoned and allowed to return. In the official pardon the emperor publicly blamed himself for punishing a loyal remonstrating official, something that he claimed would never have happened under Qianlong. It was a vital precedent; dissent could be accepted if channelled in the right way.

Rains immediately followed the imperial rituals that year, but the late imperial state had more profound structural problems. Attacks on intellectuals, book inquisitions and censorship had played a part in robbing China of intellectual vigour on the eve of her encounter with the West, while the unresolved issues of land use and population growth, together with economic stagnation, unemployment and an unfair tax system, meant that the country was heading for trouble in the next generation.

And the troubles grew in frequency and number. The most serious was the 1796–1804 White Lotus rebellion, which started as a tax protest and became an anti-Manchu revolt that led to 100,000 deaths. A millenarian rising incorporating many strange sects, in the early stages they defeated the imperial army, only later to be surrounded and crushed. For the government, however, it was a troubling event. As one Qing official reported with consternation: 'The rebels are *all our own subjects*. They are not like some external tribe ... that can be demarcated by a territorial boundary and identified by its distinctive clothing and language ... When they congregate and oppose the government, they are rebels; when they disperse and depart, they are civilians once more.'

The clampdown involved the harsh treatment of civilians. Hundreds of stockaded villages were established in disaffected areas for the mass resettlement of offenders who were brutalised by militias and mercenary forces. Then, in 1813, came the rebellion of the Eight Trigrams. Li Wencheng, a hustler and drifter, was proclaimed as the emperor, 'the True Lord of the Ming'. Another rebel, Li Qing, announced himself a reincarnation of the Maitreya, the prophesied future Buddha, his banners carrying the slogan 'Entrusted by Heaven to Prepare the Way'. Drought and floods had caused a steep rise in food prices and many in the countryside were desperate. In the summer of 1813, the rebels combined with sects like the White Lotus and the Eternal Mother. The plan was to capture the emperor on his return from a hunting trip, kill him, and proclaim a new order. The date was set for 15 September, right after the harvest, but their plans were revealed and the rising was suppressed. Although on 8 October, aided and abetted by disaffected eunuchs, seventy-five rebels did break into the Forbidden City itself and managed to hold

out for two days and a night before they were overpowered, captured or killed. First-person testimonies survive of captured rebels
interrogated before their execution; mainly illiterate hired labourers,
carters and household servants, as vivid and poignant as those from
the Luddite risings that same year in England:

> They told all the people who had joined the sect to give money
> and go with them. If you didn't give money they would kill you. I
> was afraid and paid cash ... after the village was burned I fled to
> the south and lived by begging ... I had fifty to sixty *mou* [about
> 10 acres] of land and was coming back from tending the crops ...
> then they said we all had to go to the city. In this business it was
> death if you went, and death if you stayed.

Fighting continued in the provinces until the end of year. In all,
20,000 rebels were killed and an estimated 70,000 people died
altogether. By Chinese standards the revolt was perhaps small-scale,
but the shock to the state was huge. The ease with which the rebels
had swept up the discontented and the rural poor in an eerie mix of
millenarian cult, anti-Manchu feelings and heterodox beliefs highlighted the dynasty's alarming vulnerability. Symbolically, too, they
had even penetrated the imperial compound.

We also have the view from the centre of this crisis, in the
perplexed voice of the Jiaqing emperor himself, referring to his eight-
year struggle against White Lotus after he had ascended the throne
on the death of Qianlong. A copy of this extraordinary text appeared
in translation by the East India Company press in Canton in 1815.
The self-justifying tone could not be more different from the calm
authority of Qianlong:

> My family has continued to rule the Empire during 170 years. My
> Grand Father, and Royal Father, in the most affectionate manner,
> loved the people as children. Their benevolence and virtues, I
> am unable to express! Though I cannot pretend to have equalled
> their good government and love of the people, yet I have not

oppressed nor ill-used my people. This sudden change I am unable to account for. It must arise from the low state of my virtue, and my accumulated Imperfections. Though this rebellion has broken forth in a moment, the evil has been long accumulating. Four words, 'Supine-ness, Indulgence, Sloth and Contempt' express the sources whence this great crime has arisen; and hence, also it is that affairs whether at home about Court, or abroad in the Empire, are equally in a bad state.

THE OPIUM WAR

The Jiaqing emperor died in 1820. To reform the government across the empire was perhaps beyond the powers of anyone, but certainly one without the energy, moral authority and steely will of his grandfather. He was succeeded by the Daoguang emperor, a 'well-meaning but ineffective man' who promoted officials who 'presented a purist view even if they had nothing to say about the real domestic and foreign problems surrounding the dynasty'.

As internal and external pressures grew, the first military confrontation with the imperialists took place. The problem was opium, sold by the British through Canton and other ports on the coast. From its warehouses in India, the East India Company was exporting larger and larger quantities that were being sold not only to Chinese dealers in Canton but also in illicit operations in the myriad ports and bays northwards along the indented coasts of Fujian.

The trade had begun in the late eighteenth century, when the East India Company had started smuggling opium from its Indian possessions in Bengal into China through dealers in Canton. Trading in opium was illegal; the Chinese government had passed decrees against it three times since 1799, yet the trade continued to grow regardless. From 4,000 chests of opium a year in 1787, by 1833, 30,000 chests were trafficked annually (one chest containing 170 pounds of the drug), and Chinese estimates suggest there were as many as 12 million addicts, especially in the coastal cities of Zhejiang. By the late 1830s, opium had become a serious social problem. Along the east coast and into the interior, the signs were everywhere, so much so that in the important cultural centre of Yangzhou, social-realist dramas were being acted in local playhouses which focused on the ravages of the drug. It was clear something had to be done.

The emperor appointed a new commissioner to move against the trade, Lin Zexu, a Confucian official who in retrospect has come to be seen as the quintessential loyal Confucian official. Soon after he arrived in the south in the middle of 1838, Lin wrote a famous open letter to the young Queen Victoria, who had come to the throne the previous year, urging her to put a stop to the trade:

We find that your country is sixty or seventy thousand *li* from China. The purpose of your ships in coming to China is to realize a large profit. Since this profit is realized in China and is in fact taken away from the Chinese people, how can foreigners return injury for the benefit they have received by sending this poison to harm their benefactors?

They may not intend to harm others on purpose, but the fact remains that they are so obsessed with material gain that they have no concern whatever for the harm they can cause to others. Have they no conscience? I have heard that you strictly prohibit opium in your own country, indicating unmistakably that you know how harmful opium is. You do not wish opium to harm your own country, but you choose to bring that harm to other countries such as China. Why?

Whether Victoria ever read Lin's memorial is not known, but the letter was later printed in the *Times* newspaper as a direct appeal to the British public, among whom there was widespread revulsion about the trade.

In spring 1839, Lin began his move against the sale of opium, arresting many hundreds of Chinese dealers and pressuring foreign merchants to give up their trade in narcotics in exchange for other commodities such as tea. In the early summer he seized over a million kilograms of opium and began to destroy it. But Lin's belief that Confucian morality would triumph was out of step with the times. The nature of international relations was changing, and the Chinese underestimated the commitment of the British government to protect their vital interests. Open hostilities started that same year. The British organised a task force from India with an army largely composed of Indian sepoys led by British officers. In high summer 1840, they attacked the Pearl River coastal forts, and in February 1841 blasted the Chinese forces in the south to defeat, wooden junks no match for iron-clad ships and rocket launchers.

At this point there were disagreements at the imperial court as to how to handle the situation, both militarily and politically. Some, like the strategist Wei Yuan, felt the Chinese reaction had been too confrontational, that they should have focused entirely on the opium trade and not compromised the rest of Anglo-Chinese political and trade relations, instead giving themselves time to modernise and build up their military and navy, and to open up diplomatic relations with other foreign powers like the Americans and the French who had a vested interest in containing the British. Factional fighting in the court came to a head in the summer of 1841 when Commissioner Lin was dismissed and sent into exile. The Chinese suddenly found themselves on a steep learning curve in modern realpolitik.

WEI YUAN: 'STRONG ARMY, RICH STATE'

In September 1841, in the governor's *yamen* in the old city of Ningbo, a tall Scotsman, manacled and chained around the feet, was led from the jail into an interview room. A big man, 20 stone in weight, with a shock of red hair and huge 'rufus' beard, he had a deep, rich voice and 'a sagacious, massive face, brimming over with jollity'. Captain Peter Anstruther of the Madras Horse Artillery was thirty-three years old, but looked older than his years after the wear and tear of seventeen years' fighting with the East India Company, along with a fondness for brandy and cheroots.

In the habit of exploring the hills beyond his base at Dinghai, Anstruther enjoyed sketching for pleasure (he was an accomplished artist given to painting pictures of Chinese life), but he was also making preliminary notes for a map survey. On the morning of 16 September, sketching in the hills on the island of Zhoushan, he had been seized and taken across to Ningbo. His Chinese inquisitor, the historian and scholar Wei Yuan, was one of the most brilliant intellectuals of his time. An austere Chinese mandarin wearing a long gown, with his hair in the Manchu style, Wei was a close friend of Commissioner Lin. He had already published several important works, including a modern anthology of writings on statecraft in 1826 – a text for the troubled times. Indeed, Wei, it could be said, was one of the originators of the idea of 'self-strengthening'. His doctrine that 'wealth and power was the key', and that China should 'strengthen the army to enrich the state', was the forerunner, the ideological ancestor of today's Four Modernisations. In the summer of 1841, however, Wei's concern was to build up a profile of the British, who he felt were poorly under-stood – a major failure of Chinese intelligence gathering.

In July, before he went into exile, Commissioner Lin had met Wei for the last time at Zhenjiang, on the junction of the Grand Canal and the Yangtze River. Their conversation was of the utmost importance for the story of modern China. They talked long into the night about maritime affairs, the state of coastal defences, the daunting extent of British military and naval power and technology, and the implications not just for Chinese coastal security, but for the empire itself. How could they be combated if China was so unaware of the threat?

Lin told Wei to publicise the issues as widely as possible, to awaken the Chinese to the seriousness of Western penetration of the maritime seaboard of China. To help in the task, he handed over all the materials he had put together as commissioner in Canton: government memorials, translations from English and Portuguese, maps and diagrams, and drawings of ships and guns. He also gave Wei 'The Geography of the Four Continents', a text he had based on translations from Murray's 1834 *Encyclopaedia of Geography*, which he had acquired as part of his rapid information gathering when Lin realised China was so unprepared, and so lacking in knowledge about the British. Now, 200 years and more after Ricci, and rather late in the day, the Chinese mental map of the world was about to be redrawn.

When they parted, Lin headed for exile in the far west, while Wei remained in the south. In September, hearing about the British captive, he got permission from local officials to question Anstruther. Through an interpreter he asked about England, its people, history, geography and customs, and on the basis of his notes he wrote a short essay called *A Brief Account of England*. In the book he described a tiny island sixty or seventy thousand *li* away that produced powerful ships, tough soldiers and enterprising merchants: what sort of culture was this?

That autumn Wei left the Pearl River delta and took Lin's materials back to his house in Yangzhou with a view to publishing the book he had promised to write. It was a rush job, but, as he saw it, an urgent necessity. Meanwhile, the war intensified as the British fleet moved up the Chinese coast. Following a further defeat in the estuary outside Ningbo, Wei's friend the local commander Yu Qian committed suicide, and in grief, shame and anger, Wei threw himself into his work. As the British assaults on China's coastal defences continued, he made an urgent journey to Beijing to consult the imperial archives, hoping to finish his *Military History of the Current Dynasty* in summer 1842. But by then the war had reached its crisis. On 29 August, resigned to defeat, the Qing government signed the Treaty of Nanjing on the British flagship HMS *Cornwallis* in the Yangtze River. The treaty abolished the old Canton trading system and gave the British favoured nation trading status and four 'treaty ports' – Xiamen, Fuzhou, Ningbo and Shanghai – where they could engage in commerce with whomsoever they wished. The Chinese were also to pay an indemnity of 21 million silver dollars to cover the opium destroyed by Commissioner Lin, other financial losses and war reparations, all to be paid within three years. So ended the First Opium War – the first of what the Chinese later called the unequal treaties, which would ensure a British presence on Chinese soil for the next hundred years, and in Hong Kong until 1997.

In that sombre climate Wei Yuan finished his brilliantly written and researched account of the Opium War, castigating the Qing government for its failure to look for alliances with Britain's enemies ('our ministers had no knowledge of geography'), especially the French and the Americans. He also attacked their strategic decision making:

It was the closing of trade, not the forced surrender of the opium, that brought on the Canton War. [The British Canton agent] Elliot had not wanted to fight, had agreed to the confiscation, and offered rewards for the discovery of the murderer of Chinese civilians ... Our demands on him were too great. It would have been better to sacrifice our customs interests for a time, to devote full attention to measures of defence.

Wei Yuan's overview of the First Opium War ends with a passage worthy of Thucydides:

The Barbarian Pirate War lasted two years in all, and cost us seventy million *taels*. There was always a clamour either for peace or war; but no one, strange to say, ever recommended a strictly defensive attitude. Again, fighting was neglected when fighting was proper, and indulged when out of place; so, also peace was neglected when peace was proper, and peace was decided on at exactly the wrong time. Had we fought on the defensive whilst negotiating, we could have had the benefit of other troops beside our own, for instance the French and the Americans, and also the Gurkhas, setting foreign enemy against foreign enemy ... We should have resolutely adhered to the opium interdiction ... gone down hard on the British there and allied ourselves with the other foreigners to gain their affection. Oh opportunity! It is only the true genius who can take opportunity by the forelock! But the next best thing is to repent when the opportunity has gone by. Repentance followed by the capacity to change for the better, will yet enable us to repair our errors at some future time.

In New Year 1843, only months after the Treaty of Nanjing signalled China's defeat, Wei Yuan published his *Treatise on the Maritime Kingdoms*, a book of fundamental importance in modern China. Its frontispiece in Bronze Age seal script announced its point of departure, loyalty to the Zhou, but positioned in the modern Chinese revival. With European-style world maps, it was the first work in Chinese history to take account of the expanding power of Western countries, their domination of the maritime world, and their growing threat to China. Drawing on work by Lin Zexu and from many conversations, including his interviews with Peter Anstruther, he put together as much information as he could on the nature of the new threat. Wei's work was remarkable in part because of his lack of research resources. Without the ability to travel to the West or to speak its languages, and looked upon sceptically by Confucian scholars who dismissed and derided 'barbarian studies', Wei nonetheless compiled the first piece of Chinese scholarship on Western technological advances. Through his innovative approach, he was able to devise an overarching 'foreign policy' – a programme of action connecting all corners of the Qing realm from the Pacific to Central Asia. Having always seen itself as a land power, Wei argued, China had to take control of the seas around its eastern seaboard to protect itself from the encroachments of the Europeans. For him, the assertion of Chinese influence and power in maritime East Asia was vital, both to protect China internally and to secure her global position. It was a formulation of Chinese policy that would project far into the future: today's contentious debates about the *nanyang*, the South China Sea, as a Chinese zone of influence, go back to him.

At the heart of Wei's understanding of the Opium War, though, was the traditional view that had preoccupied reformers since the days of the Donglin Academy. Political stability only came from renewed inner strength; the breakdown of the Chinese moral-political order came essentially from 'trouble in men's hearts'. One of the most interesting figures in modern Chinese history, Wei had a profound influence on all the reformers that followed. But his attempt to alert the intelligentsia and the mandarins was subverted by the onset of the Taiping rebellion, which would convulse China through the 1850s and '60s. Wei resigned from government and entered a Buddhist monastery on the shore of West Lake in Hangzhou from where he saw the sack of the city by the Taiping in 1856, the year before he died. A fierce, angry spirit, his writing encapsulated the shared experience of decline among intellectuals in the nineteenth century:

> When the state is rich and powerful, it will be effective. If it deals with traitors they will not persist in their ways; it administers revenue and there will not be waste; it acquires weapons and they will not be flawed; it organises armed forces and the troops will not be weak. What then is there to fear about barbarians anywhere?

While lobbying for a strengthening of the machinery of the state, however, Wei did not foresee the dynasty's collapse. Nor should we let the trajectory of hindsight rule our narrative at this point. In the mid-1840s, at the moment after the First Opium War, when China was poised between the old and the new, a Chinese-speaking French missionary, Père Gabet, travelled across the country and was profoundly impressed by what he saw, the fruit of two centuries of Qing rule:

> The Chinese have been able to preserve their empire for 4,000 years. Long ago they already had inventions that the Europeans proudly believed they had discovered, namely printing, gunpowder, the compass, silk weaving, the decimal system, so many other things. The Chinese have ancient classics full of the deepest wisdom, philosophical insights far superior to our classical antiquity. And unlike the Europeans they had the good sense to apply these ancient ideas to the actual practice of government which shows how intelligent they are ... They are not Christians but have hospitals for orphans ... for the old and the sick ... welfare offices where food is provided for the destitute and medicines for the sick ... along the roads they provide shelters for the free use

of travellers. How dare one say that a nation that displays such enlightenment, generosity and wisdom is inferior in any way to we Europeans?

THE VIEW FROM THE COUNTRYSIDE IN THE FIRST OPIUM WAR

Taining county lies in northern Fujian, 300 miles from the sea, in still sparsely populated, wild mountains around Dajjin Lake, where crumbling red cliffs, hung with ancient trees, are pockmarked by caves and temples of Daoist hermits. Cut off until the laying of the railways in the late 1950s, it was a world away from the offices of the Board of Finance in Beijing. It was one of countless small areas that, through the nineteenth century, were more and more prey to disorder and social dissension as the old ethos broke down and communities recorded a sense of being abandoned.

'Our County lies in midst of mountains,' wrote the community scribe in summer 1841.

> The land is lean and the people are poor. They look up to the emperor for support. For 200 years the grain tax could not be collected in full, not even one out of ten times. In recent years the tax inspectors haven't used any standard measure and taxes have been collected with flagrant abuse, unheedingly above the quotas; everywhere there is extortion and deceit. The people of the town – even the Taoist priests – have suffered endlessly with cruel exactions.

When the new local magistrate stood up to the tax gatherers, insisting on justice and accurate measures, there was joy in the village: 'The entire county felt gratitude like a hanging man cut down.' The community had his story engraved on a stone stele, 'so the memory of his virtue might be handed down forever' – it still survives today. There were many like him, for the Confucian ethos, inculcated through the exam system, was still a living code of life. However, in reports to the provincial government covered in the newly founded local newspapers, there was a sense of anxiety and gradual disillusion. Many local communities, like Taining, reported tensions; social unrest, class warfare, bandits, pirates along the coast, even private armies owned by gangsters and powerful kin groups. The impression from the periphery is one of the sheer difficulty of administering law and order in a country now of 400 million people. Loyal Confucian officials were struggling without tools and money. The old problems of Chinese history had returned to haunt them. Away from the centre, the greatest, oldest and most populous state in the world could no longer govern. The state had been fatally weakened. And at this moment came the first of three great crises that would bring the empire down.

MAKING GOD'S HEAVENLY KINGDOM: THE TAIPING CATASTROPHE

The struggles felt in little Taining could be found all over Late Qing China, and in the 1840s and '50s, new troubles began. With the concessions made after the First Opium War, the weakness of China, which Macartney had seen fifty years before, was revealed for all to see. In the countryside, even in quite isolated regions, the oppressed peasantry was increasingly coming under the influence of new ideas, millennial creeds and prophecies – some long rooted in China, some new minted through the creeping influence of foreign missionaries.

In the past, Chinese rulers had often allowed other religions into China so long as they did nothing to compromise the imperial order or the traditions of the culture. But now Western missionaries were going into China through the new treaty ports bearing the assumptions of imperialists, convinced of the superiority of their civilisation as well as of their religion. And in the 1840s, a millennial movement inspired by Christian missionaries gave birth to one of the most violent, bloody and sensational events in China's modern history, which threatened to overthrow the Qing state itself.

Not long before the First Opium War, a chance meeting had

taken place in the crowded streets outside the foreign merchants' concession in Canton between an American missionary and a young Chinese man. The American, the Reverend Edwin Stevens – Yale-educated, wearing Chinese clothes, his hair in a queue – was distributing Christian pamphlets illegally. Hong Xiuquan, a failed examination scholar, was, we may assume, looking for a new direction. The interchange was short: 'Follow the Christian God and you will reach the highest glory,' said Stevens, handing over a pamphlet printed in Chinese that included the story of Noah and the Flood. Whether Hong read it then is uncertain. But later, when he did, the message suddenly became startlingly personal – he read his own name, for 'Hong' literally means 'the flood', God's instrument to punish humanity for failing to follow the path of righteousness.

Throughout Chinese history, strange heterodox sects – White Lotus, the Red Turbans – had preached such millennial ideas; wandering preachers had been a feature of the countryside since the Ming. But in the strange, unsettling aftermath of the First Opium War, such things lodged in the mind, especially in someone whose traditional education had got him nowhere. And Hong's interests in such ideas were not just those of an inconsequential dreamer, a man out on a limb; all around there were debates about national renewal; intellectuals in the cities were in ferment. Then, in the 1840s, the Bible texts he had received years before began to work on Hong's mind, especially the words of the Prophet Isaiah: 'Your country is desolate; strangers are devouring your land before your eyes. Why be downtrodden anymore? Rise up and revolt . . .'

Hong headed to the hills, where he became a village teacher out in the wild landscape near today's town of Guiping. There he found an impoverished countryside, with mass poverty and unemployment, where corruption was all too plain to see. Even those who had a job in local government were on starvation wages, while unemployed scholars like him with years of training had no future as more graduates joined the labour market every year and unemployment steadily rose. Here was fertile ground for revolution, and Hong began to speak of a new age of justice, and of the blasphemy of the Qing empire and its 'foreign' Manchu rulers.

Hong's preaching found a willing audience. While he and his early followers earned their keep by teaching, they started to organise village meetings in the wooded hills around Guiping. Today oral stories are still told by peasant families descended from those who supported Hong and his disciples. Old Wood Village, for example, is so out of the way that it is hard to imagine much has changed since the nineteenth century. Old family houses surround a clan hall, with a big stone-lined water tank, cowsheds, stables and workshops. At the centre of the village is a giant old plane tree under which villagers meet to talk and smoke. Here, as they tell the tale, Hong stayed for a time. He and his friend Feng were educated men, and with their traditional respect for learning, the illiterate villagers listened.

Hong had identified the Christian god with the high god of ancient China, a common elision made by Christian missionaries, and he now announced that he wanted to create God's kingdom on earth by overthrowing the corrupt Qing empire. Together they would make a golden age when society lived in harmony, when justice was for the poor as well as the rich. For families like the Zengs, it was a powerful message. Nearly two centuries on, in 2016, the head of the clan proudly explained: 'They came to teach us about the Taiping religion and to preach revolution. We, the Zeng family, were the first to take part in that revolution.'

Over time the rebels created revolutionary cells in hundreds of villages. Bright Water Village over the mountains on narrow walking paths was home to Hong's right-hand man Feng right up to the eve of the uprising, and the site of the school where he taught is still remembered. Again, the landmarks of the story are still pointed out by the elders: this is where the great rebellion started that would shake the empire to its foundations.

Through the 1840s, the movement grew and gathered thousands of followers. Eventually the Qing government ordered imperial troops from the provincial governor to put down the revolt, but in such trackless and out-of-the-way places, it was too late. The rising was announced from a fortified base in Jintian, where the peasant army had gathered. Their goal was to establish the Taiping *tianguo*, 'God's Heavenly Kingdom'.

The early course of the rising was a classic rural guerrilla war inspired by clear messages. They were against Confucianism, against the Manchu emperor and the feudal landlords; they were for the peasants and the poor. They believed in a new world and even preached communal property ownership and rights for women. Their appointed leader, Hong, his mind turning on Christian missionary texts, now announced himself as Jesus' younger brother, God's Chinese Son. By 1852 he had gathered an army of 100,000 men. The rebels were joined by local people: the unemployed, miners, seasonal labourers, bandit gangs and enemies of the local elites. They armed themselves from captured munitions dumps and seized supplies of ready cash from local government offices. They even purchased armaments from foreign treaty port merchants.

The Taiping army soon defeated the Qing forces in the south, opening the path to the southern capital of Nanjing. The rebels marched north, gathering support, and in spring 1853 their combined forces attacked the southern capital in a dramatic assault. Many of the Taiping's early supporters were miners from Guizhou, expert sappers who dug tunnels under the giant walls on the northern corner of the city looking over the Yangtze. On 19 March 1853, the Taiping forces broke into the city and Hong was enthroned as ruler of God's Heavenly Kingdom in his new Jerusalem. In the hills to the east on the slopes of Purple Mountain, the rebels desecrated the tomb of the Ming founder Zhu Yuanzhang. A new age of revolutionary violence was dawning.

The Taiping had now gained power, but what would they do with it? It is a question faced by all of China's revolutionaries. Once God's kingdom on earth had been established in Nanjing, a blizzard of ideological pronouncements came pouring from the throne. In one of the book-production capitals of China they set up printing presses and a workshop for woodblock cutting; their publications included Taiping translations of the Old and New Testaments. They banned opium, tobacco, alcohol, footbinding, prostitution and gambling. Gender separation was enforced in public places and the death penalty introduced for sex between men. Most important of all, China was to be classless. Private ownership of property and land was abolished; both would be owned and distributed by the state.

All this was accompanied by a move to purge the language of foreign elements that had been introduced by the alien Manchu conquerors. It would be a new world of words for a new time, much of it uncannily prefiguring what would happen 100 years later, after the revolution of 1949. Indeed, the Taiping revolt was glorified as such by Mao in the wholesale rewriting of Chinese history in the 1950s. But in the 1850s, the task of overthrowing feudalism, redistributing land, reforming the law and moving China into a more equitable future was too great. The great Chinese divination text, the *Book of Changes*, says that there are three warnings of a coming revolution; when the third comes, it is too late to turn back. Then the moment becomes clear and cannot be deferred. And so it happened.

THE GREAT TERROR

The blow to the morale of the Chinese governing class was shattering, Taiping armies were now in control of huge swathes of the south, the richest and most populous part of the country. Their forces crossed the Yangtze and even mounted an attack on Beijing in a thoroughgoing attempt to overthrow the Qing state. But the most devastating disaster was the sacking of the rich cities of the lower Yangtze: Yangzhou, Changzhou, Suzhou, Wuxi, Shaoxing, Ningbo and Hangzhou were the cultural and intellectual powerhouses of China, the centres of trade with the West, some of them among the richest cities in the world.

Arthur Moule, a 25-year-old British missionary, had only recently arrived in Ningbo in the autumn of 1861. In his diary he describes the growing panic with the Taiping attack imminent: 'People began to leave, by junk and lorchas up the coast to Shanghai and by road up into the hills to take refuge in country villages. Half Zhejiang was on the road. November was wet and cold, and crowds of refugees were hurrying through the dripping streets with despair on their faces.' Of the city's 400,000 population, scarcely 20,000 were left as the Taiping closed in. Moule conveys the intense drama of the moment, and the sheer terror generated by the Taiping:

> We began to lay in stores as for a siege. On the 3rd of November, the news arrived of the fall of Shaoxing; on the 5th the gates of Ningbo were shut early, and so every succeeding day until they were opened by the Taipings themselves. On the 9th of November walking on the walls we observed bamboo cranes fitted with ropes and pulleys ready to let down heavy beams of wood, bristling with iron or wooden spikes on the heads of the assailants'.

On the 22nd as the Christians prepared for a grim winter, news came that Fengua, thirty miles away, had been taken by the rebels under Feng, Hong's second in command. As the panic in Ningbo grew, a gunpowder factory caught fire and in the ensuing explosion, 'thirty or forty men were fearfully burnt and scarcely any recovered ... But such sorrows and calamities were soon swallowed up in the great flood of misery coming as if in an earthquake wave'.

On 25 November, Moule noted in his diary, 'Yuyao fell ... and in a great fire three thousand houses were burned. On the 29th we suddenly saw vast columns of smoke to the north-west, evidently from the proud and rich city of Cicheng only twelve miles off. At nightfall we heard that the great Daoist temple there, the glory and the pride of all that region had been burnt to the ground.' Back at Ningbo, the authorities ordered the houses in the suburbs next to the north and east gates to be burned so as to offer no shelter to the enemy: a whole suburb from the east gate to the old bridge of boats was swept away, and the fires burned for two weeks. 'On the 7th December', Moule continues, 'the Taiping forces reached the West Gate; there was heavy firing. On Sunday 8th I attended church by the north bank ... and later the city fell'. It was an austere Christmas under Taiping rule, with a great snowstorm followed by huge downpours, which left the streets flooded. As Moule describes: 'The river was empty of ships bound for foreign and coastal markets. The harbour was usually full of clippers loaded with Ningbo cotton bound for Liverpool, the American supply being cut off by the Civil War, so cessation of the China trade only worsened the serious cotton famine prevailing in the north of England.'

Foreigners were still allowed to move about, and a Christmas service was planned for the British on a gunboat in river. Searching for holly on Christmas Eve, Moule walked into the countryside outside the walls and encountered terrible desolation: 'We saw great numbers of dead bodies ... the state of Zhejiang and most of the thirteen ravaged provinces of China could best be described in the words of Isaiah: "the city is fallen and all the graven images of gods are broken ... " Dark days indeed they were for us all.'

The New Year came with more huge snowfalls, as there had been when the English seized Ningbo in 1843 at the end of the First Opium War. 'The weather was intensely cold, standing at only thirteen degrees above zero in my room, with a fire burning all night,' reports Moule. But at least, he says, 'the severity of the weather kept the Taiping quiet for a time'.

The dramatic story of the Taiping can still be followed across China in clan records, local gazetteers and family histories, and also from living oral tradition. The Xie family in Qimen, for example (above pages 236–8), tell how the head of their family went out to the town gate with his little son to parley with rebels, asking them to spare the townsfolk, whereupon both were summarily killed; the horror of the scene was relayed to his young wife, pregnant with the child from whom the present family are descended.

Another Huizhou clan we have met in these pages, the Bao family, describe how the rebels swept into Tangyue village, looted properties and burned the family temple, whose shell still stands today opposite the women's ancestral memorial hall. The Baos' oldest son then fled to Yangzhou carrying the family's valuables and archives, including the woodblock-printed family history and a magnificent scroll painting nearly a century old depicting the salt merchant Bao Zhidao

with his family and their ancestors. Unfortunately he was caught on
the road by Taiping bandits, who seized the bags and spilled their
contents on the ground. As today's family tell the story:

'Take what we have but please do not destroy the painting,' he
pleaded. 'To my family it is worth more than gold. It was painted
for our ancestor Zhidao, a man of charity who shared his wealth
and cared for the poor ...'

'You are a filial son,' said the bandit leader, and stamped on it
with his boot. 'Take it away.'

The scroll survives today, still with the family, rolled up under
the sofa in their flat in Dongtai, complete with the faint boot mark
of a Taiping rebel.

They were lucky, but some local stories are simply terrifying. A
unique and harrowing diary by an otherwise unknown writer called
Zhang Daye, recently translated by Xiaofei Tian, gives us a child's
view of the war. Born in 1855, Zhang was only seven years old when
the Taiping sacked his native town of Shaoxing, a town with an
incomparably rich cultural and literary history. He spent two years
on the move hiding from Taiping rebels, local bandits and the imperial army and its local militias, all of whom 'preyed on the people for
money and food'. He conveys the sheer terror that descended on the
town, which had known peace and stability for many decades under
Qing rule, and also the terrible cruelty, mass killing and burning
alive of whole communities: 'From the cry of a tiny insect', he wrote,
'one can hear the sound of the vast world.'

Travelling by boat on the waterways of Zhejiang, he describes
rivers choked with the dead and covered with a thick white film of
'corpse wax' from dissolving bodies; remembering it all with a child's
clarity, he writes of massacres and terrible cruelties done to women.
In one walled town in the Zhejiang plain, local leaders mounted a
long and fierce resistance to the Taiping army. When it finally fell,
several hundred thousand people had gathered in and around the
town, including many of the wealthy families of the coastal plain
and other parts of Zhejiang who had taken refuge there. Later local
official histories speak of the deaths of up to 600,000 civilians.

Hiding in woods on Snow Shadow Peak Mountain, overlooking the town, Zhang describes Taiping armies taking the road below him, advancing like ants on Bao village, which he could see 'as big as a dinner plate' under plumes of dark smoke. He describes the roar of cannon fire, the distant cries of the people, and 'tens of thousands sank into oblivion in an instant'.

Later in life, Zhang reflected on his childhood experiences: 'And yet human beings continue to dream their great dream and none wakes up from it. From past to present they have always been busy harming and murdering one another. What ignorance! It is all very sad.'

Then came the final awful aftermath, the experience of the child still haunting the mind of the adult:

A strong wind started blowing. At dusk we looked in the direction of the village from afar: it seemed to be in great turmoil. The sound of crying and shooting, like water noisily boiling in a cauldron, continued all night. As the moon was about to go down, the morning wind blew on our wet clothes, and the cold penetrated our flesh and entered our bones. My mother and I faced each other and both burst into tears. The next day it was already noon when a villager informed us that the bandits had finally left. We went back ... there were flames and smoke throughout the village; broken body parts were strewn about, and blood was everywhere. I cannot bear to describe the awful smell of burnt flesh. Oh the cruelty of it all.

The prosperous world of Zhejiang urban society, depicted in famous works like Shen Fu's *Six Records of a Floating Life*, was wrecked. It is no exaggeration to say that the Taiping changed everything. Far more than the Opium Wars, this was a profound disruption of society. The destruction of the intelligentsia would impact on Chinese culture into the twentieth century. 'The realm of happiness in nature and that of suffering in the human world', concludes Zhang Daye, looking back on tragedies of the mid-nineteenth century, 'are as far apart as clouds and ravines.'

THE FALL

China now had rival dynasties: the Qing in the north in Beijing; and the Taiping that had spread its power and terror across the rich heartland of the south. For the British and the other foreigners, however, their stake in China was too big to jeopardise, so they lent the Chinese government advisers and the latest weaponry to help crush the rebels. The Taiping sent a northern expedition to take Beijing, but it was poorly planned and ended in disaster. Taiping expeditions between 1853 and 1863 to capture the upper Yangtze valley, Sichuan and western China also failed. The Taiping attacked Shanghai in summer 1860 but were repulsed by Qing troops supported by European officers. Eventually the Qing massed a million men against the rebels. The war ebbed backwards and forwards – Yangzhou, for example, was occupied four times – but finally, in 1864, nearly sixteen years after they left Thistle Mountain, the Taiping were forced back by imperial forces behind the walls of Nanjing, where they were decimated by disease and starvation. Hong himself fell ill and died on 30 June 1864. The following month, Nanjing fell, the leadership surrendered and were executed. Hong's body was exhumed, burned and his ashes blown from a cannon so no resting place could become a focus for commemoration by Taiping loyalists. For rehabilitation he would have to wait until the 1950s, when the Communist Party pronounced him their heroic precursor.

The war was won, though local fighting continued for seven more years, with hundreds of thousands of Taiping supporters still resisting the Qing. It was not until the summer of 1871 that the last pockets were wiped out in the border regions of Hunan, Guizhou and Guangxi.

The loss of life had been huge: it has been estimated that between 20 and 30 million died over the sixteen years of war and its aftermath in the south. If these figures are correct, then it was the worst war of the nineteenth century; indeed, the losses may have been heavier than those suffered in the First World War. In the lower Yangtze, estimates suggest that the population of 67 million recorded in the census of 1844 only recovered to 45 million by 1894. Jiangsu alone lost 6 or 7 million. Urban life in many places was wrecked. The defences around Shanghai had offered protection to foreigners and asylum for a flood of gentry, merchants and the general populace of Jiangsu and Zhejiang, but Nanjing, Changzhou, Yangzhou and Suzhou – some of the richest and biggest cities in the world in the 1830s – were decimated. Protected by foreign guns, it would be Shanghai that took off after the Taiping.

It is no exaggeration to say that the Taiping left the whole body politic traumatised; hardly any part of China proper had escaped the conflagration in one of the worst wars in history. In the end the Taiping failed, but as a rising against the empire it was a forecast, a statement that nothing would be the same. It was a sign that the whole great edifice that had grown up over 2,000 years of imperial history was now under threat. There had been breakdowns in the past, in the time of the Three Kingdoms and the Five Dynasties, in the Mongol and Manchu conquests; but now imperial China was cut to the heart. A deep tear had appeared in the gorgeous but increasingly threadbare fabric of the Chinese monarchy.

THE IMPACT ON CHINESE CULTURE

In the south, the devastation of Chinese culture over a generation put a halt to more reaching plans for cultural reform. Writers like Zheng Zhen and the Guizhou movement had hoped for a synthesis of old and new learning, but the optimism that they and many southern literati had held for the future had been broken by the war, the killing of teachers and the destruction of academies and libraries. The dreams of a new southern cultural powerhouse, already contested by the imperial government in Beijing with its hostility to the new-wave scholarship, were gone. The great scholarly movement in the Yangtze delta during the eighteenth and early nineteenth centuries, which was beginning to develop its own vision of Chinese modernity, its own Enlightenment, perished in the havoc caused by the terrifying dissolution of order during the Taiping wars.

Everyone now could see, as the *North China Herald* reported, that 'China at the present time is undergoing the throes of a transition state which in all probability may be the turning point in her destiny for future generations'. Indeed, when we look at the successive blows of the Japanese invasion, the civil war and the Cultural Revolution in the twentieth century, it could be said that China is only now recovering. The effect on schools, academies and libraries was devastating; lost lives, lost books, but especially broken links in the chains of scholarship, the scholarly lineages that had always been so important in the intellectual and cultural life of China. Hangzhou especially had been a great centre of cultural life. Sacked by the Taiping twice over 1860–61, when family and monastic libraries were lost, the city is only now recovering as a great centre of education with the new universities of the south. The losses in Suzhou were particularly severe; a gathering point for refugees at the start of the war, it has been estimated that as many as half a million people died in the city and its region in 1860. Yangzhou, which was the pre-eminent cultural centre in the eighteenth century, never recovered its position as the cultural leader in scholarship and printing. Among the losses were the leading mathematician and astronomer Luo Shilin, killed in Yangzhou in 1853, and the scholar Xu Yuren, who lost his life in the battle for Suzhou. Among the enormous number of works of literature that were lost were many unpublished writings of the historian and philosopher Zhang Xuecheng. It was as if, let us say, the scholarly heartland of Western Europe in the 1860s had been smashed from Amsterdam to Paris, its scholars killed or dispersed and its libraries destroyed.

One of the great eras of Chinese culture, the last phase of its traditional civilisation, was coming to an end. Across the world, imperialism and colonialism in the nineteenth century had accelerated the forces of modernity, both cultural and technological, shifting mental horizons, rubbing out encoded ways of seeing and doing often built up over millennia. With increasing speed, colonialism introduced secular capitalist modernity. The world of the traditional civilisations of Eurasia, which had grown up in the Iron

Age and Late Antique world, had seen its last great flowerings under the Ottomans in Anatolia and the Near East, the Safavids in Iran, the Moghuls in India, and the Qing in East Asia. Now their thought worlds were under threat as the power of the maritime nations on the Atlantic seaboard of Europe reached out across the globe. If renewal was to come, it had to begin not just with the physical fabric of the country, and new technologies, but 'in men's hearts' as Wei Yuan put it, with the rebuilding of the cultural fabric – the very ethos of the civilisation. And that was much harder to do.

17

THE GREAT CHINESE
REVOLUTION 1850–1950

The Opium Wars and the Taiping rebellion were huge blows to the Chinese empire. But the Qing state was nothing if not resilient, and could still call upon deep reservoirs of loyalty from its Confucian scholars and administrators and many of its hard-worked local officials. Under resolute leadership, renewal was still possible, and now a new generation of intellectuals and public servants grasped the nettle and pushed for major reform of the state. This movement encouraged the first embassies to the West, anxious to learn from the technological advances made in Europe, but also to understand the nature of the Western liberal mind. In the Forbidden City, however, there was resistance to real structural change, and the reformers of the late nineteenth century were unable to translate their ideas to the imperial establishment, or to the grassroots administration of the empire. Every year between the Taiping revolt and 1911 there was a rebellion somewhere in the Chinese countryside, and the unravelling of the empire began to resemble the periods of social unrest that had brought down earlier dynasties. This last phase of the imperial story begins in the aftermath of the Taiping, in the ruins of God's kingdom on earth.

At the end of the Taiping war Nanjing lay devastated, like Berlin after the Second World War. The writer Chen Zuolin, who had lived through the horrors of the Taiping, was shocked by the extent of the destruction when he returned to the city and saw 'barren encampments and abandoned ramparts ... desolation filled the scene'. The Great Ming city with its glorious architecture had been cut loose from its past, obliterating so many of its meaning-ful places, urban landscapes, temples and shrines. The Scottish photographer John Thomson witnessed 'many dreary acres of demolished streets with not a single occupant'. But by 1869 many major restorations were underway. Thomson, for example, photo-graphed the abbot of a Buddhist monastery supervising 'coolies' working in the grounds of his recently restored temple, amid piles of fallen masonry and the freshly plastered walls of newly erected brick outbuildings.

This period from the 1860s to the 1870s is known as the Tongzhi Restoration, named after the emperor who reigned from 1861 to 1875. It saw the growth of the so-called 'Foreign Matters' or 'Self-Strengthening Movement', whose origins go back to before the First Opium War. It has largely been seen as a failure because it devoted itself to material changes: importing Western technologies like armaments, ships and, later, railways, but without any meaningful political change. It did, however, keep the empire afloat for another fifty years, and sowed the seeds for many developments in twentieth-century Chinese history, including the birth of democratic ideas and the beginnings of the Chinese feminist movement. New academies, printing offices and libraries were set up in the sacked cities of the south, and a modern naval dockyard was constructed in Fuzhou. In the field of ideas, open debate began about the merits of traditional Chinese learning over Western learning, and about which direction the Chinese intellectual tradition should go. This would become the central question of the next century and a half, and the debate is still ongoing.

After the shock of the Taiping rebellion, the rebuilding was in the military, too. An arsenal was built in Nanjing in 1865 under the auspices of Li Hongzhang, one of the victorious Qing generals who had dealt with the Western powers and had advocated modernising the Qing army by bringing in Western armaments. The arsenal with its casting forges was the first in China, run on the latest scientific industrial military principles under British military advisers. Every year from now on, hundreds of tons of guns and ammunition were manufactured, ranging from heavy artillery for mounting on battery trains to field guns and carriages, howitzers, torpedoes, rockets and launchers.

One of Thomson's photographs from Nanjing in 1872 shows Chinese officials in robes and mandarins' hats standing next to stacked piles of heavy ammunition and a Gatling gun with eight rotating brass barrels mounted on a wooden carriage. First used in the American Civil War, the 'gelin gun' was the earliest automatic firearm adopted by the Chinese army. An example of the latest Western technology, it was hand-cranked and could discharge 200 shots a minute. Thomson noted the low quality of the raw materials, and the poor and underpaid workers, but it was a start.

After such a massive shock, the key was to restore the state's solidity of purpose. The victorious field commander Zeng Guofan was charged with overseeing the restoration of the structures of civil administration. He began a huge programme in Nanjing and the south: rebuilding walls, granaries, schools, governors' *yamens* and magistrates' offices. The aim was to reinstate the traditional institutions of governance and to encourage the merchants and the gentry to come back to the lower Yangtze region.

His greatest goal was to get the examinations going again in the south after the long hiatus, in the hope of producing the next generation of Confucian administrators. In winter 1864, the huge examination compound in Nanjing was inspected and the 16,000 cells were found to be still intact, but stripped of their wooden writing boards and seats, while the residences and offices for the supervisors had been destroyed. So workmen were dispatched to cannibalise wood from various Taiping palaces around the city to remake the cells and enable exams to resume as soon as possible. The old classical education system would continue as before. But for how long?

When the main restorations were completed, the emperor came to Nanjing. At that moment they must have believed that they had weathered the storms of the mid-century: the Opium Wars and the Taiping rebellion. At that moment theirs was still one of the greatest empires in history, extending from Manchuria all the way across to Central Asia, from the steppes of Mongolia down to the forests of Burma. To the Confucian bureaucrats who stood around their emperor that day, China must still have seemed the centre of civilisation. But the pressure was growing on the empire, not only from the foreign powers, but from within China itself; for in the eyes of some, the question now was not only physical rebuilding, but fundamental cultural reconstruction, and that had to begin with opening up to the world. Indeed, the first tentative steps had taken place within months of the defeat of the Taiping.

THE TONGZHI RESTORATION: FIRST MEETINGS ABROAD

In early 1866, an English clipper from Canton completed its fourteen-week journey to Europe. Among the passengers were three government-approved Chinese students and their Manchu government chaperone. One of them, Zhang Deyi, was a nineteen-year-old studying English, who later became an ambassador in England. Zhang had been one of the first pupils to attend the newly set up Combined Studies College in Beijing, which he had joined aged fifteen to study Western languages. The group was not engaged in official diplomacy; their sole mandate was to 'make a record of the geographical conditions and manners and customs of all the countries through which they pass'.

The expedition was the idea of the British inspector general of the Maritime Customs Bureau in Canton, Robert Hart, who proposed on a brief return to Britain to take the Chinese students with him. Then only thirty-one, Hart had lived in China since he was nineteen, and was destined to be one of the most influential Westerners in Qing China. He was devoted to the country, horrified by the recent disasters, and his great hope was 'to aid the Chinese in their many troubles, and ease the way for China so long isolated, to be brought into contact with the west. Moving in the direction of what we in the west are pleased to style progress, and to regard as of utility to the human family.' With this ambition, Hart submitted a memorandum to the reform-minded Prince Gong, the leader of the Qing Grand Council, with practical ideas to remedy China's international weakness; advising, for example, on the running of postal services and the proper supervision of taxes. Gong (whose charismatic portrait appears among Thomson's photographs) was a remarkably far-sighted figure, who pioneered the opening of embassies in foreign countries and established the School of Languages and Combined Learning in Beijing with a branch in Canton to encourage young Chinese students to learn foreign languages, culture and science.

The journey opened the students' eyes to the new world of the military and commercial power of the Europeans: the French ports in Indochina and the British maritime presence across the region from Hong Kong to India and on to Suez. In the courts of Europe the Chinese visitors were greeted with royal receptions, touring the key cultural, institutional and industrial sites. They thought Paris the finest city with its beautiful parks, boulevards, culture and food; there too they couldn't help but remark on the beauty of the women, and their freedom compared with women in China. In London they saw a stark reminder of the recent violent past with an exhibition of loot from the Summer Palace, sacked by the British and French in 1860. The students were fascinated by modern transport, especially by the trains and the railway engineering; so much so that one of them took home a working train model. Travelling on to the USA, they were struck by the cleanliness of the cities compared with the squalor and stench of so many of China's old towns; and again they mentioned the beauty of the women – 'the fragrant aroma of their whole bodies was so enticing' – although they were shocked by the freedom of the sexes; intimacies such as public touching and kissing, and even shaking hands, were all so un-Confucian. But these freedoms were exhilarating to the young Chinese visitors, one of whom wrote breathlessly about a group of women in Boston high society, glimpsed 'standing on a balcony lovely as fairies and lavishly clothed, beautiful enough to cause cities to fall'.

In America, the Chinese visitors found themselves in the immediate aftermath of the civil war, and they began to understand some of the key political and social issues that dominated American politics: 'the Party of Hierarchy regard blacks as slaves, but no longer dare say so. Their opposite is the Party of Equality. Democracy is a new concept: but the problem seems to be that irreconcilable self-interests lead to deadlocks.'

But it was the differences between China and the West that struck these first visitors most forcibly. China was simply the other pole of the human mind, as Zhang noted: 'There is nothing here that is not the opposite of China. In politics the people discuss and the ruler obeys; in family regulations the wife proposes and the husband follows; in writing they write from left to right; in books they begin from the back ... Customs and systems are just reversed. All of this is a mystery to us.'

THE FIRST AMBASSADOR TO THE WEST

After that first encounter, it was vital for China that light should be cast on the mystery. The way was open for a fuller official engagement with the world through diplomacy. China was increasingly part of a fast-changing world, which could not help but change China too. In earlier dynasties, diplomacy had been an important part of statecraft; the Northern Song had owed its very existence to expert and subtle diplomacy, which sought to understand the Other. But the Qing had never sent ambassadors beyond the borders of its own protectorates, and there was no suggestion of a trained corps of Manchu officials who spoke foreign languages other than Chinese, Manchu, Mongolian and Tibetan. Now it was high time the Chinese had their own representatives abroad.

On 21 January 1877, China's first ambassador to the West arrived in Britain on the P&O liner *Peshawur*. A typical workhorse of the British Empire in the East, *Peshawur* was powered by steam, not sail: a sign of the fast-changing times. At 3,782 tons and 378 feet long, she carried 112 first-class passengers, and also 106 troops returning from Calcutta in British India. And standing at the rail in his Chinese mandarin's hat and fur-lined silk coat, wrapped against the cold, was a veteran of the Opium Wars and the Taiping rebellion, Guo Songtao. The translator accompanying him was Zhang, the young man who had visited London as a student ten years before. The journey from Shanghai to Colombo through the Straits of Malacca confirmed to Guo what he already knew: the size of the British Empire in the East and its naval and mercantile supremacy, which, along with Russia's land empire, 'was surrounding China day by day ... eyes glaring like predatory lions', as he remarked in his diary. Since the start of Victoria's reign, their bruising encounters had perplexed many in Beijing. As Guo had advised the Qing government in a memo before he left, the international situation was complex, with so many foreign powers, 'which is why it is so important to understand foreign affairs. Ever since foreign trade was opened, there have been many incidents usually arising out of our dealings with foreigners ... We must create a proper foreign policy while at the same time establishing the basis of national strength and prosperity. And all this depends on one decision only on the part of our government.'

Now, on a chill and damp late winter's afternoon, *Peshawur* rounded the Needles and entered the Solent; on the port side, Hurst Castle and the soft green forests of Beaulieu; on the starboard the Isle of Wight, where a fellow traveller pointed out to Guo Queen Victoria's residence at Osborne House. Then into a bank of fog cloaking Southampton docks and arrival past a forest of masts from all over the world. After fifty days at sea, Guo set foot on British soil – the real beginning of China's modern international diplomacy. It was a journey of intellectual discovery that Guo was extraordinarily well equipped to undertake. Born in 1818, he had been educated at the prestigious Yuelu classical academy founded back in the Song dynasty (the great Zhu Xi had lectured there). In recent years the academy had broadened out its curriculum to practical subjects such as military engineering, political economy and waterworks, and its network of alumni included some of the leading progressive thinkers of the Late Qing, including Wei Yuan, author of the first treatises on Western geography and naval policy (above page 399). There Guo had befriended Zeng Guofan, the architect of the Tongzhi Restoration. As a young man he had organised defences on the Yangtze in the First Opium War, and in the second war he had built the Dagu forts only to see them taken in a firestorm by British and French assault troops. Later a commander in battles against the Taiping rebels, Guo was a man grounded in reality.

Like his friend Zeng, Guo was a vocal advocate of China's self-strengthening: even while the Taiping war raged, he had called for foreign languages to be taught in Chinese schools. But before he left China his views had become controversial among conservatives, committed as he was to the radical transformation of China. He was a well-known supporter of technological innovation and educational reform, calling for an enlightened understanding of the West. 'An apostle of progress' as *The Times* in London had called him, he had an insatiable curiosity about Britain and especially its parliamentary institutions, which he understood as a relatively modern development. Talking about Britain's political culture of parliamentary democracy, he observed:

At first the British didn't have a long and accumulated tradition of high virtue and culture. But for over a century now, their officials and their common people have collaborated in discussion of national policies, have reported these to the King and put them into application, thereby making daily progress. And now the sovereign is beloved for her wisdom, and their way of life becomes better and better.

Britain's modern progress he traced back to the scientific revolution that had paved the way for the kind of modernity that in his eyes China conspicuously lacked. In particular there was Francis Bacon's *New Science*, which Guo had had translated into Chinese before he left. He saw this as the founding text of Western modernity and, in its advocacy of a clear break with the past, a text of deep relevance to China. 'Bacon began studying the Latin and Greek classics,' Guo wrote, thinking of the status of the Confucian classics in China,

> but after a long while he realised they were empty now and incapable of practical application to the times. That's why he started to develop knowledge about natural laws that he called the 'New Science'. Within 230 or 240 years, the Europeans have become wealthy and powerful, and all this is explicable by their learning and knowledge. Western politics, education and manufacture are all based on knowledge.

Turning these things over in his diary as he travelled around Britain, Guo reflected on the comparative history of China and Europe:

> In Europe people have been competing with each other with knowledge and power for 2,000 years. Egypt, Rome and Islam have each in their turn flourished and decayed; yet the principles which formed the basis of these states still endure. Nowadays England, France, Russia, America, and Germany, all of them great nations which have tried their strength against each other to see who is pre-eminent, have evolved a code of international law which gives precedence to fidelity and righteousness and attaches the utmost importance to relations between states. Taking full cognisance of feeling and punctiliously observing all due ceremonies, they have evolved a high culture on a firm material basis. They surpass by a long way the states of our Spring and Autumn period.

So there was much to learn. Guo went to Oxford, where he attended a lecture by the great sinologist James Legge. In London he visited factories and was pained to see another exhibition of Chinese treasures looted from the Summer Palace. In July he travelled by train from Liverpool Street to Ipswich on a visit to the engineering works of Ransomes & Rapier to see the manufacture of steam locomotives. The two-hour train journey, he remarked, would have taken two or three days in his own country. This convinced him that railways would transform the life of the country: 'The railways will pass through the country rather as blood circulates in the human body,' Guo wrote to his minister back home, urging the immediate development of railway technology. He recognised that this technology could be applied to defence, too, for 'one of the ways in which Britain had taken advantage of our weak political position [was] to come to our shores as if instantly over a distance of 70,000 *li*'.

A fascinating meeting recorded by one of Guo's party took place with the seventy-year-old railway engineer Rowland Stephenson: 'On 16 March 1877 he came to visit us, and said he had built railways in England and in India. The English railways system extends over 510,000 leagues and cost £630 million. Every year they carry 507 million passengers and 200 million tons of goods.' Stephenson then unfolded a 'very workaday map' of a projected Chinese rail system: 'He could no longer at his age do the work himself,' Guo reported, 'but could direct others.' Stephenson left the map with them; this, it might be said, was the founding moment of what is today the world's most extensive and up-to-date rail network.

'Now considering the great population of China and the wealth of our products,' wrote one of Guo's companions in his diary,

if we build a railway from Canton to Swatow, Changsha, Yuezhou and Hankou, all along the Yangzi river and turn east to Nanjing, then north to Zhenjiang, Yangzhou, Huai-'an, Linqing, Qingzhou, Tianjin and up to the capital, it would involve a distance of 6000 leagues at the cost of only twenty million in gold: we are sure to gain much profit from it. When this line is up and running we can go on to open branch routes to reach every town and city, and so change the face of China.

One hundred and fifty years ago, then, Guo had articulated some of the fundamental issues on China's path to modernity, from practical engineering and long-term economic planning to the reorganisation of knowledge itself. The changes Guo and his reform-minded colleagues looked for were not just for China to modernise through technology, but to embrace modernity itself, to change the mindset of China's great tradition. But was China ready to listen?

In Britain, the press was quick to realise that the establishment of a permanent Chinese embassy in London was an 'event unprecedented in the history of the relations between China and foreign countries', and even constituted 'a proud page of British history'. But in China the reaction was more muted. As a prominent scholar, social critic and statesman, Guo had long been committed to an informed and enlightened understanding of the West. But at home such ideas were resisted by what he likened to a Chinese Oxford movement: 'a Confucian High Church Tory Revival', which aimed to purify national life and oppose the introduction of Western thought. On his return, Guo was the target of a vicious campaign organised by those scholar-officials, those 'purists' based in the government-sponsored Hanlin Academy. Criticised and marginalised after his return, Guo died disappointed and in seclusion; his brilliant journals were barred from publication and have only been published in modern times.

THE MODERNISATION DEBATE

The Qing had survived the Opium Wars and the cataclysm of the Taiping, but across China society had been stirred up. The business classes in the treaty ports had opened up to the West: from the battered intelligentsia in the cities of the delta to the scientific thinkers of the Song Literary School in Guizhou, everywhere the future of China was up for debate. And many key figures that might have helped bring in the change had been lost: the heroic Commissioner Lin had died at the start of the Taiping war; the brilliant strategic thinker Wei Yuan had died a renouncer in a monastery in Hangzhou as the city fell to the rebels; the poet and critic Zheng Zhen perished in a stockade on Mount Yumen in the bitter aftermath; and Zeng Guofan himself, the architect of the restoration, died in 1872.

A new generation would have to take the torch on now: the 'New World' theorist Kang Youwei, born during the war in 1858; the journalist, scholar, reformer and activist Liang Qichao, born during the restoration in 1873; the great writer and essayist Lu Xun (1881); and the new wave of feminists, women like Qiu Jin (1875) and He Zhen (c. 1883). This next generation would bring reform ideas into an open clash with the Qing government and eventually bring the empire down.

First, though, there was the pressure from the outsiders. In the Second Opium War towards the end of the Taiping, the British and the French had forced more concessions from the Chinese. More treaty ports were opened up on the coasts and in the interior, eventually over eighty of them. During the Taiping war, European troops had been brought in direct confrontation to protect their interests; and with their banks and villas parts of some Chinese cities began to look like corners of Europe, with the infrastructure of telegraph and banking, railways and trams. Swelled by merchants fleeing the Taiping, Shanghai was launched on its path to become the world's greatest city. China had already begun to open up, but in that lay a profound threat to the way China had seen itself and the world for so long.

For some, the whole culture needed to transform: the imperial system with its age-old rituals; its introspective Confucian culture; its feudal order; and its legal system that had never been separated from the executive. Even the traditional examinations held in the time-honoured way: in huge examination halls in cities where thousands of little brick cubicles awaited scholars immersed in the ancient classics. For the reformers, it all needed to go.

For others, however, the Chinese tradition itself was still a potential medium of revival, by combining 'Western technologies and Chinese culture'. Chinese academies had now begun to teach Western science and political philosophy, and Chinese students were being sent to the West. But to all Chinese patriots it was clear that the biggest threat to China's continuance as a unitary state was the intervention of the imperialists and all they stood for. Some modernisers argued that the only way out was to borrow from and to imitate the West; to build modern armaments, ships, guns, railways and manufacturing industries, to industrialise – and fast. But in the 1870s further clashes with the Europeans followed. No sooner were the Fuzhou dockyards built than the French destroyed them. The smell of burning was in the air.

A SMALL TOWN IN THE SOUTH

Meanwhile, the old order continued in the countryside. Out in the provinces, despite the ever-present fact of peasant unrest, banditry and piracy, loyal local magistrates educated in the old ways still tried to administer China on behalf of the Son of Heaven, and civic-minded local gentry and merchants continued to support the ideals of a Confucian society with 'acts of benevolence and virtue'. On the Fujian coast, a host of inscriptions commemorate such people. One of them from 1882 tells the story of how one small town, Anhai near Quanzhou, looked after its poor in the declining days of the Qing. Providing for the poor was an ancient tradition in China and 'relief halls' went back hundreds of years, but since the eighteenth century there had been no central legislation on poor relief, much of the burden of social welfare falling on the local communities. This included the creation and upkeep of relief halls for widows and orphans, 'long-life' halls (old people's homes) and 'infant rearing halls' for abandoned babies, who were mainly girls. Lists of such benefactors can still be found everywhere in southern temples today. One of them, the 'Clear and Benevolent Temple' in Anhai, with its ancillary buildings for the poor, had been founded in 1875 by a group of the town's gentry. But these were not wealthy people: 'their financial strength was not equal to their will', and the project stalled for lack of funds. Luckily, a prominent local clan member and 'benevolent trader', Mr Rui-Gang, returned from Shanghai and ploughed some of the fortune made in the boomtown back into founding a local benevolent society. He and his brother bought a property with a communal hall, prayer room, coffin room and office and roped in other local gentry to get behind the project. 'From then on', the inscription says, 'the widows and orphans from the poor and indigent families from the whole town had a monthly stipend, the sick had medicine, the dead had coffins, travellers in financial difficulties received help, relief was given to the destitute and support to those in danger ...'

Quoting the classics, the *Book of Changes* and the *Book of Documents*, this tale from early June 1881 shows the ethos of the old order in the countryside still in place; the old Confucian belief that goodness and virtue, not law, governance and an effective state, were the keys to social justice. But just up the coast, in the environment where Rui-Gang had made his money, the urban elites in cities like Shanghai were changing fast: imbibing European ideas of individualism and capitalism which would begin to transform the old assumptions of the ruling class. And now many critics of the government began to argue for a top-down renewal of society, some even for direct action, rebellion against the emperor and resistance to the foreigners' malign influence. And in the 1890s the next explosion came.

THE HUNDRED DAYS' REFORM

Sparked by drought and famine, poverty and class war, peasant risings were flaring up across China. Then, in 1894–5, China suffered a humiliating defeat in a disastrous war with Japan. Now the colonial powers gathered like vultures: the Russians, Japanese and Germans in the north; the French and British in the south. Mocking cartoons in Western books and periodicals showed China as a rich cake waiting to be cut up by Queen Victoria, the Tsar and the Kaiser, greedy-eyed and licking their lips. A pronounced shift in foreign attitude to China was underway, as the civilisation that the European philosophers of the eighteenth century had looked up to was now derided as a sick giant locked in its past and incapable even of defending itself.

In response, the movement for reform inside China grew more vocal. Thinkers like Kang Youwei argued that what was needed now was no longer simply 'self-strengthening', but radical institutional

and ideological change. Arguing for a constitutional monarchy like
Meiji Japan, Kang was able to persuade the young Guangxu emperor
to support his ideas, and in the summer of 1898 the emperor initiated
the Hundred Days' Reform. Guangxu issued a series of edicts calling
for comprehensive changes in a number of areas: the abolition of
the traditional exam system; the introduction of Western scientific
curricula; the establishment of a constitutional monarchy; rapid
industrialisation; and the acceptance of the principles of capitalism
in order to strengthen the economy. This was the most radical manifesto to date in Chinese history, crystallising many of the ideas that
had been debated by the opponents of despotism since the Donglin
movement nearly 300 years before. Had these edicts been put into
practice, the course of modern Chinese history might have been
very different; indeed, the country might have been spared some of
the suffering it endured in the twentieth century. But the reformers
faced opposition from the conservatives in the government, including
members of the imperial family led by the Dowager Empress Cixi.
When the reformers' plans to remove her from power were leaked,
they were defeated in a coup d'état, and the emperor was placed
under house arrest. The reformers were executed or driven abroad,
crushed by Cixi in the name of China's ancestral laws:

> All Under Heaven [China] is that of our ancestors. How dare
> you act so recklessly? The ministers have all been selected by
> me for years, to be left to assist you. How dare you willfully
> dismiss them? And then, you dare to heed demagogic and rebel-
> lious words, to change and wreak havoc upon our fundamental
> model. How can Kang Youwei be superior to the ministers I
> have selected? How can the laws of Kang Youwei be superior
> to those of our ancestors? Changing and wreaking havoc upon
> ancestral laws, and letting subjects violate them – do you know
> what a crime this is? Let me ask you: who is more important –
> your ancestors, or Kang Youwei? What can be more stupid
> and benighted than turning your back on your ancestors and
> implementing Kang's laws?

In the face of this, the Guangxu emperor 'trembled with fear and dared not respond'. It was a critical moment; had he succeeded, the path would have been open to a constitutional monarchy and fundamental changes to the political system. But it was not to be. Trapped by the weight of the ancestors and the immense burden of rulership, which he embodied in his person, the emperor caved in and submitted to house arrest. It was under these conditions that a year later, in the last days of the century, the emperor performed for the last time the most solemn of all imperial rituals, the great midwinter solstice ceremony at the Altar of Heaven with which this book began. These rituals would never be performed again. The following year, 1900, the Qing government was plunged into a catastrophe from which it would not recover, as north China was swept by a great rebellion: the Boxer Rising.

THE BOXER REBELLION

In the *I Ching*, the great Chinese book of divination whose beginnings can be traced back to the oracle bone divinations of the Bronze Age, there is a passage about great crises. It says that there are always two warnings of an impending crisis, then with the third it materialises. For China, after the Taiping, the Boxers were the second great sign.

In Shandong in the northeast, a peasant uprising broke out brought on by famine, drought, economic collapse and popular fury with the Qing government. The revolt was led by 'The Society of Righteous and Harmonious Fists', or the 'Boxers'; like the wrestling clubs in the Iranian Revolution, martial arts clubs in China had long been a hotbed of dissent, from spiritual sects like White Lotus and the Red Turbans in the fourteenth century through to the communist age. In 1899, one Boxer leader called Zhu 'Red Lantern' was a wandering healer who claimed descent from the first Ming emperor. Looking back nostalgically to the brutal fist of Zhu Yuanzhang, he proclaimed: 'Away with the Qing – restore the Ming!' Believing themselves to be possessed by the ancient spirits of China, the Boxers were thoroughly anti-imperialist, anti-colonial and anti-Christian.

Early in 1900, the Boxers swept towards Beijing in their black clothes and bandanas, calling for the killing of foreigners and the wiping out of their influence. Obscurantist and mystically driven, they were responding to a much wider sense of grievance across China. The Westerners, of course, portrayed the Boxers as violent primitives from a backward society. China's ancient civilisation, with its Confucian ideals and its beautiful and mysterious rituals, the culture beloved of the *philosophes*, of de Tocqueville and Père Gabet, was now an object of revulsion, held up for its barbarities by the 'civilised' world in a torrent of racist cartoons, postcards and pictures. For the outsiders, this was a terrifying glimpse of the irrational forces that lurked beneath the surface of an archaic civilisation that simply needed to move into the modern world and turn its back on its old self. They dismissed the Boxers as a crazed sect trapped in the past, driven by people who thought that the railways were disrupting the spirit lines of the nation; who believed that the famines were due to the displeasure of the gods; people who told their followers they would be invulnerable to bullets. But the Boxers had support from many of the peasantry and they gathered numbers in the countryside as they marched on Beijing, destroying Christian churches, killing Westerners and Chinese Christian converts. Finally the Dowager Empress held a council of the Qing government in Beijing; there they decided to support the Boxers, and they declared war against the colonial powers.

In Beijing, the foreigners resided in their own Legation Quarter. A mile by a mile and a half, it was the same size as the Forbidden City, and indeed it was another forbidden city for the ordinary citizens of Beijing, who were not allowed to enter except as service staff. Inside were Western shops and clubs, a Catholic church, the new Hôtel de Pékin, the railway officers' telegraph, the German cemetery, and French, Russian, British, German, American and Dutch legations. It was also a fortified enceinte, with high walls, embankments, berms and platforms, behind which about 900 European diplomats, soldiers and civilians were sheltered along with nearly 3,000 Chinese Christians, preparing to face a siege by the Boxers who were now supported by troops from the imperial army.

As the revolt spread, isolated Europeans in the countryside were killed and Chinese Christian communities were massacred and their properties sacked. But now a relief army of 20,000 men drawn from the eight foreign powers who had stakes in China landed at Tianjin and marched from the coast. In the height of summer 1901, the siege was broken, Beijing was stormed and the foreign powers took revenge in a rampage of looting and killing. The Boxers were crushed mercilessly with summary executions in the streets of the capital. Photographers who had previously taken society portraits of treaty-port bigwigs now captured images of Boxers with cangues round their necks, or in cages or pens awaiting their deaths. Harrowing pictures survive showing Boxers beheaded in the streets: their severed heads in bloodstained sand outside shops while cowed crowds look on, supervised by Westerners clad in pith helmets.

The acts of savagery by the Europeans and their allies, including rape and murder, were too awful to report, some Western journalists admitted, though atrocities by the Russians and Japanese were deemed to be acceptable copy. Just as Karl Marx's reports on British atrocities in India over forty years before could not be published in Britain or Europe, war crimes committed by the bearers of civilisation were not for the British public to read in their clubs or over their breakfast tables.

THE DESTRUCTION OF THE SUMMER PALACE

After the Anglo-French armies had destroyed the Yuanmingyuan Summer Palace outside Beijing in 1860 in the Second Opium War, the Empress Dowager had rebuilt the halls and gardens, and liked to spend her summers here. But now, in revenge for her support for the Boxer Rebellion, the British sent an army into the hills and smashed the restored Yiheyuan palace to pieces, even destroying the temples and desecrating the Buddhist images. For the occupying powers in 1900, nothing was sacred.

So, the imperialists wrought their havoc and the Qing state was shaken to its foundations; unable to decide which way to act, it got the worst of all worlds. The Boxer Rebellion was the beginning of the end. Even in provincial places, belief in the empire and the great edifice of Confucian values and their ritual universe had begun to ebb away, emptied of charisma. The old imperatives, including rites, rituals, allegiance to the emperor and the significance of history, were all drained of meaning. The whole vast, magical, imaginal world replete with beliefs and symbols was crumbling. The Mandate of Heaven was lost.

The indemnity imposed on the Qing government, to be paid off over forty years, was the equivalent of more than $60 billion today. What the Chinese people felt about it all can be seen through an extraordinary range of diaries and memoirs. One remarkable source is the 200-volume diary of an ordinary man in a small village near the mining town of Taiyuan in Shaanxi. His name was Liu Dapeng and he was an unlikely local hero; a kind of Chinese Everyman who gave voice to the true feelings of the people. Liu was a provincial degree holder who never held office; a teacher, farmer and mine manager who was loyal to the emperor, and to the old ways. A pillar of the traditional Confucian morality, he was not the sort to support fanatics, but he understood the root causes of the rising. In his diary Liu wrote about the spreading violence and the killing of Chinese Christian converts. He had been shocked by the brutality of the murders as the Boxers came through his village and past his front door, but all the same, despite his values as a Confucian gentleman, he understood the Boxers in their way to be patriots. The translations that follow are by Henrietta Harrison:

> The uprisings are all caused by the foreigners and Christians tyran-nising the common people ... people who oppose them are accused of being rebels, and soldiers are used to put them down. The people cannot accept this, so I suspect that the murders of officials and the killing of soldiers will continue to occur, in many places ... The indemnity is huge, and the people can scarcely survive.

As Liu saw it from his down-at-heel house on the main street of his village, the very existence of the empire was now at stake. He still believed in the old examination system; though to his disappointment he had only passed at the provincial level, twice failing the national exams in Beijing, he looked up to the gentlemen who passed the Confucian examinations with top degrees, and believed they best understood and internalised the Confucian vision of social order and public morality. For him, still most respect was due to the all-powerful and transforming image of the sage-emperor, in this case the now imprisoned Guangxu with his long, pale, drawn face. Liu believed that behind the public mask was a stern, wise, unfailing goodness. The figure of the emperor even inhabited Liu's dreams, as when he, the poor farmer, teacher and mine manager, had a chance to remonstrate before the emperor and expose the dishonest and incompetent advisers who had brought the nation to the edge of ruin:

> I stood forth to speak alone. 'The taxes in money and grain must be reduced,' I said. 'Suitable and well-qualified men should be appointed to the government, and the dishonourable should be dismissed. Schools should be rebuilt, and agriculture and sericulture should be valued. The common people's feeling for the dynasty should be confirmed and the state should be strengthened ... We need generals to drive out the Western and Japanese barbarians ... ' My words shook the room. But the emperor bent his head and listened attentively, and there was delight on his face ...

This of course was not the only culture where ordinary people dreamed of the monarch, but we can hardly have a better example of how the centuries-old image of the sage-emperor suffused the deep psychology of ordinary Chinese people. But now, as Liu wrote in his diary, speaking of his own neighbours in the coal belt of Shaanxi, the taxes to pay the indemnity of war were causing real hardship, and 'with no security an oppressed people will rise up'.

THE WOMAN'S VIEW: THE ROOTS OF
THE FEMINIST MOVEMENT

The Qing government was restored in Beijing but it was now in the power of the foreigners, and handicapped by the huge reparations bill. Exiled in Japan, survivors of the Hundred Days, reformists and revolutionaries continued to publish and speak out against China's rulers and made their plans to overthrow the dynasty. Revolution was in the air – and among women too. Their position had always been hard in such a patriarchal society, but things were now changing fast. The first women's school in China was founded in Shanghai during the Hundred Days' Reform, on 1 June 1898. Henceforth women's education would be a major priority for reform-minded intellectuals, signalling the beginnings of a women's movement across China. Establishing institutions for female education became a priority for young intellectuals and revolutionaries and many girls and women's schools opened during the first years of the twentieth century, teaching Western-inspired curricula.

As we have seen, there had been a circulation of feminist ideas among women artists, poets and writers over many centuries; speaking within the constraints of the culture but finding ways to publish their feelings and ideas. Thousands of women writers had gone into print during the eighteenth and nineteenth centuries. But a modern feminist movement arose in China during the struggle for reform in the 1890s, and a number of women's journals founded in the first decade of the twentieth century had a big impact among radicals, men and women, for whom women's liberation was central to any true revolution. Their star was the feminist poet and nationalist Qiu Jin. Charismatic, fond of wearing Western male dress, and flamboyantly keen on martial arts, today Qiu has even been recast in the cinema as a Kung Fu heroine; in reality, however, she belonged to an old family of Shaoxing literati and had been well educated in the classics. In her twenties, trapped in an unhappy arranged marriage, she came into contact with revolutionary ideas and went to Japan to join other exiles plotting the downfall of the Qing state. There she became part of the republican movement in exile, founding a radical vernacular journal for women's political voices, so long suppressed in China. In one issue she printed a scintillating manifesto: 'A Respectful Appeal to China's Two Hundred Million Women Comrades', where she attacked the traditional patriarchal system that led to unhappy marriages like her own, and to the outrage of bound feet (from which she also suffered). She spoke up for the freedom to marry and the right to education, arguing that the future would be better for women under a Western-style government than a Confucian state. Brilliant and courageous, she was the tragic protagonist of the failed revolution of 1907.

Qiu Jin went back to China to edit another radical women's journal, *China Women's News*, but it was closed by the authorities. Finally, she was arrested at the school for girls in Shaoxing where she was a teaching assistant. Despite being tortured, she refused to reveal her contacts, but she was condemned by her own writings. When the police closed in on the clan house, her family burned incriminating documents in the backyard. What they missed, which were only found later in a little niche in her bedroom, were revolutionary tracts and guns. Her last poem ends: 'My death is of no consequence at all now, all I hope is that my sacrifice will help preserve our country.'

Qiu Jin was beheaded on 15 July 1907 in the centre of Shaoxing, China's greatest literary city. A monument now marks the spot, opposite the shopping mall where the women of today's China can buy commodities from across the world. Still her words are not forgotten, as she wrote: 'Don't tell me women are not the stuff of heroes.'

A younger feminist, He Zhen, heard the news in Japan. Far less well known than Qiu Jin, yet He Zhen now seems one of the most shining, if troubled, precursors to China's modern feminist movement. The details of her lost career and some of her writings have only emerged over the past generation: the first studies on her appeared in the 1980s, but only in 2013 did a translation and study appear in the West.

Born He Ban near Yangzhou at the junction of the Grand Canal
and the Yangtze, she was another product of the stellar literary world
of Jiangnan. Educated at the Patriotic Women's School in cosmopolitan Shanghai, she became fiercely anti-Qing and in her late teens
was forced to move to Tokyo. There she joined an anarchist group
that published the magazine *Tianyi* (*Natural Justice*, 1907–08). She
wrote, too, in the Paris anarchists' journal *New Century*, one of the
pioneer magazines of modernism. There, under the pseudonym He-
Yin (her mother's family name) and Zhen ('the thunderclap'), she
was a major influence not only on the rise of Chinese feminism but
also on ideas about social revolution, and even communism in the
first decade of the twentieth century. In Tokyo she had read the first
Japanese translation of *The Communist Manifesto* in 1904, which
was reprinted seventeen times in six years. (A version in Chinese was
not completed until 1920, translated from the English.) At the very
moment the suffragettes were fighting in Britain, He Ban formed the
Association for the Recovery of Women's Rights, calling for the use
of force to end male oppression of women and to abolish the corro-
sive influence of the alliance between the ruling class and capitalism.
Among her recently rediscovered works, her essay 'On the Question
of Women's Liberation', published in *Tianyi* in 1907, and recently
translated by Lydia Liu, Rebecca Karl and Dorothy Ko, now looks
like one of the great tracts of feminism:

> For thousands of years the world has been dominated by the rule
> of man. This rule is marked by class disjunctions over which men –
> and men only – exert proprietary rights. To rectify these wrongs,
> we must first abolish the rule of men and introduce equality among
> human beings, which means that the world must belong equally to
> men and women. The goal of equality cannot be achieved except
> through women's liberation.

Other essays such as 'On Women's Labour', written in 1907, before
the end of the empire, highlighted women's economic subjection,
infanticide and prostitution. She also wrote anti-war tracts, called

for an economic revolution, and in 'The Feminist Manifesto' she made a powerful attack on patriarchy, which was read by many radicals in the period after the First World War.

Unlike many of her contemporaries, He Zhen was an internationalist; concerned less with China's fate as a nation and more with the nexus of patriarchy, imperialism and capitalism, and with gender subjugation as a global issue. We know that she returned to China after the fall of the empire in 1911, and that her husband worked at Peking University, but what happened to her after that is still a mystery. Even her face is scarcely knowable, as only one fuzzy image has so far been certainly identified. After her husband's death, there are stories that she died after a breakdown, but a friend, the poet Liu Yazi, said that she renounced the world and became a Buddhist nun, taking the name Xiao Qi – 'the one of little talent', defeated perhaps by the immensity of the task she had so boldly laid out in her writings. How long she lived, and how much she saw of the unfolding of China's twentieth-century tragedy, is not known. Suffice it to say that much remains to be discovered of her amazing tale.

THE FALL

Caught between its Confucian past and the Western future, the empire was shaking, and as belief and allegiance dissolved, power visibly ebbed away. Risings broke out all over east Jiangsu and neighbouring regions through 1900–1906 under Triad banners, while Boxer remnants were still fighting to the west. In 1907, famine broke out. The gathering disaster was big news abroad, as events in China had been for the past ten years. The *Manchester Guardian* on Tuesday 1 January 1907 headlined the famine in China with 'Four millions of starving people':

Reuter's Pekin correspondent telegraphs that owing to the excessive rains and the consequent failure of the crops the famine in the North of Anhui, the East of Honan, and the whole of the

North of Kiang-Su [Jiangsu] provinces is at present worse than
it has been at any time during the last forty years. It is estimated
that four million are starving. Tens of thousands reduced to utter
destitution are wandering over the country, and the danger arising
from this state of affairs is increased by the present activity of
the secret societies, the homeless wanderers being glad to enroll
themselves as members of these organisations in order to obtain a
little rice. The Viceroy Taunfang has been repeatedly memorialised
on the subject.

From other sources, equally black news was emerging:

Fifty thousand refugees have arrived at Nanking in a pitiable
condition. The authorities are unable to cope with the situation,
and would welcome foreign assistance. An edict has been issued
temporarily abolishing the land tax in Shantung, as the people are
unable to pay it owing to the famine.

Once the greatest power in the world, China could no longer feed
its people. Confucius was even promoted in a desperate attempt to
make the old language of loyalty and virtue speak once more:

Reuter's Pekin correspondent telegraphs that an Imperial edict
has been issued raising Confucius to the same rank as Heaven
and Earth, which are worshipped by the emperor alone. It is
believed (he adds) that this edict has been promulgated in deference to the religious scruples of the Christian students in the
Government Colleges who object to kowtow as required by
immemorial custom before the tablet of Confucius, which is
placed in all State Colleges.

The Chinese famine of 1907 was a short-lived event, but still took the
lives of nearly 25 million people. Then, while east-central China was
still reeling from the series of poor harvests, a massive storm flooded
40,000 square miles of lush agricultural territory, destroying all the

crops in the region. Food riots took place daily, and were often suppressed with deadly force by the Manchu garrisons. 'It is estimated
that on a good day', reported the correspondent of the *Manchester
Guardian*, 'only 5,000 were dying due to starvation.'

A VILLAGE IN THE SOUTH

Local society across the Late Qing world in the first years of the
twentieth century was plagued by religious and clan-based strife;
driven by population growth, high taxes and a squeeze on land.
Snapshots from local records across their vast territory show the
tensions simmering in overburdened rural societies as well as the
struggles of central and local government simply to cope. Our last
glimpse of the old Confucian order, still attempting to rule by the old
mixture of virtue and punishment, comes from the southeast coast,
the tale of Loyal Magistrate Li.

Along the shores of Fujian, facing out towards Taiwan, the
thousands of kilometres of inlets and bays with their mountainous,
wooded hinterland had been a problem for governance and policing
for the Chinese state through the ages. In the first decade of the twentieth century, in one village near the old trading city of Quanzhou, a
vicious feud between two clans, the Liu and Cai families, highlights
the gap between the aspirations of the centre and the reality out on
the periphery. The feud drew in many outlying villages, and in the
end killed hundreds of people. Finally, when the local magistrates
simply couldn't handle it anymore, they persuaded the governor of
the province to bring in a local army to put an end to the feud. Li
Wei was magistrate and acting military commissioner in the prefecture of Quanzhou. He was a man educated in the old ways, and it
was his task to stop the violent clan warfare which had broken out
when the Cais objected to the Lius' reconstruction of their ancestral
hall, which they said was too high and blocked the *feng shui* of their
ancestral graves. Eventually the feud spread across the county. The
tale is taken up by Li, whose magistrate's voice comes out in the
age-old tone of the loyal administrator:

It is written that those who live in the same village and share the same well should understand that they should care for each other. In order to guard against future consequences, people should be warned: this prohibition should be remembered forever. In the case of violent strife in the combined township of Hongtu between the Lius and the Cais, the trouble began with the Liu family's repairs to their ancestral hall. The Cai family objected because of its inauspicious location. The two sides fell out and it came to trouble, spreading over hundreds of villages and taking a toll of hundreds of deaths and injuries ... hundreds of homes burned, families broken up and everyone suffered great misery ... Fields were out of cultivation; the aggressive and the powerful looted at will, and even the spirits and ghosts were filled with grief.

From 1904 to 1907, the town went through five different local magistrates, but nothing helped, and in the end 300 people died over six years of strife. So, in autumn 1907, the local governor issued an order that the case was now so serious that the prefecture commander must bring in troops. They occupied the clan villages for five months and conducted detailed investigations. The villages 'changed mood' and raised an indemnity of 40,000 gold pieces for public relief. One core village was condemned to pay over 10,000 yuan cash indemnity, and from then on relief was provided for the homeless, houses were rebuilt, and the deep antagonisms that had grown over the past few years were 'softened and put aside'. Thirty of the most criminal elements were arrested; some were executed, others put in the cangue, their arms were handed in and fortifications demolished: 'Heavenly providence crushed the disorders and our own Quanzhou felt its impact!' The local magistrate added a coda to his account, which was set up on a stone stele that still survives in the village, to the effect that no one in government could relax: 'We must make it strikingly clear that one should live in peace but be ever mindful of the danger of conflict.'

'All of you must know', Li wrote,

that in this business of strife, the poison of hatred enters very deeply. Those who kill other people's fathers and brothers will have their own fathers and brothers killed as well ... Those who love violence endanger their own parents, in a moment of anger they forget their own personal safety and that of their family. If people cannot endure even the slightest insult but must retaliate how can there be no conflict? Don't let old hatreds rise again, don't let the weak fall prey to the strong; there must be respect and affection for one's native place.

Li then alludes to the Tang poet Bai Juyi's story of a two-clan Zhu village: a famous poem about two clans who intermarried generation after generation. And so, in the last months before the end of empire, a traditionally educated local magistrate still situated the morality of local politics by way of reference to a 1,000-year-old poem:

With covenants of peace we have unobtrusively reduced forms of aggression, helping and protecting one another, cultivating human feelings and compromise. We have changed the villages of ill repute into humanitarian places ... This then is the admirable attitude of this Prefecture! If anybody still has the audacity to persist in the past violations of the law, he will be severely punished. The network of Heaven reaches everywhere, beware of it!

Issued in the sixth month of the thirty-fourth year of the Guangxu Emperor (1908).

THE CHANGSHA RISING

After an ill-fated reign of thirty-five years, Guangxu died on 14 November 1908, one day before the Dowager Empress. He was only thirty-seven, and it was rumoured that the Dowager Empress had poisoned him, fearing that after her own death her policies would be reversed. Others speculate he was killed by the warlord Yuan Shikai, who feared his own execution if the emperor came to sole power. His reign had been the nadir of imperial power. His successor on the

dragon throne was Cixi's choice, the emperor's two-year-old nephew
Puyi, and he would be the Last Emperor.

The public mood now turned decisively against the Qing.
Conditions worsened over the next two years with more riots
across the country. A survey made by the Shanghai journal *Eastern
Miscellany* counted 113 peasant riots in 1909, and 285 in 1910.
Disorder intensified with further natural disasters, floods and bad
harvests. When riots broke out in Laiyang in Shandong in 1910,
the government brought in troops to crush the revolt with the loss
of 40,000 lives. Particularly momentous was a riot in April 1910 in
Changsha, the story of which was carried across the world in newspapers from Melbourne to Devon and which has a very special place
in the tale of modern China.

The name Changsha means 'Long Sands', and still today, though
a modern high-rise city of 10 million, opposite the tree-lined cor-
niche of the old town, is a long, sandy shore where wild horses
roam and fishermen sit in thatched huts watching the world go by.
The city lies along the Xiang River 100 miles south of the Yangtze,
whose tributaries in flood time swell into a huge lake, Dongting, 70
miles long. The capital of Hunan, Changsha had a population of
more than quarter of a million, and with its pleasant position and
climate was 'one of the best cities in China', as one Western visitor
remarked in 1910. Inside the 4-mile city wall with its seven gates was
a crowded old town – a warren of stone-flagged alleys and many
picturesque shrines and temples where one might hear a babble of
regional and tribal dialects from the hills to the south. 'Changsha
is one of the most interesting places in the empire on account of its
extreme exclusiveness,' a US railway surveyor wrote. 'Only two or
three foreigners, but no missionary, had ever been in the city, and
these few were smuggled in in closed chairs. Like all Chinese cities, it
is heavily walled, and strongly gated, the gates being locked at night,
giving a most medieval air.'

The city had opened to foreign commerce in 1904, after the
Boxer Rebellion, with an export trade seasonally dependent on
the rise and fall of the water downriver to the big treaty port of

Hankou on the Yangtze. In the past few years, a foreign settlement had rapidly grown up in the northern suburb and now there were a dozen quays along the river where steamers, junks, coal boats and huge timber rafts loaded goods and produce: coke from the local colliery, lead, antimony, tea, beans and rice. By 1910, there were even shelled, preserved eggs for export to confectioners in London: 'if this goes on, they will soon be sending lettuce and fresh strawberries with the morning dew frozen on them,' wrote the American William Giel in 1910, in an uncanny forecast of the future.

But here too tensions were rising, especially against foreign missionaries and their converts. By 1910, there were half a dozen Christian missions in Changsha, along with Western companies like Jardine Matheson and Butterfield & Swire; Yale University also had a compound with a school, hospital and college (which still exist). Now, in this subsistence-level province, there was increased agitation about rice being exported out of Changsha for profit, and there were widespread complaints about the conduct of local merchants. The key man was Ye Dehui, who had a bad reputation for being greedy and stockpiling his rice in storage warehouses in the city. In such times of dearth, grain speculation became a big thing: 'it was like buying stocks,' recalled one witness, looking back in the 1970s: 'some bosses were buying and selling grain that didn't exist and the landlords took advantage of harvest crop fluctuations to raise the prices'.

As a low-lying city on the banks of a big river, Changsha had recently had a few bad years. In the massive inundation of 1906, most of the city had been underwater, with streets flooded and people living in their roof spaces and attics. That terrible spring, the farmland of the whole plain was submerged. The city and its region had scarcely recovered when in 1909 another flood brought crowds of refugees into the city from the countryside. Outside Changsha's south gate, a huge area of open ground filled up with shanties and makeshift shelters for more than 30,000 refugees and peasants who were desperate for food. Soon known as 'Hungry Stomach Ridge', with its itinerant population of scavengers, waste collectors, clay diggers and water carriers, conditions were atrocious, and many people had frozen to death during the winter.

Here in early April 1910, a small local tragedy took place. A young woman killed herself and her two children when she tried to purchase rice from a local dealer who refused to help her. Holding her young children, she drowned herself in a pond. When he heard the news, her husband, a water carrier, also took his own life. The news spread like wildfire through the city and by evening it had become the talk of the shops and teahouses; the 'suicide pond' became a place of ill omen. Another woman who was quoted 80 in copper cash for rice was told two of her coins were not in good enough condition and that she should get better ones. When she returned, the price had gone up to 85. Rather than be browbeaten, however, she stood up to the dealer, a crowd gathered and the grain warehouse was sacked and looted. Soon such confrontations grew into major riots: one big rice dealer was beaten almost to death by a mob who pillaged his store and then marched on the government compound to demonstrate. The temperature was rising.

After the woman at the pond committed suicide on 11 April 1910, there were riots for three days. Seeing the writing on the wall, the American William Giel left the city, noting that food riots were 'affecting all in the city, and also from local masons and carpenters objecting to outside workmen coming to erect foreign houses and government buildings in foreign style . . . ' With thousands now without food, a delegation of peasants appealed to the local governor for food relief, which was refused, according to one missionary, 'with callous indifference'. Along with the starving poor, members of local craftsmen's guilds were angry at the British bringing in Hankow workers to build the new Western-style buildings. Finally the governor's walled compound was attacked, with a group of former Boxer rebels joining the rioters. Together they sacked the compound and cut down the mast with the governor's insignia. Overturning the ceremonial stone lions, they burned government buildings with kerosene and destroyed the British consular office on the riverbank.

Western homes, schools, businesses, steamboats and churches also went up in flames. The only foreign place spared was the Yale compound: the neighbouring street association posted notices saying the Americans should not be attacked because of their philanthropic and medical work. The governor responded by bringing troops in, and ten demonstrators were killed and many wounded. The story later became the subject of folk ballads and storytellers. Sixty years later, one of the participants, Zhang Liangsheng, who was twenty in 1911, remembered a local carpenter leading the crowd into the governor's compound, his *yamen*. The translation is by James Hudson:

At twilight I was standing on the old screen wall opening near the ceremonial archway bearing the inscription 'Protect the country, Aid the people' and I happened to see that there were many people outside the *yamen*. They were all yelling and cursing: 'Dog government officials, so wicked that the common people have no rice to eat.' Everyone was crying out and the emotion of the crowd was explosive. Everyone rushed towards the outer gate of the *yamen*. Suddenly I saw a short and stout fellow, 'Shorty Liu', rush out from among the crowd, in his hand he brandished a shining saw and flew as fast as an arrow towards the east facing part of the *yuanmen* [stone screen]. Liu charged forward to the gate where the sentry guards were using guns to block the crowd. One of Liu Shaoming's legs flew up and he kicked a guard to the ground, and after a few more swift steps he charged to the base of the mast located in front of the screen wall, lifted the saw high and started cutting. When the crowd saw Liu they charged in, already extremely excited, all yelling, crowding through the archway.

When order was restored, the ringleaders were executed by firing squad and some were beheaded, their heads displayed on poles. But by then parts of the city had been burned and tens of thousands had joined the protests, shouting, 'Kill the governor and drive out the missionaries.' The riot was covered in the press throughout China, and news of the 'critical situation in Hunan' spread on the telegraph wires across the world.

Among the witnesses to these events was a young trainee teacher, Mao Zedong, who forty years later would become the first leader of the People's Republic. Mao had been born in December 1893 outside Changsha in Shaoshan village, in a region of Hunan where violence and class conflict had been the norm, with peasant uprisings every year since the 1840s. Mao's father had been a smallholding peasant born into poverty and debt who had dragged himself up by his boot-straps to become relatively wealthy as a village money lender and rice dealer. (The house where Mao was born survives and, though entirely reconstructed, gives an impression of ample space for living and storage; Mao's early years were not uncomfortable.)

Given that he is one of the most famous men in history, Mao's biography still has many imponderables. The most useful account of his early life is still the interview he gave over several nights to the American journalist Edgar Snow in the summer and autumn of 1936, in the communist base at Bao'an after the Long March. Mao told Snow that he had worked on his father's farm from the age of six, and between eight and thirteen attended primary school, where he had a traditional education, reading Confucius and the classics. A vora-cious reader, he especially loved the great novels: *Monkey, The Water Margin* and *Romance of the Three Kingdoms*. Born in the last days of the empire, his teens were, however, a time of turmoil in China, and especially in his native Hunan, and young Mao was inevitably drawn into the tumultuous events of 1910 in Changsha. In his region, reformist ideas had come to the fore, for example the southern think-ers of the so-called 'Qing Dynasty Song Literary Movement' from Guizhou, who were a major influence on thinkers like Kang Youwei; writers like Lu Xun; and political leaders like Chiang Kai-shek and Mao himself. Mao in particular says he 'worshipped' the heroes of the failed Hundred Days' Reform, Kang Youwei and Liang Qichao. But the book that especially influenced Mao was *Words of Warning to a Prosperous Age*, published in 1893, the year of Mao's birth, by Zheng Guanying. Zheng was a product of the new age of Chinese professionals in the circles of the treaty ports from the 1870s onwards. Though a merchant not a scholar, Zheng was a nationalist who wrote about renewal, economic freedom from the Western powers, representative democracy and women's rights. For all the fame of celebrated reformers like Kang Youwei and Liang Qichao, Zheng would have a powerful influence on Mao's way of thinking.

Writers like Zheng gave Mao the beginning of a theoretical intellectual grounding: a 'political conscience' as he put it. But it was the politics of his youth that made the biggest mark. If we can trust the account Mao gave Edgar Snow in 1936, the inciting incident was the 1910 rising in Changsha and the subsequent waves of protest in his native Hunan. This touched the Mao family directly, as starving peasants marched into Shaoshan village and seized Mao's father's stored grain. At the time of the rising, Mao was sixteen: 'The leaders of the uprising were executed', Mao told Edgar Snow, 'and their heads were stuck on poles in town as a warning to rebels. This incident was discussed in my school for many days. It made a deep impression on me.' Though parts of Mao's account have been doubted, he had indeed started at middle school in Changsha that year, so it may well be that the memory is first hand. The town was rife with republican sentiment by then, strongly hostile to the Qing, and most of the students sympathised with the rebels, if only from an observer's point of view, as Mao observed: 'They did not understand that it had any relation to their own lives. But I never forgot it. I felt that there with the rebels were ordinary people like my own family and I deeply resented the injustice given to them.'

LEAVING CHINA: ARTHUR MOULE

The writing was on the wall for the empire. Or so it looks now. But perhaps that trajectory is only clear with hindsight. Certainly, the loyal magistrate Li in Fujian did not see it that way, even if the teenage Mao Zedong and his friends did. To many in 1910, even though pamphlets warned of the coming dismemberment of China by foreign powers, the future was not clear, and the end of the dynasty not certain. Nor was the end of empire inevitable, or even, in the eyes of many, desirable. Some thought the new emperor could still be turned into a constitutional monarch as the reformists of 1898 had proposed. Take the British scholar and missionary Arthur Moule, whom we met as a young man in the dark winter of 1858 during the Taiping siege of Ningbo. Moule was now about to retire and sail home after fifty years in China, a land he deeply loved and profoundly understood. In late 1910, after such a turbulent year, Moule climbed a hill outside Hangzhou to look over the heavenly vistas of West Lake, ringed by wooded hills topped with pagodas, and there he penned his final thoughts after so long in China. He reflected on the changes that were already apparent, from fashions and hairstyles, to Western ideas. 'I take for granted that the phenomenon of change in China is so significant as to mark a new era in the world's history,' Moule wrote. But his great fear was the over-hasty rejection of China's traditional culture; indeed, 'it may be asked whether a country and a people so ancient and stable, so highly educated and civilised, need any radical change at all'. China, he thought, should still follow the Chinese way in the new twentieth century, and not slavishly follow Western models. Even the idea of political parties, he thought, in a population ten or twenty times larger than Britain's, could never be successful. But regional assemblies, a national parliament, and a constitutional monarch, could. 'Unless events should be violently altered by revolution,' he hoped, 'some such enlargement and adaptation of the ancient government of China will be adopted, such as have been realised in some of the golden periods in her history. The emperor will still be supreme, the source of power and law, but in touch with his people through constitutional utterances in legal assemblies.' It was a verdict that perhaps came naturally to a late Victorian imperialist. But the wholesale abandonment of the old, Moule insisted, would be 'a grave error ... sure to wreck her high emprise by headlong pace and neglect of the balancing powers in a true constitution'. But as he surveyed the green hills of Hangzhou for the last time before leaving, his reflections ended on a note of anxiety: '... I cannot but regard the political future as ominous and uncertain ...'

THE XINHAI REVOLUTION

At that very moment, just before the end of 1910, the pressure across China was growing to bursting point. The peasant risings in Hunan signalled a summer of revolt, especially in the central region. The final flashpoint came in the treaty port of Hankou on the middle Yangtze, today's Wuhan, with its long, Western-style bund lined with trees; grand pillared and veranda'd houses; its foreign consulates and its bustling quaysides and floating pontoons for ocean-going steamers. Modern Hankow was the creation of Zhang Zhidong, an important reforming politician and governor of Hunan and Hubei from 1889 to 1907. He had governed with huge energy; his motto: 'Chinese learning as the foundation; Western learning for practical application.' The city was now a cutting-edge place in the textile industries; it had a new steel factory, iron and coal mines, and a government arsenal. But cultural life had not been ignored; there were important academies and schools here too, and a foreign languages institute. The British had opened a missionary school with a busy and highly regarded hospital, so Hankow was a place that now had deep links with the outside world.

On 10 October 1911, an army mutiny here launched what became known as the Wuchang Uprising. The leaders were followers of a revolutionary nationalist called Sun Yat-sen, a Chinese convert to Christianity born in Guangdong but educated in Hawaii (unusually, Sun was an English speaker). Sun had trained as a doctor, but his frustrations with the entrenched conservatives in the Qing court led to his espousal of open rebellion and the overthrow of the state. In exile in Japan, he had fomented several failed risings against the Qing, and had travelled to the USA, Europe and Britain to raise money and support for revolution. He attempted to unite the many radical movements against the Qing with his flagship 'Three Principles': nationalism, democracy and public welfare. In Hankow, rebellion finally broke through. The local army units joined the rebels and the Manchu garrison fled. Calling on other provinces to join them, the rebels declared the abolition of Qing rule in Hubei and the founding of a Republic of China.

That October in Hankow, as the fighting spread over the city, a British schoolboy took pen to paper to tell the latest dramatic news. The world was changing before his eyes. Tom Gillison was the son of a missionary family that had founded the hospital in Hankow and spent the past forty years there as doctors, teachers and missionaries. Young Tom now wrote home about the republican risings in Wuchang, Hankow and Hanyang, and the massacres of hundreds of Manchu officers and soldiers:

The fight has been fierce and hundreds have been killed and over 1000 wounded have been treated in our mission hospital and elsewhere. Bullets whistle along our street ... and the sharp rattle of the Maxim guns and the plop-plop of the rifles are heard day and night.

On 1 November, he wrote again:

They are setting fire to this great city of 500,000 inhabitants. Of course, most of the people have left: Hankow now is almost like a city of the dead. I can see the smoke rising as I write. It will destroy the trade of this place for years to come.

After a bloody siege, the Qing army recovered the city, but too late to save the empire. The rebels' call to arms had been met, and with more risings elsewhere, peace talks began. In December, a coalition of the army, bankers and the urban bourgeoisie declared China a republic. Sun Yat-sen was summoned from exile and he founded the new Republic of China on 1 January 1912. On 12 February, the boy-emperor Puyi was forced to abdicate, the papers signed by his aunt, the Dowager Empress Longyu, consort of the late Guangxu emperor. It was 2,132 years since the First Emperor, nearly 3,000 since the Zhou proclaimed the Mandate of Heaven. And now, almost overnight, that great structure of governance and ideas, that vast and resonant universe of ritual symbol and belief, was gone. But what kind of China would emerge in its place?

18

THE AGE OF REFORM: FROM
THE REPUBLIC TO MAO

The period between the end of the empire in 1911 and the founding of the People's Republic in 1949 is often seen as a broken, fragmented time of lost opportunities before the triumph of the communists. At certain moments, with warlords controlling parts of the country, China seemed about to split up again as it had at the end of the Tang and the Yuan dynasties. But with foreign investment pouring into the new China through treaty ports like Shanghai, it was a time of great possibilities, the crucible in which modern China was formed. As British Naval Intelligence reported in the Second World War, 'In spite of many vicissitudes and much current anxiety and uncertainty as to the future, the dominant note has been one of recovery and reconstruction. Perhaps no "fifty years of Europe" have seen changes so remarkable as those which have occurred in what the West used to regard as unchanging Cathay.' But in its brief life, for all its successes, the republic in the end was consumed by Japanese invasion, civil war and, finally, communist revolution.

For those attempting the giant task of building a new China, the great issues were those already outlined by the pioneers of the Hundred Days' Reform of 1898. Would the 'great tradition' of China – classical learning, Confucian ideals – provide the basis of a modern China in a modified form? Would Western ideas about capitalism and the market and democracy be the path forward? Or was root-and-branch change the only answer? A new order, as had been attempted by the Taiping revolutionaries in the century past? Shadowing these possible paths was another question: how could China escape the cycle of despotism – so deeply written into the psychology of the culture – embodied in the rule of the sage-emperor?

These crucial questions were encapsulated by China's first elected provisional president, Sun Yat-sen, in his formulation of three 'people's principles' which should guide the new republic: nationalism, socialism and democracy. And on the very complex issues surrounding the meaning of those three terms, the battles of the twentieth century would be fought.

The Chinese Republic (1912–49) was always fragile, never united; in some ways it has the appearance of a breakdown period like the Three Kingdoms or the Five Dynasties. It was a time of rival factions and warlords, of peasant risings and struggle between the nationalists and the communists, then the Japanese occupation of Manchuria in 1932 and full-scale invasion of the mainland in 1937, which was defeated after huge destruction and loss of life in 1945. After less than forty years, the republic fell apart in the civil war that followed, leading to the triumph of the communists in 1949. But the republic was also a dynamic, creative time; one of those interstitial periods between dynasties that occur in Chinese history and, though short, bequeathed many ideas that would be adopted by the longer and more successful successor regime.

Born in 1866 in the aftermath of the Taiping, Sun Yat-sen came from a peasant family from Guandong. His father, who was from the Hakka minority, was a small landowner, a Christian convert who worked as a journeyman, porter and tailor. Sun's teenage years in Hawaii (where he had joined his elder brother) gave him a different perspective with which to see his troubled native land. As we have seen, he had participated in an armed uprising in the south in 1895, and had been exiled to Japan, from where he led the republican movement. But now, though the empire was gone, from the beginning of the new republic in 1912, Sun had to deal with the old powers: the army, the warlords and the foreigners, and in its short life the republic never knew peace.

Old China was now a new republic, but it was a divided land, with whole regions under powerful warlords, especially in the southwest. Sun had no alternative but to throw his lot in with one, Yuan Shikai, who at one point was even emboldened to declare himself emperor and attempted to revive the imperial ceremony on the Altar of Heaven, though the spirits of the ancestors did not respond to him. And so, like the other parts of the globe that had endured colonial rule, poised between the old and the new worlds, ringed by treaty ports of the foreigners, with foreign troops still camped in some of its cities, the Chinese people now faced the great dilemmas of modernity.

CHINA'S FIRST ELECTIONS: THE VIEW
FROM CHIQIAO VILLAGE, SHANXI

The first assembly elections were held at the end of 1911. In Chiqiao village near Taiyuan, in the mining belt of northern Shanxi, the old Confucian farmer, teacher and mine manager Liu Dapeng found himself in a conflicted situation. He hated the idea of the new republic, which went against the very order of heaven, and hoped for the restoration of the emperor. But as a man of honour, a trustworthy Confucian gentleman who had passed his provincial examinations, even though only a farmer and mine manager, he was chosen to go around the area knocking on doors to establish the electoral roll for the first election in China's history. It took place on 29 December 1911, and saw Sun Yat-sen elected president with representatives for each of the seventeen provinces. In his diary, Liu confided that his first experience of democracy had not been edifying:

They are using the method of election by ballot, so that all the rogues and villains intrigue for office by campaigning, and the ones who have most money win. How can we possibly get decent officials from a selection process like this? Who says that elections

are a fair method? All I see is people campaigning. They have no
sense of modesty and no shame. When they tout for your vote they
treat you like a god.

In the First World War, the Republic of China initially stayed neu-
tral, but as part of its effort to join the international community,
from 1916 China provided hundreds of thousands of workers to
the Allies: 140,000 to the Western Front, along with somewhere
between a quarter and half a million more to the Russians on the
Eastern Front. After the Indians, they were the largest non-European
contingent on the Western Front: digging trenches, repairing tanks,
assembling artillery shells and transporting munitions. Photographs
and even film footage survive showing the customary celebrations
of Chinese festivals in France; with paper lanterns and flags, dragon
dances and traditional opera with dancers on stilts. Today the military cemetery at Noyelles-sur-Mer by the River Somme contains
the remains of several hundred Chinese dead, with Confucian epi-
grams on their tombstones. There are many more, from Anfield in
Liverpool to Basra in Iraq, where 227 unnamed Chinese dead are
buried by the banks of the Euphrates. Only in 2018 was the Chinese
government invited to the ceremonies at the Cenotaph in Whitehall.

In 1917, China joined the war on the side of the Allies, and when
the fighting ended, an issue arose of deep contention to the Chinese.
Among the many foreign colonies in China, the Germans had held
much of Shandong, including Qufu, the birthplace of Confucius. It
had been assumed that after the war, in recognition of its help to the
Allies, this would return to China. But they were in for a shock. At
the peace conference at Versailles in spring 1919, Shandong was not
restored to China, but given to Japan.

MAY 1919: THE NEW CULTURE MOVEMENT

The reaction in China was fury. Foreign Minister Lu left Versailles
early, refusing to sign the final treaty. Student demonstrations broke
out across China and on 4 May 1919 a huge protest took place

in Tiananmen Square, where loyal remonstrance had taken place through Chinese history. Led by the students, the demonstration was joined by many citizens of Beijing, and that hot Sunday in the city has come to be seen as a powerful symbol of the Chinese people's struggle for liberation in the twentieth century, the birth of the May Fourth or New Culture Movement. Three thousand students had gathered first in front of the gates of Peking University, outside the old library – the Red Building as they called it (which is still there). With banners made out of bamboo and cloth, they wanted the world to know about their grievances, even preparing English-language statements which they hoped to hand in to the embassies of the colonial occupying powers. The Chinese people's struggle was about to open to the world.

The 4 May demonstration in Tiananmen Square was a key moment for modern China. In a culture that gave such respect to the old, the young had spoken. And their ideas spread like wildfire. They wanted to sweep away the old and create a new culture based on Western democracy and science. With it came a powerful and creative literary movement, using the vernacular, the speech of the people, as opposed to the classical language of the old academies. A key figure in the movement was the social critic, poet and journalist Lu Xun. Lu, whose real name was Zhou Shuren, was from Shaoxing, China's pre-eminent literary city, home of the Ming essayist Zhang Dai, the Qing historian Zhang Xuecheng and the feminist Qiu Jin. Lu's family were well-to-do landowners who had fallen on hard times: his father was an invalid and became an opium addict. Lu Xun was born in 1881, so by the time the May Fourth Movement came about he was nearly forty: the age when Confucius said 'perplexities are cleared', long past the idealism of youth. Lu had trained as a doctor, and although he became a writer, through his whole life he kept that bedside manner of a world-weary, ironical but humane physician. He was, however, a pessimist, not one to let hope run away with him after the many defeats of the time. Exiled in Japan in the last years of the empire along with many other radicals (such as Qiu Jin and He Zhen, above page 438), he returned to the republic to produce a stream of essays and brilliant stories that diagnosed China's ills with a sharp lucidity; and in 1920s China, after the humiliation of the Treaty of Versailles, his was the voice.

Lu was against China's 'Great Tradition', which he felt had run its course and was now a deadening weight on people's lives; he described it as cannibalistic civilisation, 'eating its own children' – a terrible metaphor evoking a persistent dark shadow on China's history. 'The republic has failed us,' he wrote, 'we've been cheated, we were slaves before and now we're ruled by slaves. We must renew the spirit of China.' Without thoroughgoing reform, he believed, China faced tragedy.

Lu died of tuberculosis in 1936, but we might wonder what he might have felt about the Great Leap Forward, or the Great Famine, or the Cultural Revolution. He would have been in his eighties then, but, as Mao himself observed, had he survived into the communist era, he would 'either have gone silent or gone to prison'.

His most famous work, *The True Story of Ah Q*, is the bitter tale of a Chinese Everyman set at the time of the overthrow of the empire in 1911; a peasant trapped by the system who even after the empire has gone cannot free himself from its coils, or from his destiny as one of the poor masses of China struggling to find a place in the modern world. 'Hope is like a path in the countryside,' Lu wrote. 'At first there is no path, but if enough people walk in the same direction, the path appears.' But which path would China take?

SHANGHAI: METROPOLIS OF THE WORLD

China in the 1920s and '30s was a land of extraordinary extremes and hugely uneven development. In places in the deep countryside, peasants laboured barefoot with medieval implements, faced with famine and flood, selling their children into slavery while warlords and their militias extorted and murdered at will. Yet in treaty cities like Shanghai, the Jazz Age was in full swing. China's politics might have been fractured, but the '20s were a dynamic time for some. The economy was booming in cities such as Shanghai, where the splendid architecture of the Bund surpassed that of Liverpool and Manchester; a European colonial city where money was to be made and where motor showrooms, horse-racing tracks and cinemas beckoned to a rising Westernised middle class. A young Briton who came out here from Lancashire after the First World War to join the police, as there were no jobs at home, said with prophetic enthusiasm: 'It's the best city I've ever seen! The most cosmopolitan place in the world. And in time it will leave every English city a hundred years behind.'

But Westernisation was not just about material life; it was about China learning to be modern. Magazines and newspapers taught the new moneyed generation how to be; in clothes, gestures and ways of speaking. The Chinese now were to leave the old ways behind and become modern people in the way they looked, too. Adverts in 1920s Shanghai fashion magazines and shop windows in department stores juxtaposed what a traditional person was like, and what a modern person should be. There were even guidebooks on how to behave, how to wear one's hair and how to wear a suit. Sketches showed not the *ke tou* ('kowtow') or the Confucian greeting with one hand enclosed by the other, but how to shake hands – a gesture that, for a traditional person, was just not done; an inappropriate act of intimacy with a stranger.

Among the great buildings on the Shanghai Bund was the Hong Kong and Shanghai Banking Corporation, today the HSBC and one of the richest banks in the world, but founded here in China by a British trader at the end of the Taiping war. When the new building was opened in 1923, it was one of the greatest banking buildings in the world. In the foyer, murals show Shanghai alongside Paris, London and New York, with an inscription: 'All Men in the Four Oceans are Equal.' But, of course, in Shanghai and in China in general in the 1920s, they weren't. For all the transforming power of European ideas and innovation, the treaty ports were places of deeply entrenched racialist ideas on the part of the colonial powers: the British and the Americans, the French, the Germans and the Japanese who had carved out their enclaves in China in the preceding seventy years. Not surprisingly, therefore, it was here in Shanghai, the city that was most open to modern ideas, that national feeling erupted among those who believed that China's social problems were so great that only revolution offered a path forward. And one group in particular believed that history was on their side.

THE FOUNDING OF THE COMMUNIST PARTY, 1921

Among the many Western ideas coming into China was Marxism. In 1917, the fall of the Russian Empire and the October Revolution had electrified the world. At the end of the First World War, communist ideas spread across the globe; a model for the liberation of colonised societies everywhere. In British-occupied India, for example, the Bolshevik Conspiracy Case at Kanpur aimed to 'deprive King George of his empire by violent revolution'. In China, too, a strong early focus was anti-colonial and anti-imperialist. The Communist Party of China (CPC) was founded in July 1921, its first meeting in a small house which still stands in Rue Wantz, then in the French concession in Shanghai. There were only fifty-seven delegates, including the bookish peasant's son Mao Zedong, whose voracious reading had led him from Hunan to a job as an assistant librarian at Peking University. There his boss Li Dazhao had written articles about Lenin and the October Revolution. Having joined Li's group, and inspired by the May Fourth Movement, as Mao later told the story, he 'rapidly moved towards Marxism'.

At the heart of Marxism (as understood by the generation after Marx, especially Lenin with his 'scientific socialism') was the idea that human history could be divided into defined phases: from its primary stages of feudalism and capitalism to its ultimate development in a socialist society. Chinese society was so big, and suffered from such deep-rooted poverty, injustice and inequality, that Marxism offered a powerful – indeed, utopian – vision of a path forward. In the febrile atmosphere after May 1919, it is easy to see why such ideas had taken root among Chinese intellectuals, political activists and anti-imperialists, especially as utopian idealism lies at the very heart of traditional Chinese political philosophy. But it is important to see that at this point the Chinese knew very little about Marx's original ideas; none of the key texts were available in Chinese apart from *The Communist Manifesto*, which was only translated into Chinese (from English) in 1920. Far from being theoretical Marxists, then, these early Chinese followers are better described as revolutionary nationalists. Inspired by the Russian Revolution, their understanding of Marxism at first came through Stalin, who sent Russian agents (starting in summer 1921) to support the fledgling CPC. It was through them that the Stalinist model for organising society became ingrained in the minds of Chinese revolutionaries, who believed that in Russia the Soviets had initiated an age of socialism and equality under Communist Party rule. The great guides, then, were Lenin and Stalin, whose images were in every town hall and school in the Mao era, and whose pictures still look down on party conferences in the Great Hall of the People in Tiananmen Square.

So, though the Chinese revolution was one of the most significant movements in history, it came about in some sense through happenstance. Communism in China was driven above all by post-May 1919 nationalism: it was anti-foreigner and it was for the peasants. The rural problem from the beginning was seen as the key: the Chinese revolution would unfold in the countryside, not in the cities as it had in Russia. And there the grievances were by now so great (as they had been for so much of China's history) that they found wide support as the 1920s unfolded.

The rural issue was at the heart of Mao's early thinking. Briefly a librarian, and then a trainee teacher, he had read widely in such European radical literature as was available in Chinese. Back in Changsha he had formed political discussion groups and published pieces in radical newspapers. His earliest theoretical works were a short note on classes in Chinese society in 1926 and a more substantial investigation into peasant conditions in Hunan in 1927. By then in his mid-thirties, he was an experienced and hardened activist.

As for his character, much is still opaque. One of the most adored, and yet most reviled, people in the history of the world, Mao's reputation these days is enjoying a revival in China, while in the West his character has been assassinated in recent studies, which have seen him as irredeemably cruel and callous from his youth; a manipulative and ignoble person from the very beginning. It has been denied that he ever had any interest in the fate of the common people, and that he set no value on human life. But this is not how some who knew him then saw him, and it is a viewpoint hard to square with the fact that the son of well-off peasants went through such privations and personal risk for so long. As for the claim of a pathologically evil nature, how is the historian to respond if a person is irredeemable from childhood, as some modern biographers have claimed? Where is there to go? At the very least it seems perverse to deny that the young Mao was driven by idealism and feelings of sympathy for peasant oppression, to help explain the still-astounding trajectory of his life, even though he would eventually become their oppressor and must bear full responsibility for some of the greatest disasters in Chinese history, and for unleashing and encouraging the irrational cruelty and murderous violence that went with them. In this indeed, he is not so different from some of the emperors such as Hongwu, whose rule also ended in tyranny and paranoia. Even his own party admitted, in 1981, that in the end Mao had become a man who 'mistook right for wrong and the people for the enemy, and therein lies his tragedy'. But the true tragedy of course would be the one suffered by the Chinese people.

SUN YAT-SEN'S DEATH

Sun died in 1925 in a divided country, and by then the gradual modernisation of Chinese society, which he and his party had hoped for, was looking less and less likely. Or, at least, though already visible in a city of the future like Shanghai, it seemed far off in the impoverished deep countryside, where over 80 per cent of the people still lived and toiled. In this increasingly unstable situation, countless political groups, rival parties and social thinkers were now contesting the possible pathways forward into China's future.

On the verge of the Great Chinese Revolution: Beijing, the Qing capital *c.* 1900, centre of an archaic universe about to be propelled into the modern age.

The end of the empire.

Dowager Empress Cixi.

The Guangxu emperor.

The allied attack on Beijing.

Boxer prisoners await their fate.

To change the world.

Qiu Jin, the feminist poet and freedom fighter.

Lu Xun, the essayist and radical.

Mao Zedong, the revolutionary nationalist.

Sixteen-year-old Deng Xiaoping, who went to France, as he told his father, 'to help save China'.

Breakdown: the last days of the Kuomintang.

In December 1948 in Beijing the nationalist government recruits troops – mainly shopkeepers and small businessmen – to fight the communists.

A bewildered old man searches for his son as his world is left behind.

Shanghai, 23 December 1948, a panic-stricken rush on the banks. Having taken the brunt of fighting the Japanese, the KMT lost its war with the communists.

Mao Zedong declares the People's Republic on 1 October 1949: a famous and much-altered painting.

The first goal of the revolution was to transform the countryside . . .

. . . where over 80 per cent of people still lived and worked, often in the harshest conditions, here captured by Marc Riboud in 1965.

The violence of change. It is hard to believe that a mere fifteen years separates these two images. Above: Red Guards in the frenzy of the Cultural Revolution; and below, the arrival of the TV age in Deng's Reform and Opening Up after 1979.

The long memory of the Chinese people.

Xie Yercai of Qimen county Anhui in his altar room (see pp. 237–9).

Bao Xunsheng in Tangyue Anhui (pp. 280–1).

The Zhao Clan in Fujian (pp. 321–3) all carrying the traditions of Chinese local and clan culture over the great rupture of the communist era.

Restoring the world.

The Qin family of Wuxi in Jiangsu (see p. 301) praying for the ancestors on Tomb Sweeping Day at the grave of founder Qin Guan (born 1049).

A farmers' fair at Zhoukou in Henan (see pp. 24–7) at the shrine of the goddess Nüwa; a sign of the revival of traditional religion in the new China after the spiritual and cultural devastation of the Mao era.

By the late 1920s the communist movement had grown in strength, and Mao was looking to put his ideas of revolution into practice in rural Hunan, where there had been peasant rebellions every year since the First Opium War. Here was the proving ground for Mao's theory that revolution would come not through the cities, but through the rural masses. In a remarkable text written in March 1927, Mao's first major piece of writing reported on the situation of the peasantry in Hunan, where he had spent four weeks on the ground. Constructed from interviews, observations and field notes, it provided a detailed description of state oppression, clan feuds, supernatural superstition and relentless unreconstructed patriarchy, which for all the communist jargon and class war sloganising shows that the young librarian had read much and learned well. But still at this point Mao was not a Marxist; he was at root a revolutionary nationalist.

1930: THE VIEW FROM THE COUNTRYSIDE

The country he was hoping to transform was a land of extremes, with different kinds of society, different economies, and different kinds of time. In the fertile countryside of Hunan, for example, in the small river town of Nanchang, the old world still cohered, and with it the value system of traditional China. In a recent memoir, translated by Nicky Harman, one local recalled his childhood there at a time when the old lineaments of Confucian society still hung on. Born into a middling peasant family, Rao Pingru was eight in 1930 when he went through the initiation ceremony of a middle-class literatus. Woken at three in the morning, he washed, dressed and went to the main hall of the family house where everything was prepared. Such a momentous rite of passage imprinted itself on his memory; his account contains a detailed memory of the room, where scrolls hung on the walls containing Confucian injunctions and a small writing table by a shuttered window carried two big red candles and incense sticks. On the other side of the room was an old red lacquered sideboard, candles, incense, food offerings and a large painted wooden plaque honouring Confucius:

With me were my father and mother, and the gentleman who
was to initiate me into the mystery of education was standing
by the tablet that honoured Confucius. In the stillness of the
night, the candlelight lent a great air of solemnity to the occasion and I felt a thrill of excitement. But what really made me
happy were the Four Treasures of the Study, the brand new
brush, ink, paper and inkstone laid out on the writing desk. The
gentleman ... grasped my hand and together we traced the first
lesson: lines of characters dedicated to the greatest educator of
all, Confucius. He gripped my hand painfully hard, but I did not
dare make a sound.

It was a ritual still experienced by tens of millions of Chinese
people born in the 1920s and '30s. The author speaks of his love of
calligraphy, of the poetry of Du Fu and Bai Juyi, and the old stories
and songs. That traditional mental universe he would carry, like
so many Chinese, across the great divide of the Japanese invasion,
when his hometown was bombed; the civil war, in which he fought;
the Communist Revolution, when he was sent for re-education
in the countryside; and the brave new China of Deng Xiaoping's
Reform and Opening Up. Rao's tale is a measure of the almost
incredible changes that have come about in China over that time,
and the tenacity with which some of the core values of the culture
have been passed on across the ravages of the Maoist era and the
rampant materialism that has been pursued since 1979.

While, as we have seen, Rao was only eight years old in 1930,
Liu Dapeng, on the other hand, in Chiqiao village near the coal
town of Taiyuan, was nearing the end of his life that same year.
Aged seventy-three now, he had lived through the Taiping, the
Boxers, and the end of the empire. For him, the old culture meant
something more visceral, a world that inhabited even his dreams
and left him with an ache of loss and a deep uncertainty about
the future. The economy was in trouble in the mining belt, where
the old trade routes to Russia for tea and coal were closed. The
local newspapers carried news of battles to the south between the

nationalist government and the communists, while the Japanese presence in Manchuria would be compounded before his death by out-and-out invasion and the occupation of his hometown. Through it all, Liu remained a Confucian and a believer in the values of the traditional culture. In the uncertain times of the 1930s, with increasing rural impoverishment, rising taxes and grain taxes, he still made his visits by local bus from the village to the great old walled town of Taiyuan. He especially loved the magnificent Jinci temple at the foot of Xuanweng Mountain, with its garden and its ancient cypress tree, the Hall of the Holy Mother, with its fabulously intricate wooden dragon pillars, and the shrine of the Mother of the Waters over the sacred 'Never Ageing Spring'. Here in the drought-stricken early '30s, traditional people still did their prayers to the goddess for rain, and as the economy of the coal belt towns declined, they paid for a new temple to the god of mining, painting in his eyes at the dedication ceremony to bring him to life. 'In recent years', Liu wrote in his diary, 'scholars have all been divided into two groups, called "those who hold to the old" and "those who hold to the new". Those who hold to the old cleave to the way of Confucius and Mencius, while those who hold to the new seek only after Western methods.' In the 1930s, China saw the inexorable political rise of those who cleaved to the new.

Coal had been the key to the local economy in this part of Shanxi. A former mine manager, Liu had invested the money he had earned as a teacher to buy some land in the village and to pay back the loans for his children's education. He also invested more of his savings in coal, still believing that the old Confucian virtues of morality and trustworthiness should drive business. In the countryside of northern Shanxi was an isolated and (as he saw it) morally pure world of mountain villages and old mining communities; a kind of tough, hardworking pastoral idyll where a Confucian gentleman could still present himself as upholder of true values of 'civilisation'. Here, people's trust was still what made society tick, as Liu noted from his reading of the *Analects* and the standard commentary, which he had studied for the examinations forty years before:

> The superior man must be trusted before he can impose labours on the people. The word trust is at the basis of human life. In one's contacts with the world and one's dealings with people one must not lose it for a moment. Confucius said, 'I do not know how a man without trust can get on.' We can learn much from this teaching that has been handed down to us.

Through the late 1920s and '30s, however, the farming world in the north went into crisis with rising grain taxes and the Japanese occupation of Manchuria from 1931. The bottom fell out of the coal market as well as the old local industry of paper making, a back-breaking task that involved soaking the bundles of fibres in cold mountain streams, before beating and pressing the pulp. Many foreign observers remarked on the harsh times. Set in Anhui, where she lived as the daughter of missionaries, Pearl Buck's famous novel *The Good Earth* is also the tale of a farmer clinging to the old values while the world changed under his feet. In Shanxi, by the early '30s the whole rural economy once supported by the province's commerce and industry, and by coal, was sliding into poverty. Liu by now had one son dead, one mentally ill, two teaching in primary schools, and one doing well for himself as a clerk in the nationalist army in the provincial capital. Back in the village, the family was reduced to surviving on the produce from Liu's small parcel of land. But even as the nationalists and communists fought bitter battles to the south, and the Japanese armies swept into his own province and occupied his own village, Liu never lost his belief that the failures of the modern world were failures to hold onto the values of the Confucian order. By the 1930s, his commitment to orthodox Confucianism amused his younger neighbours: he would still stop in the street to pick up a windblown scrap of paper carrying writing – any writing, even on discarded cigarette papers – following the old Confucian injunction to always respect the written word.

REVOLUTION

In the south there was now savage fighting between the communists and the nationalist Kuomintang (KMT) government. In 1927, the KMT targeted the communists, murdering thousands in Shanghai and elsewhere, including Mao Zedong's wife and sister. Then, in 1931, with Russian support, the Chinese communists formed a guerrilla army in the wooded mountainous borderland of Jiangxi and Fujian, where Mao had taken refuge with the survivors of the massacres. There they declared a 'Chinese Soviet Republic', an enclave with its own administration, even printing its own money and raising taxes. Defended by an army which eventually numbered 140,000 men, the population inside the enclave grew to 3 million people. Three years later, in 1934, the nationalists under Chiang Kai-shek decided to crush the communists for good and encircled them with vastly superior forces. The communists, in five armies totalling about 87,000 fighters with 18,000 civilians, broke out of the encirclement and set out on a series of retreats to northern China. This retreat, collectively known as the Long March, in time grew to be the epic founding myth for China's Communist Party. Travelling on foot through some of the most difficult terrain in western China, in Sichuan and Gansu, they headed north into Shaanxi, reaching the region of Yan'an in late 1935. Only a tenth of the army that had escaped the encirclement survived, but it was through the march that Mao rose to leadership of the party.

The battles and struggles of the Red Army guerrillas in 1934–5 were still only the subject of rumour in the outside world, and the following year the US journalist Edgar Snow journeyed through their military lines and spent four months in autumn 1936 at the communist HQ, interviewing Mao and other leaders. It was the first insight the world had of the storm that was brewing. Published in 1937, Snow's account was the most important book on China written in the twentieth century. The first clear account of the Communist Party and its goals, it was called 'a classic' by one later critic, both as a historical record and as a 'disastrously prophetic' forecast. In ten days of talks in Bao'an, at night, over copious quantities of local brandy, Mao told Snow his life story. Snow was deeply impressed by the idealism of the predominantly youthful Red Army, though his book is criticised now for its enthusiastic account of the communists as political and agrarian reformers, rather than as radical revolutionaries bearing a totalitarian ideology. In the context of rising tension with Japan, however, one effect of the book was to show that the communists could also offer an effective anti-Japanese resistance. By far the most important single source of information about Mao's life, it is irreplaceable about his early years, not only about the facts, but about his own vision of his past.

So, two great historical factors brought China to its revolutionary moment: the actions of the imperialists, and the unresolved state of the peasantry. The course of the revolution, however, would be determined by the Japanese invasion. The Japanese had already occupied Manchuria and set up their captive – the hapless Last Emperor, Puyi – as a puppet. Then, in summer 1937, they launched a full-scale invasion of mainland China.

THE JAPANESE INVASION: THE VIEW FROM CHIQIAO VILLAGE

Liu Dapeng was eighty when the Japanese army began its advance into Shanxi. At the village bus stop, the newspapers were pasted up with the latest reports of the fighting. Soon Taiyuan, the provincial capital 12 miles to the north, was bombed, and refugees began to flood south on the old road through the village. At night, lamps were doused for fear of bombing, and soon the villagers evacuated women and children and the elderly up into the mountains, but Liu refused to go. As houses in the village were looted by retreating Chinese troops, Liu braved it out, defending his property. When the Japanese finally approached, the last local official in post, the prison warden, asked him (as the most educated man in Chiqiao) to draft a declaration of surrender. He did so, then barricaded himself in at home to await the invaders. When the Japanese entered the village, they occupied his house and beat him up, the neighbours pleading on his behalf because of his age. When they finally moved on, they left the house ransacked, the furniture burned for firewood, and Liu nursing his injuries and his wounded feelings.

For the rest of his life, Liu lived under Japanese occupation. For him it was the moral failure of China's rulers that had brought the country to such a pass; 'we are the enslaved people of a defeated land', he wrote in his diary. All the same, he kept a close eye on developments, and, critical as he was of the nationalist government, he was pleased by the successes of the Red Army in their guerrilla war. All the talk in the village was of the resistance; a Buddhist monk friend reported from the mountains that the Red Army rank and file were well behaved and did not loot or harass the local people. To his dying day, Liu remained committed to the Confucian way; as a political creed, communism would have been anathema to him, but the victories of the Red Army pleased him as a patriot, and encouraged everyone in the village. He had no doubt that in the end Japan would be defeated, though he was still 'full of remorse that I do not have the power that comes from virtue to rescue the people of my own village in this chaotic time ...'

That was how it felt in one village under occupation: not so different, perhaps, in some ways, from living in occupied Europe. Looking at the Chinese experience of the Second World War as a whole, however, it is easy to forget that, for the Chinese people, the war began in 1937 and effectively ended in 1949, and that it involved huge destruction and loss of life, running to perhaps 14 million dead. The Chinese resistance (as 'the Fourth Ally') was crucial in bringing the war to a close more quickly than it might have otherwise been: 40 per cent of all Japanese casualties were in China. For China, though, it was devastating – the worst moment perhaps the deliberate destruction of Nanjing (December 1937–January 1938), where rape was used as a weapon of war and up to 300,000 people (according to the Chinese estimate) were murdered in a prolonged massacre. In the aftermath one eye-witness recalled seeing daubed on a ruined building the famous lines of Du Fu, who through all the horrors of his day had maintained his belief in the humane Confucian values of

Chinese civilisation, and his sympathy for the suffering poor: 'The state is destroyed, but the country remains.'

The main weight of resistance fell to the armies of the KMT, while the Red Army was able to mount a guerrilla war as it consolidated its power in the northwest. It was this period that led to the rise of the communists as a plausible national leadership as well as an anti-Japanese resistance. The Communist Party's success in its dealings with the peasantry in the zones they had taken over – with land reform, the dispossession of landlords and rich peasants, and their educational and food programmes – was such that, for all their ruthlessness against 'class enemies', many people were drawn to support their ideals, convinced by their programme, and were prepared to believe in their future. Mao was only half joking when he told the Japanese years later that, but for them, he would not have become leader of China.

When the Japanese surrendered in 1945, the national front fell apart and the nationalists and the communists fought a bitter civil war. Backed by the West, especially the US, the nationalists had the manpower and equipment. The communists were outgunned, but after twelve years in Yan'an, their land reforms had gathered mass support across the countryside. Boosted by propaganda promising a golden age of social justice, in one year the Red Army swept down the length of China and broke into the south with huge battles on the Huai River. After heavy fighting, the support for the nationalists ebbed away, and they fled to Taiwan. In autumn 1949, the Chinese Red Army occupied Beijing and the People's Republic was founded.

A LAST GLIMPSE OF OLD PEKING

Beijing, 1 October 1949. The civil war almost over, the Red Army had taken over the city and the people waited with hope and trepidation to see how the new age would unfold. In the alleys of the Yu family *yamen* in the Manchu old city, lanterns burned for a wedding celebration. With its gardens and courtyards, its 100 rooms and dozen servants, the clan house had been their home for 500 years;

among their ancestors an eminent chief justice under the Qing. In the prayer room, smoke curled from antique incense burners beneath the family shrine; on the table, red lacquered boxes and bronze libation bowls; on the walls, dream stones hung beside yellowing scroll paintings bearing ancient poems and wisdom texts; in the air, the scent of the past. Outside, the gardens, with their ornamental pools and ancient cypress trees, were occupied by Red Army troops who sat around fires while the family performed the old rituals behind shuttered windows in the lamplit ancestral hall. It was a last glimpse of the old China.

On 1 October 1949, from Tiananmen Gate in Beijing, Mao announced the birth of a new China. In Tiananmen Square, the newlyweds stood on the back of a truck amid huge crowds to watch Mao's speech, then joined in the dancing and fireworks. Once again, China faced a new age; the next dynasty.

After the traumas of the Japanese invasion and the civil war, Mao's speech promised an end to the sufferings of the Chinese people. Unlike, say, Jawaharlal Nehru's speech on the stroke of midnight (15 August 1947) announcing the independence of India, Mao made no attempt at stirring flights of rhetoric, prosaically noting that 'the people throughout China have been plunged into bitter suffering and tribulation ... but now the war of liberation has basically been won and the majority of the people have been liberated'. The Communist Party, he said, was now 'the sole legal government representing all the people of the People's Republic of China ... The Chinese people have stood up.'

The moment was commemorated in China's most famous modern painting. It shows Mao on the balcony looking over the square under a blue sky (the day in fact was grey and overcast). Grouped to one side is the party leadership. Painted in 1953, the picture was repeatedly revised, first in the following year and again in 1967, when a new copy was painted to incorporate further changes. Other revisions were undertaken in 1972 and 1979; responding to whether those present had been purged or rehabilitated, and should be painted out or put back in respectively. Like the famous photograph of Lenin and Trotsky in Sverdlov Square, in its ups and downs, its changing fortunes, the painting is a mirror of the trials and tribulations of the Communist Party over the next seventy years. In a culture where history has always been a pre-eminent discipline, it would be, and still is, one of the party's biggest intellectual problems, as Sima Qian put it 2,000 years before: 'fearing the power of the past to discredit the present'.

MAO: THE VIEW FROM A SMALL TOWN

At the time of the liberation, in his memoir Rao Pingru describes the mid-autumn festival of 1949, eating mooncakes in bed as moonlight floods in: 'It was the last mid-autumn festival of the old society.' In the little southern town of Anshun in Guizhou, the Kuomintang troops retreated in early December and gentry and merchants paid local gangsters to maintain law and order. Then, two or three days later, 'one sunny cloudless winter's day', the People's Liberation Army entered Anshun. 'The streets were lined with people waving red and green streamers and welcoming placards,' Rao reports. 'And so Anshun was liberated.'

The first changes under communist rule were small, administrative reorganisations; the Highway Department, for example, was transferred to another town. 'We were all tense and nervous,' Rao wrote, 'we had no idea what [was] to happen to us.' The countryside was still lawless, full of bandits and gangs (there would be peasant rebellions here against the communists well into the 1950s). But it was soon clear one's past could count against a person. In Nanchang, Rao burned all photos of himself wearing KMT military uniform, and he threw away his green general-purpose uniform too. He and his wife Meitang started their new life as small shopkeepers struggling to make a living. As local politics grew daily more and more tense, they just about made ends meet. Their children were born and survived in the early 1950s, but there were work struggles with burglaries and business failures; a noodle bar never took off and they had to sell up and start again. Pingru's job prospects, as he feared, were marked by his KMT associations, but eventually he did an evening training course as a bookkeeper and got a job in a Shanghai hospital. This was before the party grip fastened on China. Life in Shanghai was good: Pingru had a job as a hospital accountant and also worked on hospital publications in little printing establishments for magazines like *Mother and Child Health*. Early 1950s Shanghai was still a lively, bustling place to be. Every weekend the hospitals and trade unions in many workplaces organised 'friendship dances'; private dance halls were still open, and there were foreign films to see. Though they were not wealthy, Pingru and Maitang enjoyed life with their young children.

That was in the early days of the PRC. But through the mid-'50s 'real life' changed. By 1957, Mao decided the revolution not thoroughgoing enough. Above all a revolutionary, he had always said 'a revolution is not a dinner party'; that the new world could only be born through destruction, and that loss of life was no object in achieving the goal of China's socialist utopia. He had never wavered from his view back in Hunan in 1927, that class struggle was in the very nature of the process towards a socialist China, and it would require thoroughgoing land reform with the wholesale transfer of land from the landlords, and even the middling peasants, to the poor.

The analysis had much truth in it. Historic injustices and inequalities were endemic in the countryside, where over 80 per cent of the population lived and worked. But Mao's solution was not to redistribute land gradually, using the law, but through often extreme violence against class enemies, landlords and rich peasants. Law would not even come into it. As he had written in 1949, party rule must be dictatorial: 'The right of reactionaries to voice their opinions must be deprived and only the people are allowed to have the right of voicing their opinions ... To the hostile classes, the State apparatus is the instrument of oppression. It is violent, not benevolent.'

So Mao forged a repressive state, in which words and thoughts were strictly controlled and class war was brutally waged. In 1950s China, with Russian advisers telling them how to build their ideal society, Lenin was still a god. There were considerable achievements in the early PRC: in life expectancy, health, literacy and education, especially among women. But within the first decade an increasingly totalitarian state apparatus clamped down with a far-reaching attempt to change people's minds about everything they once knew. Then, in the late 1950s, massive administrative changes began. For Mao, the very essence of communism was the commune system of agriculture, cutting across all allegiances save those owed to the collective, and through that to the state. China, then, was to be reorganised into huge collective farms and work brigades. 'Our economy will overtake Britain in a few years,' Mao announced airily.

As the move towards totalitarian dictatorship accelerated in the late 1950s, Mao also became increasingly manipulative and dictatorial. When public criticism was encouraged in the 'Hundred Flowers' campaign, the ensuing torrent wrongfooted and shocked the leadership, and a few months later Mao vindictively turned on his critics and persecuted them, sarcastically citing the First Emperor's purge of scholars with approbation. Thousands of intellectuals were jailed, tortured and in some cases hounded to death. Ideology had triumphed over morality; indeed, morality now was just another bourgeois luxury. The Chinese body politic was being hollowed out in favour of totalitarianism.

'Beginning in 1957 there was a drastic change in the political climate,' remembered Rao Pingru: 'On 28 September 1958 I was taken to Anhui province to do Reeducation Through Labour. Thus began a separation from my family that lasted twenty-two years.'

Their story echoed that of tens of millions of Chinese families. They quickly became almost destitute. 'It was during those years of turmoil,' wrote Rao, translated by Nicky Harman,

that the five children were passing through the most important period of their youth, growing to adulthood, studying and learning skills, being sent to labour in the countryside, working, and falling in love. My mother-in-law grew older, and the whole family I had left behind languished in poverty. The arduous task of holding it all together fell to my wife Meitang.

At one point the party apparatchiks came round to tell Meitang that her husband was an undesirable, a class enemy, and that she should divorce him. She refused, as Rao wrote: 'She and I saw so many families being wrenched apart by quarrels and by destitution. Fortunately, it never entered our heads to split up.'

Like so many people in Maoist China, they kept in touch by letter. Meitang took odd jobs to survive, even shifting bags of cement on a construction site, then working in a community workshop, where her friendliness and resourcefulness made her very popular, a shoulder to lean on, even though she was still often stigmatised because of her husband's status as a 'class enemy'.

Rao was sent first to the Huai River containment project to do unskilled hard labour. He became extremely resourceful: making do, mending shoes with wire and squares of rubber cut from a tyre; making socks last longer by cutting and resewing them until long socks had been cut and recut to become small socks; juggling the food coupons with his wife's advice by letter. In the late '50s things got worse for them. In the time Rao called the 'Three Years of Natural Disasters', he developed an oedema:

> My abdomen swelled up like a balloon, as if the skin had sepa-rated from the flesh, while my legs shrank to sticks, no more than twenty centimeters in diameter; it was difficult even to walk; so to keep my brain working I copied sentences from a English textbook Meitang had sent me onto scraps of paper. During the winter I kept these scraps in my jacket pocket, and in summer in my straw hat. When we took a break from labour I would take them out and recite them. At least this provided a pleasant distraction from the relentless toil.

THE GREAT FAMINE: THE 'FIVE WINDS'

What Pingru called the 'Three Years of Natural Disasters' was a giant manmade catastrophe caused by the Great Leap Forward. Up to 1956, it was possible to argue that Mao's role in the creation of the new China had had some positives. But the so-called 'first phase of socialism' was brought to a halt with the Great Leap Forward – a disastrous drive to industrialise the countryside using village forges, which ruined the environment, destroyed a household's metal utensils and made metal too poor to be of any use. All this was accompanied by giant earth-moving and dam projects conceived with military metaphors as a war on nature:

> Let's attack here!
> Drive away the mountain gods.
> Let's wage war against the great earth!
> Let the mountains and rivers surrender under our feet.
> March on Nature!
> Let's take over the power of rain and wind.

At the end of the 1950s, these misguided campaigns pushed China into the Great Famine. Recently, a period of relaxation in the opening of Chinese regional archives has revealed a flood of documentation right down to local party memos and even village petitions, and the broad picture, the scale of the disaster across China, is now clear. Needless to say, the party did not leave an honest account of its own failures, constantly contradicting itself, rewriting the record, with lies, deception and self-delusion even in the face of a human disaster of such staggering proportions. But enough evidence is there to see that even if the party's figures are underestimates, this was the worst famine in Chinese history. Chinese journalist Yang Jisheng in his *Tombstone* – a book to set beside Solzhenitsyn's *Gulag Archipelago* – estimates that 36 million people died. Others have put the figure higher still, which makes China's Great Famine by far the worst in *human* history.

Faced with such a catastrophe, it is hard for the historian to give a human scale. In a work of this kind, the events cannot be given the space they deserve, but to focus briefly on one county and one village gives us at least a sense of what actually happened at grassroots.

Fengyang in Anhui was a proverbial famine region. The town was the birthplace of the parents of Zhu Yuanzhang, the future emperor of the Ming; a man whose own peasant background led him (as we saw above page 279) to expound the idea that the peasant was the very core of society. Today in the pleasant county town, the walls of the aborted first Ming capital still stand, floodlit at night as crowds of townsfolk take their evening stroll by a lotus-covered lake and moat. But despite its brief moment in the sun in the fourteenth century, Fengyang, 'the land of the flying dragon and the soaring phoenix', was always a byword for poverty: 'nine out of ten years were famine', it was said, and beggars from the county were famous, 'carrying the flower-drum to all four corners of the country'. Pearl Buck's 1931 novel *The Good Earth*, a book which had a crucial influence on US views of China between the First and Second World Wars, portrays that world in the early twentieth century; a time of class war, rural slavery, serial famine, infanticide and warlordism. (The daughter of missionaries, Buck had lived in the Anhui countryside from 1917.) As the *County Journal* put it in the 1930s, 'Fengyang is just left to suffer on its own.'

So, famine was ingrained in these parts, and in the 1950s and '60s after the brief optimism of the new China, the itinerant rural poor of Fengyang once again picked up the flower drum and begging basket in a time of growing disillusionment about hopes for the future.

Xiaogang village lies 12 miles west of Fengyang, near the Huaihe River. The visitor approaches the village today on a new highway through rolling farmland, the green fields edged by woods with a rim of mountains to the south. A land of hot summers and wet winters, the village suffered floods throughout the early twentieth century. Life here was always hard. In the late 1950s Mao decided to make the countryside communist in the full sense, and what happened here in Xiaogang was documented three years after Mao's death in an austerely titled report, 'An Investigation of the Xiaogang Production Brigade's Household Responsibility System in Liyuan Commune in Fengyang County' – an account of the events in the village culminating in 1978, when the peasants refused any longer to work the commune system (a story told below page 507). Produced by officials of the Communist Party looking back on the history of the previous thirty years in the village, it tells an almost incredible story of the Great Famine in microcosm.

The 'Production Brigade', formerly the village, comprised 34 households, 175 people in all, with 30 head of cattle and 1,100 *mu* of farmland (1 *mu* today is 920 square yards, so the villagers had roughly 100 hectares). In the mid-1950s, every family had three hired labourers and one plough animal. The main harvest was rice, then grain, sorghum and beans. As things stood in 1955, there was still optimism about socialist China: no one was migrating; there was enough food to feed the people. The next year the changes began that would make the village part of a larger commune; but in an immediate warning sign, productivity already decreased that first year, though it would be the only time under the commune system the villagers would have a surplus to give to the state.

In 1957, the government's anti-rightist campaign came to Xiaogang. Anyone in the village questioning the superiority of socialism was persecuted. The village population comprised middling and poor peasants: there was no landlord class, and no rich peasants. But, even so, they were part of the new order now: 'large in size, collective in nature, all belonging to the public'. There were even regular searches of households, going through trunks and cupboards, with party cadres taking anything they wanted – grain, vegetables, firewood, even tiny personal belongings; 'only your teeth are yours', one farmer was told.

The next year, on 17 August 1958, the experiment began of organising the local villages into communist communes. The pilot charter was displayed in every village: 'This public commune will organise public communes across the whole county to become a cooperative federation under the leadership of the Communist Party, and gradually establish one single commune for the whole county as one political-social entity.' The commune, the people were told, 'collectively owns all the land, barren hills, rivers, lakes, woods and bamboo groves within its borders'. One third of everything produced should now go to the state; half the produce was reserved for the use of the union; the remainder controlled by the communes. Houses were now owned by the collective, whose people 'must work with enthusiasm and loyalty to build socialism'. As for rest times, 'everyone should complete 10 hours' labour; 2 hours' study; 4 hours of eating and resting, 8 hours' sleep. At busy times members may work 12 hours.'

It is astonishing to think this innovation was to be enforced tens of thousands of times across rural China. But the village was now plunged into disaster by new commands from the party, whose central planners directed the planting of crops unsuited to the local soil, sometimes appearing to the villagers to be almost on whim. The villagers now spoke of the 'Five Winds' blowing them hither and thither: the irrational diktats of the Communist Party itself; the exaggeration and deceit; the coercion; the blind commanding of production targets; and the special treatment for party cadres. By late 1958, with a poor harvest and floods, the village sank into famine.

Soon thousands across the county were dying, as was reported in the party archives, though its own cadres were still reported enjoying fine meals in the best hotel in Fengyang. With everything communally owned, the people complained, and with no private tools and animals, there was no incentive to work hard. Before long, the first young men left the land, and as labour decreased, the fields were left barren and livestock began to die. The people were soon starving while the 'Five Winds' blew ever stronger. In an effort to keep in favour with the party hierarchy and deliver their quotas, however, local officials continued to exaggerate the grain production figures, and were then ordered by Beijing to requisition higher amounts for state use, and even for export. In reality, there was a 15 per cent drop in grain production nationally in 1959, and another 10 per cent in 1960. By then in the village, only 100 *mu* of farmland, less than 20 acres, were still under cultivation, and ten families remained on the land – a total of thirty-nine people. In those three years, sixty villagers died of famine, to be marked down as 'unnatural deaths' in party records in the county office. Six households disappeared altogether, with seventy-six people leaving the village hoping to find a way of making a living in cities to the south, especially over the river in Nanjing.

So, Anhui, the 'epicentre of reform', became 'a disaster zone of leftist mistakes'. And if Anhui stood for the country, then Fengyang was the epitome of Anhui. Figures from the local party archives suggest that during the Great Famine a quarter of the county's population, 90,000 people, died of starvation; some estimates suggest one third. In Xiaogang village alone, between 1958 and 1960, sixty-seven villagers died of starvation out of a population of 120.

This terrible manmade suffering was made worse by the 'Four Nos' issued by the party in dealing with so many unnatural deaths: there should be no burials less than a metre deep (as crops must be planted on top); no burials by the roadside (so as not to advertise funerals everywhere); no mourning ceremonies; and no crying over the dead.

Gradually, therefore, the old bonds of Chinese society – of kinship and ancestors, parents and children, which had given the peasantry solidarity and sustained them through the hard times they had known so often through Chinese history – were deliberately and cruelly broken down in the name of an ideology that went against everything Chinese culture stood for. By the end of the Great Leap Forward, Xiaogang village was half in ruins; there were weeds everywhere, and the areas planted with useless crops had gone to waste. Scarcely a decade after the party took over, with all its utopian plans for socialism, the village was destitute.

In the late 1960s, thousands migrated from the county. One farmer who stayed in Xiaogang was Yan Jichang, a 21-year-old newlywed in 1968. He grew ginger, red chili peppers, onions and leeks next to the walls of his farmhouse, from which he raised a small amount of cash. By the house were a dozen persimmon trees which, against the rules of the commune, he and his wife picked in the late autumn, baked and sold. With their surplus they bought two pigs, which brought them an income of about 800–900 *yuan* a year:

most of which went on buying food for the family to avoid going on midwinter trips with the children south into Jiangsu 'counting doors', as they put it – that is, begging in the street. For selling the fruit of the trees they were publicly criticised by some party officials and even by some neighbours as 'capitalist roaders'. As Yan recalled looking back in 2018, 'it was as if, if only we all starved together, then we would be equal'.

So, in a village with no landlord, and no wealthy peasants, by 1975, younger members of all twenty families had migrated away to beg or work. By then the Cultural Revolution had further broken communal solidarity; the end result of constant denunciations and accusations was a land left barren, poverty-stricken families, and social and spiritual division. Even then, though, people still maintained some sense of gratitude to the party (as if their travails were not mainly their fault), as for the whole period from 1966 to 1978 they still depended on grain handouts and ration stamps. But, as one commune member reported,

We are all people of the fields, and we have worked our lifetime on farmland. Seeing such long-term shortage of crops brings the heart to a boil. We feel ashamed for not giving a single gram of grain in surplus; yet year after year we have to eat the food given by the state. We know how to harvest more grains, but their 'policies' don't allow it.

By the late 1960s the situation in Anhui and in China as a whole had eased, but the Cultural Revolution brought back the feeling of crisis. Between spring and winter 1967, the local government archive says over 18,000 people left Fenyang county, mainly heading south across the Yangtze to Nanjing hoping to find work or to beg. Over a third of the rural population of Anhui was on the move. Even into the '70s, starvation remained a serious problem and Fengyang became known again far and wide as the 'town of the flower drums'. The lyric of the song is still remembered by all Fengyang folk today:

To talk of Fengyang
Fengyang was once a fine place
The first Ming emperor was born here;
But since then nine out of ten years were famine.
The big families sold land
Small families sold their kids.
And I who have no kids to sell,
Must roam around with my flower drum.

THE GREAT PROLETARIAN CULTURAL REVOLUTION

By the early 1960s, the imposition of Russian-style communism on
the Chinese people had clearly failed. While still upholding Mao's
pre-eminent role in the civil war and the revolution, a reform-minded
group including the future paramount leader Deng Xiaoping, himself
a veteran of the Long March, wanted now to demote him to a ceremonial role of chairman and take economic policy out of his hands.
In 1961, Mao was sidelined as leader of the party, and in early 1962
the new leadership denounced the Great Leap Forward as the main
cause of the Great Famine; some of the more restrictive rules on the
peasant communes were loosened, and emergency supplies of grain
were imported from Canada and Australia to alleviate starvation.
But Mao wouldn't let go. Now in his early seventies, in 1964 he
regained control of the party and two years later launched what he
called the Great Proletarian Cultural Revolution.

In summer 1966, Mao mobilised millions of young people – Red
Guards – to reignite the nation's revolutionary fervour, attacking
all figures of authority, whether the party, the universities, teachers
or intellectuals in general. The causes are still debated. Mao feared
the revolution had lost its impetus, that the party itself had become
another privileged elite and that liberal bourgeois elements were
still thwarting the growth of socialism. In part, too, he was clearly
motivated by revenge against those who had opposed the Great Leap
Forward and who had pushed him aside in 1961. Frustrated also by
the Chinese people's loyalty to their traditional culture and beliefs,

he called on the young to smash the 'Four Olds': old customs, old culture, old habits and old ideas – the structures of thought that had 'poisoned the minds of the people for thousands of years' – an idea which, as we have seen, had already been espoused by Lu Xun and the New Culture Movement after 4 May 1919.

The Cultural Revolution was another bitter time for the Chinese people, for the deliberate destruction of their past meant the severance of deep emotional attachments to what it had meant to be Chinese. Traditional festivals were banned, along with the old rituals of birth, marriage and death; the destruction of family altars, genealogies and spirit tablets commemorating the ancestors was aimed at breaking the old spiritual link with earlier generations. It was a time, one outside observer said, when the Chinese people 'lost the warmth of home'. Hundreds of thousands died tortured and brutalised in mock trials and summary executions by the Red Guards and the mobs they incited. Virtually all temples, mosques and churches were closed and vandalised. In a gruesome symbolic attack on the hated 'feudal' past, the tomb of the Ming emperor Wanli outside Beijing was opened and his remains, with those of his chief consorts, were dragged out, denounced and burned. In Confucius' hometown Qufu, the local people saved some architectural treasures by boarding them up and painting them with Maoist slogans; the family cemetery of Confucius, however, was wrecked and some of the bodies within dug up, though the tomb of the Master himself was found to be empty when the Red Guards opened it. Religion was banned: by 1971, one foreign visitor reported that it was possible to travel right across eastern China and see no sign of religious practice of any form.

Today, the Cultural Revolution is still difficult to talk about in China. Though there are now websites where victims and oppressors can communicate with each other, what one did in the Cultural Revolution is still a very contentious and painful topic. Every Chinese family has its memories. In Dongtai near Yangzhou, the Bao family, originally from Tangyue in Anhui (whom we met above page 250) faced a terrifying dilemma the night before the Red Guards descended

on their town. Loyal village officers in the Ming dynasty, philanthropic salt merchants in the Qing, they now faced the destruction of
their treasured documents, paintings and calligraphy – or vicious punishment if they tried to conceal them. During the Taiping rebellion, the
family had risked their lives to save a great eighteenth-century painting
of their ancestors (above page 412), and now they went through it all
again. As Bao Xunsheng tells the story:

> That night Grandma came in – 'The Red Guards are coming,'
> she said. 'Come with me now!' We wrapped the picture up with
> the woodblock-printed family genealogy, and we went out and
> buried it in the vegetable patch: we put the turf back on top,
> patted it down – we did really a good job! The next day we got
> out some books and calligraphy and burned them in front of the
> Red Guards, and they were satisfied with that.

Others weren't so lucky. In the old clan villages of Huizhou, tons
of family documents were loaded on carts to be burned in the town
square. In Qimen county, the Xie family (above page 237) were able
to save their precious ancestral plaques, their spirit tablets, by hiding
them in the roof. But the worst loss was in ruined lives. In some
places the mass hysteria of the time snapped all bonds of humanity,
as if violence took on a life of its own. In Daoxian in Hunan, one
horrific massacre was the subject of an official investigation years
later by a Chinese journalist, Tan Hecheng, who pursued the story
further after the case was closed. The story he uncovered was truly
shocking. Over nine weeks in 1967, over 9,000 'class enemies' in the
town were massacred with sickening brutality. Local party bosses
caught up in the hysteria of the Cultural Revolution, and paranoid
about imagined counter-revolutionary insurgencies, instigated the
murder of people who were branded as 'landlord class' or simply
'bad elements'. Many of the dead were women and children, old
people and even infants. The ideological labels were mere excuses;
most of the killings in fact were motivated by local enmities and by
greed. The atrocities of the Daoxian story, which cannot have been

unique at that time, strongly recall accounts of wanton cruelty in the wars at the fall of the Tang, or during the Five Dynasties – or, indeed, accounts from the Second World War in Eastern Europe: it was not just in China that people in our own time turned with such savagery against their old neighbours in a world where, just as in Nazi Germany, language itself was debased by totalitarianism. For modern China, it was, however, the darkest period.

One of the few detailed contemporary journalistic records that came out of China was by an official photographer of the Communist Party in Harbin in the northeast. Tragic and often heart-rending, the photographs reveal how everyday cruelty and persecution happened on the ground, also giving us haunting images of the oppressed crowds which should be scrutinised by all who wish to understand the tortured psychology of the time: the collective hysteria, the mass condemnations of 'capitalist roaders', the shootings of class enemies, even lovers, condemned for their affair, still trying to hold hands as they face the firing squad. As one of the condemned said: 'This world is too dark.'

TIBET

Of all the regions under Chinese rule, none suffered more in the Cultural Revolution than Tibet. For most of its history an independent kingdom, from the eighteenth century Tibet had been a protectorate under the Qing dynasty, which had freed it from the Djungar Mongols. From 1920, Tibet had functioned as a de facto independent country. In 1949, it was invited to join the PRC by Mao, but the Dalai Lama's council refused. It was invaded by the Chinese army in 1950 and in 1959–60 a rebellion was brutally crushed. Then, during the Cultural Revolution, the rift tearing China apart was exported to the Tibetan plateau. Busloads of Red Guards were brought in to devastate what remained of the old culture, and with widespread torture and murder, Tibet became a theatre of cruelty. On 25 August 1966, the Guards destroyed the famous Jokhang temple in Lhasa; its bronze statuary, manuscripts and textiles thrown into its central courtyard to be smashed or burned. Then they spread out across Tibet even to the far west with gunfire and dynamite. By the end, 90 per cent of the monasteries and nunneries were destroyed along with their artistic treasures and libraries built up over a thousand years. In 1980, a fact-finding mission found all the great shrines in ruins: Ganden, Sera, Gyantse, Drepung, the Jokhang in Lhasa – great centres of learning from the medieval heyday of Tibetan Buddhism which, especially in the eighteenth century under the Qing emperors, had played such a role in Chinese civilisation.

In western Tibet, the Red Guards rampaged through the shrines around Mount Kailash and continued on to the far west, a region with virtually no surfaced vehicle roads. Here was an important place in the story of Buddhism: the monastery of Tholing. Founded in 996 by King Yeshe-O, Tholing was the mother house of 108 monasteries in Tibet, Nepal and the Himalayan regions. Most of these were now destroyed, though some survive outside Tibet, like Halji in Nepal, and Tabo, a glorious survival of Indo-Tibetan art and sculpture just inside India.

To go to Tholing today by road is a 300-kilometre drive westwards from the region of Mount Kailash on dirt roads as far as the ravine of the Sutlej River, which flows down to India. The first Chinese military base behind the mountain passes on the edge of India, the town stands on a steep-sided plateau, a tiny 'wild west' town with a population of a few hundred, with a street of shops and restaurants and the inevitable nightclub for the Chinese troops. It is so far from anywhere that it is hard to believe the Red Guards came out here, but the existence of a drivable road sealed its fate.

Tholing has a very special place in the story of Tibetan Buddhism: the centre of the second great dissemination of Buddhism into Tibet in the early eleventh century, when the scholar Richen Zangpo went to India to learn Sanskrit and came back to translate many Buddhist texts into Tibetan, another great historical moment in the long story of rich exchanges between India, the Tibetan plateau and China.

At the centre of this great complex was the temple of Yeshe-O: a three-dimensional mandala with a central hall and eighteen subsidiary chapels, which made this one of the most splendid buildings in Asia. It was a memory room of Tibetan culture; a labyrinth full of magnificent bronzes, giant painted and gilded Buddhas and Bodhisattvas, and a great cycle of medieval wall paintings by travelling Kashmiri masters; in sum, a literal representation of the Tibetan world of the spirits. All of it was destroyed in the Cultural Revolution save for two chapels, later used as grain stores, which preserve exquisite murals. In the main temple, dismembered heads and limbs of broken statues still lie in bare side chapels. All that is left is a few precious photos taken in 1939, and written Tibetan inventories from the twentieth century, 'setting down in writing everything that was here, to make it easier for future ages to understand ... ' The 1870 inventory of the greatest monastery in the 'Kingdom of the West' is eerily prophetic: 'The times are bad. In the long run the images and the vessels and the property, large and small, will eventually be taken away. Since then there will be no chance of retrieving them. It will surely happen that one day in the future there will be nothing virtuous left outside and inside the monastery, in any place, and it will be like an empty paradise ...'

THE CULT OF MAO

From Tibet to Harbin, Xinjiang to Shanghai, and from Confucius' Qufu to the Temple of the Eastern Peak in Beijing, the devastation of China's traditional culture involved an almost unquantifiable loss of cultural heritage, for the whole world as well as for China – the longest-lived continuous civilisation in the world. And all of it driven by the personality of Mao himself, centre of a ruler-cult that in some respects recalls that of the sage-emperors of the past. As a Peking Radio broadcast put it in the summer of 1967 in the first frenzy of the Cultural Revolution:

All rivers flow into the sea, and every Red heart turns towards the sun. O Chairman Mao, Chairman Mao, the mountains are tall, but not as tall as the blue sky. Rivers are deep, but not as deep as the ocean. Lamps are bright, but not as bright as the sun

and moon. Your kindness is taller than the sky, deeper than the
ocean, and brighter than the sun and moon. It is possible to count
the stars in the highest heavens, but it is impossible to count your
contributions to mankind.

This rhetoric has many predecessors in Chinese history, from
Empress Wu declaring herself the 'all-powerful emperor' in the
seventh century to the Rites controversy of the Ming period, when
the Jiajing emperor announced that 'none but the Son of Heaven
has the right to discuss the rites of state ... To measure it [the Way]
according to Heavenly principle and human heart, to fix it according
to fairness, correctness, benevolence, and righteousness: this can be
done exclusively by the emperor.'
   Such are the deep continuities of political ideas at the centre of the
Chinese tradition. In sum, the emperor has the supreme authority 'to
determine the nature of Heavenly principle, the human heart, centrality, correctness, benevolence, and righteousness!' The supreme
power, then, is also the supreme ideological authority. After Mao's
death, his successor Hua Guofeng pronounced two cardinal principles: 'Whatever Mao commanded; whatever Mao taught' – the
ancient cult of the sage-monarch harnessed by the Marxist-Leninist
state ...
   Seen in this light today, we can see that Mao's appeal was on
many levels. His credentials as a revolutionary spoke for themselves.
His utopian dreams, which chimed with ancient currents of Chinese
thought, were at first hugely popular among the lower classes who
had always been downtrodden. He came to power after a long
period of 'national humiliation' and the breakdown of the modern
state, so strong rule was much desired. In that light, the adoration of
Mao can be understood. But as historians see it now, the traditional
figure of the sage-ruler involved not just adoration but the creation
of an overreaching political structure that controlled people's lives
from cradle to grave. The natural outcome was the dictatorship
of a single man which, in the words of a contemporary Chinese
historian who lived through the Cultural Revolution, became 'very

frightening, where terror envelops the entire society, suffocating the entire nation's ability to think', and in the end 'the attempt to create utopia on earth by using these dictatorial powers brought about disastrous consequences'.

Steered by the 'Great Helmsman', Mao's China was directed by the rigid and secretive mind of the Chinese Communist Party, at first with its Russian advisers, which set out to regulate every aspect of people's lives. Viewed from the perspective of seventy years, certain features of its rule, already evident in the 1950s, have now become clear. Though the party claimed to have liberated the people from 'feudalism' and all its ills, the new regime after 1949, as it has turned out, has reproduced many of the most repressive features of the imperial despotism: a centralised bureaucracy; an entrenched and self-protecting elite; ideological conformity and the control of history; corruption and nepotism.

That said, it would be a great mistake – and a Western-centric one – to view all of Chinese civilisation and history as a story of unrelieved totalitarian oppression. Such generalisations do not reflect the reality we have encountered in these pages. As we have seen, in the Mao era too, there were real achievements. The unification of China under one rule after a long period of division is central to Mao's legacy. Great advances were made in public health, education and literacy. There was also a big improvement in the role and status of women, on which Mao had written from the beginning of his career. All of this undeniably helped shape today's China. It is a huge paradox, then, that Mao's achievement was the liberation of the Chinese people, one of the greatest events in history, and yet he also engineered a tragedy of unbelievable proportions, the greatest disasters in Chinese history – namely the Great Famine, the Cultural Revolution, and the devastating war on nature in the name of material progress. The balance sheet on his rule is still contested; perhaps it is too early to tell. As an interim verdict, the party stalwart Chen Yun put it succinctly: 'Had Mao died in 1956 he would be an immortal; in 1966 still a great man, but flawed. But he died in 1976. Alas, what can one say?'

In the great Chinese divination text, the *Book of Changes*, whose origins are to be found back in the oracle bone divinations of the Bronze Age, there is a hexagram entitled 'Revolution'. The commentary says this:

> In a revolution two things must be avoided: You must not move with excessive haste; and you must not use excessive ruthlessness against the people. The revolution must correspond to a higher truth. A revolution not founded on inner truth will come to grief for in the end the people will support only what they feel in their hearts to be just.

19

THE RISE OF THE NEW CHINA

By the late 1970s, the Chinese people had been worn down and impoverished by thirty years of communist rule, by economic mismanagement and environmental disaster, by class war and by devastating famine. But in 1979, their new leader Deng Xiaoping announced a 'Reform and Opening Up' policy, turning his back on communism. So began an unparalleled economic and social transformation. The past forty years have seen the biggest lifting of people out of poverty which has ever taken place in history, a huge rebuilding of the nation's infrastructure and a massive economic lift-off. On many reckonings China already has the biggest economy on the planet, and is back on the world stage as a great power. These astonishing achievements are not without their downside: in key ways, China's rulers have remade the bureaucratic autocracy of imperial times; the rule of law is still a dream rather than a reality; the headlong pursuit of materialism has undermined spiritual life in ways still to be quantified. But, all in all, China's Age of Reform already looks like one of the greatest events in world history. This final chapter, which of course can only offer an interim judgement, begins with the drama of the fateful year that saw the death of the 'Great Helmsman' Chairman Mao.

Halfway between Beijing and the coast, Tangshan today is a city of shining high-rise business districts and an eco-park. Back in 1976, it was a shoddily built city of a million people, based

on industry and coal mining, which had been busily and chaoti-
cally expanding since the 1950s. This part of Hebei has a humid
monsoon climate, with summers often sweltering in the mid-30s,
but in late July 1976 the weather was abnormally stifling. That
summer, which turned out to be the last of Mao's Great Cultural
Revolution, was already a 'cursed year'. Prime Minister Zhou
Enlai, who through all the madness had been loved and trusted
by the people, had died. According to the rumours, Mao had been
incapacitated for many months, and his health was now failing.
So, the stifling air was also thick with political tension, caused by
paralysis in the leadership as the court closed its ranks around the
dying emperor.

In Tangshan, however, a different kind of anxiety had come to
the surface. Scientists from the Bureau of Seismology met in the city
that July with a growing sense of disquiet. The previous year there
had been a number of huge earthquakes elsewhere in the world, and
now they had started picking up seismic anomalies in China: changes
in atmospheric electricity and high levels of radon in a plummeting
water table. Something was happening underground. On 23 July
came disturbing news from monitoring stations in Hebei: four sites
had recorded serious seismic activity. A day later, as the unnaturally
oppressive weather continued, sudden changes in the temperature of
water drawn from wells were reported and nocturnal animals were
seen in daylight. The local county earthquake team, sleepless now
as they frantically tried to get the measure of what was going on,
began to suspect a major quake was on the way. Some, anxiously
assessing the risks, put their beds outside in the open air. For the
Tangshan municipality, however, the evidence that something was
going to happen had no timescale and therefore, unable to plan when
the information was so vague, they did not act at all. The earthquake
team knew that the predictions indicated a quake of five or six on
the Richter scale during the next few weeks, or perhaps months,
and they debated mass evacuation, encouraging people to set up
temporary accommodation in the fields. But still no plan of action
came from the authorities.

In the last hours, the omens came thick and fast. Village ponds dried up in some places and overflowed in others; a pale, yellow fog blurred the air in mining areas and radio stations detected strange magnetic waves. Later it was said that 'Nature' knew; that dogs attacked their owners and horses broke loose from their stables. There were swarms of dragonflies, pet cats fell into a frenzy and, just as in the old European plague legends, clusters of rats with tangled tails were found in the fields. But the strangest phenomena were seen in the sky, eerily mirroring the omens in the 1330s that announced the fall of the Yuan. On the night of 27 July, farmers reported red lights in the night and fireballs over the coast to the northeast; fishermen out at sea saw a sudden band of light under the water, 'like a procession of torches', that vanished in a second. Then, just before midnight, a sudden burst of rain drove people indoors.

At 3.43 am on 28 July, the Tangshan earthquake struck. It lasted twenty-three seconds. Witnesses more than 60 miles away saw a red glow in the sky and heard a distant roar. In Tangshan's main park, those up early for tai chi reported a loud rumbling and the sky in the northeast turning a livid red. Then the earth started to shake. The walls surrounding the park collapsed and the buildings across the road crumbled, filling the air with choking dust and dirt. At the hospital, nurses on the late shift who had gone into the grounds to take the air heard a shrill screech, 'like a knife cutting through the sky', followed by 'the roar of a thousand trucks'. Where the nurses stood, a huge chasm opened up as the hospital collapsed, the workers' dormitories 'shaking like birdcages swinging in the air'. The seismic wave of energy was, it was said, 400 times that of the atomic bomb at Hiroshima. Within minutes the centre of the city was a scene of total devastation, looking as if it had indeed suffered a nuclear blast. Streets were torn up, the night train from Manchuria was thrown on its side and the station flattened. Then there was silence, the darkness before dawn lit only by fires in the ruins. In the air, a gauzy haze, full of dust, smoke, dirt and pulverised debris, deadened the shouts of the survivors. Tangshan, whose buildings were largely made of wood, brick and cheap concrete, had been obliterated. That day, 85 per cent of the buildings were demolished, and more went in a series of aftershocks through the next day and into the autumn. The death toll has never been established; the official estimate was at least a quarter of a million; others put it at more than 655,000.

The force was felt right across northeastern China into Korea and northwards into Mongolia. More than 100 miles away in Beijing, 10 per cent of the buildings were damaged and many people died. The biggest earthquake in China since the ill-omened catastrophe of 1556, this was one of a series of natural disasters over those few months which were widely seen as signs that the government had lost its legitimacy, that the 'Mandate of Heaven' had been lost; for, as the saying went, 'When the heavens crack, the earth shakes.' Whether the dynasty was done though, was still to be seen; Chinese history, after all, moves in longer, slower rhythms than any other. Some had foreseen the fall of the Qing already in the 1840s, after the First Opium War, but it still took another seventy years to come about.

In Beijing that night, Mao was staying in the leadership compound on the lake by the Forbidden City. Visibly shaken and confused, he was wheeled through the warm rain to a quake-proof shelter. Parkinson's and motor neurone disease had left him unable to function properly, with brief moments of lucidity before falling back into incoherence. Protected and shielded by an inner clique, the Chairman had long ceased to have a realistic grip on the world. 'No one outside of Mao's inner circle knew this,' one of Deng Xiaoping's close associates later recalled: 'the outside world, the Chinese people, and even senior party cadres, were all in the dark.' Mao was still worshipped 'like a god' and his remarks still taken as the 'supreme directives', while the state of his health was kept strictly confidential.

Mao died on 9 September 1976 aged eighty-three, mourned as 'the esteemed and beloved great leader of our Party ... the great teacher of the international proletariat and the oppressed people'. Corrupted by power and his messianic personality cult, he was too central to the narrative of the party for his legacy to be realistically assessed after his death. Mao never underwent – and has still never undergone – the thoroughgoing public criticism that followed the death of Stalin in Russia, in part because in China there was no way to separate Mao from the party; he *was* the party. Before he died, Mao had summed up his legacy to his inner circle with a mixture of clarity and terrifying self-delusion:

> I have accomplished two things in my life. First, I fought Chiang Kai-shek for decades and drove him out to a few islands. After eight years of war with the Japanese they were also sent home. We fought our way to Beijing and at last entered the Forbidden City. There are not many people who do not recognise these achievements. The second matter you all know about. It was the launch of the Cultural Revolution. On this matter, few support it, many oppose it, but it is not finished, and its legacy must be handed down to the next generation.

It was said that in the days before his final decline, he was reading Sima Guang, the famous historian of the Song dynasty (above page 213–4). And, indeed, there were many lessons for rulers, from all periods in Chinese history, in that great historian's work. Sima's message was that the history of China had been a story of violence and chaos in which periods of good order had been short. Harmony in the state, he said, was a very difficult thing to establish and 'needed to be very carefully tended once it had been achieved'.

Today, Mao is still a hero for many in China and is undergoing a major rehabilitation under President Xi Jinping. There are Mao shrines in houses once more; Mao-themed restaurants play Cultural Revolution songs while you eat; and in the book market in Beijing, Mao memorabilia are everywhere. What you could buy for next to nothing in the 1980s – magazines, posters, badges and, of course, the Little Red Book – now fetch high prices. Many in China still think that, for all his mistakes, Mao made the nation great again.

Within years of his death, however, slowly the party began the process of facing up to history, moving in a subtle – one might say distinctly Chinese – fashion. Mao's greatness was undeniable, they said, but for the party and its historians, the writers of the current textbooks in school, the balance sheet of history was perhaps 70/30 per cent in his favour. In June 1981, the eleventh party congress issued this historic resolution:

> Practice has shown that the Cultural Revolution did not in fact constitute a revolution, nor was it social progress in any sense. Chief responsibility for the grave error of the Cultural Revolution, an error comprehensive in magnitude and protracted in duration, does indeed lie with Comrade Mao Zedong. In his later years ... far from making a correct analysis of many problems, he confused right and wrong, and confused the people with the enemy. Herein lies his tragedy.

It was China's tragedy too. But, the party added, 'they were the faults of a great revolutionary', and as the dust settles in today's boom-time China, his place in history is uncontested – if deeply shadowed by the memory of those dark times half a century or so ago. Some modern accounts have presented a truly terrible image of a despot who descended into tyranny, a man with no mitigating features; but that is not, in the main, how the Chinese people see it. The emperor had lost, and then regained, the Mandate of Heaven, and then – with staggering losses – clung on to it. But the dynasty, if we may so call it, survived.

THE RETURN OF DENG XIAOPING

Mao's funeral took place in September 1976, the memorial speech made by his appointed successor, Hua Guofeng, a Mao loyalist and a colourless and mediocre party man. It was a speech designed to continue Mao's legacy of factionalism:

> Under Chairman Mao's leadership, the Chinese people, who had long suffered oppression and exploitation, won emancipation and became masters of the country. It was under Chairman Mao's

leadership that the disaster-plagued Chinese nation rose to its feet.
The Chinese people love, trust and esteem Chairman Mao from
the bottom of their hearts.

As for the future, Hua concluded: 'We must deepen the struggle to
criticise Deng Xiaoping and repulse the right deviationists' attempt
to reverse correct verdicts, consolidate and develop the victories of
the Great Proletarian Cultural Revolution and combat and prevent
revisionism.'

For anyone watching, after the savagery and terror of the Cultural
Revolution, such words only showed how China's self-deluding
inner circle was still in the grip of Mao's charisma. In the nation at
large, society was battered and exhausted by hardship, riven with
social conflict and worn down by the corruption and institutional
disorder caused by the virulent leftist policies of the Mao era. The
countryside was in ruins, the environment devastated, and the rural
population in poverty or starving. The educational system was in
chaos; the closure of universities and schools meant that a whole
generation had lost ten years of education. Industry had stagnated
or collapsed. Worse still, across the country, group feeling had been
fragmented. Hard as it was to admit, Mao's policies had amounted to
a systematic attack on the very core ideas that had sustained Chinese
society for so long.

The turning point came in 1978, a moment historians now see as
China's second revolution, and one of the most significant events in
modern world history. After Mao's death, his clique, the so-called
'Gang of Four', were defeated, and in the following two years of
party infighting, Hua Guofeng was sidelined and a new leader
emerged – the very man condemned by name in Hua's funeral ora-
tion for Mao: Deng Xiaoping.

A chain-smoking veteran of the Long March and the civil war,
the diminutive Deng Xiaoping was of peasant stock from Sichuan.
His family were originally from the Hakka ethnic minority and
had migrated from Guangdong in the seventeenth century. With a
strong Sichuan accent 'that some found difficult to follow', he was a

caustic, steely man, possessed of an astonishing memory and formidable self-control. Deng had joined the Communist Party in France
at the age of fifteen, telling his father he hoped 'to learn knowledge
and truth from the West in order to save China'. He spent five
years there working in a Renault tractor works and a shoe factory,
where he became convinced that Western education was the key to
modernisation. In 1927, he returned to China to participate in the
guerrilla wars of the Jiangxi Soviet and was on the Long March,
becoming a military leader in the civil war. He had supported the
anti-rightist campaign in the late 1950s that had ruined many lives
(he would later admit it was unjust and excessive, though never
conceded it was wrong). He had also supported the initiatives that
led to the disasters of the Great Leap Forward, although privately,
as we now know, it was at that time that he felt the direction of
China's socialist reconstruction started to go wrong, and was particularly disturbed by the personality cult in which he felt 'Mao was
worshipped as a deity'.

Deng presents us with a paradox, then, which none of his modern
biographers has been able to resolve, perhaps because he left no
diaries or letters, let alone a personal memoir. Deng toed the line
but, like others in the leadership from the late 1950s through the
'60s, though he had blood on his hands, he saw where Mao's policies were leading and challenged them. He was eventually sent to
the countryside to do manual labour, purged for his 'rightist' views
and his opposition to Mao's concept of permanent revolution. As
for the Cultural Revolution, that was 'an unprecedented disaster'
in which 'political chaos, social turmoil, sabotage of production
and hardship in daily life, had brought our economy to the brink
of collapse, and hurt countless individuals in every walk of life,
in innumerable ways'. For him, as reported by his daughter Deng
Rong, it was a 'tremendous catastrophe ... whose scars might never
heal, a miasma of confusion in which political, economic, scientific,
cultural and educational life were severely damaged in the name of
revolution and class struggle that went on without end to the great
detriment of the people'.

Purged twice by Mao during the Cultural Revolution, Deng's amazing career would have three comebacks. That said, however, Deng was a diehard communist with unswerving loyalty to the party, despite his criticisms, and despite the way it had treated him and his family. Throughout his life he never doubted the one-party state and was opposed to any whiff of democracy outside what the party imposed on itself – a multi-party system on the Western model could not, he thought, be China's path. During the Cultural Revolution, his son was imprisoned by the Red Guards, tortured and thrown out of a fourth-floor window leaving him paralysed (he later become an important fighter for disability rights in China). Deng and his wife were sent into exile for four years, during which he worked in a tractor factory in Nanchang in rural Jiangxi. There they lived in an old school building, in a bare room furnished with just a table and chairs; outside was a woodshed, a privy and a vegetable patch. (Deng's walk to work along a 'little red gravel path' is now a tourist attraction.) But it was a time to think, and Deng was a thinker. According to his daughter, he was a great student of history and spent much time reading Chinese historians as well as Marxist texts in an attempt to understand Chinese history, the fruits of which reading we will attempt to untangle below.

GAIGE KAIFANG: THE REFORM AND OPENING UP

So how did the biggest change in China's history begin? In 1973, Premier Zhou Enlai had brought Deng back to Beijing from exile to focus on reconstructing the Chinese economy, and in 1974 Deng flew to New York and spoke at the UN, arguing that a new epoch was beginning in China's foreign policy towards the world. On his fact-finding missions he was shocked by how far China had fallen behind the rest of the world. He became convinced of the value of study tours, crash courses and learning from the developed world. For Deng already had a plan to reverse the policies that had led to class war: 'wherever I see a communist economy I see poverty', he said, and 'wherever I see the American system I see people's lives enriched'.

In early 1976, Deng had been savagely criticised and then removed from power shortly before Mao's death by the Chairman's old comrades, the 'Gang of Four', but in July 1977 he was reinstated and, from then on, all eyes were on him. He never became premier, chairman or president, but he was the de facto leader, even though his conservative opponents still feared he would betray the revolution. With the help of a group of allies and using his prestige as a longstanding revolutionary and veteran of the Long March, he immediately began planning for sweeping change.

His goal was to use capitalism to build a socialist society, while not loosening the dictatorship of the party. His focus was on economics, science and technology; the planned reform would not be political. Whether it is possible to have one without the other has become one of the great questions of current Chinese history and no doubt will dominate the next few decades too. For Deng, the key was to face what had happened since 1949 with a clear eye, as a close associate remembered, reflecting on their conversations:

> China had not been a socialist society from 1956 to 1978. It was a period characterised by economic stagnation, political turmoil, cultural decay, and a population living in poverty and distress. In the twenty years after 1957 China's destiny was in great danger and China was travelling along a path that was leading our party and our state to perdition.

Deng understood this and was not so blinded by ideology that he did not see the need for fundamental change. He began to push through reform in several areas, including the law, while being careful not to criticise Mao directly. His first moves had been long considered during his exile, and were shared in private conversations with close friends and trusted colleagues. One of these discussions in late May 1977 is especially revealing of his reading while in exile: 'The key to modernisation', he told his ally Yu Guangyuan, is the development of science and technology. But unless we pay special attention to education it will be impossible to develop these areas. We must have knowledgeable and trained people; without them how can we develop? China is now at least twenty years behind developed countries in science, technology and education. As early as the Meiji Restoration, the Japanese began to spend a great deal of effort on them, right now we must work in the spirit of the Meiji restoration and Peter the Great. To promote science and technology we must improve education.

In line with this thinking, Deng first asked to be put in charge of education, and a few days later the party leadership approved. It would be quite a task. The education system was broken. During the Cultural Revolution, only Communist Party members had access to higher education, though there was a nationwide system of peasant scholarships. Most universities were closed and intellectuals, including many teachers, had been purged. In 1977, only 47,000 pupils were in higher education where there had been 675,000 in 1960. So, in August that year, Deng held an education conference in the Great Hall of the People in Beijing, an imposing and frankly terrifying environment for many of the delegates, who had been summoned at short notice. The mood was extremely cautious, and at first none of the attendees felt able to speak – not surprisingly given the way dissent had been handled under Mao. Deng had to cajole those in the hall to 'speak freely and without fear'. Then one of the youngest delegates, a chemist called Wen Yuankai, stood up and broke the silence: 'This is my opinion. University exams should be restarted as soon as possible. They should be open to all, free and fair, and judged on merit, although the party should of course approve the candidates.' Deng agreed to the first three suggestions and dismissed the need for party vetting. An announcement was placed in the *People's Daily* that university exams would be organised before the end of the year. When the news came out, 5.8 million people from all over China applied to take the exams.

It is hard to exaggerate the meaning of this moment to ambitious

young people with a thirst for education; people who, even during
the Cultural Revolution, had tried to keep up their studies in the
hope that one day things would improve. It is a moment etched into
the memories of that generation: 'When I finished high school I went
to work in a factory in Shanghai. I didn't have any hope of entering
university,' recalls Professor Zhang Weiwei of Fudan University.
'The exam was very tough; less than 5 per cent passed. The ages
of the candidates varied from eighteen to thirty-five in my class;
we were coal miners, farmers, soldiers, workers, young apprentices
like me. That exam changed the lives of so many people.' In exile
in the countryside at that time, for Professor Xue Lan, the current
dean of Tsinghua University, it meant liberation: 'I thought I would
spend my life in that village, so when we heard the news we were
so happy, just exhilarated. It was a life-changing moment for us.'
Within ten years there would be an incredible fiftyfold increase in
college intake.

Deng now sponsored a series of fact-finding tours to Hong Kong,
Japan and Europe, the last led by his reformist ally Gu Mu. This
crucial mission of 2 May–6 June in 1978 has been compared by
Western historians to the Iwakura mission in the 1870s, which
opened up Japan to the US, Britain and Europe; or Peter the Great's
Grand Embassy from Russia to Western Europe in the 1690s, when
he inspected new naval technologies at the Chatham dockyards.
Indeed, as we have seen, these examples were precisely the ones on
Deng's mind.

Deng hoped the thirty people who went with the mission would be
future leaders of the economy. With so little knowledge of the West,
they had much to learn. They went to a Swiss power plant and to
Charles de Gaulle airport in France (air-traffic control in China was
still not computerised in 1978). They were amazed at the size of the
container port in Bremen and the level of French agricultural productivity. They were not only shocked by how far China lagged behind,
but by how willing the Westerners were to share knowledge and
technology, having been taught for so long that they were 'the enemies'. 'Our eyes were opened,' said one. 'Everything we saw shocked

every one of us. We were enormously excited. We were taught the capitalist West was decadent and corrupt and treated their workers brutally but we saw with our own eyes that this was not true.' On their return, they reported that the 'Four Modernisations' (industry, agriculture, defence and science and technology) first propounded by Zhou Enlai in the early 1960s, were at last a realistic prospect. It was the beginning of a new age of openness for China.

WATCHING THE NEW AGE ON TV

Things now moved fast. In mid-September, Deng, who was nearly seventy-five years old, went on a tour of northeast China to 'light the spark'. In Liaoning in Manchuria, Deng surprised local officials by announcing that the leaders of the Chinese Communist Party, including himself, should admit their mistakes: 'We have let down the wonderful Chinese people who had been very patient.' To those who were fluent readers of subtext, it could not have been clearer that the Mao era was in the dock: 'Our nation's system is basically taken from the Soviet Union,' Deng said. 'It is backward, deals with issues superficially and piles on bureaucracy. It needs to be thoroughly reformed.' On 22 October, Deng himself went to Japan, visiting the most modern steel works and the latest electronics factories. He travelled on the high-speed train and commented that although the Japanese had lost the war, they were now decades ahead of China. He took a CCTV crew with him to record what he was seeing: 'Don't film me,' he ordered, 'film what's out there, to show the people back home.'

As Deng intended, the impact on the Chinese public was huge; they heard the news reports on the radio, but also through the new medium of TV. In 1978, there was only a handful of local stations; the national broadcaster CCTV had been formed that year and fewer than 10 million, mostly urban, Chinese had a TV set. In her tiny apartment in a block of flats in Shanghai, for example, Rao Meitang, now a canteen worker, wrote a letter to her husband, who was in the twentieth year of his re-education in the Anhui countryside: 'We've rented a TV; the screen is nine inches wide but fine if you are just watching at home.' The payments were being made by her son, and she reported the neighbours all coming round to watch films. Charles Laughton's *Hunchback of Notre Dame* (1939) was a favourite, and there was a full house for the old 1962 serialisation of *Dream of the Red Chamber*, which really thrilled the children: 'they can't get enough of it'. With the advent of TV, the world was literally opening before their eyes: 'They're showing Japanese films too!' she wrote. 'And I've been watching all the satellite broadcasts of Vice Chairman Deng Xiaoping's visit to Japan.'

Reading Meitang's letters, one feels the astonishing patience and stoicism of the Chinese people, and the optimism in the air of the post-Mao age. A world stifled for so long was beginning to open up. On 12 November, Deng went to Singapore and was shocked to see modern, well-equipped workers' housing. Again he compared this to China, where the condition of the peasantry in places was no better than it had been in the 1920s. At this point Mao's follower Hua Guofeng was still premier, but Deng was preparing his path; his allies seeding articles in the newspapers which were avidly read on the factory floor. Writing from Shanghai on 17 November, Meitang sent another letter to her exiled husband: 'On October 7th in the *Liberation Daily* there was an article about professionals getting their old jobs back. It says that there are provisions for releasing anyone who's served their term doing "Re-education Through Labour". Get hold of a copy and look!'

Now articles about the 'Wind of Change' came thick and fast. In her tenement behind the Bund in Shanghai, Meitang was now a daily visitor to the news stand:

On the 14th there was a very good article in the *Wenhui News* which said 'democracy must be strengthened and the rule of law must be instituted'. And another yesterday said: 'We must seek the truth from facts, wrongs must be righted.' You must have a look at them, there are articles like this every day now.

Letters like this catch the new mood of the times. The way was being prepared for a major shift by the party. The next stage as Deng manoeuvred for power was to get his reform ideas accepted at a plenum meeting scheduled for December. Deng decided that the first step was to air the ideas at the Works Conference that November, but as the delegates started arriving in Beijing, events in the countryside were starting to overtake them. As so often in history, while the leadership likes to take credit for change, in reality it is driven by the grassroots.

XIAOGANG: THE VIEW FROM THE VILLAGE

Less than twenty years on from the Great Famine, we return to Xiaogang village in Fenyang county, Anhui, just south of the Huai River. The approach to the village today is on the new highway, G36, which goes all way down from the Yellow River to Nanjing through rolling farmland. As you drive through the emerald green rice paddies with their network of reservoirs and irrigation canals, it is hard to imagine the famine-stricken world of the early 1960s and '70s, when some farmers still had wooden ploughs and harrowing boards. Even in 1978 the village was still a straggle of mud-brick farmsteads along a tributary of the Huai. It's been rebuilt now and only one old house has been saved, complete with its old farm gear; relics from forty years ago that would not look out of place in a Tudor husbandman's toft. That was the material culture of Xiaogang after thirty years of communism.

In the early 1960s, during the Great Leap Forward, as we have seen, Fengyang county, along with much of the rest of the country, was plunged into famine. In Xiaogang village, half the inhabitants died of starvation between 1958 and 1960. Then, with the outbreak of the Cultural Revolution, a new generation of children was born into hunger and near destitution. After a poor harvest in 1978, things became desperate, as Guan Youjiang, a young farmer then in his twenties, recalls: 'I had four children, they all went out begging, even the youngest. There was not enough food for sure. Life was so hard.'

On 24 November, eighteen of the local farmers, heads of families, met in that mud-brick farmhouse at the far end of the village to sign a secret agreement to divide the land of the local people's commune into family plots. For one of the farmers, Yan Jinchang, 'it was just heart-breaking. If we didn't do so, we would starve to death. If we did, we'd take a risk. Eventually we chose to go down this road. Even with the threat of prison or death, we divided the land. To end starvation.' It was against the law and against one of the very foundational ideas of the revolution. Now, each plot was to be worked by an individual family who would turn over their allotted quota to the government but would keep the surplus for themselves and sell or barter it where they could. The villagers agreed that, should the ringleaders be caught and executed, their neighbours would raise their children until they were eighteen years old. Faced with the renewed threat of famine, and the possibility of more deaths, it was, said Yan, 'a life or death contract'. The document was signed with thumbprints in red ink as if in blood.

After this hidden mutiny, the following year, Xiaogang village produced a harvest larger than the previous five years combined with a grain output increasing to 90,000 kilograms. 'Income for each household shot up eighteen times in one year from 22 *yuan* to 400,' says Yan Jinchang. When they found out, local government officials turned a blind eye. Facts on the ground had outflanked the hardliners in Beijing and the innovation was soon held up as a model to other villages across the country. Within two years, collective farming right across China was abandoned, resulting in a huge increase in agricultural productivity.

The secret contract in Xiaogang in November 1978 is now seen as the symbolic beginning of the period of rapid economic growth and industrialisation that mainland China has experienced in the years since. Communism had proved to be against the grain of Chinese civilisation. Today, Xiaogang is largely rebuilt, still surrounded by rice fields and woods. At one end of the village there is a monumental heroic frieze and a small museum, where the 'life or death contract' is proudly on show. Mr Yan now has a thriving restaurant, and students from local sixth-form colleges arrive with questionnaires about Deng's Reform and Opening Up. When they ask him what happened, he simply replies, 'We had no choice. We had to sign or starve.'

THE TURNING POINT

At the very moment when these events were unfolding in the countryside, the Party Works Conference was underway in Beijing. The arcane workings of the Communist Party and its plenums are dry as dust, and wearisome in their jargon and self-serving mendacity; to go back over their pronouncements is to read through decades of rhetorical self-delusion, enough to wear the historian's patience thin. But this conference is worth a moment's pause, as it inaugurated one of the most important events in modern history: China's opening up and reform after the traumatic three decades of Maoism.

The Communist Party Works Conference took place from 10 November to 15 December 1978. It was held in the Jingxi Hotel close to the Defence Ministry, 4 miles west of Tiananmen Square. A drab, concrete, Soviet-style building with heavily guarded high-perimeter walls, the car park crammed with black Audis favoured by party high-ups, it is still there today – still not open to outsiders – though its current entry in TripAdvisor recommends the hotel and praises the attentive and good-looking staff. Back in 1978, 200 or so delegates gathered in the big conference room, representatives from every region of the country. There were conservative hardliners, party ideologues, and new wave allies of Deng, including Gu Mu, who had led the science and technology mission to Europe; Hu Yaobang, later chairman and general secretary of the party; and Zhao Ziyang, a pioneer of rural reform and a future premier who would play a central role in the crisis of 1989. Deng sat on the platform flanked by other party officials while speaker after speaker outlined their own personal experiences of the Mao years: disastrous food shortages, famine, chaos and social conflict. This was the reality of the past twenty years of life for the Chinese people. Speaking freely for the first time, sixteen provincial leaders reported real rather than exaggerated figures for grain output – the situation in Anhui, for example, was desperate, with production nowhere near that of 1955; indeed, it was more like the 1949 level. One participant later recalled: 'It was heart-breaking that farmers in the old revolutionary base areas of the Dabie mountains were so poor that they didn't have trousers to wear or quills to use.' The scenes described left the delegates 'deep in thought'. Deng now became the advocate for change and paradoxically found himself the guardian of the party's (and the nation's) bruised soul.

In a still rural civilisation, agriculture was the great question, and reformers like Hu Yaobang were keen to scrap the commune system altogether and try family quotas; an experiment already being tried in Sichuan and, unbeknown to them, at that very moment in Anhui. But many in the party felt they couldn't go against Mao's key directives, that they had to 'uphold Mao's prestige for fear of much greater impact within the party and in society as a whole'. At the end of the conference, Deng spoke. He had been thinking about the issues of the speech since at least the late '60s, when he was banished by Mao, and probably since the disasters of the Great Leap Forward. While never directly attacking Mao, everything he said in the speech was an implicit rebuke. He decried the personality cult and slavish adherence to ideology, which had suffocated the entire nation's ability to think. Most of all, what concerned him was the closing of the Chinese mind. 'Today', he began, 'I mainly want to talk about one question, how to emancipate our minds ... seek the true path from facts and form a united view on how to face the future.'

Three pages of notes in his calligraphy survive, about 1,600 characters, 800 words. 'He wanted the speech to be pithy and forceful and spoken in short sentences,' said a friend: 'he wanted to talk about the backwardness of China and give an overview of his approach for a new era.' The headline topics in his handwritten notes can be reduced to certain key ideas which together form the blueprint for today's China:

1. Free our minds from ideology
2. Promote democracy inside the party and in the legal system
3. Review the past to guide the future
4. Curb excessive bureaucracy
5. Allow some regions and enterprises to get rich first

The key to modernisation, Deng said, was to lay out a clear, practical course. China's lack of the necessary knowledge and technology was obvious to all, so it must start to learn again. The answer to it all was education in economics and science. As for the party's historic errors, only later, 'at an appropriate time', he added, 'we will need to sum up Mao's errors and draw lessons from them ... with the Cultural Revolution everything wrong should be redressed ... but without settling of scores'.

Spoken in a flat, unemotional monotone, after the past twenty years of class warfare, hardline ideology, centralised economic planning and the hysterical ruler cult, Deng's words signalled a fresh start, and for many in the room there was huge optimism. Deng even had to restrain the confident mood: 'It won't happen overnight; some problems will be for the next generation to solve.'

The plan was put to the party's Third Plenum in Beijing, the following week, when the contents of Deng's speech were ratified. The Third Plenum was really just a confirmation of the Work Conference, but it announced changes so momentous that when a Chinese person today speaks of 'the Third Plenum', everyone knows what they mean.

For Deng, rapid development of China's civil law code was one important path away from the excesses of Maoism and the burden of two millennia of imperial ruler cult; what he called 'feudal think-ing', and what current Chinese historians call 'monarchism'. But the weight of history, as it turned out, was not so easy to throw off. At every point Deng trod carefully, concerned to show he was not dis-missing the whole of Mao's legacy, and when he spoke of democracy it is important to understand that he was not talking about a multi-party system, but reforming a one-party state whose functionaries he thought should be subject to democratic scrutiny to make the state machinery function better. The party, importantly, should still have a monopoly of power.

CHINA OPENS UP

The pace of events now accelerated. The week following the plenum, *Time* magazine put Deng Xiaoping on the front cover and declared him their Man of the Year. Then, on 1 January 1979, after months of secret diplomacy, the US announced a major change in foreign policy, downgrading its relationship with Taiwan and recognising the People's Republic of China, thus ending three decades of antagonism. Fifteen days later, China began its new international age with Deng's visit to the US seeking American help for his reforms. As President Jimmy Carter remembered it, Deng was above all 'a man in a hurry'. On the White House lawn, he summed up the moment: 'China has taken the bold and momentous decision to open up.' Standing by his side, Deng replied, 'We share the sense of being on a historic mission ... a single spark can cause a prairie fire.'

Deng visited Seattle, Atlanta and Houston, where he even had the time to get down-home at a Texas rodeo, posing for the cameras with a Stetson – an image that went down well with TV audiences East and West. As the anchorman Jim Laurie said on ABC news: 'Premier Deng Xiaoping not only went west, he went Western!' But behind the fun was a cool, calculating brain; Deng needed the US to help his great reform, while the US realised that China could be a huge market, and helping China to develop would open opportunities for their economy too. Meanwhile, back home on TV, Americans who had been demonised during the Cold War were shown as welcoming and keen to help China, and America's lifestyle, culture and standard of living became something the Chinese could aspire to.

In early 1979, therefore, the stage was set for the reforms. Guangzhou on the Pearl River in south China was to be the testing ground. China's historic commercial capital, the city had gone into a steep decline since the revolution of 1949. Visitors to the area in the 1970s saw an economy in ruins: few buses, old factories with outdated plants and no spares, and a demoralised workforce. Ezra Vogel, who first visited the city in 1973, recalls that 'in Guangzhou there were still dog carts, there were a lot of people without clothes, who were so thin that you wondered if they were going to make it'. The head of the party in Guangdong province at the time was an old revolutionary comrade of Deng's, Xi Zhongxun, the father of the current president Xi Jinping, who, like Deng, had been purged in the Cultural Revolution. When he first arrived, the region was struggling to prevent a tide of young men fleeing to Hong Kong in search of a better life, hundreds of whom drowned trying to swim across the narrow straits. Xi called for greater autonomy for Guangdong, saying it should be allowed to pursue its own trade policies and let in foreign investment. 'If Guangdong was an independent country', he told Deng, 'and I was the leader left to get on with it, I could make huge changes in a few years.' Deng agreed and, although he couldn't supply funding, he was happy to sign off on a policy giving Guangdong the status of 'Special Economic Zone'. Xi Zhongxun was then free to broker deals between Hong Kong and local industry, unleashing the potential of this newfound economic freedom. Subsequently, three more Special Economic Zones were set up near Hong Kong and Macau in which market forces were permitted to operate. The zones were wildly successful – in large measure because Hong Kong took advantage of the cheap labour available on the mainland and moved their production facilities into these special zones – and in a short time they became the model for the entire country.

Thus China embarked on an economic and social experiment mixing the communist command economy with the energy of capitalist entrepreneurship. The Communist Party could push through big construction projects, providing the infrastructure for growth. But they also liberated talents lower down the chain of command, as Deng put it, to democratise economic production.

By the early 1980s, the signs of reform were everywhere, from the schoolroom to the marketplace to the cars on the streets where once there were only bicycles. The number of television stations rose from a dozen or so in 1978 to around a hundred in the '80s. A huge demographic change began. A key feature of China's modernisation process was urbanisation; the rural population moved into the cities at a rapid pace, increasing the country's productivity twentyfold. In just a few years, therefore, China's agriculture was de-collectivised, education and industry were reformed and private business allowed to flourish. The Communist People's Republic of China even opened a stock exchange.

THE DEMOCRACY MOVEMENT

Deng's concept of democratic reform was still only within one-party rule, however. He embraced only economic liberalisation and rejected Western-style political liberalisation. Within a decade, this tension reached breaking point. By early 1988, the reform stalled and economic indicators were poor. The production of staple crops was declining and prices were on the rise. Rationing of key food items like pork, sugar and eggs was reintroduced and inflation rose to more than 20 per cent in the cities. Eight million people a year were moving into the urban areas, with 30,000 migrant workers arriving daily in Shenzhen railway station. The floating population of unemployed workers was over 1 million in both Beijing and Guangzhou and nearly 2 million in Shanghai. Meanwhile, mechanisation and a freeze on capital construction projects led to a worsening situation in the countryside, where 180 million farm workers were now reported as 'redundant'.

The new entrepreneurial developments, therefore, were taking place in an increasingly tense and problematic economic situation, with real splits in the ideology at the top of the party, and in early 1989 these issues were being aired openly in the Chinese press. Inflation was now at 26 per cent and grain production continued to drop. Labour unrest, party corruption, rapid population growth and unregulated movement, together with the continuing failure of educational reform to combat illiteracy, formed a toxic mix. Living standards fell in the cities as big capital projects were put on hold, and many people were put out of work. Shortages led to panic buying and the hoarding of a whole range of products from grain and cooking oil to soap and toothpaste. The push to modernise, some said, had been too fast, and too unregulated. The dream of reforming China's economy and modernising the whole nation now teetered on the edge of disaster. Among the hardliners, the main issue was what they saw as Deng's betrayal of the Marxist utopian dream.

The breaking point came early in 1989, as calls for more political openness grew louder. Reformers on public platforms in the universities now spoke openly of freedom of expression and democratisation as the keys to scientific and economic progress; real reform and opening up, they said, was impossible without *political* reform. There was unrest in many Chinese cities – in some places it was suppressed, in others it was defused without violence; but it was widespread and supported in many places by working people. Then, in April 1989, a student demonstration occupied Tiananmen Square in the heart of Beijing, precipitating the biggest crisis of the post-Mao era.

Tiananmen Square 1989 is still a controversial event in the history of modern China, one that remains very difficult to talk about in official circles or in the Chinese media. When a 48-episode TV biography of Deng Xiaoping was launched by CCTV in 2014, it ended with the events of 1988. 'It is too early for 1989,' the director said at the press launch. As always in China, the time will come, probably in the not-too-distant future, when the Tiananmen Square massacre can be talked about, and when authenticated sources are released to show precisely what happened inside the Politburo. As things stand, the account of this signal event in modern Chinese history must be reconstructed from eyewitness accounts and from five key documentary sources, two of which were published only in 2019. First are the Tiananmen Papers, which purport to contain the deliberations of the Politburo. There are still issues, however, over the way these have been redacted, and not all historians are sure they are genuine; it is a question that will remain until the original documents become available. The second key source is undoubtedly

what it claims to be: the memoir of Zhao Ziyang, the former premier
and general secretary of the party. A reformer ousted by Deng and
placed under house arrest after supporting the students, Zhao smuggled out cassette recordings of his own view of the disaster in his own
voice. Third is the diary of the hardliner Li Peng, which he prepared
for publication in 2003 but was refused publishing permission. Li's
book is a self-justification: 'I would sacrifice my life and that of my
family to prevent China going through a tragedy like the Cultural
Revolution,' Li claims to have written on 2 May 1989. Finally published illicitly in 2010, again there are issues about its genuineness,
given that Li Peng was on the side of the crackdown and redacted
his own diaries with self-serving motives.

A fourth crucial dossier concerns the aftermath. In a meeting
of the Politburo two weeks after the massacre, sympathisers were
compelled to sign self-criticisms designed to establish the party's
united line on these events. A smuggled copy was published only in
summer 2019. A fifth collection of internal documents unearthed by
a Chinese investigative journalist, also in summer 2019, includes an
unpublished letter by six army generals opposing the deployment of
the military in the crackdown. From these sources the historian may
now have some certainty about what happened, when and where;
though it is still not entirely clear why.

TIANANMEN SQUARE, JUNE 1989

On 15 April, Hu Yaobang died suddenly. A reform-minded mod-
erate, Hu had been forced to resign as general secretary in 1987,
after being blamed for being too lenient on student protesters. His
resignation had only garnered him more support from progressives
and intellectuals, who saw him as a force for change. In the wake of
his departure, the hardliner Li Peng had been promoted to premier.
With that, the party appeared to be turning away from the path to
reform, so Hu's death was the spark for the student demonstration
in Tiananmen Square. There were calls for reform, an end to corruption and for more democratic participation in decision making. The

protests continued for a month, bolstered by new protesters arriving to mark the seventieth anniversary of the May 1919 movement.

Meanwhile, the central government had made the fateful error of adopting a hardline stance. In April, the student movement was attacked in the *People's Daily* in an article from the leadership, which is presumed to have been authorised by Deng. The editorial called the movement an anti-Communist Party conspiracy and declared that the students were 'counter-revolutionary and unpatriotic'. Inevitably this only caused fury, and the protests grew. Soon a million protesters massed in the square demanding change. The students were backed by many citizens of Beijing, including factory workers, and the occupation of the square continued for seven weeks. One witness, then a twenty-year-old working for a machine tool company, who had spent three years in the army, recalled the mood of the time:

> To this day I am proud of what the people of Beijing did back then. All those people exposed themselves to the heat in the dog days of summer. To support the students in the heat, many old women brought with them mung bean soup every day on their flatbed three-wheeled carts. My family was the same way. Almost every day my mother sent a free box of eggs, cucumbers and tomatoes. She mumbled as she went, 'Mustn't let those kids get sunstroke in this awful hot weather ...' We didn't know anything about politics, much less overthrowing the government. All we thought was that the words and actions of the students in Tiananmen Square represented the feelings and aspirations of the people. Doesn't everyone want their own country to be healthier? The Communist Party says the same thing, but that's like a cancer patient announcing that cancer is what they wanted all along and calling it perfect health.

In mid-May, a highly publicised state visit took place by the Soviet premier Mikhail Gorbachev, who was engaged in what was to the Chinese communists an ominous process of opening up and reform of the Soviet state, moving towards *glasnost* – democratisation and freedom of speech. On 13 May, Chinese student protesters began hunger strikes in Tiananmen Square, where the welcoming ceremony had been due to be held. Attempting to avert the crisis, the government offered to hold a dialogue with the students, but the meetings quickly fell apart in antagonism and recrimination. When Gorbachev arrived, he was welcomed instead in the airport, a moment of huge embarrassment to the Chinese government. Moreover, there had been a relaxing of press restrictions over this period, allowing many foreign journalists into China to witness Gorbachev's historic visit, and the protests now began to receive a huge amount of coverage in the international media.

So how would the leadership react? Deng Xiaoping was old and frail now; at eighty-five, the same age as Emperor Qianlong when he abdicated. Qianlong had stayed for two more years as the power behind the throne, and Deng had made the same mistake. He had wanted to retire at eighty, but the situation in the country was too unstable, and his name and authority were still needed. Among hardliners like Li Peng, there seems to have been a fear of major disorder breaking out on the lines of the Cultural Revolution – at least that is how Li presented it in his published diaries. The anarchy of the Cultural Revolution was also Deng's nightmare. 'If all one billion of us undertake multi-party elections,' he had told President Bush that spring, 'we will certainly run into a full-scale civil war. Taking precedence over all China's problems is stability.'

In an emergency meeting of five senior party members, martial law was declared. A dissenting voice in the meeting was the general secretary of the party, Zhao Ziyang, a well-known reformer who had represented the country on the international stage in Washington alongside Ronald Reagan with charm and humour, and not a little style. Zhao had urged that the *People's Daily* article be withdrawn, but the hardliner Li Peng argued in Deng's name that to do so would mean a loss of face. Zhao left the meeting refusing to support martial law. Before dawn on 19 May, in a scene of intense drama, Zhao went down to the square to talk to the students through a megaphone in a speech of almost Shakespearean intensity:

You are still young, we are old, you must live healthy and see the day when China accomplishes the Four Modernisations ... You are not like us. We are already old; we do not matter anymore ... All the vigour that you have as young people, we understand as we too were young once. We too protested and we too laid on the tracks without considering the consequences. I beg you once again, think about the future calmly.

The next day Zhao was stripped of his office and put under house arrest. Pressure to intervene now became intense inside the Politburo, but local PLA military units were unwilling to attack their fellow citizens: 'You had these ... touching moments', said one civilian witness, 'of the people appealing to the army to join them, and feeding them, and giving them water, and saying, you know, "Could be your son. Could be your daughter."' So the residents of Beijing effectively took over the city, setting up checkpoints to keep the army out of the centre, as another eyewitness remembers: '"We'll never let them in," [the locals] told me, "only the old people and the children are asleep. The rest of us are in the streets ... the army and the people should be united," so they were rallying now to prevent the army from attacking the people.'

With the PLA troops stationed in Beijing reluctant to confront the demonstrators, the leadership now brought in units from distant provinces who were told the demonstrators were agitating to overthrow the state. Six generals protested, but their letter was suppressed. Finally, on 3 June, after Deng had agreed to the use of force, the army moved in on the centre of Beijing. Foreign eyewitnesses say the main casualties took place not in the square but at the roadblocks on the boulevards to the west. Many died at the Muxidi intersection 4 miles out where electric buses had been placed across a bridge and set on fire to block the army's advance. Chinese eyewitnesses describe panic and terror amid indiscriminate shooting in the streets:

In shock, I turned around and started running back to Tiananmen Square to warn my fellow students of what was coming. I remember reaching one of the main crossings and seeing a man in a white coat heading towards a wounded man. He put up his hand, shouting, 'Don't shoot, I'm a doctor.' They shot him anyway. As I passed one of the main road junctions, people were shouting, 'Fascists!', 'Murderers!' and some were shot.

Dozens of soldiers were also killed, the *Wall Street Journal* reporting shocking scenes: 'At an intersection west of the square, the body of a young soldier, who had been beaten to death, was stripped naked and hung from the side of a bus. Another soldier's corpse was strung up at an intersection east of the square.'

Tiananmen Square itself was cleared in the early hours of 4 June. A column of students left the square under armed guard at 5am, then at 9am the debris of their occupation, the tents and belongings and the famous replica of the Statue of Liberty built by the students, was destroyed by tanks and bulldozers. The loss of life across the city ran into hundreds, according to the government, but may have been two or three thousand, mainly ordinary working-class citizens of Beijing.

According to the account of the British ambassador Richard Evans, Deng was angered and dismayed by the scale of the bloodshed, accusing Li Peng of 'bungling the military operation appallingly'. Nonetheless, as always in his career, he would justify the killings. As for how it looked from the wider ranks of the leadership, in summer 2019 a memoir was published by a high-ranking party member, Li Rui, then retired but one-time secretary of Mao himself. Li had spent twenty years in prison and exile for criticising the Maoist order. During 1989 he lived in an apartment block reserved for party elites near Muxidi junction in western Beijing, where the army began its attack on the demonstrators, and was confronted by hundreds of angry citizens. His diary describes wild gunfire that even killed someone in his block, then panic-stricken phone calls from outraged friends and former colleagues including an old general, Xiao Ke, who had earlier tried to dissuade Deng from bringing the army in:

[My friend] Han Xiong's call was deeply dejecting. What has the party been reduced to? When I hung up, my tears could not stop flowing. An Zhiwen [another friend] called to ask about the situation; he sighed and wondered how it could be that the party did this! The whole day I felt restless and constantly wanted to wail. Xiao Ke predicted: the party will be condemned through the ages and this event will go down in history as a byword for infamy.

On 9 June, Deng reappeared to make his only major public statement about the crushing of the protest: a speech to the troops, part of which was shown on CCTV's main network news that evening. It had been, he said, a 'counter-revolutionary rebellion' intended to overthrow the state, and its suppression had been fully justified. He admitted many troops had been killed, and 'several thousand' injured. Given the mood of the times – in Europe the first moves towards the dismantling of the Iron Curtain were underway – he suggested that the crisis had been 'bound to come sooner or later' and dismissed the ringleaders as 'bad people ... the dregs of society' who had mixed in among the students. In an uncharacteristic moment of self-doubt, Deng also admitted that some of the leadership had not agreed with the actions taken, but he had faith that in the long run they would change their minds. Remarkably, though, most of his speech was devoted to the question of whether the 'Reform and Opening Up' policy of the past ten years was the right course. Inviting the TV audience to ponder that, he then looked to the future. China's goal was to become a moderately prosperous nation by 2050, Deng said, but this was only achievable under the rule of the Communist Party. The events of 4 June had been caused by the party's failure to enforce control; it had been too open-minded in pandering to Western values. Western-style democracy, Deng asserted, was a bourgeois ideology not suited to 'Chinese conditions'. Restrictions would inevitably follow, curtailing freedom of speech, the press and rights of assembly. With that, the party's path to the twenty-first century was laid down.

A week or so later, as we now know from top-secret documents published only in summer 2019, a meeting of thirty senior members of the leadership and elders of the Politburo was held to affirm that the 'turmoil' (*dongluan*) had been a 'counter-revolutionary riot' and to draw a line under the crackdown. Those who had supported Zhao Ziyang were peddling 'ill-considered advice to make whole-sale use of Western theories, put forward by people whose Marxist training is superficial and who don't have a deep understanding of China's national conditions'. Blame for the disaster lay with foreign powers and imperialist interference; even Voice of America radio had fomented discord 'so that China would stay in chaos'; all part of the West's continuing post-Cold War efforts to overthrow communism. Those who had sympathised with the students were compelled to make grovelling mea culpas, though no apology was offered for the killing of so many people. A few days later, these confessions were copied to a larger meeting of 500 members of the central committee and other party officials to study and internalise as the true account of what happened.

This was intended to be the last word on the Tiananmen tragedy. Four important pointers for the future emerge from the records of this meeting. First, the party saw itself as under permanent siege from opponents at home, backed by enemies abroad. Secondly, the weapons in this siege were Western liberal democratic values, which were contrary to the Chinese way. Thirdly, economic reforms were needed to keep the party in power. And, finally, ideological discipline must be enforced; if the party is allowed to become internally divided by factions, it will fall. These remain the party's credo today.

The brutal crushing of the protest in Beijing marked Deng's career forever and stalled the reform process. He retired almost immediately. Afterwards, playing his cards close to his chest, like the expert bridge player he was, he would always justify the military action as essential to prevent China from descending into chaos. As we have seen through the whole story of China, in the grand narrative, the greatest fear is disorder.

Deng died aged ninety-two in 1997. Like Mao, he had over-stayed his welcome. Had he retired in 1985, as he had intended and wished, he would be remembered as one of the greatest figures in modern world history, if not the greatest. A complex, tenacious man, on whom more will come out if his daughters, or his loyal secretary Wang Ruilin, who was with him from the 1950s, produce their own accounts. His legacy has been overshadowed in the West by the events of 1989, but of all national leaders in the twentieth century, he did most to improve the lives of his people, who, let us not forget, make up one fifth of humanity. Indeed, more than any other individual perhaps, he changed the course of history. Today in the grounds of the Communist Party School in Beijing there are two larger-than-life statues. One is of Mao at Yan'an – the young revolutionary; the other, Deng, coat over his shoulder, striding briskly forward – 'the chief engineer'. A third plinth as yet has just a spurt of fire made of red moulded plastic, awaiting the new *hexin*, the next 'core' leader.

CHINA RISING: 1989–2020

After Tiananmen Square, the compromise candidate Jiang Zemin came to power, but the spirit of Deng Xiaoping was still in play. Urged by Deng to accelerate the reform process, Jiang introduced the term 'socialist market economy' in a speech at the 14th National Congress. Meanwhile, China's new premier, Zhu Rongji, proposed that the experiment of the Special Economic Zones be extended to Shanghai – the richest, best-educated and most advanced area of the country, which Deng himself had regretted leaving out of the first wave.

Across the river from Shanghai were nearly 200 square miles of flat land running along the coast: Pudong. Much of it was open country then, with factories and warehouses on the river, housing and desultory blocks of flats in the hinterland. Here the government planned a spectacular programme of development. Today's forest of futuristic skyscrapers accommodates businesses in trade and finance, modern tech companies and industries; there is a huge international airport and even a Disneyland. With a population of over 24 million people, Shanghai is now one of the largest cities in the world, and the single richest urban economy.

Together Jiang and Premier Zhu – a capable economist with a dry sense of humour – presided over double-digit growth in China through the 1990s, and they brought the Chinese people with them. As Zhu said: 'I always considered the social and psychological effect on people. At the end of the day, no matter how many economic theorists were involved, if you can't get people to buy into it, it doesn't stick. Then it fails.'

Their era saw the return to China of Hong Kong and Macao from British and Portuguese rule respectively. By now new forces were in play that would shape the next phase of China's future. In 1999, a self-made internet millionaire, Jack Ma, founded Alibaba, a company specialising in e-commerce, retail, internet sales and the first of China's 21st-century online giants. With a website in English, the global market was Ma's goal from the beginning, with the strap line 'Open Sesame'. Today Alibaba is one of the richest ten companies on the planet, rivalling Google, Apple and Amazon. And at the start of the new millennium, as new Chinese tech companies like Alibaba, Huawei and Tencent reached out across the world, increased prosperity at home saw the growth of a huge Chinese middle class. History was on the move.

In 2002, Jiang was replaced by Hu Jintao, a bureaucrat who had been groomed for the leadership by Deng. By now the reform model had triumphed over the conservatives, completely transforming Chinese society and its economy. But with it came huge divisions in society between rich and poor, and corruption on an unimaginable scale. The political opening up promised in the 1980s, and stifled in 1989, did not develop, and the considerable progress made in developing a workable legal system slowed after 2004 and had stalled by 2008.

It was at this moment, on 10 December 2008, the sixtieth anniversary of the Universal Declaration of Human Rights, that a remarkable document was published online in China and across the world, calling for an independent judiciary, freedom of association, free speech, and the end of one-party rule. Charter 08 was signed by over 300 Chinese intellectuals, human rights activists, lawyers, poets and artists, most of them living inside China. The authors began with a brief but incisive overview of Chinese history from the nineteenth-century 'Self-Strengthening Movement', through the end of empire, the attempts to build a constitution, the New Culture Movement and then, after Japanese invasion and civil war, the descent into totalitarianism under Mao with its huge human cost. Deng's Reform and Opening Up policy, the charter acknowledged, had 'extricated China from the pervasive poverty and absolute total-itarianism of the Mao Zedong era' and increased the standard of living, partially restoring freedoms so that civil society had begun to grow. But the authors spoke of the 'accumulated discontents' of the population at large, in a 'modernisation bereft of universal human values that in the end corrodes human nature and destroys human dignity'. Among the world's great states, they said,

> China alone still clings to an authoritarian way of life and has, as a result, created an unbroken chain of human rights disasters and social crises, which have held back the development of the Chinese people, and hindered the progress of human civilisation. This sit-uation must change. We cannot put off political democratisation reforms any longer.

The charter met with a swift, nervous reaction from China's rulers. State media were forbidden to report it, arrests and interrogations followed, and one of the authors, Liu Xiaobo, was later sentenced to eleven years in prison for 'inciting subversion of state power' (Nobel Peace Prize winner in 2010, Liu would die in custody in 2017). In a speech only days later, President Hu Jintao pointedly conceded the need for more democracy, though not a Western-style multi-party system. The chairman of the National People's Congress said that 'without the single Communist Party in control, a nation as large as China would be torn apart by strife and be incapable of achieving anything'. The facts of the charter's historical analysis, however, were irrefutable, and the challenge to the continued rule of the party was plain. With communism abolished, and Marxist theory discarded, what did the Communist Party actually stand for? If its only goal was to keep power by fostering the pursuit of materialism, was this not indeed the betrayal not only of the people, but of the greatness of Chinese civilisation itself? The authors of Charter o8 concluded:

> Where will China head in the twenty-first century? Continue a 'modernisation' under this kind of authoritarian rule? Or recognise universal values, assimilate into the mainstream civilisation, and build a democratic political system? This is the major decision that now cannot be avoided.

The question was, how would the party respond?

THE AGE OF XI JINPING

In late 2012, a new Chinese leader was appointed – a hitherto unremarkable provincial administrator, Xi Jinping, son of Xi Zhongxun, who had been Deng's ally in Guangdong in 1979. Born in 1953, young Xi had seen the chaos and cruelty of the Cultural Revolution close up; his father had been purged and humiliated, their home wrecked, his mother forced to publicly condemn her husband and sentenced to hard labour; his half sister committed suicide. Xi himself was sent to the Yan'an countryside for 're-education' in 1969 after his father's fall, a time now seen as part of his myth. There, he later claimed, his consolation had been the poetry of Du Fu, and his hero Song Jiang, the bandit leader from the novel *The Water Margin* who was 'neither brilliant nor handsome', but a charismatic team leader. (An admirer of American popular culture, Xi has also named *The Godfather* among his favourite films.) He started his political career as local party chief in the same region and remained there until leaving for Beijing in 1976. Later he held top government jobs in Fujian and Zhejiang where he made his name as a loyal party man willing to pursue corruption and to attract investment.

To the outside observer in late 2012, when Xi took over, it was not clear which way the new leadership would take the country, whether indeed Deng's path of economic reform might at last continue into the realm of politics. But within a year or two the signs became clear. Xi himself, as characterised by one US diplomat, was 'repulsed by the all-encompassing commercialization of Chinese society, with its attendant nouveaux riches, official corruption, loss of values, dignity, and self-respect'. For Xi, the party itself faced an identity crisis; it had lost its way through corruption and a lack of meaningful ideology – a failure of belief in its historic role. So Xi saw his essential job as a rescue mission: 'The tasks our Party faces in reform development and stability are more onerous than ever', he told the Politburo in 2014, 'and the dangers and challenges are more numerous than ever.' Behind this was the question of what the party stood for. 'Ever since Mao's day, and the beginning of Reform and Opening Up,' Xi said, 'we have talked about a "crisis of faith", the sense that rapid growth and political turmoil have cut China off from its moral history.' The answer was to renew the ideology, and the source of renewal would not be Western liberal ideals; it lay, Xi thought, in a re-energised party and in the rediscovery of the greatness of Chinese civilisation. Under Xi, China was to seize back the grand narrative.

Since then Xi has pursued this goal, deploying both hard and soft power to assert the pre-eminence of the party, and backing the massive growth of internal security and surveillance technology. He has articulated a muscular nationalism to glorify the Chinese story on the world stage and has also pursued global influence and regional leadership on several fronts. In 2013 the Chinese occupied islands in the South China Sea through which a third of all global maritime trade flows, building bases and landing strips in the Spratly Islands between Vietnam and the Philippines, uninhabited dots to which China had no historic claim. Wei Yuan's warning to the Qing government in 1844 to pay attention to the *nanyang*, the southern sea (above page 402), was finally being heeded.

The same year, President Xi announced the 'Belt and Road' initiative, a trillion-dollar infrastructure project to link China to the world by land and sea, focused especially on the land routes of the old Silk Road. It has been characterised by observers as 'a Chinese Marshall Plan, a state-backed campaign for global dominance, a stimulus package for a slowing economy, and a massive marketing campaign for something that was already happening – Chinese investment around the world'. It is an infrastructure project of extraordinary scale and ambition.

At home, the state has become more and more intrusive in people's lives, particularly so in places like Xinjiang, where the current clampdown on the Uighur minority has seen a massive assault on Muslim culture and local languages, with blanket facial recognition technology and mass incarceration disturbingly similar to Mao's prison and re-education camps. In daily life in the big cities of mainland China, the visitor is rarely aware of the coercive power of the state, whether army or police. But behind the scenes the pressure has been ratcheted up with censorship and surveillance. Forbidden topics for the nation's students, journalists, lawyers and intellectuals focus on the 'Seven Taboos'. Announced in 2013 in a secret memo known as 'Document Number 9', these take the form of explicit rejection of the main demands of Charter 08, including not only universal human rights (which had been guaranteed in the constitution in 2004), press freedom, citizens' rights, and the independence of the judiciary, but also any discussion of the idea of civil society. Also ruled out is discussion of 'the Communist Party's historical disasters' and of the 'Privileged Capitalistic Class', by which they mean the 'red aristocracy' who have made fortunes out of the recent growth of China's economy. The memo was condemned by one Chinese commentator as a 'stunning retrogression in ideology'. The president, it turns out, is not so much the son of Xi Zhongxun but the grandson of Mao – or, as one joke doing the rounds in Beijing has it, 'Mao's revenge on Deng'.

Among the seven 'unmentionables', by forbidding intellectuals, journalists and the media to dwell on the party's past disasters, Xi was paving the way for the resuscitation of Maoist ideals, especially the Maoist-Leninist tradition of 'democratic centralism' and the ruthless suppression of dissent. The party's biggest disasters – the Great Leap Forward, the Great Famine and the Cultural Revolution – were in no small part the product of the mentality of Mao himself. But now Xi has reiterated that 'if we give up Maoism, the foundation of the party will be gone'. In 2018, indeed, Xi put forward his now famous theory that, looking at events since 1949 as a whole, the party should not differentiate between the pre-reform and post-reform periods: 'While socialism with Chinese characteristics was initiated during the time of Reform and Open Door [i.e. post 1978], it was established on the basis of more than twenty years of socialist construction beforehand. These two periods should not be arbitrarily cut off one from the other – and one period should not be used to negate the other.'

Politically, therefore, the absolute power of the Communist Party has been reaffirmed. China today, we might say, is a hybrid Confucian–Leninist state with a market economy enriching its middle-class support. China's middle class, estimated to be around 400 million strong and growing, has now overtaken in size the entire population of the United States. But while the economic prosperity of so many citizens is improving, the government in parallel has articulated an authoritarian conception of 'right behaviour'; uncannily resonating the edicts of the Qing emperors, but this time with the aid of modern technology. In an almost direct lineal descent from the registration system first enacted under the First Emperor, today the tax records and social value indices of each citizen are encoded onto the national ID cards, which are needed for most operations, even booking a train. In 2018, facial recognition technology was introduced at all major airports, and in many public places. Such high-tech surveillance capitalism reaching into everyone's lives encourages people to do as the government wishes without recourse to open threats, but with the ever-present warning of punishment behind it. It is an apparatus of control of a size and complexity unmatched in human history, but one that has so far been accepted by the mass of the people in exchange for stability, prosperity, good public services, leisure and jobs. In 2017, Xi abolished Deng's time limits on the tenure of party leadership and put the creation of a professional bureaucracy further on hold.

THE CHINA DREAM?

The new dynasty founded by Mao, if we may call it that, for now seems relatively secure. Like the Manchus, after a period of immense disruption and suffering, and the brutal enforcement of an allegiance maintained by wide-ranging coercive powers, it has brought stability and a huge leap in the standard of living, accompanied by an unparalleled demographic shift from the countryside to the cities.

The next stage of national revival will have three main planks; the continued pre-eminence of the party, the sustaining of economic growth, and a major push to assert the historic greatness of Chinese civilisation and identity. But all will depend on the government's continuing balancing act. Today the top 1 per cent of the population own half of the national wealth; so, as Deng knew it would, the 'get rich quick' policy has skewed in favour of the party and the rich, who are often the same people. So far, the general public have accepted that imbalance in exchange for better governance, management, public services and infrastructure, and less corruption. But the party must continue to deliver these in order to be seen as legitimate. The middle classes are being given the perks of a successful economy, good food and housing, holidays, foreign travel, high-quality education for their children, commodities and luxuries that were unimaginable forty years ago. But those who step out of line will be in trouble, even when expressing casual online opinions, and the repression of journalists, lawyers and human rights protesters will get smarter and tighter. China spends more money on internal security than on external defence, and certain minorities will be repressed even more harshly: whether Xinjiang Uighurs, Tibetans, or religions deemed to be 'non-Chinese'. But the vast majority will see a China with more freedoms. Responding to the people's desires may not mean more democracy in Western terms, but there will be more consultation. And for Chinese people the world is opening up, too; in 2017, more than 600,000 students studied abroad and 130 million Chinese people travelled to foreign countries; in 2018, the figure for the latter was 160 million. The prediction for 2025 is an almost unbelievable 730 million. Such enormous numbers will change Chinese attitudes more than previous generations could ever have imagined.

The inherent danger of continuing growth on this scale, of course, is a further phase of environmental disaster when the country has yet to deal with the catastrophic pollution caused by Mao's war on nature, which left massive problems in the loss of cultivable land and failures of the food chain. This is the biggest single concern openly voiced by the Chinese public. A recent TV documentary on the issue had 200 million online views before it was taken down by the government. In the past forty years China's GDP has increased almost seventy times and carbon emissions are up ninefold. China has 20 per cent of the world's population but only 11 per cent of its land is arable. It is estimated that between 15 and 20 per cent of that land is heavily contaminated. Just how serious this is can be seen everywhere today: half the rivers fouled with industrial effluent; the pollution of the water table and of huge swathes of farmland. The cost of cleaning up the soil alone is estimated to be well over a trillion dollars. Hence President Xi's commitment to the Davos climate accords, and his stated ambition for China to develop an 'ecological civilisation', is serious. Here too the party believes that only a centrist one-party state can mobilise the resources to tackle the massive and rapid changes needed in the next thirty years to save the environment. And they may be right: paradoxically, after becoming an environmental disaster zone in the second half of the twentieth century, China is already making great steps forward in solar power and low-emission technology, and intends to become the global leader in environmental protection by 2030. If the planet is to be saved from climate breakdown, then China will have to be in the forefront.

THE MANDATE RENEWED?

Over the past three centuries, the era of Western colonialism and imperialism has wrought both dynamic change and immense destruction across the world, rubbing out cultures that have often taken millennia to evolve. The great traditional civilisations of China, India and Islam, whose peoples make up the bulk of the population of the planet, have responded in different ways to the traumatic impact of colonialism and the challenges of modernity, with its new technologies and new ways of seeing. With no tradition of a common political culture and such wide regional, cultural and linguistic diversity, Africa (which is three times the size of China, with a comparable population) was hit hardest by the impact. India, which will soon surpass China in population, is only now beginning to recover from the colonial era and the deliberate impoverishment of the country, while still wrestling with profound questions of cultural identity and its own huge linguistic and cultural differences. China, on the other hand, always had the great advantage of its long-nurtured sense of a common Han culture and the Chinese language and script, as well as its common political traditions. But even then, after the long period of tentative 'self-strengthening' in the nineteenth century, China too was rocked by the impact of modernity in the twentieth, and is still negotiating its own path out of the multiple crises it has faced during its 150-year age of revolution. Now, though, as Mao put it in October 1949, 'China has stood up'.

China's story, which we have traced in these pages over four millennia, is one of almost incredible human drama; the greatest such story in history, one is tempted to say. It is a tale of the efforts of the Chinese people and their rulers to build stable societies, to create justice, order and beauty; to make art, literature and poetry; and to nurture the pleasures of life while struggling with the demons as well as the benefits bequeathed by the ancestors. In the 1670s, in what is still China's greatest manifesto against despotism, Huang Zongxi looked at the pattern of Chinese history and concluded that the necessary reform of China's mechanisms of government centred on the rule of law: 'Without government by law there can be no government by men.' If he were alive today, Huang would no doubt still hold to that opinion; admiring the remarkable achievements of the modern Chinese state, yet seeing uncanny parallels with the imperial order of the Late Ming and Early Qing. For today's centralised bureaucratic state in some ways has not escaped certain deep-seated historical tendencies in Chinese history, and has reproduced the despotic structures of the past whose development we have traced in this book.

The People's Republic celebrated its seventieth anniversary in 2019. Now the party has set its sights on 1 October 2049, the 100th anniversary of the Revolution, a date to mark the consolidation of China's latest dynasty. The pattern of Chinese history has its own rhythms, longer and slower-moving than in other cultures. To end, then, perhaps it is appropriate to reflect on that different order of time. Since prehistory the Chinese saw those rhythms mirrored in the patterns of the cosmos, in the movements of the stars and planets, and especially in the rare five-planet clusters that were seen to mark the changes of dynasties: the founding of the Xia in 1953 BCE, the Shang in 1576 BCE and the Zhou in 1059 BCE, or the later conjunctions that inaugurated the Han and the Song. While few today believe the heavens intervene directly in our earthly affairs, perhaps it is still worth noting, as the ancients would have done, the timing of the next five-planet gathering in the sequence of 516-year cycles that were held to affirm Heaven's Mandate – or to take it away. The date is 8 September 2040.

By then, no doubt, the path of the next cycle of history will have become clear – for China, as indeed for the entire world.

AFTERWORD

In October 2019 when the Peoples Republic celebrated its 70th anniversary, it remained confident in its international standing, the second largest economy in the world, despite growing concern over the economic impact of its trade war with the US. But at that moment events were overtaken by a sudden and unexpected crisis. By mid-November, a mysterious pneumonia-like infection had been reported in the city of Wuhan in the central province of Hubei. Through the summer of 2020, the coronavirus became a global pandemic with an enormous loss of life and huge and ongoing damage to economies across the world.

In China, the epidemic exposed both the weaknesses and the strengths of bureaucratic centralism. The outbreak was initially covered up by the local communist party in Hubei, who fatefully delayed lockdown of the city until late January 2020. For a time the central government in Beijing also prevaricated, clamping down on reporting of the outbreak. By the time China shared the genetic sequence of COVID-19 with the World Health Organization on 12 January, the infection had already spread to Europe and America, and subsequent outbreaks there were soon followed by a surge of anti-Chinese feeling across the world, to heights not seen since the 1989 Tiananmen Square democracy protests, and causing great damage to China's reputation in the world. The obvious questions followed: if the PRC could not be honest about a matter of such vital importance to global health, how could it be trusted in other fields, such as the controversial role of the telecoms giant Huawei in the development of an international 5G network?

Within China, the initial local and state reaction was treated by the general public as an epitome of the party's secrecy and suppression of free speech. On 30 December 2019 Dr Li Wenliang at Wuhan Central Hospital had attempted to warn his colleagues in his private WeChat social media group of a potential outbreak of a SARS-like respiratory illness, but he was accused by the party in Wuhan of making false statements and disturbing public order, and he was swiftly forced to retract his statement by the party in Wuhan. On 8 January he published his letter of admonition online, telling the Beijing-based media group *Caixin*: 'a healthy society should not just have one voice,'

After Dr Li's death due to the virus, millions of people responded with fury on WeChat and other online platforms; over the night of his death there were 1.5 billion views of the story on the microblogging site Weibo. One group of middle school teachers in Chengdu cited the novel *La Peste* by Albert Camus: 'Without truth, the plague cannot be fought.' In a culture uniquely alert to symbolic meanings, the disease had become a metaphor. On 4 February Professor Xu Zhangrun of Tsinghua University published an extraordinary online attack on the party and on President Xi himself, in language full of classical allusions whose subtext was familiar to all. In it he spoke of the 'volcanic' popular fury against a totalitarian system that had 'hollowed out the moral fabric of the nation' and had spread the crisis by blocking vital public information. In doing this Professor Xu belonged to the tradition of loyal remonstrance that we have observed through this book.

Meanwhile, with public anger growing, the central government in Beijing changed track and the sweeping powers of the party were brought into play. On 23 January, a lockdown was imposed on Wuhan and other cities in Hubei-affecting about 57 million people. Local party officials organised food drops on a street by street basis, medical staff were flown in from around the country, the army was mobilised and hospitals built from scratch in a matter of days.

So central power and control, enforced through local party structures, brought planning, coordination and mobilisation unimaginable in the West. The mood of the people on social media changed from fury to compliance and cooperation – although in reality there was no possibility of opting out as track and trace is part of everyday life in China, where even buying a train ticket requires an identity card and all journeys are recorded on government databases. But still, news bulletins carried a myriad stories of social solidarity and mutual help typical of a culture which has traditionally asserted the primacy of the collective over the individual.

In Wuhan, a city of over 11 million people, the lockdown lasted 76 days. By May 2020, although movement was still controlled, China was working again, but with massive disruption to the economy, and many tens, possibly hundreds, of millions unemployed. A new outbreak in Beijing towards midsummer underlined that without a vaccine there were no guarantees that the plague had been fully contained.

So the disease threw a harsh light into the workings of the regime. The Chinese system had responded to the pandemic by deploying the full powers of the centralised state; the Leninist PRC reacted in accordance with what we might call its political DNA. But the crisis could not have more clearly demonstrated that, as one commentator put it, 'when China sneezes, the world catches a cold'.

How then will the long-term effects of the coronavirus crisis play out? With the world's main economic blocs reeling, the international balance of power is in a particularly unstable and unpredictable moment. The COVID-19 outbreak has left China's main economic rivals badly wounded, and they will take time to recover. In many eyes, this has presented China with a historic opportunity. Since 1979 China's view of foreign policy had been the 'crouching tiger hidden dragon' principle of Deng Xiaoping. China, Deng counselled, should lie low and bide its time, repairing the damage of the Mao years and slowly building up its economic strength while reforming its structures of governance and its legal system. But since 2013 President Xi's muscular and nationalistic brand of politics has seen

China vie for global leadership with aggressive foreign initiatives from the South China Sea to the Himalayas, and from Africa to the Belt and Road in Central Asia. Could 2020 then mark a tipping point in the balance of power?

As the disease took its grip on the world through the summer of 2020, this question became the subject of intense debate in the West. Was the visible erosion of US leadership, wealth and reputation the sign that American global dominance which had lasted unchallenged for over a century, was now on the wane? In the decades ahead would the PRC take its place again as the leading world power, as it had been under the Qing in the eighteenth century? And would China be able to rise to the huge responsibilities that come with such a role, not only political and economic, but moral? Open minded and outward going, as it had been for example under the Tang, embracing a vision of positive interdependence and enriching both itself and other cultures with its civilisation?

The signs in summer 2020 were not good: under cover of COVID-19, a confrontation in the Himalayan borderland with India was followed by renewed threats towards Taiwan and a long-planned move against the judicial independence of Hong Kong, which has sent alarm bells ringing around the world. Reneging on a treaty it no longer regards as binding, China it appeared was not concerned with how it is seen, taking its lead from what President Xi is fond of describing as the 'Chinese Way', a term which is used specifically to justify the party's bureaucratic dictatorship over the norms of Western liberal democracy.

But as with all dynasties through Chinese history, the path to the future is contingent on the continuance of its system: in this case the Leninist party bureaucracy and the ideas that underwrite it. To maintain its position, the system needs to continue to deliver growth. Big as its economy is, China's per capita income is still that of a middle-level nation, Gabon or the Dominican Republic. Its achievements to be sure have been astonishing; according to the World Bank, since 1979 850 million Chinese people have been lifted out of extreme poverty, and the party has set its sights on eradicating it by 2020. But many are still struggling and the gap between rich and poor is enormous and growing, with wealth concentrated in the hands of a small elite. With economic problems deepened by COVID-19, in summer 2020 the party abandoned its growth targets for the first time in the thirty years since it set them. But then in spring 2021 China announced a return to strong post-Covid growth, the only major global economy to do so. Forceful central control coupled with the solidarity and collective ethos of the Chinese people had pulled them through the epidemic.

The second great issue for the party is the matter of allegiance, and the continuing debate about democratisation. Can China's rise as a world power continue without further political and legal reform to match the economic opening up which has taken place since 1979? Many observers, both Western and Chinese, think not. Since 2011 there has been debate inside China about the role of constitutional democracy and rule of law, including voices inside the party who have criticised the leadership for its denial of free speech and impartial justice, and the failure of its anti-corruption campaign. The party's powerful Central Commission of Discipline and Control has even admitted that their anti-corruption drive with its Legalist punishments ('kill a chicken to scare the monkeys') has been thwarted because cadres have not internalised the essentially Confucian principles of benevolence honesty and virtue. And that, of course, brings us back to the ancient ideals of Chinese civilisation that we have followed through this book. Here too, at this moment in 2021 the signs are hard to read, with the government of Xi Jinping not only reinforcing its Leninist order at home, but with increasing stridence promoting its idea of a new global order abroad with 'alternative global normal and standards." The stated mid century goal of Xi Jinping's government is 'a rejuvenation of China as a global leader in terms of composite national strength and international influence" through the dictatorship of the Communist Party- almost a 21st century version of the ancient 'all under Heaven" when the 'Great Way' will prevail-though now an authoritarian Leninist path. The direct challenge to the USA is now plain.

To conclude this afterword, in the middle of COVID-19, let us then return to the remarkable British Naval Intelligence account of China during the Second World War, the Civil War, and the Communist victory of 1949, out of which today's China has emerged (above page 455). In their vision of China's future, the authors chose to highlight not disorder or despotism, but the deep enduring characteristics of the Chinese world view, for example, the 'strong democratic element in Chinese institutions and outlook on life', in which 'the rights of the people and the obligations of rulers have been the themes of China's greatest sages from the Classical age'. Looking ahead beyond the immediate postwar world, they suggested that a 'liberal-minded intelligentsia' driven by China's national self-consciousness, and 'strong tendency to cultural unity', would lead in a future democratic republic to 'a new and perhaps even greater China'. The Chinese intelligentsia has taken many blows since then, but despite the devastating attacks on civil society – even in the last few years – it has not been broken, and after the thirty tumultuous years of the communist experiment, and the Reform and Opening Up period that followed, that hope remains. For China, there are still many paths to the future.

Despite current pessimistic views of the short term, then, it would be foolish in the long term to underestimate the Chinese people. Their traditional civilisation, 'this culture of ours,' was above all else in its ideals a moral order. And as Confucius said long ago, an order that is not moral will, in the end, lose the allegiance on which all effective governance depends.

ACKNOWLEDGEMENTS

I would like to thank the many friends and colleagues in China with whom I have worked over the past eight years, especially Mandy Bueschlen Li and David Tong. I would also like to thank the many Chinese people whose interviews, conducted between 2013 and 2019, have given my text such a sense of the living culture; my main debts there are cited in the notes. In the UK, I would first like to thank the staff at the SOAS Library who were unfailingly kind and helpful: it is a delight to work there. I am grateful too for the generous support of the University of Manchester. At Maya Vision, Tina Sijiao Li, Suzanna Thornton and John Cranmer, who worked on *The Story of China* series, have continued to give their expertise, help and advice. For their assistance in editing and cutting down my longer first draft, my special thanks are to Rebecca Dobbs, Fotini Papatheodorou and Mina Wood, and to Mina at a later stage for her many acute observations and criticisms, and her improvements both to my text and the bibliography. At Simon and Schuster, Iain MacGregor was behind the project from the start, Ian Marshall took it on, and my unflappable editor Kaiya Shang saw it through with tremendous patience, skill and care. Bea Joubert found the pictures and Martin Lubikowski drew the very clear and informative maps. I'd also like to thank my wonderful agent Catherine Clarke at Felicity Bryan – the historian's dream agency! PBS, CPNB, BBC and BBC Studios commissioned the original film series – thanks, too, for their support. Finally, I am especially grateful to Frances Wood, Rana Mitter, Tom Holland, Peter Frankopan and William Dalrymple, who very generously read my draft. It cannot be too strongly stressed that all errors of facts or interpretation that remain are mine.

NOTES

These notes cite texts mainly in English, and also contain acknowledgements to numerous interviews conducted in China between 2013 and 2019.

PREFACE

1   **novel of the millennium:** Hawkes (trans.) (1973).
2   **'this culture of ours':** the phrase comes from a famous passage in Confucius's *Analects*, 9.5, Leys (1997), 39 – on which see Bol (1992), 1–6.
        Simon Leys: in *The Burning Forest* (1988), 42; his books from *Les Habits neufs du président Mao* (1971) to *Chinese Shadows* (1978) were a bracingly sceptical orientation for my generation of students, journalists and historians, and remain so; for a great and profoundly humane collection of essays, see Leys (2013).
        Chinese attitudes to the past: Leys (2013) 285–301; Mote (1973).
        Shimao: see below, 30–31; for **Taosi**, below 32–5.

PROLOGUE

7   **midwinter 1899:** my account of the ceremony relies on Bredon (1922), 132–49, with a plan of the disposition of the ritualists for the ceremony at 134; Arlington and Lewisohn (1935), 105–13; Soothill (1913, 274, and 1951, 66–8); plus the brilliant and indispensable guide to today's Beijing, Aldrich (2006), 229–31.
        the Guangxu emperor: for the edicts quoted here, J. Chang (2013), 175–90.
8   *Peking Gazette:* https://digital.soas.ac.uk/content/AA/00/00/06/08/00017/AA00000608_1899.pdf; https://primarysources.brillonline.com/browse/the-peking-gazette/translation-of-the-peking-gazette-for-1899;pkga1899; see in general Harris (2018): https://brill.com/view/book/9789004361003/BP000036.xml?language=en
9   **the situation is perilous:** J. Chang (2013), 307–8.
10   **deprived childhood:** for details, J. Chang (2013), 175–81.
11   **'radiant in its isolation':** Bredon (1922) 132, for whom the altar was 'close to the secret wonders of the earth', 149.

12   **English missionary**: Soothill (1913), 274.
13   **terraces**: for the layout of the ritual, Bredon (1922), 134.
        Qianlong: Rawski and Rawson (eds) (2005), 118.
14   **the antecedents**: Granet (1926), 242–51; G. F. Hudson in Soothill
        (1951), xiii–xviii; on the prehistoric roots of the myth of Sage Kingship
        which will be a theme in this book, the essays of Liu Zehua (2013–14),
        with the commentary of Yuri Pines.
15   **Cixi edict**: for the text, J. Chang (2013), 307–8.
16   **'swarming with … discontented … idlers'**: https://eu.desmoinesregister.
        com/story/opinion/columnists/2017/05/26/amazing-adventures-iowas
        -first-ambassador-china/344105001/

1: ROOTS

Overviews: for histories of early China in general, Ebrey (2010),
10–35; Hansen (2015), 19–55; Li Feng (2013), 15–40; for a richly
illustrated overview of the prehistory, Allan (ed.) (2005). On the broad
interpretation of the path to political authority, K. C. Chang (1983);
on historiographical issues of the early kingship, Liu Zehua's essays
(2014); for further remarks on the replication of China's despotic
pattern, de Bary (1993), 1–3; Levenson (1958), 162–3. For primary
texts across the whole story, de Bary, *Sources of Chinese Tradition*, 2
vols (1960 and later eds), cited henceforth in these notes as *Sources*.
Online, key early sources are also available in the Chinese Text
Project, https://ctext.org. For a guide to the sources, Wilkinson (2017).

21   **Yellow River Power**: Keightley (2000), 113–14.
        Will there be floods?: Keightley (2000), 114; on flood myths in general,
        Lewis (2006).
        oracle bones: Li Feng (2013), 90–111; Keightley (2000); and the first
        remarkable publication in the West, Chalfant (1906).
        the flood of 1048: see Zhang Ling (2016); on 1099–1102, 198–9.
22   **Zhongguo**: on the meaning and antiquity of the term, Wilkinson
        (2017), 4,1 Box 2.
24   **Zhoukou temple festival**: my account is based on a visit in April 2015;
        my thanks to the temple management for their hospitality; on the
        survival of local religion, Overmyer (ed.) 2003, Overmyer (2009) and
        Yang (2005); on temple fairs and markets, Cooper (2013); for a recent
        account of the return of religion in China, Johnson (2017).
25   *Bai Hu Tong*: Loewe (ed.) (1993), 347–56
        the goddess Nüwa: Yang (2005) 170–75; Lewis (2006), 110–45;
        Pankenier (2013), 383–403; on her connection with fertility myths,
        Lewis (2006), 121–5, and with marriage, 134–7.
26   **Nüwa town**: interviews conducted at the Huaiyang shrines near
        Zhoukou in April 2015. My recording of the song has been augmented
        by the lyric collected in 1993 by Yang Lihui and printed in her
        pathbreaking *Handbook* (2005). Nüwa's temple at Nieduzhen Henan
        was massively restored in 2016. Aspects of women's culture there and

at Zhoukou include writing resembling Nüshu, the 'women's writing' unique to Jiangyong County in the southern tip of Hunan, where the remarkable thread-like lines were transmitted through 'sworn sisters' or mothers and daughters: https://en.unesco.org/courier/2018-1/nushu-tears-sunshine. The last native practitioner of Nüshu in Hunan died in 2004: https://web.archive.org/web/20121104181654/http://news.xinhuanet.com/english/2004-09/23/content_2012172.htm. For a study, see Idema (2009).

28–9 **Gu Zuyu:** K. C. Chang in Allan (ed.) (2005), 126.

30 **Yangshao and Longshan cultures:** Li Feng (2013); Liu Li (2004).
Shimao: Jaang Li et al.(2018), 1008–22.

32 **Taosi:** Li Feng (2013), 31–5; Pankenier (2013), 17–37; He Nu (2018), available online at https://www.sciencedirect.com/science/article/pii/S2352226717300247

34 **Sima Qian:** on king Yao and astronomy, Pankenier (2013), 218.

35 **the myth of King Yu:** summary by Sima Qian, Watson, *Records* (1969), 230–31; Lewis (2006), 28–43. On recent discoveries in archaeo-astronomy, Pankenier (2013); on the antiquity of 'the tribute of Yu' story, 401–8; for a new extraordinarily ambitious survey, Li Min (2018), 396–448.
Yu's tracks: the tradition in the Book of Documents is said to have been compiled by Confucius from older texts; for the text online with the translation of James Legge: https://ctext.org/shang-shu/tribute-of-yu

36 **the story of King Yu:** interview at Yu temple, Yuwang Tai, Kaifeng, April 2014 (a temple built after the flood of 1517 on a site going back to the Western Han).

37 **bronze tureen:** Li Feng (2013), 50–51; discussed by Li Min (2018), 309–401.
Marcel Granet: *Fêtes et chansons* (1929), 155–74; on forms of recital, *Festivals and Songs* (1932), 207–23.

38 **flood myths:** Yang (2005) 21–3, 73–4, 114–16; Lewis (2006), 104–5, 191–2; on Yu the Great, 38–9.
Jishi Gorge discoveries: Qingling Wu et al. (2016); summary ref to article: https://science.sciencemag.org/content/353/6299/579; photos, and for aerials: https://blogs.agu.org/landslideblog/2016/08/05/jishi-gorge-landslide1/
flood impact: Chen Yunzhen (2012) with: https://www.ncbi.nlm.nih.gov/pmc/articles/PMC3472015/

39 **the Xia and Erlitou:** Li Feng (2013), 41–65; Pankenier (2013), 122–48; Allan (2007a); Liu Li and Xu Hong (2007), 886–901; my thanks to Dr Xu Hong for showing me around the site and the finds store at Erlitou.
carbon dates: compare with Pankenier (2013), 193–204.

40 **the Forbidden City:** on extraordinary architectural continuity from the Bronze Age, R. L. Thorp in Steinhardt (1984), 59–68.

41 **Anyang:** there is an enormous literature: the key texts in English are Li Chi (1975) and K. C. Chang (1980); summary by K. C. Chang in

Allan (ed.) (2005), 150–171. See too now Li Feng (2013), 66–89. On more recent discoveries such as Lady Fu Hao's tomb, Allan (ed.) (2005) and Ebrey (2010), 26–7; Fu Hao's itineraries, along with those of the last king, Di Xin, were untangled by Dong Zuobin (1945); for images of the dig, *Yin Xu Fa Jue Zhao Pian Xuan Ji 1928–1937* ('Historic Photos from the Anyang Excavations 1928–1937'), Taipei (2012): http://archeodata.sinica.edu.tw/1_2/HPftAE/index.html

42   **the climate:** Keightley (2000), 1–8.
    the wind: Creel (1937), 181; Keightley (2000), 3, note 10, and 125–8.

43   **divination survivals:** Keightley (1978), 9.
    the origins of the script: Goepper (1996) and Boltz (2011).

44   **first ancestors:** the phrase is Keightley's (2014), 87–99 and 155–206.
    offerings: Keightley (2000), 113–14; on beheading sacrifices, 26–8, 88–9.
    survivals in folk religion: S. Allan, 'The Shang Foundations of Modern Chinese Folk Religion' in Allan and Cohen (1979), 1–21; Keightley (2014a), 155–206, and (2014b), 87–99.

46   **So with the Shang:** the broad picture, K. C. Chang (1983); Keightley (2000), 129.

2: THE GREAT WAR OF THE SHANG

47–8   **the Zhou background:** Li Feng (2013), 112–39; Ebrey (2010), 30–37; Hansen (2015) 38–55.

48–49   **chronology:** for new discoveries in archaeo-astronomy, Pankenier (2013), 196–202.

49   **key account:** the 'Lost Book' is analysed by Shaughnessy (1980).
    Li Gui: Li Feng (2013), 120–21.

50   **chariot warfare:** Shaughnessy (1988); in Anatolia, NE Syria, Mycenaean Greece and Rig Vedic India, the introduction of chariot warfare technology is also Late Bronze Age.

50–53   all quotations are from Shaughnessy (1980), 57–60.

52   **'King Wu descended':** translation by Shaughnessy (1980–81), 59; on violence and blood sacrifice as a root of Shang civilisation, Campbell (2018), which came to my attention after this book went to proof stage.

53   **Shangqiu:** Murowchick (2001) and Des Forges et al. (eds) (2010), a very useful look at three ancient cities of the Henan heartland. My visit to the sites in and around Shangqiu was in April 2014.

54   **the word *shang*:** on the wide contemporary semantic range, K. C. Chang (1995), 69–77.

55   **'Great City Shang':** Murowchick (2001), 1–2.

56   **itineraries:** Dong (1945). My thanks to Suzanna Thornton for her translations and deciphering the journeys on Dong's sketch maps.

57   **Ebo Tai:** Hu Zhongwei (1999), 231–4.

58   **resistivity survey:** Murowchick (2001), 10–12.

59   **Changzikou:** 'A Western Zhou Tomb at Taiqinggong, Luyi Henan',

Henan Provincial Institute of Cultural Relics and Archaeology: https://
www.degruyter.com/view/j/char.2001.1.issue-1/char.2001.1.1.137/
char.2001.1.1.137.xml

3: THE MANDATE OF HEAVEN

60   **Luoyang:** new finds on the Zhou, Li Feng (2013), 112–61.
61   **horses and chariots:** Shaughnessy (1988).
       Zhou inscription: Ibid.; on the Iron Age aristocracy in China in
       general, Li Feng (2013), 169–82.
62   **'The hero Fang-shu ...':** adapted from Waley (trans.) (1954), 128–9.
       'the ages before the Qin ...': Burton Watson (1958) 182–6.
63   **the rise of bureaucratic despotism:** Li Feng (2013), 195–206.
       the classics: these are *The Book of Changes* (trans. R. Wilhelm); *The
       Book of Songs* (trans. A. Waley); *The Book of Documents* (trans. C.
       Waltham); https://ctext.org/shang-shu; *The Book of Rites*: https://
       ctext.org/liji; and the *Spring and Autumn Annals*, a chronicle from
       Confucius's native Qufu (trans. B. Watson 1989).
64   **the Mandate of Heaven:** on the idea of the mandate, Allan (2007a),
       1–46; Li Feng (2013), 143–4; on the cosmo-political background,
       Pankenier (2013), 193–219.
65   **monarchism:** fundamental are the essays by Liu Zehua (ed. Yuri Pines)
       (2014); see too the suggestive essay of Liu Zehua (2015) on the Sage
       King and Mao.
66   **Master Kong:** Leys (trans.) (1997); Li Feng (2013), 207–207; for a
       cautionary view on the question of the authenticity of *The Analects*,
       a recent review by C. Harbsmeier: https://www.cuhk.edu.hk/ics/
       journal/articles/v68p171.pdf
67   **Qufu town digs:** Lu Liancheng in Allan (ed.) (2005), 213–14.
68   **the origins of Confucius:** Eno (2003), 1–11; Li Feng (2013), 210–16.
69   **'When the Way prevails':** *Analects* 16.2, Leys (trans.) (1997), 81; Pines
       (2009), 28.
71   **Canetti:** *Analects*, Leys (trans.) (1997), xxi; as Sima Qian
       remarked: 'whenever I read Master Kong I see him before me as the
       person he was.'
72   **the Axial Age:** Jaspers (1953); on Duperron, Waley (1963), 11–29.
       Bellah and Joas (2012) is a recent major overview, but we await a
       convincing account from Iron Age specialists as opposed to historians
       of comparative religion and philosophy.

4: THE FIRST EMPEROR

75   For background, Li Feng (2013), 229–56; for a fresh overview of recent
       archaeology, Lewis (2009a); on the rise of the Qin, an illustrated
       survey, Xu Pingfang in Allan (2005), 249–88; R. Yates in Portal (ed.)
       (2007), 30–57; 'Qin History Revisited', Pines *et al.* (eds) (2013), 1–34.
76   **Mozi and Lao Tzu:** Pines (ed. & trans.) (2017), 15–16.

76-7   *the Book of Lord Shang*: See now Pines (ed. & trans.) (2017), 19-24.
78   **the Qin annexed the Zhou**: Dawson (ed.) (1994), 67.
        the rise of the Qin: Li Feng (2013), 245-8; R. Yates in Portal (ed.)
        (2007), 36 (map) and 53-6 (roads); on the king himself, Dawson (ed.)
        (1994), 3-9; on his deeds, *Annals of Qin*, Dawson (ed.) (1994), 63-97.
79   **'the Qin took over all within the seas'**: Pines (2012), 20.
        'The house of Zhou is destroyed': Pines (2009), 19.
        roads and long walls: Portal (ed.) (2007), 79, with map; Dawson (ed.)
        (1994), 55-61; Li Feng (2013), 229-56.
80-81   **burying the scholars and burning books**: Dawson (ed.) (1994), 77
        (book burning) and 80 (burials); the story has been doubted, but on
        legalist book burning, see de Bary, *Sources* I, 140-41.
81   **Mr Tui the benevolent magistrate**: Barbieri-Low and Yates, Vol. II
        (2015), 1332-58.
82-4   **The Case of the Murderer Tong**: Lau and Staack (eds & trans) (2016),
        228-46, whose translation I have gratefully used.
84   **the finding of the Liye strips**: Yates (2012-13), 291-329.
85   **Nanyang householder**: C. Sanft in Pines *et al.* (eds) (2015), 249-72,
        at 251; on Han scribes, see the discussion in Barbieri-Low and Yates
        (2015), 1084-1109.
86-8   **Qin soldiers' letters**: translation by E. Giele in Richter (2015), 457-63.
88   **Mrs Qing's cinnabar factory**: R. Yates, 'Soldiers, Scribes and Women'
        in Li Feng and Branner (eds) (2011), 367.
89   **'Whenever Qin wiped out'**: Dawson (ed.) (1994), 77-8.
        Epang Palace: Dawson (ed.) (1994), 67 and 77-8; on the archaeology:
        Hiromi Kinoshita in Portal (ed.) (2007), 83-93. For the texts of the
        inscribed edicts, Dawson (ed.) (1994), 67-74.
89-90   **Inspired by the Greeks?**: J. Rawson in Portal (ed.) (2007), 129;
        Nickel (2013).
91   **the twelve bronze figures**: Dawson (ed.) (1994), 66; J. Rawson in Portal
        (ed.), 128-9, Nickel (2013).
92   **Belle the Potter**: on literacy among the lower orders, R. Yates in Li
        Feng and Branner (eds) (2011), 339-69, with 'Belle' at 367; on male
        and female artisans' literacy, A Barbieri-Low in Li Feng and Branner
        (eds), 370-399.
92-5   **the tomb**: Li Feng (2013), 250-6; J. Rawson in Portal (ed.) (2007),
        124-5, 129-135.
93   **the slave Yu**: J. Rawson in Portal (ed.) (2007), 131-4; Sima on the
        tomb, Dawson (ed.) (1994), 85-6.
94   **the layout of the tomb**: Dawson (ed.) (1994), 85-6; Rawson (ed.)
        (1996), 136-45.
95   **geophysical surveys**: Portal (ed.) (2007), 205-7.
95-6   **the story of the meteor**: Dawson (ed.) (1994), 81.
96   **Du Mu poem**: there are many translations of this famous poem: for
        a full version see e.g. John Minson, http://chinaheritage.net/journal/
        the-great-palace-of-chin-a-rhapsody/
97   **on the idea of the sage ruler**: Li Zehua in Pines *et al.* (eds) (2015).

5: THE HAN

98   For overviews of the Han: Lewis (2009a); Ebrey (2010), 60–85; Hansen (2015), 118–57; Li Feng (2013), 257–82; on the rise of the bureaucracy, Li Feng, 283–303; on organisation and material culture, Wang (1982) and Loewe (1986); for interesting comparisons with the Roman Empire, not least in the embracing of Buddhism in China and Christianity in the West, Poo *et al.* (eds) (2017).

99   **story of the two rebels:** de Bary, *Sources* I, 53–6; Li Feng (2013), 258–60.

100   **the risings … coalesced:** on Xiang Lu, Dawson (ed.) (1994), 109–40; and Chen Sheng, 141–8.

102   **wars with the Xiongnu:** Yap (trans.) (2009).

103   **in spring 110 BCE:** Yap (trans.) (2009), 207–9.
       Sima Qian: On Sima, Watson (1958 and 1969); Dawson (1994).

104   **recent finds in Han tombs:** Barbieri-Low and Yates (2015).

105   **'I was born at Longmen':** adapted from the translation by Watson (1958), 48.

106   **'Don't forget!':** Watson (1958), 49–50.

107   **the Silkworm Chamber:** Watson (1958), 57–67; 'A man has only one death. That death may be as weighty as Mount T'ai, or it may be as light as a goose feather. It all depends upon the way he uses it.' (Watson, 63).

108–9   **history and filial piety:** on the writing of history, Nylan (1998–99).

110–11   **in Zheng village:** von Glahn (2016), 108–13.

111–13   **Franklin King:** on the perseverance of this way of life there are many studies in the twentieth century from personal memoirs such as Graham Peck's *Two Kinds of Time* (1950) to anthropological accounts like the evocative field study of country life by Lake Tai in the Yangtze delta: *Peasant Life in China* by Fei Hsiao-tung (London: Kegan Paul, 1939).

113   **a European traveller:** Keyserling (1925), 71.

114–16   **Hu Sheng the slave:** for the inscribed bricks, Wang (1982), 212–13.

116   **scribes:** Barbieri-Low and Yates (2015), 1084–111.

117   **the Silk Road:** Yü Ying-shih(1986); Wood (2002); Hill (2009); and latterly Hansen's brilliant documents- and archaeology-based narrative (2012) and Frankopan's sweeping overview (2015).
       Polybius: *The Histories*, 1.3.

118   **Sima Guang on the Xiongnu:** Yap (trans.) (2009).

119   **the postal system:** Hansen (2012), 83–11; on reconstructing the postal system of the Han period, Y. Edmund Lieu in Richter (2015), 17–52.

120   **letters from Xuanquan relay station:** E. Giele in Richter (2015), 403–74.

121   **'the shoes':** E. Giele in Richter (2015), 432–5.
       'dear Yousun': E. Giele in Richter (2015), 454–5.

122   **'Zheng sends his best regards':** E. Giele in Richter (2015), 442–3.

123   **the Red Cliff:** centre of the novel *The Romance of Three Kingdoms* and latterly of many movies including John Woo's 2008 film, video games and apps. The supposed Tomb of Cao Cao has recently been

found and excavated in 2016–17 (http://www.chinadaily.com.cn/china/2009-12/28/content_9234640.htm) but that it is his is still contested. The excavation was reported in the *South China Morning Post*: https://www.scmp.com/news/china/society/article/2138951/archaeologists-confident-they-have-found-body-fabled-chinese

124   **Emperor Wen of Sui**: For an overview, Wright, 'The Sui Dynasty (581–617)' in Twitchett (1979), 48–149; Lewis (2009a), 248–58, offers a wide-ranging survey of the period after the Han.

125   **Grand Canal**: Edwards (2009a), 21–5; (2009b), 254–6; Bishop (1997); cf. T. Brook (1998); see too Heng (1999), 74–5, with maps, 75 and 76.

126   **Theophylact Simocatta**: Yule (ed. & trans.) (1915), 29–31.

6: THE GLORY OF THE TANG

127   overviews: for introductions to the Tang, Benn (2004); Ebrey (2010); Lewis (2009b); Hansen (2015).

       Xuanzang: for his life, Beal (1911); Li Yongshi (trans.) (1959 and 1995); and Devahuti (2001); for the story of the journey, A. Yu (ed. & trans.) (1980). My account is informed by journeys in his footsteps in Xinjiang in 1984, 1989–90, 2006 and 2015; in Uzbekistan in 1996; and in 2005–07 to Buddhist sites in Afghanistan, Pakistan and Varanasi Bodhgaya Lumbini and Patna in the Ganges Plain.

128   **Buddhism in China**: de Bary, *Sources* I, 266–86.

130   **Bamiyan manuscript finds**: https://www.schoyencollection.com/news-items/bamiyan-buddhist-thailand-exhibition-2010; and now Salomon (2018).

       Gandhara: on the culture: https://www.classics.ox.ac.uk/gandhara-connections

131   **Kanishka's stupa**: for the stupa site today see Wood (2007), 126–9.

133   **Silk Road in the Tang**: Lewis (2009b) 145–78; Hansen (2012).

       Suyab: Clauson (1961); Forte (1994); Abe (2014); Yamafuji *et al.* (2016).

134   **Cen Shen**: Waley (1963), 30–46 – a typically delightful evocation.

135   **'Here in the camp'**: Waley (1963), 38.

136–8   **Xi'an/Chang'an**: Heng (1999), 1–29, map, 8; Thilo (1997); Shi (1996).

138–9   **city wards**: Heng (1999), Benn (2004), 50–53 and 64–7; Souen (1968), 24–8, 63–9 with maps; for a famous Tang novel set in these streets, Dudbridge (1983).

139   **biography of Xuanzang**: as in 127n; Devahuti (2001), 1–16, adds an invaluable collection of biographical material from Uighur Chinese and Korean sources.

140   **Xuanzang's works**: inventory in Devahuti (2001), 151–67, from a Korean text.

140–41   **translation projects**: for a scintillating overview of the role of Buddhism in the East and South Asian 'Sanskritic cosmopolis' of the early Middle Ages, Pollock (2006).

141 **Xuanzang's letters to India:** Devahuti (2001), 17–22, the first publication in English of letters preserved in later printed texts in Uighur and Chinese, a remarkable insight into Xuanzang's life after his return.

142 **Nara:** for the Tang in Japan and 'the emergence of East Asia', Lewis (2009b), 153–6.

142–3 **the Shoso-in:** Hayashi (1975).

143–5 **Nestorian Inscription:** Saeki (1916), 162–80, including the poem at 172–4.

145–6 **Tang historical writing:** on Liu Zhiji, Beasley and Pulleyblank (eds) (1961), 136–51; with Liu's autobiographical reflections, 137–8; the self-reflexiveness of the culture was not confined to poetry.

146 **the move to the south:** Lewis (2009b), 18–21; on the agricultural revolution, 129–36; on Yangzhou, 113–17; Heng (1999), 73–83, with the Grand Canal, 74–5, and maps, 75 and 76. The later history of this fascinating city has generated a huge and continuing literature; for the model of how to explore the many pasts of a Chinese city see e.g. Finnane (2004) and Olivová and Børdahl (eds) (2009); my thanks to Vibeke Børdahl for putting me in touch with the living storytelling tradition of Yangzhou.

147 **Li Bai:** Waley (1958), 34–5.

150 **the War of An Lushan:** Lewis (2009b), 40–44.

150–53 **Du Fu:** for his biography, Hung (1952a) and A. R. Davis (1971); for translations, Watson (trans.) (2002), Owen (2013) and Owen (trans.) (2016). My thanks to Professor Owen and Professors Zeng Xiangbo and Yang Yu and Dr Liu Taotao for sharing their thoughts on Du Fu's rich legacy and continuing significance in today's culture. The later view of the poet as a Confucian prophet (Schneider, 2012) still holds today: President Xi has said his consolation in the countryside was classical poetry and especially Du Fu: https://www.nytimes.com/2015/09/25/world/asia/xi-jinping-china-cultural-revolution.html; Xi has also quoted him in speeches: http://www.chinadaily.com.cn/a/201801/01/WS5a495ef6a31008cf16da4738_2.html.

151 **'I remember ...':** Ballad of Pengya Road, Owen (trans.) (2013), 236–7.

153 **'Weeping in the wilderness':** Night in the Tower, Owen (trans.) (2013), 255.

7: DECLINE AND FALL

154 **overview:** on the events Lewis (2009b), 70–71, 272–3; on the Late Tang mood, Graham (1965), Owen (1986) and Owen (2006), 19–40; on the crisis of culture after 755, Bol (1992), 108–47.

156 **the *Tongdian*:** de Bary, *Sources* I, 437; Twitchett (1992), 104–7; Foot and Robinson (2015), 32–3 and 485–93; on Du You's family culture, the estate and the Tongdian, Owen (2006), 258–60.

157 **Han Yu:** de Bary, *Sources* I, 369–82; on Han Yu as a precursor of the Song Confucian revival, 371–2.

158   **Wuzong Edict:** de Bary, *Sources* I, 379–82; my narrative is based on
Reischauer (1955), 321–6.

158–60   **the clash with Buddhism:** Reischauer (1955); no source gives a better
sense of what it was like to travel through Tang China.

160   **Du Mu:** the first Tang poet translated into English, in 1819: see
Graham (1965) and Burton (trans.) (1990); for an account of his
career, Owen (2006), 254–314.

162   **'Once you were a novice':** Burton (trans.) (1990), 20: see too 38 ('the
monastery is abandoned') and 61 ('an old monk sent back to the
secular world'); and Owen (2006), 297.

            200 million coins: Reischauer (1955), 346.

            mass executions: Reischauer (1955), 348–9.

163   **A meeting on the road:** Reischauer (1955), 370–71.

164   **'The poet of lost idyll':** Owen (2006), 306–14; on the Red Slope
poems, 298–302.

165   **the Huang Chao rebellion:** Lewis (2009b), 70–71 and 272–3;
Dudbridge (2013), 42–5.

168   **cannibalism:** in general in the Tang, Benn (2004), 123–4.

            the poet Wei Zhuang: Lewis (2009b), 272–3.

169   **the Li family:** Johnson (1977).

8: THE FIVE DYNASTIES

172   This period has recently attracted huge interest; for an overview,
an older study: Schafer (1954); new surveys include Davis (trans.)
(2004); Kurz (2011); Lorge (2010); Dudbridge (2013); Davis (2015);
and Tackett (2017).

            Jing Hao: on this 'supreme moment in classical Chinese landscape
painting', Sullivan (1967), 179–80.

173   **Wang Renyu:** my thanks to the late Glen Dudbridge for discussing
Wang's story; all the translations that follow are his. Thanks too to
Tina Li for advice on the grave inscription at Lixian.

174   **Eric Teichman:** 'Routes in Kan-su', *Geographical Journal*, Vol. 48
(1916), 474, quoted by Dudbridge (2013), 8.

            the 'Spirit Road Epitaph': Dudbridge (2013), 192–9.

175   **the dream of pebbles:** Dudbridge (2013), 12.

176   **the story of the monkey:** Dudbridge (2013), 186–8; on the feelings of
primates, 183–5.

178–9   **Wang's grandson recalled:** Dudbridge (2013), 192–9.

180   **Twin Dragon Alley:** interview recorded spring 2014.

181   **Battle of Gaoping:** on the military events, Lorge (2015), 53–61.

183   **the conjunction of 967:** Pankenier (2013), 425; confirmed by the five
planets in 1007, Pankenier (2013), 422.

            on the rise of the Song: Kuhn (2009), 10–28; Lorge (2015);
Tackett (2017).

184   **cannibalism:** Lorge (2015), 124.

9: THE SONG RENAISSANCE

185   For broad accounts, Ebrey (2010), 136–63, and the excellent and readable overview by Kuhn (2009); also Lorge (2015); Tackett (2017); Twitchett and Smith (2009).

187   *How to Have a Happy Healthy Retirement*: the latest edition is 2013.

188   **Song Kaifeng**: Heng (1999), 87–90; on the Song cityscape, 117–39; map, 118; the streets of Kaifeng, 151, with map at 153; also Kracke (1975); West (1985); Wu Pei-yi (1994).

188   **the Jews of Kaifeng**: A. E. Moule (1911), 403ff; Smith (1851); Leslie (1965–67 and 1982); Malek (ed.) (2000).

189   **Jewish Silk Road letters**: Hansen (2012) 211–18.

190   **Muslims**: Leslie (1986 and 2006).

191   **Qingming scroll**: Heng (1999); West (1985); for a discussion with map of the city in relation to the scroll's depiction, Zhang Zeduan (2008).

193   **food**: for a broad picture, M. Freeman in K. C. Chang (ed.) (1977), 141–194; the 'Pure Eating' cookbook was printed as *Shanjia Qinggong* (Shanghai Commercial Press, 1936); for a current edition, *Zhonghua Shuju* (2013).

194   **Dreams of Splendour**: Wu Pei-yi (1995).
        Sima Guang on food: see Ebery (2009) 241.

195   '**The people ... were kind and friendly ...**' Meng in Wu Pei-yi (1995), 51.

196   **the examinations**: Bol (1992), 48–75.

197–9   **printing books**: Dudbridge (2000); on Taizu's instructions, 2–12; on print technology, 13–14.

199–200 **Song science**: Needham (ed.), *Science and Civilisation*, Vol. IV, Part 2 (1965): on Su Song's clock, 446–81, with reconstruction, 449; see too Needham's essay in *The Great Titration* (1969), 78–83.

10: THE FALL OF THE NORTHERN SONG

202   overview: Ebrey (2010), 136–63; Kuhn (2009); Twitchett and Smith (eds)(2009).

203   **armies**: Lorge (2011).
        Su Dongpo: R. Egan, 'Su Shi's Informal Letters in Literature and Life' in Richter (2015), 475–507.

204   **the 1048 environmental disaster**: I am here indebted to the recent pioneering study by Zhang Ling (2016) on which my account relies: my thanks to Dr Zhang and to Tina Li for advice on the tomb memorial inscription to Linghu Duanfu, which is quoted in my text.

205   '**the people were swept away like fish**': Zhang Ling (2016), 1–3; for a vivid reconstruction, 107–8; on the long term impact, 248–79, and Chen Yunzhen (2012).

207   '**yellowish dead soil**': Zhang Ling (2016), 221–2.

208–12 **Wang Anshi**: the fullest account in English is still Williamson (1935–7); for texts, de Bary, *Sources* I, 409–35; Bol (1992), 212–53.

209 'Before I ever took up office': Yang Xianyi and Young (trans.) (1984), 221–2.

212 'Reading History': Hinton (trans.) (2015), 85.

212–15 Sima Guang: texts: de Bary, *Sources* I, 448–51; see Pulleyblank's essay in Beasley and Pulleyblank (eds) (1961), 151–66, with fascinating material on Sima's editing process, 160–66; the first full-length study in English is Ji (2005); see Yap (trans.) (2009) for a great sense of his powerful narrative history. My special thanks to current members of the Sima clan, custodians of his ancestral temple and tomb at Guangshan, Henan, for their generosity.

214 'You will see in these pages': for Sima's overarching interpretation of Chinese history, de Bary, *Sources* I, 448–52.

216–18 Li Qingzhao: like many readers in the West the present author was introduced to the poet by Kenneth Rexroth's translations (1972 and 1979); there are later versions in K. S. Chang and Saussy (eds) (1999) and Idema and Grant (2004), and now Ronald Egan's magisterial and moving biography (2014), whose translations I have used with grateful thanks.

216 women in the Song: See Ebrey (1993); on Li, 158–60; and the marriage 'idyll', 117.

217 'Insight, they say': Egan (2014), 178–9. on her autobiography, Owen (1986), 80–98.

218 'I arrived in Laizhou': Egan (2014), 310–12.
the Song emperor: Ebrey (2014).

219 the stone tablet: Vermeer (1991), 107–9.
the Jurchen invasion: Ebrey (2014), 421–48; Egan (2014), 130–36 and a map of the route of Li's flight, 138.

221 the march north: Ebrey (2014), 476–503; her translation of the diary, 480–81.
'Deep chasms of evil': Rexroth (trans.) (1979), 56–8.

223 'you should have been more cautious': Rexroth (trans.) (1979), 57.
'A million people': Zhang Zeduan (2008).

II: THE SOUTHERN SONG

224 For broad guides, Kuhn (2009); Ebrey (2010); on society, material culture and the city, Gernet (1962): on the growth of Song patriotism, Trauzettel (1975), 199–213.
Li Qingzhao: again the translations are by Egan (2014); on Li's remarriage, 153–8.

225 'the crossings of the Yangtze would soon be blocked': Egan (2014), 140.

226 'All my life': Egan (2014), 147–50; the poem to the emissaries, 166–71.

227 'Since crossing the Yangtze': Egan (2014), 178.

229 Mulan poem: Egan (2014), 184–5.
Hangzhou: Gernet (1962) and Heng (1999), 139–42; map, 142. My thanks to Suzanna Thornton, who shared her research on the merchant clans of Hangzhou in the Southern Song.

230   **'unbelievable beauty'**: Naval Intelligence Division (1944–5), vol. 3, 291.
       Zhao clan: interviews in the Zhao family village, Zhangpu
       Fujian, 2015.

231   **Lu You**: Watson (trans.) (1973), 68; and his diary, Watson
       (trans.) (2007).

232   **'Our dynasty'**: Elvin (1973), 205
       Hangzhou: Gernet (1962); A. C. Moule (1957); Heng (1999), 139–
       42, map 142.

234   **merchant ships**: on maritime technology in the Song, Needham (ed.),
       Science and Civilisation in China, Vol. IV, Part 3 (1971), 460–77; on
       the rapid urbanization of open port cities in the South, Heng (1999),
       183; on Quanzhou, 186–9; and on the 'new urban paradigm', 205–9.

235   **Lu You poem**: Watson (trans.) (1973), 33.

236   **the Huizhou gentry**: in general, see McDermott (2013). My thanks to
       Xie Yercai for discussing his family history with me at his home in
       Qimen County, Anhui, in spring 2014 and for answering my further
       questions in summer 2019. I am especially grateful to Zhang Jianping,
       author of a wonderfully evocative photographic study of local lineages
       and their traditions: *Huizhou* (2013), who in 2014 introduced us to
       local clans such as the Xie of Qimen and the Wu of Wan'an. Thanks,
       too, to Daniel Kwok for sharing his ongoing research on the Bao family
       in Tangyue. My translations from the Tangyue local gazetteer and the
       Bao family history are by Suzanna Thornton. In Tangyue, my thanks to
       Bao Shumin, and to Bao Xunsheng and his family in Dongting Jiangsu.

237   **Mr Xie**: interview in Qimen County, 2014; for Xie lineage
       photographs, Zhang Jianping (2013), 173–89.

239   **The Confucian revival**: de Bary, *Sources* I, 383–435; and on the Neo-
       Confucian 'School of Reason' in general, 455–502.

239–41 **Zhu Xi**: the literature is truly enormous, no less than for Aristotle.
       Crucial for our purposes is Ebrey (ed. & trans.) (1991); for a selection
       of texts, de Bary, *Sources* I, 479–502; for a very accessible overview,
       Thompson (2017); for wider portraits of Zhu Xi, Munro (1988)
       and Zhu (2019); for the broad conception of Confucian learning
       on the 'Moral Heart-Mind', Ivanhoe (2016); on Zhu's 'Universal
       Heart-Mind', de Bary, *Sources* I, 503–513, and the important essay
       by Klein (2018).

240   **'Your filial son'**: Ebrey (ed. & trans.) (1991), 173.

241–44 **the Mongol invasion**: for a brisk narrative, Brook (2010); for a detailed
       account of the naval war of 1279, Lo (2012); with battle of Yaishan
       at 237–45.

12: YUAN

On the Mongol period: Chan (ed.) (1982); on visual arts, Watt (2010);
Brook (2013); Rossabi (2014); Jackson (2018).

246   **Ma Duanlin**: de Bary, *Sources* I, 444–7: Chan and de Bary (eds)
       (1982), 27–88.

247 **Xu Heng:** a peasant and refugee from war, Xu Heng rose to the highest levels of the Yuan court; on him, see Klein (2018), 91.

248 **Mongol Beijing:** Watt (2010), 41–63.

249 **Yuan drama:** Ebrey (2010), 186–90; for an overview, Mackerras (1990).

250 **Tangyue in Anhui:** thanks to Bao Shumin and to Daniel Kwok. My translations from the Bao family book and the Tangyue local gazetteer are again by Suzanna Thornton; for photos of the Bao lineage in Tangyue, Zhang Jianping (2013), 142–55.

251–2 **Christians under the Mongols:** for Pegolotti, Rossabi (2014).

252 **maps:** Smith (1996).

252–5 **Marco Polo:** Wood (1998); Vogel (2013); my quotation on 254 is adapted from Moule's update of Yule: https://en.wikisource.org/wiki/The_Travels_of_Marco_Polo

255 **Yangzhou:** there is now a visitor pavilion and a memorial hall for Marco Polo in Yangzhou. On Katerina Ilioni's family, Rouleau (1954), 346–65. My thanks to the director of Yangzhou Museum for allowing inspection of the original stone.

257–8 **Rabban Sawma:** Budge (trans.) (1928); Rossabi (1992).

259 **Black Death:** my thanks to Timothy Brook's *Troubled Empire* (2010), from which I have gratefully borrowed the dragons! On the Black Death, a controversial subject among scientists of disease, Sussman (2011); Drancourt *et al* (2006), 234–41; and Drancourt and Raoult (eds) (2008).

261 **Manichaeism:** a fascinating footnote to Chinese history. A still active temple at Cao'an near Quanzhou preserves a stone cult image of Mani. In that part of Fujian some kind of cult survival has been reported as a secret society, the 'Religion of Light'. Dan (2002), 17–18.

262 **Macheng:** my account is from Rowe (2007).

265 **Suzhou:** Marmé (2005).

266 *An Illustrated Guide to Suzhou:* medieval gazetteers of Suzhou are translated by Milburn (2015), 133–6.

267–72 **Zheng Yunduan:** Idema and Grant (2004), 269–80; a modern edition of *Suyong ji* (Solemn Harmonies) is in Sun Yuxiu (ed.), *Hanfenlou miji* (Shanghai: 1921); see K. S. Chang and Saussy (eds) (1999), 131–9, with her autobiographical preface, 677–8. Translations and biographical details are by Peter Sturman. On writing and illness as a feminine condition, in later literature, Grace Fong in Fong and Widmer (eds)(2010), 17–47. My thanks to Zheng Yangwen for her information about living family traditions of the poet among the women of the Zheng clan.

13: THE MING

274 Broad introductions: Ebrey (2010); Dardess (2012); Brook (2013); Hansen (2015); and the sumptuously illustrated Clunas and Harrison-Hall (eds) (2014).

275 *Story of a Dream:* for a suggestive comparison of the peasant rebel founding emperors Hongwu and Mao, Andrew and Rapp (2000).

278   **new order**: most evident in the Great Ming Code, Younglin (2005 and 2011).

279   **Nanjing bricks**: my example is transcribed from an example in the brick museum in the Zhonghua Gate, Nanjing.

280–82   **Yellow Registers**: Brook (2010), 43; Zhang Wenxian (2008), 148–75; for a new survey which came out after this book went to print, Will (2020).

280   **Tangyue in the Ming**: interviews with Bao Shumin in Tangyue, spring 2014.

283   **Yongle**: for a vivid recreation of the 1421 celebrations for Yongle's new Beijing, Levathes (1994), 151–3.

284   **'The countries beyond the horizon'**: excerpt from the full inscription from the Changle temple, Fujian: Needham (ed.), *Science and Civilisation in China*, Vol. 3 (1959), 557–8.
           Zheng He: Ma (1970) is the key text; on the size of ships, Church (2005); and on the archaeology of the dockyards, Church, 'Two Ming Dynasty shipyards in Nanjing and their infrastructure': http://www.shipwreckasia.org/wp-content/uploads/Chapter3.pdf. On wider issues of the voyages, Dreyer (2007), and on Ming foreign policy towards Central Asia and the Amur River region before Zheng He, the important essay by Rossabi (2014).

286   **Yemeni accounts**: Yajima (1974); for an online translation: https://en.wikipedia.org/wiki/Chinese_treasure_ship#Yemen

287   For modern junks and Pechili traders, Worcester (1947), 114–15, with a folding plan of an eighty-foot trader: 'The large Kiangsu trader seldom to be seen nowadays ... was occasionally as long as 170 feet.' On technical matters of the construction of large wooden junks my thanks to T. J. Jia at the Dragon Boat Development Company, Nanjing.

288   **'Documents ... were removed ... and destroyed'**: Dreyer (2007), 173.

289   **A Ming writer**: T'ien (1981), 186–97, at 194.
           Five planets: Pankenier (2013), 426–32.
           Confusions of Pleasure: the phrase is from Brook (1998).

290–91   **On Ming Suzhou**: Marmé (2005).

291–2   **the Bao family of Tangyue**: text from Bao Shumin, translation by Suzanna Thornton.

292   **Matteo Ricci**: my thanks to the library of former Leal Senado in Macau, who made available to me the 1617 edition of *De Christiana expeditione apud Sinas*, a Latin translation of the original Italian text, on which see Ricci, Trigault (ed.) and Gallagher (trans.) (1953); the latest biography is by R. Po-Chia Hsia (2010).

293   **'It seems worthwhile to record'**: translated from Ricci's diary, 1617.

294   **'this strange and shallow creed'**: for Zhang Dai's essay on Christianity, Spence (2008), 128–9, 131–3; 'this religion has spread across the world, yet its teachings are often both strange and shallow'; on another critic, Li Zhi, de Bary (1970), 145–225; for a Chinese account of Ricci, Ye (trans.) (1999), 60.
           Ricci's map: on the four editions of Ricci's map, see Smith (1996),

42–9. The Vatican's 1602 copy was reproduced by Pasquale d'Elia in *Il mappamondo cinese del P Matteo Ricci, S.I.* in 1938. For the copy in the James Ford Bell Library, University of Minnesota: https://www.wdl.org/en/item/4136/#q=Ricci&qla=en

295   **responses to Ricci:** Li Zhi in de Bary (1970), 223; Xu Guangxi, Brook (2010), 176–8; and Zhang Dai, Spence (2008), 128–33.

     the Ming decline: Huang (1981) is a classic account; 130–55 for a portrait of a model late Ming local official; in general Brook (2010), 238–59.

296   **'The emperors in modern times':** Ricci (1953).

297–304   **Donglin Academy:** Dardess (2002): in Wuxi, my thanks to Qin Baoxin and the Qin family for their great hospitality on memorable visits in 2013 and at the Qingming Festival, April 2014; to Frank Ching for discussions on family history in Wuxi and London: my account is drawn from conversations with Frank and from his book *Ancestors* (1988).

301   **'Our ancestor Qin Ercai':** interview, Wuxi, April 2015; Ching (1988), 184–98.

303   **'the rationale for public officials':** de Bary (1993), 94–5; de Bary, *Sources* I, 530–42; on the significance of Huang Zongxi, de Bary (1993), 52–85; Struve (1988), 474–502.

14: LAST DAYS OF THE MING

305   For the broad picture: on the culture, Brook (1998); and on the decline Brook (2010), 238–59; Ebrey (2010), 21–16; He (2013).

306   **cultural movements:** on the book publishing industry, He (2013); on the Ming as the great age of the novel, Plaks (1987). *Romance of the Three Kingdoms, The Water Margin* and *Journey to the West* are the three famous classics; the fourth, circulated in manuscript in the 1590s and printed c.1610, is the notorious and scandalous *The Plum in the Golden Vase* (Roy, trans., 1993–2013): a complete annotated version of the 1610 printing with extraordinary insights into late Ming society, manners and sexual mores.

306–7   **Mrs Wang's boat journey:** translated by Grace Fong (2008), 169–78.

307–8   **a European traveller:** for a vivid picture of the late Ming urban landscape, Escalante tr Frampton (1579) (2008 ed) 44–9.

308   **Zhang Dai:** see Kafalas (2007) and Spence (2008); for texts: Zhang Dai (1995); for Zhang's 'Epitaph for Myself', Ye (trans.) (1999), 98–103; for Zhang's visit to Taishan I have used the translation of Richard Strassberg (1994), 338–9. Zhang's *Night Ferry (Yehang chuan,* ed. Liu Yaolin, Hangzhou, 1987) is untranslated: my thanks to Tina Li for her excerpts. In general on Zhang's 'remembrance of things past', Owen (1986), 134–40. My thanks too to the doyen of Zhang scholars, Professor She Deyu, for sharing his thoughts in Zhang's native Shaoxing.

308–9   **ferries:** this river life survived into the 1940s, Worcester (1959), 33 and 58–9.

0

312   **Zhang Dai in Tai'an:** Strassberg (1994); Ye (trans.) (1999).

313   **Xu Xiake:** the fundamental Western study is Ward (2001), to which
            I am indebted for my translations of Xu's journeys into Yunnan;
            Strassberg (1994), 317–19; for his earlier travel diaries I have
            also used Xu (2010) and Xu (2001), which has a fascinating and
            informative series of maps. My thanks to the custodian Ma Li for her
            help and her insights at Xu's ancestral home at Jiangyin outside Wuxi
            in April 2014.
            'The last day of the third lunar month' Xu (2010), 5.

314   **'The rain had just stopped':** Xu (2010), 5.

315   **'When I questioned him':** translations by Ward (2001).

316   **Xu Xiake in Yunnan:** Ward (2001), 131–56; with the Mu
            family, 138–40.

317   **'The Mu family have been here for 2,000 years':** Ward (2001), 138–9;
            'The boy ... has been unable to get even a glimpse of the culture of
            the Central Plains', 140.

318   **'Many local chiefs ... oppress the ... people':** Ward (2001), 138.

318–19   **Mr Zao:** Ward (2001), 142–3.

319   **rebellions in the south:** Ward (2001), 143–4.

320   on **landscape as sacred space:** Ward (2001), 187–9.
            'My greatest regrets': Ward (2001), 204.
            with the Zhao family: My thanks to the Zhao family for their
            hospitality in 2015 at the clan village near Zhangpu County, Fujian.
            The 1619 stele on which this story is based, and which is still standing
            in the village, is published in Vermeer (1991), 28–32.

322–3   **'Recently I received a petition':** Vermeer (1991), 30–31.

324   **the tale of the Fang family:** I have relied on Willard Peterson's moving
            biography (1979) from which comes my paraphrase of Yiji's poetry on
            285–7. For Tongcheng County in the Ming, see in general Beattie (1979).
            I would like to thank the Fang family of Tongcheng Anhui for sharing
            with me their traditions of Aunt Weiyi and their seventeenth-century
            ancestors; Tao Du'an of Tongcheng was my contact and kindly provided
            me with information and photographs of Weiyi's grave.

325   **the Nanjing pleasure quarter in Yiji's youth:** see Levy (trans.) (1966),
            who includes a translation of 'Diverse Records of Wooden Bridge'
            by Huai Yu (1616–96). For a wonderful collection of Ming stories
            from this period originally published in 1628: Yang Shuhui and Yang
            Yunqin (trans.) (2018).

328   **Aunt Weiyi:** K. S.Chang and Saussy (eds) (1999), 284–8, to which I
            am indebted for the translations of her poetry by Paula Varsano. Her
            preface to her sister's poetry, 687–8, is translated by Dorothy Ko. On
            the riches of women's writing in the 17th century see in general Ko
            (1994), 29–67; for a parallel to Weiyi as a literary patron see Ellen
            Widner in Mann and Cheng (eds) (2001), 179–94 on the writer editor
            and anthologist Wang Duanshu.

332   **Sack of Changshu:** Struve (ed. & trans.) (1993), 73–92.

333   **the death of the actor Laojiang:** Struve (ed. & trans.) (1993), 80.

the tale of Madame Liu: Struve (ed. & trans.) (1993), 93–113, to whose translation I am indebted; on women and letters, Widmer (1989), 1–43, and Ko (1994), plus the essays on women's letters in Mann and Cheng (eds) (2001); see too Widmer in Richter (2015): '20 Letters as Windows on Ming/Qing Women's Literary Culture', 744–74.

336 The Hunting of Fang Yiji: Peterson (1979), 160–66, and for the translation of Fang's poem.

15: THE GREAT QING

341 For a brilliant and readable overview, Rowe (2012). The Grandeur of the Qing website is full of interest and illumination: http://afe.easia. columbia.edu/qing/site-index.html; on material culture, Rawski and Rawson (eds) (2005), the catalogue of the magnificent RA exhibition in London in 2005–06; for the grand narrative, Wakeman (1986).

342 Zhang Dai at West Lake: Ye (1999), 102–3; Spence (2008), 250–52.

342–3 'I've lived as a tenant': Ye (1999), 102.

345 the restoration of Chinese culture: Wakeman (1986), Rowe (2009); in the recovery of cities in the south, the example of Yangzhou was famous: Meyer-Fong (2003), 14–24; see the Dutch traveller Nieuhof (1655): 'The salt trade has so enriched the inhabitants of this town that they have rebuilt their city since the last destruction by the Tartars, erecting it in as great a splendour as it was at first; https://archive.org/ details/McGillLibrary-126081-3026/page/n63

346 On the expansion of Manchu hegemony over Xinjiang, Perdue (2005). The issue of when China's GDP was overtaken by the British, and why, is controversial: Pomeranz (2000) is the classic account, on which see Rowe (2009), 149–65; for a Western-centric view, Jones (2003).

347 'heart and eye are gladdened': Spence (1974), 12.
'That's all there is to it': Spence (1974) 143–4.

348 'Giving life to people and killing people': Spence (1974), 29.
'Errors are inexcusable': Spence (1974), 32–3.

349 Chen Hongmou: Rowe (2007), a magisterial account of eighteenth-century *paideia*.
on the *Sacred Edict*: Milne (trans.) (1817); Herbert Giles and Guo Moruo are quoted by Victor Mair, 'Language and Ideology in the Sacred Edict' in Nathan *et al.* (eds) (1985), 55.

351 Chen Hongmou in Yunnan: Rowe (2007), 61–7; on the educational campaign, 417–26.

352 the *Kangxi Dictionary*: Kangxi also published *The Complete Works of Zhu Xi* in 1713 and a huge philosophical compilation in 1715, Rowe (2009), 81.

352–3 the execution of Da Mingshi: Spence (1974), 85–6.

353–67 a Qing family saga: on the thorny question of Cao family chronology I have followed Spence (1966); but see Zhou Ruchang (2009); on Cao Yin and the Complete Tang Poems, J. S. Edgren in Olivová and Børdahl (eds) (2009), 117–19.

354   **the sketch of Cao Xueqin:** by Wang Nanshi (Wang Gang, 1679–1770)
           who knew him; it is dated February 1744. http://bbs.tianya.cn/
           post-help-490338-1.shtml

355   **'Reminders of my poverty':** Hawkes (trans.) (1973), 21.

357–8   **the southern tours:** for illustrations, Rawski and Rawson (eds) (2005),
           86–97; my thanks to the Qin family for sharing their vivid oral
           traditions of Qianlong's visits to Wuxi.

357   **Yangzhou printing:** J. S. Edgren in Olivová and Børdahl (eds)
           (2009), 109–30.

359   **the fall of the family:** Spence (1966), 282–92; Zhou Ruchang
           (2009), 66–75.
           Yongzheng: 'I had 40 years in the real world', Spence (1966), 286.
           inventory of the house: Spence (1966), 290.

360   **Cao Fu letter:** 'Your respected eminence', Zhou Ruchang (2009) 35;
           and the emperor's reply, 46.

361   **the family house in Beijing:** Zhou Ruchang (2009), 76; for the street
           map: Qianlong's Peking Map of 1750 (at 14 x 13 metres, the oldest
           and most detailed map of Peking) was published in Peking in 1940
           in 17 vols: (Vol. 11) http://dsr.nii.ac.jp/toyobunko/II-11-D-802/
           index.html.en

362   **Old Beijing:** Bredon (1922).

363   **Temple of the Eastern Peak (Dongyue):** the key study is Goodrich
           (1964); Bredon (1922), 234–7; Arlington and Lewisohn (1935),
           257–63; Naquin (2000), 506–17; it was opened again in 1999; on its
           state today, Aldrich (2006), 256–9; for a vivid account of a visit to the
           shrine in 1895, and the visceral 'awe-inspiring' power of its imagery of
           crime and punishment, 'like being in a magistrate's court', the diary
           of Liu Dapeng, Harrison (2005), 51–2.

364–5   **Literary Inquisition:** Guy (1987), 159–200; J. S. Edgren in Olivová
           and Børdahl (eds) (2009), 120–21.

365   **Qing high culture:** Rowe (2009), 81–8.

367   **A proscribed book:** Cornaby (1919); Cornaby (1901), 223–4 ('one of
           the most remarkable works China has produced').

367–8   **censorship:** Guy (1987), 159–200.

368–9   **'Having made an utter failure of my life':** Hawkes (trans.) (1973), 20.

369–75   **Goodwife Xun:** Mann and Cheng Yu-yin (2001), 217–30.

374   **Zhang Xuecheng as a historian:** Nivison (1966); Zhang's essays
           are translated by Ivanhoe (ed. & trans.) (2010) and his essay 'On
           Women's Learning' by Susan Mann in K. S. Chang and Saussy (eds)
           (1999), 783–99.

375   **18th-century women writers:** on Gan Lirou, see Fong (2008), 161–6,
           and on Shen Cai 85–120; for an overview, Fong and Widmer (eds)
           (2010) with Gan Lirou at 37–43.

375–6   **Civil society?** Rowe (1993), 139–57; Elman (1990), 319ff.

376–7   **Waiting for the barbarians:** on the versions of the treatise on tributary
           peoples: http://www.icm.gov.mo/rc/viewer/20023/1080

16: OPIUM WAR TO THE TAIPING

Macartney: his letters and papers are quoted from Singer (1992); Macartney's journal is online: *Some Account of the Public Life, and a Selection from the Unpublished Writings, of the Earl of Macartney* (London: 1807), 163–410: https://archive.org/details/someaccountofpub02barr/page/370/mode/2up

381–2   **the embassy:** Singer (1992); Bickers (ed.) (1993).

382   **Qianlong poem:** Singer (1992), 85.

385   **edict:** Singer (1992), appendix A, 180–81; the second edict answering the six requests, 183–6.

386   **'The common people of China':** Singer (1992), 121–2.

387   **'an old, crazy ... Man of War':** Singer (1992), 172.

388   **'The aim is gradually to mould the China trade':** Singer (1992), 172.

389   **Shen Fu:** *Six Records* (1983), 25.

389–90 **Matsu temple in Meishan:** Vermeer (1991), 71–3.

391–4   **intellectual movements:** on early nineteenth-century Guizhou intellectuals and the beginnings of Chinese modernity, Schmidt (2013), 19–40; on the Changzhou school, Elman (1990 and 2001).

392   **Hong Liangji:** on Hong see the essay by B. Elman, 'The Failures of Contemporary Chinese Intellectual History' (2010): https://www.princeton.edu/~elman/documents/Elman%20--%20Failures%20of%20Chinese%20Intellectual%20History.pdf; and Helen Dunstan, 'Official Thinking on Environmental Issues and the State's Environmental Roles in Eighteenth-Century China' in Elvin and Liu (eds) (2009), Vol. 1, 585–616.

394   **White Lotus rebellion:** Naquin (1976); confessions of the rebels, 271–79.

395–6   **East India Company press:** Morrison (1815), 4–7.

396   **the Opium War:** on the background, Greenberg (1951) drawing on the Jardine Matheson papers is crucial; Wei (1888) and Waley (1958); recent works include Lovell (2011); a new study from a Chinese perspective by Mao Haijian (2016) offers some important revisions and new detail on the military events.

396   **the Canton trade:** Greenberg (1951); statistics on the opium trade, 220–21.

397   **Yangzhou in the 1830s:** for a novelist's response, *Courtesans and Opium* (Hanan trans., 2009) is a city novel exposing the violence corruption and decadence of the elites at the time of the Opium War by an author who lived in Yangzhou's pleasure quarters for thirty years; on opium in nineteenth-century Yangzhou, S. Kuzay, 'Life in the Green Lofts of the Lower Yangzi Region' in Olivová and Børdahl (eds) (2009), 304–10.

        'We find that your country': Commissioner Lin, de Bary, *Sources* II, 5–9.

398   **Wei Yuan:** the introduction to Wei Yuan's *1843 Illustrated Gazetteer of the Maritime Countries* is translated in de Bary, *Sources* II, 10–17.

The fundamental study in English is still that of Leonard (1984). The last chapter of Wei Yuan's *Military History of the Qing* is translated by Parker (1888).

401   'It was the closing of trade': Parker (1888), 38.
        the Barbarian Pirate War: Parker (1888), 79–80.

403   Père Gabet: see the essay by Simon Leys in *The Burning Forest* (1988), 53–95.

404   the view from the countryside: 'the stone record of virtue and love' from Taining Fujian is published in Vermeer (1991), 79–81.

405   Taiping: for background, Spence (1996); my thanks to families in the Guiping countryside at Flower Island Village and Rushing Water Village, Guangxi, interviews conducted by Suzanna Thornton in 2015: especially Zeng Yongfu and Zeng Chuipeng and the Zeng family in Old Wood Village, Guangxi.

407   interviews conducted in spring 2015, Guangxi.

408   sack of Nanjing: Spence (1996), 171–91.

409–11 Moule diary: A. E. Moule (1911), 21–94; on Ningbo and its pagoda, 82–5, with plate at 86.

411   Xie family: Thanks again to Xie Ercai (interview, Qimen, 2014); and in Dongting, to Bao Xunsheng for access to the painting of his eighteenth-century ancestors; for a photo, Zhang Jiangping (2013), 152–3.

412–13 Zhang Daye: the diary is translated by Tian Xiaofei (2013), 83–103; 'A strong wind', 105.

415   the poet Zheng Zhen: hitherto little known outside China, but J. Schmidt's rich and provocative study (2013) has brought into full light one of the great Chinese poets.

415–17 impact of the Taiping: on the destruction of libraries and scholarly lineages, see the important account by Elman (1990), 287–95, and Meyer-Fong (2013), esp. 175–202.

17: THE GREAT CHINESE REVOLUTION 1850–1950

Some guides: Fairbank (1987); Spence (1991); Ebrey (2010); Chesneaux (1973); Bianco (1971); and a sparkling overview, Fenby (2013).

419   Nanjing: for images, Yao (ed.) (2010), plates 81 and 82 (Gatling guns) and 83 (rebuilding).
        Tongzhi Restoration: Ebrey (2010); Spence (1991), 194–215; on the rise of Shanghai, Johnson (1993).

421   In early 1866: the journey to Europe, Biggerstaff (1937), 307–20; on the cleanliness of Paris, 316.
        Robert Hart: on this remarkable figure see Bredon (1910); Guo Songtao, 9–16.

422   The journey opened the students' eyes: Biggerstaff (1937), 316–20.

423   'All of this is a mystery': Ho and Kuehn (eds) (2009), 148–9, 'everything in England is the opposite of China'; and 171–2, Chang's journal, 'all this remains a mystery to us'.

424   **Guo Songtao:** Frodsham (ed.) (1974), 74–7; Tong (2009), 45–61.
        'eyes glaring': Frodsham (ed.) (1974), 73.

425   **At first the British:** Frodsham (ed.) (1974) 97; 'and yet if we look back,
        the work of their building up their national strength really began only
        after the Qianlong period'. Guo is especially interesting on the growth
        of a system of international law and China's need to join it, 72.

425–6 **Francis Bacon:** Qingsheng, 'Guo Songtao in London: an
        Unaccomplished Mission of Discovery' in Ho and Kuehn (eds)
        (2009) 49.

426   **'In Europe people have been competing':** Frodsham (ed.) (1974), 72.

427   **'If we build a railway':** Liu journal in Ho and Kuehn (eds) (2009),
        129; Guo on railways, Frodsham (ed.) (1974) 98–9, 102–3; Liu's
        journal, 114–15; for the meeting with Rowland Stephenson, 102–3;
        Liu, 128–9.

429   **Shanghai rises:** Johnson (1993).

430   **a small town:** inscription published by Vermeer (1991), 47–51.

432   **100 Days' Reform:** Spence (1990), 224–30; on Cixi as a woman of
        power, in part a feminist reaction to misogyny and orientalising
        stereotypes, Warner (1972) and Seagrave (1992). Most recent
        is the compelling account of Jung Chang (2013), though her
        rehabilitation of Cixi as the 'concubine who launched modern
        China', taking her almost to the level of Mao as a maker of
        modern China, has not found favour with mainstream scholarship;
        see e.g. Pamela Kyle Crossley's review https://docs.google.com/
        file/d/0By7Ajg4xYgVqYklQR296bl9lOGs/edit

432   **'All Under Heaven':** Liu Zehua (2013), 284.

433   **the Boxers:** Spence (1990), 230–35; on the historiography, and the
        racism of the West, Elliott (2002), xxi–xliii; for the 'deep-seated
        resentment' of common people towards missionaries in the late
        nineteenth century, Guo Songtao's memo of 1877 published in Chien
        (trans.) (1993), 33–4.

436   **Liu Dapeng:** Harrison (2005), 85–6. My thanks to Professor Harrison
        for putting me in touch with the Liu Family at Chiqiao Taiyuan in
        2015, where they still live in the family house. My translations are from
        her haunting book (2005), one of the most memorable microhistories
        from modern China, which recalls Ida Pruitt's extraordinary portrait
        in *Daughter of Han* (1945) of a poor working woman who was a
        contemporary of Liu Dapeng.

437   **dreaming of the emperor:** Harrison (2005), 84.

438   **feminism and the women's movement:** for Qiu Jin's manifesto and her
        poetry, Idema and Grant (2004), 770–808; 'To My Sisters', 796–9;
        and K. S. Chang and Saussy (eds) (1999), 632–57; for her famous
        last poem, 656–7: 'I only hope my sacrifice will help to preserve
        our country'.

439–41 **He Zhen:** see the path-breaking study by Zarrow (1988) and now L.
        Liu et al. (2013).

441   *Manchester   Guardian:*   https://theguardian.newspapers.

com/search/#query=Four+Millions+of+Starving+People&
ymd=1907-01-01&lnd=1&t=5077

443 **A village in the South:** on the loyal Confucian magistrate Li, Vermeer (1991), 101–6.

445 **Changsha rising:** Geil (1911); Esherick (1976), 123–42; Lewis (1976); McDonald (1978).

446 **revolts in Hunan:** Chesneaux (1973), 44.

449 **'At twilight':** translation by J. J. Hudson, 'River Sands/Urban Spaces: Changsha in Modern Chinese History', doctoral thesis (University of Texas at Austin, 2015), 127.

450 **biography of Mao Zedong:** for Mao's own account, Snow (1937), 126–46; on the rising, 131–2 (in the revised and enlarged Penguin edition, 152–74). For other insights into the young Mao, see the revealing relationship with the philosopher and rural reformer Liang Shuming, Alitto (1986), 283–92, and Lynch (2018), 195–214, both of whom had long interviews with Liang. My thanks to Liang Peikuan and Liang Peishu for talking with me about their father in October 2014 in Zouping.

451 **leaving China:** A. E. Moule (1911), 335–7.

453 **Wuchang Uprising:** Esherick (1976); Rowe (1992); Esherick and Wei (2014).

454 **missionaries:** Clemmow (2016), 234–5.

18: THE AGE OF REFORM

Some background: for a dazzling overview, Mitter (2004); for a powerful and searching survey of the communist era, Walder (2015); for a rich narrative, Fenby (2013); and for a provocative glimpse into the future which leaves much to ponder, Jacques (2012).

455 **Naval Intelligence:** Vol. II (1945), 4; this brilliant survey over more than 1,500 pages compiled in the 1940s is perhaps the greatest single account of China written in the twentieth century. It is worth remembering how things appeared at that moment: despite civil war and Japanese invasion, the authors saw the longer-term outlook for China very positively: her 'powers of recuperation and reconstruction are shaping the emergence of a new and *perhaps even greater China*' (Vol. 1, July 1944, 364). In June 1945, the last volume highlighted the 'strong democratic element in Chinese institutions and outlook on life' and suggested that a 'liberal-minded intelligentsia' driven by China's national self-consciousness, and strong tendency to cultural unity, as opposed to European disunity, would lead to 'a much higher degree of integration' (Vol. II, 152–4).

456 **Sun Yat-sen:** a portrait by Mitter (2004), 38–9, 140–42.

457 **Liu Dapeng on the elections:** Harrison (2005), 101–2 ('who says that elections are a fair method?') and 106–7; on Western learning coming in, 87–91.

459 **the New Culture Movement:** Mitter (2004), 3–68; for older studies on

May Fourth: Chow (1960); Bianco (1971), 27–52; Schwarcz (1986); and Spence (1990), 300–333.

459–60 Lu Xun: Mitter (2004), 57–61; Davies (2013); Pollard (2002); and Julia Lovell's introduction to her pathbreaking Penguin translation of Lu Xun's stories (Lovell, 2009).

460 Republican Shanghai: Harrison (2000); Mitter (2004), 49–53.

461 the best city: Mitter (2004), 42.

462 Communist Party: Ladany (1992) is still essential; but see now Lam (2018).

463 on Mao: on his early life above, see p.450 and the note on p.559; Chang and Halliday (2005) gained worldwide publicity, but was criticised by specialists for its tendentious use of sources and at times misleading or inaccurate citation; for a sample of academic reviews, see Benton and Lin (2009). Much nonetheless remains: as his former secretary Li Rui put it: 'Mao's way of thinking and governing was terrifying. He put no value on human life'; https://www.theguardian.com/world/2005/jun/02/china.jonathanwatts

the rural movement: Bianco (1971), 82–107; Merkel-Hess (2016); Mao (1967), 23–59, prints his 1927 report from Hunan. The same year Liang Shuming began an alternative vision of peasant reform: (de Bary, *Sources* II, 187–91). The parallels between their careers (and their personal relationship) have given rise to an extensive literature since the pioneering study of Alitto (1979, new ed. 1986): Liang is now seen as an founder figure of the New Confucianism; see for example the essays in Lynch (2018). My grateful thanks to the Liang family, for inviting me to their anniversary ceremonies in 2013 at his tomb near Zouping Shandong.

465 the view from the countryside: Rao (2018), 16–17. This moving and delightful book gives a wonderful sense of a Chinese family enduring untold hardships by resilience, good humour, deep affection and loyalty, and also a profound attachment to the enduring values of the culture. Rao Pingru died in spring 2020, aged ninety-eight, as this book went to print.

466–8 Liu Dapeng in the Japanese invasion: Harrison (2005), 159–60.

469 the Long March: Harrison Salisbury (1985) was still able to interview survivors and eyewitnesses; for a recent retracing, Sun (2006).

469–70 Edgar Snow: first published in 1937; revised and enlarged edition, 1968; with further revisions by the author, 1972.

470 the Japanese war: see now Mitter (2013); Liu Dapeng's local experience is told by Harrison (2005), 159–65.

471–2 famous lines of Du Fu: Li Chiu Tien of Midland Michigan recorded 2008, https://www.youtube.com/watch?v=6Y-yV8qWOIM

472 Peking, October 1949: Kidd (2003), 3–15.

473 the painting: 'The Founding Ceremony of the Nation', Andrews (1994), 75–85.

474 a small town: Rao (2018), 205–11. For Meitang's life in Shanghai, 236–49; for another perspective on everyday life in Shanghai under

Mao: Brown and Johnson (2015), which looks at the tension between the state culture and the rise of an unofficial culture below the 'propaganda state' in Shanghai, which included a youth culture and 'a mania for Hong Kong films' (199–229).

475   'revolution is not a dinner party': Mao (1967), 28, writing in March 1927.

Mao forged a repressive state: Dikotter (2013) on the early days of the liberation, 39–62; the beginning of the clampdown, 82–101; and the Great Terror, 84–102.

476   Hundred Flowers: Dikotter (2013), 275–95.

'the five children': Rao (2018), 249.

477   'my abdomen swelled up': Rao (2018), 257.

478   on Mao's war against nature: Shapiro (2001). As Liang Shuming had noted in 1917 (de Bary, *Sources* II, 188), the idea of the conquest of nature in the name of material progress was alien to Chinese traditional civilisation.

the Great Famine: the opening up of the archives in the 1980s made it possible to gather written and oral testimonies, e.g. Becker (1996) and Zhou Xun(2013); Dikotter (2010) and Yang Jisheng (2012) make powerful use of regional Party archives.

479   Report on Xiaogang: see Wu (2016), 1–12. I am grateful to Yan Jichang and Guan Youjiang of Xiaogang village, Fengyang, for their hospitality in summer 2018 and for discussing with me the events in their village during the Great Famine and in the dramatic crisis of autumn 1978.

482–3   Yan Jichang: interview, July 2018.

483   'We are all people of the fields': quoted by Wu (2015).

484   Cultural Revolution: Dikotter (2016) is a recent summary; though too late for this book, new light is cast by Walder (2019) highlighting the virulent factionalism at the local level.

485   one foreign visitor: https://www.nytimes.com/1971/05/19/archives/china-transformed-by-elimination-of-four-olds.html

486   'That night Grandma came in': interview with Bao Xunsheng in Dongtai, summer 2014. For Huizou clan experiences at this time, Zhang (2013).

murder of 'class enemies': on the massacre at Daoxian in Hunan, Tan (2017).

487   Harbin photographs: Li Feng (2003), perhaps the greatest single record of the Cultural Revolution? 'This world is too dark', 193.

Tibet under the PRC: Detailed discussion of Tibet is out of the scope of this book; see Purdue (2005) on the history of Tibet under the Qing empire, and a recent survey of its modern history by Schaik (2011); on the position in international law, McCorquodale and Orosz (eds) (1994). The account of the destruction of Buddhist shrines was produced by the Tibet Foundation through Phuntsog Wangyal's 1980 fact-finding mission: see the Minority Rights Group report in 1983: https://minorityrights.org/wp-content/uploads/old-site-downloads/

download-1462-The-Tibetans-two-perspectives-on-Tibetan-Chi
nese-relations.pdf

Ganden: a monastic city, home to more than 5,000 monks
before 1959; after partial restoration, about 500 live there today
under close supervision: https://tibet.net/revisiting-the-cultural
-revolution-in-tibet/

488   **on Tholing:** Vitali (1999). My visit was in 2004 but I am informed
that much of the complex is still in ruins.

489   **photographs:** for images taken in 1939 at Tholing: Govinda (1979),
plates 147–51.

     'an empty paradise': Vitali (1999), 4.

489–90   **Mao cult on Peking radio:** 6 December 1967, quoted in Urban (ed.)
(1971), 139. On the antiquity of these ideas, Li Zehua essays in Pines,
Yuri *et al.* (eds) (2015); compare e.g. the cult of the first emperor
documented by Sima Qian, Dawson (ed.) (1994), 68–70; on exporting
these ideas worldwide, Lovell (2019).

490–1   **a contemporary Chinese historian:** Li Zehua (2015), 288.

491   **'Alas, what can one say?'** https://www.economist.com/
books-and-arts/2006/08/31/big-bad-wolf

492   **the *Book of Changes*:** Hexagram 49, Wilhelm (trans.) (1968), text and
commentary, 189–92.

19: THE RISE OF THE NEW CHINA

494–6   **Tangshan earthquake:** I have relied on the Tangshan Report and on
James Palmer's gripping account (2012).

497   **'I have accomplished two things':** Walder (2015), 313.

498   **1981 CP statement:** https://www.marxists.org/subject/china/
documents/cpc/history/01.htm, para 22.

     Deng Xiaoping: I have relied on Vogel (2011) but consulted Pantsov
(2015) and Dillon (2015); on his life in France (he didn't learn French),
Wang (1982), 698–705.

500   **Deng on the Cultural Revolution:** as reported by his daughter Deng
Rong (2005), 443, 448 and 450ff.

501   **Reform and Opening Up:** No account of the inception of 'Reform and
Opening Up' in autumn 1978 can neglect Yu Guangyuan (2004), the
fundamental inside witness.

502   **'China had not been a socialist society':** Yu Guangyuan (2004), 211–14.

503   **'development of science and technology':** Yu Guangyuan (2004), 12.

     education conference: my thanks to Professor Yuan Wenkai and, for
memories of the first exams, Professors Zhang Weiwei and Xue Lan
(interviews conducted August 2018).

504   **examinations:** my thanks to Professor Zhang Weiwei for sharing with
me his memories of the Reform and Opening Up period, and his time
in the 1980s as Deng Xiaoping's translator.

     fact-finding missions: on Gu Mu, Vogel (2011), 221–7, with an
interview with Professor Vogel at Harvard, September 2018;

conversation with Professor Xie Chuntao, Chinese School of the Central Committee of the Communist Party, who conducted an extensive interview with Gu Mu before his death in 2009.

505   **Party officials at Liaoning:** Vogel (2011), 228.

Japan: Vogel (2011), 297–310, and interviews with Zhang Weiwei in Shanghai and Xie Chuntao in Beijing, July 2018.

505–6   **the arrival of TV:** Rao (2018), 337, 340–41, 344–6 (watching Deng on TV, 346).

507   **Return to Xiaogang 1978:** Wu Xiang (2016), 51–6. My thanks again to Yan Jichang and Guan Youjiang of Xiaogang for their hospitality in summer 2018 and for discussing with me the events in their village during the crisis of autumn 1978.

509   **the Communist Party:** Ladany's forensic dissection (1992); on the Third Plenum, Yu Guangyuan (2004); for Deng's speech as published: https://dengxiaopingworks.wordpress.com/2013/02/25/emancipate-the-mind-seek-truth-from-facts-and-unite-as-one-in-looking-to-the-future/

511   **monarchism:** Liu Zehua (2014 and 2015).

512   **China opens up:** Vogel (2011), 333–48; my thanks to Ambassador J. Stapleton Roy for sharing his reminiscences of the rapprochement with China under the Carter administration; to the late Jack Fensterstock for recalling his role in the secret UN deals reaching out to China in 1978; and to Ezra Vogel for his insights into the beginning of Deng's reforms (Washington and Harvard, September 2018).

513   **Guangzhou:** for the background, Vogel (1989); interview with Ezra Vogel, September 2018; on Xi Zhongxun, Vogel (1989), 395–7; 739–40; and interview with Chen Kaizhi, July 2018, in Guangzhou.

514–15 **the Democracy Movement and Tiananmen Square:** the key texts are Zhang Liang (2001); Zhao (2009), Liao (2019) and Li Peng (2010); the latest documents are in Bao (ed.) (2019); for the preface by Andrew Nathan, https://www.foreignaffairs.com/articles/china/2019-05-30/new-tiananmen-papers; see too the valuable review by Ian Johnson: https://www.nybooks.com/articles/2019/06/27/tiananmen-chinas-black-week-end/

517   **'to this day I am proud':** for Chinese witnesses, Liao (2019), 80; on the lack of a mechanism for dialogue with the people, see the interview too with Li Hai, 141–54.

519   **Zhao Ziyang's speech** and video broadcast on CCTV: https://en.wikipedia.org/wiki/Zhao_Ziyang and https://www.youtube.com/watch?v=P7icb6H2XMw; images: https://www.youtube.com/watch?v=JRshth1Nyb4

foreign witnesses: for example Evans (1993), 272–97, and John Gittings' 'China through the Sliding Door' website, Chapter VIII, the Beijing Massacre: http://www.johngittings.com

519   **'In shock, I turned':** https://www.theguardian.com/lifeandstyle/2009/may/23/tiananmen-square

520   **Richard Evans:** (though his information came from a Party contact).

520–21 **Li Rui diary:** see Ian Johnson: https://pulitzercenter.org/reporting/chinas-black-week-end; on Li himself: https://www.nytimes.com/2019/02/15/obituaries/li-rui-dead.html

521 **Deng speech on CCTV:** http://www.tsquare.tv/chronology/Deng.html

523 **Zhu Rongji:** https://www.scmp.com/article/407635/history-will-smile-zhu-rongji

524 **legal progress stalled:** these developments, which it should be said included major developments in education and in women's rights, can be followed in the instructive comments in successive introductions to the four editions of Albert Chen's introduction to PRC law since 1992.

524–5 **Charter 08:** For the text of Charter 2008, http://www.charter08.com/charter08.php

525 **Liu Xiaobo:** see the essay by Simon Leys: https://www.nybooks.com/articles/2012/02/09/liu-xiaobo-he-told-truth-about-chinas-tyranny/

527 **on the 'Belt and Road':** see e.g. Frankopan (2018), plus https://www.theguardian.com/cities/ng-interactive/2018/jul/30/what-china-belt-road-initiative-silk-road-explainer

528 **Document Number 9:** for Xi Jinping's Seven Taboos, http://www.chinafile.com/document-9-chinafile-translation; https://www.dw.com/en/opinion-xi-and-chinas-seven-taboos/a-16870412
Xinjiang repression: for a representative introduction, https://www.cfr.org/backgrounder/chinas-repression-uighurs-xinjiang

529 **Xi's 2018 speech:** https://www.nytimes.com/2018/12/18/world/asia/xi-jinping-speech-china.html

532 **China's story:** for a challenging long view, Pollock and Elman (eds) (2018).

532–3 **Huang Zongxi 'without government by law there can be no government by men':** de Bary (1993), 99.
8 September 2040: for the next conjunction, Pankenier (2013), 442–3.

AFTERWORD

535 **Dr Li Wenliang:** https://www.scmp.com/news/china/politics/article/3049606/coronavirus-doctors-death-becomes-catalyst-freedom-speech
Chengdu teachers on Camus: https://www.nytimes.com/2020/02/14/opinion/china-coronavirus-social-media.html
Xu Zhangrun's protest: http://www.china le.com/reporting-opinion/viewpoint/viral-alarm-when-fury-overcomes-fear; for his archive: http://chinaheritage.net/xu-zhangrun許章潤/; for Xu's essays that appeared after this book went to press: *Six Chapters from the 2018 Year of the Dog* by Hong Kong City University Press (2020).

536 **China's historic opportunity:** for examples see eg Peter Frankopan https://www.theguardian.com/commentisfree/2020/may/14/china-global-leadership-beijing-coronavirus and Kurt Campbell and Rush Doshi https://www.foreignaffairs.com/articles/china/2020-03-18/coronavirus-could-reshape-global-order

537   **Hong Kong:** for a recent summary with links: https://www.theguardian.
com/commentisfree/2020/may/22/the-guardian-view-on-hong-kong-
a-broken-promise For the drafting of the impending new security
laws: https://www.theguardian.com/world/2020/jun/18/china-table
s-draft-hong-kong-security-law-in-sign-it-intends-to-rush-legislation
As for the reasons behind this, the insecurity of the leadership in
Beijing should not be forgotten: Hong Kong is an enormous conduit
of information to the mainland: the TV news for example is seen in
Guangzhou and Shenzhen: reaching an economic zone of nearly 25
million who are affluent and well informed. The new security law
for Hong Kong law was passed by the National People's Congress on
30 June 2020; the legislation to give Beijing control of Hong Kong's
electoral system was approved by the NPC on 11 March 2021, vetting
all candidates for patriotism and loyalty to the Party.

538   **the downturn of the Chinese economy:** for a sample reaction taking
into account Covid 19 https://www.foreignaffairs.com/articles/
united-states/2020-04-03/chinas-coming-upheaval
denial of free speech: Article 35 of the 1982 State Constitution states
that the people of the PRC 'enjoy freedom of speech, of the press, of
assembly, and of association and demonstration.'
internalising Confucian virtue and benevolence: 'Those who succeed
in mighty undertakings are always open minded and willing from
the bottom of their hearts to hear different views" said the head of
the Committee the influential Wang Qishen, now Vice-President of
the PRC: https://www.wsws.org/en/articles/2016/03/26/chin-m26.
html The specific discussion of the importance of Confucian values
appeared on the homepage of the Committee's website (reported 20
April 2020 ccdi.gov.cn).
the signs are hard to read: for a pithy summary of the current
state of play by a seasoned observer, Rana Mitter: https://www.
newstatesman.com/international/china/2020/05/china-and-attraction
s-authoritarianism
Naval Intelligence: see above page 560 note 455.
a global leader: see e.g. Daniel Tobin's article https://www.csis.
org/analysis/how-xi-jinpings-new-era-should-have-ended-us-debate
-beijings-ambitions

539   **the moral order of Chinese civilisation:** Keightley (2014), 37–74;
Roel Sterckx, *Chinese Thought,* Penguin (2019) 163–227. As Zhang
Xuecheng wrote in 1797, 'for the people of a century hence, we too
will be men of old. Let us therefore put ourselves in their place. How
then will it fare with us?' Nivison (1966), 272.

BIBLIOGRAPHY

BOOKS

Aldrich, M. A., *The Search for a Vanishing Beijing: A Guide to China's Capital Through the Ages* (Hong Kong: Hong Kong University Press, 2006)

Alitto, Guy S., *The Last Confucian: Liang Shu-ming and the Chinese Dilemma of Modernity* (Berkeley: University of California Press, 1979; new edition 1986)

Allan, Sarah, *The Shape of the Turtle: Myth, Art and Cosmos in Early China* (Albany: State University of New York Press, 1991)

Allan, Sarah (ed.), *The Formation of Chinese Civilization: An Archaeological Perspective* (New Haven: Yale University Press, 2005)

Allan, Sarah and Cohen, Alvin P., *Legend, Lore and Religion in China* (San Francisco: Chinese Materials Center, 1979)

Altenburger, Roland *et al.* (eds), *Yangzhou, a Place in Literature: The Local in Chinese Cultural History* (Honolulu: University of Hawai'i Press, 2015)

Andrew, Anita M. and Rapp, John A. (eds), *Autocracy and China's Rebel Founding Emperors: Comparing Chairman Mao and Ming Taizu* (Lanham: Rowman & Littlefield, 2000)

Andrews, Julia Frances, *Painters and Politics in the People's Republic of China 1949–1979* (Berkeley: University of California Press, 1994)

Arlington, L. C. and Lewisohn, William, *In Search of Old Peking* (Peking: Henri Vetch, 1935)

Bao Pu (ed.), *The Last Secret: The Final Documents from the June Fourth Crackdown* (Hong Kong: New Century Press, 2019)

Barbieri-Low, A. J. and Yates, Robin D. S., *Law, State and Society in Early Imperial China* (Leiden: Brill, 2015)

Beal, Samuel (trans.), *The Life of Hiuen-Tsiang by the Shaman Hwui Li* (London: Kegan Paul, Trench, Trübner, 1911)

Beasley, W. G. and Pulleyblank, E. G. (eds), *Historians of China and Japan* (London: Oxford University Press, 1961)

Beattie, Hilary J., *Land and Lineage in China: A Study of T'ung-ch'eng County, Anhwei, in the Ming and Ch'ing Dynasties* (Cambridge: Cambridge University Press, 1979)

Becker, Jasper, *Hungry Ghosts: Mao's Secret Famine* (New York: Free Press, 1996)

Bellah, R. N., *Religion in Human Evolution: From the Paleolithic to the Axial Age* (Cambridge, MA: Belknap Press, 2011)

Bellah, R. N. and Joas, H. (eds), *The Axial Age and Its Consequences* (Cambridge, MA: Belknap Press, 2012)

Benedictow, Ole J., *The Black Death 1346–1353: A Complete History* (Woodbridge: Boydell Press, 2004)

Benn, Charles, *China's Golden Age: Everyday Life in the Tang Dynasty* (Oxford: Oxford University Press, 2004)

Benton, Gregor and Lin Chun, *Was Mao Really a Monster?* (Abingdon: Routledge, 2010)

Bianco, Lucien, *Origins of the Chinese Revolution 1915–1949* (Stanford: Stanford University Press, 1971)

Bickers, Robert A. (ed.), *Ritual and Diplomacy: The Macartney Mission to China 1792–1794* (London: British Association for Chinese Studies/WellSweep Press, 1993)

Bishop, Kevin, *China's Imperial Way* (Hong Kong: Odyssey, 1997)

Bol, Peter K., *'This Culture of Ours': Intellectual Transitions in T'ang and Sung China* (Stanford: Stanford University Press, 1992)

Bol, Peter K., 'Government, Society, and State: On the Political Visions of Ssu-ma Kuang (1019–1086) and Wang An-shih (1021–1086)' in Hymes, Robert P. and Schirokauer, Conrad (eds), *Ordering the World: Approaches to State and Society in Sung Dynasty China* (Berkeley: University of California Press, 1993)

Boltz, William G., 'Literacy and the Emergence of Writing in China' in Li Feng and Branner, D. P. (eds), *Writing and Literacy in Early China* (Seattle: University of Washington Press, 2011), 51–84

Bredon, Juliet, *Sir Robert Hart: The Romance of a Great Career*, 2nd edition (London: Hutchinson, 1910)

Bredon, Juliet, *Peking: A Historical and Intimate Description of Its Chief Places of Interest*, 2nd edition (Shanghai: Kelly & Walsh, 1922)

Brook, Timothy, *The Confusions of Pleasure: Commerce and Culture in Ming China* (Berkeley: University of California Press, 1998)

Brook, T., 'Xu Guangqi in His Context: The World of the Shanghai Gentry' in Jami, Catherine *et al.* (eds), *Statecraft & Intellectual Renewal in Late Ming China: The Cross-Cultural Synthesis of Xu Guangqi (1562–1633)* (Leiden: Brill, 2001)

Brook, Timothy, *The Troubled Empire: China in the Ming and Yuan Dynasties* (Cambridge, MA: Belknap Press, 2010)

Brown, J. and Johnson, M. (eds), *Maoism at the Grassroots: Everyday Life in China's Era of High Socialism* (Cambridge, MA: Harvard University Press, 2015)

Budge, Sir E. A. Wallis (trans.), *The Monks of Kublai Khan* (London: Religious Tract Society, 1928)

Burton, R. F. (trans.), *Plantains in the Rain: Selected Chinese Poems of Du Mu* (London: Wellsweep Press, 1990)

Campbell, Roderick, *Violence, Kinship and the Early Chinese State: The Shang and Their World* (Cambridge: Cambridge University Press, 2018)

Chalfant, Frank H., *Early Chinese Writing: Memoirs of the Carnegie Museum, Vol. IV, No. 1* (Pittsburgh: Carnegie Institute, 1906)

Chan Hok-lam and de Bary, W. Theodore (eds), *Yüan Thought: Chinese Thought and Religion under the Mongols* (New York: Columbia University Press, 1982)

Chang, Jung, *Wild Swans: Three Daughters of China* (London: HarperCollins, 1991)

Chang, Jung, *Empress Dowager Cixi: The Concubine Who Launched Modern China* (London: Jonathan Cape, 2013)

Chang, Jung and Halliday, Jon, *Mao: The Untold Story* (London: Jonathan Cape, 2005)

Chang, K. C., *Early Chinese Civilization: Anthropological Perspectives* (Cambridge, MA: Harvard University Press, 1976)

Chang, K. C. (ed.), *Food in Chinese Culture : Anthropological and Historical Perspectives* (New Haven: Yale University Press, 1977)

Chang, K. C., *Shang Civilization* (New Haven: Yale University Press, 1980)

Chang, K. C., *Art, Myth, and Ritual: The Path to Political Authority in Ancient China* (Cambridge, MA: Harvard University Press, 1983)

Chang, Kang-i Sun and Saussy, Haun (eds), *Women Writers of*

Traditional China: An Anthology of Poetry and Criticism (Stanford, CA: Stanford University Press, 1999)

Chen, Albert, *Chinese Law: An Introduction to the Legal System of the People's Republic of China* (Hong Kong: LexisNexis, 2011)

Chen Ji, *Shouqin Yanglao Xinshu* (c. 1085; current edition 2013)

Chesneaux, Jean, *Peasant Revolts in China 1840–1949* (London: Thames & Hudson, 1973)

Chien, Helen Hsieh (trans.), *The European Diary of Hsieh Fucheng: Envoy Extraordinary of Imperial China* (New York: St Martin's Press, 1993)

Ching, Frank, *Ancestors: 900 Years in the Life of a Chinese Family* (London: Harrap, 1988)

Chou, Eva Shan, *Reconsidering Tu Fu: Literary Greatness and Cultural Context* (Cambridge: Cambridge University Press, 1995)

Chow Tse-tsung, *The May Fourth Movement* (Cambridge, MA: Harvard University Press, 1960)

Chu Hsi, *The Philosophy of Human Nature*, trans. Bruce, J. Percy (London: Arthur Probsthain, 1922)

Church, Sally K., 'Two Ming Dynasty Shipyards in Nanjing and Their Infrastructure' in Kimura, Jun (ed.), *Shipwreck Asia: Thematic Studies in East Asian Maritime Archaeology* (Adelaide: Maritime Archaeology Program, Flinders University, 2010), http://www.shipwreckasia.org/wp-content/uploads/Chapter3.pdf

Clemmow, Frances, *Days of Sorrow, Times of Joy: The Story of a Victorian Family and Its Love Affair with China* (Sandy: Gottahavebooks, 2016)

Clunas, Craig and Harrison-Hall, Jessica (eds), *Ming: 50 Years That Changed China* (London: British Museum Press, 2014).

Cooper, Gene, *The Market and Temple Fairs of Rural China: Red Fire* (Abingdon: Routledge, 2013)

Cornaby, W. A., *China under the Searchlight* (London: T. Fisher Unwin, 1901)

Creel, Herrlee Glessner, *The Birth of China: A Study of the Formative Period of Chinese Civilization* (New York: Reynal & Hitchcock, 1937)

Creel, Herrlee Glessner, *Studies in Early Chinese Culture* (London: Kegan Paul, 1938)

Dan, Jennifer Marie, 'Manichaeism and Its Spread into China', honours thesis, University of Tennessee, 2002

Dardess, John W., *Blood and History in China: The Donglin Faction and Its Repression 1620–1627* (Honolulu: University of Hawai'i Press, 2002)

Dardess, John W., *Ming China 1368–1644: A Concise History of a Resilient Empire* (Lanham: Rowman & Littlefield, 2012)

Davies, Gloria, *Lu Xun's Revolution: Writing in a Time of Violence* (Cambridge, MA: Harvard University Press, 2013)

Davis, A. R., *Tu Fu* (New York: Twayne, 1971)

Davis, Richard L. (trans.), *Historical Records of the Five Dynasties* (New York: Columbia University Press, 2004)

Davis, Richard L., *From Warhorses to Ploughshares: The Later Tang Reign of Emperor Mingzong* (Hong Kong: Hong Kong University Press, 2015)

Dawson, Raymond (ed.), *The Legacy of China* (London: Oxford University Press, 1971)

Dawson, Raymond (ed.), *Sima Qian: Historical Records* (Oxford: Oxford University Press, 1994)

de Bary, W. Theodore, *Sources of Chinese Tradition*, 2 vols (New York: Columbia University Press, 1960; new editions, Vol. I: 2000, Vol. II: 2001)

de Bary, W. Theodore, *Self and Society in Ming Thought* (New York: Columbia University Press, 1970)

de Bary, W. Theodore, *East Asian Civilizations: A Dialogue in Five Stages* (Cambridge, MA: Harvard University Press, 1988)

de Bary, W. Theodore, *Waiting for the Dawn: A Plan for the Prince* (New York: Columbia University Press, 1993)

de Bary, W. Theodore, *Asian Values and Human Rights: a Confucian Communitarian Perspective* (Cambridge, MA: Harvard University Press, 1998)

Deng Rong, *Deng Xiaoping and the Cultural Revolution: A Daughter Recalls the Critical Years* (Beijing: Foreign Language Press, 2002)

Des Forges, Roger *et al.* (eds), *Chinese Walls in Time and Space* (Ithaca: Cornell University Press, 2010)

Devahuti, D., *The Unknown Hsüan-tsang* (New Delhi: Oxford University Press, 2001)

Dikotter, Frank, *Mao's Great Famine: A History of China's Most Devastating Catastrophe 1958–1962* (London: Bloomsbury, 2010)

Dikotter, Frank, *The Tragedy of Liberation: A History of the Chinese Revolution 1945–1957* (New York: Bloomsbury, 2013)

Dikotter, Frank, *The Cultural Revolution: A People's History 1962–1976* (New York: Bloomsbury, 2016)

Dillon, Michael, *Deng Xiaoping: The Man Who Made Modern China* (London: I. B. Tauris, 2015)

Dong Zuobin (Tung Tso-pin), *Yin-li-p'u (Tabulated Data of the Yin Dynasty According to Chronology of Recorded Events Found in the Oracle Bone Inscriptions)* (Peking: Academia Sinica, 1945)

Drancourt, Michel and Raoult, Didier (eds), *Paleomicrobiology: Past Human Infections* (New York: Springer, 2008)

Dreyer, Edward L., *Zheng He: China and the Oceans in the Early Ming Dynasty 1405–1433* (London: Pearson Longman, 2007)

Dudbridge, Glen, *The Lost Books of Medieval China* (London: British Library, 2000)

Dudbridge, Glen, *The Tale of Li Wa* (London: Ithaca Press, 1983)

Dudbridge, Glen, *A Portrait of Five Dynasties China: From the Memoirs of Wang Renyu (880–956)* (Oxford: Oxford University Press, 2013)

Ebrey, Patricia Buckley (ed. & trans.), *Chu Hsi's 'Family Rituals'* (Princeton: Princeton University Press, 1991)

Ebrey, Patricia Buckley, *The Inner Quarters: Marriage and the Lives of Chinese Women in the Sung Period* (Berkeley: University of California Press, 1993)

Ebrey, Patricia Buckley, *The Cambridge Illustrated History of China*, 2nd edition (Cambridge: Cambridge University Press, 2010)

Ebrey, Patricia Buckley, *Emperor Huizong* (Cambridge, MA: Harvard University Press, 2014)

Egan, Ronald C., *The Burden of Female Talent: The Poet Li Qingzhao and Her History in China* (Cambridge, MA: Harvard University Press, 2014)

Elliott, Jane E., *Some Did It for Civilisation, Some Did It for Their Country: A Revised View of the Boxer War* (Hong Kong: Chinese University Press, 2002)

Elman, Benjamin A., *From Philosophy to Philology: Intellectual and Social Aspects of Change in Late Imperial China* (Cambridge, MA: Harvard University Press, 1984)

Elman, Benjamin A., *Classicism, Politics, and Kingship: The Ch'ang-chou School of New Text Confucianism in Late Imperial China* (Berkeley: University of California Press, 1990)

Elvin, Mark, *The Pattern of the Chinese Past* (Stanford, CA: Stanford University Press, 1973)

Elvin, Mark and Liu Ts'ui-jung (eds), *Sediments of Time: Environment and Society in Chinese History*, 2 vols (Cambridge: Cambridge University Press, 2009)

Esherick, Joseph W., *Reform and Revolution in China: The 1911 Revolution in Hunan and Hubei* (Berkeley: University of California Press, 1976)

Esherick, Joseph W. and Wei, C. X. George (eds), *China: How the Empire Fell* (Abingdon: Routledge, 2014)

Evans, Richard, *Deng Xiaoping and the Making of Modern China* (London: Hamish Hamilton, 1993)

Fairbank, John King, *The Great Chinese Revolution 1800–1985* (London: Chatto & Windus, 1987)

Farrer, R. J., *On the Eaves of the World*, 2 vols (London: Edward Arnold, 1926)

Faure, David, *Emperor and Ancestor: State and Lineage in South China* (Stanford: Stanford University Press, 2007)

Fenby, Jonathan, *The Penguin History of Modern China: The Fall and Rise of a Great Power, 1850 to the Present*, new edition (London: Penguin, 2013)

Finnane, Antonia, *Speaking of Yangzhou: A Chinese City 1550–1850* (Cambridge, MA: Harvard University Press, 2004)

Foccardi, Gabriele, *The Chinese Travelers of the Ming Period* (Wiesbaden: Otto Harrassowitz, 1986)

Fong, Grace S., *Herself an Author: Gender, Agency, and Writing in Late Imperial China* (Honolulu: University of Hawai'i Press, 2008)

Fong, Grace and Widmer, Ellen, *The Inner Quarters and Beyond: Women Writers from Ming through Qing* (Leiden: Brill, 2010)

Foot, Sarah and Robinson, Chase F., *The Oxford History of Historical Writing, Vol. II: 400–1400* (Oxford: Oxford University Press, 2015)

Frampton, J. (trans.), *Bernardino de Escalante A Discourse of the Navigation which the Portugales Doe Make to the Realmes and Provinces of the East Partes of the Worlde* (London, 1579)

Frankopan, Peter, *The Silk Roads: A New History of the World* (London: Bloomsbury, 2015)

Frankopan, Peter, *The New Silk Roads: The Present and Future of the World* (London: Bloomsbury, 2018)

Frodsham, J. D. (trans.), *The First Chinese Embassy to the West: The Journals of Kuo Sung-t'ao, Liu Hsi-hung and Chang Te-yi* (Oxford: Clarendon Press, 1974)

Gardner, Daniel K. (trans.), *Learning to Be a Sage: Selections from the Conversations of Master Chu, Arranged Topically* (Berkeley: University of California Press, 1990)

Geil, William Edgar, *Eighteen Capitals of China* (London: Constable, 1911)

Gernet, Jacques, *Daily Life in China, on the Eve of the Mongol Invasion 1250–1276* (Stanford: Stanford University Press, 1962)

Goepper, Roger, 'Precursors and Early Stages of the Chinese Script' in Rawson, Jessica (ed.), *Mysteries of Ancient China: New Discoveries from the Early Dynasties* (New York: George Braziller, 1996)

Goodrich, Anne Swann, *The Peking Temple of the Eastern Peak: The Tung-yüeh Miao in Peking and Its Lore* (Nagoya: Monumenta Serica, 1964)

Govinda, Li Gotami, *Tibet in Pictures, Vol. II: Expedition to Western Tibet* (Berkeley: Dharma, 1979).

Graham, A. C., *Poems of the Late T'ang* (Harmondsworth: Penguin, 1965)

Granet, Marcel, *Danses et légendes de la Chine ancienne* (Paris: Félix Alcan, 1926)

Granet, Marcel, *Fêtes et chansons anciennes de la Chine*, 2nd edition (Paris: Ernest Leroux, 1929)

Granet, Marcel, *Festivals and Songs of Ancient China* (London: George Routledge, 1932)

Greenberg, M., *British Trade and the Opening of China 1800–42* (Cambridge: Cambridge University Press, 1951)

Guy, R. Kent, *The Emperor's Four Treasuries: Scholars and the State in the Late Ch'ien-lung Era* (Cambridge, MA: Harvard University Press, 1987)

Haeger, John Winthrop (ed.), *Crisis and Prosperity in Sung China* (Tucson: University of Arizona Press, 1975)

Hanan, Patrick (trans.), *Courtesans and Opium: Romantic Illusions of the Fool of Yangzhou* (New York: Columbia University Press, 2009)

Hansen, Valerie, *The Silk Road: A New History* (Oxford: Oxford University Press, 2012)

Hansen, Valerie, *The Open Empire: A History of China to 1800*, 2nd edition (New York: W. W. Norton, 2015)

Harris, Lane J., *The Peking Gazette: A Reader in Nineteenth-Century Chinese History* (Leiden: Brill, 2018)

Harrison, Henrietta, *The Making of the Republican Citizen: Political Ceremonies and Symbols in China 1911–1929* (Oxford: Oxford University Press, 2000)

Harrison, Henrietta, *The Man Awakened from Dreams: One Man's Life in a North China Village 1857–1942* (Stanford: Stanford University Press, 2005)

Hawkes, David with Minchin, John (trans.), *The Story of the Stone*, 5 vols (Harmondsworth: Penguin, 1973–86)

He Yuming, *Home and the World: Editing the 'Glorious Ming' in Woodblock-Printed Books of the Sixteenth and Seventeenth Centuries* (Cambridge, MA: Harvard University Press, 2013)

Heng Chye Kiang, *Cities of Aristocrats and Bureaucrats: The Development of Medieval Chinese Cityscapes* (Honolulu: University of Hawai'i Press, 1999)

Hessler, Peter, *Oracle Bones: A Journey between China and the West* (London: John Murray, 2006)

Hill, John E., *Through the Jade Gate to Rome: A Study of the Silk Routes during the Later Han Dynasty, 1st to 2nd Centuries CE* (Charleston: BookSurge, 2009)

Hinton, David (trans.), *The Late Poems of Wang An-shih* (New York: New Directions, 2015)

Ho, Elaine Yee Lin and Kuehn, Julia (eds), *China Abroad: Travels, Subjects, Spaces* (Hong Kong: Hong Kong University Press, 2009)

Hsia, R. Po-chia, *A Jesuit in the Forbidden City: Matteo Ricci 1552–1610* (Oxford: Oxford University Press, 2010)

Hsiao Chi'en, *Etching of a Tormented Age: A Glimpse of Contemporary Chinese Literature* (London: George Allen & Unwin, 1942)

Huang, Ray, *1587, a Year of No Significance: The Ming Dynasty in Decline* (New Haven: Yale University Press, 1981)

Hudson, J. J., 'River Sands/Urban Spaces: Changsha in Modern Chinese History', doctoral thesis, University of Texas at Austin, 2015

Hung, William, *Tu Fu: China's Greatest Poet* (Cambridge, MA: Harvard University Press, 1952)

Hung, William, *A Supplementary Volume of Notes for 'Tu Fu: China's Greatest Poet'* (Cambridge, MA: Harvard University Press, 1952)

Hayashi, Ryoichi, *The Silk Road and the Shoso-in* (New York: Weatherhill, 1975)

Idema, Wilt L., *Heroines of Jiangyong: Chinese Narrative Ballads in Women's Script* (Seattle: University of Washington Press, 2009)

Idema, Wilt and Grant, Beata, *The Red Brush: Writing Women of Imperial China* (Cambridge, MA: Harvard University Press, 2004)

Ivanhoe, Philip J. (ed. & trans.), *On Ethics and History: Essays and Letters of Zhang Xuecheng* (Stanford: Stanford University Press, 2010)

Ivanhoe, Philip J., *Three Streams: Confucian Reflections on Learning and the Moral Heart-Mind in China, Korea, and Japan* (New York: Oxford University Press, 2016)

Jackson, Peter, *The Mongols and the West 1221–1410*, 2nd edition (Abingdon: Routledge, 2018)

Jacques, Martin, *When China Rules the World*, 2nd edition (London: Penguin, 2012)

Jaspers, Karl, *The Origin and Goal of History* (New Haven: Yale University Press, 1953)

Jen Yu-wen, *The Taiping Revolutionary Movement* (New Haven: Yale University Press, 1973)

Ji Xiao-bin, *Politics and Conservatism in Northern Song China: The Career and Thought of Sima Guang (AD 1019–1086)* (Hong Kong: Chinese University Press, 2005)

Jiang Yonglin (trans.), *The Great Ming Code* (Seattle: University of Washington Press, 2005)

Jiang Yonglin, *The Mandate of Heaven and the Great Ming Code* (Seattle: University of Washington Press, 2011)

Johnson, Ian, *The Souls of China: The Return of Religion after Mao* (London: Penguin, 2017)

Johnson, Linda Cooke, 'Shanghai: An Emerging Jiangnan Port 1683–1840' in Johnson, Linda Cooke (ed.), *Cities of Jiangnan in Late Imperial China* (Albany: State University of New York Press, 1993)

Jones, Eric, *The European Miracle: Environments, Economies and Geopolitics in the History of Europe and Asia*, 3rd edition (Cambridge: Cambridge University Press 2003)

Kafalas, Philip A., *In Limpid Dream: Nostalgia and Zhang Dai's Reminiscences of the Ming* (Norwalk: Eastbridge, 2007)

Keightley, David N., *Sources of Shang History: The Oracle-Bone Inscriptions of Bronze Age China* (Berkeley: University of California Press, 1978)

Keightley, David N., *The Ancestral Landscape: Time Space and*

Community in Late Shang China, ca. 1200–1045 BC (Berkeley: Center for Chinese Studies, University of California, 2000)

Keyserling, Hermann, *Travel Diary of a Philosopher*, 2 vols (London: Jonathan Cape, 1925)

Kidd, David, *Peking Story: The Last Days of Old China* (New York: New York Review Books, [1988] 2003)

King, F. H., *Farmers of Forty Centuries: or, Permanent Agriculture in China, Korea and Japan* (Madison: Mrs F. H. King, 1911)

Ko, Dorothy, *Teachers of the Inner Chambers: Women and Culture in Seventeenth-Century China* (Stanford: Stanford University Press, 1994)

Kracke, E. A., 'Sung K'ai-feng' in Haeger, John Winthrop (ed.), *Crisis and Prosperity in Sung China* (Tucson: University of Arizona Press, 1975)

Kuhn, Dieter, *The Age of Confucian Rule: The Song Transformation of China* (Cambridge, MA: Belknap Press, 2009)

Kurz, Johannes L., *China's Southern Tang Dynasty 937–976* (Abingdon: Routledge, 2011)

Ladany, Laszlo, *The Communist Party of China and Marxism 1921–1985: A Self-Portrait* (Hong Kong: Hong Kong University Press, 1992)

Lam, Willy Wo-lap, *Routledge Handbook of the Chinese Communist Party* (Abingdon: Routledge, 2018)

Lau, Ulrich and Staack, Thies (eds & trans), *Legal Practice in the Formative Stages of the Chinese Empire: An Annotated Translation of the Exemplary Qin Criminal Cases from the Yuelu Academy Collection* (Leiden: Brill, 2016)

Leonard, Jane Kate, *Wei Yüan and China's Rediscovery of the Maritime World* (Cambridge, MA: Harvard University Press, 1984)

Leslie, Daniel, *The Chinese-Hebrew Memorial Book of the Jewish Community of Kaifeng* (Leiden: Brill, 1965–67)

Leslie, D., *The Identification of Chinese Cities in Arabic and Persian Sources* (Canberra, 1982)

Leslie, Donald Daniel, *Islam in Traditional China: A Short History to 1800* (Canberra: Canberra College of Advanced Education, 1986)

Leslie, Donald Daniel *et al.*, *Islam in Traditional China: A Bibliographical Guide* (Sankt Agustin, Germany: Monumenta Serica, 2006)

Levathes, Louise, *When China Ruled the Seas: The Treasure Fleet of* the Dragon Throne 1405–1433 (New York: Simon & Schuster, 1994)

Levenson, Joseph R., Confucian China and Its Modern Fate (London: Routledge & Kegan Paul, 1958)

Levy, Howard S. (trans.), A Feast of Mist and Flowers: The Gay Quarters of Nanking at the End of the Ming (Yokohama, 1966)

Lewis, Charlton M., Prologue to the Chinese Revolution: The Transformation of Ideas and Institutions in Hunan Province 1891–1907 (Cambridge, MA: Harvard University Press, 1976)

Lewis, Mark Edward, The Flood Myths of Early China (Albany: State University of New York Press, 2006)

Lewis, Mark Edward, The Earliest Chinese Empires (Cambridge, MA: Harvard University Press, 2009)

Lewis, Mark Edward, China's Cosmopolitan Empire: The Tang Dynasty (Cambridge, MA: Belknap Press, 2009)

Leys, Simon, The Chairman's New Clothes: Mao and the Cultural Revolution (London: Allison & Busby, 1977)

Leys, Simon, Chinese Shadows (London: Penguin, 1978)

Leys, Simon, Broken Images: Essays on Chinese Culture and Politics, trans. Cox, Steve (London: Allison & Busby, 1979)

Leys, Simon, La Forêt en feu: essais sur la culture et la politique chinoises (Paris: Hermann, 1983),

Leys, Simon, The Burning Forest: Essays on Chinese Culture and Politics (London: Paladin, 1988)

Leys, Simon (trans.), The Analects of Confucius (New York: W. W. Norton, 1997)

Leys, Simon, The Hall of Uselessness: Collected Essays (New York: New York Review Books, 2013)

Li Chi, Anyang (Seattle: University of Washington Press, 1975)

Li Feng, Early China: A Social and Cultural History (Cambridge: Cambridge University Press, 2013)

Li Feng and Branner, David Prager (eds), Writing and Literacy in Early China (Seattle: University of Washington Press, 2011)

Li Min, Social Memory and State Formation in Early China (Cambridge: Cambridge University Press, 2018)

Li Peng, The Critical Moment: Li Peng Diaries (n.p.: West Point Publishing House, 2010)

Li Rongxi (trans.), A Biography of the Tripiṭaka Master of the Great Ci'en Monastery of the Great Tang Dynasty (Berkeley: Numata Center for Buddhist Translation and Research, 1995)

Li Tang and Winkler, Dietmar W., From the Oxus River to the

Chinese Shores: Studies on East Syriac Christianity in China and Central Asia (Zurich: LIT, 2013)

Li Yung-hsi (trans.), *The Life of Hsuan Tsang : the Tripitaka-Master of the Great Tzu En Monastery* (Beijing: Chinese Buddhist Association, 1959)

Li Zhengsheng, *Red-Color News Soldier: A Chinese Photographer's Odyssey through the Cultural Revolution* (London: Phaidon, 2003)

Liao Yiwu, *Bullets and Opium: Real-Life Stories of China after the Tiananmen Square Massacre* (New York: One Signal/Atria, 2019)

Liu Kwang-ching, *Orthodoxy in Late Imperial China* (Berkeley: University of California Press, 1990)

Liu Li, *The Chinese Neolithic: Trajectories to Early States* (Cambridge: Cambridge University Press, 2004)

Liu, Lydia, *et al.* (eds), *The Birth of Chinese Feminism: Essential Texts in Transnational Theory* (New York: Columbia University Press, 2013)

Liu Zehua, 'Political and Intellectual Authority: The Concept of the "Sage-Monarch" and Its Modern Fate' in Pines, Yuri *et al.* (eds), *Ideology of Power and Power of Ideology in Early China* (Leiden: Brill, 2015)

Lloyd, G. E. R. and Zhao, Jenny (eds), *Ancient Greece and China Compared* (Cambridge: Cambridge University Press, 2018)

Lo Jung-pang, *China as a Sea Power 1127–1368: A Preliminary Survey of the Maritime Expansion and Naval Exploits of the Chinese People during the Southern Song and Yuan Periods* (Hong Kong: Hong Kong University Press, 2012)

Loewe, Michael, 'The Former Han Dynasty' in Twitchett, Denis and Loewe, Michael (eds), *The Cambridge History of China, Vol. I: The Ch'in and Han Empires 221 BC–AD 220* (Cambridge: Cambridge University Press, 1986)

Loewe, Michael, *Early Chinese Texts: A Bibliographical Guide* (n.p.: Society for the Study of Early China, 1993), http://starling.rinet.ru/Texts/Students/Loewe%2C%20Michael/Early%20Chinese%20Texts%2C%20A%20Bibliographical%20Guide%20%281993%29.pdf

Lorge, Peter A., *Five Dynasties and Ten Kingdoms* (Hong Kong: Chinese University Press, 2010)

Lorge, Peter, *The Reunification of China: Peace through War under the Song Dynasty* (Cambridge: Cambridge University Press, 2015)

Lovell, Julia (trans.), *The Real Story of Ah-Q and Other Tales of China: The Complete Fiction of Lu Xun* (London: Penguin, 2009)

Lovell, Julia, *The Opium War: Drugs, Dreams and the Making of China* (London: Picador, 2011)

Lovell, Julia, *Maoism: A Global History* (London: Bodley Head, 2019)

Lynch, Catherine, *Liang Shuming and the Populist Alternative in China* (Leiden: Brill, 2018)

Ma Huan, *The Overall Survey of the Ocean's Shores* (Cambridge: Cambridge University Press, 1970)

McCorquodale, R. and Orosz, N. (eds), *Tibet: The Position in International Law* (London: Serindia, 1994)

McDermott, Joseph P., *The Making of a New Rural Order in South China, Vol. I: Village, Land, and Lineage in Huizhou 900–1600* (Cambridge: Cambridge University Press, 2013)

McDonald, Angus W., Jr, *The Urban Origins of Rural Revolution: Elites and the Masses in Hunan Province, China 1911–1927* (Berkeley: University of California Press, 1978)

Mackerras, Colin, *Chinese Drama: A Historical Survey* (Beijing: New World Press, 1990)

Mackerras, Colin, 'Yangzhou Local Theatre in the Second Half of the Qing' in Olivová, Lucie and Børdahl, Vibeke (eds), *Lifestyle and Entertainment in Yangzhou* (Copenhagen: NIAS Press, 2009)

Malek, Roman (ed.), *From Kaifeng to Shanghai: Jews in China* (Sankt Augustin: Monumenta Serica, 2000)

Mann, Susan and Cheng Yu-yin (eds), *Under Confucian Eyes: Writings on Gender in Chinese History* (Berkeley: University of California Press, 2001)

Mao Haijian, *The Qing Empire and the Opium War: The Collapse of the Heavenly Dynasty* (Cambridge: Cambridge University Press, 2016)

Mao Zedong, *Selected Works of Mao Tse-tung, Vol. I*, 2nd edition (Beijing: Foreign Languages Press, 1967)

Mao Zedong, *Mao Tse-tung Unrehearsed: Talks and Letters 1956–71* (Harmondsworth: Penguin, 1974)

Marmé, Michael, *Suzhou: Where the Goods of All the Provinces Converge* (Stanford: Stanford University Press, 2005)

Meyer-Fong, Tobie S., *Building Culture in Early Qing Yangzhou* (Stanford: Stanford University Press, 2003)

Meyer-Fong, Tobie S., *What Remains: Coming to Terms with Civil*

War in 19th-Century China (Stanford: Stanford University Press, 2013)

Milburn, Olivia, *Urbanization in Early and Medieval China: Gazetteers for the City of Suzhou* (Seattle: University of Washington Press, 2015)

Milne, William (trans.), *The Sacred Edict* (London: Black, Kingsbury, Parbury and Allen, 1817)

Mitter, Rana, *A Bitter Revolution: China's Struggle with the Modern World* (Oxford: Oxford University Press, 2004)

Mitter, Rana, *China's War with Japan 1937–1945: The Struggle for Survival* (London: Allen Lane, 2013)

Morrison, Robert, *Translations from the Original Chinese* (Canton, 1815).

Moule, A. C., *Quinsay: With Other Notes on Marco Polo* (Cambridge: Cambridge University Press, 1957)

Moule, Arthur Evans, *Half a Century in China: Recollections and Observations* (London: Hodder & Stoughton, 1911)

Munro, Donald J., *Images of Human Nature: A Sung Portrait* (Princeton: Princeton University Press, 1988)

Mutschler, Fritz-Heiner (ed.), *The Homeric Epics and the Chinese 'Book of Songs': Foundational Texts Compared* (Newcastle upon Tyne: Cambridge Scholars, 2018)

Naquin, Susan, *Millenarian Rebellion in China: The Eight Trigrams Uprising of 1813* (New Haven: Yale University Press, 1976)

Naquin, Susan, *Peking: Temples and City Life 1400–1900* (Berkeley: University of California Press, 2000)

Nathan, Andrew J. *et al.* (eds), *Popular Culture in Late Imperial China* (Berkeley: University of California Press, 1985)

Naval Intelligence Division, *China Proper*, 3 vols (London, 1944–45)

Needham, Joseph (ed.), *Science and Civilisation in China*, 25 vols (Cambridge: Cambridge University Press, 1954–present)

Needham, Joseph, *The Grand Titration: Science and Society in East and West* (London: George Allen & Unwin, 1969)

Nivison, David S., *The Life and Thought of Chang Hsüeh-ch'eng (1738–1801)* (Stanford: Stanford University Press, 1966)

Olivová, Lucie and Børdahl, Vibeke (eds), *Lifestyle and Entertainment in Yangzhou* (Copenhagen: NIAS Press, 2009)

Ouyang Xiu, *Historical Records of the Five Dynasties*, trans. Davis, Richard L. (New York: Columbia University Press, 2004)

Overmyer, Daniel (ed.), *Religion in China Today* (Cambridge: Cambridge University Press, 2003)

Overmyer, Daniel, *Local Religion in North China in the Twentieth Century: The Structure and Organization of Community Rituals and Beliefs* (Leiden: Brill, 2009)

Owen, Stephen, *Remembrances: The Experience of the Past in Classical Chinese Literature* (Cambridge, MA: Harvard University Press, 1986)

Owen, Stephen, *The Late Tang: Chinese Poetry of the Mid-Ninth Century (827–860)* (Cambridge, MA: Harvard University Press, 2006)

Owen, Stephen, *The Great Age of Chinese Poetry: The High Tang*, revised edition (Melbourne: Quirin Press, 2013)

Owen, Stephen (trans.), *The Poetry of Du Fu*, 6 vols (Berlin: De Gruyter, 2016)

Palmer, James, *Heaven Cracks, Earth Shakes: The Tangshan Earthquake and the Death of Mao's China* (New York: Basic, 2012)

Pankenier, David W., *Astrology and Cosmology in Early China: Conforming Earth to Heaven* (Cambridge: Cambridge University Press, 2013)

Pantsov, Alexander V., *Deng Xiaoping: A Revolutionary Life* (New York: Oxford University Press, 2015)

Peck, Graham, *Two Kinds of Time* (Seattle: University of Washington, [1950] 2008)

Perdue, Peter C., *China Marches West: The Qing Conquest of Central Eurasia* (Cambridge, MA: Belknap Press, 2005)

Peterson, Willard J., *Bitter Gourd: Fang I-chih and the Impetus for Intellectual Change* (New Haven: Yale University Press, 1979)

Pines, Yuri, *Envisioning Eternal Empire: Chinese Political Thought of the Warring States Era* (Honolulu: University of Hawai'i Press, 2009)

Pines, Yuri, *The Everlasting Empire: The Political Culture of Ancient China and Its Imperial Legacy* (Princeton: Princeton University Press, 2012)

Pines, Yuri (ed. & trans.), *The Book of Lord Shang: Apologetics of State Power in Early China* (New York: Columbia University Press, 2017)

Pines, Yuri *et al.* (eds), *Birth of an Empire: The State of Qin Revisited* (Berkeley: University of California Press, 2013)

Pines, Yuri *et al.* (eds), *Ideology of Power and Power of Ideology in Early China* (Leiden: Brill, 2015)

Plaks, Andrew H., *The Four Masterworks of the Ming Novel* (Princeton: Princeton University Press, 1987)

Pollard, David E., *The True Story of Lu Xun* (Hong Kong: Chinese University Press, 2002)

Pollock, Sheldon, *The Language of the Gods in the World of Men: Sanskrit, Culture, and Power in Premodern India* (Berkeley: University of California Press, 2006)

Pollock, Sheldon and Elman, Benjamin (eds), *What China and India Once Were: The Pasts That May Shape the Global Future* (New York: Columbia University Press, 2018)

Polo, Marco, *The Travels of Ser Marco Polo*, ed. Cordier, Henri, trans. Yule, Henry, 2 vols (London: John Murray, 1903)

Polo, Marco, *The Description of the World*, ed. & trans. Moule, A. C. and Pelliot, P., 2 vols (London: George Routledge, 1938)

Polo, Marco, *The Description of the World*, ed. & trans. Moule, A. C. and Pelliot, P., revised edition (London: Routledge, 2010)

Pomeranz, Kenneth, *The Great Divergence: China, Europe, and the Making of the Modern World Economy* (Princeton: Princeton University Press, 2000)

Poo Mu-chou *et al.* (eds), *Old Society, New Beliefs: Religious Transformation of China and Rome, ca 1st–6th Centuries* (Oxford: Oxford University Press, 2017)

Portal, Jane (ed.), *The First Emperor: China's Terracotta Army* (London: British Museum Press, 2007)

Pruitt, Ida, *A Daughter of Han: The Autobiography of a Chinese Working Woman* (Stanford: Stanford University Press, 1945)

Rao Pingru, *Our Story: A Memoir of Love and Life in China*, trans. Harman, Nicky (London: Square Peg, 2018)

Rawski, Evelyn S. and Rawson, Jessica (eds), *China: The Three Emperors 1662–1795* (London: Royal Academy of Arts, 2005)

Rawson, Jessica (ed.), *Mysteries of Ancient China: New Discoveries from the Early Dynasties* (London: British Museum Press, 1996)

Reilly, Thomas H., *The Taiping Heavenly Kingdom: Rebellion and the Blasphemy of Empire* (Seattle: University of Washington Press, 2004)

Reischauer, Edwin O., *Ennin's Travels in T'ang China* (New York: Ronald Press Company, 1955)

Rexroth, Kenneth (trans.), *Complete Poems of Li Ch'ing-chao* (New York: New Directions, 1979)

Rexroth, Kenneth (trans.), *Women Poets of China* (New York: New Directions, 1982)

Ricci, Matteo, *China in the Sixteenth Century: The Journals of Matthew Ricci 1583–1610*, ed. Trigault, Nicolas, trans. Gallagher, Louis J. (New York: Random House, 1953)

Richter, Antje, *A History of Chinese Letters and Epistolary Culture* (Leiden: Brill, 2015)

Rossabi, Morris, *Voyager from Xanadu: Rabban Sauma and the First Journey from China to the West* (Tokyo: Kodansha International, 1992)

Rossabi, Morris, *From Yuan to Modern China and Mongolia* (Leiden: Brill, 2014)

Rowe, William T., *Hankow: Conflict and Community in a Chinese City 1796–1895* (Stanford: Stanford University Press, 1992)

Rowe, William T., *Saving the World: Chen Hongmou and Elite Consciousness in Eighteenth-Century China* (Stanford: Stanford University Press, 2001)

Rowe, William T., *Crimson Rain: Seven Centuries of Violence in a Chinese County* (Stanford: Stanford University Press, 2007)

Rowe, William T., *China's Last Empire: The Great Qing* (Cambridge, MA: Belknap Press, 2012)

Roy, David Tod (trans.), *The Plum in the Golden Vase*, 5 vols (Princeton: Princeton University Press, 1993–2013)

Salisbury, Harrison E., *The Long March: The Untold Story* (New York: Harper & Row, 1985)

Salomon, Richard, *The Buddhist Literature of Ancient Gandhara* (Somerville, MA: Wisdom, 2018)

Sanft, Charles, 'Population Records from Liye: Ideology in Practice' in Pines, Yuri, *et al.* (eds), *Ideology of Power and Power of Ideology in Early China* (Leiden: Brill, 2015)

Schafer, Edward H., *Empire of Min: A South China Kingdom of the Tenth Century* (Tokyo and Rutland, VT: Charles E. Tuttle, 1954)

Schaik, Sam van, *Tibet: A History* (London: Yale University Press, 2011)

Schmidt, J. D., *The Poet Zheng Zhen (1806–1864) and the Rise of Chinese Modernity* (Leiden: Brill, 2013)

Schneider, David K., *Confucian Prophet: Political Thought in Du Fu's Poetry 752–757* (Amherst, NY: Cambria Press, 2012)

Schwarcz, Vera, *The Chinese Enlightenment: Intellectuals and the Legacy of the May Fourth Movement of 1919* (Berkeley: University of California Press, 1986)

Seagrave, Sterling, *Dragon Lady: The Life and Legend of the Last Empress of China* (New York: Knopf, 1992)

Shapiro, J., *Mao's War against Nature: Politics and the Environment in Revolutionary China* (Cambridge: Cambridge University Press, 2001)

Shen Fu, *Six Records of a Floating Life*, trans. Pratt, Leonard and Chiang Su-hui (Harmondsworth: Penguin, 1983)

Shi Nianhi, *Xi'an li shi di tu ji / The Historical Atlas of Xi'an* (Xi'an, 1996).

Singer, Aubrey, *The Lion and the Dragon: The Story of the First British Embassy to the Court of the Emperor Qianlong in Peking 1792–1794* (London: Barrie & Jenkins, 1992)

Smith, George, *The Jews at K'ae-Fung-Foo* (Shanghai: London Missionary Society's Press, 1851)

Smith, R. J., 'Rituals in Qing Culture' in Liu Kwang-ching (ed.), *Orthodoxy in Late Imperial China* (Berkeley: University of California Press, 1990)

Smith, Richard J., *Chinese Maps: Images of 'All Under Heaven'* (Hong Kong: Oxford University Press, 1996)

Snow, Edgar, *Red Star over China* (London: Victor Gollancz, 1937; revised and enlarged edition, 1968; further revisions, Harmondsworth: Pelican, 1972)

Soothill, W. E., *The Three Religions of China* (London: Hodder & Stoughton, 1913)

Soothill, W. E., *The Hall of Light: A Study of Early Chinese Kingship* (London: Lutterworth Press, 1951)

Souen K'i, *Courtisanes chinoises a la fin des T'ang entre circa 789 et le 8 janvier 881* (Paris: Presses universitaires de France, 1968)

Spence, Jonathan D., *Ts'ao Yin and the K'ang-hsi Emperor: Bondservant and Master* (New Haven: Yale University Press, 1966)

Spence, Jonathan D., *Emperor of China: Self-Portrait of K'ang-hsi* (London: Book Club Associates, 1974)

Spence, Jonathan D., *The Gate of Heavenly Peace: The Chinese and Their Revolution, 1895–1980* (Harmondsworth: Penguin, 1983)

Spence, Jonathan D., *The Search for Modern China* (New York: W. W. Norton, 1991)

Spence, Jonathan D., *God's Chinese Son: The Taiping Heavenly Kingdom of Hong Xiuquan* (New York: W. W. Norton, 1996)

Spence, Jonathan D., *Return to Dragon Mountain: Memories of a Late Ming Man* (New York: Penguin, 2008)

Steinhardt, Nancy Shatzman, *Chinese Traditional Architecture* (New York: China Institute in America, 1984)

Strassberg, Richard E., *Inscribed Landscapes: Travel Writing from Imperial China* (Berkeley: University of California Press, 1994)

Struve, Lynn (ed. & trans.), *Voices from the Ming–Qing Cataclysm: China in Tigers' Jaws* (Yale University Press, 1993)

Sullivan, Michael, *A Short History of Chinese Art* (London: Faber & Faber, 1967)

Sullivan, Michael, *The Three Perfections: Chinese Painting, Poetry, and Calligraphy* (London: Thames & Hudson, 1974)

Sun Shuyun, *The Long March: The True History of Communist China's Founding Myth* (New York: HarperCollins, 2006)

Tackett, Nicolas, *The Origins of the Chinese Nation: Song China and the Forging of an East Asian World Order* (Cambridge: Cambridge University Press, 2017)

Tan Hecheng, *The Killing Wind: A Chinese County's Descent into Madness during the Cultural Revolution* (New York: Oxford University Press, 2017)

Teichman, Eric, *Travels of a Consular Officer in North-West China* (Cambridge: Cambridge University Press, 1921)

Thilo, Thomas, *Chang'an: Metropole Ostasiens und Weltstadt des Mittelalters 583–904, Vol. I: Die Stadtanlage* (Wiesbaden: Otto Harrassowitz, 1997)

Thompson, Kirill, 'Zhu Xi' in *Stanford Encyclopedia of Philosophy*, ed. Zalta, Edward N., Summer 2017 edition (Stanford: Stanford University Press, 2017), https://plato.stanford.edu/archives/sum2017/entries/zhu-xi

Tong Qingsheng, 'Guo Songtao in London' in Ho, Elaine Yee Lin and Kuehn, Julia (eds), *China Abroad: Travels, Subjects, Spaces* (Hong Kong: Hong Kong University Press, 2009), 45–61

Trauzettel, Rolf, 'Sung Patriotism as a First Step toward Chinese Nationalism' in Haeger, John Winthrop (ed.), *Crisis and Prosperity in Sung China* (Tucson: University of Arizona Press, 1975)

Twitchett, Denis (ed.), *The Cambridge History of China, Vol. III: Sui and T'ang China 589–906, Part I* (Cambridge: Cambridge University Press, 1979)

Twitchett, Denis, *The Writing of Official History under the T'ang* (Cambridge: Cambridge University Press, 1992)

Twitchett, Denis and Smith, Paul Jakov (eds), *The Cambridge History of China, Vol. V: The Sung Dynasty and Its Precursors 907–1279, Part 1* (Cambridge: Cambridge University Press, 2009).

Urban, George (ed.), *The Miracles of Chairman Mao: A*

Compendium of Devotional Literature 1966–1970 (London: Tom Stacey, 1971)

Vermeer, Eduard B., *Chinese Local History: Stone Inscriptions from Fukien in the Sung to Ch'ing Periods* (Boulder: Westview Press, 1991)

Vitali, Roberto, *Records of Tho.ling: A Literary and Visual Reconstruction of the 'Mother' Monastery in* Gu.ge (Dharamshala: Amnye Machen Institute, 1999)

Vogel, Ezra F., *One Step Ahead in China: Guangdong under Reform* (Cambridge, MA: Harvard University Press, 1989)

Vogel, Ezra F., *Deng Xiaoping and the Transformation of China* (Cambridge, MA: Belknap Press, 2011)

Vogel, Hans Ulrich, *Marco Polo Was in China: New Evidence from Currencies, Salts and Revenues* (Leiden: Brill, 2013)

von Glahn, Richard, *An Economic History of China: From Antiquity to the Nineteenth Century* (Cambridge: Cambridge University Press, 2016)

Wakeman, Frederic, Jr, *The Great Enterprise: The Manchu Reconstruction of Imperial Order in Seventeenth-Century China* (Berkeley: University of California Press, 1986)

Walder, Andrew G., *China under Mao: A Revolution Derailed* (Cambridge, MA: Harvard University Press, 2015)

Walder, Andrew G., *Agents of Disorder: Inside China's Cultural Revolution* (Cambridge, MA: Belknap Press, 2019)

Waley, Arthur, *The Poetry and Career of Li Po 701–762 AD* (New York: Macmillan, 1950)

Waley, Arthur (trans.), *The Book of Songs* (London: Allen & Unwin, 1954)

Waley, Arthur, *The Opium War through Chinese Eyes* (Stanford: Stanford University Press, 1958)

Waley, Arthur, 'A Chinese Poet in Central Asia' in *The Secret History of the Mongols and Other Pieces* (London: Allen & Unwin, 1963)

Waltham, Clae, *Shu Ching: The Book of History* (Chicago: H. Regnery, 1971)

Wang Zhongshu, *Han Civilization*, trans. Chang, K. C. *et al.* (New Haven: Yale University Press, 1982)

Ward, Julian, *Xu Xiake (1587–1641): The Art of Travel Writing* (Richmond upon Thames: Curzon Press, 2001)

Warner, Marina, *The Dragon Empress: Life and Times of Tz'u-hsi, 1835–1908, Empress Dowager of China* (London: Weidenfeld & Nicolson, 1972)

Watson, Burton, *Ssu-ma Ch'ien, Grand Historian of China* (New York: Columbia University Press, 1958)

Watson, Burton (trans.), *Records of the Grand Historian* (New York: Columbia University Press, 1969)

Watson, Burton (trans.), *The Old Man Who Does as He Pleases: Selections from the Poetry and Prose of Lu Yu* (New York: Columbia University Press, 1973)

Watson, Burton (trans.), *The Tso Chuan: Selections from China's Oldest Narrative History* (New York: Columbia University Press, 1989)

Watson, Burton (trans.), *The Selected Poems of Du Fu* (New York: Columbia University Press, 2002)

Watson, Philip (trans.), *Grand Canal, Great River: The Travel Diary of a Twelfth-Century Chinese Poet* (London: Frances Lincoln, 2007)

Watt, James C. Y., *The World of Khubilai Khan: Chinese Art in the Yuan Dynasty* (New York: Metropolitan Museum of Art, 2010)

Wei Yuan, *A Chinese Account of the Opium War* (Shanghai: Kelly & Walsh, 1888)

Wilhelm, Richard (trans.), *The I Ching, or Book of Changes*, 3rd edition (London: Routledge & Kegan Paul, 1968)

Wilkinson, Endymion, *Chinese History: A New Manual*, 5th edition (n.p.: Endymion Wilkinson, 2017)

Will, Pierre-Etienne, *Handbooks and Anthologies for Officials in Imperial China*, 2 vols (Leiden: Brill, 2020)

Williamson, H. R., *Wang An Shih: A Chinese Statesman and Educationalist of the Sung Dynasty*, 2 vols (London: Arthur Probsthain, 1935–37)

Wood, Frances, *Did Marco Polo Go to China?* (Boulder: Westview Press, 1998)

Wood, Frances, *The Silk Road: Two Thousand Years in the Heart of Asia* (Berkeley: University of California Press, 2002)

Wood, Michael, *The Story of India* (London: BBC, 2007)

Worcester, G. R. G., *The Junks and Sampans of the Yangtze: A Study in Chinese Nautical Research, Vol. I: Introduction and Craft of the Estuary and Shanghai Area* (Shanghai: Statistical Department of the Inspectorate General of Customs, 1947)

Worcester, G. R. G., *The Junkman Smiles* (London: Chatto & Windus, 1959)

Wu Xiang, *Contemporary Chinese Rural Reform* (Singapore: Springer, 2016)

Xu Xiake, *Randonnées aux sites sublimes*, ed. & trans. Dars, Jacques (Paris: Gallimard, 2001)

Xu Xiake, *The Travels of Xu Xiake* (Shanghai: Shangai Foreign Languages Education Press, 2010)

Yajima, Hikoichi, *On the Visit of a Division from Zheng He's Expedition to Yemen* (1974)

Yamafuji, Masatoshi *et al.*, 'In Pursuit of the Tang Outpost Suyab: An Archaeological Expedition at Ak-Beshim site, 2015 Autumn Season' in *Archi-Cultural Interactions through the Silk Road: 4th International Conference, Mukogawa Women's Univ., Nishinomiya, Japan, July 16–18, 2016, Proceedings* (Nishinomiya: Mukogawa Women's University Press, 2016)

Yang Jisheng, *Tombstone: The Untold Story of Mao's Great Famine* (London: Allen Lane, 2012)

Yang Lihui and An Deming: *Handbook of Chinese Mythology* (New York: Oxford University Press, 2008)

Yang Shuhui and Yang Yunqin (trans.), *Slapping the Table in Amazement: A Ming Dynasty Story Collection by Ling Mengchu, 1580–1643* (Seattle: Washington University Press, 2018)

Yang Xianyi and Young, Gladys (trans.), *Poetry and Prose of the Tang and Song* (Beijing: Panda, 1984)

Yao, Betty (ed.), *China: Through the Lens of John Thomson 1868–1872* (Bangkok: River Books, 2010)

Yap, Joseph P. (trans.), *Wars with the Xiongnu* (Bloomington: AuthorHouse, 2009)

Yates, Robin, *Qin Legal Texts* (Leiden: Brill, 2017)

Ye Yang (trans.), *Vignettes from the Late Ming: A Hsiao-P'in Anthology* (Seattle: University of Washington Press, 1999)

Young, David and Lin, Jiann I., *Out on the Autumn River: Selected Poems of Du Mu* (Akron: Rager Media, 2007)

Yu, Anthony C. (ed. & trans.), *The Journey to the West, Vol. III* (Chicago: University of Chicago Press, 1980)

Yu Guangyuan, *Deng Xiaoping Shakes the World* (Manchester: Eastbridge, 2004)

Yü Ying-shih, 'Han Foreign Relations' in Twitchett, Denis and Loewe, Michael (eds), *The Cambridge History of China, Vol. I: The Ch'in and Han Empires 221 BC–AD 220* (Cambridge: Cambridge University Press, 1986), 377–462

Yule, Henry (ed. & trans.), *Cathay and the Way Thither: Being a Collection of Medieval Notices of China, Vol. I: Preliminary*

Essay on the Intercourse Between China and the Western Nations Previous to the Discovery of the Cape Route (London: Hakluyt Society, 1915)

Zhang Dai, *Night Ferry (Yehang chuan)*, ed. Liu Yaolin (Hangzhou, 1987)

Zhang Dai, *Souvenirs rêvés de Tao'an*, trans. Brigitte Teboul-Wang (Paris: Gallimard, 1995)

Zhang Daye, *The World of a Tiny Insect: A Memoir of the Taiping Rebellion and Its Aftermath* (Seattle: University of Washington Press, 2013)

Zhang Jianping, *Huizhou: Discovering a Culture in Photos* (Hangzhou: Zhejiang Photographic Press, 2013)

Zhang Liang, *The Tiananmen Papers* (New York: Public Affairs, 2001)

Zhang Ling, *The River, the Plain, and the State: An Environmental Drama in Northern Song China 1048–1128* (Cambridge: Cambridge University Press, 2016)

Zhang Zeduan, *Scenes along the River during the Qingming Festival* (Shanghai: Shanghai Press, 2010)

Zhao Ziyang, *Prisoner of the State: The Secret Journal of Premier Zhao Ziyang*, ed. & trans. Bao Pu *et al.* (New York: Simon & Schuster, 2009)

Zhou Ruchang, *Between Noble and Humble: Cao Xueqin and the Dream of the Red Chamber* (New York: Peter Lang, 2009)

Zhou Xun, *Forgotten Voices of Mao's Great Famine 1958–1962* (New Haven: Yale University Press, 2013)

Zhu Xi, *Selected Writings*, ed. & trans. Ivanhoe, Philip (New York: Oxford University Press, 2019)

JOURNAL ARTICLES

Abe, Masashi, 'Results of the Archaeological Project at Ak Beshim (Suyab), Kyrgyz Republic from 2011 to 2013 and a Note on the Site's Abandonment', *Intercultural Understanding*, Vol. 4 (2014): 11–16

Allan, Sarah, 'On the Identity of Shang Di and the Origin of the Concept of the Celestial Mandate', *Early China*, Vol. 31 (2007): 1–46

Allan, Sarah, 'Erlitou and the Formation of Early Chinese Civilization: Toward a New Paradigm', *Journal of Asian Studies*, Vol. 66, No. 2 (2007): 461–96

Biggerstaff, Knight, 'The First Chinese Mission of Investigation Sent to Europe', *Pacific Historical Review*, Vol. 6, No. 4 (1937): 307–20

Caldwell, Ernest, 'Social Change and Written Law in Early Chinese Legal Thought', *Law and History Review*, Vol. 32, No. 1 (2014): 1–30

Chang Kwang-chih, 'The Meaning of "Shang" in the Shang Dynasty', *Early China*, Vol. 20 (1995): 69–77

Chen Yunzhen, 'Socio-Economic Impacts on Flooding: A 4000-Year History of the Yellow River, China', *Ambio*, Vol. 41, No. 7 (2012); 682–98

Church, Sally K., 'Zheng He: An Investigation into the Plausibility of 450-ft Treasure Ships', *Monumenta Serica*, Vol. 53 (2005): 1–43

Clauson, Gerard, 'Ak Beshim – Suyab', *The Journal of the Royal Asiatic Society of Great Britain and Ireland*, Vol. 93, No. 1–2 (1961): 1–13

Cornaby, Arthur W., 'The Secret of the "Red Chamber"', *New China Review*, Vol. 1, No. 4 (1919): 329–39

Drancourt, Michel *et al.*, '*Yersinia pestis* as a Telluric, Human Ectoparasite-Borne Organism', *Lancet Infectious Diseases*, Vol. 6, No. 4 (2006): 234–41

Eno, Robert, 'The Background of the Kong Family of Lu and the Origins of Ruism', *Early China*, Vol. 28 (2003): 1–42

Forte, Antonino, 'An Ancient Chinese Monastery Excavated in Kirgiziya', *Central Asiatic Journal*, Vol. 38, No. 1 (1994): 41–57

He Nu, 'Taosi: An Archaeological Example of Urbanization as a Political Center in Prehistoric China', *Archaeological Research in Asia*, Vol. 14 (2018): 20–32.

Hu Zhongwei *et al.*, 'A Chinese Observing Site from Remote Antiquity', *Journal for the History of Astronomy*, Vol. 30, No. 3 (1999): 231–5

Hudson, James J., 'Confronting Modernization: Rethinking Changsha's Rice Riot of 1910', *Journal of Modern Chinese History*, Vol. 8, No. 1 (2014): 43–62

Islam, Gazi, and Keliher, Macabe, 'Leading through Ritual: Ceremony and Emperorship in Early Modern China', *Leadership*, Vol. 14, No. 4 (2018): 435–59

Jaang Li *et al.*, 'When Peripheries Were Centres: A Preliminary Study of the Shimao-Centred Polity in the Loess Highland, China', *Antiquity*, Vol. 92, No. 364 (2018): 1008–22.

Johnson, David, 'The Last Years of a Great Clan: the Li Family of

Chao Chün in Late T'ang and Early Sung', *Harvard Journal of Asiatic Studies*, Vol. 37, No. 1 (1977): 5–102

Klein, Esther S., 'Spreading the Word of Zhu Xi: Xu Heng's Vernacular Confucianism under Mongol Rule and Beyond', *Parergon*, Vol. 35, No. 2 (2018): 91–118

Liu Li and Xu Hong, 'Rethinking Erlitou: Legend, History and Chinese Archaeology', *Antiquity*, Vol. 81, No. 314 (2007): 886–901

Lin, Justin Yifu, 'The Needham Puzzle: Why the Industrial Revolution Did Not Originate in China', *Economic Development and Cultural Change*, Vol. 43, No. 2 (1995): 269–92

Liu Zehua, 'Monarchism: A Historical Orientation of Chinese Intellectual Culture', *Contemporary Chinese Thought*, Vol. 45, No. 2–3 (2014): 21–31

Ryckmans, Pierre, 'The Chinese Attitude towards the Past', *China Heritage Quarterly*, No. 14 (2008)

Mote, F. W., 'A Millennium of Chinese Urban History: Form, Time and Space Concepts in Soochow', *Rice Institute Pamphlet – Rice University Studies*, Vol. 59, No. 4 (1973): 35–65

Murowchick, Robert E., and Cohen, David J., 'Searching for Shang's Beginnings: Great City Shang, City Song, and Collaborative Archaeology in Shangqiu, Henan', *Review of Archaeology*, Vol. 22, No. 2 (2001): 47–61

Nickel, Lukas, 'The First Emperor and Sculpture in China', *Bulletin of the School of Oriental and African Studies*, Vol. 76, No. 3 (2013): 413–47

Nylan, Michael, 'Sima Qian: A True Historian?', *Early China*, Vol. 23–4 (1998–99): 203–46.

Wu Pei-yi, 'Memories of K'ai-feng', *New Literary History*, Vol. 25, No. 1 (1994): 47–60

Pines, Yuri, 'Liu Zehua and Studies of China's Monarchism', *Contemporary Chinese Thought*, Vol. 45, No. 2–3 (2014): 3–20

Rouleau, Francis A., 'The Yangchow Latin Tombstone as a Landmark of Medieval Christianity in China', *Harvard Journal of Asiatic Studies*, Vol. 17, No. 3–4 (1954): 346–65

Rowe, William T., 'The Problem of "Civil Society" in Late Imperial China', *Modern China*, Vol. 19, No. 2 (1993): 139–57

Saeki, P. Y., 'The Nestorian Monument in China', *Journal of the Royal Asiatic Society of Great Britain and Ireland*, Vol. 49, No. 1 (1916)

Shaughnessy, Edward L., '"New" Evidence on the Zhou Conquest', *Early China*, Vol. 6 (1980–81): 57–79

Shaughnessy, Edward L., 'Historical Perspectives on the Introduction of the Chariot into China', *Harvard Journal of Asiatic Studies*, Vol. 48, No. 1 (1988): 189–237

Shaughnessy, Edward L., 'New Sources of Western Zhou History: Recent Discoveries of Inscribed Bronze Vessels', *Early China*, Vol. 26–7 (2001–02): 73–98

Struve, Lynn A., 'Huang Zongxi in Context: A Reappraisal of His Major Writings', *Journal of Asian Studies*, Vol. 47, No. 3 (1988): 474–502

Sussman, George D., 'Was the Black Death in India and China?', *CUNY Academic Works* (2011)

T'ien Ju-kang, 'Cheng Ho's Voyages and the Distribution of Pepper in China', *Journal of the Royal Asiatic Society of Great Britain and Ireland*, Vol. 113, No. 2 (1981): 186–97.

Wang, Nora, 'Deng Xiaoping: The Years in France', *China Quarterly*, Vol. 92 (1982): 698–705

West, Stephen, 'The Interpretation of a Dream', *T'oung Pao*, Vol. 71, No. 1 (1985): 63–108

Widmer, Ellen, 'The Epistolary World of Female Talent in Seventeenth-Century China', *Late Imperial China*, Vol. 10, No. 2 (1989): 1–43.

Wu Qingling *et al.*, 'Outburst Flood at 1920 BCE Supports Historicity of China's Great Flood and the Xia Dynasty', *Science*, 5 August 2016, 579–82

Yates, Robin D. S., 'The Qin Slips and Boards from Well No. 1, Liye, Hunan: A Brief Introduction to the Qin Qianling County Archives', *Early China*, Vol. 35–6 (2012–13): 291–329

Zarrow, Peter, 'He Zhen and Anarcho-Feminism in China', *Journal of Asian Studies*, Vol. 47, No. 4 (1988): 796–813

Zhang Wenxian, 'The Yellow Register Archives of Imperial Ming China', *Libraries and the Cultural Record*, Vol. 43, No. 2 (2008): 148–75

INDEX